102 153 751 9

Theatre in Europe:

This is the fourth volume to be published in the series Theatre in Europe: a documentary history. This book charts the development of theatrical presentation at a time of great cultural and political upheaval. It is, for today's theatre practitioner, historian and theoretician, the most important period in the evolution of our art. The mid-nineteenth century witnessed the start of self-awareness and self-reflection among theatre artists. Putting on plays was no longer an end in itself, but the creation of imaginary worlds had to be justified on ethical, sociological and political as well as aesthetic grounds. The first great debate, which goes on to this day, especially in television, concerned the notion of realism/naturalism. It became more fascinating when artists, towards the end of the century, rebelled in the name of poetry before rejecting all conventions, in an assertion of total freedom of creation. Our documents chart the growth of naturalism throughout Europe and its gradual rejection and replacement by symbolism and expressionism. The second half of the nineteenth century saw also the assertion of the director (*metteur en scène*) and his unstoppable ascension, which resulted in the displacement of the star performer and the playwright.

For the first time in European theatre history, the training of actors – in schools or within professional companies (the 'ensemble') – mobilized the energies of the best practitioners. The documents show how in France, Germany, Russia and Scandinavia, directors, playwrights and theorists searched for more professional ways of staging plays with actors who had undergone a thorough technical training. The growing importance of sets and integrated set designs is also illustrated, alongside the new technologies (for example, electric lighting). Then, as now, the majority of actors were struggling to eke out a living and we reproduce some eye-opening contracts that were forced on would-be performers. Throughout the period, and in all countries, censorship prevented the free expression of ideas; rules and regulations were imposed which resulted in many a protracted battle opposing the authorities to playwrights and theatre directors. The period, 1850 to 1918, was, in theatrical terms, the most colourful, the most turbulent, and the most inspiring of our theatre history. It is also a period which still affects every aspect of play-making today. With few exceptions, our documents are unavailable to an English-reading public and many are out of print (or unpublished) in their original language. The volume contains numerous illustrations, the source location for each document and a substantial bibliography.

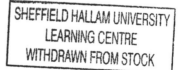
SHEFFIELD HALLAM UNIVERSITY
LEARNING CENTRE
WITHDRAWN FROM STOCK

Theatre in Europe: a documentary history

General Editors

Glynne Wickham
John Northam
W.D. Howarth

This series presents a comprehensive collection of primary source materials for teachers and students, and serves as a major reference work for studies in theatrical and dramatic literature. The volumes focus individually on specific periods and geographical areas, encompassing English and European theatrical history. Each volume will present primary source material in English, or in English translation, relating to actors and acting, dramatic theory and criticism, theatre architecture, stage censorship, settings, costumes, and audiences. These sources include such documents as statutes, proclamations, inscriptions, contracts, and playbills. Additional documentation from contemporary sources is provided through correspondence, reports and eyewitness accounts. The volumes also provide not only the exact source and location of the original documents, but also complementary lists of similar documents. Each volume contains an Introduction, narrative linking passages, notes on the documents, a substantial bibliography and an index offering detailed access to the primary material.

Published

Restoration and Georgian England, 1669–1788, compiled and introduced by David Thomas and Arnold Hare, edited by David Thomas

National Theatre in Northern and Eastern Europe, 1746–1900, edited by Laurence Senelick

German and Dutch Theatre, 1600–1848, complied by George W. Brandt and Wiebe Hogendoorn, edited by George W. Brandt

French Theatre in the Neo-classical Era, 155–1789, edited by William D. Howarth

English Professional Theatre, 1530–1660, edited by Glynne Wickham, Herbert Berry and William Ingram

The Medieval European Stage, 500–1500, edited by William Tydeman

Romantic and Revolutionary Theatre, 1789–1860, edited by Donald Roy

Theatre in Europe: a documentary history

Naturalism and symbolism in European theatre 1850–1918

Edited by
CLAUDE SCHUMACHER

Université Rennes 2
Haute-Bretagne

CAMBRIDGE
UNIVERSITY PRESS

CAMBRIDGE UNIVERSITY PRESS
Cambridge, New York, Melbourne, Madrid, Cape Town, Singapore, São Paulo, Delhi

Cambridge University Press
The Edinburgh Building, Cambridge CB2 8RU, UK

Published in the United States of America by Cambridge University Press, New York

www.cambridge.org
Information on this title: www.cambridge.org/9780521230148

© Cambridge University Press 1996

This publication is in copyright. Subject to statutory exception
and to the provisions of relevant collective licensing agreements,
no reproduction of any part may take place without the written
permission of Cambridge University Press.

First published 1996
This digitally printed version 2008

A catalogue record for this publication is available from the British Library

Library of Congress Cataloguing in Publication data

Naturalism and symbolism in European Theatre, 1850–1918 /
  edited by Claude Schumacher.
      p.   cm. – (Theatre in Europe)
    Includes bibliographical references.
    ISBN 0 521 23014 4 (hardback)
      1. Theatre – Europe – History – 19th century – Sources.   2. Theatre –
  Europe – History – 20th century – Sources.   I. Schumacher, Claude.
  II. Series.
PN2570.N43   1996   96-19086
792'.094'09034 – dc20   CIP

ISBN 978-0-521-23014-8 hardback
ISBN 978-0-521-10079-3 paperback

Contents

Scandinavia, 1849–1912
Edited and translated by Inga-Stina Ewbank

England, 1850–1914
Edited by Louis James and Marion O'Connor

Italy, 1868–1919

Edited and translated by Laura Richards

Iberian Peninsula, 1884–1913

Edited and translated by David George

Select bibliography

List of documents

Asterisks before titles indicate illustrated documents

V Symbolism and the 'Crisis in the Theatre', 1902–1908

VI Kommissarzhevskaya and Meyerhold, 1905–1907

VII New directions for the Moscow Art Theatre, 1909–1917

III The Catalan dimension

General editors' preface

In appointing appropriately qualified editors for all the volumes in this documentary history it has been our aim to provide a comprehensive collection of primary source materials for teachers and students on which their own critical appraisal of theatrical history and dramatic literature may safely be grounded.

Each volume presents primary source documents in English, or in English translation, relating to actors and acting, dramatic theory and criticism, theatre architecture, stage censorship, settings, costumes and audiences. Editors have, in general, confined their selection to documentary material in the strict sense (statutes, proclamations, inscriptions, contracts, working-drawings, playbills, prints, account books, etc.), but exceptions have been made in instances where prologues, epilogues, excerpts from play texts and private correspondence provide additional contemporary documentation based on authors' authority or that of eyewitnesses to particular performances and significant theatrical events.

Unfamiliar documents have been preferred to familiar ones, short ones to long ones; and among long ones recourse has been taken to excerpting for inclusion all passages which either oblige quotation by right of their own intrinsic importance or lead directly to a clearer understanding of other documents. In every instance, however, we have aimed to provide readers not only with the exact source and location of the original document, but with complementary lists of similar documents and of secondary sources offering previously printed transcripts.

Each volume is equipped with an introductory essay, and in some cases introductory sections to each chapter, designed to provide readers with the appropriate social background – religious, political, economic and aesthetic – as context for the documents selected; it also contains briefer linking commentaries on particular groups of documents and concludes with an extensive bibliography.

Within this general presentational framework, individual volumes will vary considerably in their format – greater emphasis having to be placed, for example, on documents of control in one volume than in another, or with dramatic theory and criticism figuring less prominently in some volumes than in others – if each volume is to be an accurate reflection of the widely divergent interests and concerns of different European countries at different stages of their historical development, and the equally sharp differences in the nature and quality of the surviving documents volume by volume.

Glynne Wickham (Chairman)
Bristol University

Editor's preface

This volume has been fifteen long years in the making, and many a time one had the feeling that it would never reach completion. It was first entrusted to James Arnott, who, on his retirement, asked me to take over, promising that he would go on working on the project. Sadly, it was not long before I had to labour without his kind and expert advice as he died after having enjoyed only a year or two of a very busy retirement. To his memory, we dedicate this volume.

Two of the original section contributors left the project for personal reasons and new colleagues had to be recruited at a time when Laurence Senelick, Michael Patterson and Laura Richards had all but completed their work. To these three collaborators *extraordinaires* I owe an immense debt of gratitude: their expert contributions showed the way to the rest of the team and their diligence ensured the survival of the project.

We are all deeply grateful to Sarah Stanton and Glynne Wickham for their initial help and encouragement. We are most particularly indebted to John Northam and Victoria Cooper for their close reading of earlier drafts, their detailed and constructive criticism, and their generous support throughout.

We should like to thank the staff of the Bibliothèque historique de la Ville de Paris; the Archives de la Comédie-Française; the Archives nationales; the Bibliothèque de l'Arsenal; the Musée Carnavalet, all in Paris; the Teatervitenska-pelig institutt, Universitetet i Bergen; Universitetetsbiblioteket, Oslo; Statens Teaterhøyskole, Oslo; the Strindberg Museum, Stockholm; Drottningholms Tea-termuseum, Stockholm; the British Library; the Biblioteca Burcardo, Rome; Kathy Hale, Leela Meinertas, Barry Norman, Anne Rosher and Sarah Woodcock, the Theatre Museum, London; Jill Davis (Eliot College), Steve Holland (Library), Jim Styles and Spencer Scott (Photographic Unit), University of Kent at Canterbury.

I am more personally grateful to David Walker and Richard Hand for their help in translating many of the French documents. As for all other translations in each section they have been made by the given editors, unless otherwise stated.

Finally we want to express very special thanks to Helen Southall, our hawk-eyed copy-editor, for her patience and consummate skill in giving the volume such an immaculate look.

General introduction

This volume charts the development of theatrical presentation from the middle of the nineteenth century to the end of the First World War. These were times of great cultural, social and political upheaval; for today's theatre practitioner, historian and theoretician in the European theatrical tradition, they represent by far the most important period in the evolution of our art.

The mid-nineteenth century witnessed the start of a new kind of self-awareness and self-reflection among theatre artists. Putting on plays was no longer an end in itself: the creation of imaginary worlds had to be justified on ethical, sociological, political and aesthetic grounds. The first great debate, which goes on unabated to this day, in television as well as in the theatre, concerned the notion of realism/naturalism. The debate grew more fascinating still when artists, towards the end of the century, rebelled against the tyranny of 'materialistic truth' in the name of poetry and of a higher idea of what constitutes ultimate reality, before rejecting all conventions in an assertion of the total freedom of the creative mind. Our documents follow the growth of naturalism throughout Europe and its gradual (and almost contemporaneous) rejection and replacement by symbolism and expressionism.

For the first time in European theatre history, the training of actors mobilized the energies of the best practitioners. The documents show how in France, Germany, Russia and Scandinavia, directors, playwrights and theorists searched for more professional ways of staging plays with actors who had undergone a thorough technical training and acquired some intellectual and aesthetic culture. The growing importance of scenography (i.e. of integrated set designs) is also illustrated, alongside the new technologies (for example, electric lighting).

Then, as now, the majority of actors were struggling to eke out a living and we reproduce some eye-opening contracts that were forced on would-be performers who were treated, in some cases, as slave labourers. This was also the time when theatre became 'show-biz': while some idealistic men and women strove to give their art a spiritual and aesthetic grandeur rarely achieved in the past, others were only motivated by financial considerations.

But beyond all these contradictory pulls an earnest debate on the nature of theatre was beginning. That debate was not conducted on the level of abstract ideas, but pursued concretely in the very act of creating the theatrical event. That debate continues and will go on for as long as we are drawn to the creation of fictional lives to try to make sense of our own lives.

THE *METTEUR EN SCÈNE*

The rich creativity that was unleashed in the second half of the nineteenth century and the early years of the twentieth century on the European stage was made possible by the assertion of a number of far-sighted men of their 'directorial' prerogatives within the organization of the theatrical event. The notion of *mise en scène* (for which there is no adequate translation in English: the meanings of 'production', 'staging', 'direction' are not as all-encompassing as the French term) was only really developed in the 1880s, when the 'director' (*le metteur en scène*) asserted his 'dictatorial' authority over the minutest aspect of the theatrical creation, including his 'reading' of the playwright's text. Whereas in the past the author, the leading actor or a 'stage manager' were vaguely responsible for blocking a show, the modern 'director' came to proclaim the theatrical specificity of the theatrical creation. A play produced on the stage was no longer to be considered as the mere physical illustration of a literary text that happened to be a play, but the production (the play in space and time) was to be seen as a work of art in its own right and had to be conceived as such, not only by its creators but also by the spectators.

It so happens, and it is no coincidence, that the rise of the director came about at the time when, in literature and in painting, artists were striving for ever greater realism – a striving inspired by positivist philosophy and encouraged by an unshakeable faith in scientific progress. The faithful and perfectly exact reproduction of social, psychological and material reality, as advocated by the avant-garde of the 1880s and 1890s, called for the emergence of a controlling authority, and, therefore, the rise of the director was a development that had to happen. The first modern director was Ludwig Chronegk (1837–91) who worked at the Meiningen Court Theatre and who influenced the conceptions of André Antoine in Paris and Konstantin Stanislavsky in Moscow. But, in many ways, the real father of our modern stage was not a man of the theatre at all, but a cantankerous critic and a failed playwright: the French novelist Emile Zola (1840–1902). From 1865 until 1880, Zola, also a theatre critic and an influential political journalist, was not so much writing reviews of the shows he saw professionally night after night as he was building, more and more impatiently, the theory of the 'new theatre'. In 1880 he collected together his most important texts and published them in book form under the title, *Le Naturalisme au théâtre*. Zola's ideas were often misconstrued at the time, and are still too often presented in a caricatured fashion; nonetheless their impact cannot be overstressed.

Rejecting centuries of obsolete conventions, Zola called for truth and reality in the creation of the theatrical event. Life itself – and not 'eternal' rules of dramatic construction – was to be the inspiration of writers, directors, designers and actors. Everyday life, everyday situations, ordinary people, colloquial speech, real environments, truthful feelings: this, for Zola, is the stuff of true theatre.

Opponents to naturalism, then and now, have repeated with nauseating monotony that Zola's aesthetics in theatrical matters was nothing but the translation into predictable images of the hegemonic materialist bourgeois ideology. In this context, much is made of Zola's fascination with photography. That Zola was a keen and superlative photographer is a well-known fact: how could it have been otherwise since the writer was excited by every new technology and new idea, and his life and art were devoted to observing the reality around him? What is wrong (wilfully wrong) is to equate photography with passivity, boredom and meaningless reproduction of a superficially beheld reality. With naturalism the essentialist vision of the world, and of man's position in the world, gives way to an analytical and critical perception of Darwinian man in an ever-changing environment. Antoine and Zola were not so naïve as to think that the task of the director, actor and designer was to put reality on the stage, but to *represent* reality as honestly and as truthfully as possible.[1] This, obviously, entailed a three-dimensional construction of sets resembling as closely as possible real locations, filled with real objects, and for flesh-and-blood characters to behave in these re-created spaces as naturally as possible. In his preface to *Miss Julie* (1888), Strindberg expresses most fully and succinctly the 'illusionistic' programme of the entire naturalist movement in the theatre. But what cannot be stressed enough is that Chronegk, Antoine, Strindberg, Stanislavsky, Brahm, Grein, all these men who created 'free theatres' (i.e. theatres free from stultifying conventions) were not thoughtless children unaware of the meaning of their actions, but artists trying, at a given time and in a given place, to realize for their publics what theatre people have always tried to do, namely to animate a reliable picture of *man in the world*. Their ideal was to achieve the most consummate '*effet de réel*'.[2] What Barthes named the *effet de réel*, i.e. the 'artistically created impression of reality', must not be confused, as it too often is, with reality itself. Everyone in the theatre, the actor on the stage and the spectator in the auditorium, knows that some fiction is being performed: the actor *may* in a

---

[1] Anachronistically Zola/Antoine/Stanislavsky et al. are accused, implicitly, of having ignored Brecht, or are berated for not having been Brecht. It is doubtful whether, without their example, even Brecht could have become Brecht.

[2] Expression coined by Roland Barthes in *Communication*, 11 (1968). See Patrice Pavis, *Dictionnaire du théâtre* (Paris: Messidor, 1987).

paroxysm of emotion 'lose' himself for a fleeting moment; the spectator *may* feel, equally fleetingly, that a real event is 'being enacted' – but, fundamentally, no one is duped, unless it be narrow-minded academics who choose to deny any intelligence to the theatrical creators of the late nineteenth century and to their spectators.

'The impression of reality' was most passionately sought in the art of the actor – and, ironically, that quest of total identification between actor and role, that desire to affect emotionally each spectator in the deepest recesses of his being, will be most exacerbated in those twentieth-century directors, actors and theorists who most vehemently reject the lessons of naturalism, from Artaud to Grotowski to performance artists. One example must here suffice. To hostile critics – in all the countries represented in this volume – Ibsen was the epitome of everything that was bad in naturalism, the quintessence of decadence, of bad taste, of immorality. It goes without saying that all those who undertook to perform the Norwegian's plays were worse than the man himself, since they should have had the good sense not to touch his distasteful creations. When Antoine came to stage *Ghosts* (30 May 1890) he lavished all his naturalist know-how on the *mise en scène*: the set was fully constructed and, on their first entrance at the opening of the play, the characters coming from outside the house were dripping with rain (and what could be more boring, naturalistic, meaningless, i.e. 'photographic', than water sprinkled on actors?). Yet, according to those critics who were not systematically hostile to the Théâtre Libre, the play produced a profound and lasting effect. George Moore, an English writer residing in Paris, wrote that he had 'lived through a year's emotion' during Oswald's confession of his need for Regina (*Ghosts*, Act III), and he concludes: 'Antoine, identifying himself with the simple truth sought by Ibsen, by voice and gesture, casts upon the scene so terrible a light, so strange an air of truth, that the drama seemed to be passing not before our eyes but *deep down in our hearts in a way we had never felt before.*'[3] It is the measure of the greatest acting that it can achieve such a powerful effect on a knowledgeable spectator.

The term 'naturalism' is used in the title of this volume because the 'naturalist movement' is deeply ingrained in the history of Western theatre, but the contributors to the various sections would be deeply disappointed if readers were to get the impression that the notion of naturalism is a closed notion. For theatre artists, then and now, there is no such thing as 'naturalist fundamentalism': even the preface to *Miss Julie* insists on a set which represents only the corner of a room, leading the eyes of the spectators 'into unknown perspectives' and thus haunting their imagination. In October 1888, for instance, André Antoine staged a one-act

---

[3] George Moore (1852–1933), *Impressions and Opinions* (London, 1913), pp. 162–7; quoted in Jean Chothia, *André Antoine* (Cambridge University Press, 1991), p. 51. Emphasis added.

play, *Les Bouchers* (The Butchers), by Fernand Icres (1856–88) who had recently died of consumption. The play, and its production, are often cited to deride the entire naturalistic endeavour: imagine, Antoine hung a carcass of beef on the stage![4] What nonsense, what bad taste! What is generally overlooked is that the play is written in impassioned verse and that Antoine, far from re-creating the neat and clinical aspect of a village butcher's shop, had strewn the stage with offal: offal everywhere, even on the ground. There is a term to describe such heightened theatrical imagery, and that term is 'expressionism'. Emile Faguet, a particularly astute critic, wrote as early as December 1888 that the Théâtre Libre was a very eclectic institution, open to a rich variety of experiences where there is something for all tastes: 'The Théâtre Libre is the free tribune of the theatre … They are accused of being monopolized by a very closed, imperious and intolerant school … I am pleased to see it is nothing of the kind.'[5] Antoine himself insisted, again and again, that he was not the prisoner of one school of thought, the slave of one exclusive aesthetics, and that the door of his theatre was as wide open to symbolism or any innovation in theatrical writing or style of presentation as to naturalism. With *Les Bouchers*, its supercharged acting and its gory set, Antoine behaved like a distant forerunner of the theatre of cruelty, assaulting mercilessly his spectators' senses and peace of mind.

A similar open, ecumenical attitude was to be found in the actions of all leading practitioners of the time: in Paris, the 'naturalist' Antoine welcomed and trained the 'symbolist' Lugné-Poe; in Berlin, Brahm called Reinhardt to his side; in Moscow Meyerhold learned his craft under Stanislavsky, who invited the 'avant-gardist' Craig to direct Shakespeare in his theatre, and so on. For the sake of convenience, the careers of the greatest playwrights writing in the second half of the nineteenth and the beginning of the twentieth centuries are divided into 'periods', and even more conveniently Strindberg had the kindness to follow a perfect trajectory from naturalism to expressionism through symbolism. But such a superficial approach to the work of the writers, directors and actors of the time is dangerously reductive. For example, Strindberg's *The Father* (1887) was presented to Zola by the author himself as a 'naturalist tragedy' and it is cited, again and again, as a masterpiece of the naturalist school and of Strindberg's naturalist period. Yet for the Intimate Theatre in 1908 Strindberg wanted an expressionist production, with the wife acted 'like a fury from hell'. And indeed the text of the play is redolent of symbolism, the well-observed claustrophobic set is a symbol in itself, many actions (like the final swaddling of the Captain into a strait-jacket) are more symbolic than factually correct, and, here and there, especially with the

---

[4] The beef was in reality mutton, and its use was highly symbolic as Francis Pruner so eloquently describes it in his *Les Luttes d'Antoine – Au Théâtre Libre*, Tome 1 (Paris: Minard, Bibliothèque des Lettres modernes, 1964), pp. 250ff.   [5] Cited in Chothia, *André Antoine*, p. 87.

throwing of a burning oil lamp, the heightened atmosphere of expressionism is achieved. The same wealth of meanings can be observed, to a greater or lesser extent, in the entire *œuvre* of playwrights like Ibsen, Strindberg or Chekhov, and their best interpreters at the time rose perfectly to the challenge.

THE SYMBOLIST REACTION

Why such a subtitle if I am arguing that the division into separate schools is largely artificial? Because a fundamental shift occurred 'away from naturalism' at the very time naturalism was establishing itself and promoting a new approach to the art of the theatre. The Meiningen, Antoine, Stanislavsky, all had faith in the materiality of the stage (the set, the props, the actors) as they had a positivist certainty of the *pérennité* (durability) of the world. Coupled with a strong humanism, such an optimistic certainty guided them towards the establishment of a solid theatrical craft which still is – and the statement bears repetition – the foundation of today's performance culture in the Western world.

But there were those who doubted, and questioned in the most fundamental manner, the very existence of the material world. Contemporaneously with Antoine's work at the Théâtre Libre, the most innovatory French symbolist poet, Stéphane Mallarmé (1842–98), was refining a theatrical 'anti-theatricalist' theory. For Mallarmé, Shakespeare's *Hamlet* represents not only the highest peak of theatrical art but also the highest achievement of human artistic creativity (which, for him, was the only creativity worth considering). *Hamlet* is a unique masterpiece because the tragedy is a *monodrama*: *Hamlet*, says Mallarmé, is a play consisting of a single 'soliloquizing' character surrounded by inconsistent shadows. For Mallarmé the fascination of the play lies in Hamlet's interior monologue, the innermost encounter of a man with himself, the confrontation of a human being with the ultimate metaphysical questions. What, for the ordinary spectator, creates the excitement of a theatrical performance – namely the action, the unfolding of a plot in time, expectation and suspense, the reversal of the main character's fortune, the confrontation of an actor with his character – Mallarmé rejects as inessential and vulgar materiality. Indeed, a performance can only destroy the perfection of the writer's creation. For Mallarmé and his disciples, a theatrical performance could, at best, take the form of a public reading, if it is given the solemnity of High Mass: 'The ultimate Work of Art [*l'Œuvre totale*] is a book, read and commented by Mallarmé in front of a chosen public, according to a sophisticated ritual in order to transmit a certain metaphysical teaching which would take the place of existing religions.'[6] Mallarmé was dreaming of a theatre

---

[6] Jacques Scherer, *Le 'Livre' de Mallarmé* (Paris: Gallimard, revised edition, 1977), p. 37.

which would be pure music, pure colour, pure song and pure dance: a theatre of dreams dreamt by and for disembodied souls.

Needless to say, such an extremist attitude is the very rejection of theatre and no man of the theatre could follow such a programme, since it signifies, purely and simply, the abolition of theatre. But less extreme symbolists were disheartened by the naturalists' insistence on the corporeality of the stage and they saw in the material presence of sets and actors a denial of the spiritual dimensions of art and of human life. Such creators were anxious that the spiritual dimension and the dream element should never be forgotten.[7]

The *Zeitgeist*, as usual, has a lot to do with changing attitudes. On the one hand, older writers (again: Ibsen, Zola, Strindberg . . .) who had not only followed the principles of naturalism as an aesthetic path to theatrical creation, but had firmly believed in the notion of progress inscribed in the positivist philosophy of their youth, became disillusioned by the lack of results and by the appropriation of their techniques by second-rate playwrights and theatre-makers who applied their methods mechanically and, thereby, debased naturalism by producing shows that were nothing but a collection of trite clichés. On the other hand, the young generation, for whom naturalism appeared to be the only approach their predecessors had ever known, and who judged the failure of the 'scientific age' with a harshness bordering on rage, made the rejection of materialism a question of dogma. Their search for spiritual values, their desire to express the inexpressible, became highly polemical. Poets of the theatre such as Maeterlinck, Jarry or Quillard, Wedekind or Hofmannsthal, Blok or Andreev, Synge or Yeats, wanted to effect a total break with the dominant artistic trend and, therefore, their rejection of naturalism was total and the discredit they cast upon it knew no bounds. It is they who first dismissed naturalism as mere surface photography – the gibe which lazy critics have repeated ever since. Now that a full century has passed, now that we can cast a more informed and dispassionate eye on the history of our art, it becomes obvious that naturalism and symbolism are as indissociable as the fingers on one's hand, and these age-old traditions (renewed by generation after generation) enrich each other in every successful work of art.

THE ADVENT OF THE 'SAVAGE GOD'

After the first night of Alfred Jarry's *Ubu roi* (Paris, 9 December 1896) Yeats wrote

---

[7] The list of post-naturalist, symbolist or even spiritualist writers and playwrights is inexhaustible, and should begin with Zola himself who, at the time of his death, was working on a messianic novel (*Vérité*, Truth, published posthumously, 1903). As stated earlier, naturalist playwrights like Ibsen, Strindberg and Chekhov can easily be classified among symbolists, and most directors (Antoine included) should be mentioned as symbolist as well as naturalist creators, even if their personal inclinations led them more readily towards one rather than the other direction.

in his diary: 'After us, the Savage God!'[8] The Irish poet saw (rightly, as it happens) in Jarry's monstrous character the harbinger of genocidal times. *Ubu*'s two performances both caused a stir among the Parisian literati and exploded all theatrical conventions (naturalist as well as symbolist): in *Ubu* Jarry rejects all notions of character, time, coherence, causality, plot, decorum or literary composition. The play is a firebrand thrown into twenty-five centuries of Western theatrical tradition. Its first reluctant director, Lugné-Poe, disowned the production the day after its première, only to reclaim it many years later when realizing its seminal importance. Jarry's example was to be followed in Italy by the futurists who proclaimed in 1909, through Marinetti's 'Manifesto of Destructive Incendiary Violence': 'Poetry must be a violent onslaught. There is no masterpiece without aggressiveness ... '.[9] A little later, in 1916, in Switzerland, Germany, France (and the United States), the anarchist and nihilist Dada, through manifestos, anti-establishment exhibitions and wild cabaret performances,[10] announced the end of art and civilization. As Glynne Wickham so aptly writes: 'for if the war had done nothing else for art, it had revealed all too clearly how feeble modern man actually was, and *how frail was his continuing hold on civilized life*.'[11] In Russia a somehow less pessimistic reaction against naturalism made itself felt in Meyerhold's and Evreinov's insistence on the theatrical nature of theatre: the art of the performer is not to pretend that what he is doing is an ordinary everyday action, but 'to proudly exhibit' his histrionic skills for all to admire. Their actors were to be the ultimate performance artists – tragedian-comedian-impersonator-dancer-singer-clown-tumbler-juggler, whose aim was to affect the mood of the spectator, to work directly and physically on his emotions, to thrill and to enthral by their virtuosity. Before the October Revolution (and that is the only period that interests us here), the question of conveying a message, of instructing the audience, of having any moral impact on the spectator was mostly rejected as irrelevant by such theatricalists who excelled in parody and experimented in all possible theatrical forms.

Although Aristotle is still being studied in universities (and more and more practitioners gain a university training before launching their careers), the idea that there are dramaturgical rules that must be followed for a play to be a play has lost its currency. Today's creators do not have to resort to youthful anarchistic revolt in order to be able to express themselves: they express themselves in total

---

[8] Cited in Roger Shattuck, *The Banquet Years: The Origins of the Avant-Garde in France from 1885 to World War I* (London: Jonathan Cape, 1969; first published 1955), p. 209.

[9] F. T. Marinetti (1876–1944), 'The Founding and Manifesto of Futurism', *Le Figaro*, Paris, 20 February 1909.

[10] Most memorably at the Cabaret Voltaire, in Zürich (1916–17), inspired by Jean Arp (1887–1966) and Tristan Tzara (1896–1963).

[11] Glynne Wickham, *A History of the Theatre* (Oxford: Phaidon Press, 1985), p. 223. Emphasis added.

freedom. They are free to create form and content as they go along, and they have the avant-garde of a hundred years ago to thank for that hard-won freedom. The activities of the likes of Jarry, Blok, Wedekind, Marinetti or even Strindberg (marginal, shunned and dismissed at the time by the 'Pillars of Establishment Art') have laid the foundation of the best of twentieth-century theatre, in playwriting, directing and design. A roll-call of post-Second World War artists directly inspired by the iconoclastic visionaries of the late 1890s and the early years of our century would fill a volume, from Edward Albee to Leonid Zorin, through Arrabal, Artaud, Beckett, Bergman, Brecht, Brook, Dürrenmatt, Fo, Frisch, Grotowski, Handke, Ionesco, Littlewood, Mnouchkine, Pinter, Planchon, Rame, Ronconi, Stein, Strehler, Svoboda, Weiss, Bob Wilson, Zadek, and so on and so forth. To which we should add the names of designers, theatre architects, theorists and theatre companies – all of whom found and continue to find their inspiration in the work of their forefathers of the turn of the century.

THE VOLUME'S ORGANIZATION

A volume dealing with a European overview of theatrical activity from 1850 to 1918 calls, quite obviously, for a division in national entities. The second half of the nineteenth century was the time of the nation-state *par excellence*: not only were European nations strongly affirming their individual identities, but they were also (politically and economically) affirming their singularity as never before, with the disastrous consequences that were to follow. It is natural, in a compilation like this, to give the reader a strong picture of how each nation chose to organize its theatrical activity. We are, therefore, presenting the documents in chronological order within each section, and each national entry has been divided into subsections which best represent the main emphases of the theatrical development in these countries.

But another, thematic, option could also have been adopted. If, on the political level, nation-states were asserting their individuality, theatre artists were constantly criss-crossing the continent ignoring the strict boundaries enforced by politicians. In that sense, it was tempting to devote a section to, say, the Théâtre Libre and another to Stanislavsky; one to *mise en scène* and another to financial considerations; yet another to international touring, and so on. It is, however, impossible to find a satisfactory solution to the complexity of the task as the majority of documents could be listed under many different headings.

To allow our readers to find a path through the whole volume and to encourage a 'thematic' reading, 'subject' entries have been included in the traditional name index.

France, 1851–1919

Edited by JOHN McCORMICK *and* CLAUDE SCHUMACHER

Translated by RICHARD HAND, JOHN McCORMICK, CLAUDE SCHUMACHER *and* DAVID WALKER

Introduction

Ominously, in France, the second half of the nineteenth century opened with two pieces of bad theatre. In real life, Louis Napoléon Bonaparte, the Prince-Président, overthrew the Second Republic and crowned himself emperor Napoleon III (2 December 1852); on the stage, earlier that same year, Alexandre Dumas *fils* triumphed with *The Lady of the Camellias*. The two events are in no way interconnected, yet they both testify, each in its own way, to the corrupt nature of French bourgeois society, and they both contrive to conceal the truth of what was really happening. The political *coup d'état* and the theatrical *coup d'éclat* both give the impression of a 'new beginning' when, in reality, they fit neatly into an uninterrupted flow of conservative thinking. No change for the better was brought about as a result of Napoleon's self-elevation or the public incarnation of Dumas's whore: French bourgeoisie remained firmly in power, in government as well as in cultural affairs.[1]

The undisputed master of the French stage was then Eugène Scribe (1791–1861), the creator of the 'well-made play' (*la pièce bien faite*) and purveyor of over 500 vaudevilles, comedies and dramas. His reign, begun at the time the first Napoleon met his comeuppance, continued, undiminished, until his death. The successful formula was also being exploited by Emile Augier (1820–89), who scored his first hit with *Hemlock* in 1844, soon to be joined by Dumas *fils* (1824–95) and Victorien Sardou (1831–1908). The triumvirate Augier–Dumas–Sardou exerted a stranglehold over French theatrical life for almost fifty years and managed to stifle new talents until the turn of the century.[2] They were seconded in their negative attitude by the uncritical support of conservative critics hostile to any true innovation, the most powerful of whom was Francisque Sarcey (1827–99), drama and literary critic of the influential *Le Temps* for over thirty years.

Augier, Dumas and Sardou had the ambition to be 'realists', to be the truthful observers and reliable painters of contemporary mores; they aspired to be thinkers and philosophers, and even, in Dumas's case, stern moralists. But their so-called thesis or problem plays (the problems being money, marriage, sex . . .), written

---

[1] See Zola's series of *Les Rougon-Macquart*, especially *La Curée* (The Kill) and *Nana*.
[2] See Zola, *Nos auteurs dramatiques*.

according to the timorous tastes of their public and following outmoded conventions, lacked life. If the successful well-made play testifies to its author's mastery of stage techniques (intricate intrigues; witty, aphoristic dialogue; clever *coups de théâtre*; neat dénouements), it also shows up his lack of true inventiveness and poetic powers. The only Augier–Dumas–Sardou play to survive in the modern repertory is the notorious *Lady of the Camellias*: not because it is an outstanding example of the well-made play, but because it belongs to the older, yet ageless genre, the sentimental tear-jerker, also known as melodrama.

Napoleon III's Second Empire (1852–70) produced only one dramatist whose plays are still staged today: the prolific Eugène Labiche (1815–88), author of charming comedies, dazzling vaudevilles and biting comedies of manners in which he dissected the petite bourgeoisie with great gusto, yet without indulgence. He denounced the crass stupidity, the cynical egoism, the self-satisfaction, the hypocritical lies and the platitude of his contemporaries in theatrical and surrealist flights of fancy that announce the Ionescos or Boris Vians of a century later: the regularly revived *Chapeau de paille d'Italie* (The Italian Straw Hat, 1851), *Le Voyage de M. Perrichon* (Monsieur Perrichon's Holiday, 1865) or *Le plus heureux des trois* (The Happiest of the Three, 1870) continue to delight French audiences to this day, and tell us far more about nineteenth-century society than any ponderous thesis play could ever manage.

However, if the names of Dumas *fils*, Augier, Sardou, Scribe and Labiche have found their way into the history of dramatic literature (as perceived by the bourgeoisie) and their plays have been performed at relatively up-market theatres, it is important to remember that there was also a large popular audience that remained faithful to the Ambigu-Comique, to the Château d'Eau, and also to the various local theatres (*théâtres de quartier*), such as the Bouffes du Nord and the ring of suburban theatres from Montparnasse to Montmartre. These audiences thronged to see melodramas in the same way that the previous generation had done on the Boulevard du Temple (better known to play-goers as 'le boulevard du crime'). The subjects might have changed from Gothic horrors to the more sensational contemporary crimes reported by the newspapers, but the audience was largely the same. (The Théâtre du Grand-Guignol, founded in 1895, and catering for a more middle-class public, also exploited sensational crime, as the tabloid press does today.)

Long before Zola, the popular theatres were pioneering naturalism in terms of reproduction of reality, and particularly the reality of life amongst the poorest sections of society and in the most sordid conditions. In the 1820s already we find such plays as Antier's *La pauvre famille* (The Poor Family), and many others described as 'tableaux populaires', which set out to do little more than provide a genre picture of low life (sometimes attached to such social questions as alcoholism). By the 1870s Noël and Stoullig, who provided an annual account of the activities of Parisian theatres, were complaining of the excess of naturalism in the popular theatre, especially at the Ambigu-Comique.

Most of the dramatists for the popular theatres have disappeared in much the same way as scriptwriters for television, who are rarely remembered beyond the episode they have written, if at all. If Guilbert de Pixérécourt[3] is remembered as the author of the 'first' melodrama, Anicet Bourgeois and Adolphe Dennery,[4] two of the most prolific purveyors of melodrama through the century, are virtually unknown today. Yet Dennery (with Cormon, one of his many collaborators) was responsible for *Les deux orphelines* (The Two Orphans, 1872), a piece which would continue well into the twentieth century, being staged by Stanislavsky himself, and providing the basis for Griffith's film, *The Orphans of the Storm*. The number of plays written and performed in the first half of the century at the popular theatres was phenomenal. A huge proportion of these were vaudevilles (i.e. slight comic plays, interspersed with songs), many of which received only a handful of performances and served as curtain-raisers to the main programme. By the 1860s the appetite for theatre had not declined, but successful plays were now running for a considerable time, and some of these – for example, Dennery's adaptation of Jules Verne's *Le Tour du monde en quatre-vingts jours* (Around the World in Eighty Days) – had an immensely expensive staging and ran from one season to another. The long run changed the face of French theatre (as it did in England) and also contributed to the demise of provincial theatre and the stock company, with road productions of successful Paris plays being sent out on tour around France.

The nineteenth century may not have been a century of great dramatic literature, but it was a century of enormous theatrical and technical development. Already a dramatist such as Pixérécourt paid great attention to the overall staging of his plays and some of the better melodramas received far more attention in terms both of scenery and costumes on the one hand, and of interpretation by the actors on the other, than was the rule at the Comédie-Française or the fashionable theatres concerned with churning out comedies and vaudevilles in stock set to entertain the more affluent classes. Even here, however, there were exceptions, such as Montigny – at the Gymnase from 1844 – who is generally credited with introducing what might be described as 'upholsterer's' theatre in France. By 1820 it was already common practice to publish the *mise en scène* (then restricted to the 'blocking' and careful description of the scenery) of successful Parisian productions for the benefit of the provincial theatres. Acting editions of plays, which became popular from the late 1830s, and printed stage-directions based on the prompt-copy of the original production were also published. From the 1860s, the

---

[3] René Charles Guilbert de Pixérécourt (1773–1844) was also a successful theatre director.
[4] Adolphe Dennery (1811–99, also known as d'Ennery).

popular theatres accelerated their attempts to reproduce reality on the stage, and in this they were helped by the upsurge of theatre-building that followed the demolition of the Boulevard du Temple in 1862 (followed by the subsequent comprehensive rebuilding of the boulevards under Haussmann), and the 1864 Act which freed the theatres from the previous restrictive legislation.

Gas lighting, although introduced around 1820, had been slow to develop, but it did allow for a hitherto unknown control of light, and was exploited by some of the great scene-painters, such as Daguerre (1789–1851) and Ciceri (1782–1868). Electric lighting, timidly introduced from the 1880s, was at first used in the same way as gas, and it was only with the art theatre movement, towards the end of the century, that it began to become a serious means of theatrical expression. Stage machinery and technical effects, especially at the larger theatres, such as the Châtelet, became more and more important. The primary effect was usually sensation, and in some cases critics suggested that the play itself might as well be forgotten about. This was the triumph of visual theatre, which should not be underestimated because of its literary shortcomings.

This was also a period of actors' theatre, and in many cases a play could only acquire its true importance in performance. This was particularly true for some of the great vehicles for actors, such as *Le Courrier de Lyon* in which starred Paulin Ménier, not to mention the string of plays that Victorien Sardou turned out for Sarah Bernhardt. Such pieces may not have produced an intellectual's theatre, or even set out to do more than entertain, and their *raison d'être* was certainly not art theatre.

The actors of the large popular theatres, such as the Ambigu, had developed in the tradition of the melodrama and were used to projecting their performances to audiences in the topmost galleries. There is no doubt that they were aiming at a form of realism in their playing, but it had to be magnified. A part of the importance of the Théâtre Libre, and other art theatres, was their small size. Seating only a few hundred people (as opposed to 1,500 or even over 2,000), these theatres allowed the actor a much closer contact with the audience and removed the need to magnify every effect. It was this, as much as anything, that helped bring about the development of the 'naturalistic' actor. In order to put the new Théâtre Libre actors in perspective, it is also important to contrast them with the actors of the Comédie-Française, who had a long and rather fossilized tradition, including a special way of speaking, which was quite unlike that which had developed in the more popular theatres of the capital.

To counteract what they perceived as being an unacceptable decline in artistic and literary standards of mainstream theatre, the foremost novelists of the nineteenth century (from Balzac to Zola) all turned to playwriting with apostolic zeal: they may have altered the course of French theatre for the better in the long run, but had to resign themselves to seeing their plays fail on the stage with predictable regularity. Even if, as theatrical 'librettists', they achieved a measure of success and financial wealth, they did not possess the creative power to regenerate the stage in the way, as novelists, they had reinvented narrative writing.

Emile Zola, born in 1840, started his 'theatrical' career as a drama critic in 1865. Over the years he published a wealth of articles which appeared in book form in 1881. His *Naturalisme au théâtre* (Naturalism in the Theatre) and *Nos auteurs dramatiques* (Our Dramatists) are powerful manifestos calling for a new theatre: new writing, new acting, new directing, new 'spectating'. Alas ... Zola was not to be the Shakespeare of the new era, nor were any of his disciples. The stage adaptations of his novels were among the greatest successes of nineteenth-century French theatre, but they did not embody his lofty ideals. The writer did not adapt his novels himself, but turned to professional hacks who manufactured huge melodramatic spectaculars out of *Nana* or *L'Assommoir*, appealing to a public ever hungry for sensationalism and slightly *risqué* situations. The lone 'naturalist' playwright, Henry Becque (1837–99), author of *Les Corbeaux* (The Scavengers, 1882) and *La Parisienne* (1885), became the model of the new naturalist school, but he refused steadfastly to ally himself to Zola and kept aloof of the exciting theatrical ventures of the late 1880s and 1890s.

Despite his inability to become the longed-for naturalist playwright, Zola was nonetheless one of the main catalysts of the most momentous theatrical revolution of modern times: the advent of the *metteur en scène*, the director. The rise of the director in the theatre was in no way a French phenomenon, but it found in Zola its foremost theorist, and in the director of the Théâtre Libre (1887–94), André Antoine (1857–1943), its most enthusiastic practitioner. Antoine's ambition was to reform the theatre by following many of Zola's precepts. He started by abolishing the star system and replacing it with ensemble playing. His actors had to learn to speak naturally; their gestures and movements had to be justified by the logic of the situation and dictated by the author's text and the layout of the set. Antoine demanded that the actors make a profound psychological as well as physiological study of their characters, in order to vanish behind the author's creations. He also insisted on total control over the production which, in its minutest details, should correspond to his own vision of the play. Antoine, of course, started by staging naturalist plays which he presented with painstaking accuracy, but it would be wrong to confine the director of the Théâtre Libre to naturalist clichés. Another of Antoine's ambitions was to encourage established writers as well as new playwrights to write for the stage. In the seven years of his

Théâtre Libre's existence, he put on over a hundred new plays (either French or foreign translations): sad to say only one (minor) French playwright has remained in the repertory of contemporary theatres, the comic writer Georges Courteline; but Antoine can take credit for having introduced to the French stage the best of European drama with plays by Ibsen, Strindberg and Hauptmann.

When naturalism eventually reached the French stage, it had already been rejected by the other arts (painting, prose writing, poetry, music) and the symbolist reaction in the theatre happened almost simultaneously with Antoine's effort to establish his Théâtre Libre. Symbolism in the theatre was championed by a youthful poet of seventeen, Paul Fort (1872–1960), who founded the Théâtre d'Art in 1890. The young man's aim was resolutely *anti-theatrical* and unashamedly elitist: his ideal theatrical performance was to be an ethereal dream induced by a subtle combination of evocative words, sounds, colours and perfumes. He staged Maeterlinck's first plays, but his most unorthodox (and final) experiment was his adaptation of *The Song of Songs* (11 December 1891). The intention of this production was to realize a Baudelairian synthesis of the senses. In fact it was the first attempt at total theatre, and as such is highly significant, although, in practice, a bewildered audience was doused with perfume and left choking in fumes of incense which the ventilation system of the theatre was unable to cope with.

One of Fort's collaborators, Aurélien Lugné-Poe (who had previously worked with Antoine), had a better grasp of things theatrical and created a more permanent and lastingly influential symbolist theatre in 1893: the Théâtre de l'Œuvre, on the occasion of his production of Maeterlinck's *Pelléas et Mélisande*. In subsequent years Lugné-Poe revealed the greatest contemporary European playwrights to the Parisian public: Maeterlinck (already mentioned), Hauptmann, the later plays of Ibsen and Strindberg, Synge and Shaw, Gogol, Jarry and Paul Claudel. Lugné-Poe staged at the turn of the century not only the best the world repertoire could offer, but also the works of the few playwrights who would shape the drama of the twentieth century, and beyond.

If Antoine and Lugné-Poe helped to shape the future, they had precious little direct impact on the 'theatre industry'[5] of the time. The theatrical activity had been frenetic throughout the nineteenth century, especially after 1864, when Napoleon III 'freed' the theatres. It has been calculated that more than 32,000 *new* plays were performed in Paris between 1800 and 1900, the annual average rising from about 200 (1800–30) to over 400 (1831–50) before settling down to around 300. When revivals are added to these figures, one finds that a staggering number of plays were being performed annually in Paris. In 1852, the 20 Parisian

---

[5] See F. W. J. Hemmings, *The Theatre Industry in Nineteenth-Century France* (Cambridge University Press, 1992).

theatres staged 932 plays (610 revivals, 322 creations).[6] The more plays shown, the more spectators were attracted to the theatre. The box-office receipts quadrupled from around 5 million francs in the early nineteenth century to over 20 million in 1903 (despite a remarkable stability in the price of theatre tickets, and the cost of living).[7]

Unfortunately, the 'art of the theatre' did not share in this commercial wealth, nor did the vast majority of the actors who still suffered the indignity of having to sign draconian contracts enslaving them to theatre managements. To counteract, on the social level, this sorry state of affairs, several attempts were made, during the 1890s and the first years of this century, to create a 'popular theatre'. Idealistic notions of a popular theatre had been floating around since the middle of the century. Several short-lived popular operas came into existence, particularly at Alexandre Dumas's former Théâtre Historique (today's Théâtre de la Ville, Place du Châtelet), then a municipal theatre, and at the Château d'Eau, where summer seasons of popular opera ran during the later 1860s and through the 1870s. At that time, the prominent architect, Viollet-le-Duc, also proposed turning the enormous Châtelet Theatre into a people's theatre, with low seat prices. In the 1880s and 1890s, the notion of improvement of the popular classes through culture led to performances at cheap prices by the Comédie-Française and the Opéra in some suburban theatres. The real impetus for a people's theatre, however, came with the increase of literacy amongst the popular classes, thanks partly to the cheap press and partly to the development of public libraries. As workers became more organized in the 1870s, the notion of a working-class that might accede to power through education began to develop, and this led to the formation of the Universités Populaires at the turn of the century. The thinking behind the ideas of a Romain Rolland, a Maurice Pottecher or a Jean Jaurès needs to be seen against this background. The fact that the ideal of a 'people's theatre' was, and remains to this day, a utopia, does not detract from its importance. The various Parisian experiments (Théâtre du Peuple in Clichy, Théâtre Populaire in Belleville) were not only short-lived, but they also attracted the 'wrong' kind of audience with over-long and over-ambitious programmes which opened with a lecture at 7.30 p.m., followed by a curtain-raiser, a full-lengh play and miscellaneous scenes, songs or sketches, and never closing before midnight. Firmin Gémier (1869–1933), who worked with Rolland in 1902, founded his own Théâtre National Ambulant, a vast touring company, in 1911, but the enterprise was doomed from the start as local and national authorities refused to support it. Heroic as the short-lived Théâtre National Ambulant was, Gémier's real contribution to the people's theatre movement was, first, his championing of a class-free

---

[6] Dominique Leroy, *Histoires des arts du spectacle en France* (Paris: L'Harmattan, 1990), p. 242.
[7] Leroy, *Histoires des arts*, p. 279.

theatre, no longer divided up by a wide range of price categories, and, secondly, his success in persuading the government to set up a Théâtre National Populaire at the Trocadéro in the 1920s. The basic idea was one of democratization of culture, making quality theatre available to large audiences at popular prices. Unfortunately, Gémier never received the budgets needed for running such a theatre, and so it was only after the Second World War, with the appointment of Jean Vilar as director in 1951, that the Théâtre National Populaire, in the Trocadéro, now rebuilt as the Palais de Chaillot, could become a reality.

Theatre has always been a business. However, in the first decades of the nineteenth century, the owners of the secondary theatres were often the people who ran them. Gradually theatre became more of an industry, with shareholders looking for profit on their investment. The 'popular' theatres of the early part of the century were made more comfortable and transformed into places where the popular classes seldom ventured. The popular audiences were to be found mostly in the theatres away from the centre (also due to the demographic development, the expansion of the capital and the incorporation of former suburbs into 'greater Paris') and in these theatres the melodrama continued to flourish long after it had disappeared from the more sophisticated stages. From the Second Empire onwards the theatre industry went through a period of boom. After 1864 many new theatres were built, catering for the most part for an affluent middle-class public. The very term 'théâtre de boulevard' lost its association with popular drama and became associated with relatively worthless and insignificant entertainment for the well-off (which is still the current meaning of the disparaging expression). The new opera house, designed, but not completed, under the Second Empire, and known after its architect as the Palais Garnier, symbolized the notion of theatre as a luxury trade and illustrated only too well the passage of theatre from popular entertainment at the beginning of the century to the *fin-de-siècle* elitist social gathering.

The twentieth century started in confusion. The old favourites continued to satisfy the traditional audiences until the outbreak of the First World War, but theatre practitioners became increasingly unhappy with the dispiriting and cheap routine of contemporary theatre practice and dramatic literature. No one felt the need for a new departure more keenly than Jacques Copeau, whose words provide a fitting epitaph for most of nineteenth-century French theatre:

> Most theatres have been snapped up by a handful of entertainers in the pay of unscrupulous impresarios; everywhere, most of all in those places where great traditions should safeguard some integrity, there is the same mountebank, speculative attitude, the same vulgarity; one finds fakery everywhere, excess and exhibitionism of all kinds, all the usual parasites of a dying art that no longer pretends to be otherwise; everywhere one finds flabbiness, mess, indiscipline,

ignorance and stupidity, disdain for the creative and abhorrence of the beautiful; what is produced is more and more extravagant and self-congratulatory, criticism is more and more fawning and public taste more and more misguided: that is what has roused our indignation.[8]

Copeau's Théâtre du Vieux-Colombier, founded in 1913, was extremely short-lived. It performed for only eight months before the outbreak of war; it was in New York for two seasons (1917–19) and closed down, in 1924, less than five years after Copeau's return to Paris. But these few short years and Copeau's subsequent activity as a teacher (today we might call him a 'guru') with the Copiaus in Burgundy have had a seminal influence on French theatre – an influence that is still felt today. Louis Jouvet and Charles Dullin started their highly successful careers as actors and directors with Copeau. Almost all the directors of the new 'decentralized' theatres set up by the French government immediately after the Second World War had been, directly or indirectly, his pupils: Jean Dasté (Saint-Etienne), Hubert Gignoux (Rennes, Strasbourg), and so on. The founder of the modern Théâtre National Populaire and creator of the world-famous Avignon Festival, Jean Vilar, who was the incarnation of living French theatre during the 1950s and 1960s, not only trained with Dullin, but adopted the same ascetic aesthetics as Copeau had advocated at the beginning of the century. Ariane Mnouchkine, the highly innovative and imaginative director of the Théâtre du Soleil, acknowledges with gratitude the influence of Copeau on her conception of theatre (although she was just fifteen when the 'master' died). And thanks to the Anglo-American connections of his nephew (Michel Saint-Denis), his influence was also felt in England (London Old Vic), where he established a drama school, before moving to the United States (Juilliard School, Lincoln Center, New York) and Canada (National Theatre School, Montreal).

More radical even in its negative approach than Copeau's reconstructive action on theatre was Dada, and Dada too was destined to produce a rich progeny. In the best iconoclastic tradition, vociferously inaugurated by Jarry's *Ubu roi* (Ubu Rex, 1896), Dada believed, in the middle of the horrors inflicted by 'civilized' men upon other civilized men in the trenches of the Somme, that the only way to bring about a renewal of 'art' and a regeneration of humanity was to destroy the cultural and intellectual heritage that led to this unprecedented carnage. If Dada itself is best remembered for its thundering manifestos, and failed to propose a viable alternative, it inspired the theorists, playwrights and directors who would create the new theatre ('le nouveau théâtre') which started to flourish towards the end of the Second World War and, eventually, shaped the theatre of the second half of

---

[8] Jacques Copeau, 'On Dramatic Renovation', *Nouvelle revue française*, September 1913, quoted in John Rudlin, *Jacques Copeau* (Cambridge University Press, 1986), pp. 3–4.

the century throughout the Western world, namely, Artaud, Beckett, Genet, Ionesco, Arrabal, Pinter, Albee, and so on, and so on.

The story which is documented here continues ... and therefore we shall not conclude.

I The business of theatre

I On acting, casting, directing and rehearsing in the 1880s

E. Meignen et E. Fouquet, *Le Théâtre et ses lois*, n.d. [late 1880s], pp. 29–30, 158–9, 318–20 and 322

The authors of *Le Théâtre et ses lois* (The Laws of the Theatre) had the ambition to write an encyclopaedic treatise on every aspect of the theatre, aesthetic and administrative, artistic and technical. Yet they show little historic perspective and assume that the 'laws' they have uncovered will be true for all times and all genres.

ACTORS Actors must possess certain physical qualities: expressive face and eyes; ease of manner and bearing; precision and restraint in gesture; verve; brightness; sensitivity; and grace. They must also possess qualities which they acquire through the practice and study of their art and its traditions, such as expansiveness, tenderness, passion, spirit, warmth, liveliness: these should be natural, sincere, and proportionate to the feelings to be conveyed.

Their articulation must be sharp and clear; their pronunciation free from any accent; their voice sonorous. Their 'r' must be neither guttural nor rolled. [...]

Bombast and declamation have now been replaced by simple and natural delivery, best achieved when the actor has the gift of identifying with his character.

The actor should not overdo his effect by indulging in loud outbursts or excessive gesticulation; it is sometimes in bad taste to 'knock them in the aisles', and the catch in the voice performed for dramatic effect is nowadays out of place everywhere except in certain provincial theatres. [...]

Certain unconscientious or tired actors neglect sections of their role, concentrating only on emphasizing a number of specific effects or the end of long speeches, in order to win applause.

It would constitute a lack of taste on the part of actors to fall into familiarity, exaggeration or caricature. They must prepare comic effects with care; utter artfully, stressing slightly, the lines intended to provoke laughter; put across the asperities of the dialogue by dint of tact and restraint; they should also laugh in a natural and infectious manner.

CASTING When the decision has been taken to stage a given play, the author casts the parts, including understudies, from within the company. [. . .]

Authors have the final say in casting. They have the right to prevent their play being performed by actors of whom they have not approved. [. . .]

Actors cannot presume to judge their personal merit or the value of the work they are called upon to perform by refusing a part, on the grounds that it is beneath their talent. The exception is that if they are assigned a certain type of role in their contract and the part in which they are cast does not come into the category.[1] [. . .]

In the provinces, actors engaged to play a specific type of part have the right to demand certain roles which must be reserved for them.

REHEARSALS [. . .] The first rehearsals take place in the greenroom or the public foyer. Their main purpose is to determine the positions the actors must take up, their moves, their entrances and exits. [. . .]

Duty rosters calling actors for rehearsals, readings and performances are sent, in the evening, to their dressing-rooms if they are working or to their home the following morning if they are not.

The notice posted each evening in the greenroom will give all the information relating to their duties, and actors will have to adhere to that.

Rehearsals always begin a quarter of an hour after the time indicated on the roster or on the notice, 'on the hour for quarter past'.

No one may be present at the rehearsals of a play without the consent of both the author and the director. [. . .]

The day after a first performance, the author has the right to ask for an extra rehearsal. [. . .]

DRESS-REHEARSALS [. . .] Nowadays, dress-rehearsals are really 'first nights', put on for the benefit of drama critics giving them twenty-four hours to write their reviews. [. . .]

However, dress-rehearsals must only be considered as rehearsals, and are not in the nature of public performance.

[1] i.e. the 'category of types' which falls outside their 'emploi': see 11.

2(a)   An actor's contract in a private boulevard theatre, 1896

Standard contract offered to actors working at the Théâtre de l'Ambigu-Comique[1] in 1896. Bibliothèque de l'Arsenal (Rt 1214)[2]

Art. 1. – In order to ensure the smooth running of the theatre, every Artiste or employee, whatever his duty, is bound:

1. To live not more than one kilometre away from the Theatre (*if the Theatre were to suffer from a breach of this clause,* even if such a breach had been agreed, *the Director will have the absolute right to withdraw permission and to impose the clause rigorously*). Such an agreement with the Director can in no way liberate the Artiste from such obligations [. . .] even in the case of a road or rail accident, nor from any other clauses regarding hours of attendance;

2. Never to leave Paris, even on rest days, without the Director's written permission;

3. To attend all rehearsals [. . .] at the appointed time, even after a performance, if necessary;

4. To be at the Theatre at least half an hour before each performance, even if he is not due to perform in the advertised programme, in order to allow the Management to implement a change at short notice;

5. To make do with the lighting and heating, as provided by the Theatre, in the dressing-room or *seat in a dressing-room* allocated to dress, such room or seat being liable to change for each new production;

6. To contribute, in all circumstances, and in the most complete and absolute manner, by *any* means, gifts, or talents appreciated by the Director, to the general good of the enterprise and the particular demands of the performance; at the Director's command, to compose his physiognomy (make-up and costume) with great care according to the age and status of the character he is entrusted to perform;

7. Not to delay the performance of a play, due to lack of memory, having had time to learn fifty lines a day, not counting cue lines, under penalty of deduction of a month's wages for every additional day of delay;

8. To submit himself to all the imperatives of the *mise en scène,* and all special effects [. . .];

9. To take part, alone or with the company, by day or night, even outside Paris, in costume, evening or city dress, in every public or private ceremony, such as fêtes, balls, galas, charity sales, club or private performances, or on any other stage, without asking for any extra payment or compensation, beyond travelling and carriage costs;

10. To consent that all his parts, in repertoire or not, be given by the Management to whomsoever it pleases, as understudies or shared roles, if it is deemed to be advantageous to the enterprise; and to resume the said parts whenever the Management commands;

11. Never to make use of his talents as Artiste, Teacher or Director [*metteur en scène*] on any other Stage, paid or unpaid, and never to appear in any ordinary, special or benefit performance, without the Director's written authorization; [. . .]

13. To provide all contemporary costumes (city dress) with all accessories, i.e.

gloves, shoes, hats, as well as jewels, canes, umbrellas, etc., *without any exception,* and without requesting any item from the wardrobe; [...]

15. To wear, without the right to refuse under any pretext, any historical attire or fancy costume provided by the Management. [...]

Art. 2. [...]

1. Any artiste, ill or unable to perform, must, whatever the length of his illness, inform the Stage Manager of his state of health before noon. Failing that, the Management will consider him as capable of performing [...] and he will be liable for all fines and deductions applied to the Artiste able to work normally;

2. In the case of illness, the Artiste will only be officially relieved from duty when the *Theatre's own physician* has certified that the said Artiste is genuinely incapable of working. No other doctor's opinion will be accepted. If not deemed ill by the Theatre's physician, the Artiste will forfeit his entire month's salary. In any case his wages will be suspended for each day of illness, and if he should be ill for more than a week [...] or if repeated absence should deprive the Theatre of his services for more than two weeks in any one year, his contract can be instantly terminated, by decision of the Director, without any compensation. [...]

Art. 3.

1. If the Artiste is due leave, the Director may subtract from the said leave any period of time, however short, during which the Artiste, either deliberately, or through accident, military service or illness, had been unable to work. [...]

3. If, through unforeseen circumstances (fire, riots, etc., etc.), the Theatre should close, the Artiste acknowledges that he will not be paid [...] and that he will not be free to sign a long-term contract with another Theatre until six months after the aforementioned closure.

Art. 4.

1. The 'theatre year' starts on 1 September and ends on 31 August the following year. The 'performing year'[3] starts on the opening day of the theatre season[4] and ends on the day of the annual closure, which can occur any time after 15 May; but it can be indefinitely postponed due to the weather or a running success. It can even be cancelled.

2. Consequently contracts are signed for the 'performing year': i.e. the Director guarantees a *minimum* of eight months' employment to the Artiste. Seven of these

eight months are full months (*October to April*) and will be paid as laid down in the contract, as *Winter* [or full] *wages*. The other months, known as *Summer wages*, will be reduced by 20 to 30 per cent, as well as the *feux*.[5] The wages, guaranteed by the Director, for the second fortnight in September and the first fortnight in May, complete the guarantee of a minimum of eight months' employment. [...]

No further fees are due for matinées, except *feux* as agreed in the contract. [...]

4. As the Director guarantees eight months' employment per annum, he is free, whenever he decides, to suspend the contract for four months, in a single or in several periods, summer closure included, without, of course, paying any wages or compensation during such time. [...]

6. Finally, the Artiste agrees to rehearse, without wages, for at least two weeks, and at most one month, before the opening of a season. [...]

If, through illness, the Artiste should be unable to perform, he will repay whatever he would have received for the rehearsals.

Art. 5.

Any engagement can be cancelled *by decision of the Director alone*, and without any compensation to the Artiste who, hereby, renounces any claim, first (as is the custom) at the end of each theatrical year, then at any other time:

1. If the public showed disapproval of the Artiste;
2. In the event of pregnancy;
3. If the Management considers that the Artiste's talent is declining, or if he becomes unable to play the parts in which he is usually cast (lack of memory, aphonia, deafness, aphasia, obesity not present at the moment of engagement, etc.);
4. If more than four fines had to be levied in a single month;
5. If he came to the Theatre in a state of drunkenness. [...]

Art. 10.

1. Fines. – In fairness to the Artistes, fixed-rate fines have been abolished and replaced by a percentage of each Artiste's *monthly wages*:
2. **During rehearsals:**
Quarter of an hour late: $\frac{1}{4}$ per cent
Half an hour: $\frac{1}{2}$ per cent
Three quarters of an hour: 1 per cent
One hour: 2 per cent

Full rehearsal: 5 per cent

For each scene missed during a rehearsal: 1 per cent

[...]

Fines are doubled and trebled for afternoon and evening dress-rehearsals, respectively.

During performances: To have caused delay during an interval or a quick scene-change: 1 per cent per additional minute.

To have delayed the start of the performance: 2 per cent per minute, without prejudice to the damages to the Director and for which the latecomer is obviously responsible. [...]

4. For wilful damage or unauthorized alterations to costumes, additions to or cuts in the play text, changes to the *mise en scène*, for refusing an encore, for refusing to take a bow,[6] for giggling or chatting on stage, for signalling to spectators, for indecent or untoward gestures, or generally for causing any kind of disturbance, according to the gravity of the offence and at the sole discretion of the Director: from 1 to 10 per cent.[7]

---

[1] See p. 46, note 1.

[2] Individual contracts are hard to come by, but the Comédie-Française has in its archives a contract signed on 19 August 1900 between Jules Claretie, the General Administrator, and a modest actress, Jeannine Fayolle (born 17 July 1872). The various clauses of the contract are as draconian as in the above document, although the language is slightly less harsh. Article VII guarantees that 'the General Administrator of the Comédie-Française [will pay], out of the Theatre's treasury, the sum of *eighteen hundred francs* for each year in which this present engagement remains in force, payable in twelve monthly instalments'. This is a very low salary (for comparison, see 7(a)).

[3] 'L'Exercise théâtral': the management makes a clear distinction between 'the "calendar" year' (1 September to 31 August) and the 'contractual time' during which the theatre more or less guarantees the payment of wages.

[4] i.e. on the night of the first performance.

[5] The *'feux'* (literally 'the fires') are extra payments per performance negotiated on a personal basis between actor and management for each appearance on stage. This system was introduced at the Comédie-Française on 28 September 1682. The allowance was originally meant to cover costs of candles and firewood for the dressing-room. In 1885 the level of *'feux'* ranged from 5 to 100 francs. But many actors received only the basic wage agreed by contract.

[6] i.e. during the performance, at the end of a monologue or after an exit. After the last word of the monologue the actor would step forward and take a bow or he would return if his exit was accompanied by applause. In either case the scene could be repeated for the delight of the spectators.

[7] Pougin writes in his dictionary that provincial actors were forced to sign contracts that were even more 'draconian', *Dictionnaire historique et pittoresque du théâtre et des arts qui s'y rattachent* (Paris: Firmin-Didot, 1985), pp. 331–3. See 4(a), 42(n) to 42(q) and 202.

2(b)   Honoré Daumier's caricature: 'A stage-manager fines an actor', 1856

Le Charivari, 15 December 1856

CROQUIS DRAMATIQUES

THE STAGE-MANAGER: Vous avez beau jouer les rois, je ne vous en flanque pas moins à l'amende d'un franc cinquante, pour avoir manqué votre entrée.
(King or no king, you're fined one franc fifty for missing your entrance.)

3   Actors and their costumes, 1881

Archives of the Comédie-Française

Until the beginning of the twentieth century, and in some theatres until the 1950s, actors were responsible for providing their own costumes, unless they were acting in a 'period' or 'fantastic' play (see 2(a) and 4). The Comédie-Française was, in fact, very generous in giving financial assistance to its actresses, but, even so, the situation was most unsatisfactory and grossly unfair. It also led to abuse since, according to their own wealth or – more often – to the generosity of their male 'admirers', actresses dressed up to impress the audience, regardless of the part they had to perform. Outside Paris it was expected that each actor possess a complete wardrobe of historical costumes (antique, medieval, Renaissance, Louis XIII to Louis XVI, romantic and, of course, modern), together with all 'accessories'.

Rules governing costumes and town toilettes for lady artistes

As from 1 March 1881

The town toilettes which the lady artistes of the Comédie-Française will be authorized to have made by outside dressmakers will be divided into four categories each with its own price range, namely:

1. Ball gowns and evening toilettes, in satin or in Flemish silk with embroidery, lace, flowers, etc ... must not exceed 1,000 or 1,200 [francs].[1]

2. Rich town toilettes, in velvet or Flemish silk, with matching overcoat or cloak will be reimbursed from 800 to 1,000.

3. Afternoon dresses, in cashmere or light Flemish silk, with – if required – overcoat or cloak: 500 to 700.

4. Lastly, ordinary outfits or travelling suits in wool, cloth, linen or any such fabric must not exceed 300 to 500, according to the material.

These prices include all accessories which dressmakers traditionally supply, i.e. muslin underskirts, matching material for shoes, corsage, etc ...

Town hats must not exceed 80 to 100 francs for the 2nd category, 40 for the 3rd, or 50 to 70 for the 4th category.

Ankle boots made of material matching the toilette will be reimbursed from 24 to 26. Shoes in satin or Flemish silk, with wooden heels, must not exceed 22 to 24.

Boots made of black canvas or black kid are the actresses' own responsibility.

The General Manager will issue an order form specifying the category of costume to be ordered and bills will only be refunded if they comply with the said order form.

[1] In other words, the cost of an evening gown could exceed the annual wages of a lesser-paid actor.

4(a)   Actors and agents, 1891

Auguste Germain, *Les Dessous du théâtre – Les Agences dramatiques et lyriques* (Paris: Perrin, 1891), pp. 8–19

For engagements in the provinces, except in special cases, the theatrical agent takes 2.5 per cent of the artistes' salaries. For Paris and abroad, he takes 5 per cent. But don't think that this percentage of the artistes' salaries is deducted at the end of the month or season. No, the agent deducts his fees *at the outset.* Let me explain how the system works. Usually, in the provinces or abroad, the season is considered to be seven months long. Suppose, therefore, that an artiste is engaged in Italy and is to be paid 500 francs a month. The agent takes his commission on the seven-month period when the contract is signed. So the artiste who receives his first month in advance – i.e. 500 francs – is forced to pay up $25 \times 7 = 175$ francs. He's got 325 francs left to buy the required clothing and to meet his numerous initial expenses.

If the artiste is successful in the town he is sent to, he will earn a decent living. But we shall see how some people want to make him fail and how it is in the agent's interest to get as many unsuccessful artistes as he can.[1] [...]

[Another trick] requires the agent to make an agreement with the director for whom the artiste is going to work. I hasten to add that not all directors enter into such agreements. Unfortunately there are some who don't refuse.

An agent says to a singer: 'I've got a job for you in some provincial town. Through me, you'll get 800 francs. Are you interested?' The artiste accepts, pays the commission and off she goes. At the end of the first month, she happens to be remarkably successful. Her *'débuts'*[2] have been well received by the local audience. The newspapers have praised her. Encouraged by all this adulation, she considers herself securely established and takes her season for granted when the director sends for her. Then the following little comedy unfolds:

—'Well, my dear director,' enquires the artiste, 'are you happy with me?' The director makes a vague gesture, shakes his head, and purses his lips.

—'Happy? You ask me if I'm happy? Aren't you pushing it a bit?' The singer's enthusiastic face turns gloomy. What? She got cheers, flowers, rave reviews; everyone in the company agrees that her début was superb and the director's not happy?

—'Well, my dear child,' he goes on, 'don't get carried away; you've only been here a month!'

—'Yes, but the first month's the hardest.'

—'What do you know about it?'

—'Well, in the provinces, the three statutory débuts are the most difficult. The rest is plain sailing.'

The director is still shaking his head and pursing his lips; he assumes his most serious expression and says in a hollow voice:

—'I repeat, don't get carried away. You've been successful. Good! But what does the future hold? God only knows, and we don't even know that for sure. Do you know what I was thinking as you came in?' Bewildered, the singer listens on ...

—'I was thinking that the theatre can't afford your salary. The season won't be as good as I had hoped. Times are hard and so is the audience ... I offered you 800 francs, I can't keep you at this rate ... Just think: if you're a failure in the play I'm putting on for you next month, I shall be completely ruined. I'm offering 400 francs to keep you. Is that settled?' [...]

What could she do if she refuses the offer? Go back to Paris, look for a new contract? The season has already started, all the jobs have gone. No matter what the director says, she has been successful here. Who knows if in another town she would be as lucky? She must accept the wage cut and go on singing. She gets poorer while the director and the agent, who got his commission on 800 francs,[3] get richer. But our latter-day Pontius Pilates don't give a damn... [...]

[1] There follows an anecdote about an actress who fell ill before taking up her employment. The director of the theatre claimed back the 500 francs deposit, out of which only 375 francs were left. The agent kept the 175 francs commission and the artist's wardrobe was seized so that the director could claw back the missing 175 francs.

[2] On joining a provincial company a new actor had to undergo three 'trial' performances (débuts). If the spectators protested, booed or whistled (which they did with gusto if they did not like the actor) or if the reviews were hostile, the contract would be null and void.

[3] i.e. a commission of 2.5 per cent on 800 francs over seven months which was paid when the contract was signed.

4(b)   Daumier: 'An artist's engagement', 1845

Honoré Daumier's caricature was published in *Le Charivari*, 29 September 1845: 'Un engagement d'artiste'

So, you'd like a job in my theatre ... but that's wonderful, my dear, ... as you're so pretty, it'll only be twelve hundred francs ... which you can pay me each year without fail ...

—Agreed ... but on condition that I'll never get a pay rise ...

5(a)   The 'claque', or hired applauders, 1900

La Gazette des Tribunaux. Theatre Archives, Bibliothèque historique de la Ville de Paris

A major feature of French theatre in the nineteenth century was the 'claque', or hired applauders, whose business it was to ensure the success of a show or of a particular actor or actress (rival 'claques' were sometimes a problem). Generally the 'chef de claque', or 'cheer leader' would come to an arrangement with the theatre, whereby he would receive a given number of seats for every performance, which would be available for him to resell or dispose of as he thought fit, provided that the occupants of those seats would provide suitable applause. This fits into a wider context of tickets which were not sold through the theatre box-office, and which thus avoided taxes (such as the poor tax) or authors' royalties. Many people seem to have had access to such tickets, ranging from the owners of theatres (who often stipulated in the lease that they should have so many tickets for each performance) to the theatre refreshment seller. Theatre managements themselves sometimes resorted to the illegal sale of tickets. In the middle of the century this was a source of constant correspondence between the police authorities and the Minister of the Interior.

In 1892, Lagoanère, director of the Théâtre des Menus-Plaisirs (subsequently the Théâtre Antoine), signed a contract with Bergère, a *chef de claque*, for 1000 performances. The bankruptcy of Lagoanère prevented his honouring the contract, and in 1896 the Commercial Tribunal of the Seine decided in the director's favour on the grounds that the whole idea of the 'claque' was dishonest and immoral. Bergère persisted, and on 5 April 1900, the Court of Appeal overthrew the previous judgement, and condemned Lagoanère to pay the *chef de claque* the 26,800 francs outstanding, plus interest of 6 per cent from the date Bergère originally took his case, as well as legal expenses for the original case and the appeal.

'Considering: that by the contract registered on 26 September 1892, it was agreed between de Lagoanère and Bergère that the latter would subscribe 14 orchestra stalls, 2 dress-circle seats in the centre of the first row and two in the second row, 4 seats in the second gallery[1] and 35 seats in the first row of the gallery[2] for the "claque" service. This agreement was made for a thousand performances at the Théâtre des Menus-Plaisirs, of which de Lagoanère was then director, against a sum of 50,000 francs (50 francs per performance[3]) payable in advance and in instalments;

'Considering: that de Lagoanère gave only 224 performances (and not the agreed 1000); that when he gave up the management of the Théâtre des Menus-Plaisirs, he had received the sum of 38,000 francs from Bergère; that Bergère has claimed the sum of 26,800 francs paid by him without having received in exchange the seats for performances, according to the terms of the agreement mentioned above; that there are grounds to observe that Bergère, at the same time as being responsible for the "claque" at the Théâtre des Menus-Plaisirs, sold theatre tickets, and was fully licensed to carry out this profession; [...]

'Considering: that the first judges were wrong in declaring that the service provided by the "claque" is essentially based on dishonesty and corruption; that expressions of appreciation bought in advance by purveyors of success, hinder or destroy the paying public's freedom to enjoy and appreciate the work; that they disrupt public order and morality; and that the contract in question is null and void because it is illegal, and cannot serve as a basis for claiming repayment of the sums paid by Bergère, the latter not being allowed to profit from his own moral depravity; [...]

'Considering: that, in fact, as far as public order is concerned, it is accepted practice in nearly all the theatres in Paris to have a "claque"; and that the authorities ... responsible for the maintenance of public order, have not expressed any opposition to the organization of this special service [...];

'Considering: that the "claque" cannot be regarded as contrary to public order or damaging to the paying audience's freedom to watch; that in fact ... applause at certain predetermined moments, usually with the aim of giving prominence to a passage to which the audience's attention should be more particularly drawn, in no way harms the audience's free appreciation of the performance; [...]

'That, in addition, it is recognized that for the performers of dramatic works, the "claque" is necessary to help them overcome the stress and difficulties inherent in a public performance; that applause occurring at certain points gives the actors a few moments' indispensable rest when this break in the action cannot have a bad effect or damage the audience's appreciation in any way; [...]

'Considering: that the obligation to carry out the terms of the agreement is to be settled by the payment of damages, should the debtor not fulfil his part; that in this case Lagoanère has not fulfilled the whole of the agreement in question; that he is obliged to pay damages as a consequence of failing to honour an agreement which he had freely and regularly signed; that there are grounds for condemning the aforesaid Lagoanère to pay Bergère the sum of 26,800 francs, with the interest due since the date he took his case, and, this by way of additional damages in compensation for the difficulty in which he placed Bergère by not providing him with the seats which he had agreed to make available to him.'[4]

[1] Unusually, in this theatre, seats in the second circle were known as the 'fauteuils du foyer', presumably because the foyer was at this level.
[2] These seats, priced at one franc at the box-office, represented half the front row of the gallery, applause from the 'gods' obviously being seen as the most important.
[3] The box-office cost of these seats would normally be nearly three times this amount.
[4] Lagoanère was also condemned to pay all costs.

5(b)   The Emperor victim of a silent 'claque', January 1853

On a lighter note, Edmond Got[1] recorded the following anecdote in his diary (entry for 13 January 1853):

A few days ago, a ministerial decree ordered the total abolition of the 'claque' in every state-aided theatre.

It would be a welcome measure if it were possible, given on the one hand the vanity of actors, and on the other their self-interest. At the very least the intention is good. Most of my colleagues are only too happy to declare that the audience needs that extra stimulus and that it provides a necessary rest and break.

But tonight when the Emperor entered his box in the theatre there wasn't a single cheer from the audience.

What a flop, my friends! The 'claque' was promptly re-established.

[1] Edmond Got (1822–1901) was one of the top actors of nineteenth-century French theatre. He chose to spend his entire career at the Comédie-Française, which is why his fame died with him. He was the 'doyen' (dean) of the company from 1873 until his retirement in 1894.

5(c)   Daumier: 'The claqueur', 1842

published in *Le Charivari*, 13 February 1842

'Bloody hell! I'll be sweating it tonight with the new three-act play: the comic wants me to burst out laughing; the heroine wants me to sob; the author wants me to stamp my feet, not forgetting the old dear who wants to be cheered on her entrance . . . quite a job on my hands!'

6(a)   The rule of the usherette in Parisian theatres, 1901

Gustave Bienaymé, *Le Coût de la vie à Paris: Profits, étrennes, pourboires* (Paris: Berger-Levrault, 1901), pp. 11–12

Usherettes – It is usually with an air of resignation that Parisians hand over the small taxation levied on them in theatres or other places of entertainment by usherettes.[1] These women have paid dearly[2] for the right to sell the programme, which they often force upon the spectator, and to receive a gratuity for the cloakroom service or simply for pointing out the seat.

The profits of that industry can be quite high in theatres that are in vogue and where rich patrons, particularly men in gallant company, spend freely. Seclusion in a latticed box is easily bought by the male palm; but in less patronized theatres, where no successful show is drawing the crowds and where usherettes can only count on the stinginess of the regulars, they do not earn much and can make a loss even when the house is fairly full. [. . .]

Provincial and foreign spectators, often ignorant of our way of life, either give far too much for fear of not giving enough, whereas others give the minimum or just flatly refuse.

We have, of course, among us, grumpy spectators determined to add nothing or as little as possible to the cost of their tickets and, above all, those who would be sorry to spoil the gratuity of their complimentary ticket.

On the whole Parisian spectators are aware that 'they buy at the door' the right to consider usherettes as being momentarily in their service and that they have, therefore, the duty to reward them with a coin. They know that before leaving their seat, it will cost 50 centimes, if they are alone or accompanied by one person only; in a box one franc will just do, but two francs will astonish; in a cheaper seat, too far from the stage and too close to the chandelier, one can get away with a copper. [. . .]

The rate has long been steady at 2 per cent, but, in line with the increasing cost of tickets, it has gone up to 5 per cent.

---

[1] The custom has survived to this day, the gratuity being paid before sitting down. Theatre-goers are expected to tip usherettes in all but the subsidized theatres. One is even expected to give one or two francs to the cinema usherette, although seats are never numbered!

[2] Usherettes were not paid employees but private licencees who bought the privilege from the previous incumbent and by payment of a concession to the theatre itself. The amounts varied according to the theatres and to the allocated areas in the theatres.

6(b)   Daumier: 'The usherette', 1864

Le Charivari, 3 February 1864

'Only five seats are taken, sir! There's a spare one … if you lean well forward, you'll catch a glimpse of the stage.'

7(a)   General expenditure at the Comédie-Française, 1880–1897

Comédie-Française Archives, document IVA, 4CF, HP 1894–1898

As stated in the document itself, a large artistic institution like the Comédie-Française is also big business which can only survive with strict accounting. During the seventeen years under consideration, total annual expenditure averaged 2 million francs, and box-office receipts were in the region of 1.9 million. Thanks to the government's grant of 240,000 francs and accrued interest on capital, the theatre made a healthy profit, to be distributed among the *sociétaires*, i.e. the privileged actors who had received tenure and become shareholders of the company. Between 1880 and 1897, the share was never less than 15,000 francs, and reached 42,000 francs in 1889. Such payouts, on top of comfortable basic salaries, meant that the *sociétaires* were very well off. Compared to the lowly paid *pensionnaires* who had to struggle on a basic wage of less than 2,000 francs (see 2(a)), they were indeed extremely rich. (See also 42, 166, 167, 168 and 202.)

[page 1]

Fixed overhead expenses at the Comédie-Française (after deduction of poverty relief contributions,[1] and royalties which vary greatly) amount to an annual average of 1,587,000 francs, i.e. a daily average of 4,347 francs.

> In 1880, the daily average was 3,666.44
> In 1885, ,,   ,,   ,,   ,,   3,724.57
> In 1886, ,,   ,,   ,,   ,,   3,962.57
> In 1890, ,,   ,,   ,,   ,,   4,154.66
> In 1891, ,,   ,,   ,,   ,,   4,481.38
> In 1892, ,,   ,,   ,,   ,,   4,347.00
> In 1893, ,,   ,,   ,,   ,,   4,326.92
> In 1894, ,,   ,,   ,,   ,,   4,357.61
> In 1895, ,,   ,,   ,,   ,,   4,313.05
> In 1896, ,,   ,,   ,,   ,,   4,293.75
> In 1897, ,,   ,,   ,,   ,,   4,524.40

These amounts show that expenses have steadily increased over the past 17 years. They include:

Staff salaries (actors, *sociétaires*,[2] *pensionnaires*,[3] and other employees)	613,000 frs
Pensions for retired *sociétaires*	112,000 frs
Pensions for [retired] *pensionnaires*	16,000 frs

Pensions for [retired] employees   17,000 frs
Annual solidarity fund   18,000 frs
                                         to be carried forward 776,000 frs

[page 2]

                                    Amount carried forward   776,000 frs
Production expenses (lighting, heating, costumes, sets, security
men and firemen, etc.)   811,000 frs
                                              TOTAL   1,587,000 frs

If we add child-welfare contributions and royalties which amount in an average
year:

the former to   174,000 frs
the latter to   233,000 frs
                                                               407,000 frs
Or an annual expenditure budget: 1,994,000 frs

Box-office receipts   1,900,000[4] frs
Grants   240,000 frs
Interest on social fund deposits   60,000 frs
Interest on reserve and annuities   130,000 frs
                                                         336,000 frs profit
From this must be deducted
$\frac{1}{10}$ for the reserve   33,000 frs
$\frac{1}{2}$ share which is usually   7,000 frs   40,000 frs
                                       which leaves 296,000 frs

This puts the share at no more than 15,000 francs because a certain amount must
always be reserved for working capital.

[page 3]

The average expenses during the last 17 years were:

In 1881, 1,727,000 frs
In 1882, 1,854,000 frs
In 1883, 1,717,000 frs
In 1884, 1,666,000 frs
In 1885, 1,811,000 frs

In 1886, 1,874,000 frs
In 1887, 1,891,000 frs
In 1888, 1,756,000 frs
In 1889, 2,124,000 frs*
In 1890, 1,930,000 frs
In 1891, 2,070,000 frs
In 1892, 2,021,000 frs
In 1893, 1,974,600.90 frs
In 1894, 2,043.475.55 frs
In 1895, 2,038,565.90 frs
In 1896, 2,050,812.20 frs
In 1897, 2,119,401.65 frs

* Year of the Exhibition when expenses were considerably increased by royalties
and child-welfare contributions.

[page 4]

This makes it clear that an artistic institution, like any other enterprise having to
rely on fashion, requires strict financial management. The Comédie-Française is,
indeed, a temple, but it is also a factory. Depending on the success of our
productions, the profits are high or low, and the dividend handsome or derisory.
Over the past 18 years the lowest full-share dividend paid out was 15,000 francs
and the highest 42,000 francs (Exhibition year). We have never again reached
such an amount.

Let us suppose that the theatre had been deprived of its subsidy in 1872 and
1873 (years when the share was 15,000 francs). The most fortunate artistes
would have received a 2,000 francs dividend. It is easy to calculate what half-
share or quarter-share *sociétaires* would have got.

It must be stressed that in poor years, the subsidy does not only increase the
sociétaires' profit but it represents also a working capital in itself. It allows the
budget to be more flexible, it gives security to the administration and this makes
artistic management easier. It also encourages the Comédie-Française to put on
new plays which other theatres would not produce.

It must be remembered that the Comédie-Française pays back part of its subsidy
in child welfare.[5]

[1] Known as the 'droits des pauvres', this tax was 11 per cent of the gross box-office receipts at the end
of the nineteenth century. The tax was introduced before the creation of the Comédie-Française.
Under Louis XIV the rate was even higher: one sixth of the receipts. In the seventeenth century, the
tax was paid to the Hôtel-Dieu; in modern times to the Exchequer (mainly used to cover the cost of
looking after orphans in state-run institutions).

² The Comédie-Française, created by Royal Decree in 1680, has retained the administrative structure of Molière's company: each permanent actor (or *sociétaire*) is a shareholder in the company. The smallest remuneration is one twelfth of a share, but *sociétaires* are usually allocated a minimum of a quarter of a share. It is the assembly of all *sociétaires* that decides on the level of remuneration of each member. *Sociétaires* receive a fixed salary, plus the dividend paid out by the share. The number of *shares* has always been, and still is, 18, but the number of *sociétaires* is variable (18 in 1872; 22 in 1876; 25 in 1882; 27 in 1894). Presently it stands at around 30.

³ *Pensionnaires* are hired actors, on fixed-term contracts.

⁴ In 1883 ticket prices ranged from 1 to 10 francs. In 1822 the cheapest seat cost 1.80 and the most expensive 6.60.

⁵ To enable readers to compare nineteenth-century prices in a meaningful way, we are reproducing here some basic facts about cost of living and levels of income during the period 1850-1914. France experienced some inflation during the Second Empire (1852-70). Thereafter, prices reached a peak around 1880, followed by a general deflation which continued until the turn of the century. The average prices given here for *c.*1885 are valid (as averages) throughout our period.

Basic expenditure: (from Gustave Bienaymé, *Le Coût de la vie à Paris* (Nancy: Berger-Levrault et Cie, 1897)

[price per kilo, or *c.*2.2 lb]

rice	0.50 franc	potatoes	0.07	fresh vegetables	0.35
fresh fruit	0.50	dried beans	0.30	jam	1.00
sugar	1.00 to 1.35	salt	0.25	coffee	4.00
butter	2.50	cheese	1.20	meat	1.20 to 1.40
fish	0.60 to 0.70	bread	0.87	eggs	0.08 each
oysters	0.09 each			litre of good wine	0.55

According to Bienaymé the average annual expenditure on food for an adult male would have been, in Paris, just short of 600 francs. The figure includes: bread, meat, fish, butter, cheese, fruit and vegetables; but also wine, beer, cider and spirits which alone came to 250 francs.

Cost of some non-food items:

daily newspaper	0.15	illustrated dictionary	3.90 (hard cover)
gent's haircut	0.50		
and shave	0.25		

Theatre tickets 1.00 to 15.00 francs

Accommodation: In Paris, basic 'working-class' accommodation would cost around 200 francs per annum. Small flats with an annual rent of 300 francs would already attract 'middle-class' tenants.

Income: (from Emile Chevallier, *Les Salaires au XIXᵉ siècle* (Paris: Arthur Rousseau, 1887))

In the 1880s the daily average working day was 12 hours long (a 10-hour day was considered to be 'short').

In Paris, in 1881, the average daily salary for a trained workman, working 12 hours, not living on his employer's premises and not fed by him, was 5.66 francs (or a maximum of 1,700 francs per annum for 300 working days). For the same job a provincial workman would have earned a daily average of 3.37 francs (annual equivalent: 1,000 francs).

The highest daily wage of 10 francs was earned by jewellers.

According to Chevalier, in 1885 'a daily salary of 3 to 4 francs guarantees a decent standard of living, even in Paris'.

In other words, even the cheapest theatre tickets were very expensive by today's standards.

7(b)   Detailed running costs at the Comédie-Française for 1882

Arthur Pougin, *Dictionnaire historique et pittoresque du théâtre et des arts qui s'y rattachent* (Paris: Firmin-Didot, 1885; reprinted 1985). Article: Frais

Administration	63,216.60
Hired actors	164,371.55
Front-of-house employees	38,000
Stage-hands	27,000
Workshops employees	35,989.80
Stage-managers, machinists	40,354.50
Pensions for the *sociétaires*	85,649.65
Pensions for actors and actresses	17,800
Pensions for employees	11,477.50
Food aid[1]	20,560.20
Extras and chorus members	25,086.85
Extraordinary stage expenses	3,843.25
Appearance fees and supplementary payments	38,600
Literary commissions, fees, *ex gratia* payments	25,000
Administrative reserve fund	36,400
Tax and licence	4,688.55
Insurances	11,657.60
Posters and programmes	19,553
Lighting	89,092.85
Heating	13,000
Costumes, refunds of dressmaking expenses	142,003
Poor tax	186,954.70
Playwrights' royalties	268,621.80
Guard	8,161
Firemen	12,181.90
Sets and properties (painting)	33,292.45
Wood, canvas, ropes, ironmongery (sets)	15,016.30
Auditorium: carpet and seats	7,285.35
Printing	5,744.50
Office supplies	2,162.40
Archives, libraries, gallery, portraits	875.35
Miscellaneous supplies and expenses	19,119.80
Building upkeep, cleaning	23,108.55
Stage carpet and furniture	24,047.15
Dividends distributed to the *sociétaires*	199,207.65
Reserve for the ministry	48,000

Reserve for repairs	10,000
Benefit performance	22,000
Matinées	24,609.50
Funeral costs	800.75
Sarah Bernhardt affair	81.69
Subscription to the Barrière[2] Monument	500
Top-up payment for the 3 per cent annuity	6,876.15
Total	1,853,906.79

representing a 'fixed cost' average of 4,878.70 francs per performance (there were 380 performances in the year, including the matinées).

---

[1] Throughout its history the Comédie-Française has enjoyed the reputation of a very caring 'mutual society' looking after all the workers, sometimes long after retirement. The *sociétaires*, generally, lived on generous pensions, but less well-off workers (stage-hands, cleaners, and so on) did, on occasion, receive *ex gratia* payments after retirement, and low-paid workers were given 'food aid', either in cash or kind. In some wretched cases, the Comédie had to help with funeral costs.

[2] Théodore Barrière (1823–77), a minor dramatist who cashed in on the dubious taste of his contemporaries for 'studies of courtesans' in the wake of the success of *The Lady of the Camellias* with his *Les Filles de marbre* (The Marmoreal Girls, 1853).

8   Salaries: a wage sheet, Ambigu-Comique, 1862

Paris, Archives Nationales F21 1050

The accounts of a theatre give a useful picture of the personnel and their functions, as well as relative monthly salaries. The wage sheet is for the Ambigu-Comique[1] in May 1862.

Salaries for the administration

		francs
M. Edmond	accountant	300
M. Albert	stage-manager	333.30
M. Monet	assistant stage-manager	166.65
M. Debreuil	boilerman[2]	150
M. Langlois	clerk	83.35
M. Laitier	office messenger	83.35
M. Auguste	properties	85
M. Bondeville	armour	50
Mme Ferret	cleaner	110
Mme Janvelle	laundry	110
MM. Cheret and Chanet	scenery	1,666.70
M. Bertucchee (*sic*)	costumes	533.35

M. Panelle	'machiniste'[3]	1,200
Mme Hanquez	wardrobe	225
M. Lesage	upholsterer	50
M. Mercier	shoemaker	50
M. Moreau	'garçon de théâtre'[4]	60
M. Princet[5]	hire of horses	70
M. Thétiot	caretaker	60
M. Thomas	hairdresser	100
M. Raynaldi	floor polisher	40
M. Verdier	water carrier	10
M. Masson	prompter	90

Various salaries

Orchestra:

| M. Alex. Artus | conductor | 300 |
| The Orchestra[6] | | 990 |

Box-office:

| M. Savigny | cashier (*contrôleur en chef*) | 175 |
| Box-office employees | | 425 |

Chorus:

| M. Nerant | director of the chorus and for the members of the chorus | 587.50 |

Salaries for the artistes

M. Berret	100
Mme Blanchard	100
M. Bondois	953.35
M. Bosquette	125
M. Castellano	560
M. Clèves	100
M. Desormes	100
Mlle Jane Essler	601.65
M. Faille	166.65
M. Hosten	125
Mme Gilbert	125
Mme Eudoxie Laurent	200
Mme Laurent	200

Mlle Mêa	129.15
M. Machanette	112.50
M. Metreme	208.30
M. Moretteau	100
M. Nérant	83.35
M. Omer	166.65
M. Regnier	120
Mlle Marie Lambert	112.50
Mlle Tissier	60
M. Dornay	100[7]

---

[1] Built in 1769 the Théâtre de l'Ambigu was one of the most famous theatres of the 'boulevard du crime' and one of the most successful. In 1845 Dumas's *Three Musketeers* broke all box-office records; in 1879 Zola's *L'Assommoir* was rapturously received. The theatre was less successful in our century and property speculation demolished it in 1965.

[2] The boilerman was not employed in the summer.

[3] The term today implies a stage-hand – in fact it means a deviser of machines and trick effects much appreciated in melodrama theatres.

[4] Combination of odd-job man and messenger boy.

[5] In 1858 Princet was listed as 'carrier'.

[6] This particular wage sheet does not indicate how many musicians were involved, but an 1848 account sheet for the same theatre lists 16 players.

[7] It is interesting to compare this pay-roll with that of a small suburban theatre: Belleville (July, 1862). At Belleville there were 11 actors listed, with a monthly salary ranging between 10 francs and 55 francs (the main actors of the troupe receiving between 30 and 40 francs per month, approximately the same as the daily wage of a female manual worker). Administration and stage staff numbered a dozen, and there were four box-office employees. The conductor received 580 francs (presumably he was responsible for payment of musicians). There were also some additional fees for outside performers.

In neither case are stage-hands mentioned, and one wonders who actually paid them.

II Censorship

9 Imperial decree granting freedom to French theatre, 1864

Bulletin des lois, vol. XXIII, pp. 52ff., Hôtel de Ville, Paris

From the late seventeenth until the mid-eighteenth century, the number of theatres in Paris was limited by a system of patents similar to that operating in London. The imperial decree of 6 January 1864 establishing the freedom of the theatres is thus directly comparable to the English Act of 1843. In 1807 Napoleon had tightened up the situation of patent theatres, whose monopolies had been severely eroded since the late eighteenth century. In addition to the four subsidized theatres (Comédie-Française, Odéon, Opéra and Opéra-Comique), four secondary theatres were allowed (with particular specification as to the dramatic genres permitted), and the Cirque Olympique, which presented equestrian entertainments of an increasingly dramatic nature. The Gaîté and the Ambigu-Comique were officially designated the home of the melodrama, whereas the Variétés and the Vaudeville became that of the lighter genres. The patent to manage a theatre was allocated to an individual for a certain period and, theoretically at least, was not tied to a particular building. Further patents were issued as the century progressed and by 1864 the concept of restrictive patents had become obsolete. However, the change in the law did result in the construction of a number of theatres in Paris in the later years of the century, and generic distinctions according to theatre became less and less obvious.

Declaration of the freedom of the theatres, 6 January 1864

Art. 1. Any individual may build and exploit a theatre, provided he make a declaration to our Minister for the Arts, to the Parisian police authority,[1] and to the relevant provincial authorities. Theatres which appear particularly worth encouraging may be subsidized either by the State or local authorities.

Art. 2. Theatre managers must conform to all ordinances, decrees and rulings for everything to do with order, safety and public health. The existing laws on policing and closing of theatres will continue to operate, as will the percentage levied for the benefit of the poor and hospitals.

Art. 3. According to the terms of the decree of 30 December 1852, every dramatic work, before being performed, according to the terms of the decree, will have to be examined and authorized by the Minister of our Household and of the Arts, for the theatres of Paris, and by the Prefects for the theatres of the *départements*. This authorization can always be withheld for reasons of public order. [...]

Art. 5. Theatres with child actors continue to be forbidden.

Art. 6. Sideshows, puppet shows and cafés known as *cafés chantants*, *cafés concerts* and other similar establishments will remain subject to the laws currently in force. [...]

Art. 7. Existing theatre managements, with the exception of the subsidized theatres, are and remain freed, as far as the stage is concerned, from all clauses and conditions on their schedule in so far as such clauses and conditions are contrary to the present decree. [...]

6 July 1864

---

[1] Préfecture de Police, Paris.

10   Theatre censorship and Dumas *fils's Lady of the Camellias*, 1851

Anon., *La Censure sous Napoléon III*, and an interview with Edmond de Goncourt,[1] Paris, Albert Savine, éditeur, 1892 (Bibliothèque de l'Arsenal)

Napoleon I instituted official theatre censorship in France, and with one or two breaks (notably in 1830), it remained in place until the fall of the Second Empire. The system was a preventative one which required that all manuscripts of plays be submitted to a group of censors, whose recommendations would then be passed on to the Minister of the Interior. Occasionally the performance of a play could give offence and the play might have to be taken off (this happened in the case of Musset's *Le Chandelier* at the Comédie-Française in 1850), but theatre managers operated a sort of self-censorship to avoid this expensive risk. Generally the censors watched for political references (criticisms of the government or heads of friendly governments) and for anything that might undermine the basic principles of bourgeois sexual morality (notably the 'family'). Alexander Dumas *fils's La Dame aux camélias* (The Lady of the Camellias) was submitted three times to the censors in 1851 and was rejected three times. When it was eventually performed on 2 February 1852, after Napoleon III had appointed a new Minister of the Interior, it aroused a considerable storm. The document is particularly interesting in that it demonstrates clearly the hypocritical double standards of the censors.

First report, dated 28 August 1851, on *La Dame aux camélias*, a drama in five acts and six scenes, Théâtre du Vaudeville.

The play puts on the stage the hectic, unrestrained and shameless life of courtesans who are prepared to sacrifice everything, including their health, to the intoxications of pleasure, luxury and vanity; women who sometimes, when they are sated, find a love which will lead them to extremes of devotion and self-denial.

Such a woman is Marguerite, known as The Lady of the Camellias, because this unscented flower is the only one she likes and wears. Since her humble beginnings as a seamstress she has managed to acquire an old duke as her protector and, as her official lover, a wealthy count whose generosity each year is to the tune of 50,000 francs (without counting presents from other parties). She spends this all the more recklessly because she believes she has an unknown and incurable disease and wishes her life to be *short and enjoyable.*

During a party at which she receives her most intimate gentlemen friends in her boudoir, a new worshipper is introduced. He is Armand Duval, son of a senior tax official, who is overwhelmed with a burning passion for her. His reserve, his blushes and his modesty are an immediate source of mockery for the lady of the house and her joyous crew. But soon, with the first steps of a 'schottische', Marguerite stops dancing in a fit of coughing and her handkerchief becomes red with blood. Nothing is wrong. She is used to it, and when she asks her friends to leave her alone, they stroll nonchalantly into the salon *to light a cigarette.* But Armand, pale with fear and emotion, is alarmed and stays with her. Tenderly he tries to make her aware of the dangers of the excessive life she leads, begging her to give it up and receive proper medical attention, and offering to look after her like a brother and to cure her. At first the astonished Marguerite can only respond to his devotion and to the confession of ardent love *by asking him to leave and save himself from her.* He is too young and sensitive to live in a world like hers. With his kind heart he needs to be loved, and she, *thank God! has never loved anyone.* These words exalt Armand even more, and Marguerite, out of a kind of pity, ends by telling him *to come and see her and not despair too much.* This is not enough for him – let him ask what he *does* want and *make up his own programme.* What he wants *is for her to dismiss everyone and remain alone with him! 'This evening – no, it isn't possible',* but she gives him a flower from her bouquet – *he is to bring it back to her in twenty-four hours, at midnight when it has wilted, but he must be good and obedient.* Armand promises to do as she asks, and departs, drunk with hope and happiness. Marguerite then thinks she will join her friends, but when she opens the salon door she finds a note on the threshold, with the words *Good Night!* They have heard everything, guessed everything, and have left. *So be it! no one is going to say they made a mistake.* So she orders her maid to call back M. Duval.

After four days, when Armand *has returned each evening at midnight, only to leave in the morning at the time when people one loves, and receives at midnight, leave,* Marguerite asks her lover to leave her free on the fifth night. But Armand, *mad with love and already as jealous as a tiger,* suspects that she is expecting someone. *She says not,* but she is tired and *one can't live it up every day, or rather night. Promise me you're not expecting anyone. I swear that I love you and only you – isn't that enough?* Armand leaves unwillingly and the count, *whom she also thought she loved,* replaces him. Marguerite has dreamt of going and spending two or three months in the country alone with Armand. She has already asked the old duke for 6,000 francs, and he has sent her the money. She needs another 15,000 francs and, as the count is rather short of ready money at the moment, she asks him to let her have a draft for 18,000 francs. At this very moment a letter is brought in from Armand. On his way out he noticed the count go in to Marguerite and dismiss his carriage. He asks her to forgive his one offence – that he does not have an income of 100,000 francs, and announces that he is leaving Paris immediately. *Here's a piece of good news, my dear Julien – this letter has saved you 18,000 francs. I'd fallen in love and that was the sum I was going to make you pay, my poor count, so as to be able to lead a quieter life. With the other one? Yes. Let's go and have supper. I need to go out.*

However, Armand has not gone. In his despair he has rushed to a friend of Marguerite living in the same house. He wants to see his faithless mistress again. But this friend, who is afraid that there may be trouble with the count, sends a message to Marguerite that she wishes to speak to her immediately. The latter, who is still at the door, waiting for a pelisse to keep her warm, comes up and, upon learning that Armand is there, sends a message down to the count that she is unwell and dismisses him. Armand appears and throws himself at her feet. She reminds him that: *She is not her own mistress, that she hasn't a sou, and that she spends 100,000 francs a year. One must accept people as they are and understand their position. 'I am a woman, I'm pretty, I'm good company. You are an intelligent young man. Take from me what is good, leave what is bad, and don't bother about the rest. I had dreamt of spending two months in the country with you, but in order to make that dream reality I had need of that man. At the end of that time, which would have been enough to calm and even exhaust our great passion, we would have come back to Paris, shaken hands, and converted the remains of our love into good friendship. That humiliates you. You have a noble heart. Let's not talk about it any more. You have been my lover for four days. Send me a piece of jewellery and that will be that.'*

But Armand listens only to his passion. He begs and entreats her, and Marguerite, overcome and transformed, finally gives in, exclaiming: *Let's not think or argue any more. We're young, we're in love – let's go ahead and follow our love wherever it may lead us.*

The two lovers have spent two months at Bougival in a state of ever-increasing bliss. But the old duke and the count have ceased to provide money, and Marguerite, who does not want to ask Armand for it, has been able to cover the expense only by selling her horses, carriage, shawls and jewels. Moreover, her creditors, no longer having the count and the duke as guarantors, have demanded payment, seized the furniture in Paris and are about to sell it.

In addition, Armand's father has cut off his allowance. Marguerite is preparing to dispose of her magnificent furniture at a ridiculously low price and to move with her lover into the cheapest type of accommodation, when M. Duval appears.

First he tries to exert his paternal authority over his son. When he fails, he turns to Marguerite and, finally, by appealing to her love, gets her not only to leave her lover, but also to persuade him she no longer loves him. The wretched woman makes this deplorable sacrifice, and, so as to deprive him of any uncertainty or hope, accepts the offers of one of her richest admirers. But such an effort exhausts her courage and strength. Her disease makes rapid progress – she is dying, and soon does so in the arms of Armand, who has come back to her, more in love than ever. His pardon, at the end, absolves and consoles her.

This report, although extremely incomplete, on the plot and the scandalous details which constitute the play, nonetheless shows just how shocking it is from the point of view of morality and general decency. It is a picture in which the choice of characters and the crudity of the colouring go beyond the furthest limits of what is acceptable on the stage. What makes the subject and the idea of producing it even more shocking, is that it re-creates the life of a recently deceased courtesan, who has already provided a novelist and a clever critic with a book and a biography which have become popular and which explain everything that might not be clear about certain situations or details.

For these reasons, we are all in agreement to propose that the Minister should not allow this play to be performed.[2]

---

[1] In a letter to the Censorship Commission (Commission de censure), Edmond de Goncourt protests against some of the more absurd cuts imposed on his own stage adaptation of *Germinie Lacerteux*, a play set among the Parisian underclass and prostitutes. Even an innocent joke like: 'ce pays sera toujours un pays où le derrière des gens est le premier à s'asseoir' ('this country will always remain a country where the people's behind is the first to hit the seat') had to be cut.

[2] The second report, dated 1 September 1851, and the third, of 1 October, confirmed the terms of the original condemnation despite Dumas's claim that he 'had cut all the passages that gave most offence'.

11   A 'try-out' theatre to beat censorship, 1886

Claude Michu, *L'Abolition de la censure* (Paris: E. Dentu, 1886)

In this substantial, well argued and passionate pamphlet against censorship, Michu puts forward a most original proposal: to create a try-out theatre (Théâtre d'Essai) where new plays would be performed for a limited period, free from all administrative interference. Not only would such a theatre, argues Michu, liberate the theatre but it would give young playwrights the opportunity to learn from the staging of their plays and it would give actors a greater chance of employment as well as an opportunity of escaping from the shackles of typecasting. Needless to say, the proposal came to nothing.

Let us open up a free theatre as one might open up a free market where the first to arrive set out their merchandise without trimmings, and let the public choose.

It may be thought that it would be impossible to find the personnel for a theatre where each play would only be performed four times. Over and above the necessarily numerous actors engaged as a permanent company, we shall offer a multitude of actors employment in *twelve hundred and sixty new acts* to be performed *four times* each, (i.e. five thouand and forty acts per annum in 360 daytime performances and 360 evening performances).

All actors in employment, along with the multitude of unemployed actors languishing in Paris or the provinces, would have the right to enrol at the Théâtre d'Essai, each indicating the type of role they played.[1] The authors would be free to agree matters with these actors and could therefore choose particular artists to perform their plays, without restricting themselves to the regular troupe, from among whom they could always employ one or more individuals. [. . .]

Though it is highly likely that the trial run would be of little use to established authors who would have to submit to it as a legal formality, it is plain that it would be all the more beneficial to inexperienced authors in that the latter might on occasion be exposed to ridicule. Moreover, by attending the trial run, a theatrical manager on the look-out for new material would be able to choose a play with greater certainty than if he simply read it; and he could buy for next to nothing a work which was apparently a failure, and with very few alterations make it into a highly successful play. [. . .]

No more censorship, then; no more crossing out of words. But since 'every society must keep a watchful eye on its morals and institutions', and must oppose anything which might disrupt law and order within it, the government of the Republic would have the legal right to forbid the performance of obscene or libellous plays, for fear that, having had proof of their impact at the Théâtre d'Essai, some theatre manager with a fondness for scandal might want to stage them.

Consequently, the Minister for Arts would designate a certain number of WITNESSES who would be appointed to the Théâtre d'Essai. These WITNESSES would attend, in groups of three, all four performances of each work. After each performance they would produce a very brief report indicating if the dramatic work was well received by the audience or if the audience booed such and such a passage.

Thus we would achieve the protection of all dramatists in absolute equality; a rebirth of the dramatic art, from all points of view, through relative freedom. It would mean a new source of work and profit for the printing industry and the book-selling trade, for all the plays whose performance had been permitted would form a repertoire which would soon be immense.

---

[1] The French term translated here as 'type of role' is *emploi*. Since the seventeenth century, and in some traditional theatres even to this day, every French actor, male or female, was generically cast into a fixed type of role: comic servant, villain, juvenile lead, noble father, king . . ., for actors; comedy maid, juvenile lead, mother, queen . . ., for actresses. See pp. 119, 126 and 429, note 2.

12   Becque on censorship, 1888

Henry Becque, 'La Censure', *Le Figaro*, 17 November 1888. Reprinted in *Querelles littéraires* (Paris, E. Dentu, 1890), pp. 252–60

This is the kind of thing the government says to dramatic authors: 'We haven't changed our views on censorship and we still find it absolutely despicable. We are only retaining it for your sake. You are the most dissolute people on earth, your plays are profoundly revolting, and no one would agree to stage them, if it wasn't for the Censor who authorizes them and gives them his blessing.'

[...] The republican government intends to keep control over the theatre; it intends that every word spoken shall be known in advance and be capable of being suppressed if the need should arise. There, on the stage, it once again becomes authoritarian and conservative through and through. [...]

Our fine dramatic art, so justly admired, for all the qualities it demands and all the talent expended on it, remains superficial. It is productive and unvarying; it is brilliant and limited; it succeeds in cameos and gives up all thought of great paintings. Let us look back over the history of our time, over these last forty years. We have had the Empire and the end of an Empire; we have had the war [the Franco-Prussian war of 1870], the invasion and the Commune; no less than three Republics; all kinds of worlds have collided and all kinds of passions have come out into the open. [...] This body of material has passed us by; from all these events we have not taken the action of a single drama, not one; hundreds of characters have crossed the stage of public life, they surface in novels and chronicles, memoirs and correspondences, but the theatre will be seen to have failed to give them precise features which would have fixed them definitively as types.

If people should say to us that the fault lies with the playwrights themselves, that there was nothing to stop them applying their talent to all these great events, we shall reply that there was everything to stop them: today's censorship, the one that preceded it, centuries of censorship. [...] In order to expound and enclose a set of facts in a dramatic composition it is not enough to reflect upon them for six months or a year; an accumulated store of observations has to be brought to bear. Our faculties of observation are currently directed quite naturally towards subjects which are admissible and which we will be able to make use of... In spite of ourselves, we stick to banal passions, to comic foibles of a trivial kind; or else we dramatize matters of only passing interest, which appear daring but don't seriously alarm anyone.

[...] When M. Zola, with his admirable talent, studies a special class of worker; when he shows us their heart-rending wretchedness, the barbarity by which they are oppressed and the repression which lies in store for them, he is directly involved in democratic and social issues; he is constructing a play, whether good or bad does not concern us here, which the Republic ought to reward, and if the

Republic bans it, what government will allow it? Today, more than a century after the first performance of *Le Mariage de Figaro*, current events prove Beaumarchais right, and playwrights can adopt the words of their great ancestor [. . .]: In the theatre, 'provided that I don't mention the authorities, or religion, politics, morality, or people in power, influential bodies, the Opéra, other shows, or anybody who is somebody, I am free to stage whatever I like, as long as two or three censors have examined my play.'[1] [. . .] But when everyone around me is free, I insist on being free as well. When everyone thinks, speaks and writes what he likes, I want to do likewise. I do not wish to lose what is perhaps the only benefit derived from living in a country which has had a revolution.

[1] Freely adapted from Figaro's famous monologue in Act V of *The Marriage of Figaro* (first performed in 1784, after a long struggle against royal censorship).

III   Spectacular theatre

13(a)   The theatre of Eugène Labiche (1815–1888)

Engraving by Michelet, Musée Carnavalet, Paris, Mœurs PC 09012

Eugène Labiche (1815–88) was arguably the most successful and most original French comic playwright of the nineteenth century. His first comedy, *Monsieur de Coyllin*, was presented at the Théâtre du Palais-Royal in 1838 and Labiche supplied this theatre with tens of highly entertaining and successful plays well into the 1870s.

Labiche's heyday was the Second Empire, and his plays were written for the entertainment of the bourgeoisie of that period. This same bourgeoisie forms the basic subject-matter for all the plays, and is closely observed and constantly caricatured by Labiche in the tradition of Henri Monnier and Honoré Daumier. Labiche's career as a dramatist began in 1838, with his first real success in 1848, *Un jeune homme pressé* (A Young Man in a Hurry), for which he defined *vaudeville* as 'the art of making the girl's father, who first said no, say yes'. *An Italian Straw Hat* (1851) was one of his most popular plays (and survived into the twentieth century with René Clair's classic film). A full-length play, it takes a popular device of farce and melodrama, the chase, but instead of keeping it for the end of the play uses it as a leitmotiv running throughout, as the hapless hero is pursued by an entire wedding party. The play abounds in wickedly accurate observations of the bourgeoisie, and moves at breakneck speed from situation to situation and misunderstanding to misunderstanding.

Le Voyage de Monsieur Perrichon (Monsieur Perrichon's Holiday, 1860) showed a more developed sense of characterization, its hero being the epitome of the Second Empire bourgeois. Much of the action hinges on the simple psychological mechanism that we are much more grateful to those we help than to those who help us. In *Célimare le bien-aimé* (Célimare the Beloved, 1853), a play that seems to anticipate the work of Anouilh, the hero causes consternation to two husbands he has cuckolded when he decides to get married. This theme of the *ménage à trois*, previously thought of more as the subject for a drama, was fully developed by Labiche in one of his last plays, *The Happiest of the Three* (1870), in which the husband is the happiest (and ultimately prefers domestic bliss with the wife's lover rather than the wife). In 1864 Labiche was accepted into the Comédie-Française with his harsh comedy about an egotist, *I*, but this was not one of his more successful pieces. *Three Cheers for Paris* (*La Cagnotte*, 1864) is the *Italian Straw Hat* in a darker vein, bringing a group of provincials to Paris, where they experience a variety of discomforts. Labiche was admitted to the French Academy in 1880 and spent his last years on the estate purchased with the proceeds of his plays.

The engraving pays tribute to Labiche's inventiveness and illustrates his best-known plays.

13(a)

13(b) The public at the Bouffes-Parisiens, late 1850s

Engraving by Bayard, Musée Carnavalet, Paris, Mœurs PC 088/7

A lively caricature of the public in Offenbach's highly successful theatre during the Second Empire. Jacques Offenbach (1819–1900), the master of light operettas during the Second Empire, opened his own theatre, which he lavishly redecorated and renamed Bouffes-Parisiens, on 29 December 1856 with *Ba-ta-clan*, a 'chinoiserie' set to music by Offenbach himself, on a canvas by Ludovic Halévy. The partnership scored further run-away successes with *Orphée aux enfers* (Bouffes-Parisiens, 1858), *La belle Hélène* (Variétés, 1864) and *La Vie parisienne* (1866). Offenbach's greatest 'fan' was the Emperor himself and his music is seen as the very embodiment of the Second Empire frivolous taste.

14   A spectacular play at the Châtelet: Jules Verne's *Michel Strogoff*, 1880

Theatre Archives, Bibliothèque historique de la Ville de Paris

Adaptations of Jules Verne (1828–1905), staged with numerous scenes and breathtaking effects, were highly popular. *Michel Strogoff* was performed at the Châtelet[1] in 1880, in an adaptation by A. d'Ennery (1811–99), one of the most prolific and popular writers of spectacular melodrama in the late nineteenth century. It is worth noting not merely the huge number of extras and horses, but also the use of a moving panorama (a device that had been introduced earlier in the century, which allowed a long scene to unroll progressively on the backcloth) and magic lantern projections.

MICHEL STROGOFF

A spectacular drama in 5 acts and 17 scenes by MM. A. d'Ennery and J. Verne.
Music by M. Alexandre Artus[2] – ballets devised by M. Balbiani
Scenery by MM. Carpezat[3], Bard and Maréchal – Machines and special effects by M. Bertillon[4]
Fireworks by Ruggieri[5]
Armour by M. Ernest Dieudonné – Properties by M. Masse
Stage machinery by Decauville's – Hairdressing by Charles Aimé's
Projections by Molteni's[6]

Dramatis personae

Harry Blount	Marfa Strogoff
Jollivet	Nadia
Ivan Ogareff	Sangarre
Michel Strogoff	The Emir M.
The Grand-Duke	Captain Tartar
The Governor of Moscow	THE POSTMASTER
Vasili Feodor	A Sergeant
Telegraph employee	An aide de camp ...
A traveller. ... M. Rainal	

List of scenes

1. The New Palais
2. Moscow illuminated (grand ballet)
3. The Torchlight Tattoo
4. The Post Relay Station
5. The Telegraph *Isba*
6. The Battlefield of Kolyvan
7. Ivan Ogareff's tent
8. The Emir's camp
9. The Tartar feast
10. The Clearing
11. The Raft
12. The Banks of the Angara ⎫
13. The River of Naphta ⎬ Moving Panorama
14. The Town in Flames ⎭
15. The Grand Duke's Palace
16. and 17. The Franco-Russian alliance

In the second scene

MOSCOW ILLUMINATED

Grand ballet danced by the principal dancers and one hundred ladies of the corps de ballet.

Torchlight tattoo by the horse guard, drummers, pipers and brass band.

In the ninth scene

THE TARTAR FEAST

Grand ballet devised by M. Balbiani – Music by M. Guilhaud

Mlle J. Laurent: star dancer   Mlle L. Mireveau: 1st dancer

Mlles Briant, Paulin, Dumond, Pierra, Gaillard, Bossi, Martelluci, 50 ladies of the corps de ballet and 50 *figurantes* – procession of 250 persons.

In the sixteenth and seventeenth scenes

THE FRANCO-RUSSIAN ALLIANCE

Grand military and allegorical scene, the French and Russian armies.

New music by MM. Gabriel Pares and T.-H. Pares – Russian national anthem and the Marseillaise, sung by a choir of 150, accompanied by 80 musicians, 20 trumpets, 10 drums – 300 characters – 40 horses.

---

[1] Inaugurated in 1862, the Théâtre du Châtelet (built opposite the Théâtre de la Ville, see **15**) specialized, until the end of the century, in huge spectaculars. In the twentieth century it hosted Strauss's *Salomé* (1907), the Ballets Russes (1909–12), Cocteau's *Parade* (1917) ... Presently its programme consists mainly of musical theatre, ballet and concerts.

[2] Artus had been conductor and principal composer for various boulevard theatres, notably the Ambigu-Comique, where the orchestra was an indispensable part of all performances.

[3] Carpezat was the major scene-painter of the later nineteenth century. The nineteenth-century habit of employing a number of scenic artists, each executing a different scene, is well illustrated here.

[4] In the popular theatres of the nineteenth century the designer of machines was highly esteemed, especially in the spectacular melodrama, and was often one of the most highly paid people in the theatre.

[5] The eighteenth-century tradition of pyrotechnics was still important in the late nineteenth-century theatre. Earlier in the century, Ruggieri had written a treatise on pyrotechnics.

[6] It is sometimes forgotten that projections had been used in the nineteenth-century theatre long before Erwin Piscator gave them a new currency in the 1920s.

15   The Sarah-Bernhardt Theatre: a theatre directory entry, 1908

Annuaire des artistes, de l'enseignement dramatique et musical, ed. Emile Risacher (Paris: A. Maréchal, 1908)

These directories, despite being obviously intended for publicity, are useful in any comparative study of theatres, repertoires, seat prices and general artistic policy. They are also useful to show modifications in the interior seating arrangements.

The 1860s saw the building of four 'municipal' theatres in Paris: the Châtelet (1862), the Gaîté (1862), the Lyrique (1862) and the Vaudeville (1869). The first three replaced theatres of the Boulevard du Temple, demolished to make way for the Place de la République, and the Vaudeville moved to the Chaussée d'Antin from the Place de la Bourse in 1869 to make way for the rue du 4-Septembre.

The Théâtre Lyrique, built by the architect Davioud, looking across the Place du Châtelet to the slightly larger, but very similar Châtelet Theatre, changed its name several times (Théâtre Lyrique-Dramatique, Historique, des Nations, de Paris). It was burned down during the Commune of 1871 (as was the Porte-Saint-Martin) and rebuilt. More recently, during the German Occupation, the theatre was known as the Théâtre de la Cité, and today as the Théâtre de la Ville (reminding us that it is still a municipal theatre).

Sarah Bernhardt (1844–1923), 'la divine Sarah', epitomizes the nineteenth-century star. She made her (unsuccessful) *débuts* at the Comédie-Française in 1862, left under a cloud, returned in 1872, and left again in 1880, after eight triumphal years. Artistically, her subsequent career was mediocre, but it brought her international fame and financial rewards no actor at the Comédie-Française could dream of. She managed the Ambigu and the Porte-Saint-Martin (1884), then, after a period at the Théâtre de la Renaissance (1893–8), she took over the direction of the smaller theatre of the Place du Châtelet – the Théâtre Lyrique, which had become the Théâtre des Nations in 1880 – and baptized it Théâtre Sarah-Bernhardt. Her direction ran from 1899 until her death in 1923, and was then continued for a few years by her son, Maurice Bernhardt.

86

SARAH BERNHARDT

PLACE DU CHATELET
ADMINIST- AVENUE VICTORIA, 15 Téléphone 2??.??

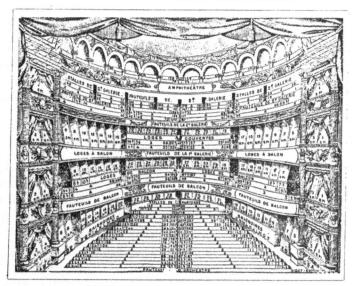

Directrice : Mme Sarah Bernhardt.
Administrateur : Victor Ullmann.
Secrétaire : Georges Loiseau.
Régisseur : Rebel

1699 PLACES

Bureau de location ouvert de 11 h. à
6 h. 1 2, et les jours de matinée à partir
de 10 h.

	Bur. et Loc.
Avant-scènes .... la place	15 fr.
Loges de balcon.... . . —	12 »
Baignoires.... ...... —	12 »
Faut. de balcon 1er rang. —	12 »
— — 2 rang. —	10 »
Faut. d'orchestre........ —	10 »
Avant-scène, 1re galerie. —	7 »
Loges à salon — . —	7 »
— couvertes — . —	6 »
Fauteuils — . —	6 »
Avant-scène, 2e galerie. —	4 »
Fauteuils —	4 »
Stalles de parterre..... —	3 50
— 2e galerie..... —	2 50
— d'amphithéâtre.. —	1 »

*Les dames sont admises sans chapeau
aux fauteuils d'orchestre.*

Clôture annuelle de juillet à septembre.

Le théâtre Sarah-Bernhardt. —
Une des salles les plus élégantes de Paris.

C'est dans l'ancien *théâtre des Nations*
que Mme Sarah-Bernhardt a élu domicile.
Le monument appartient à la ville de
Paris, comme le Châtelet d'ailleurs. Le
théâtre des Nations subit des fortunes
diverses, on y joua successivement le
drame et la comédie.

Après le terrible incendie de l'Opéra-
Comique qui coûta la vie à près de deux
cents personnes (15 mai 1887), sa troupe
vint prendre possession du théâtre des
Nations et y resta jusqu'en 1898, époque
à laquelle elle put rentrer dans la salle
Favart reconstruite.

C'est au mois de janvier 1899 que Mme
Sarah-Bernhardt s'installa place du Châtelet; elle quittait le théâtre de *la Renaissance*, dont les dimensions restreintes
ne lui permettaient pas la mise en scène
qu'elle rêvait pour les œuvres qu'elle
voulait interpréter.

L'illustre tragédienne fit installer une
salle et une scène merveilleuses où le
confort et l'élégance se sont donné ren-
dez-vous. Le *théâtre Sarah-Bernhardt*
était fondé, il devait être digne du nom
qu'il portait.

Les créations ou les reprises qu'y fit
sa directrice sont autant de succès : *Hamlet* de Morand et Schwob, *L'Aiglon*
d'Edmond Rostand, qui fut joué pendant
toute l'année de l'Exposition et repris
deux fois depuis; *Francesca da Rimini*
de Marion Crawford et Schwob, *La
Dame aux Camélias* d'Alexandre Dumas
fils, *La Samaritaine* d'Edmond Rostand; *Théodora, La Tosca* et *Fedora* de
Victorien Sardou; *Théroigne de Méricourt*
de Paul Hervieu.

Le talent déployé par Mme Sarah Bernhardt dans ses diverses créations, son
goût sûr et le grand souci d'art qui pré-
side à toutes ses tentatives, le soin qu'elle
a eu de grouper autour d'elle les artistes
les plus aimés, ont vite classé son théâtre au premier rang des scènes parisiennes.

HUNYÁDI JANOS LA MEILLEURE EAU PURGATIVE NATURELLE
Exiger le nom ANDRÉAS SAXLEHNER sur l'étiquette et le bouchon.

Director:	Mme Sarah Bernhardt
Administrator:	Victor Ullmann
Secretary:	Georges Loiseau
Stage director:	Rebel

1,699 seats

Booking is open from 11.00 a.m. until 6.30 p.m. and from 10.00 a.m. on matinée days.

Ladies without hats are admitted to the orchestra stalls. Annual closure of the theatre: from July to September.

The Théâtre Sarah-Bernhardt

One of the most elegant theatres in Paris. Mme Sarah Bernhardt has taken up residence in the former Théâtre du Châtelet. The Théâtre des Nations had a chequered history, with both serious drama and comedy being performed there.

After the terrible fire at the Opéra-Comique (15 May 1887) in which nearly 200 people perished, the company took over the Théâtre des Nations, and remained there until 1898, when it moved back into the rebuilt Favart Theatre.

In January 1899 Madame Sarah Bernhardt moved to the Place du Châtelet, leaving the Renaissance, whose smaller size did not allow the *mise en scène* which she dreamt of for the plays she wished to perform.

The celebrated tragic actress refurbished both stage and auditorium, according to the highest standards of comfort and elegance. The Théâtre Sarah-Bernhardt was established, and it had to be worthy of the name it bore.

The director's new productions and the revivals have all been successes: Morand and Schwob's *Hamlet*; Edmond Rostand's *L'Aiglon*, which played throughout the year of the Exhibition, and has since been revived twice; Marion Crawford and Schwob's *Francesca da Rimini*; Alexandre Dumas *fils*'s *La Dame aux camélias*; Edmond Rostand's *La Samaritaine*; Victorien Sardou's *Théodora*, *La Tosca* and *Fédora*; Paul Hervieu's *Théroigne de Méricourt*.

The talent displayed by Mme Sarah Bernhardt in her various new productions, her good taste and the great attention to artistic quality in all her ventures, as well as the care she has taken to gather around her the most beloved performers, have rapidly made her theatre one of the foremost in Paris.

16   Sarah Bernhardt on tour, 1905

If the 1890s and the first two decades of the twentieth century saw the flowering of avant-garde theatre, it was also the era of massively organized tours by star performers. Sarah Bernhardt travelled with the great plays of her repertoire, in this case visiting German-speaking 'Strassburg' with *The Lady of the Camellias*, in which she was now a somewhat elderly Marguerite Gautier, and Edmond Rostand's *L'Aiglon* (The Eagle's Son) in which she played the breeches part of Napoleon's ill-fated son, the Duke of Reichstadt, who died at the age of 21. Sarah Bernhardt created the role in 1900, aged 56.

17   *Cyrano de Bergerac* cut to size, 1 February 1898

Jules Lemaître[1], *La Revue des Deux Mondes*, 1 February 1898

Cyrano de Bergarac by Edmond Rostand (1868–1918) was the greatest box-office success of the 1890s. When it opened at the Théâtre de la Porte-Saint-Martin in 1897 critics used up all the superlatives they could find to praise the play, full of swashbuckling heroism, of bombastic and patriotic sentiments. Although its rhetoric is hollow, the language was highly appreciated and Rostand was hailed as the greatest French playwright since the heyday of the seventeenth century.

Cyrano de Bergerac is far and away the greatest success that I have seen in nearly thirteen years as drama critic. The day following the first night and for a whole week thereafter the press proclaimed *Cyrano* a masterpiece. [...]

I shall be bold and ungrateful enough to consider *Cyrano* as an event which is no doubt marvellous, but not, strictly speaking, supernatural. M. Rostand's play is not only delightful: it had the wit to appear at the right moment. I can see two reasons why it was so amazingly successful: the first is its excellence. The second reason is doubtless a weariness on the part of the spectators: they'd had enough of all those psychological studies, trivial tales of Parisian adultery, of all those feminist, socialist and Scandinavian plays. I have nothing against such works; some of them contain perhaps as much moral and intellectual substance as this radiant *Cyrano*; but they are certainly less delectable, and we have been somewhat depressed by them recently. *Cyrano* even benefited from our civil dissension.[2] One eloquent journalist wrote that *Cyrano* 'burst upon us like a fanfare of red uniform trousers': it heralds the awakening of French nationalism. [...]

But it is true that this comedy 'opens a new century', or, more modestly, that it 'is the beginning of something', – like *Le Cid, Andromaque, L'Ecole des femmes, La Surprise de l'amour, Le Mariage de Figaro, Hernani, La Dame aux camélias?*

For me, if I may venture an opinion, the merit of this ravishing comedy consists, not in 'opening' anything at all, but in extending, in combining and blending in itself effortlessly, and certainly with brilliance, and even with originality, three centuries of 'home-grown' comic fantasy and moral graciousness. [...]

Everything in *Cyrano* is retrospective; everything, even the modern romanticism which adapts itself with such ease to the romanticism of 1630. Nothing, I say, belongs to the author, except the great and intelligent love which he has devoted to these bygone visions; except that voluptuous melancholy which, in his last three acts, makes him so artful a dramatist and so rare a poet.

Many people, who were not all fools, resisted the charms of *Le Cid, Andromaque,* ... plays which did indeed introduce 'something new' and whose moral content may well have been more considerable, after all, than that of *Cyrano de Bergerac.* This is no doubt why no discordant voice troubled the universal applause which greeted M. Rostand's play. This all-too-fortunate work therefore lacks at least one of those accessory features which permit us empirically to discern innovatory works. It lacks the virtue of having been misunderstood (I imagine the author will get over this without too much difficulty). [...] Everything charms us in *Cyrano*; nothing is shocking. But by the same token nothing in the play addresses our most serious intellectual and moral preoccupations. If it were true that this very brilliant romantic comedy 'opens the twentieth century', then the twentieth century will be condemned to a certain amount of tedious reiteration.

[1] Jules Lemaître (1853–1914): open-minded, anti-doctrinaire theatre critic and university lecturer.
[2] *Cyrano* was the perfect antidote against the prevailing gloom generated by the Dreyfus scandal and Zola's bitter attack (in his famous open letter to the French President: 'J'accuse', early in 1898) on corruption in the army. The 'red trousers' refer to the 'anti-dreyfusards' who rallied around Cyrano's nose.

18(a) Theatre of thrills: the Grand-Guignol, 1890s

Camillo Antona-Traversi, *L'Histoire du Grand-Guignol – Théâtre de l'épouvante et du rire* (Paris: Librairie théâtrale, 1933), pp. 28, 714

The Grand-Guignol, originally a chapel in the rue Chaptal, was founded in 1895 by Oscar Méténier (1859–1913), an author of ultra-naturalistic plays for the Théâtre Libre. The Grand-Guignol represented the trend towards more intimate theatres. Closer contact with the audience led to even more meticulous attention to realism of detail in staging. The Grand-Guignol is particularly associated with a theatre of terror, of strong dramas with maximum emphasis on the macabre and on the more repugnant details of crimes (André de Lorde [1871–1942] was a major author in this genre). Doctors, judges and madmen figure most prominently in the repertoire of this theatre, which did not cease business until 1962. In Méténier's *Lui* (*Him*), for instance, a prostitute recognizes a customer suffering from hallucinations as the author of a gory murder. Plays were short: generally full of emotion and bloody terror packed into two acts. There were a number of plays on the bill every night, including short farces or comedies sandwiched between the sensational 'dramas'. The comedies themselves became a genre celebrated almost as much as the dramas.

They were wonderful days. At the Grand-Guignol it was guaranteed that we'd tremble to the marrow or laugh until we cried. Beautiful women swooned, unable to control their nerves during the most terrifying scenes. [...]

How many horrifying dramas were performed on the tragic stage of the rue Chaptal! How many murders were committed! I won't attempt to mention all the gun shots, the knife and razor attacks, which happened non-stop while we heard gushing cascades of blood!

Engraved in my memory is Robert Scheffer and Georges Lignereux's horrifying play *La petite maison d'Auteuil* [The Little House in Auteuil].[1] A man, bound hand

and foot, had his beard, teeth and fingernails torn out; his face was slashed with a knife and his eyes burnt out with a red-hot poker.

And *Le Baiser de sang* [The Kiss of Blood]?[2] A jealous man murders the woman he adores. Nightly her Ghost returns to haunt him and – in revenge – kisses the hand that killed her. The unfortunate man is tortured by a most atrocious grief: he, first, cuts off one of his fingers and then hacks through his wrist with an axe!

The public got very used to watching the Grand-Guignol's displays of terror. The only outcry I ever heard of was over a play entitled *Au petit jour* [At Dawn]. The play ended with the staging of an execution: a condemned man was dragged up to the guillotine and the blade did its work.

At first, a deathly silence reigned in the auditorium; then a little timid applause was heard, drowned out by whistling. A spectator began to protest from the balcony that it was a scandal. M. Félix Gandera, in the orchestra, told the protestors that they were just 'guests' and had no right to create such an uproar. Cries of 'Lout!' and 'Scoundrel!' were exchanged. It was quite riotous!

Shrieks of horror also rang out from the public at the sight of the head covered in leprous and disintegrating scabs. But as the play was written by Lorde and Bauche, we expected as much.

Despite' some unfortunate exceptions, the fast-moving plays at the Grand-Guignol were always poignant and real. They did not depend on convention. *Reality* and *Life* were presented there, with all their violence, ardour, rage, brutality, but also – we must not forget – the *Beauty* that is inherent in *Truth*.

Each time a new work was performed, Choisy, the director, was in agony, and it was not a good idea to go near him. He took refuge in the corner of the wings and listened to what was happening in the auditorium, watching the reactions of the public.

One evening, after many curtain calls for *Laboratoire des hallucinations* (a play in three scenes by A. de Lorde and H. Bauche), I heard Choisy ask his stage-manager, Jean Bernac: 'How many women have fainted?'

'Three, sir!' came the reply. Choisy exclaimed in complete delight: 'It's a triumph, my boy!'

---

[1] A horror play by Robert Scheffer and Georges Lignereux, 1907.
[2] Two-act horror play by Jean Aragny and Francis Neilson, 1929.

18(b)   A 1904 caricature of the Grand-Guignol
Le Journal, 11 December 1904

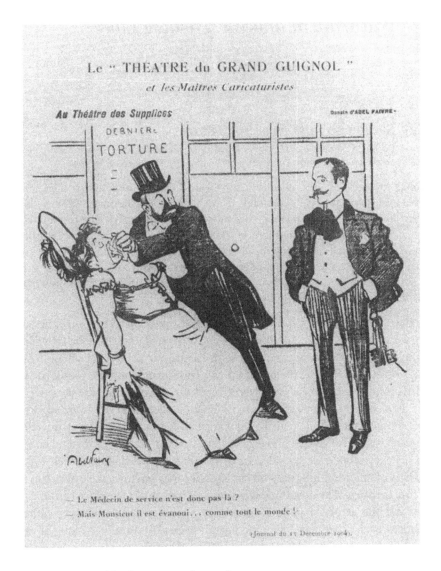

'At the torture theatre'
'–Is there a doctor in the house?'
'–Yes; but he's fainted, like everybody else!'

IV Naturalism and the Théâtre Libre

19(a) Sardou on *mise en scène*, 1870s

Quoted in Germain Bapst, *Essai sur le théâtre: la mise en scène, le décor, le costume, l'architecture, l'éclairage, l'hygiène* (Paris: Imprimerie Lahure, 1893), p. 584

Although the term *mise en scène* entered into theatrical jargon in the 1830s, it originally referred exclusively to stage decoration. It was only much later in the century, after Antoine had begun on his reforms, that *mise en scène* gradually came to acquire its contemporary meaning of an all-embracing (intellectual, ideological, aesthetic, theatrical) interpretation of a stage play. Note that Sardou's[1] text, written in 1874, was approvingly quoted twenty years later, and that Becq de Fouquières's essay (**19b**), considered at the time as the most authoritative study on the subject, proposes a very retrograde view of the art of *mise en scène*.

In Scribe's[2] time, the door was upstage, facing the prompter's box; on either side there were chairs in a row, just like we used to have in our living-room. Nowadays the stage represents a proper salon, furnished as are our fashionable salons. I must say it's not I who deserve the credit for this transformation but Montigny,[3] the man who has been such a skilful director at the Gymnase for the past twenty years. In a comedy, you would have a number of individuals who were supposed to be acting scenes from real life, looking like four musicians in a travelling orchestra: instead of speaking to each other, each would address the audience in turn, as they stood side by side, lined up along the footlights. Struck by the absurdity of this, Montigny effected his first reform by having a table placed in the centre of the stage. The next thing was that the chairs had to be placed around the table, and the actors, instead of remaining standing and conversing without looking at each other, sat down and began to speak naturally, looking at each other as people do in real life. Once the table and chairs were in place, the décor was arranged as you have arranged your own living-room; pedestal tables, chiffoniers, all manner of seats were set out more or less everywhere, in keeping with today's fashion. Such credit as I can claim is for having applied Montigny's theories to historical plays: I have tried to introduce truth into theatre. In *La Haine* [Hate],[4] for example, the portrayal of the mob breaking open the castle gate is rigorously exact. The men who lifted up the beams and broke down the walls were performing real actions, as might have been carried out by workers given such a job to do.

---

[1] Victorien Sardou (1831–1908): with Scribe (see below), the undisputed master of the well-made play. He knew what pleased his audience and tailor-made play after play for the French society of the second half of the century. His successes stretch from *Les Premières Armes de Figaro* (1859, *Figaro's First Arms*) to *L'Affaire des poisons* (1907). He was also well received in England, but Shaw dismissed his formula by coining the term 'Sardoodledom'.

[2] Auguste Eugène Scribe (1791–1861): the creator of the well-made play. He wrote some 500 plays, either alone or in collaboration.

[3] Montigny (Auguste-Adolphe Lemoine, 1805–80, known as) became director of the Théâtre du Gymnase in 1844 and introduced a more realistic approach to acting and stage design. To prevent actors from 'standing and delivering' in front of the prompter's box, he arranged furniture 'naturally' on the stage, moving chairs and tables into the centre, away from the walls where they had traditionally been placed.

[4] Théâtre de la Gaîté, 3 December 1874.

19(b)   Louis Becq de Fouquières's opposing point of view, 1884

Louis Becq de Fouquières, *L'Art de la mise en scène, Essai d'esthétique théâtrale* (Paris: G. Charpentier, 1884), pp. 20–21

In the performance of a play, everything which a director adds, beyond a certain limit, for the pleasure of the eye or the ear, destroys the integrity of a pleasure which ought to be intended for the mind only. The spectator whose eyes are captivated by the splendours of the *mise en scène* has ceased to be in a state of receptivity that enables the appreciation of either the work's literary beauty, or the profundity and psychological truth of the emotions it portrays. Our attention is distracted from its main object, and in that case the pleasure which we enjoy, in effect a pleasure of the senses, is inferior to that which we ought to have experienced. It can therefore be categorically asserted that the misuse and overuse of *mise en scène* tends to produce a decline in dramatic art.

[...] The need for *mise en scène* becomes all the greater if the work is weaker. Without the help of décor, costumes and large numbers of extras, many plays, denied these artificial means of distraction, could not face up to the judgement of fair-minded critics.

20   Conventional staging at the Comédie-Française: Emile Augier's *Les Fourchambault*, 1878

Archives of the Bibliothèque nationale, Paris

A prime example of conventional 'theatricality': the attitudes are wooden and the set is made of flimsy flats. Note the absence of furniture. Augier's work has never been revived.[1]

20

¹ Emile Augier (1820–89), social playwright, considered as a forerunner of naturalism, was successful in his lifetime. Most of his plays were staged at the Comédie-Française.

21   A naturalist manifesto: Zola's *Thérèse Raquin*, 1873

Emile Zola, Préface to *Thérèse Raquin*, dated 25 July, 1873, in *Œuvres complètes*, ed. Henri Mitterand, vol. xv (Paris: Cercle du livre précieux, 1969), pp. 121–5

Emile Zola (1840–1902) first published his novel *Thérèse Raquin* in 1867. He was, then, already a well-known drama critic and he found more to blame than to praise on the contemporary stage. He was particularly irked by what he saw as the outmoded conventions preventing new talents from expressing themselves freely. Despite his disingenuous disclaimer, Zola wrote his adaptation as a 'naturalist manifesto'. The production, first performed on 11 July 1873 at the Théâtre de la Renaissance, had a mixed reception, but it achieved a very respectable run of thirty-seven performances. Marie Laurent[1] played Madame Raquin (a 'chilling' performance by all accounts), a part which she revived, with Antoine as Laurent, at the Théâtre Libre (Vaudeville) on 20 May 1892. Antoine staged it again at the Théâtre de l'Odéon (21 May 1910). There are also two notable film adaptations: Jacques Feyder (1926) and Marcel Carné (1953).

To tell the truth, I have committed a villainous deed in adapting *Thérèse Raquin* for the theatre. I did hesitate for a long time; and, if I finally yielded, it was in submission more to some personal questions which interest me than to external circumstances. Some critics were extremely severe towards the novel when it appeared, and formally defied me to dramatize it; the book, for them, was filth. They happily dragged it through the gutter, declaring that the day such horrors were displayed on stage, the spectators would extinguish the footlights with their whistling. I am very curious by nature and I like a good fight: I promised myself that I would see if the critics' threat would come true. [...] *Thérèse Raquin* contained an excellent subject for drama, which would allow me to conduct a theatrical experiment I once thought of. I found in it the environment I had searched for, good enough characters; in short, all the elements I needed were ready for use. That made my mind up.

I have no ambition to wave my play like a flag. It has some major faults, and no one judges it more severely than I do. If I undertook its critique myself, all that would remain is my desire to bring the sweeping movements of truth and experimental science to the theatre, which, since the last century, have spread and grown in all other fields of human intelligence. The impetus was given by new scientific methods. Hence naturalism has renovated criticism and history, subjecting man and his actions to exact analysis, concerning itself with social circumstances, milieu and physiology. [...] In the continuing creation of humanity, we are giving birth to truth. That is the strength of our century and all knowledge must progress relentlessly. I am determined to see the naturalist movement impose itself on the theatre, and impose on the stage the power of reality, the new life of modern art.

In the theatre all innovation is sensitive. Literary revolutions are slow to make their impact felt on the stage. It is the last citadel of lies, and truth must besiege it. [...] Theatre will die if a new spirit does not rejuvenate it. The corpse needs a blood transfusion. Operetta and *féerie* are said to have killed drama. That is false, theatre died a natural death: it was murdered by extravagance, lies and platitude. Comedy still stands amidst the ruins of our stage because it is more rooted in real life, and is often genuine. I challenge the last romantics to put heroic drama on the stage. [...] Now that everything has collapsed, cloak and swords have become useless; it is time to produce works of truth. To replace the classical with the romantic tradition would be a betrayal of the freedom our predecessors won for us. There is no need for schools, for theories, for clichés of any kind; there is nothing but life, an immense field where each is able to study and create at will.

I do not mean to write a manifesto. I have the profound belief that the experimental and scientific spirit of our century will win over the theatre, and that it is the only possible renovation for our stage. [. . .] The past is dead. We must look to the future; and the future lies in the study of the human predicament within the framework of reality, the rejection of all myths: people living in their true environment, a drama free from old wives' tales and tattered histories, from grand meaningless words and conventional foolishness and bragging. The rotten structure of yesterday's drama is collapsing. We must wipe the slate clean. The well-known recipes for developing and concluding an intrigue had their day; today we need a large and simple painting of man and his world, a drama that Molière could have written. [. . .]

Naturalism is taking its first steps on the stage. Either theatre will become modern and real or it will die.

---

[1] Marie Laurent (1825–1904): an excellent, but conventional actress, Marie Laurent became the 'doyenne' of naturalist theatre. Aged 77, she appeared in Antoine's production of Zola's *La Terre* (1902). In 1880 she founded an orphanage for children of artists. She was awarded the Légion d'honneur in 1888.

22   A naturalist performance: Zola's *Nana* at the Ambigu-Comique, 28 January 1881

Arnold Mortier,[1] *Les Soirées parisiennes, par un Monsieur de l'orchestre* (10 vols. Paris: E. Dentu, 1875–84), vol. VIII (29 January 1881), pp. 42–9

Well before Zola became the inspiration for the Théâtre Libre, his novels – along with those by such contemporaries as Jules Verne – were providing exciting melodramas for the boulevard theatres. The emphasis was on grandiose staging with fully constructed sets for each scene. In Busnach's[2] adaptation of *Nana* the novel was divided into ten 'dramatic' moments. To the modern reader this account may appear to be a 'send-up' of the production, but it is, in fact, a typical piece of journalistic criticism of the time. It also allows us to get a sense of the production and of the taste of the theatre public, especially at the popular Ambigu-Comique, towards the end of the nineteenth century.

Nana is, without doubt, the most eagerly awaited première of the year. The reactions stirred up by the novel, the fearsome scenes it contains, the ill report of those who have not read it, [. . .] the powerful effect of certain tableaux at yesterday's public dress-rehearsal, all that is more than enough to justify the interest aroused by the play. Emile Zola's talent challenges even its most sworn enemies. And yet we have only been dished out a revised, watered-down, and considerably weakened Zola in M. William Busnach's adaptation: an edited, rearranged, 'genteelified' *Nana*; a sweetened *Nana* who would not have upset even the prudest of prudes. But this did not stop the Parisian audience acclaiming last night's performance as a great theatrical event.

1. The morning after a first night

Nana's bathroom. Walls covered in Persian carpets. Mlle Leriche, who has left the Variétés, plays the maid, Zoe, and she has been translated into a little poppet, with traditional costume and bonnet. Very sweet, Mlle Leriche. She projects her lines with lots of verve, and she has plenty to project, much of it very daring. Hers is the most 'naturalistic' role in the play. [...]

Nana rolls a cigarette and lights it – which is the height of audacity. [...]

3. The blonde Venus

The greenroom at M. Bordenave's theatre. Green furnishings. Nothing could be less naturalist than these wings. This tableau offers incontrovertible proof that it is impossible to break with convention in the theatre. [...]

Everyone knows that Nana undresses on stage to put on her Venus costume. Nothing could be more chaste than this scene which had been announced as extremely daring.

4. The ruins at Chaumont

A marvellous creation by Chéret. This is where we begin to see the great and justified success which greeted *Nana*'s charming *mise en scène*. The landscape has a delightful poetic quality. The ruins of the abbey on the hill, the paths which wind through the vines, the mossy dells, the little bridge and the stream which flows with a gentle murmur, and above all a ray of sunlight which strikes a gleam from the water on the stones of the bridge, all this has an exquisite truthfulness and charm. [...]

We are in the midst of an idyll. Nana wants some apples, and the young Georges Hugon (a seventeen-year-old actor, M. Emile Hébert, who dresses very badly), shakes a cardboard tree from which real apples fall. [...]

The most striking effect in the tableau was when Dailly fell in the little stream. This cold bath caused indescribable joy in the auditorium. We have had the wash-house scene in *L'Assommoir* [see 23]. Here is its counterpart. Natural water decidedly plays a leading role in the naturalist dramas at the Ambigu. [...]

5. Avenue de Villiers

[...] Mlle Honorine's entrance, as a rag-and-bone woman, was roundly applauded. This is the first truly naturalist character in the play. Mlle Honorine got her costume from a real rag-and-bone woman. In exchange she gave her a splendid new outfit and two tickets for *Rose Michel*.[3]

6. *The weighing-in enclosure*

A faithful reproduction. Racehorses, among which is 'Guerrière', who has come in last in several handicap races at Longchamp. It was Franconi who went out and hired the thoroughbred ridden by Dailly. He even had him take a few riding lessons: the donkey rides which Dailly performed in *Strogoff* [see **14**] had been judged unsatisfactory. [. . .]

10. *Room 206 in the Grand Hôtel*

An ordinary sort of hotel room. Nana's death. A bedside table cluttered with potions. The final scene surpasses in horror anything previously seen in the theatre.

When Nana, alone and abandoned in her hotel room, opened the curtains of her bed and appeared in her shift, dishevelled, her face ravaged by smallpox, a long shudder of horror ran throughout the auditorium.

Apparently, to achieve the desired effect, long consultations took place between the theatre doctors and the make-up dealers.

Eventually they used the following ingredients:

– A mixture of red and burnt umber;
– Four dabs of burnt umber for the smallpox pustules;
– White lipstick;
– Black beneath the eyes, and, to dull the brow, white in the roots of the hair.

I hope I will do my lady readers a service by giving them the recipe. It might come in useful for next winter's masked balls.

---

[1] Arnold Mortier (1843–85): journalist and playwright. Drama critic of *Le Figaro*.
[2] William Busnach (1832–1907): playwright, librettist and theatre director (Théâtre de l'Athénée, 1867–8). Best known for his stage adaptations of contemporary novels, especially Zola's. His main successes were *L'Assommoir* (1879), *Nana, Pot-Bouille* (1883), *Le Ventre de Paris* (1887) and *Germinal* (1888). In 1906 his adaptation of Flaubert's *Madame Bovary* was staged.
[3] Comedy by E. Blum, first performed in the same Ambigu-Comique on 21 January 1875.

23   An early naturalist set: Zola's *L'Assommoir*, 1879
Bibliothèque nationale, Paris

Zola's novel, adapted in ten 'tableaux' by Busnach and Gastineau, was a huge popular success, but a great disappointment for anyone hoping to see the emergence of a realist (or naturalist) theatre of quality. Judging the failure of the previous generation of novelists (1860–90) to write any play of quality, a younger author declared: '[The great realists of the last 30 years] ... sliced up their most *masterpiece'ish* novels and refrained from rewarding virtue in the last act; they brought on to the stage a few shreds of reality, but they could not, or dared not, sweep away conventions, give up string-pulling, scorn the contrived solution, or, indeed, show themselves to be realists in any context other than that of sexual passion' (Paul Bonnetain, in Henderson, *The First Avant-Garde* (London: Harrap, 1971), p. 41). Sad to say, Zola's novels – once adapted to the stage – were turned into hugely spectacular melodramas, and were absolute denials of everything he had ever written about regenerating French theatre.

The engraving depicts the famous wash-house scene of *L'Assommoir* culminating in the spanking inflicted by Gervaise on Virginie's bare bottom (according to Zola's description of the catfight in the novel). Many a spectator will have been disappointed as the climactic moment was prudishly set at the back of the stage, behind the large crowd of shrieking washerwomen. Staging the scene, *naturalistically*, as it is graphically described in the novel, would have been unthinkable.

24   Poster for the 1900 revival of Zola's *L'Assommoir*

Designed by A. Steinlen: Musée Carnavalet, Paris

The production was directed by Lucien Guitry (1860–1925) at the Théâtre de la Porte-Saint-Martin and, according to the press, 'was seen by the Tout-Paris'.

25   Jean Jullien's theories of naturalism in the theatre, 1890

Jean Jullien,[1] *Le Théâtre vivant* (Paris: Charpentier et Fasquelle, 1892), pp. 8–22. Text written in 1890 as a preface to his play, *L'Echéance*[2]

1. WHAT THE LIVING THEATRE CONSISTS OF – [...] There have been attempts to revive serious theatre, certain authors, in line with the evolution of literature, endeavour to create a naturalistic theatre; but their efforts have not, and could not, achieve any result. Indeed, the naturalist theatre drew on the old conventions [...] not only as regards the organization of scenes and dialogue, but also in acting and *mise en scène*; it was as if our engineers were to try using gas pipes to conduct electricity! Reform cannot consist of injecting brutality into the action and putting foul language into the mouths of the characters, nor of using props from real life. If a play, performed by actors of the traditional school, is to evolve, after a vapid exposition, towards a humdrum crisis only to conclude with a happy or tragic dénouement, using (on the way) all the devices, subterfuges, cases of mistaken identity and implausibilities of the old form of theatre, then it really is not worth taking the trouble to change anything. A new genre calls for a new play structure, a new approach to *mise en scène*, new actors, and critical appraisals need to be formulated from a new *perspective*. I believe that, as art is not simply nature, so *theatre should not be simply life*.

2. SERIOUS THEATRE IS A LIVING IMAGE OF LIFE – The principal aim of theatre is to interest the spectator and above all to move him, and for this reason it should remain as close as possible to life. The characters will be human beings and not creatures of fantasy; the players straightforward folk, speaking as they would speak in real life, but raising their voices slightly – not actors overdoing the grotesque or the odious, ranters delivering a lecture or developing a thesis while displaying showy qualities of diction. For theatre to achieve its aim, everything that smacks of technique or special effects must disappear, as must everything that points to the author's presence; so much the worse for the style of the former and the tricks of the latter, everything must merge in the character; *an actor may be interesting – but a man is impressive*.

The spectators must temporarily cease to be aware that they are in a theatre and, to this end, I think it necessary for the audience to be in darkness as soon as the curtain is raised; the stage picture will stand out more forcefully, the spectator will remain attentive, will no longer dare to chat and will become almost intelligent. This is the only way to stage serious theatre.

Apart from concessions to time, place and distances, which are indispensable given that infinity cannot be contained within three walls, there are no conventions from which one cannot break free. I shall mention a few examples among many. We have preserved a fondness for those footlights which mean that the actors are lit from below whereas in life we are lit from above. Why not get rid of the footlights, increase the number of battens and enhance the lighting on stage? It also seems a good idea to me to do as the English do and put an end to the use of painted props; a plain unadorned backdrop is better than childish daubings which fool no one. And as regards *mise en scène* and acting style, it is irrational to have everything converge on the prompter's box. If the actor must always be listening out for responses from the auditorium, he must never let this be apparent; he must act as if he were in his own home, without paying undue attention to the emotion he arouses, to the applause or calls for silence; in place of the curtain there must be a fourth wall, transparent for the audience, opaque for the actor.

3. A PLAY IS A SLICE OF LIFE ARTISTICALLY SET ON THE STAGE – People are forever telling us that theatre is the art of preparation and that the audience must above all be let into the secret; I consider this principle false and the technique utterly misconceived. *Theatre is action*; the spectator is struck much more by what he sees than what he hears; dialogue in action grips him, monologues bore him; and he is right, monologues belong in books. The action must send its vibrations through the play from beginning to end: action is the play's breath, as it were, its pulse, its blood, its life. [. . .]

4. CONCERNING THE SYNTHESIS OF LIFE IN THE PLAY – [. . .] A play is a synthetic version of life achieved through art.

5. LIFE MUST EXIST IN THE MISE EN SCENE – [. . .] The author must determine the way his characters walk as he determines the way they speak and he must personally concern himself with everything involved in the *mise en scène*: with the costumes (which will not be some fashionable designer's display), with the props, with the décor – and here he will not leave it to the manager, who always answers, 'Don't worry, it'll be all right on the night'. [. . .]

6. THE INTERPRETATION OF LIFE ON THE STAGE – [. . .] Tartuffe, being a living person, must be multifaceted in the way he expresses himself, while of course maintaining the fundamental consistency of his character and temperament which emerge through the naturalness of the acting style and not through contrived effects. But nowadays the actor is not meant to enter into a role, the role has to be adapted to suit the actor, to his speciality,[1] his mannerisms, his weaknesses; it has become a costume designed to show him at his best and which he slips on like a garment.

---

[1] Jean Jullien (1854–1919), playwright and drama critic closely associated with the naturalist movement.

[2] First performed at the Théâtre Libre (Théâtre des Menus-Plaisirs), 31 January 1889.
[3] 'emploi': see 11, note 1.

26   Antoine against Sarcey, 25 June 1888

Francisque Sarcey,[1] *Quarante ans de théâtre* (Paris: Bibliothèque des Annales politiques et littéraires, 1900-2), vol. VIII, pp. 250-8

In his review of 18 June 1888 of the Théâtre Libre's previous night's performance of Salandri's *La Prose*, Georges Ancey's *Monsieur Lamblin*[2] and Paul Alexis's *La Fin de Lucie Pellegrin*, Sarcey roundly attacked all three plays and ended with a typical outburst: 'Oh naturalism! What horrors are written in thy name!' The following week (25 June) he reproduced Antoine's response.

I am not writing to discuss what you chose to say about the last performances at the Théâtre Libre. Questions of literature are of no concern to me. The author alone is responsible for what he writes. If you are kind enough to find the acting adequate and the *mise en scène* passable, I have achieved my goal and the honour of the theatre is safe.

On behalf of the theatre I must remark on your comment that 'M. Antoine knows well enough that there is no art in *Lucie Pellegrin*'.

Lucie Pellegrin was published as a novel two years ago and widely acclaimed as a masterpiece; it is frequently quoted and the reading public is familiar with it. When Alexis said to me: 'I'll give you *Lucie Pellegrin*', how could I refuse? Alexis is a member of the Médan[3] group which, rightly or wrongly, attempts to bring about on the contemporary stage the evolution which has been brought about in the novel. Directors closed their doors to him. In accepting such a significant work I was setting myself a great challenge. Did Alexis fail? That's not my concern. You said that the performance was adequate; so I fulfilled my job.

If we performed these works publicly, and if I were responsible for presenting these plays to unsuspecting spectators coming to the theatre with their wives and daughters, you'd have a point. But that's not the case. Everyone knew what would be shown on the stage last Friday. Everyone in the auditorium had read the novel. We knew where we were going and what we were doing. I only did my duty, and the Théâtre Libre achieved its goal, which is to perform works by new writers or experimental works by established authors. This is impossible on any other stage. [...]

I have been called a crook, a pornographer, a money-grabber ... But those kindnesses left me unperturbed. I'd be more hurt if you were to say that a play was inadequately produced at the Théâtre Libre, than if I were accused of minting 300,000 francs per annum there.

¹ Francisque Sarcey (1827–1899), drama critic of *Le Temps*, from 1867, of conservative and 'academic' taste.
² Georges Ancey (1860–1917), playwright closely associated with the Théâtre Libre.
³ The 'group of Médan': five naturalist writers who, with Zola, published a volume of short stories, *Les Soirées de Médan* (1880). They are Alexis, Céard, Hennique, Huysmans and Maupassant.

27   Antoine assesses the Meininger, 23 July 1888

Francisque Sarcey, *Quarante ans de théâtre*, vol. VIII, pp. 258–63 (23 July 1888)

As in 26, Sarcey reproduces a letter that Antoine had sent him on the subject of *mise en scène*. In July 1888 Antoine spent two weeks in Brussels to see the Meininger season and to study their performance style. See also 51, 52, 53, 80, 81.

I've always disliked the way we deal with crowd scenes in our theatre. [...] I've never seen anything which has given me a convincing sense of the crowd. But I've seen it at the Meininger! [...] Their productions aren't made up of people picked at random like ours. They don't employ extras just for the dress-rehearsal, people who are dressed badly and aren't used to wearing bizarre or cumbersome costumes, especially if they are authentic. *Immobility* is nearly always the best advice we can give our extras, but the Meininger's can act and display character. They don't overdo it nor do they divert attention from the lead actors. The tableau they create is complete and wonderfully effective.

There are about seventy actors in the Meininger troupe. Each performer appears on stage every night whether or not he has got a speaking role. If there are twenty acting roles in a play, the other fifty actors, without exception (not even for the company's most important members), appear in crowd scenes. Established actors are in charge of groups of extras whom they direct and control.¹ [...]

The Meininger thus create extraordinarily convincing crowd scenes. How can we achieve this in our theatre? How can we ask even a fifth-rate actor to furnish the Princesse de Bouillon's salon!? Our work is held back by people who don't understand what to do or why they should do it. I know this only too well. I used to be an extra myself at the Comédie-Française. [...]

There was a superb moment in *William Tell*:² the murder of Gessler. Gessler was stopped by a poor woman and her two children, begging with their backs to the audience, while Tell aimed at him. You would agree that if an actor turns his back to the auditorium at the right moment, he gives the impression that he is oblivious to the presence of the public and thus creates the perfect illusion. [...]

In group tableaux, a protagonist can create total silence with a gesture, a sound or a movement. If the extras watch and listen to the actor instead of looking into the audience or, as at the Comédie-Française, looking at the performer with silent awe, the spectator will be convinced that the crowd is listening and that 200 people are interested by a towering character. [...]

Please don't think that I'm utterly enraptured by the Meininger. Their décor may be very colourful, but it is always curiously placed and no way near as well painted as ours. They overuse rostra, putting them everywhere. The costumes are splendid, when they are purely *historical*. When historical documents are missing or when they have to produce a work of fantasy or imagination, their costumes are usually in shocking taste, and foolishly expensive.

Their lighting effects are very conventional and reveal a naïvety of epic proportions. Thus a clear sunbeam shining on the head of a dying man suddenly becomes the light shining through a church window at the very moment the gentleman dies, only to create a good tableau. Also, it was sad to see an amazing effect of torrential rain (achieved with electric projectors) suddenly stop without any transition. [...]

The actors were no more than adequate. Many wore their costumes badly. The mountain-dwellers had clean hands and knees, just like at the Opéra-Comique.

It seems to me they've employed performers with strong voices and broad shoulders perfect for draping marvellous fabric around (which the extravagant Duke bought himself). I read that they spent 75,000 thalers on Schiller's *Mary Stuart*.

For the most part, their actors have had nothing more than a superficial training. [...]

Their repertoire is extremely varied. They even performed Ibsen's *Ghosts* at Meininger (I have a translation of it).[3] The Duke had the idea (very *théâtre-libre!*) of giving a private performance of it in front of the author and select critics from the German press. The play's too subversive to be performed publicly: I think next October you'll be a little shocked yourself!

Another Meininger hallmark is their strict regulation forbidding actors and extras to step beyond the proscenium arch. [...] In a dozen nights I didn't see anyone step within two metres of the prompter. Neither are they allowed to look at the audience, which is, I should add, in the dark. All the extras turn their backs to the audience and watch the central performers upstage where nearly all the main scenes are played.

---

[1] The obligation made on its performers is such that when Madame Hans de Bulow – one of the Meininger's stars – refused to be in a crowd scene because she felt it a duty beneath her talent, she was instantly dismissed.

[2] Friedrich von Schiller (1759–1805): *Maria Stuart* (1800), *Wilhelm Tell* (1804).

[3] See **193, 214**. Antoine himself staged *Les Revenants* (Ghosts) in 1889.

28   A programme design for the Théâtre Libre, 29 November 1892

Henri-Gabriel Ibels (1867–1936). Collection Samuel Josefowitz

Antoine's name is intimately associated with naturalism, but the director of the Théâtre Libre had catholic taste and staged plays which, at first sight, would not seem to fit easily into his repertoire, like François de Curel's *Les Fossiles* (Théâtre des Menus-Plaisirs, 29 November 1892). *Les Fossiles* is a philosophical problem play dealing with a kind of abstract, even mythical, aristocratic family completely out of touch with the real world. Ibels's design captures neatly the stiffness and lifelessness of Curel's society.

These programme designs, by some of the best artists of the time, are the only extant pictorial documents of these rich theatrical decades.

During the 1892/93 season Ibels produced lithographs for eight Théâtre Libre programmes. The subjects of these lithographs were freely chosen by the painter and did not necessarily relate to the plays themselves: fairground artists, marching soldiers, customers in cafés, singers or spectators at the opera . . . The figures, strongly silhouetted, are in line with Antoine's search for grand realism, and the overall composition is bold, simple and innovatory. The lithographs, pregnant with a strong theatrical atmosphere, are testimony to Antoine's incessant search for new means of expression and belie his reputation as a 'narrow-minded naturalist'.

29   Antoine interviewed, 5 February 1889

George Moore, 'The Patron of the Great Unacted', interview with André Antoine in London, published in the *St. James's Gazette*, 5 February 1889

'I always wanted to be an actor, but my parents would not hear of it, and having no money of my own I was obliged to accept a clerkship in a gas company. But in the evening I used to act. [. . .] One day it occurred to me that it would be far more interesting to play new roles than old ones; and to have my way I undertook the entire financial responsibility. Paul Alexis[1] found a play among his papers, *Mademoiselle Pomme*, Hennique gave me *Jacques Damour*. We invited the press, but only Fouguer and another came. *Jacques Damour* was a success; but I had to live on bread and cheese, for the performance cost me £6, and I only received £7 a month from the gas company. I had therefore to wait two months before I could give another performance. To induce the press to come I asked M. E. Bergerat[2] for a play. He gave me *La Nuit bergamasque*, and brought the entire press. I read the articles that appeared, and found that my debts exceeded £20. Every afternoon at five o'clock when my work was done at the gas company I went my rounds calling on men of letters, asking them what plays they could give me. I only asked for their plays; I did not ask them for money. At the same time, I sent circulars to rich people whom I had reason to think were interested in art, asking them to subscribe £4 apiece for a dozen performances; but no one answered my appeal, and had it not been for M. Jamid, of *Le Cercle des Mirlitons*,[3] who alone brought me fifteen subscribers, my scheme would have collapsed. [. . .]'

'The aim of Le Théâtre Libre is to encourage every writer to write for the stage and, above all, to write what he feels inclined to write and not what he thinks a manager will produce. I produce anything in which there is a grain of merit, quite irrespective of any opinion I may form of what the public will think of it, and anything a known writer brings me, and exactly as he hands it to me. If he writes a monologue of half a dozen pages, the actor must speak those half-dozen pages word for word. His business is to write the play; mine to have it acted. If the public like it, so much the better; if they don't, they hiss or leave the theatre. I never play any piece more than once.'

'Is it not,' I asked, 'very difficult to find thirty plays a year in which there is in each a grain of merit?'

'It is difficult, no doubt; but I am always on the watch. Paris is the art centre of the world. The Germans are a race of sages and soldiers, you are a race of shopkeepers, we are a race of artists. The spring of French art is inexhaustible.'

'And your actors. Where do you find them?'

'Everywhere, like the plays, I give every one a chance. I have discovered as much histrionic as I have literary genius. The worst of it is I am robbed of my geniuses as fast as I find them. Several of the young men and women whom I rescued from the drudgery of commercial life are now earning handsome salaries in the leading theatres. I have not one professional actor or actress with me; everyone in my company is practising a trade. They are now on their holidays, and tomorrow night you will see how they act – no screaming, no taking the stage, no playing to the gallery; real life is the art of the Théâtre Libre. We shall play *Jacques Damour* and *La Mort du Duc d'Enghien*. Both are by Hennique[4] and they are our two most successful pieces – that is to say, among those which your censor of plays will license. Ah! if he would only license *La Puissance des ténèbres*.[5] During the week we shall probably give, but with closed doors, *En famille* by Oscar Méténier,[6] and *L'Amante du Christ*.'[7]

'You have spoken about everything except yourself!'

'I am young, I have plenty of time before me; for the present I am devoted to art. After the success of *Le Baiser*[8] I could have entered the Comédie-Française; but what good would that have done me? I should have made £80 a month instead of making £20. But I prefer my position as director of the Théâtre Libre, and every 100 francs I spend on myself I look upon as a cartridge less in its arsenal.'

Then I thought of my country, where actors aspire only to be gentlemen, and where plays are written by those who can write nothing else. We are charitable barbarians, nothing more; thousands are subscribed yearly for the maintenance of indigent nondescripts who call themselves actors; but not a pound could be collected were the object an artistic one – for instance, to found a free theatre in England.

---

[1] Paul Alexis (1847–1901): playwright and novelist, friend and disciple of Zola. Contributed to the *Soirées de Médan* (1880), the manifesto volume of short stories by Zola and another five naturalist writers (see **26**, note 3).

[2] Auguste-Emile Bergerat (1845–1923): journalist, novelist and playwright. Bergerat did not belong to the naturalist school. *La Nuit bergamasque* is written in verse.

[3] An amateur theatre company.

[4] Léon Hennique (1851–1935): playwright and novelist, friend and disciple of Zola. Also a contributor to the *Soirées de Médan*.

[5] *The Power of Darkness*, by Tolstoy.

[6] Oscar Méténier (1859–1913) had been personal secretary to a Parisian commissioner of police from 1883 to 1889. In his subsequent career as a naturalist playwright he drew heavily on his experience of life among the lower and poverty-stricken classes. In 1895 he founded the Théâtre du Grand-Guignol. See **18**.

[7] One-act 'mystery play' in verse, by R. Darzens, Théâtre Libre, 19 October 1888.

[8] One-act play in verse, by Théodore de Banville. Premièred in quick succession at the Théâtre Libre (23 December 1887) and the Comédie-Française (14 May 1888).

30   Antoine on the director, 1 April 1903

André Antoine, 'Causerie sur la *mise en scène*', *Revue de Paris*, 1 April 1903, pp. 603–4 and 609–11. Reproduced in *Esthétique théâtrale*, eds. Monique Borie et al (Paris: CDU & SEDES, 1982)

It is the set which dictates the actor's movements, rather than the actors creating the scenery by their actions. This simple idea does not seem to be strikingly new. However, it is the whole secret of the novel impact which the Théâtre Libre has made on the theatrical scene.[. . .]

For a set to possess originality, ingenuity and character, it must first be based on a familiar place, be it a landscape or an interior. If the scene represents the inside of a house, it ought to be built completely, with its four walls and without regard to the one which will eventually disappear to let the audience see the action.

Then, taking into account architectural imperatives, one must clearly indicate doorways and windows. Plans should be drawn showing the layout of the house, even if other rooms and hallways will only be glimpsed at through half-open doors; spectators should feel the presence of the whole house surrounding the scene of the action.

Do you see how much easier and more convenient it will be, having considered the set from every angle, to determine exactly where the celebrated fourth wall should come off, ensuring that the most striking and the most telling features will be retained? [. . .]

The second part of the director's work begins. The characters can now be introduced into a *milieu* which breathes life and is full of light. But new problems arise! The actors' old routines, the in-built resistance bred by a stultifying tradition, all that gets in the way. We require active, living actors, and all we get are walking statues. Our aim is to breathe life into ordinary people and we are supposed to do it with men and women who have been taught that in the theatre one must never walk and talk at the same time. Just as it was 250 years ago. They continually step out of character to address the audience directly, to emphasize or comment on the playwright's text. [. . .]

With the exception of the Comédie-Française, whose artists have been specifically trained to play the classics, our best actors are those who have come up through the ranks. They have learned their craft the hard way in daily contact with the public after painstaking rehearsals. They might occasionally mumble, like Dupuis, Réjane and Huguenet; but they never 'declaim'[1]: they live their parts and are the wonderful interpreters of today's dramatic literature. Such actors know:

 - that movement is an actor's most intense means of expression;
 - that their whole physical being belongs to the character they are portraying and that, at certain times, their hands, their backs, their feet are more eloquent than speech;
 - that every time an actor is seen underneath the character the dramatic illusion is broken;
 - that by stressing a line, they spoil its impact.

They know that each scene of a play has its own rhythm, which contributes to the overall shape of the work, and that nothing – neither the need for a prompt nor a desire to upstage the rest of the cast – must be allowed to interfere.

They live their parts before us, faithfully representing all their physical and moral aspects.

[1] 'Ils ne "disent" pas . . .': Antoine makes a firm distinction between 'dire' (to say) and 'causer' (to chat). *Dire* is 'histrionic'; *causer* is familiar.

31   A hypernaturalistic set: Zola's *La Terre* at the Théâtre Antoine, 21 January 1902

Bibliothèque nationale, A.S.P., Paris

The play, adapted by Ch. Hugot and R. de Saint-Arroman, opened in Antoine's own theatre on 21 January 1902. The photograph shows the farmhouse of Act II. Note the feeding chicken in the foreground.

V The symbolist reaction

32(a) A symbolist production: Quillard's *La Fille aux mains coupées*, 20 March 1891. Programme note: 'the drama of the human soul'

Marcel Collière, [Quillard's] *La Fille aux mains coupées: argument de la mise en scène.* Programme du Théâtre d'Art, 20 March 1891, Collection Rondel, Bibliothèque de l'Arsenal. Reprinted in *Deux pièces symbolistes*, Textes littéraires XXII (University of Exeter, 1976)

As a reaction against the perceived hegemony of naturalism in the theatre, the young Paul Fort set up the Théâtre d'Art in 1890, forerunner of Lugné-Poe's Théâtre de l'Œuvre. Pierre Quillard's (1864–1912) *La Fille aux mains coupées*, published in 1886, was a 'manifesto' performance and its aim was to establish a new aesthetics on the stage.

The intention of this production is to emphasize the lyricism of the verse. The human voice is a precious instrument: it vibrates in the soul of each spectator. We have rejected the imperfect illusions of décor and other material means. Such devices are useful if you want a precise depiction of contemporary life. They are useless in 'dream' works, that is to say, in works of *real truth*.

We rely on speech to create the set within the spectator's mind. Through the magic of the human voice, we hope to achieve *complete* illusion. No material detail will be allowed to spoil the abstract concept.

Therefore, the verse has a continuous prose accompaniment which explains the changes in time and space, indicates different entities, reveals the facts. Thus the verse is freed to fulfil its essential and exclusive function: the lyrical expression of the characters' souls. The prose is an ever-present chorus: it follows the action, and nothing impedes the flight of the verse. Songs should only involve singing.

What set could imprison the drama of the human soul? The human soul is unchanging and true to itself: it is unaffected by useless succession of time sequences and meaningless geographical changes.

32(b) Paul Sérusier's lithograph for the programme

Paul Sérusier's[1] programme lithograph was reprinted in the short-lived art journal,
Théâtre d'Art, season 1891–2. Collection Samuel Josefowitz, Pully-Lausanne, Switzerland

[1] The set was designed by Paul Sérusier (1865–1927), a symbolist painter who was very closely
associated with Lugné-Poe's anti-naturalistic Théâtre de l'Œuvre.

32(c) *La Fille aux mains coupées* (extracts)

Pierre Quillard, *La Fille aux mains coupées*. Reprinted in *Deux pièces symbolistes*

The action takes place anywhere, but preferably in the Middle Ages.

*In a silent room, where the radiant silk of the dawn floats in through the glaucous
stained-glass windows, the GIRL is kneeling and praying in her adorable lily whiteness.*

The large blouse of white damask, embroidered with the star and silver chalices snowing on her breast, is hardly stirred by the breath of her pale body sculpted in white marble.

She reads from a heavy jewel-encrusted prayer book, in such a low voice that it seems the murmur of sumptuous fabrics which distant princesses rustle in heaven.

She drops the book and her eyes turn towards a bloodless Christ against a blood-stained sky; she seals her half-open lips and prays speechless dreams. [...]

THE MANSERVANT[1]

Oh my daughter, your hands are like fine corollas;
Your hands are a bouquet of may-blossom;
Your flesh exhales the breath of spring:
I do not harvest flowers with the blade.
You are delirious.

THE GIRL

Be quiet, the ulcer of unexpiable caresses
Bites into my flesh and melts my tallow.
Obey, without the mortal horror of confession:
The terror of which would break thy ears.
(She raises her hand in an awesome gesture.)
                                        I command!

(Without fear the willing martyr puts her hands which appeared from her sleeves on the porphyry table decorated with mosaic chimeras.
Her fixed eyes do not blink when the steely blue glaive comes down, gushing drops of purple on the heraldic beasts.
Brandishing in the twilight the twin torches of her mutilated arms she orders that a gilded crystal ewer be presented to her.
Horrifying and radiant a double water-lily with scarlet stems floats on a pink foam of trodden oriental grapes.)

Oh! The basin where the soul is cleansed!
Go take the ewer to my good father. Go.

[1] The heroine's father's old and trusted servant.

32(d) Quillard's aesthetic credo, 1891

P. Quillard, 'De l'inutilité absolue de la mise en scène exacte' (On the Absolute
Pointlessness of Precise *Mise en scène*), *La Revue d'art dramatique*, 22 (1 May 1891)

Nowhere does the inanity of naturalism appear more clearly than in the theatre.
Think of the splendour of the Théâtre Libre. There we have seen M. Antoine die
many a time with consummate art (I write art for want of a better word); on his
stage, men and women, whores and pimps hold the most banal conversations and
exchange the most vulgar remarks, *as in life*. Each of their remarks, taken in
isolation, is true and might have been said by the author's concierge, his lawyer,
by the man in the street, in fact by any anonymous, colourless individual you like.
Yet such dialogue in no way reveals how a character differs from his neighbour or
what constitutes in him the *quid proprium* which distinguishes one monad from
another. To give the complete illusion of life, it is thought clever to establish
scrupulously exact décors, real fountains murmur on the stage and meat drips
blood on the butcher's stall.[1] Yet, despite the meticulous care with which the
exterior of things is presented, the drama is enigmatic if not absent, and illusion
entirely lacking. This is because naturalism, the exploitation of trivial details and
of slight and contingent documents, is the very opposite of theatre.

Every dramatic work is above all a synthesis: Prometheus, Orestes, Oedipus,
Hamlet, Don Juan are examples of humanity in general, in whom an exclusive
and imperious passion is embodied with extraordinary intensity. The poet has
breathed supernatural life into them; he has created them by the power of
language [...] and the simple backdrops of fairground booths conjure up for the
spectators the poet's dream architecture. *The word creates the décor as well as
everything else.*

[...] The *mise en scène* should not disturb the illusion and, therefore, must be
very simple. If I say a 'marvellous palace', and if the scene-painter were to produce
the most beautiful and sophisticated creation he could devise, the effect would
never be the equivalent of a 'marvellous palace'. These two words will conjure up
in every soul a personal, private image, which will clash with the crude stage
representation. Far from aiding the free play of the imagination, the painted
canvas will impede it. *The décor must be a pure ornamental fiction which complements
the illusion through analogies of colour and line between it and the drama.* In most
cases, a backdrop and a few movable drapes will suffice to give an impression of
the infinite multiplicity of time and place. [...]

This aesthetic is not new; on the contrary it is as old as time. [...] Let's simply
recall the masks of Greek theatre or the anonymous antechamber of classical
tragedy. These are similar devices by means of which the informed spectator
collaborated in the drama. [...]

It can confidently be asserted that such an art-form has no place for trickery, since the poet rejects artifice and requires only the word and the human voice.

[1] Reference to *Les Bouchers*, a one-act 'expressionistic' play in verse, by Fernand Icres [see p. 5].

32(e)   A critic's judgement, 1891

Pierre Veber, 'Au Théâtre d'Art', *La Revue d'art dramatique*, 22 (15 April 1891)

On Thursday 26 March 1891, at the Théâtre d'Art, the symbolists had their *memorable evening*, a miniature version of the 'soirée of *Hernani*'.[1] [...] Mme Rachilde's[2] play and M. Quillard's mystery did not give rise to any incident. [...]

With M. Quillard's mystery, *La Fille aux mains coupées*, we are dealing with the most hermetic kind of symbolism. It would be boldness indeed on our part to undertake a detailed exposition of this mystery; the more so as the essence of a symbolist work is that it lends itself to all possible explanations. In a vaguely Byzantine décor a young girl is praying (in medieval costume). She aspires exclusively to divine love. A choir of invisible angels warns her that she must not cut herself off from the other kind of love. Enter a warrior who covers the girl's hands with kisses and departs. To eradicate the stain, she has her hands amputated. Abandoned in a boat, she reaches land in the domain of the Poet-King, who charms her. She would like to resist – but the angels, who have restored her hands so that she can embrace, order her to yield: 'The hell of kisses is the equal of our paradise.'

The impression produced is interesting, but rather fragmentary. The overall idea – or rather, the symbol – does not emerge clearly. Is the fault in us? Or is M. Quillard to blame? Apparently he has sought to represent the eternal drama of the soul aspiring to divine love, offended by the brutality of the real, and finding refuge in pagan love. [...]

All in all, M. Quillard's experiment can be summed up as a drastic simplification of dramatic devices; a narrator, placed in a corner of the proscenium arch, describes the scene, the décor and the action. The dominant role is given over to a lyrical text. The theatre disappears completely, so to speak, to make way for an intoned dialogue, a kind of poetic decoration. Even Maeterlinck does not go that far.

[1] A reference to the stormy first night of Victor Hugo's drama at the Comédie-Française in 1830 which assured the pre-eminence of Romantic over neo-classical aesthetics in the highbrow French theatre.
[2] Rachilde (1860–1953) was close both to the naturalist and the symbolist writers. She befriended Alfred Jarry and, later, wrote a study on the author of *Ubu: Jarry, ou le Surmâle des lettres* (1928). The play which the Théâtre d'Art performed on that memorable evening was *Madame la Mort* (Dame Death), described by Veber as 'a cerebral drama'.

33   Maeterlinck on symbolist theatre, 1896

Maurice Maeterlinck,[1] 'Le Tragique quotidien', in *Le Trésor des humbles* (Paris: Mercure de France, 1896). Translated by Alfred Sutro as 'The Tragical in Daily Life', in *The Treasure of the Humble* (London: George Allen, 1897), pp. 95–119

There is a tragic element in the life of every day that is far more real, far more penetrating, far more akin to the true self that is in us than the tragedy that lies in great adventure. [. . .]

Is it beyond the mark to say that the true tragic element, normal, deep-rooted, and universal, that the true tragic element of life only begins at the moment when so-called adventures, sorrows, and dangers have disappeared? Is the arm of happiness not longer than that of sorrow, and do not certain of its attributes draw nearer to the soul? Must we indeed roar like the Atrides, before the Eternal God will reveal Himself in our life? When we think of it, is it not the tranquillity that is terrible, the tranquillity watched by the stars? And is it in tumult or in silence that the spirit of life quickens within us? Is it not when we are told, at the end of the story, 'They were happy', that the great disquiet should intrude itself? What is taking place while they are happy? Are there not elements of deeper gravity and stability in happiness, in a single moment of response, than in the whirlwind of passion? Is it not then that we at last behold the march of time – aye, and of many another on-stealing besides, more secret still – is it not then that the hours rush forward? [. . .]

I admire Othello, but he does not appear to me to live the august daily life of a Hamlet, who has the time to live, inasmuch as he does not act. Othello is admirably jealous. But is it not perhaps an ancient error to imagine that it is at the moments when this passion, or others of equal violence, possess us, that we live our truest lives? I have grown to believe that an old man, seated in his armchair, waiting patiently, with his lamp beside him; giving unconscious ear to all the eternal laws that reign about his house, interpreting, without comprehending, the silence of doors and windows and the quivering voice of the light, submitting with bent head to the presence of his soul and his destiny – an old man, who conceives not that all the powers of this world, like so many heedful servants, are mingling and keeping vigil in his room, who suspects not that the very sun itself is supporting in space the little table against which he leans, or that every star in heaven and every fibre of the soul are directly concerned in the movement of an eyelid that closes, or a thought that springs to birth – I have grown to believe that he, motionless as he is, does yet live in reality a deeper, more human and more universal life than the lover who strangles his mistress, the captain who conquers in battle, or 'the husband who avenges his honour'.

[. . .] I do not know whether it be true that a static theatre is impossible. Indeed, to me it seems to exist already. Most of the tragedies of Aeschylus are tragedies without movement. In both the *Prometheus* and the *Suppliants*, events are lacking; and the entire tragedy of the *Choephorae* – surely the most terrible drama of antiquity – does but cling, nightmare-like, around the tomb of Agamemnon, until murder darts forth, as a lightning flash, from the accumulation of prayers, ever falling back upon themselves. [...]

Indeed, it is not in the actions but in the words that are found the beauty and greatness of tragedies that are truly beautiful and great. [...] One may even affirm that a poem draws the nearer to beauty and loftier truth in the measure that it eliminates words that merely explain the action, and substitutes for them others that reveal, not the so-called 'soul-state', but I know not what intangible and unceasing striving of the soul towards its own beauty and truth. And so much the nearer, also, does it draw to the true life. To every man does it happen, in his work-a-day existence, that some situation of deep seriousness has to be unravelled by means of words. Reflect for an instant. At moments such as those – nay, at the most commonplace of times – is it the thing you say or the reply you receive that has the most value? Are not other forces, other words one cannot hear, brought into being, and do not these determine the event? What I say often counts for so little; but my presence, the attitude of my soul, my future and my past, that which will take birth in me and that which is dead, a secret thought, the stars that approve, my destiny, the thousands of mysteries which surround me and float about yourself – all this it is that speaks to you at that tragic moment, all this it is that brings to me your answer. There is all this beneath every one of my words, and each one of yours; it is this, above all, that we see, it is this, above all, that we hear, ourselves notwithstanding.

---

[1] Maeterlinck (1862–1949) was a poet of the theatre. Like Jarry and Mallarmé (1842–98), he looked upon stagecraft with suspicion, convinced as he was that the performance of a play could never be as rich and as satisfying as its reading. 'I cannot say that any theatrical representation, whether of my own plays or of others, gives me real pleasure ... I think that almost all plays that are not mere stage-carpentry can be better appreciated in reading than on stage' (quoted in Jonas Barish, *The Antitheatrical Prejudice* (Berkeley: University of California Press, 1981), p. 339).

34   Theatre ticket for Maeterlinck's *Intérieur*, 15 March 1895

Ticket for Maeterlinck's *Intérieur*[1] by the Théâtre de l'Œuvre, 1895. Bibliothèque historique de la Ville de Paris

Like Antoine's Théâtre Libre, Lugné-Poe's Théâtre de l'Œuvre did not originally have its own theatre. Lugné-Poe's policy was to present new and foreign authors to the French public. His repertoire was eclectic, ranging from symbolism to naturalism, without disdaining the occasional less serious piece. Maeterlinck's very simple drama shares this bill, Lugné's fifth production at L'Œuvre, with an unperformed one-acter, *La Scène*, by André Lebey, a slight eighteenth-century play, *La Vérité dans le vin* (Truth in One's Cups) by Collé[2] and *Les Pieds nickelés* (Obstinacy) by the popular boulevard writer, Tristan Bernard.[3] The Théâtre de l'Œuvre spearheaded the symbolist anti-naturalist reaction and Lugné-Poe's *mises en scène* were characterized by stylized (almost non-existent) décors, artificial and monotonous delivery and an all-pervasive atmosphere of unreality.

THÉATRE DE " L'ŒUVRE "

SALLE DU NOUVEAU-THÉATRE, 15, RUE BLANCHE

(Deuxième Saison)
5ᵉ Spectacle

LA SCÈNE, de M. LEBEY

La Vérité dans le Vin   Les Pieds Nickelés
de COLLÉ   de Tristan BERNARD

INTÉRIEUR
de MAURICE MÆTERLINCK

FAUTEUIL D'ORCHESTRE Nᵒ 120

M

RIDEAU A 8 H. 1/4.

[1] The venue for this performance was the Eden Théâtre.
[2] Charles Collé (1709–89): eighteenth-century 'realist' playwright. *La Vérité dans le vin* was first performed at the Comédie-Française in 1747.
[3] Tristan Bernard (1866–1947): wit, journalist and playwright. He was very successful at the turn of the century.

35   Jarry's anti-naturalist manifesto, 1896

Alfred Jarry, 'De l'inutilité du théâtre au théâtre' (1896), in *Tout Ubu*, Le livre de poche (Paris: Librairie générale française, 1962), pp. 139–45. Translated by Barbara Wright as 'Of the Futility of the "Theatrical" in the Theatre', in *Selected Works of Alfred Jarry*, eds. Roger Shattuck and Simon Watson Taylor (London: Methuen, 1965), pp. 69–75

What follows is a list of a few things which are particularly horrifying and incomprehensible to the five hundred,[1] and which clutter up the stage to no purpose; first and foremost, the *décor* and the *actors*.

Décor is a hybrid, neither natural nor artificial. If it were exactly like nature it would be a superfluous duplication ... It is not artificial, in the sense that it is not, for the five hundred, the embodiment of the outside world as the playwright has seen and re-created it.

And in any case it would be dangerous for the poet to impose on a public of artists the décor that he himself would conceive. In any written work there is a hidden meaning, and anyone who knows how to read sees that aspect of it that makes sense for him. Every spectator has a right to see a play in a décor which does not clash with his own view of it. For the general public, on the other hand, any 'artistic' décor will do, as the masses do not understand anything by themselves, but wait to be told how to see things.

There are two sorts of décor: indoor and outdoor. Both are supposed to represent either rooms or the countryside. We shall not revert to the question, which has been settled once and for all, of the stupidity of *trompe-l'œil*. Let us state that the said *trompe-l'œil* is aimed at people who only see things roughly. That is to say, who do not see at all: it scandalizes those who see nature in an intelligent and selective way, as it presents them with a caricature of it by someone who lacks all understanding. Zeuxis is supposed to have deceived some birds with his stone grapes and Titian's virtuosity hoodwinked an innkeeper.

Décor by someone who cannot paint is nearer to abstract décor, as it gives only essentials. In the same way simplified décor picks out only relevant aspects.

In the conditions we are advocating, each piece of scenery needed for a special purpose – a window to be opened, for instance, or a door to be broken down – becomes a prop and can be brought in like a table or a torch.

The actor adapts his face to that of the character. He should adapt his whole body in the same way. The play of his features, his expressions, etc., are caused by various contractions and extensions of the muscles of his face. No one has realized that the muscles remain the same under the make-believe, made-up face, and that Mounet[2] and Hamlet do not have the same zygomatics, even though in anatomical terms we think that they are the same man. Or else people say that the difference is negligible. The actor should use a mask to envelop his head, thus replacing it by the effigy of the CHARACTER. His mask should not follow the masks in the Greek theatre to indicate simply tears or laughter, but should indicate the nature of the character: the Miser, the Waverer, the Covetous man accumulating crimes. [...]

By slow nodding and lateral movements of his head the actor can displace the shadows over the whole surface of the mask. And experience has shown that the six main positions (and the same number, in profile, though these are less clear) suffice for every expression. We shall not cite any examples, as they vary according to the nature of the mask, and because everyone who knows how to watch a puppet-show will have been able to observe this for himself.

They are simple expressions, and therefore universal. Present-day mime makes the great mistake of using conventional mime language, which is tiring and incomprehensible. An example of this convention is the hand describing a vertical ellipse around the face, and a kiss being implanted on this hand to suggest a beautiful woman – and love. An example of universal gesture is the marionette displaying its bewilderment by starting back violently and hitting its head against a flat.

Behind all these accidentals there remains the essential expression, and the finest thing in many scenes is the impassivity of the mask, which remains the same whether the words it emits are grave or gay.

---

[1] For the elitist Jarry (1873–1907), author of the notorious *Ubu roi*, the world was peopled by no more than 500 aesthetes capable of understanding 'high art'.

[2] Jean Mounet-Sully (1841–1916): one of the greatest tragic actors of the second half of the nineteenth century. Joined the Comédie-Française in 1872. Received the Légion d'honneur in 1889.

VI   Popular theatre

36   A citizens' theatre for a socialist society, December 1900

Jean Jaurès,[1] 'Le Théâtre social', *La Revue d'art dramatique*, 10 (15th year, December 1900), pp. 1065–77

CITIZENS! [...] On the day that socialist theatre is established, the social Revolution will nearly be accomplished. The theatre is not, and by its very nature cannot be, a force in the forefront of change ...

[...] Why? In the first place because the powers that be, society at large, are more frightened by new ideas set out on the stage than by new ideas propagated through books. When new ideas are expressed on the stage, when the demands of the suffering resurgent classes are voiced on the stage, it is no longer just a question of a new idea seeking out the individual in the tranquil meditation of solitary reading. What happens is that the proletariat, the exploited, the down-trodden, rise up physically, as it were, and demand their liberation. (*Applause.*)

This is what has always frightened the ruling classes, and that is why new ideas – revolutionary ideas – only reach the stage after they have attained a position of dominance over people's minds. That is why if the social theatre is destined to assert itself, it will be an excellent symptom of the progress of our ideas; the drama is already to a certain extent the prelude to Revolution itself, since, like the Revolution, it mobilizes the masses.

[...] Over the last century and a half, from the middle of the eighteenth century to the present, we can distinguish, from the social point of view, three principal phases in the theatre. First, during the second half of the eighteenth century, it contributes to the preparation of the French Revolution and the coming of bourgeois society; then, during virtually the entire nineteenth century, it can be seen as a partial critique to which bourgeois society, overwhelmed by the evidence of its own evils and its own contradictions, is obliged to subject itself. This can be observed in part, inadequately, with Dumas *fils* [see 10]; in a bolder and more extensive fashion with Ibsen [see 133]; – and finally we enter, with the dramatic works of Hauptmann, *Before Sunrise, The Weavers* [see 55], with Zola's banned *Germinal* (*Applause. – Cries of 'Long Live Zola!'*) we enter the period when we no longer see bourgeois society timidly criticizing itself, but the proletariat, the working masses, making their way on to the stage. [...]

97

Now at last we see the advent of the proletariat, the advent of the working-class depicted on the stage, in *Germinal*, and in the plays of Hauptmann. I hardly need tell you that in *Before Sunrise* the peasants and miners of Silesia make up almost all the characters, and that in *The Weavers* the main character is that mass of Silesian weavers with its unbelievable suffering and its unbelievable torments, which only revolts when spurred on by extremes of pain. [...]

It is only a few years since the proletariat began to figure on the stage and moreover it still speaks very timidly, for *The Weavers* of Hauptmann are the weavers of half a century ago. Hauptmann depicts the great strikes of 1840 and 1855 in Silesia, strikes in which the weavers don't have a single socialist idea, not a single idea of how to organize. It is simply the human animal driven beyond its limits. [...] This is not as yet an organization which is conscious, deliberate, motivated by an idea: that proletariat has not yet made its way on to the stage.

[...] What strikes me is that today's playwrights, in the criticism which they aim at bourgeois society, go more boldly, more profoundly, more cruelly to the very core of falsehood. Thus, for example, the criticism levelled at the laws of the Church and of the family is far harsher, more far-reaching, more corrosive, more revolutionary in the work of Paul Hervieu[2] than in that of Alexandre Dumas *fils*. And a simple study of apparently objective and impartial facts – which Brieux[3] in *La Robe rouge* (The Red Gown) applies to the judiciary – leaves not a stone of these institutions standing. I do not know what Brieux thinks personally, but I say that he has created a revolutionary work, because, at the very moment when he sliced his scalpel into society, the Revolution itself, unknown to him, pushed his arm so that he would drive the blade in.

[1] Jean Jaurès (1859–1914): historian and university professor of philosophy; sat as a socialist MP from 1893. A right-wing fanatic assassinated him in 1914 because of Jaurès's internationalist and pacifist convictions.

[2] Paul Hervieu (1857–1915): *Point de lendemain* (Cercle de l'Union artistique, 14 January 1890), *Les Paroles restent* (Variétés, 17 November 1892), *Les Tenailles* (Comédie-Française, 28 September 1895), *La Loi de l'homme* (Comédie-Française, 15 February 1897).

[3] Eugène Brieux (1858–1932): a born crusader. Brieux started his career as a journalist in Rouen. His first play was *Ménages d'artistes* (Théâtre Libre, 21 March 1890). If, theatrically, his plays are uninspiring, many had a direct impact on French social life (particularly *Les Avariés* (Damaged Goods), 1902, dealing with the taboo question of syphilis).

37   Popular theatre in Paris: a project, 1899

'The Popular Theatre in Paris', *La Revue d'art dramatique*, 8 (October–December 1899), pp. 321–3[1]

In Paris there are theatres for all sections of the public, but there is no theatre aimed at the people, that is to say the nation as a whole.

In Paris there are as many tendencies and forms of dramatic art as there are intellectual categories corresponding to social divisions: each of these forms of art appeals to one group of individuals, and remains inaccessible, or a matter of indifference, to the others. No dramatic art exists which might create between individuals a sense of beauty they can experience in common.

Fragmented people and fragmented art. The more they are divided, the smaller they become. This fragmentation ultimately produces scorn or mistrust between them, and barbarism or sterility within them.

We believe that the ideal for a people is to become a fraternal whole; that the ideal for art is to be a complete art.

Between the elite playhouse, where thought is refined to the point where it ceases to exist, and the entertainment of the populace, where feeling is amplified to the point of crudity, we want to create a theatre dedicated to all, open to all, in which thought and feeling might be reconciled, where social solidarity will be strengthened by equal access to beauty.

Is such a theatre possible? Yes. In former times it was a reality. Art is only great art when it is the expression of the feelings, ideas and dreams of a people: and it only achieves harmony if it speaks for all.

Conceived with the aim of educating the people, a popular theatre will also bring about a liberation and rebirth of art. The people's hunger has until now been staved off with crude fare. We intend to satisfy it with an art matured through human thought, enabling such an art to draw youthful vigour and eternal freshness from popular imagination.

What we have to do is find a means of rapidly establishing this new theatre and a plan for its practical organization. We hereby appeal, in the name of an undertaking which will be the work of all, to the imagination, the labour and the resources of everyone.[2]

---

[1] The signatories of the manifesto, all members of the steering committee of this aborted attempt at setting up a 'popular theatre' in Paris at the turn of the century, were made up of prominent novelists, playwrights and critics. They were: Henry Bauer, Lucien Besnard, Maurice Bouchor, Georges Bourdon, Lucien Descaves, Robert de Flers, Anatole France, Gustave Geffroy, Jean Jullien, Louis Lumet, Octave Mirbeau, Maurice Pottecher, Romain Rolland, Camille de Saint-Croix, Edouard Schuré, Gabriel Trarieux, Jean Vignaud and Emile Zola.

[2] The readers of the journal were invited to send in ideas which would enable the committee to draw up the perfect plan for a popular theatre in Paris. The deadline was set for 1 February 1900. A prize of 500 francs would go to the best submission. In March 1900, the journal's editorial (p. 193) stated that twenty-three manuscripts had been received and that some of them were such 'major contributions' that a decision had to be postponed until April to allow more time to evaluate the various schemes. In the event, three prizes were awarded: a first award of 300 francs to Eugène Morel, and two of 100 francs each. Morel's project, 'Projet de théâtres populaires', was published in the *Revue d'art dramatique*, December 1900, pp. 1115–86. Morel advocated the creation throughout France of a network of weekly repertory theatres which would operate for twenty-five weeks each year. He proposed cheap season tickets, free access for children, cheap catering facilities, an early

evening start, easy transport to and from the theatre, a mixture of classical and new plays, and so on. Many of his ideas were to be adopted by the Théâtre National Populaire after the Second World War and in the many new theatres (Centres dramatiques, Théâtres nationaux) created throughout France in the 1950s and 1960s. In 1900 the project was sent, with a petition, to the Minister for Education and Culture (Ministre de l'Instruction publique et des Beaux-Arts) but was ignored by the authorities.

38   A popular audience in a 'Theatre for the People', c.1900
Bibliothèque historique de la Ville de Paris

The audience attending the ninety-seventh popular gala of *Thirty Years of Theatre*, at the suburban theatre of Belleville. The bill was made up of a play by Molière (*Les Femmes savantes* (The Learned Ladies) performed by the Comédie-Française), a ballet (*L'Invitation à la valse* from Weber's *Freischütz*, by the Paris Opéra), extracts from an opera (Verdi's *Le Trouvère*), a song recital and a lecture by a music and drama critic. This concept of bringing art to the people had an important role in the early years of the people's theatre movement. Popular prices ranged from three francs in the few boxes available to fifty centimes in the upper gallery (top prices in Paris at the time were between ten and fifteen francs, the gallery being one franc or one franc fifty centimes usually) and advance booking did not cost more between noon and 6.00 p.m., as was the case then in most theatres.

Many French theatre workers, from the mid-nineteenth century to the present, are uneasy about the bourgeois, elitist nature of their art and business. So, regularly, one sees initiatives whose primary aim is 'to bring the theatre to the people'. Firmin Gémier, strongly influenced by the intellectual climate of the time, attempted such an experiment with his Théâtre National Ambulant (1911). Jean Vilar made the Théâtre National Populaire (TNP) world-famous in the 1950s and 1960s, continuing in the tradition of 'making culture available to all'.

39   Popular theatre: family ticket for a suburban theatre

Theatre Archives, Bibliothèque historique de la Ville de Paris

This concessionary ticket, valid for 'one or several persons', gives a useful indication of the genuinely popular nature of the suburban theatres of the period. These theatres, which included Montmartre, Montparnasse, Grenelle, the Batignolles and Belleville, catered for local audiences. It was at such theatres that melodrama survived into the second decade of the twentieth century.

40   Call for a nationally subsidized popular theatre, 1899

Maurice Pottecher,[1] 'Le Théâtre populaire à Paris', *La Revue d'art dramatique*, 7 (April–September 1899), pp. 405–23

The people's theatre cannot partake of the general, eternal life of art, if from the start it condemns itself to be merely a political manifestation with subjects limited to a certain number of themes: social demands, cries of anger, calls for revolution – however justified these calls and demands may be in other respects – and if it addresses one class – however important that class may be – to the exclusion of the rest of the nation and the rest of humanity. [...]

Being aimed at spectators who have little culture, whose taste has been kept in a state of almost complete barbarity, there is every chance that it would not always refrain from pandering to that crude taste, if it were not helped by a minority of intellects to fight against such a taste and school it.

The Theatre of the People must be conceived of as aiming to bring together in a common emotion all those elements which go to make up a people. [...] It has no reason to exist and no chance of surviving unless it truly creates a sense of brotherhood between spectators of all classes. In the mass of these people, experiencing emotion together through the creative force of poetry and influenced by the nervous energy which constitutes the collective soul of a crowd, one section must communicate to the other its intelligence and the other must communicate its sincerity.

It must limit neither the field of its concerns nor the choice of its subjects; equally, it must not restrict to a certain category of citizens the aesthetic pleasure and moral teaching which it sets out to offer.

Just as the bourgeois theatre has been reproached for increasingly coming to resemble a place of ill repute, so the Theatre of the People must not expose itself to the reproach that it is principally an offshoot of the meeting hall or political platform.

[...] It is important that the Theatre of the People should have a serious and solemn character and that the laughter it provokes should have nothing in common with the casual after-dinner diversion audiences expect from a facetious or smutty show. [...]

In founding the first Theatre of the People in Lorraine [Bussang], we expressed the hope that our venture would not be an isolated instance.

It was our wish that throughout the different regions of France ventures similar to ours would soon be set up, offering the prospect of theatrical pleasure and education to the section of the people which has remained deprived of them, and at the same time opening up for art a path towards truth.

It was a question of creating provincial theatres, making use of the resources of each region, drawing on the particular riches of those customs, legends and history which together comprise the heritage of France, calling upon the particular genius of each place and arousing that life which lay dormant but not dead in the limbs of this great body. All those concerned with the problem of decentralization[2] quickly associated this endeavour with the ideas they uphold, and – from that point of view – emphasized its particular importance, which an overriding principle had prohibited us from insisting upon: the emphasis on the artistic element of our work before all else, and the avoidance of areas where politics and contemporary events are dominant. [...]

It will be through the spirit that sustains it that the Theatre of the People will differ from all its predecessors; it will be a modern creation, drawing its life from contemporary life; it will interest all men of today by speaking their language, appealing to their concerns, their memories and their hopes. In a word it will be for French people of the twentieth century not what Greek theatre is for us, but what it was for the contemporaries of Aeschylus, Sophocles, Aristophanes and Euripides. [...]

How in practical terms can we manage to found, organize and maintain this theatre? [...]

I. THE PREMISES Can the Theatre of the People be set up in an already existing theatre? [...] No. [...] I believe that in order to achieve something truly new and to demonstrate that it is new, it is necessary to have a *new* theatre. [...]

The old auditoria are completely at odds with the very idea of a Theatre of the People. The way these auditoria are divided into stalls, grand circle, upper circle, lower and upper galleries, etc., sanctions the division of the audience into castes and harshly affirms social inequality.[3] Furthermore, this layout is inadequate regarding sightlines and acoustics. Among the spectators, one section seems to be there in order to be seen: the others can see only with difficulty or not at all. The foyers take up almost half of certain buildings. This is all very well for that conception of the theatre which sees it as a place for the pleasures of fashionable society, a place to meet people and chat while occasionally watching a scene, a speech or a famous actor. Wagner understood this and pointed out that such an arrangement was inappropriate to the theatre of true art and serious thought: at Bayreuth, as everybody knows, the auditorium is laid out in tiers: all the seats are alike, except for the distance that separates them from the stage: one can see and hear well from all of them. In essence this is the layout of the ancient amphitheatres. [...]

2. THE ACTORS Michelet thought that the dramatic work which was born of the people, inspired by the people, would find amongst the people its interpreters.

Indeed it was actors from the people whom we called upon in the provinces to make up our rustic theatre company. They were not members of the acting profession, but were motivated by a common desire and inclination to bring to life the characters conceived by the imagination of the poet. Experience has proved that the historian was right, and that one can find, without too much difficulty, even in a far-flung village, young people capable of turning themselves informally into tragic or comic actors. Some of them possess a surprising instinctive gift, talents for imitation, an admirable verve or demeanour; what the interpretation lacks in trained skills, it makes up for in freshness and sincerity. [...] But as a rule it is advisable to entrust the tragic characters to the more cultured and experienced of the committed unpaid actors. We must not forget that the Theatre of the People company must include such actors as these alongside its more humble players. [...]

3. SOLEMNITY [...] This theatre is intended to provide festive occasions for the

people: currently only society people and those who have nothing to do can enjoy such events all the time, not the people who have their living to earn first.

Dates will be chosen for these dramatic performances like those the Greeks chose for their theatrical celebrations: seasonal festivals, anniversaries, important events in the life of the community. [...]

Why should we not institute a public competition, along the lines of those held in Greece, featuring the works accepted by a selection committee? The public would then be called upon, each year, to decide for itself and to award a prize to one of the three or four works performed before it. Under these circumstances, the authors, even those who did not win an award, could not, in all good faith, dispute the competence of the people's judgement, since it would no longer be to one section of the public, but to the people in its entirety that they had addressed themselves: and even if they think that the judgement is mistaken, they will have to bow to it. [...]

5. RESOURCES [...] Over a million francs will be required to found this undertaking. Where shall we get the necessary funds? [...]

(Certainly not from speculative investment.) The Theatre of the People should be considered as a national institution: it presents to the people the lesson of art. It will be for France a veritable sanctuary dedicated to the veneration of the French – that is to say the human – genius in its most noble traditions and its most ardent expectations. So the Theatre of the People should be a national asset and the property of the nation, as is the Louvre, as are the *lycées*, as are still, all in all, the Opéra, the Opéra-Comique, the Comédie-Française and the Odéon, which were built at the nation's expense, and which are maintained and subsidized by the nation.

---

[1] Maurice Pottecher (1867–1960): journalist, writer, playwright and champion of 'popular theatre', or 'theatre for all', or 'theatre for the people'. In the early 1890s he organized 'popular' theatre performances in his native Bussang (Vosges) and in 1895 he launched there a summer festival, 'Le Théâtre du Peuple' with his own *Le Diable marchand de goutte* (The Devil Liquor Peddler). 'Le Théâtre du Peuple de Bussang' is still thriving today, showing plays performed by local amateurs working with a professional director during the summer months and attracting large numbers of spectators.

[2] Since the seventeenth century France has become a highly centralized country and, as far as artists are concerned, their fame can only be established if their work is seen in Paris. Since the end of the nineteenth century various movements of 'decentralization' have taken place, with little success, in all fields of French life. Although, since the 1950s, there are 'national theatres' dotted throughout the country, Paris is still the 'centre of excellence' and *real* decentralization a long way off.

[3] See also 158.

VII The uncertain future

Dada was a short-lived movement (c.1916–22) which changed the direction of twentieth-century European art, in general, and theatre, in particular. Dada was born out of the frustration of the generation that came of age at the beginning of the First World War; out of frustration with the state of the world and with artists' perceived inability to effect any positive change. Marcel Raymond: 'Dada appears as a desperate systematic scepticism leading directly to negation.' So, Dada said 'NO'. No to logic, to social hierarchies, to received ideas . . .; no to a world that made possible the horrors of the First World War. Dada stood for the 'abolition of memory, of archaeology, of prophets, of the future . . .', but stated its faith 'in every god that is the immediate product of spontaneity'. Dada's rejection of all traditions on which Western art is founded and its championing of anti-art (whatever that means) paradoxically laid the foundation of later twentieth-century developments in theatre. In Zurich (Cabaret Voltaire, 1916), and then in Paris, Berlin and New York, Dada, under the impulse of Tristan Tzara,[1] mounted a number of subversive events, undermining the visual (as with Marcel Duchamp's 'ready-mades') as well as the performing arts.

Dada treats language, psychology, interpersonal relationships – if such traditional concepts may be evoked at all – with derision. Theatrical communication – in effect, any kind of communication – is deemed to be illusory. Language, characters, actions, comedy or tragedy – all these theatrical ingredients which had achieved such a high degree of sophistication – were excluded from their dramatic writing and theatrical performance. Of his play, *The Gas Heart*, Tzara writes: 'I beg my interpreters to treat this play as they would a masterpiece like *Macbeth*, but to treat the author, who's no genius, without any respect . . .' The characters, Nose, Mouth, Ear, Eye, Neck and Eyebrow, speak nonsense ('The void drinks the void: air was born with blue eyes, that's why it endlessly swallows aspirin') and dance bewildering ballets. With its daring innovations and total disregard for public approval, Dada opened the way, after a second universal cataclysm, for Ionesco's *Bald Prima Donna*, Beckett's *Waiting for Godot* or Pinter's *Homecoming*. Twenty-five centuries of constant striving for more rationality were to bring forth the irrational. As Ubu said, 'Hornstrumpot! We shall not have succeeded in demolishing everything unless we demolish the ruins as well. But the only way I can see of doing that is to use them to put up a lot of fine, well-designed buildings.'

---

[1] Tristan Tzara (1896–1963): French poet of Romanian origin and founder of Dada. He was the most dedicated exponent of Dadaism, first in Zurich (Cabaret Voltaire, 1916) before moving to Paris in 1920. See *La Première Aventure céleste de M. Antipyrine* (1916–19), *Vingt-cinq poèmes* (1918). Tzara's first manifesto, *Monsieur Antipyrine*, was read at the first Dada event in Zurich (Salle Waag) on 14 July 1916; and the last, *On Feeble Love and Bitter Love*, in Paris, on 12 December 1920.

41   Dada rejects all tradition, 1919

'Proclamation sans prétension', read at the eighth Soirée Dada in Zurich (Salle Kaufleuten), 9 April 1919. Published in *Anthologie Dada*, 1919 (reprinted in *Sept manifestes Dada, lampisteries* (Paris: J. J. Pauvert, 1963); see also *Seven Dada Manifestos and Lampisteries*, tr. Barbara Wright (London: John Calder, 1977)

un-
pretentious
proclamation

Art is falling asleep as a new world is being born "ART" — *a parrot word* — replaced by **DADA**, **PLESIOSAURUS**, or handkerchief

Talent WHICH CAN BE LEARNT *turns a poet into a chemist* **TODAY** *the fingering critic no longer lingers on*

Hypertrophic and hyperesthesic painters and hypnotized by the hyacinths of seemingly hypocritical muezzins

LET'S CONSOLIDATE THE PRECISE HARVEST OF CALCULUS

HIPPODROME OF IMMORTAL CERTAINTIES : *Nothing is important nothing is transparent nor apparent*

MUSICIANS GO SMASH YOUR BLIND INSTRUMENTS on the stage

The **SYRINGE** is only there to help me understand. **I write as naturally as I piss or puke**

Art requires surgery

Art is nothing but a CONCEIT stocked by the TIMIDITY of the bedpan, **hysteria** bred in the artist's **studio**

We are looking for a straight **pure sober unique** strength we are looking for NOTHING we assert the ENERGY of every **instant**

anti-philosophy of spontaneous acrobatics

Presently I detest the man who whispers before the interval — eau de cologne — rancid theatre. ECSTATIC FART.

IF EVERYONE SAYS THE OPPOSITE, IT'S
BECAUSE HE'S RIGHT

Get the geyser of our blood gushing —
underwater squadrons of transchro-
matic aeroplanes, cellular and digital metals for
somersaulting images

above the regulations of

Beauty and its tests

It's not for cretins
who contemplate their navel

Germany, 1850–1916

Edited and translated by MICHAEL PATTERSON

Introduction

For most of the nineteenth century, German-language theatre was in a state of stagnation. The last third of the eighteenth century had been a period of intense theatrical activity and progress: the pioneering work of Lessing, especially at the new if short-lived National Theatre in Hamburg; the translation of Shakespeare into German by Wieland; the establishment of impressive court and municipal theatres under the directorship of former touring actor-managers like Schröder, Seyler and Koch; the extraordinary and seminal experiments of the 'Storm and Stress' dramatists; the bold theatrical style of the National Theatre at Mannheim, which dared to première Schiller's *Die Räuber* (The Robbers); and the personal involvement of Germany's two greatest writers, Goethe and Schiller, in the Court Theatre at Weimar. Indeed, it was during this period of ferment that Germany could be said finally to have developed a native theatre tradition in place of the slavish imitation of French models, which had formed the basis for Gottsched's proposals for theatre reform earlier in the century.

Within a few years of the start of the nineteenth century, Schiller was dead, Goethe had given up his directorship of the Weimar Court Theatre, and German theatre entered a period of unadventurous consolidation.[1] The formal, classical style of Weimar had its imitators, but generally the more realistic style of Berlin, Mannheim and Hamburg prevailed, the so-called 'realism' often providing the pretext for historical pageant and spectacle. The repertoire became safe, performances routine. Major dramatists were given little or no support: Goethe's *Faust II* had to wait twenty-two years for its première; Kleist's finest play, *Prinz Friedrich von Homburg*, was not performed until ten years after the writer's death; neither of Büchner's masterpieces, *Dantons Tod* (Danton's Death) and *Woyzeck*, was performed in the nineteenth century at all. Ludwig Tieck, who had become Dramaturg in Dresden in 1825 and had been responsible for the staging of *Homburg* there in 1821, was one of the very few theatre practitioners who were

---

[1] For a much fuller discussion of this period, see especially Marvin Carlson, *The German Stage in the Nineteenth Century* (Metuchen: Scarecrow Press, 1972); Heinz Kindermann, *Theatergeschichte Europas*, vols. VI–VIII (Salzburg: Müller, 1964–8); Michael Patterson, *The First German Theatre: Schiller, Goethe, Kleist and Büchner in Performance* (London: Routledge, 1990).

prepared to take risks with new material or unfamiliar styles – in his case, above all by experimenting with a revival of the multi-levelled Shakespearian stage (*A Midsummer Night's Dream*, 1843).

On the positive side, the first two thirds of the nineteenth century saw the theatre established in Germany as an indispensable part of cultured living. Theatres became big business, catering for the needs of the growing middle class, and the phenomenon of the full-time theatre critic made its appearance. None of this was particularly conducive to the aesthetic development of the theatre (the critics offering journalistic appraisals rather than critical judgements), but it did accord the theatre the social and economic status which would make any later progress much more significant.

The 1870s witnessed this long-awaited progress, which was associated with four major impulses. In 1869 a new Trade Law (*Gewerbeordnung*) was passed to promote economic growth. One of its effects was to remove almost all restrictions on the establishment of new theatres, ushering in a new era of 'Theatre Freedom' (see 45). Within eighteen months, ninety new theatres had opened in North Germany alone, making for a huge upsurge in theatrical activity, even if, predictably, it was not of a very consistent quality.

The second important event was the unification of Germany in 1871, providing a strong central government under Bismarck, and a period of colossal economic expansion and relative social stability (see 44). In the world of theatre itself, the two significant dates were 1873, the year the Meiningen troupe first toured to Berlin, and 1876, when Wagner staged *Der Ring der Nibelungen* in Bayreuth. Their respective contributions were fundamentally different, almost opposed. The Duke of Saxe-Meiningen can be recognized as a major forerunner of naturalist theatre (see 51 and 53); Wagner as an inspiration to anti-naturalistic and symbolist practitioners at the turn of the century (see 60).

The achievements of the Meininger are well documented.[2] Among them were: the revival of the classics, above all the plays of Shakespeare, but also those of Schiller, Goethe, Lessing, Molière, Sophocles and Euripides; the restoration of scenes, like the murder of Macduff's family, previously thought too violent to be staged; the striking authenticity of costumes, settings and properties; the detailed care given to all elements of performance, especially in the handling of crowd scenes; the importance given to the overall stage-picture; the careful use of off-stage sound effects; the favouring of the realistic box-set, even for the classics, in

---

[2] See especially, Ann Marie Koller, *The Theater Duke. George II of Saxe-Meiningen and the German Stage* (Stanford University Press, 1984); Steven DeHart, *The Meininger Theater 1776–1926* (Michigan: UMI Research Press, 1981); Max Grube, *The Story of the Meininger*, trans. A.M. Koller, ed. W. Cole (Coral Gates: University of Miami Press, 1963); John Osborne, 'From Political to Cultural Despotism: the Nature of the Saxe-Meiningen Aesthetic', *Theatre Quarterly*, 5, 17 (1975), pp. 40–54, and ed., *Die Meininger. Texte zur Rezeption* (Tübingen: Niemeyer, 1980).

place of painted wings and backdrop; and, perhaps most impressive of all, the emphasis on ensemble playing.

As an opera-composer, Wagner's influence on the theatre was predictably less specific. Nevertheless, his vision of the *Gesamtkunstwerk*, the total work of art,[3] was to have a profound influence on Adolphe Appia and thence on much theatrical experimentation of the early twentieth century. Wagner viewed opera as an almost religious experience to be shared by pilgrims journeying to out-of-the-way Bayreuth, sitting in a darkened auditorium (the first in Germany), and submitting themselves to colour, light and sound in mystic harmony. The reality fell far short of his vision: the 'pilgrims' were wealthy socialites, few with a genuine interest in opera, and the scenery, costumes and lighting were inadequate and generally tawdry.

While it took a couple of decades for Wagner's ideas to achieve full recognition in the theatre (Appia's *Die Musik und die Inscenierung* was published in 1899), the effects of the Meiningen style were much more immediate. There had already existed in Germany a tradition of the 'middle-class tragedy', notably in Lessing and Schiller, and continued by Hebbel with his *Maria Magdalene* (1844). In the 1890s, with the popularity of Ibsen on the German stage and with impulses coming from Antoine's Théâtre Libre in Paris, naturalism became for a while the dominant new style in German theatre, its leading exponents being the director Otto Brahm (see **58**) and the playwright Gerhart Hauptmann (see **55** and **56**).

Naturalism was soon abandoned by more progressive elements, however, including eventually Hauptmann himself. The theatre turned to a less representational style, whether in the *Neuromantik* with its chief representative Hofmannsthal (see **64** and **65**) or in the less important *Neuklassik*, especially in the work of Paul Ernst (see **63**).

Towering over this theatrical activity was the young Max Reinhardt, one of the most prolific and arguably the most important European theatre director of this century, himself too much of an eclectic to be closely identified with any particular school or movement (see **66**, **67(a)** and **67(b)**). Reinhardt was in the forefront of the small theatre movement, founding with his Kammerspiele in Berlin the first ever studio theatre attached to a main-house auditorium (see **46**). A similar development could be observed with the growth of the literary cabaret, a theatre form peculiar to the modern period, in which both Reinhardt and Wedekind were deeply involved (see **66** and **68(a)**).

In Wedekind's plays and theories (**71**, **72(a)** and **72(b)**), and in the bold experiments of the Munich Art Theatre under Fuchs (**69** and **70**), the way was prepared for the expressionist revolution in theatre. But this radical reassessment

[3] See Hans Gal, *Richard Wagner* (London: Gollancz, 1976), esp. pp. 158ff.

of theatrical communication in German expressionism, from which strands as diverse as the theatre of Bertolt Brecht and Samuel Beckett were to emerge,[4] would not have been possible without the exploration of so many different theatrical possibilities in the two decades leading up to the First World War.

[4] See Michael Patterson, *The Revolution in German Theatre 1900–1933* (London: Routledge, 1981).

I General situation of the theatre in German-speaking countries, 1850–1914

42 A survey of German-language theatres, 1911

Charlotte Engel Reimers: *Die deutschen Bühnen und ihre Angehörigen. Eine Untersuchung über ihre wirtschaftliche Lage* (Leipzig: Duncker & Humblot, 1911)

We are fortunate indeed that a carefully researched investigation into virtually all aspects of contemporary German-language theatre practice was undertaken towards the end of the period under consideration, and Dr Reimers's work will form a substantial introduction to this section. Her study was based on a questionnaire circulated in the theatre season 1907/8. Replies were received from 237 theatres and 13 touring groups.

(a) Foreword [pp. xv–xvi]

There is no other nation that takes its theatre so seriously as we, or brings to it such enormous financial sacrifices. The Latins may have greater talent for acting; the Germans certainly make better audiences. They inject German seriousness and German thoroughness into the theatre, and actors, in their turn, respond to this. Only Germans regard their theatre as a means of educating the people. The Latin peoples want to be excited and amused; for the puritanical English the theatre is a source of sinful pleasure. Both these nations pay more attention to the music hall than they do to the theatre. [...] We alone regard theatre as a moral institution.[1]

[1] Reference to Schiller's essay, 'Die Schaubühne als eine moralische Anstalt betrachtet' (1784).

(b) Types of theatre [pp. 26–30]

According to the Stage Almanac[1] for 1908/9, there are 592 theatres in German-speaking areas (i.e. the German Empire,[2] Austria,[3] German Switzerland,[4] and including the Russian towns of Lodz,[5] Riga[6] and St Petersburg, where there are German theatres, but excluding the German theatres in America).

First, there are 32 *court theatres*. [...] They are the property of a prince or an emperor, a luxury which they permit themselves and in which they invite their subjects to participate. The costs are covered by private means, if the takings are insufficient. Their existence is therefore secure. Their Directors[7] are civil servants with fixed salaries. The munificence of the princes often provides their courts with theatres, whose artistic achievements and splendid facilities far excel theatres of commercial and industrial centres ten times bigger. Consider Weimar or Meiningen, where since touring has ceased each performance costs the Duke 600 Marks.[8] [...] If the taste of the prince is less lofty, the institution can suffer artistically for years despite the best will of the Director. On the other hand, through their financial security and their dependence on only one mind, the court theatres are more capable than any other of breaking with traditions that have become routine and of risking artistic experiments and striving for the extraordinary.

Freer in their work but more tied in their finances are the *municipal theatres*, which depend primarily on public taste. The larger towns usually own their own theatres which are leased out. Of the 206 theatres which call themselves 'municipal theatres', in fact only 149 are the property of the town. Of these 149, those that receive subsidies from the town are a special case. The town usually exercises influence on the management of the theatre by setting up a theatre committee, presided over by the mayor, or to which at least councillors belong, so that the municipality has a voice in the way money is spent. In this way the lessee of the municipal theatre is not, like the Director of a court theatre, responsible to one individual but to a many-headed sovereign, the theatre committee. At the same time, because he is working at his own risk, he is forced to fill his theatre, that is to attract the public by every possible means. This sets limits on his best artistic intentions. Only a few towns manage their own theatres. Then, instead of a lessee, there is a Director with a fixed salary, who can attempt truly artistic work because he is not working at his own risk. [...] Such theatres are the municipal theatres of Brünn, Colmar, Freiburg im Breisgau, Graz, Mulhouse, Kiel and the Court and National Theatres of Mannheim.

In addition to the court and municipal theatres are the *private theatres*, whose numbers have grown enormously from year to year. The Almanac for 1909 lists 205, of which 57 call themselves 'municipal theatres'. [...] These private theatres often cultivate specialities – like French farce, French comedy of manners, operetta, or dialect play – or confine themselves to a local catchment area and with low prices try to win that part of the populace which cannot afford to go to the municipal theatre. [...] Vienna has 18 private theatres, Berlin no less than 37. [...]

Amongst the private theatres, mention must be made of *café theatres*. Here the public sit at small tables, drink beer and smoke. These are the theatres where the craftsman and his family or the skilled worker enjoy their Schiller, the theatres to which working-men's clubs organize their outings. Some have a garden where the audience relaxes in the intervals; often the performances take place in the garden.

Actual *summer theatres* and *spa-town theatres* perform exclusively light material, operetta, farce, light comedy. [...] Of 101 summer theatres, 52 are situated in spa towns.

Where the town is too small, and the theatre-goers too few, the Director may combine two or more places where his company plays in the course of a season. There are 60 of these *combined town theatres*. [...]

The *touring theatres*, of which there are 45, remain in one place only as long as the attendances at performances allow, and then travel on, hoping for the best, often covering vast distances. They play at small towns and even villages.

[1] *Bühnen-Almanach*, published annually from 1873, originally *Almanach der Genossenschaft deutscher Bühnenangehöriger*, renamed *Bühnen-Almanach* in 1889. Despite further renaming (1890–1914) as *Neuer Theater Almanach*, it is still usually referred to as *Bühnen-Almanach*.
[2] The German Reich then included Alsace-Lorraine and East Prussia with Danzig and areas now part of Poland.
[3] Austria boasted some forty German-language theatres, over half of which were in Vienna. Austro-Hungary also incorporated Bohemia, Moravia, Croatia and Slovenia.
[4] The German-speaking area of Switzerland had about a dozen theatres.
[5] Now in Poland.
[6] Capital of Latvia. There were also German-language theatres in Libau in Latvia and in Czernowitz, capital of the Ukraine.
[7] Throughout this section, the term Director (capital D) is used to designate the person who runs a theatre (*Intendant*), and director (lower-case d) to refer to the person who directs a play (*Regisseur*).
[8] In 1873, 1 Mark was set at 0.3584 g of pure gold. In 1910, 10 eggs cost 1 Mark, ½ kilo of butter 1.40 Marks, ½ kilo of coffee 1.35 Marks, ½ kilo of mutton 1 Mark, 1 litre of milk 20 Pfennigs. Rents for an apartment in a working-class tenement were 30–50 Marks a month. A skilled worker earned about 150 Marks a month (men) and 30–60 Marks (women). For each performance, the Duke of Saxe-Meiningen was therefore personally paying out roughly the equivalent of half a year's wages for the average worker. For further information on the Meininger, see 51 and 53.

(c) Capacity of some municipal theatres [pp. 34–5]

Stadttheater Bremen	built 1843,	renovated 1899		1,600 seats
Stadttheater Düsseldorf	,, 1875,	,,	1906	1,700 seats
Stadttheater Hamburg	,, 1827,	,,	1874 and 1900	2,000 seats
Schauspielhaus Cologne	,, 1872,			1,600 seats
Altes Theater, Leipzig	,, 1766,	,,	1817	1,200 seats
Neues Theater, Leipzig	,, 1865–8			1,900 seats

The most recent theatres, namely those that cultivate modern drama, are being built smaller than ever:

Lessing Theater, Berlin	built 1888		1,000 seats
Kleines Theater, Berlin	,, 1901		400 seats
Kammerspiele, Berlin	,, 1906		300 seats

(d) Equipment [pp. 36–41]

The *fly-tower* is now generally in use in all our larger theatres. [...] It permits for the first time a generous use of the box-set. This is lowered like a folded screen, then opened up into its three walls. On to this the ceiling is lowered. The advantages for the dramatic effect are obvious. The spoken word is thrown back from the walls, the illusion is total; even from side seats one can no longer see into the wings where actors lounge about waiting for their cues. The Meininger showed how box-sets, which until then had been used only for drawing-room dramas, could also be used for classical drama.

However great the advantages of the fly-tower, it still did not solve the problem of achieving set changes fast enough to avoid lengthy intervals which destroyed the tension in the audience. The intervals remain unbearably long; the noise behind the curtain is annoying. It was the brilliant Lautenschläger[1] who managed to circumvent this difficulty with his *revolving stage*. [...] This new, colossally improved facility for changing sets now at last makes it possible to perform the classics in full. Until now so much time was wasted on the intervals, that a complete rendering of the text was impossible. The blue pencil, scissors and paste-pot were the indispensable tools of the director. Productions like *Faust* failed because of frequent set changes. Cuts had to be found, scenes run together, changes made, so that some of it totally lost its original character. With the revolving stage, first installed in Munich by Lautenschläger, we have reached the summit of technical achievement. Its great disadvantage, which is shared by the Asphaleia system,[2] is its cost. Some theatres, like the Schiller Theater in Berlin, have therefore confined themselves to the *turntable*, whereby only the middle section of the stage revolves. There are, however, only a few very modern theatres that have revolving stages or turntables. [...]

It is no exaggeration to say that the modern art of theatre production became possible only through electric light. [...] It is almost as bright as daylight and it is soft and constant. It does not flicker or exude heat. [...] Electric light can be taken wherever one wants. If the castle in *Kätchen of Heilbronn*[3] is to go up in flames, then wires are attached beforehand, and the collapsed structure will glow at the appropriate moment. For an elfin dance little bulbs can be placed in the hair of the dancers. [...] By using the so-called multi-colour system – at most theatres: green, red and white, to which especially luxurious theatres can also add blue – varying effects can be achieved which make the finest nuances possible. [...] Colour effects accompany the action like music in the opera, they interpret for the eye what is heard by the ear. Productions like *Pelléas et Mélisande*[4] would be impossible without the wonderful symphonies of light achieved with modern technical equipment. In addition, this equipment operates with lightning speed and precision.

¹ Karl Lautenschläger (1843–1906) is best known for inventing the modern revolving stage, first installed at the Munich Court Theatre in 1896.
² This system permitted sections of the stage to be hydraulically raised and lowered, so that set changes could take place beneath the stage. In 1911 it was in use only in Halle and Pest (Hungary).
³ The play by Kleist (1808).
⁴ The play by Maeterlinck (1893). No doubt the reference here is to Reinhardt's production at the Kleines Theater, Berlin (1903).

(e) Number and categories of staff [pp. 42–56]

Königliches Theater, Berlin	approx.	1,000	employees
Stadttheater Hamburg		469	,,
Stadttheater Düsseldorf		139*	,,
Stadtheater Göttingen		85	,,

* excluding orchestra and front-of-house staff

Executive personnel: artistic director (*Regisseur*); musical director (*Kapellmeister*); leader of the orchestra (*Konzertmeister*); répétiteur (*Korrepetitor*); conductor of the chorus (*Chordirigent*); choreographer (*Ballettmeister*); director of crowd scenes (*Statisteninstrukteur*)

Actors: In modern theatres in Berlin the custom of typecasting actors has been dropped. In the rest of the Reich the traditional categories are maintained. The Stadttheater Düsseldorf has, for example: 1 first hero and lover; 2 juvenile heroes; 1 bon vivant; 1 timid lover; 1 character actor; 3 comic actors; 4 second fathers, character and supporting roles; 1 heroine and first lover; 1 first grande dame; 1 young character actress; 1 tragic–sentimental lover (f.); 2 comic ingénues; 1 farcical soubrette; 1 actress for minor roles; 1 classical mother; 1 comic old woman and mother

Artistic assistants:¹ prompter; dressers; chief wardrobe master and mistress; armourer; hairdresser; stage-manager; chief technician; flyman; trapman; property man

Technical personnel: stage-hands; scene-painters; paint-mixer; scenery moulder; lighting technician

Front-of-house personnel: box-office clerks; commissionaires; cloakroom attendants; ushers and usherettes; cleaners

¹ It will be noted that this category does not include set or lighting designers. Cf. sections (k) and (l), below.

(f) Conditions of lease [pp. 60–5]

Cost of leasing municipal theatres, 1902:
Aachen – 4,500 M.; Breslau – 300 M.; Cologne (three theatres) – 60,000 M.;
Düsseldorf – 17,000 M.; Hamburg – 70,000 M.; Leipzig – 51,175 M.; Augsburg,
Mainz, Metz and Stettin – free of charge

In a questionnaire of 1902, the following questions were asked: (a) Was a
probationary period of successful management required of the applicant before
final granting of the lease? (b) Was any proof of relevant experience required?
Negative replies to both questions were received from Aachen, Breslau, Cologne,
Hamburg and Leipzig. To (b), Breslau replied: 'not required, but voluntarily
supplied by applicant'.

(g) Outgoings [pp. 75–7]

Annual budget 1907/8 for the municipal theatres of Cologne (Altes Theater,
Neues Theater, Bonner Theater):

Artistic personnel:	*Marks*
opera – 95 solo and choral singers	355,988
theatre – 18 gentlemen from 1,800 M. to 10,400 M.	77,485
14 ladies from 1,400 M. to 6,600 M.	52,000
ballet – 18 dancers	19,440
stage-managers and prompters	7,215
non-contractual fees	33,500
stage-extras	18,000
guest performances	12,910
orchestra – 74 musicians (partly paid by municipality)	102,500
occasional musicians	5,196
	684,234

Technical and administrative personnel:	
chief technicians, scene-painters, wardrobe, caretaker	69,660
technical personnel – approx. 124 with minimum wage of 125 M. per month	147,610
ushers	20,587
box-office and administration	33,905
	271,762

Lighting and fire precautions:

lighting	47,900
fire watching	15,800
heating	21,500
water	2,275
	87,475

Running costs:

materials for technical departments	20,000
administrative costs	6,500
travel	4,250
taxes	850
handbills and printed material	24,989
sickness and liability insurance	7,762
fire insurance (paid by town)	32,900
	97,251

Purchase and maintenance of building, stage machinery, scenery, etc.:

paid by the town	135,263
paid by the lessee	31,600
	166,863

To authors for purchasing and borrowing scripts and for royalties:	50,500
Grand Total	1,358,085

(h) Ticket prices[1] [pp. 105–15]

Neues Theater, Cologne		Altes Theater, Cologne
Box:	5–6 M.	3.75–4.50 M.
Front stalls:	3–5 M.	3–3.75 M.
Rear stalls:	1.50 M.	1.20 M.
Balcony:	5–6 M.	3.75–4.50 M.
Lower circle:	1.50–3.50 M.	1.20–2.75 M.
Upper circle:	1.50 M.	1.20 M.
Gallery:	0.75 M.	0.50 M.

[1] The figures given here are based on a survey conducted in 1902. By 1911 the prices of more expensive seats had risen by about 25 per cent; lower prices had remained constant.

(i) Municipal subsidies [pp. 120–1]

	1900 Marks	1905 Marks	1908 Marks
Aachen	44,291	51,756	69,092
Breslau	72,500	66,405	66,355
Cologne	–	311,200	497,900
Düsseldorf	21,133	23,217	51,130
Frankfurt am Main	200,000	290,500	237,000

(j) Repertoire [pp. 123–4]

Authors whose plays received more than 150 performances in 1910:
1. Schiller[1] (1,909); 2. Sudermann[2] (1,026); 3. Shakespeare (961); 4. Kadelburg[3] (957); 5. Bahr[4] (850); 6. Schönthan[5] (784); 7. Ibsen (725); 8. Blumenthal[6] (723); 9. Goethe[7] (589); 10. Hauptmann (579); 11 =. Thoma,[8] Bisson[9] (534); 13. Bjørnson[10] (465); 14. Wildenbruch[11] (459); 15. L'Arronge[12] (437); 16. Kraatz[13] (420); 17. Meyer-Förster[14] (383); 18. Anzengruber[15] (369); 19. Moser[16] (358); 20. Rössler[17] (335); 21. Dreyer[18] (327); 22. Bataille[19] (323); 23. Lessing (317); 24. Schnitzler (307); 25. Grillparzer (299); 26. Hardt[20] (297); 27. Molière (277); 28. Birch-Pfeiffer[21] (238); 29. Fulda[22] (223); 30 =. Hebbel, Skowronnek[23] (222); 32. Kleist (214); 33. Benedix[24] (199); 34. Shaw (186); 35. Ernst[25] (180); 36. Halbe[26] (177); 37. Hartleben[27] (176); 38. Beyerlein[28] (158); 39. Sardou (154); 40. Freytag[29] (153); 41. Nestroy (151).

[1] *Wilhelm Tell* was performed 381 times, *Maria Stuart* 240. It is predictable that Schiller should head the list. Notable omissions from the most frequently performed authors are Chekhov, Gorki, Wedekind and Strindberg, the last of whom became very popular after 1910.

[2] Hermann Sudermann (1857–1928): writer of naturalistic domestic dramas.

[3] Gustav Kadelburg (1851–1925): actor and writer of farces, often in collaboration with Schönthan and Blumenthal.

[4] Hermann Bahr (1863–1934): essayist, critic and director. Best known play: *Das Konzert* (The Concert, 1909). See also 61.

[5] Franz Schönthan (1849–1913): actor, director and writer of farces.

[6] Oskar Blumenthal (1852–1917): founder of Lessing Theater, Berlin, and writer of comedies, e.g. *Im weissen Rössl* (White Horse Inn, 1898) in collaboration with Kadelburg.

[7] *Faust*, Part I, was performed 208 times.

[8] Ludwig Thoma (1867–1921): writer of satirical comedies, often in dialect, e.g. *Moral* (1909).

[9] Alexandre Bisson (1848–1912): French writer of farces.

[10] Bjørnstjerne Bjørnson (1832–1910): Norwegian novelist and writer of realist dramas. See also pp. 265–6.

[11] Ernst von Wildenbruch (1845–1909): writer of historical dramas.

[12] Adolph L'Arronge (1838–1908): director and founder of Deutsches Theater, Berlin, and writer of comedies. See also 45 and 51.

[13] Curt Kraatz (1857–1925): writer of farces.

[14] Wilhelm Meyer-Förster (1862–1934): author of romantic comedy, e.g. *Alt Heidelberg* (Old Heidelberg, 1901).

[15] Ludwig Anzengruber (1839–1889): author of Austrian folk plays.
[16] Gustav von Moser (1825–1903): writer of some seventy farces and comedies.
[17] Carl Rössler (1864–1948): writer of comedies.
[18] Max Dreyer (1862–1946): writer of realist dramas.
[19] Henry Bataille (1872–1922): French writer of light comedies.
[20] Ernst Hardt (1876–1947): writer of neo-Romantic pieces.
[21] Charlotte Birch-Pfeiffer (1800–68): actress and adaptor of sentimental novels for the stage.
[22] Ludwig Fulda (1862–1939): translator and writer of comedies.
[23] Richard Skowronnek (1862–1932): writer of comedies.
[24] Roderich Benedix (1811–73): writer of comedies.
[25] Paul Ernst (1866–1933): chief theorist and playwright of the *Neuklassik*. See 63.
[26] Max Halbe (1865–1944): writer of naturalist dramas, e.g. *Jugend* (Youth, 1893).
[27] Otto Erich Hartleben (1864–1905): writer of naturalist dramas, e.g. *Rosenmontag* (Rose Monday, 1900).
[28] Franz Adam Beyerlein (1871–1949): writer of dramas about military life.
[29] Gustav Freytag (1816–95): see 56, note 3.

(k) Rehearsals [pp. 129–31]

In every well-managed theatre, rehearsals for a new piece last several weeks. The first rehearsal is devoted to blocking (*Arrangierprobe*). [...] With the stage half-lit, the auditorium in darkness, the actors work through the play, wearing everyday dress and with their scripts in their hands. The director sits by the prompter's box, with a small table and a bell in front of him. At this rehearsal discussion takes place about entrances and exits and about what should be performed standing or sitting, in order to instil life and variety into the performance. Only gradually, after several rehearsals, when the actors have mastered their roles, are finer nuances introduced. It is now the task of the director to guide the actor with skilful suggestions and instructions without upsetting the actor's conception of the role. [...] It is said that Eduard Devrient[1] never interrupted a scene, so as not to destroy the mood, but noted down his comments as he sat quietly in the corner. At the end of the scene he would then quietly make his points to each actor individually. In good theatres, some acts, some scenes even, are rehearsed for hours, namely crowd and battle scenes and processions, until the director is completely satisfied. Besides these are the technical rehearsals (*Dekorationsproben*), in which the director, the chief technicians and the chief electrician choose, examine, erect and take away, until they have found what they want. The process is completed with the dress-rehearsal (*Generalprobe*), in which everything must run as smoothly as in performance and the actors appear made up and in costume. [...]

But there are only a handful of theatres that work in this way. Nearly everywhere there is simply not enough time – even at the bigger theatres. The public demand variety; new plays and new productions follow hard on one another. Farces and operettas, which depend on 'slickness' for their effect, are still carefully rehearsed. For performances of the classics, often a single rehearsal must suffice, even for a guest performance, despite the fact that no one knows the visiting performer's style of playing nor whether he is used to the same cuts in the text as the resident actors. Because of the lack of time and personnel, all the smaller theatres are reduced to holding three rehearsals. A blocking rehearsal, a dress-rehearsal, and 'the play must go on'.

---

[1] Eduard Devrient (1801–77): actor in Berlin, director in Dresden and Karlsruhe, 'a grand old man' of nineteenth-century German theatre.

(l) Décor [pp. 131–4]

Our age has developed a sense of history, 'a feeling for the authentic', as the slogan goes. [...] Even in its search for historical accuracy the nineteenth century held fast to the pleasant and dainty – what we would nowadays call the 'operatic'. Peasants appeared in velvet jackets, spotlessly white stockings and patent leather shoes; Kosinski[1] could spend days roaming with the robbers without getting a speck of dirt on his smock or boots. [...] No one minded that crowds consisted of a handful of untrained extras who, if they had no lines, stood as immobile as blocks of wood, taking no part in the action. [...] If a rose was to be picked, then an artificial rose protruded from a painted hedge, which was obvious even to the back row of the audience.

This tawdriness, which could still be seen in the 1880s at the biggest municipal theatres, was banished by the Meininger.[2] [...] And when naturalism became the watchword, the pursuit of authenticity knew no bounds. Indeed, plays like Hauptmann's *Die Weber* [Weavers, 1892],[3] Sudermann's *Die Ehre* [Honour, 1889],[4] or Gorki's *Nachtasyl* [Lower Depths][5] would have lost their effect without the accurate reproduction of externals. But now things have gone so far that on the occasion of a new production of *Rienzi*[6] lengthy negotiations have taken place between the Director of the Court Theatre in Berlin and Bayreuth on how to solve the problem that in the Wagnerian opera Rienzi's house lies in a different part of Rome from that in which, according to the researches of the Director, it actually lay.

Fortunately, such extravagances only occur in Berlin. But the capital sets the tone, and so the theatres of other big towns have to make colossal efforts in this direction. A memorandum of the Theatre Union speaks of 40,000 Marks, which is often spent by municipal theatres that are not particularly large, even when it is doubtful whether the play is worth it or not. In part, this expenditure is merely a correlative of the general growth in the need for luxury and hence a direct result of the rising standard of living, which can be observed everywhere in the fashion for extravagant colours and shapes. The public do not want to go to a theatre that does not offer them what they can see around them every day. On the contrary, the world of illusion must always offer a heightened reality. [. . .]

So the art of décor has gradually acquired a significance on which the success of a play depends. In fact it is now not uncommon to speak of the 'staging' (*Inszenierung*) rather than of a 'performance' (*Darstellung*). Major artists are commissioned to produce designs to be followed by scenery-painters and wardrobe masters. [. . .] Painted back-cloths are seen now only at small theatres; at the bigger ones there are three-dimensional trees, furniture and houses that cast natural shadows, so that the shadows of the actors and of the scenery do not fall in different directions, as sometimes happened with painted scenery. Shadows now play an especially important role in set decoration; through the use of adjustable electric floods, shadows can be shortened or lengthened, for example to suggest the fall of dusk by gradually lengthening shadows. [. . .]

Even small theatres can no longer risk having a temple façade that gives way when the hero leans against it. The old canvas frame door that used to swing open as the actor aproached it, as though controlled by some ghostly hand, is banished. Now the actor has to open the door himself with a wooden handle. [. . .]

There are now firms, the largest of which are in Berlin, which carry out the production of the complete décor and then hire it out. Even the bigger theatres make use of this facility, especially with respect to costumes.

[1] A character in Schiller's play, *Die Räuber* (The Robbers, 1781).
[2] See section (d), above, and 53.
[3] First performed 26 February 1893 at Freie Bühne, Berlin.
[4] First performed 27 November 1889 at Lessing Theater, Berlin.
[5] First performed 23 January 1903 at the Kleines Theater, Berlin.
[6] The opera by Wagner (1840).

(m) Training[1] [pp. 162–3]

Category	Length of training	Cost of training (Marks)	Cost of providing own costumes etc.[2] (Marks)
Ingénue	None–1½ yrs	0–800	700–1,500
Tragic heroine	—	500	500
Sentimental lover (f.)	1 yr	200–600	600–800
Comic lover (f.)	½–1 yr	300–1,000	3,000–5,000
Comic old woman	2 yrs	500	—
Male actor	3 months	90	300
Character actor	1½ yrs	1,000	1,500–2,000
Hero	½–1 yr	100–300	1,000
Chief director	6 hours	30	600–700

[1] This information is based on only twenty replies, but there is no reason to suppose that they were not typical.

[2] Men were provided with historical costumes but had to furnish their own contemporary dress; women had to costume themselves entirely at their own expense. See 3.

(n) Novices and trainees [pp. 164–7]

The lot of the novice is not an easy one. [...] A young lady of my acquaintance was 'trained' by a very famous actress of the Thalia Theater in Hamburg. [...] The Director of the theatre in X agreed to let her perform but demanded a 'sum of guarantee' of 50 Marks for each appearance. This was duly paid, and the young actress received good notices. The Director then offered to engage her for his theatre, and she asked to be allowed to play Judith[1] for her début. The Director agreed, she studied the role and acquired beautiful costumes, but weeks passed without the play's being put into the programme. She finally challenged the Director and received the reply: 'My dear lady, I can't possibly let you play the role for a mere 50 Marks. I shall have to insist on a larger sum of guarantee.'[2] [...]

Many novices are accepted only as trainees (*Volontäre*). They receive either minimal payment or none at all, usually no regular wage but a remuneration of 2–5 Marks for each performance. [...] The trainees depress wages considerably; for a theatre manager who has filled a category[3] with a trainee actor will hardly decide in the following year to engage a properly paid performer. [...] In the questionnaire, fifty-eight theatres indicated that they employed trainees. [...] The gloomiest example is Mainz; of fifty-one members of the company, seventeen are trainees!

[1] The heroine of Hebbel's tragedy, *Judith* (1840).

[2] Eventually 500 Marks were paid, so that she might perform the role. See 4(a) and 4(b).

[3] The term 'category' is used here – like the French '*emploi*' – to indicate stock-roles common to most European theatre companies of this period. See 11, note 1.

(o) Working conditions [pp. 174–82]

Since most actors spend eight or nine hours every day in the theatre, the conditions there are more important for them than in their own lodgings, which are only used for sleeping and for quickly packing together costumes and props in the afternoon. [...] It is only in the last ten years that any thought has been given to dressing-rooms when a theatre is built. [...] Apart from the completely new theatres, the dressing-rooms of even the bigger theatres literally break the law, that is to say they do not fulfil the building and sanitary regulations required of all other dwelling and work places. [...] The most outrageous conditions obtain in Bremerhaven,[1] especially outrageous when one considers that this is no small town: 'The dressing-rooms are quite terrible, hardly ever heated and with an atmosphere that contravenes sanitary regulations. To get to the stage you have to negotiate two staircases and a corridor, in which the doors to the garden are left open! The dressing-rooms are in the cellar, constructed out of old scenery, the gentlemen's and ladies' dressing-rooms separated only by a tattered flat. Very bad lighting, we have to make up by candlelight. No mirror. Very cold and dirty. When masked balls are held, the dressing-room is used as a *chambre séparée*. Vomit from the drunks which stank out the dressing-rooms was not cleared up until it had dried. Cat and dog excrement and a smoking stove sometimes made it impossible to stay there.'

[1] The Bremerhaven Stadttheater was at this time the property of an innkeeper. Fortunately, a new theatre was built shortly afterwards.

(p) Frequency of performances[1] [pp. 187–227, 241]

[1,584 performers were asked about frequency of performance:]

On	average	4–10	appearances	each	month	245	[15.5%]
,,	,,	10–15	,,	,,	,,	291	[18.4%]
,,	,,	15–20	,,	,,	,,	329	[20.8%]
,,	,,	20–25	,,	,,	,,	294	[18.6%]
,,	,,	25–30	,,	,,	,,	327	[20.6%]
More than		30	,,	,,	,,	98	[6.2%]

A member of the Stadttheater Aachen reports: '[...] The working time of the individual actors and of the company, in which no category is filled twice, can best be seen from the following statistics. From 14 September 1907 to 11 April 1908, 272 performances were given on 210 working days (137 theatre performances, 114 opera, 21 operetta). Of the 137 theatre performances, 66 plays were performed, most of them only once. [...] Every week two to three new plays are rehearsed! [...]'

Large court and municipal theatres have their own company of extras, which can be supplemented if necessary with non-contracted actors, unemployed craftsmen, soldiers and students. At smaller theatres, however, each actor in the ensemble is required to perform as an extra when needed.

[1] This information was based on 1,584 individual cases and is averaged over the whole season. In December 1907, when Christmas matinées were common, 124 out of 385 replies (32.2 per cent) indicated more than thirty stage appearances, in three cases quoting a figure in the seventies!

(q) Income[1] [pp. 347–498]

The income of 2,112 theatre workers[2] for the season 1907/8:

under 400 M.	56	[2.7%]
400–1,000 M.	770	[36.5%]
1,000–2,000 M.	782	[37.0%]
2,000–3,000 M.	220	[10.4%]
3,000–5,000 M.	166	[7.9%]
5,000–10,000 M.	102	[4.8%]
over 10,000 M.	16	[0.8%]

Of the 2,082 replies that indicated the length of season, the monthly income averaged as follows:

up to 50 M.	66	[3.2%]
51–100 M.	412	[19.8%]
101–200 M.	918	[44.1%]
201–300 M.	294	[14.1%]
301–500 M.	265	[12.7%]
501–1,000 M.	108	[5.2%]
over 1,000 M.	19	[0.9%]

Singers receive on average considerably higher wages than actors; men much more than women. [...] The heroic tenor is at the top of the wages' league. Even at smaller theatres like Augsburg he receives 9,200 Marks for the seven-month season. [...] The top categories in the theatre are similarly graded. At the Mannheim Court Theatre the first hero receives 7,500 Marks annually. [...] The young member of a category is always worse off than the first member. Weimar pays the first lover (female) 5,500 Marks and the young lover (female) 2,400 Marks. [...] Very famous performers can ask what they want and they get it too. It is said that Edith Walker[3] receives 56,000 Marks at the Stadttheater Hamburg.

---

[1] Even at these meagre salaries, theatre workers could count themselves fortunate to be regularly employed. Only theatres in Berlin and certain court theatres remained open all year. As a result, of 19,742 actors listed in the Stage Almanac for 1907/8, at least 12,000 (over 60 per cent) had no income during the summer months. Since the 'winter' season at theatres was usually only six months and rarely exceeded eight months, most actors received no income for one third to one half of the year. By comparison, unemployment at this period varied from about 2 per cent (building trades in the summer) to about 17 per cent (building trades in winter), with only a few trades rising over 20 per cent (e.g. seamen at 27.5 per cent during winter). See 2, 8, 176, 202.

[2] These included mainly actors, actresses and operatic singers, with a very few (not statistically significant) replies from directors, chief technicians and administrative posts.

[3] Despite her evident success, posterity has been less favourable to Edith Walker. I have traced only one mention of her, in an illustration caption in Kindermann, *Theatergeschichte Europas*, p. 255.

(r) Family background [pp. 660–94]

Of 1,703 replies, the occupation of father was given as follows:

Businessman	500	[29.4%]
Civil servant	291	[17.1%]
Theatre worker	246	[14.4%]
Craftsman or worker	239	[14.0%]
Legal, academic or medical profession	141	[8.3%]
Officer	50	[2.9%]
Other	236	[13.9%]

(s) Former employment before going on stage [pp. 695–714]

Of 825 replies, former occupation was given as follows:

Businessman or commercial employee	321	[38.9%]
Craftsman or worker	157	[19.0%]
Profession (including 64 students)	129	[15.6%]
Musician	44	[5.3%]
Civil servant	30	[3.6%]
Army	8	[1.0%]
Theatre employee	7	[0.8%]
Theatre director	1	[0.1%]
Other	128	[15.5%]

(t) Conclusion [p. 714]

Here ends the chapter on the economic situation of theatre employees: penury, anxiety and deprivation for thousands; for a few, fame and a reasonable standard of living, and amongst them a few hundred who can enjoy a comfortable life with an adequate income in a secure situation. Heavy working demands for the majority, the inability to continue working at an early age, and seldom sufficient financial provision in illness or old age. A superfluity of applicants to the profession, so that the situation of everyone who fails to become a star grows more and more difficult, more and more desperate.

43   Poster advertising the farce *Reisewuth!* (Travel Madness!), 1877

In Ruth Eder, *Theaterzettel* (Dortmund: Harenberg, 1980), p. 161. Original in German Theatre Museum, Munich

The late nineteenth-century theatre's pursuit of authenticity encouraged the creation of exotic settings, making performances into virtual travelogues. In this poster for *Reisewuth!* (Travel Madness!), it is significant that the main attraction is the 'entirely new scenery'.

44   An appeal to Bismarck to support the theatre, 1882

Heinrich and Julius Hart, 'Offener Brief an den Fürsten Bismarck', *Kritische Waffengänge*, Berlin, 1882, Heft 2, pp. 4–6. Reprinted in Erich Ruprecht, ed., *Literarische Manifeste des Naturalismus 1880–1892* (Stuttgart: Metzler, 1962), pp. 24–5

The Hart brothers (Heinrich, 1855–1906, and Julius, 1859–1930) were among the leading theoreticians and propagandists of naturalism, especially in their journal, *Kritische Waffengänge* (Critical Forays), which appeared irregularly in Berlin from 1882 to 1884. In this extract, they appeal to the Imperial Chancellor to remove theatre censorship and to provide state subsidies. It was to take thirty-six years, until after the end of the First World War, for these demands to be fulfilled.

It is true that our fathers created magnificent literature without worrying about support from the state. But why? They had no state, no fatherland. They felt this cruelly enough, when Klopstock had to emigrate to Denmark, when Schiller and Wieland and the rest were forced to seek refuge in the confines of princes' courts. [...]

But we have become children of a nation and so we demand what they lacked, for the state owes to literature the same respect and support as it already pays [...] to religion and education and in part to the arts and sciences.

There are in fact already the beginnings of such state support in Germany, for the laws of copyright and literary conventions with foreign countries may be regarded as such. But that is all there is.

How little respect the state has for literature and related arts is shown by the fact that theatre is controlled by trading laws. This is a confusion of the practical with the cultural and has been responsible for many of the problems that beset the theatre. No doubt it is to make up for this lack of consideration that the greatest care is devoted – in Prussia at least – to the maintenance of theatre censorship, although there is no reason for separating the censorship of books from that of theatre by removing the one and keeping the other. Theatre, which should mirror not so much the external conditions of our times as their spirit, suffers especially from such trivial supervision, above all when it is administered by a police force that is not always sensitive in aesthetic matters. It may indeed be possible for a play to have a violent and disturbing effect, but that is not the fault of the writer but of the situation which is portrayed, so it is the situation which should be censored.

At the very least, the right which the state assumes through censorship should be balanced by a duty, namely that of providing subsidies. We know what dreadful associations the term 'state theatre' [Staatstheater] conjures up. On the other hand, as things stand at present, we can see no healthy future for German theatre without proper state support. Court theatres which enjoy regular subsidies from their princes are obliged to remain exclusive and to tread carefully in a way that affects new playwriting like a poisonous mildew.[1] That is why the state should support and consolidate those private companies that reveal a truly artistic policy and a firm, creative Directorship. We cannot pursue this question further and examine all the arguments for and against, since our letter is not intended as a final statement but only as a means of generating public discussion.

---

[1] As an example, one could cite the Kaiser's own court theatre in Berlin, where it was impossible to stage new naturalistic plays on the grounds that one does not 'plant potatoes in a vineyard' (see Patterson, *The Revolution in German Theatre*, p. 25).

45   Adolph L'Arronge condemns 'theatre freedom', 1896

Adolph L'Arronge, *Deutsches Theater und deutsche Schauspielkunst*, Concordia Deutsche Verlags-Anstalt, Berlin, 1896

Adolph L'Arronge (1833–1908) was the leading founder of the Deutsches Theater, Berlin, which was dedicated to the presentation of serious theatrical work by a co-operative society of actors. It opened on 29 September 1883, and established L'Arronge as the leading director of the capital, until he appointed Otto Brahm as his replacement in 1894. Here L'Arronge gives a personal account of the problems outlined by Dr Reimers in 42, and traces their source to the free trade laws of 1870 which abolished the need for theatres to be licensed. Unlike the Hart brothers (44), he concludes by urging some form of state control and the retention of theatre censorship.

(a) Theatre freedom [pp. 22–33]

Before 1870, the management of a theatre in Germany was dependent on the issue of a licence from the police, a licence which was granted only to that one theatre and which laid down the limits of the repertoire. At that time there were privileges. So, for example, in Berlin, only the Court Theatre had the right to stage performances of serious plays, above all of our classical masterpieces. [...] These privileges also protected the theatres themselves; for any public entertainment that so much as had the appearance of a theatrical performance was forbidden. In the circus, neither ballets nor processions were allowed, in beer-halls songs could not be performed in costume. These privileges were abandoned with the introduction of free trade. [...]

In 1870, the first year of the new law (*Gewerbeordnung*), about 90 new theatres were founded. [...] There are now about 600 theatres in Germany. [...]

As long as licences and privileges were the order of the day, as long as the opening of a new theatre was primarily dependent on the question of need, that is as long as there were relatively few theatres in Germany, it was not easy to find employment as an actor, and it was much more difficult even for talented actors to gain a secure contract with a large theatre. For this reason, and because of the prevailing social prejudice against actors, each young person who wished to devote himself or herself to the theatre had to fight a hard struggle with the family, a struggle that often led to expulsion from home. This may be the reason why traditionally so many actors use a false name. [...]

How very different since the new theatre freedom! Numerous new theatres appeared, and in order that their presence could be justified, the search began for performing artists. Most good actors were naturally already bound by contract to the existing larger theatres. Admittedly a few were tempted with grand promises to join the new enterprises. But initially the new sun shone into the hidden corners, where the so-called neglected talents waited to receive the protection and good fortune that had eluded them until then. Now the barriers were down, privilege had ceased, now the German public was to discover how much artistic power and greatness had been held back by the former restrictions! But there were so many new theatres that the neglected veterans alone were not enough to fight the new battle, no, above all new talents would have to be promoted.

And these young talents were easy to find. Why not? The art of acting is not hard, is it? So long as you know the tricks – it's as easy as lying, as Hamlet says.[1] Then the theatre freedom gave birth to countless tutors who offered dramatic instruction, their fees ranging from the modest to the excessive, depending on what their name was worth. Pupils who were well off had to study longer; those who were badly off were trained in a short time. From all walks of life, people turned to the theatre, and all who possessed a modicum of ability were accepted and were soon earning money. Youngsters who only a few months previously had been sitting at their school desks or had been studying at a university, young clerks and others who had only recently been shaving faces had suddenly become artists. Anyone who could wear a dark suit with tolerable grace became a youthful lover with a monthly salary of 150 to 200 Marks. [...] So the social prejudice against the theatre has rapidly given way to practical considerations, and today it is the exception for a family not to have someone on the stage. [...]

It is not true that we needed so many theatres; what is true is that the theatre was hindered from progressive development by the limitations and privileges that were imposed on it. The extension of free trade to the theatre opened the way to its free evolution: [...] new theatres, comfortably and tastefully furnished; the best available actors even if at excessive salaries; the most successful new plays, even if acquired only at considerable financial sacrifice; productions of the classics – in short, nothing was missing to make an attractive programme. The one thing that was missing was the audience. [...] The productions of great dramas, of even the most worthy in our literature, met with no or very little response in the audience. [...] This is easily explained. These productions in the new theatres were not only no better than in the old; on the contrary, they were often far worse. [...] With a few unsatisfactory rehearsals, hardly enough to allow the parts to be learned, without doing justice to the spirit of the piece, these works were rattled off and not only in the smaller theatres, but – and it is embarrassing to admit it – also in the larger theatres that had until then enjoyed the protection of privilege. The classics had become the Cinderella of dramatic literature.

[1] *Hamlet*, Act III, sc. ii. The reference in Shakespeare is not to acting but to playing a pipe.

(b) The directors [pp. 46–54]

The art of directors who today enjoy a certain reputation in the German theatre often consists of nothing more than the taste and skill of an interior decorator. They know how to fill rooms and other sets with all sorts of little items, play with lighting effects of sun and moon and organize everything according to the 'mood'. [...] It should, however, be their primary aim to clarify for the actors the content and atmosphere of the play, to support them according to need in the conception and execution of their roles, to stimulate them and if necessary to be of active help to them. [...] The director should not hold literary lectures for his actors on stage; nor is it necessary for him to show off his knowledge by learning whole encyclopaedia articles and reciting them to the actors. And this does happen. [...]

And finally a little harmless story from a provincial theatre, just to illustrate what some people imagine directing to be.

It is the first rehearsal of a play set at the time of the French Revolution. The director has just sat down. He rings his bell and the curtain rises. During the first scene he does not speak; nor in the second. A few more scenes are played under this mild and indulgent direction. Then backstage a noise starts which grows louder and louder. At first the mild-mannered gentleman merely listens and shakes his head. Finally, however, it becomes too much for him. He jumps up angrily and shouts with a stentorian voice: 'Quiet, backstage, quiet! Stage-manager, take down the names of the people making that row!' The stage-manager sticks his head out of the wings and says: 'I'm sorry, but that is the Revolution.' 'Oh, I see, the Revolution?' the director replies. 'All right, we'll keep it in.'

Nevertheless, I do not wish to maintain that there is no one of taste and education in the German theatre who cannot do justice to the position of director. Most directors, however, are also engaged as actors, and this is a mistake, since such a double role gives rise to jealous quibblings; or theatre managers themselves direct very often without any ability and only because they assume the rank of director. [...] Every actor, even the best, needs a director. [...]

(c) Plans for the improvement of our theatrical situation [pp. 90–110]

Having offered a truthful picture of our theatrical situation and having identified as the cause of the evils I see around us the extension of free trade to the theatre, I now wish to name the means which might benefit the theatre. [...]

My reactionary ideas really do not go so far that I want to see the restoration of privileges, limitations of concessions and the favouring of individuals. Definitely not! But even if everyone should have the same rights, does this mean that the practice of a serious and beautiful art, which is to be considered a means of education, should be reduced to the level of a manual trade without state protection? [...] Above all the question of the actual *need for theatres* must be considered. And it is inappropriate that the police should have control over the theatre and its profession, as though they were involved in peddling goods like beer and schnapps. [...] A commission of men with literary sensitivity, who could be relied on to have understanding and interest for the aims and needs of the stage, and under the chairmanship of the Minister himself, would have to decide about theatrical questions. This commission would control censorship and the allocation of licences.

The lifting of theatre censorship does not seem at all desirable to me. For if theatres could perform every play without prior approval of the authorities, then they would be exposed to the danger of a state prosecution banning the performance of a play, just as books can be impounded after publication, until the court reaches its verdict. In this way much greater damage would be caused to theatre managers and writers than if a play had never been granted a licence for performance. [...]

Just as important for the commission would be the task of judging who is suitable to manage a theatre, with regard to the following questions: first, are the personal qualities of the applicant such as to guarantee a reliable and artistic management of the theatre? Secondly, is the sought-after founding of the theatre a need, or can one at least reckon on the viability of the undertaking in the future? [...]

Today, things are so bad that small towns of 30,000–40,000 inhabitants have not only one theatre but two, even three, not counting the so-called speciality theatres. That these theatres have no permanence and can only run on quite inartistic lines, needs no explanation. The season lasts usually from 1 October or 15 October to Palm Sunday, so long as some row has not put an end to things sooner.

The actors, who have flocked to the theatre without any justification and have just managed to survive for five or six months on their miserable wages, now face the question of how they can continue to live. There are a number of summer theatres, but not many and their existence is even more desperate. And if they are overtaken by fate and the manager can no longer pay any wages, then the staff have to beg for their bread. [...]

An improvement in our theatrical situation must begin at the bottom; we must start in the small towns. Several such towns should be covered by one licence – three, four or more places according to the number of their inhabitants. This licence should be awarded to one manager who would be responsible for performing for some months in each town. Meanwhile, no other theatre should be licensed in this area. [...]

Admittedly, this would mean that since so many little theatres would cease to exist, many untalented actors would be out of a job. This would not be a misfortune, I think; on the contrary, it would be better for the theatre and better for those it affected, who would then have to turn to other employment which would offer them better prospects than if they continued as bad actors. [...]

Moreover, the German Empire should follow Vienna's example and open theatre schools in our larger cities and appoint suitable staff. This might put an end to much nonsense and create institutions that could have the most beneficial effects on the future of acting. The establishment of state schools would rid us of those many weeds of theatre freedom, those self-styled teachers who have no right whatsoever to give dramatic instruction, who lure young people with the promise of an engagement, take their money, and then, heedless of their fate, send them off into a state of destitution.

The free trade law, that was intended to bring with it a free development of theatre, has missed its aim completely. We have taken wrong turnings and have landed in a swamp. We must turn back if our theatres, not only in solitary cases but as a general rule, are to be homes of beautiful art, an inspiration and joy for both mind and soul.

46   *Censorship:* Max Reinhardt applies for permission to perform Wedekind's *Spring Awakening*, 1906

Max Reinhardt, *Schriften. Briefe, Reden, Aufsätze, Interviews, Gespräche, Auszüge aus Regiebüchern,* ed. H. Fetting (Berlin: Henschelverlag, 1974), pp. 97–9

From the two preceding documents it is clear that theatre censorship was a major concern of the day, and here is an example of a specific request for a licence to perform a controversial piece. Max Reinhardt (1873–1943), unquestionably the leading German director of the first third of this century, had taken over the Deutsches Theater in Berlin from Otto Brahm in 1904, and there in 1906 he introduced the revolutionary concept of appending to the main auditorium a studio theatre, which he called the Kammerspiele on an analogy with *Kammermusik* ('chamber music'). It is interesting to note that one of the major arguments to the censor is that of the very exclusiveness of the audience at the Kammerspiele. *Spring Awakening* was, both in content and style, arguably the most revolutionary work to be performed in Germany in the decade preceding the First World War.

To Councillor von Glasenapp,
Theatre Department I,
Royal Police Headquarters,
Berlin.   16 October 1906

Dear Sir,
The management of the Deutsches Theater herewith requests you to grant permission to perform in the Kammerspiele of the Deutsches Theater the enclosed play, *Spring Awakening*,[1] a children's tragedy in five acts. Since the performance is to take place in the near future, we would ask you to be kind enough to treat this application as a matter of urgency. [. . .]

We consider it to be the duty of an artistic institution, a duty which it would be impossible to take too seriously, to make it possible to perform works which abandon conventional patterns and which open up new forms of theatre. This is the case here. In this work it is not just a question of new subject matter, but also of quite new forms of psychological portrayal, and the problems (the intellectual and sensual struggles of adolescent youth) are treated with so much moral serious-ness, honesty, grandeur and tragic impact, so completely free of any unpleasant speculation, that the possibility of causing moral offence seems out of the question. Finally, theatre should not pass over such serious problems, which are at the root of so many tragedies;[2] and furthermore, the writer has succeeded in elevating the specific problems of three individual cases to a tragic experience of such profound general implications that for the sake of the magnificent final act alone it would be an artistic sin to withhold this play from the stage.

We can call upon a number of testimonials from outstanding authorities in support of our evaluation of the play. Professors like Privy Councillor Dr Erich Schmidt, writers like Gerhart Hauptmann,[3] men of such deep artistic seriousness and of such diverse beliefs as the Director of the National Gallery, Professor Dr von Tschudi, and Maximilian Harden,[4] publicists of all shades of political opinion have expressed themselves similarly about Wedekind's *Spring Awakening*.

The play has been available in bookshops for about fifteen years, has gone through several editions and has always been favourably discussed and reviewed in literary circles and journals. In addition to these literary considerations, we believe that there are other points that arise from the specific nature of our planned production, which may be of decisive importance in the release of this work:

First, we are not performing for the general public, but in the Kammerspiele, a theatre which seats only some 300 and which, owing to the high prices,[5] will draw its public from the most exclusive social circles. Performances of the proposed play are initially intended only for subscribers to the Kammerspiele.

Secondly, commercial considerations are of major importance to us, since we have promised our subscribers an as-yet-unperformed work by Wedekind and we would risk losing subscriptions if we had to abandon this project.

Thirdly, we hope that by filling all the roles with adult actors we shall avoid any possibility of causing embarrassment.

Fourthly, we believe that the work of our ensemble to date has proved that we take for granted a performance style that is discreet and devoid of any coarse or drastic effects, a style concerned only with artistic and noble qualities. The management of the Deutsches Theater has often, and again recently, proved that it has concurred with the wishes of the censor,[6] even where this has involved great artistic and financial sacrifice. [...] In the case of *Spring Awakening*, we are convinced that the authorities will pay heed to our genuinely serious arguments. For all these reasons we request that this work be released for performance. [...]

Yours faithfully,
Max Reinhardt

¹ *Frühlings Erwachen* (1891) was premièred at the Kammerspiele on 20 November 1906. Wedekind himself played the Man in the Mask.

² The kind of adolescent suicide portrayed by Wedekind in his play was a not-uncommon occurrence: in Prussia alone 110 schoolboys took their lives between 1883 and 1889.

³ Hauptmann's brief testimonial read: 'Frank Wedekind's drama, *Spring Awakening*, is a serious, rigorous artistic work, a public performance of which would in my view have nothing but a purifying effect.'

⁴ See 54.

⁵ Initially, all tickets at the Kammerspiele cost 20 Marks.

⁶ No doubt this is a reference to agreement reached over Ibsen's *Ghosts*. No record remains of the precise conditions under which *Spring Awakening* was granted permission to be performed. One may speculate that the two scenes of masturbation and the whipping scene were definitely cut, but there were no doubt petty conditions imposed regarding the text. Ten years later a letter to Reinhardt from the censor contained the following requirement to change the text of Lenz's Storm and Stress play, *The Soldiers*: 'The terms "officer" and "good soldier" [*braver Soldat*] are to be replaced with "militia officer" and "reliable soldier" [*tüchtiger Soldat*]'.

47   *Acting*: Adolph Winds's acting techniques, 1904

Adolf Winds, *Die Technik der Schauspielkunst* (Dresden: Heinrich Minden, n.d. [1904])

After five documents dealing with various aspects of the general theatre situation in Germany during this period, we turn our attention to a central consideration, that of acting style, first in a standard handbook, then in the case of one of the leading performers of the age. Adolf Winds (1856–1927) was an actor at the Saxon Court Theatre in Dresden and tutor at the Royal Conservatory there. In many respects his guide to acting is conventional and formal in its rigid categorizing and in its use of external formulas for creating various emotions. On the other hand, his recommendations to employ emotion memory (see section (c) – 'Dignity' and 'Jealousy') and to use careful obervation, as in 'Illness' and 'Madness', are close to Stanislavskian techniques, as is the suggestion of the 'as-if metaphor' proposed in 'Contempt'. Despite this, Winds sneers at naturalism in acting (section (b)).

(a) General introduction [pp. 4–6]

This work is based on two laws:

1. Expressions of emotion are basically the same in people of all types.

> I have attempted to show by reasonably detailed analysis that all the principal forms of expression employed by man are the same throughout the whole world.
>
> Darwin, *The Expression of the Emotions in Man and Animals*

2. The tone of verbal expression always depends on facial expression and gesture. [...] It has always been a rule of acting that gesture precedes the word; more precisely, the gesture is the preparation for the word.

(b) Voice training [p. 25]

Without secure speech control even great acting talent remains trapped in naturalism, just as passionate expression can only be ennobled by thorough training of the voice.

(c) Examples of states of mind and emotions

Dignity [pp. 33–5] The representation of dignity and decorum requires the acquisition of a measure of bearing and physical control. But its true quality can only find appropriate expression through inner feelings and not through the dancing instructor alone. [...] All acting can be achieved only by working from the inside outwards, only through the power of imagination. Dignity, it would seem, can be represented through imitation, and certainly the observation of people who possess a dignified bearing will enrich the imagination, and again the posture and stillness of gesture that are acquired through physical training are essential to the portrayal of dignity and decorum; but both these are only means to an end. [...] The posture is upright, the look mild, the lips gently pressed together, the facial expression broad and relaxed rather than long and stern. [...] Often this is accompanied by a light nodding of the head as though in greeting, while the corresponding movement of the hand, the gesture of command, is firm. [...] Even as a boy ... you sometimes became close to a pupil in a lower class, went around with him and helped him with his exercises. A strain of condescension showed in this. [...] Recall this feeling.

Anger [p. 79] In anger the eyes sparkle, the eyebrows are drawn together, the face becomes red, the nostrils flare, the jaw juts, the body assumes a tense pose as though in attack, and the fists are clenched. Anger, which can develop into weeping, also affects the tear ducts. The actor must possess a certain control over these.

Astonishment [p. 94] In astonishment not only are the eyes opened wide, but also the mouth. [...] The arms are held apart, the palms of the hands turned inwards, the body leans backwards. With regard to body posture, let the following point be made here. The posture can be totally upright only in a state of calm; when emotions are involved, a slanting posture is adopted, and the body leans either backwards or forwards, and in most cases the whole body, not just the torso.

Love [p. 119] While the main characteristic of speech is a quavering and mellow voice, in facial expression it is the 'light' in the eyes. [...] The gait of the fortunate lover is elastic, his head is raised, his face suffused with a smile.

Jealousy [p. 160] One's own experience is always the best and most effective basis.

Remember some incident or other [. . .], recall people and circumstances as well as the words and the intonation with which you approximately spoke or would have spoken.

Contempt [pp. 197–8] Imagine you are taking some medicine, you taste something bitter and unpleasant, and your face will assume the expression appropriate to this emotion: 'Ugh, that tastes disgusting!' Then say the words: 'He is a thoroughgoing rogue!' In expression and tone the two sentences will look and sound the same.

Stupidity [p. 206] In a state of mourning the eyes are clouded; in stupidity they are pronouncedly dull, and the eyebrows are raised.

Illness [p. 219] Admittedly a conventional portrayal is frequently offered: continuous groaning, a flat tone, occasional grasping of the chest are often the only means by which illness is represented. The intelligent actor may study illness at sick-beds and discover what symptoms are especially appropriate in any given case.

Madness [p. 221] Go to lunatic asylums and be aware of different symptoms, only be careful in their use, reject whatever is repugnant.

48   Josef Kainz on his performances in *Don Carlos* (1883) and *Ghosts* (1894), and on his forthcoming guest-performance in Berlin (1909)

Josef Kainz, *Briefe*, ed. Hermann Bahr (Vienna: Nicola Verlag, 1922)

Josef Kainz (1858–1910) was arguably the leading actor of his day. Born an Austrian, he began his career with the famous Meiningen troupe (1877–80), was at the Munich Court Theatre (1880–3) before moving to Berlin, where apart from one season at Barnay's Berliner Theater (1889), he regularly performed at L'Arronge's Deutsches Theater (1883–99), from 1894 under the directorship of Otto Brahm. For the last ten years of his life he returned to his homeland to work at the Burgtheater in Vienna. This selection of letters spans two and a half decades of his career, from his first great success in Berlin to his powerful performance as Oswald in Ibsen's *Ghosts*, and finally to his proposals for his forthcoming guest-performance in Berlin, including the insistence on performing Hamlet in Elizabethan costumes – a rejection of the contemporary trend towards obsessive historical accuracy.

(a) To his mother [letter no. 6]

Berlin, 11 November 1883

Dearest Mother-heart,

[. . .] Oh, if only you could have been in the theatre yesterday! My big scene beside

Posa's corpse[1] was interrupted after the first paragraph with such a thunderous burst of applause that I could not continue speaking. This tumult lasted for several minutes right in the middle of the scene – for several minutes, I'm telling you. Only by using my voice at full power could I penetrate the cheering, finally silence it and then continue speaking. At the end of the speech the rumpus was repeated; it was extraordinary, Berlin has never seen the like. The success exceeded my wildest dreams. Even the weakest scenes were met with tumultuous applause. The Crown Prince again stayed in the theatre to the end. He leant forward out of his box and applauded wildly. The greatest success I have had since being in the theatre. It was overwhelming. [...]

Seppl

[1] Schiller's *Don Carlos* (1787), Act V, sc. iv. Kainz played the title role in L'Arronge's production, which was performed twice in November 1883.

(b) To Frau Bertha Böhm[1] [letter no. 36]

Brunswick, 11 July 1894

Well, yesterday we performed *Ghosts*[2] for the first time. Thank God it is over, and the production went off brilliantly. I had done excellent work on my part, I was very calm and had fun observing in cold blood the colossal impression exerted by this play on the public. During the second act, however, which was performed with quite terrible oppressiveness, various members of the audience, ladies and children, left the theatre.

One lady fainted. It was during Oswald's confession to his mother. After the second act we were called out tumultuously four times, and when the curtain fell at the end of the last act the audience sat silent for quite a while under the terrible impact, then at last the applause burst forth, and I was called out five or six times.

Well, now that is over. Hanns Land[3] says it is a brilliant role of mine, but he would not like to see it a second time, it affected him too deeply. [...]

[1] Kainz's cousin.
[2] Ibsen's *Ghosts* had been the production with which Otto Brahm's Freie Bühne had opened in 1889 and remained one of the most controversial and influential pieces of German theatre at this time.
[3] Pseudonym for Hugo Landsberger (b. 1861, d. in Third Reich), a writer and close friend of Kainz.

(c) To Dr Paul Lindau[1] (letter no. 125)

Rigi-Kaltbad, 17 August 1909

Dear Paul,

[...] I should like to ask you to let me know when I can send my own prompt-copy of *The Robbers*[2] and to whom. Can I send it to you to pass on to the director in question? I told you the last time I was in Berlin how concerned I am that the royal Directorate of the Court Theatre should condescend to accept my instructions for *The Robbers* and *Hamlet*. It is only a few years ago that a new staging of *The Robbers* was prepared here in Vienna. I had terrible trouble forgetting the old text and the conventional groupings and tableaux, and I would get into an awful muddle if I had to adapt now to yet another staging. God knows what might happen on the night! I might end up hanging old Daniel and jumping out of the window myself.[3] I therefore beg you earnestly – I mean, in the staging of the Franz Moor scenes – to let me have my way.

While in *The Robbers* it is a matter of purely external groupings, the request that now follows, and which relates to the guest-performance of *Hamlet*, arises from an artistic conception which I have taken a year to arrive at. It might also appear to be a merely external consideration, but it is one of those which exerts a profound influence on the whole presentation and on the nature of the play and the character of Hamlet. It is the costume. Since my last guest-performance in Berlin I have been playing Hamlet in the costume of the Elizabethan period, that is in Shakespearian costume. It makes a huge difference whether Hamlet's lines are spoken by a man dressed as a fourteenth-century knight or wearing a courtier's doublet of the sixteenth century. One could write a book about it, but you will be much more easily convinced by a single performance in the costume of the Shakespearian age. To name only two or three obvious things that have always otherwise appeared anachronistic: the players' scenes! duelling with foils! the firing of cannons! Philosophical reflection is also quite different in a ruff and with a rapier at one's side than in a knight's collar and with a broadsword. In this play words strike home like the thrusts of a rapier or a foil – they do not fall like the blows of a broadsword or rattle like chain-mail. I beg you to insist on my costume and you will be rewarded. At first my fellow actors will perhaps find the idea strange, but they will soon feel happier in their roles than before. The so-called Spanish costume is the dress of court intrigue, and *Hamlet* is full to the brim with it. The costumes of earlier ages are for simpler natures. One thing more. The actors of Shakespeare's time, and it is they that appear in this piece, were gorgeously dressed. They spent vast amounts on their royal cloaks and their breeches. 'A forest of feathers' and 'Provincial roses' on high shoes are actual descriptions from the play itself.[4] So, now I have told you what I would like to have. In *Richard II* I will fit in with all the instructions of the Court Theatre, so long as Shakespeare's text does not suffer. Perhaps I could receive your prompt-copy in advance, so that I can inform myself in good time. I have heard that this is a brilliant production by the Court Theatre. [. . .]

Josef

[1] Paul Lindau (1839–1919): director of Meiningen Court Theatre (1895–9), director at Berliner Theater (1899–1903) and at Deutsches Theater, Berlin (1904–5), finally Dramaturg at the Court Theatre, Berlin. See also 53.
[2] Kainz played the villain, Franz Moor, in Schiller's play.
[3] In Act V, sc. i, Daniel runs from the burning room, as Franz strangles himself.
[4] *Hamlet*, Act III, sc. ii. The reference to high shoes is based on a misunderstanding of 'razed' (i.e. slashed) shoes.

49   Kainz performs Hamlet, 1905

Ferdinand Gregori,[1] 'Josef Kainz: Hamlet', *Jahrbuch der deutschen Shakespeare-Gesellschaft*, 41 (1905), pp. 13–21

From the cool detachment described in the second letter above (48), and from the desire to play Hamlet in Shakespearian costume, one can deduce that Kainz was no thoroughgoing naturalist. However, the naturalness, psychological subtlety and physical mobility of his performance as Hamlet at the Burgtheater, Vienna, described below, show that he had progressed beyond the static and declamatory style of the dominant theatrical tradition, still influenced by the Weimar Court Theatre (see 56).

Act III, sc. i Hamlet enters slowly, his hands behind his back, he is thoughtful. Near the door he briefly looks round the room, because he is looking for the person who has sent for him. Since he does not see anyone, he continues on his way and returns to his thoughts. Thus he reaches the middle of the stage and says, as though it were the result of lengthy reflection, 'To be, or not to be, that is the question.' On this line he lowers himself quite mechanically on to a couch, and during the next lines he pulls his legs up equally mechanically and meditates, lying on his back, speaking up into the air. On 'perchance to dream!' he changes his position and sits. He fills the first two thirds of the monologue with infinite melancholy but does not relate it specifically to his personal fate. However, he emphasizes the last word of the line, 'Thus conscience does make cowards of us all!' in a tone of bitter self-accusation, a feeling he sustains until he hears a noise behind him. He glances round quickly and espies Ophelia. The expression on his face becomes gentler, because he assumes that it was she who had sent for him, driven by her love of him. He softly says to himself, while his hands almost fold in prayer, 'Nymph, in thy orisons/Be all my sins remembered.' Ophelia sees and hears nothing of this. But when she poses her first conventional question, he forces himself to indifference and begins to leave. As she hands him her love tokens, he has already reached the door, but something holds him back. Turned away from her, he listens to her reminiscences, which he too recalls, and he fights back his tears when she mentions the 'sweet breath' of his declarations of love. After her 'There, my lord' he has to pause while he collects himself. But then he hurls at her face almost the same mockery and scorn that he flings at the world. [. . .] But Ophelia is the only being towards whom he cannot maintain his contemptuous tone; we keep on hearing his fractured soul cry out, he softens all his hard accusations with overtones of injured love. After the second admonition to go to a nunnery, which he says with total sincerity, sitting beside her, he gets up to leave. Then he sees the tapestry behind which Claudius and Polonius are hiding. At once Hamlet, so used to being spied on, is seized with suspicion. He immediately perceives that he is the victim of a minor conspiracy and that it is the obedient daughter, not the unhappy lover, who is sitting in front of him. So he moves, after he has studied her closely from the side, firmly towards her. Pulling her head towards him, he almost pierces her with his look: 'Where's your father?' And when her eye avoids his gaze and she utters the lie, 'At home,' he turns away full of disgust and delivers his final speeches coolly and with embitterment. The warm tones from before are dissipated. He intends his loud words of abuse partly for the eavesdroppers, partly for the weak beloved.

Act V, sc. ii At the end he stands before us as he was at the beginning, the perfect nobleman. But his pessimism has given way to fatalism. Unsuspecting, amiable, full of alacrity he goes into the dishonourable combat. Kainz knows how to fence properly. It is a joy to watch how he wins the first two rounds; the third is a draw. [...] Then Laertes threatens him, 'Have at you now!' and actually scratches his arm with the poisoned rapier. Hamlet hesitates a moment and one can see that he grows suspicious. But even though he fears that his opponent's weapon is not blunted, he does not imagine it to be poisoned and fights on. In order to find out the truth of the matter, he attempts a disarming manoeuvre, so as to get hold of the rapier himself. The manoeuvre succeeds, he twists the rapier out of his opponent's hand, places his foot on it and seizes it then with his right hand. With his left hand he gives his own weapon to Laertes and goes into the attack again with the poisoned blade. Laertes is unprepared for this, he drops his guard and Hamlet strikes. [...] Laertes collapses, Hamlet is surprised and examines the sharpened rapier. Since he as yet knows nothing of the poison nor feels its effect in his own body, his only care is not for himself but for the dying queen, and he orders all the doors to be shut in order to trap her murderer. Then Laertes tells him of the true state of affairs and names the instigator of all these treacherous deeds. Hamlet cries out, 'The point envenomed too', emphasizing 'envenomed' in the sense of 'not only sharpened' (while others put the stress on 'too' and so refer to the queen's poisoning). He then leaps at Claudius, runs him through with his bloody rapier, forces the goblet of poison to his lips and finally lands him a decisive blow with a dagger. It is touching how shortly afterwards, as he struggles with death, he pleads with Horatio to stay alive and wrenches the goblet from his grasp. Then he drags himself to a couch at the side of the stage, feels the effect of the poison growing stronger and stronger, hurriedly nominates Fortinbras as king and begins to give further instructions, but his voice fails. He opens his mouth, signals with his hand that he can speak no more and groans softly as a smile flickers across his noble features: 'The rest is silence.'

---

[1] Ferdinand Gregori (1870–1928): actor at Deutsches Theater, Berlin, (1895–8); Burgtheater, Vienna (1901–10); Director of Mannheim National Theatre (1910–12); then until 1921 director at Reinhardt's theatres in Berlin.

50   Poster for Kainz's *Hamlet*, 1909

In Erich Kober, *Josef Kainz* (Vienna: Neff, 1948), facing p. 305

This programme is for a later performance in Berlin than that referred to in Kainz's letter (48). Note that, while set and costume designs are credited, the director's name is not mentioned.

Neues Schauspielhaus in Berlin

Gastspiel Josef Kainz

Hamlet

von Shakespeare

(am 29. und 31. Januar, 1., 4., 7., 9., 11. und 14. Februar 1909).

Personen:

Claudius, König von Dänemark	Hans Siebert
Hamlet, Sohn des vorigen und Neffe des gegenwärtigen Königs	Josef Kainz
Polonius, Oberkämmerer	Ernst Arndt
Horatio, Hamlets Freund	Erich Kaiser-Titz
Laertes, Sohn des Polonius	Hermann Romberg
Voltimand	Otto Wollmann
Cornelius	Fritz Georg Metzl
Rosenkranz } Hofleute	Franz Höbling
Güldenstern	Karl Vogt
Osrik, ein Hofmann	Alfred Kühne
Marcellus } Offiziere	Robert Garrison
Bernardo	Otto Hertel
Francisco, ein Soldat	Hans Baumann
Reinhold, Diener des Polonius	Alfred Felden
Ein Edelmann	Paul Koerner
Ein Hauptmann	Karl Diehl
Ein Priester	Otto Grünberg
Erster Totengräber	Albert Borée
Zweiter Totengräber	Fritz Kleinke
Erster Schauspieler (König im Schauspiel)	Karl Machold
Zweiter Schauspieler (Königin im Schauspiel) . . .	Helene Burger
Dritter Schauspieler (Lucianus im Schauspiel) . . .	Robert Garrison
Der Geist von Hamlets Vater	Adolf Klein
Fortinbras, Prinz von Norwegen	Carl Wilhelm
Gertrude, Königin von Dänemark und Hamlets Mutter	Gertrud Arnold
Ophelia, Tochter des Polonius	Clara Goericke

Herren und Damen vom Hofe, Offiziere, Soldaten, Schauspieler, Boten u. a.

Die Dekorationen nach Entwürfen von **Svend Gade** hergestellt im Atelier für Theatermalerei von Nicolei, Janowitz & Co., Berlin.

Die Kostüme nach Zeichnungen von **Prof. Lefler** angefertigt im Atelier von Alexander Blaschke & Co., Wien.

Rechts und links (wo sich diese Bezeichnungen nicht unzweideutig auf die Person des Darstellers beziehen) vom Zuschauer aus verstanden.

II Naturalism

51 L'Arronge declares his debt to the Meininger, 1896

Adolph L'Arronge, *Deutsches Theater und deutsche Schauspielkunst* (Berlin: Concordia Deutsche Verlags-Anstalt), 1896

Adolph L'Arronge (see **45**) here clearly declares the importance of the Meininger for the development of German theatre and, specifically, as an impulse to his own founding of the Deutsches Theater in Berlin (1883). The theatre enthusiast, Duke George of Saxe-Meiningen, had created at his Court Theatre an ensemble of actors, which, largely through their European tours from 1874 to 1890, were to revolutionize the course of European theatre. With their attention to realistic detail in properties, costumes and set, and with their impressive ensemble playing, they prepared the way for naturalist theatre, not least through their influence on Stanislavsky on their second visit to Moscow in 1890, and on Antoine, when they performed in Brussels in 1888.[1]

Overnight, after the first performance of *Julius Caesar* in Berlin,[2] the Meininger became world-famous. The artistic use of every technical device to create the setting was a revelation: set, furniture, costumes, weapons, props – everything was exactly reproduced according to the time of the Roman Empire. Who in the last few decades would have even thought of risking so much expense on the design of a Shakespearian drama gathering dust on a library shelf?

Those who were envious of this or shamed by it tried to criticize and minimize the unparalleled success of the Meininger by ascribing this success solely to the imposing décor, which they claimed was splendid but overdone, and which sought to impress with particularly ingenious and obtrusive details, by which the attention of the audience would be distracted from the text. I remember reading the following complaint: When in the first act of *Macbeth*[3] Duncan enters the courtyard and Banquo indicates the swallows as a sign of peace, most of the audience – so the review said – turned their opera-glasses on the set to look for swallows' nests and so completely missed hearing the important scene that precedes the murder of Duncan. Naturally I cannot say that the critic was lying about what he saw or how he interpreted it, but I know from my own experience that neither in this *Macbeth* production, nor in any other of the Meininger, did the quality and interest lie only in the décor. The carpers and the grudgers maintain this, however, and refer to the authority of Laube,[4] who declared such magnificent décor in a serious play to be nonsense. [...]

The Meininger have also presented ensemble work, the like of which was unknown in Germany until now. Never have crowd scenes been so effective. One only has to think of the mobs in *Julius Caesar* or the charge of the cuirassiers in *Wallenstein's Death*.[5] When a director previously had driven weary, overworked chorus-members or apathetic, stupid extras on to the stage, the result was always a hoot of laughter from the audience. How did the Meininger manage? They engaged a large number of actors, admittedly no great talents, who only received relatively low wages. But some of these were intelligent and diligent young people and they all at least could grasp what was required of them. Besides this, all the actors who had been engaged for larger roles were obliged to take part in crowd scenes if they were not cast in a leading role. From this intelligent and willing material the directing skill of the Meininger formed a quite new element for the stage, a chorus that not only participated in the action so that effects were produced which no doubt the writer had dreamt of but which until now no theatre had achieved.

And now to get to the main point, to the interpretation of individual roles. I must admit that the actors that came with the Meininger were not always of great importance, that we have seen this and the other role played by famous performers more rivetingly, more brilliantly and more effectively. [...] Nevertheless the critics were all agreed [...] that intelligence, artistic sense and untiring hard work had managed without especially outstanding stars to create an ensemble in which each character was at least as conceived by the writer and in which the spirit and intention of the work were central.[...]

In the history of the theatre the Meininger have erected a monument which will not quickly weather away. Unfortunately I have to add that their instructive and convincing example of priding themselves on their ensemble productions has found a response in only a few theatres. With the exception of some large theatres (e.g. the Court Theatre in Berlin), most theatres continue to deny serious drama the attention it deserves. But the impression the Meininger made on me has remained, and the desire to extend what I have learned from them and to try out my own skills in this area, has lent courage to me and to several important theatre practitioners to risk founding the Deutsches Theater in Berlin.

---

[1] See 27 and 'Antoine and the Meiningen crowd scenes', in A. M. Nagler, *A Source Book of Theatrical History* (New York: Dover Publications, 1959), pp. 580–2.

[2] On 1 May 1874, at the Friedrich-Wilhelm-Städtisches Theater. *Julius Caesar* was the most popular of their productions, performed 330 times out of a total of 2,591 performances.

[3] *Macbeth* was performed only ten times.
[4] Heinrich Laube (1806–84): writer, politician and Director of the Burgtheater, Vienna (1849–67) and of the Viennese municipal theatres (1875–80). Although himself an opponent of a hollow declamatory style, his concentration on the spoken word made him suspicious of the elaborate realism of the Meininger.
[5] Schiller's *Wallensteins Tod* (1799) was also a popular item of the repertoire, being performed 140 times.

52   Spectacular Meiningen crowd scene: Schiller's *Wallenstein's Death*, 1882 production

Drawing by Julius Ehrentraut from *Illustrierte Frauen-Zeitung*. Original in Cologne Theatre Museum. Reproduced from Max Grube. *The Story of the Meininger*, trans. A. M. Koller, ed. W. Cole (Coral Gables: University of Miami Press, 1963), Plate XIIIA

53   The Duke of Saxe-Meiningen expounds his principles of staging, 1895–1899

Paul Lindau, 'Herzog Georg II von Sachs-Meiningen', *Die deutsche Bühne*. Reprinted in Grube. *The Story of the Meininger*, pp. 40–46, translated by A.M. Koller.

When, in 1895, Paul Lindau (see **48**(c), note 1) succeeded Ludwig Chronegk and Paul Richard as Director of the Meiningen Court Theatre, the Duke of Saxe-Meiningen felt obliged to communicate his basic ideas on staging to Lindau in notes sent to him after various performances. Here the 'Theatre Duke' is concerned with two major consider-ations: what is visually pleasing on stage and what 'gives the appearance of life and naturalness'. It is interesting that, despite the Meininger's own frequent and innovative use of box-sets, instructions and warnings are still being given with regard to perspective scenery. Cf. 1.

We should take into consideration in the composition of a stage picture that the middle of a scene does not correspond with the middle of the stage. If the composition proceeds from the geometric middle, two halves result. From this the danger follows that in the arrangement of groups, disposing them to the right and left will result in a somewhat symmetrical balance. This will appear wooden, stiff, and boring. [. . .]

The actor should at no time stand in the middle of the stage directly in front of the prompt-box, but instead he should always stand a little to the right or left of the prompter. The middle of the stage, reckoned as about as wide as the prompt-box and extending from the footlights to the perspective in the background, should serve for the actor only as a passageway from right to left or vice versa. He has no business there for any other reason. It is also best, if possible, to avoid having two persons standing at an exact distance from the prompt-box.

More attention should be paid to a pleasing relationship between the actors' positions and the set decorations. [. . .] For example, an actor should not approach the scenery in the upstage wings so closely that the disproportion becomes striking. He should not – as one often sees – stand immediately in front of a painted house, the door of which reaches up to his hips, where he, without stretching, can look into a window on the second floor, and where, if he raised his hand, he could touch the chimney. [. . .]

The balcony of *Romeo and Juliet* is usually placed much too low. There is one disadvantage that in a really correct placement of the balcony, Juliet stands somewhat high, but that is less important than the customary mistake – that with a balcony of moderate height, there is always one disturbing thought: even if he were not a really good gymnast, Romeo could with only one leap reach his 'inaccessible' sweetheart and fold her in his arms.

The actors must never lean against the painted scenery. If the movement is vigorous, the contact will shake the painted piece and any illusion is lost. Yet if the actor uses the necessary caution not to joggle the canvas scenery with his movements, this lack of freedom restricts his actions until they are offensive in their rigidity.

Scenic pieces against which an actor may lean or upon which he can support himself must be made of sturdy materials and must be solid.

With the simultaneous use of painted and three-dimensional objects on stage, all possible care must be taken so that differences in these materials are not readily apparent. The shading, for example, from real or artificial flowers and leaves to those which are openly painted must be so finely achieved that the audience can scarcely distinguish the painted from the real. [...]

Borders made of cut strips of linen painted blue to represent the sky, and running crosswise above the stage, must never be used. In scenes depicting country landscapes, trees with widely extending boughs may be employed. These extended arches can usually be used for town scenes, streets and market places, too. Sometimes the action presents a place in such a way that above the streets and squares garlands or banners, flags or pennants, can be stretched. If this is impractical and the sky must appear above the scene, even then cloud borders are preferable to the painted blue linen. There is no place in an artistically decorated set for this tediously ugly blue border.

At the first rehearsal of a new play with crowd scenes and a large personnel, the hair of the director usually stands on end. He almost despairs of the possibility of enlivening and moulding the stiff, inflexible mass. A great help in solving this problem is to have the scenery up permanently from the very beginning. Any change in the setting, such as hanging or shifting scenery or moving furniture during rehearsals slows them terribly, upsets the nerves, and wearies and enervates the actors.

In costume plays everything should be tested as early as possible with the weapons, helmets, armour, swords, etc. Then during the play the actors will not be hindered in their actions by the unfamiliarity and ponderous weight of the weapons.

In these plays it is essential even before dress-rehearsal, which should differ from the opening performance only in the absence of the public, that the artists should rehearse in costume – either the proper one or, if this is not yet ready or must be kept fresh, in one of the corresponding cut. [...]

It is a real mistake to place the actors in positions parallel to one another. If it is necessary to place groups parallel to the footlights, then a direct face-to-face position is not attractive; this is especially true when two actors of the same height stand parallel to the footlights. If the actor has to move from the right to the left, he should avoid moving directly across; that is not the best way on stage. Instead, he should move unobtrusively at an angle to break the straight line.

If three or more actors in a scene are on the stage at the same time, they should avoid above all else standing in a straight line. They should always stand at an angle. The distances between the individual actors should not be equal. If they stand at equal intervals, they will become uninteresting and as lifeless as figures on a chessboard. It is always attractive if the actor can unaffectedly touch a piece of furniture or some other suitable object on the stage. This gives the appearance of life and naturalness.

If the stage has different levels – steps, hilly ground with rocks, and the like – the actor should not let the opportunity escape to display a harmonious line by making his movements rhythmical. He should also, for example, when ascending a flight of steps, avoid standing on one step with both feet at the same time. If he climbs down from an elevation and has to stop to say something or to make an observation, he should place one foot a little lower than the other. By this, his whole body gains in freedom and attractiveness. 'One leg high' is the usual command from the director in this instance.

The management of masses on the stage demands special and different attention during rehearsal. [...]

The extras should be divided into smaller groups, each of which is separately trained. Each of these groups should be led by a skilled, thoroughly trained actor or by a clever member of the chorus, who 'covers' the others and who therefore stands conspicuously in the foreground. To some extent, this leader must carry the responsibility that subordinates entrusted to him obey the orders he gives. He himself is responsible to the director for such subordinates and must see to it that positions, movements, etc., are produced on cue. These leaders receive partial scripts with cues, in which the directions are often only generally given by the author as 'noise', 'tumult', 'murmurs', 'cries', 'shrieks', and the like; these the director has to put into words to be committed to memory by the performers. Such insertions must naturally be presented in different forms and must not be given simultaneously by all the groups in the same manner.

The problems which devolve upon the leader of a group of walk-ons are not simple. It is a regrettable error and one very harmful to artistic efforts when members of the company engaged as 'actors' consider these roles valueless and unworthy of real artists, and try to avoid them whenever possible; or if they are required to play such parts, they make no effort to hide their disinclination.

In Meiningen all artists without exception are required to do duty as extras.

The lack of beauty resulting from poor placement of individual artists in relation to one another is especially disturbing in crowd scenes. The principal charm of grouping lies in a beautiful line of actors' heads. Just as uniformity of carriage is to be avoided, absolute uniformity in the height of those placed next to each other is to be avoided. If it occurs that several of the same height are placed together, then they should stand on different levels. Depending on the situation, some might kneel, some stand, some bend over, others remain erect. It works out very well if an irregular semi-circle can be built around the person or the object on which the gaze of the group is fixed.

The director must also ensure that all those standing nearest the audience, and therefore most prominently in the eyes of the audience, be placed and arranged so that their shoulders are not all at the same angle to the footlights. It should be impressed upon every extra that he must alter his position if he notices he is standing in exactly the same position as his neighbour. In no well-composed picture would one find many figures standing together at the same height and in the same position. This order should be repeated to the actors and extras at almost every rehearsal of the mob scenes, because they always forget it.

The extras must be forcefully instructed not to look out into the audience. It is natural that they should do this; for many, 'play-acting' is new and unusual, and it excites their curiosity to look into the dark auditorium.

Action that is not really attractive – for example, dragging off the dead and wounded – must be 'covered' and thus be hidden as much as possible from the eyes of the audience. But this should not be done in such a way that a thick and impenetrable wall of men hides the action; that is ridiculous. The masking should be somewhat patchy; the viewer should not see everything that is happening, but he should see enough so that he can surmise what the action is all about.

To give the impression that a very large crowd is on the stage, groups should be so arranged that those standing on the edge of the group extend into the wings. From no place in the auditorium should anyone see the edge of the crowd. To the members of the audience it should be believable that farther off stage still more of the crowd are thronging.

B. NATURALIST THEORY

54   Maximilian Harden's definition of naturalism, 1886

Maximilian Harden, 'Die Wahrheit auf der Bühne', *Der Kunstwart*, 1, 1887–8, Heft 15. Reprinted in Ruprecht, ed., *Literarische Manifeste des Naturalismus*, p. 108

As one of the founders of the Freie Bühne and editor of the literary weekly *Die Zukunft*, Maximilian Harden (1861–1927) was one of the leading champions of naturalism in Germany. The following concise description reflects the prevalent desire to base naturalistic theatre on the objectivity of scientific observation.

What is naturalism? Naturalism demands the rejection of all convention, the ruthless search for truth free of any compromise; it seeks to represent a piece of nature as it reveals itself in its temperament,[1] without painting a layer of prettifying varnish over the picture. Just as science has recourse to analytical experiments and history turns to a study of source material, so literature should collect 'human documents'. These should present human beings as the result of their living conditions and environment, not as the accidental products of an imagination thirsting after beauty – human beings of solid flesh, perceived by the writer, involved in the sort of relationships, conflicts and passions that occur in the everyday life of each individual – that is the most noble article of faith in the gospel of naturalism.

[1] Clearly based on Zola's dictum: 'L'œuvre d'art est un coin de la nature, vu à travers un tempérament' ('A work of art is a corner of nature seen through the temperament [of an artist]'). But Harden, either deliberately or unwittingly, changes the sense to exclude the subjectivity of the artist by using 'temperament' to refer to nature itself. See 150, note 4.

55   Gerhart Hauptmann: aphorisms of a leading naturalist

Gerhart Hauptmann, *Sämtliche Werke*, Centenar-Ausgabe, ed. Hans-Egon Hass (Berlin: Propyläen Verlag, 1963), vol. VI, pp. 1036–45

Gerhart Hauptmann (1862–1946) was unquestionably the leading dramatist of German naturalism. His first play, *Vor Sonnenaufgang* (Before Sunrise, 1889), caused a furore when it was performed at the Freie Bühne. His play on the revolt of the Silesian weavers, *Die Weber* (The Weavers), also premièred at the Freie Bühne (1893), was initially banned from performance on public stages. But like many naturalists, Hauptmann soon also turned to more symbolic and mystical writing, as in his 'dream play', *Hannele* (1893). The aphorisms below, first published in this arrangement in 1942 but almost certainly formulated before 1914, reflect this dual approach. Some stand as pronouncements on naturalist theatre; others, like the reference to the 'inner being' of the actor or the desire to restore a sacral quality to theatre, point in a quite different direction. Of the eighty-five original aphorisms, only a selection concerned with the practice of drama and theatre is given here.

In almost every respect I should like Lessing to speak for me, especially with regard to [. . .] acting: 'This young woman possesses feeling and vocal quality, a fine appearance and grace; she has not yet been contaminated by the false tone of the theatre . . .'[1]

A drama that is not exposition from the first word to the last is not truly alive.

Time in drama: the natural succession of the psycho-biological. Space in drama: the position and movement of human beings relative to one another.

There is such a thing as the psychic nude. A dramatist must above all be able to draw nudes. Many so-called dramatists are unfortunately, at best, costume designers.

The art of acting: not imitation, but heightened language; the richest expression of the personal becomes more conscious in the actor than in anyone else.

In the actor, too, it is the inner being that emerges.

The relationship of the actor to the text must be more than that of the horse to harness and carriage.

The theatre will not be fully and deeply effective, until it has for us, as in Ancient Greece, the sanction of a divine service. In itself, it is still powerful, but it is only tolerated, not cultivated. It stands under the pressure of hostile prejudice, not under the protection of sanctity.

To trace someone's way of thinking is easy. To trace their way of feeling, of empathizing, which is my sole concern, difficult.

Drama rules the world, not theatre.

What is called healthy and normal is overstepped in the emotions. A drama without emotions is unthinkable, so it must always to some extent move into the pathological.

What is given to the action is taken from the characters.

Ibsen sees the tragic usually only in so-called failed lives. The tragedy of a full life is the higher form.

The writer who takes flight to the realms of the pathological has failed, says Paul Ernst.[2] Is the writer not permitted to have a universal view of man? Is he required to make a medical diagnosis between sick and healthy and then eliminate sickness?

[1] G. E. Lessing, *Hamburgische Dramaturgie* (1767–9).
[2] See 63.

C. NATURALIST ACTING

56   Hauptmann satirizes the classical style of Weimar, 1911

Gerhart Hauptmann, *Sämtliche Werke*, vol. II (1965), pp. 774–9

In most of the court and municipal theatres of Germany the classical style of Weimar had remained dominant in the nineteenth century, at least for the performance of classical works. In his 'Berlin tragi-comedy', *Die Ratten* (The Rats), Hauptmann parodies the worst aspects of this style: its preoccupation with heroic figures, hollow declamation and formal movement. Through the figure of Spitta he speaks for naturalist theatre: the portrayal of the non-heroic protagonist and a natural acting style devoid of bombast.

Director Hassenreuter is giving instruction to his three pupils, Spitta, Dr Kegel and Käferstein. He himself is sitting at the table, is constantly opening letters and is beating out the metre with the paperknife on the table. At the front to one side stand Kegel and Käferstein, on the opposite side Spitta as the two choruses of The Bride of Messina.[1] *Their feet are placed within a grid, which is marked in chalk on the floor and which is divided into the sixty-four squares of a chess-board. (...)*

DR KEGEL and KÄFERSTEIN   (*with enormous pathos*)
    Thee I greet in awe,
    Venerable hall,
    Thee, oh royal cradle
    Of my kings,
    Splendid roof on pillars borne.
    Deep in its sheath –

DIRECTOR HASSENREUTER   (*shouting furiously*) Pause! Full-stop! Full-stop! Pause! Full-stop! You're not playing a barrel-organ! The chorus from *The Bride of Messina* is not written for the barrel-organ! 'Thee I greet in awe' again from the top, sirs! 'Thee I greet in awe. Venerable hall!' That's the way to say it, sirs! 'Deep in its sheath / Let the sword rest'. (...) Full-stop! You may as well continue.

DR KEGEL and KÄFERSTEIN
    Deep in its sheath
    Let the sword rest (...)
    For the inviolate threshold
    Of the hospitable house
    Is protected by oath, son of the Erinyes –

DIRECTOR HASSENREUTER   (*leaps up, roars, dashes around*) Oath, oath, oath, oath! Stop! Don't you know what an oath is, Käferstein? 'Is protected by oath!! – son of the Erinyes'. The oath is the son of the Erinyes, Dr Kegel! Lift your voice! Then dead silence! The audience, down to the last usherette, is a mass of gooseflesh! A shudder of terror passes through every frame! Now listen: 'For the threshold of the house is protected by the oath!!! – son of the Erinyes, the most terrible of the gods of hell!' – Don't go back, carry on! Just take note that there is a difference between an oath and a pickled onion.

SPITTA   (*declaims*) Within my breast my heart grows wrathful –

DIRECTOR HASSENREUTER   Stop! (*He runs to Spitta and twists his arms and legs to achieve the desired tragic pose*) In the first place you have lost your statuesque pose, my dear Spitta. You simply do not express the dignity of a tragic figure. And then you failed to move your right foot from square ID to IIC, as I required you to! [...] Eh bien, my friend, begin again.

SPITTA   (*recites according to the sense and without pathos*)
    Within my breast my heart grows wrathful.

My fist is clenched to start the fight.

For lo! the Gorgon-visaged train

Of the detested foemen nigh.

Hardly can I command my boiling blood.

Shall I now to parley deign?

Or shall I obey my raging soul? [...]

DIRECTOR HASSENREUTER   (*has sat down and listens, his head resting on his hand, full of devotion. Only when a few seconds have elapsed after Spitta has finished, he looks up as though coming to himself*) Have you finished, Spitta?! – Thank you very much! – You see, dear boy, I am now in a very complicated position with regard to you: either I tell you bluntly to your face that I like your manner of recitation – and then I will have perpetrated the most despicable mendacity – or I say that I find it horrible, and we will have another awful row.

SPITTA   (*growing pale*) I'm afraid I can't stand anything stilted or rhetorical. That's why I gave up Theology, because I hate the affected style of the pulpit.

DIRECTOR HASSENREUTER   So you want to rattle off tragic choruses the way a clerk of the court reads out the records or a waiter tells you the menu?

SPITTA   I really don't like all the sonorous bombast of *The Bride of Messina*. [...]

DIRECTOR HASSENREUTER   My God, right now your face is a study in arrogance and audacity. [...] You deny the art of speaking, the vocal organ, and wish to replace it with organ-less squeaking! You deny action in the drama and maintain that it is worthless and incidental, something for the groundlings. [...] You know nothing of the heights of humanity. Recently you asserted that in certain circumstances a barber[2] or a cleaning woman from Corporation Street might be as much an object of tragedy as Lady Macbeth and King Lear.

SPITTA   (*pale, cleans his spectacles*) Before art, as before the law, all men are equal, Herr Hassenreuter.

DIRECTOR HASSENREUTER   Really! I see! Where did you pick up this platitude?

SPITTA   (*unperturbed*) This sentence has become second nature with me. It may be crossing swords with Schiller and Gustav Freytag,[3] but not with Lessing[4] and Diderot.[5] I have spent the last two terms studying these truly great theorists, and, as far as I am concerned, they have spelled the end of stilted French pseudo-classicism, not only in literature but also in the utterly silly 'Rules for Actors' of the older Goethe,[6] which are nothing but mummified nonsense.

DIRECTOR HASSENREUTER   Really?

SPITTA   And if the German theatre wants to renew itself, then it must look to the young Schiller, the young Goethe of *Götz*[7] and again and again to

Gotthold Ephraim Lessing. There you will find ideas that match the fullness of art and the richness of life and which are commensurate with nature.

¹ *Die Braut von Messina* (1803) was Schiller's major attempt to write tragedy in the neo-classical style and contains a chorus, composed of two warring factions.
² Almost certainly a reference to one of Hauptmann's favourite plays. Büchner's fragment *Woyzeck* (1835), in which early editors thought that Woyzeck was a barber.
³ Gustav Freytag (1816–95): primarily a writer of realistic novels, e.g. *Soll und Haben* (1855). Spitta's antipathy is no doubt based on Freytag's *Die Technik des Dramas* (1863), a schematic work on dramatic technique, and on his sententious historical tragedies, e.g. *Graf Waldemar* (1858), *Die Fabier* (1859).
⁴ Lessing (1729–81) introduced the genre of middle-class tragedy to Germany, notably in *Miss Sara Sampson* (1755).
⁵ Denis Diderot (1713–84), whose 'drames bourgeois' Lessing translated into German in 1760, was, together with Nivelle de la Chaussée (1692–1754), one of the progenitors of middle-class tragedy in Europe.
⁶ Goethe's 'Regeln für Schauspieler' (noted down 1803, published 1824), were ninety-one hints for the guidance of actors, deriving from Goethe's own work at the Court Theatre of Weimar. Many of them, including the suggestion that the actor might imagine the stage divided into sixty-four squares, seem curiously formal, but were not intended for rigid application.
⁷ *Götz von Berlichingen* (1771) was the major drama of Goethe's youthful Storm and Stress period.

57   Non-verbal communication in naturalist acting, 1898

Johannes Schlaf, 'Vom intimen Theater', *Neuland*, 2, 1 (1898), pp. 35–8. Reprinted in Ruprecht, ed., *Literarische Manifeste des Naturalismus*, pp. 104–6

Johannes Schlaf (1862–1941) is now best remembered for his collaboration with Arno Holz (1863–1929) on the seminal naturalist works *Papa Hamlet* (1889) and *Die Familie Selicke* (1890). Here Schlaf makes one of the earliest and clearest statements about the non-textual levels of communication inherent in naturalist drama. In this sense, this essay stands as an early contribution to the semiotics of theatre. The title, 'On intimate theatre', points to the need, already expressed by Strindberg, for a theatre building small enough to allow the actor to use subtle signs which could be followed only by an audience physically close enough to 'read' them. Such a theatre was first realized by Reinhardt (see 66).

If we attentively follow the progress of a real conversation, then it is nothing short of astonishing how the spoken word is often of secondary importance, how it is often merely a stepping-stone in the communication between two or more people. We can observe how obscure, ambiguous, clumsy and brittle it is, how it stammers and stutters, how it misses the precise expression of an idea or of an emotion, and how gesture, facial expression, body movement and emotional colouring are the main element if not everything. We may observe too how all these factors often enough represent a second parallel language which betrays, often in very comic fashion, what the spoken word is trying to conceal, or unmistakably expresses what the word can or may only suggest.

We know that drama of the old style did not possess this intimate sense for dialogue. In order to express what is most intimate and, as one might say, the inexpressible, that was often of such great importance, traditional drama had to resort to such crude means as the monologue or in special cases was obliged to use the aside, a device whose unnaturalness would provoke our laughter in a modern play. Today we can reveal more inner life of a character in a minute of silent action than was earlier possible with page-long monologues or endless asides.

The drama of which we speak has taken a decisive step in this direction. It has abandoned the last remnants of schematic exposition, if one can still speak of exposition at all. It has replaced everything that was once achieved by the dead conventions of dramatic devices with subtlety of dialogue, milieu, gesture, posture and silent action, and attempts with these free and natural means to achieve what the conventions spoiled rather than attained: a living and immediate effect and convincing illusion of meaningful life.

This drama will also extend the domain of the actor, as no other modern drama can. Here, he will have the opportunity to develop a new intimate art of the soul in the living, differentiated shading of the word, in gesture, posture and in silent action.

D. THE FREIE BÜHNE

58   The manifesto of the Freie Bühne, 1890

Anon. [Otto Brahm], 'Zum Beginn', *Freie Bühne für modernes Leben*, ed. Otto Brahm, I, I (1890), pp. 1–2. Reprinted in Ruprecht, ed., *Literarische Manifeste des Naturalismus*, pp. 155–7

Modelled on André Antoine's Théâtre Libre, founded in 1887, the Freie Bühne was established two years later in Berlin by a group of writers and critics, notably Theodor Wolff, Maximilian Harden, Paul Schlenther and Otto Brahm.[1] Possessing neither theatre company nor theatre premises, the Freie Bühne presented modern works, otherwise banned by the censor, in closed performances for its members, beginning with a production of Ibsen's *Ghosts* in 1889.[2] As can be seen from this manifesto, they were advocates of the naturalist movement, while still insisting on the importance of the subjectivity of the artist – 'individual truth'. It is also clear that the commitment to naturalism was provisional, and by the 1890s they had begun to perform new works of symbolism and neo-Romanticism. Meanwhile, the establishment of the Freie Bühne had provided a model for the people's theatre, the Volksbühne, which was founded in 1890. See 25, 29, 30, 149, 213, 214.

We are opening a free theatre for modern living – the Freie Bühne.

At the centre of our efforts will stand art – the new art that contemplates reality and the life of today.

Once there was art which fled from daylight and sought poetry only in the twilight of the past, striving for those idealized spheres, where something that has never existed continues to bloom in eternal youth. The art of today clings desperately to what is alive, to nature and society. Hence modern art and modern living are bound by the strongest and finest strands of interaction. Whoever wishes to seize hold of modern art must penetrate modern living in its thousands of ramifications, in all the life-drives that cross and conflict with one another.

The slogan of the new art, inscribed in golden letters by leading minds, is the one word: Truth. And it is Truth, Truth in every sphere of existence, which we too are demanding and striving for. Not objective truth, which is not part of the struggle, but individual truth, which is freely born of inner conviction and is freely expressed: the truth of the independent mind who does not have to beautify or conceal anything. And who therefore knows only one opponent, its deadly arch-enemy: the lie in every form.

We shall not record any other programme on these pages. We do not swear by any formula and will not dare to chain the eternal movement of life and art with the dead coercion of rules. We are committed to change, and we look more intently towards what is to come than towards the eternal past, which tries to tie the endless possibilities of humanity to conventions and precepts. We bow in respect before all the great things that past epochs have handed down to us, but they do not supply us with the model and norms of existence. [...]

Modern art, in its liveliest forms, has taken root in the soil of naturalism. Obeying a basic impulse of our age, it has focused on the awareness of the natural forces of existence and shows us with ruthless pursuit of the truth the world as it is. Friends of naturalism, we want to walk a good part of the way with it. But we shall not be surprised if in the course of our wanderings, at a point which we do not yet see, the road suddenly turns a corner, and surprising new views of art and life are revealed. For the endless development of human culture is tied to no formula, not even to the most recent; and in this conviction, in the belief in eternal change, we have opened a free theatre for modern living – the Freie Bühne.

[1] Otto Brahm (1856–1912): from 1894 Director of the Deutsches Theater, Berlin; from 1904 of the Lessing Theater, Berlin; the leading director of German naturalism and the mentor of Max Reinhardt. See also Horst Claus, *The Theatre Director Otto Brahm* (Michigan: UMI Research Press, 1981). For Maximilian Harden, see **54**.
[2] See **48**(b), note 2. For a full list of the plays performed by the Freie Bühne, see John Osborne, *The Naturalistic Drama in Germany* (Manchester University Press, 1971), p. 173.

E. WORKERS' THEATRE

59   Workers' theatre in Leipzig

Heinrich Lange, *Aus einer alten Handwerksburschen-Mappe*, Leipzig, n.d., pp. 162–4. Reprinted in Friedrich Knilli and Ursula Münchow, *Frühes deutsches Arbeitertheater 1847–1918. Eine Dokumentation* (Munich: Hanser, 1970), pp. 175–7

Of the amateur theatre movement in Germany, that of the workers was the most significant. It provided a focus for working-class consciousness, the setting for the founding of the Volksbühne, and a preparation for the later developments in workers' theatre, most notably the 'Proletarian Theatre' of Piscator and the didactic theatre of Brecht in the 1920s and early 1930s.

In the Society for the Further Education of Workers things became much worse under the Socialist Laws.[1] When Manfred Wittich[2] was to give a talk on Ulrich von Hutten,[3] the police prevented him from speaking. Then the Society asked him to set down his ideas in the form of a festival drama. So the members of the drama section said on stage what the author had been forbidden to utter. In 1881 the drama section had rehearsed a play, *J. J. Rousseau*, by a certain Müller.[4] However, it did not reach performance, because the day before the leading performers were arrested and deported. [...] Stimulated by the new German writing, we set our sights still higher. So, for example, we gave several performances of Ibsen's *Pillars of Society*. Admittedly, the productions would not have stood up to serious criticism. When we performed scenes from *William Tell* on Schiller's birthday in the Society club-rooms, our secretary Georg Gieseler, playing Stauffacher, wandered over the Swiss Alps in carpet-slippers, because Sporbert, the caretaker, had to mend his boots during the performance, since it was raining hard that evening. No one laughed though. Schiller belonged to us, even if the town council had refused us permission to lay a wreath in Schiller's house in Gohlis, while allowing Dr Gensel's Society for Popular Welfare[5] to do so.

Anyway, it was impressive what our drama section achieved. Its Director, the master cobbler August Scheibe, did not have an easy task rehearsing parts, obtaining costumes, doing the make-up, and as a rule acting himself. Rehearsals could be held only after work, but the members were totally committed. Take, for example, the case of two young market-porters, Zschocher and Massias. One day I saw them coming down the Petersssteinweg, one pushing, the other pulling their barrows, so that they could walk side by side. They were so absorbed they did not notice me, and then I heard that they were rehearsing a scene out of the play they were both in – in the midst of the city bustle.

[1] The so-called *Sozialistengesetz*, which was passed on 21 October 1878, banned all 'social-democratic, socialist, and communist' political activity and dissemination of ideas, and was Bismarck's attempt to contain the political aspirations of the proletariat. It was repealed in 1890.

[2] Manfred Wittich (1851–1904) was one of the leading Social Democrats in Leipzig. Wittich's play, *Ulrich von Hutten*, was published in Berlin in 1911 (see Knilli and Münchow, *Frühes deutsches Arbeitertheater*, pp. 177–85).

[3] Since Herder's rediscovery of him, Ulrich von Hutten (1503–52) had been adopted as a proto-revolutionary for his uncompromising opposition to the Papacy and the German Princes.

[4] Hugo Müller's play, *Rousseau*, was published in Leipzig in 1894.

[5] Verein für Volkswohl, a nationalistic organization.

III Alternatives to naturalism

60 Wagner's influence: the 'total art-work', 1849

Richard Wagner, 'Das Kunstwerk der Zukunft' §4, *Gesammelte Schriften und Dichtungen* (2nd edn., Leipzig: Fritzsch, 1887), vol. III, pp. 150–8

The influence of Richard Wagner (1813–83) on the development of German theatre may have been indirect, but it was nonetheless certain. Perhaps his major contribution was to elevate theatre from what was generally regarded as, at best, a craft, not merely to a legitimate art-form but to the highest of all the arts. His vision of a total art-work (*Gesamtkunstwerk*) which would bring together all art-forms in harmonious excellence was, by way especially of Appia and Craig, to have a profound influence on anti-naturalist tendencies at the turn of the century. No matter that Wagner himself did not get very close to his ideal 'art-work of the future'; the concept itself fired the imaginations of theatre-practitioners for half a century.

The artist can achieve fulfilment only in the unification of all art-forms in the communal art-work. If the artist's abilities are subjected to specialization, then he is no longer free, not completely what he might be. [...]

Art therefore strives to be all-embracing. Anyone genuinely inspired by art will not develop talents in order to celebrate those special talents but in order to celebrate humankind itself.

The highest communal art-work is drama. It fully achieves its potential richness only when each individual art-form achieves its fullest potential. [...]

Illusion in the fine arts becomes truth in drama. The painter and sculptor lend a helping hand to the dancer and the mime, so as to be absorbed in them by becoming dancer and mime themselves. The dancer and mime will, as far as they are able, communicate the feelings and aspirations of humankind to the eye. The scenic space in all its breadth and depth belongs to the performer for the plastic representation of a figure and its movements, either as an individual or together with fellow performers. When the limits of the performer are reached, when the performance goes beyond inner feelings and aspirations and so has recourse to language, [...] the performer will become a poet, and in order to be a poet, will become a composer of music. As dancer, composer and poet, he is, however, one and the same, nothing other than a performing artist, who achieves the fullest potential by communicating to the finest level of response.

In the performing artist the three sister-arts [movement, music and writing] are united in common effectiveness, which allows each art to achieve its highest development. [...] The mime/dancer overcomes his limitations as soon as he can speak and sing. The creations of musical art gain generally intelligible meaning by being taken up into the movement of the mime and the words of the poet. The poet, on the other hand, becomes truly human only by entering into the flesh and blood of the performer; [...] poetic intention is realized in the ability of the performer.

None of the possibilities inherent in different art-forms will remain unused in the total art-work of the future; on the contrary, they will here finally achieve their full effect. [...]

So the three united sister-arts, sometimes together, sometimes in twos, sometimes singly, will make their appearance according to the demands of the dramatic action. Now mime will listen to the cool reflection of thought; now the decision reached by thought will be expressed by a gesture; now music on its own will express the flow of feeling or the shudder of awe; and now all three in communal embrace will transform the intention of drama into immediate and effective realization. For there is only one medium, in which all these united art-forms can transform their intentions into glorious reality, and that is the drama.

61   Hermann Bahr on non-naturalistic (stylized) stage design, 1905

Hermann Bahr, 'Über Dekorationskunst', *Der Weg*, 5, Vienna, 1905. Reprinted in *Die Schaubühne* (later *Die neue Weltbühne*), Berlin, 1905–14 (reprinted Königstein: Athenäum, 1979–80), 1979, pp. 289–91

The Austrian Hermann Bahr (1863–1934) worked at the Burgtheater as Dramaturg and was later a director with Reinhardt. A declared opponent of naturalism, he wrote articles and essays proposing a less realistic form of theatre, reliant on the creativity of the imagination, as in his long essay *Die Überwindung des Naturalismus* (The Conquest of Naturalism), published as early as 1891. In his dream of a 'dramatic architect' he approaches closely to the vision of Wagner and Craig.

Suddenly in the nineteenth century the imagination of the audience was no longer to be trusted. This would be another whole chapter, on the psychological history of the middle classes: how they had hardly achieved power, when they began on all sides to lose faith in their strengh and sought aids to sustain it. So when previously a stage-set had only said to the audience, 'Imagine a castle or forest', it is now filled with doubt about its ability to achieve this and instead tries to reproduce such settings. The sign is replaced by a panorama. It becomes 'authentic'. Just go to the Burgtheater! Lefler and Goltz.[1] You will not see such design better done, such inferior design. And this brings us to another whole chapter, the psychology of performance. The imagination of the audience is totally excluded from the performance so that their imagination becomes idle and redundant and so turns against the performance itself. When imagination is no longer allowed to participate, it becomes critical; [...] it turns in vengeance on the artist, because the latter refuses to let the imagination play a part in art. And the result is that for anybody with a little taste conventional stage designs have become unbearable. And, as is the way of things, some shout: 'Go back!', others cry: 'Go further!' ... That was the point we arrived at six or seven years ago. Everywhere. That is what is so remarkable, that when the time is ripe, things start happening everywhere as if by agreement, and people who hardly know one another all appear to obey an unspoken order. Here in Austria: Kolo Moser, Roller, Olbrich.[2] The book by Appia.[3] The young Fortuny.[4] Then in Berlin Reinhardt's designers. Now Craig. All of them filled with antipathy, with disgust towards panoramic scenery. And all of them grimly determined to find a new form of stage design. So a new word has been coined, 'stylized', by which everyone means something different. The only thing they agree about is that a stage-set should no longer pretend to be this or that, a castle or a forest, but that its function is to assist in creating the dramatic mood. It should achieve with lines and colours what the writer achieves with words: to compel the audience to feel the same as the author or director. [...] All drama has only ever been suggestion. [...] When in the drama the word 'castle' or 'forest' appears, the writer never has a real castle or forest in mind, but is concerned only with the evocative quality which the word possesses, and now the stage designer seeks to discover the same quality through lines and colours. This was the meaning of the 'stylization' that was talked about. Olbrich in Darmstadt made the first radical attempt, then Moser in Salten's Jung-Wiener Theater.[5] [...] Olbrich now says that for him it is enough to have a curtain, which he will illuminate differently whenever the feeling changes, using a different colour to reflect the mood and feeling of the scene. [In *Hamlet*] we know that we are on the battlements or in the palace, or in the Queen's closet because the words have told us so and it is unnecessary to be shown what we have already been told. We should not see the battlements, which everyone can imagine for themselves, we should see the feeling of the scene [...] – the décor as the expression of spiritual emotion. [...] Then there is Reinhardt who in *A Midsummer Night's Dream* has finally dispensed with the 'boards' altogether; the whole stage has become dramatic. And now Craig's achievement; to wrest control from the writer and to give it to the designer. Finally – somewhere in the future – my favourite figure, the 'dramatic architect', the great conductor, obeyed by writer, musician, designer, actor, singer and dancer alike.

---

[1] Heinrich Lefler (1863–1919) and Alexander Demetrius Goltz (1857–1944): designers at the Burgtheater, Vienna.

[2] Kolo Moser (1868–1918): designer at the Jung-Wiener Theater, Vienna. Alfred Roller (1864–

1935): designer with Mahler at the Vienna Court Opera, then with Max Reinhardt in Dresden and Berlin (*Der Rosenkavalier, Faust, The Oresteia*). Joseph Olbrich (1867–1908): primarily an architect, co-founder of the Wiener Secession, leader of *Jugendstil* movement.

[3] *Die Musik und die Inscenierung* (Music and the Art of Production), published in Dresden in 1899.

[4] Mariano Fortuny (1871–1949): designed the sky-dome or 'Kuppelhorizont' illuminated by indirect lighting, in place of the conventional backdrop and borders. First installed in Germany at the Krolloper in Berlin in 1907.

[5] Felix Salten (1869–1947): now most widely remembered as the author of *Bambi* (1923)! Also a playwright and Theatre Director. Founded the progressive Jung-Wiener Theater.

62   Reinhardt's revolving woodlands: *A Midsummer Night's Dream*, 1905

In Edda Fuhrich and Gisela Prossnitz, eds., *Max Reinhardt* (Munich: Langen Müller, 1987), p. 52

The play was performed at the Neues Theater, Berlin. Designer: Ernst Stern.

63   Paul Ernst on neo-classicism or *Neuklassik*, 1906

Paul Ernst, 'Unsere Absichten', *Masken*, 1, 6 (1905–6), pp. 8–11. Reprinted in Erich
Ruprecht and Dieter Bänsch, eds., *Literarische Manifeste der Jahrhundertwende 1890–
1910* (Stuttgart: Metzler, 1970), pp. 450–3

Paul Ernst (1866–1933), initially a naturalist, soon became the leading proponent of
Neuklassik (neo-classicism). This movement represented a reaction against the perceived
platitudinous imitation of the naturalists in an attempt to restore the tragic impact and
sacral quality of classical Greek drama to the German stage. Though short-lived and
producing few plays of any merit (e.g. Ernst's own *Demetrios*, 1905, *Canossa*, 1908),
Neuklassik helped to prepare the ground for expressionist theatre by abandoning naturalistic psychological characterizations in favour of representative figures, by embracing a
stylized performing style and by seeking to give its audience a profound emotional
experience. Cf. 32.

Both our dramatic literature and our theatre arts have reached an important
watershed. Unless we are deceived, we are standing at the beginning of a
significant period, which, if everything develops according to expectation, must
lead to an outcome that will later appear one of the high points of theatre. [. . .]
   The path which naturalistic art can follow from its inception to its climax is
extraordinarily short. In German naturalism the climax was also soon reached,
and a second stage should have followed. Instead we witnessed, on the one hand,
the stultification of naturalism in mannerisms, and on the other hand, a groping
around in every imaginable style by second-rate imitators. 'Stylization' became a
word to describe all sorts of dramatic dilettantism. [. . .]
   It became apparent in the naturalist period that it was nothing more than the
effect of being true to life which was created, but that the cathartic experiences
[*Erschütterungen*] which we expect today, were not possible. At best, the audience
experienced sentimental stirrings in their souls. The naturalistic hero, when not
actually boring, excites our compassion, no more. Not one work of this period
achieves tragic catharsis. Thus modern art cannot through realistic detail
generate the truth which it demands; it must seek other means.
   These other means are usually named by the misused term, 'stylization'. Since,
thanks to modern dilettantes and hacks, this term has acquired a hollow ring, it is
better to avoid it and replace it with what it actually means: namely, instead of
gathering realistic detail, we must discover the essential quality of life, or that
which we regard as essential, and to portray this. If the composition is successful,
then we shall also create the illusion of being true to life; and from our earlier great
periods of art we know that in this process the desired catharsis is possible. Our
slogan of the 'great line'[1] implies this process.
   This is the starting point of the work of the [Düsseldorf] Schauspielhaus.[2]
   We hope that we shall soon see a dramatic work which creates a construct of

life which both seems true for us today and also achieves catharsis. It would arise from insights deriving from the will of the age. We intend to produce such works in their appropriate staging; that is to say, we wish alongside developments in dramatic literature to evolve a new classical style of performance from that of naturalism. Our theatrical style also strives to be true to life but not with naturalistic means; and just as the truth of future dramatic writing will be a higher truth than that of naturalism, then so shall the truth of our actors be higher truths. We seek new emotions, emotions that grow out of the will of our age and which affect the will of our age.

This is all merely a hope, a desire, a plan, and will only gradually assume a shape. If our intentions come to fruition, then we would hope, too, to awaken our classical writers to new life on the stage. We shall not render them unpalatable through the emotionalism of their imitators [Epigonen],[3] nor drag them down with the banality of the naturalists,[4] but we shall endeavour to clothe their eternal truth in such a performance style that they will not only seem true for our time, they will seem modern.

[1] The 'grosse Linie' of the Neuklassik implied a rejection of the incidental details of naturalism in favour of 'tragic monumentality' (Ruprecht and Bänsch, Literarische Manifeste, p. 450).
[2] Ernst was for a while Dramaturg at the Schauspielhaus, Düsseldorf.
[3] In terms of writing, this would refer to the adaptations of the classics in the Neuromantik (e.g. Hofmannsthal's Elektra, 1903, Eulenberg's Kassandra, 1903).
[4] e.g. Gerhart Hauptmann's Der Bogen des Odysseus (1912).

64   Hofmannsthal calls for neo-Romanticism (Neuromantik): the stage as dream image, 1903

Hugo von Hofmannsthal, 'Die Bühne als Traumbild', Das Theater, Berlin, 1903. Reprinted in H. von Hofmannsthal, Prosa II (Frankfurt/Main: Fischer, 1951), pp. 75–80

Hofmannsthal (1874–1929) was the leading writer of the Neuromantik (neo-Romanticism). Like Paul Ernst and the writers of the Neuklassik, he pursued an anti-naturalist path by turning his attention from the imitation of external detail; but, unlike the Neuklassik, and in the style of the symbolists (e.g. Maeterlinck), he did not so much seek to discover the eternal truths and 'great line' of the Neuklassik as to explore the individual human psyche in states of crisis. To this end the stage should no longer attempt to give the illusion of real life, but should attempt to reproduce the logic of the dream, as in the manner of Strindberg's note to his Dream Play (1901; see p. 316 and 157(b)):[1]

> In this dream play the author has [...] attempted to imitate the inconsequent yet transparently logical shape of a dream. Everything can happen, everything is possible and probable. Time and place do not exist; on an insignificant basis of reality the imagination spins, weaving new patterns; a mixture of memories, experiences, incongruities and improvisations.

Let us never forget that the stage is nothing and worse than nothing if it is not something full of wonder. It must be the dream of all dreams, or it becomes a wooden pillory on which the naked dream of the poet is horribly prostituted. Whoever creates the stage-set must know how to, and must believe at the deepest possible level that there is nothing fixed in the world, nothing that exists in isolation and only for itself. He must know this from dreams and must see the world in this way; the power of dreams must be strong in such a person, and he must be a poet amongst poets. [. . .] The economy of dreams is indescribable; who can forget how in dreams terrible violence arises from utter bareness and simplicity? We are about to be flung from a tower. We are aware of nothing about this tower except for the terrifyingly sheer drop and the fatal vertical line of naked walls. [. . .]

And the lighting master, who controls the beams of light, who can hurl one from above, a beam of terror, a sparkling sword, into the soul of the praying Gretchen, while the horrifying chords of the organ bind themselves around her like chains, and who can then cast a ray of bliss, honey-coloured and other-worldly, into the pale and deathly air of the formless mass of her prison cell[2] [. . .] – he, who can command such light, should he forget to cast these beams and instead erect a cathedral, a specific Gothic structure with wood carvings on a painted back-cloth and with massive arches that sway when a costume brushes against them, and then a prison-cell, a 'real' one, with straw on the wooden planks of the stage, with cardboard prison-bars? Instead the lighting master will cast forth his light, bearing the unutterable power of dreams, and let it fall into the mysterious space, vague and shrouded in darkness, inhabited with the magic of the unknown.

[1] August Strindberg, *The Plays*, trans. Michael Meyer (London: Secker & Warburg, 1975), vol. II, p. 553.

[2] The reference is to Goethe's *Faust I*, in which Gretchen, pregnant with Faust's child, is obsessed with her guilt in the Cathedral Scene and receives a sign from heaven in the final Prison Scene that she will be saved.

65   Neo-Romantic staging: Hofmannsthal's *Elektra*, 1903

Hugo Hofmannsthal, 'Szenische Vorschriften zu "Elektra"', *Das Theater*, Berlin, 1903. Reprinted in Hofmannsthal, *Prosa II*, pp. 81–4

Hofmannsthal's first major work for the theatre was his free adaptation of Sophocles' *Electra*, now best known in its operatic version by Richard Strauss. Impressed by the success of Oscar Wilde's *Salomé* (1893), premièred by Reinhardt in Berlin in 1902, the young Austrian poet Hofmannsthal rewrote the Greek original to accentuate the morbid aspects of Electra's obsession with the unavenged murder of her father, Agamemnon. It was to be the first of many successful collaborations with Max Reinhardt. In his 'Directions for staging *Elektra*', Hofmannsthal reveals a strong visual imagination in his opposition to the conventional anaemic staging of Greek dramas. Instead we are in a world full of powerful dream-like images, a world of bold colour, shadows and mystery.

The stage The set should entirely dispense with those pillars, those wide flights of steps, and all those banal classical imitations, which only succeed in being tedious rather than evocative. The set should be claustrophobic, enclosed, isolated. The designer will – as a point of departure – come closer to what is needed if he considers the mood of a busy yard in a town-house on a summer's evening rather than yielding to the image of conventional temples and palaces. It is the courtyard behind the royal palace, surrounded by outbuildings which contain the slaves' quarters and workrooms. The back wall of the palace has that quality which makes great houses in the Orient so uncanny and mysterious; it contains very few and quite irregular windows of differing dimensions. [. . .] Above the low roof of the house on the right spreads from outside a gigantic, heavy, crooked fig tree, whose trunk cannot be seen and whose thick foliage, strangely shaped in the evening light, lies across the roof like an animal in wait. Behind this roof the sun stands very low in the sky, and deep spots of red and black are cast from this tree across the whole stage.

The lighting Initially as in the description of the stage-set. [. . .] At first the interior of the house lies in darkness, the door and windows seem like mysterious black hollows. [. . .] During Elektra's monologue great spots of blood seem to be glowing on the walls and ground. During the scene between Chrysothemis and Elektra the red fades, the whole courtyard sinks into twilight. The procession, which heralds the appearance of Clytemnestra within, first fills the big window, then the second window to the left of the door, with a changing aspect of torchlight and black shapes sweeping past. Clytemnestra appears with her two confidantes in the broad window, her pale face and her splendid gown brightly lit – almost like a wax image – by torches to either side. Clytemnestra steps into the doorway, two torchbearers follow her into the dark courtyard, flickering light falls on Elektra. Clytemnestra dismisses her companions and they exit into the house, the torchbearers also leave, and only a very faint flickering light spills from an inner room down the hallway into the yard. One confidante returns, a torch carried behind her; at Clytemnestra's command several torch-bearers return, and for a moment it becomes quite bright. They exit, it is now dark in the courtyard, but the evening sky to the right, as far as it can be seen, remains bright in its changing colours. It is an element of the prevailing mood that it is dark in this dreary courtyard, while it is still light in the world *outside*. The brightest spot is the open door on the right. In this open doorway appears the dark shape of Orestes.[1] Now everything is played in deepening darkness, the length of the piece is exactly the duration of a slow nightfall. [...]

The costumes also exclude all pseudo-classical imitation as well as all ethnographic tendencies. Elektra wears a pitiable wretched tunic that is too short for her. Her legs and arms are bare. The costumes of the slave-girls require no instructions other than that they should appear worn and threadbare; they are not an operatic chorus. [...] Clytemnestra wears a magnificent garish red robe. It looks as though all the blood of her pale face has drained into her costume. She has covered her throat and arms with jewellery. She is weighed down with talismans and precious stones. Her hair colour is natural. She carries a stick set with jewels. [...] Orestes and the old man, his tutor, are clothed as wandering merchants. It must be clear that they belong to a foreign nation, they must appear as foreigners. Their costume must, without being too outlandish, have nothing of the conventional and pseudo-antique, and might suggest the mood of oriental fables but in dark though by no means dead colours.

[1] cf. the stage-direction in *Elektra*: 'Orestes stands in the courtyard doorway, silhouetted against the last brightness of the evening sky.' (*Gesammelte Werke*, S. Fischer, Berlin, 1934, vol. II, p. 160). The significance of Orestes' arrival is emphasized by the lighting: he has come from the world of light – at the bidding of the sun-god Apollo – into the dark place of unavenged murder, where he will wrench Clytemnestra and Elektra from their obsession with the past into the flux of time present.

66   Reinhardt's 'impressionistic' style, 1901

Arthur Kahane, *Tagebuch eines Dramaturgen*, Berlin, 1926, pp. 115–21. Reprinted in Reinhardt, *Schriften*, pp. 64–7

Max Reinhardt, described by the contemporary critic Ihering as 'the most colourful theatre talent of all time', already in 1901 had a clear conception of the kind of theatre he wished to create. In style he wished to go beyond naturalism to what has since been variously described as 'stylized realism' or 'impressionism'; in terms of repertoire he intended to breathe new life into the classics; with regard to performance spaces he sought to establish both an intimate theatre and a vast amphitheatre. All these undertakings proved successful: Shakespeare's *A Midsummer Night's Dream* (1905) and Sophocles' *Oedipus* (1910) were in the truest sense revivals of the classics. His Kammerspiele (see 46) was opened in 1906, and his Grosses Schauspielhaus, the so-called Theatre of Five Thousand, in 1919, although the latter admittedly proved a financial failure.

What I conceive of is a theatre that people can enjoy once more. A theatre that transports them beyond their grey and dreary everyday lives to a serene and pure world of beauty. I sense how people are tired of encountering their own misery in the theatre and how they yearn for brighter colours and a higher plane of existence.

This does not mean that I wish to abandon the major achievements of naturalistic theatre with its hitherto unattained truth and authenticity. I could not, even if I wanted to. I have trained in this school and am grateful that I have been able to. The rigorous education to uncompromising truthfulness can no longer be removed from the development of modern theatre. But I should like to carry this development further, to apply it to other things than the depiction of social conditions and milieu. I should like to go beyond the stench of the poor and the problems of social criticism and apply the same high degree of truth and authenticity to the purely human, in a profound and refined art of the soul. I should like to show life from another side than that of pessimistic negation, but that is just as true and authentic in its serenity and full of colour and light.

I have no intention of following a definite literary programme, whether it is naturalism or anything else. Admittedly I feel that the highest art of our time, that of Tolstoy, has grown far beyond naturalism, that abroad Strindberg, Hamsun, Maeterlinck and Wilde have gone in quite different directions, that in Germany Wedekind and Hofmannsthal are breaking into new areas; and I sense everywhere new young talents maturing in their own ways. Whatever new talents appear in our age, from whatever side they emerge, I will welcome them. I shall not be afraid to experiment if I believe it is valuable to do so.

What I shall not do is experiment for the sake of it, stage literature for its own sake. I can only do what I believe in. A failure or a *succès d'estime* serves neither the author nor the theatre; a writer is helped not by having his work performed but by having it performed in such a way that the public is won over to it. Indeed for me the theatre is more than an art supporting other arts. There is only *one* aim of theatre: *the theatre*, and I believe in a theatre that belongs to the actor. No longer should purely literary considerations be the main ones, as in recent decades. They have been, because writers dominated the theatre. I am an actor, I identify with the actor, and for me the actor is central to theatre. This has been so in all the great ages of theatre. The theatre has a duty to let the actor show himself from all sides, to work in many styles, to indulge his joy in play and transformation. I know the playful and creative powers of the actor, and I sometimes really would not mind restoring something of the old *commedia dell'arte* to our overdisciplined age only in order occasionally to give our actors the opportunity of improvising and kicking over the traces.

I shall make the greatest demands on my actors. Truth and authenticity are taken for granted; but I demand more. I want to have beautiful people around me; and above all I want to hear beautiful voices. The cultivation of the art of speaking, as was once the case in the old Burgtheater, without, however, the pathos of those days but with the pathos of today. I shall employ the best speech instructor I can find, and I myself shall not weary of this task until I have got to the point where the music of the word is heard once more.

I conceive of a small ensemble of the best actors. Intimate plays whose quality one can take for granted. Even the smallest part filled not only with a good actor but with the best possible actor for the role. So carefully rehearsed that the strongest and most divergent individuals work together in complete harmony. That is the goal I have set myself.

Do you remember those delightful evenings in the Bösendorf Hall in Vienna, when the Rosé Quartet played chamber music by Haydn, Mozart and Beethoven? I should like to achieve something similar. I imagine some sort of *theatrical chamber music*. One must arrive at the point where the best members of the public say to themselves: you can go to this theatre, whatever is being performed; you can depend on it that only the best will be offered and in the best possible way.

And then when I have perfected my instrument like a violinist who has tuned his valuable old violin, when it obeys me like a good orchestra blindly trusting in its conductor, then I shall move on to the main task: I shall perform the *classics*. You are surprised? Yes, I consider the classics to be the theatre's most sacred property. In the works of the classical writers I recognize the natural bedrock of the repertoire. And for me the art of acting is nothing if it cannot meet the demands of the classics. Everything else is child's play in comparison. You have no idea how easy it is to perform naturalistic plays well. I would feel confident of getting talented dilettantes up to that level. You cannot be an actor until you have proved that you can play Shakespeare. I want to perform Shakespeare and I feel certain of my ground. Certainly, I know the smell of boredom that rises from conventional productions of the classics, and I understand the public when it stays away. I know what a patina of pathos and empty declamation has been spread over these works by the ossified tradition of the court theatres. This dust must go. We must play the classics anew; we must play them as though the writers were alive today, as though their works reflected the life of today. [...]

From the classics the stage will gain a new lease of life: colour and music and splendour and joy. The theatre will once more become a celebration which is its actual purpose. Theatre means richness and fullness. We shall have the courage once more to spread our wings, we shall breathe again, be freed for a while of our strict austerity, of the narrow art of having to do without. I cannot tell you how much I yearn for music and colour. I intend to call on the best painters, I know how they are waiting for this and how much they are involved in theatre. And just as the most suitable director is selected for each production, the most suitable actor for each role, I should like to find the most suitable painter, perhaps the only suitable painter, for each work.

In fact one would have to have *two theatres side by side*, a big one for the classics and a smaller, intimate one for the chamber art of modern writers. If only so that actors do not become set in one style and so that they can work alternately in both types of performance. And because it will sometimes be necessary to stage modern writers like classics and certain classical works with the whole intimacy of the modern art of the soul.

And actually one would need a third theatre, don't laugh, I am quite serious, and I can imagine it already, a really large theatre for great art of monumental effects, a *festival hall*, freed from the everyday, a house of light and consecration, in the spirit of the Greeks, but designed n˙ ˙ only for Greek works but for the great art of all times, in the form of an amphitheatre, without curtains or wings, perhaps without sets, and in the centre the actor, dependent alone on the pure effect of his personality and on the word, in the midst of the audience, and the audience itself, a community once more, participating as an element in the action, in the play. For me the frame that separates theatre and reality has never been fundamental and my imagination has never submitted itself willingly to its despotic rule. I regard it merely as a makeshift of illusionistic theatre of the peep-show stage, which developed from the specific needs of Italian opera and is not valid for all time. Everything that breaks out of this frame, that extends and increases effectiveness, that strengthens contact with the audience, whether in an intimate or a monumental style, has my approval. Just as anything that is liable to add to the unsuspected possibilities of theatre will meet with my approval.

In between times we shall naturally have to tour, we shall have to affirm in other towns, countries and continents, what we have achieved in narrower circles. So that we do not grow lazy and stultify in the secure recognition of our all-too-familiar audience; so that we are forced to renew ourselves through the responses of new audiences who know nothing of us but our immediate effect; so that we hear the echo of foreign tongues which the art of theatre needs when it feels itself mature enough to conquer the world. And then, too, because personally I never feel so happy as when I am travelling.

67(a) Reinhardt on designing the Kleines Theater, 1901

Max Reinhardt, Letter to Berthold Held, 4 August 1901. Reprinted in Reinhardt, *Schriften*, pp. 68–72

Originally called the 'Schall u. Rauch' ('Sound and Smoke'), the Kleines Theater was opened in Berlin on 9 October 1901, under the management of Berthold Held and Dr Hans Oberländer. It was here that the work of many important new writers was premièred (e.g. Strindberg, Wedekind, Hofmannsthal, Wilde, Schnitzler), including *Elektra* in 1903. Previously the same year Richard Vallentin's production of Gorky's *Lower Depths* caused a major sensation. Officially, Reinhardt managed the Kleines Theater only from 1903 to 1905, but his involvement clearly predated this. In some of his more outrageous proposals concerning the décor (footlights like fools' caps, complete with bells), Reinhardt shows himself to be as much the showman as the serious artist.

> 4 August 1901
> The Spa Hotel,
> Fanø,
> Denmark

Dear Held,[1]
[...]
Arnold[2] As last resort agree to 600 Marks. *Got* to have him. But I'm sure we'll get him for 500 if we approach him in the right way and make it clear what opportunities he'll have with us. He mustn't think that we're some sort of vulgar cabaret. [...]

Liebmann is worth only 80 Marks. Even the best theatres work with trainee actors [*Volontäre*]. Liebmann, about whose talents we know nothing and who could find no other engagement, should be regarded as a trainee. The Deutsches Theater pays the same salary to some of its *actors*. He hasn't even asked for that much, so it must be enough for him to exist on. Nowhere in the world do people get more than they ask for. [...] 20 Marks difference is a trifle and hardly worth bothering about, but it is a matter of principle. When I *started*, I received 30 *Guilders a month* and had to live off that. [...]

The *stage-manager* must *definitely* be a useful *actor*. How about asking Liebmann if he'd like to take it on? It's just an idea. Then we could – and would have to – pay him more. [...]

Walde We're going to lose her too? Well, what ladies are left? We cannot just have older and serious ladies. We're not setting up a home for elderly gentlefolk. We need youth, joy and vitality. You can't overdo that. It's easier to give a serious part to a lightweight actress or singer than the reverse. In all our efforts let's guard against the menacing ghost of boredom. [...]

Great simplicity in the interior decoration is always an advantage, so long as it is tasteful and not just shabby. Kayssler[3] knows exactly what we want. It should not look dreary; on the contrary, bright, cheerful and elegant. [...] Smoke-grey paling into brilliant white, stylized clouds of smoke rising upwards. In between individual bulbs suggesting sparks, which if possible can be switched off during the performance. The proscenium arch simply in straight lines, using Kayssler's excellent suggestion of imitating the shape of a Greek temple. The solemnity of this will be relieved by the two pillars which will enclose the stage like two shafts of smoke. [...]

The prompter's box should represent the back of a head and its two lamps should look like hands. [...]

I consider we must *definitely* have steps leading down from the stage into the audience. They could be very useful and they would add to the intimacy. [...]

The shades of the footlights might perhaps suggest fools' caps. Perhaps their bells might really ring electrically to signal the start of the performance. It would be very nice and surely easy to do (bicycle bells). In the design of the stage just make absolutely sure that lightning-quick scene-changes are possible, that there is as much playing space as possible for crowd scenes (as in *The Oresteia*) and that scene-changes in the dark are possible with the curtain open. Above all, the lighting must be flexible, lots of colours, spots as well. The lighting will have to replace sets, which initially we shall have to dispense with altogether. [...]

For the rest, greetings to everyone and all the best to you, dear Held,[4] you tapeworm-slayer! Work, work, d'you hear? We've got to work.

Reinhardt

[1] Berthold Held (1868–1931) began his career as an actor, then worked with Reinhardt as actor, director and manager. Later head of the Acting School at the Deutsches Theater.
[2] Victor Arnold (1873–1914) came to Reinhardt from the Residenztheater in Berlin in 1902. Best known for his comic roles, he was particularly memorable as Flute/Thisbe in *A Midsummer Night's Dream*.
[3] Friedrich Kayssler (1874–1945) left Brahm to join Reinhardt. Later a major director, e.g. at the Volksbühne 1918–23. See 74.
[4] 'Held' in German means 'hero'.

67(b) Plan of Reinhardt's Kleines Theater

In Heinrich Huesmann, *Wettheater Reinhardt* (Munich: Prestel, 1983), p. 114

The auditorium of Reinhardt's Kleines Theater (formerly Schall u. Rauch), Berlin.

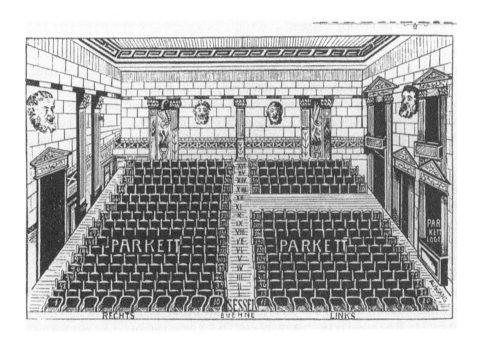

68(a) Ernst von Wolzogen: in praise of cabaret, 1901

Ernst von Wolzogen, 'Das Uberbrettle', *Das litterarische Echo*, 3, 8 (1900–1), cols. 542–8. Reprinted in Ruprecht and Bänsch, eds., *Literarische Manifeste*, pp. 120–7

In the theatre practice of the day one of the most important impulses towards innovation came from the much-maligned variety theatre. Wedekind was an experienced cabaret performer; Reinhardt founded his own cabaret 'Schall u. Rauch' ('Sound and Smoke', originally 'Die Brille') in Berlin in 1901; it was an important reference point for the expressionists and, of course, the Dadaists; and it influenced the style of both Piscator's and Brecht's theatres.

Ernst von Wolzogen (1855–1934) combined within himself the varied talents of the cabaret style. He had gained experience of public performance at Weimar as Grand Ducal Reader, and was a composer, director, and short story and novel writer. In his proposals for transplanting the cabaret style to Germany he hoped to assuage the doubts of police censorship, reduce the sense of alienation of the artist and bring all classes together in communal appreciation of art that would be both elevated and popular. The reality turned out differently: of the attempts, mainly in Berlin and Munich, to set up cabarets, only the 'Elf Scharfrichter' in Munich, where Wedekind performed, preserved Wolzogen's intentions. For the rest, Wolzogen's recognition of a lack of suitable performers and of a Bohemian element in the German public proved prophetic: those cabarets that survived degenerated into erotically toned variety shows, and Wolzogen himself was driven from his own enterprise by his financial backers.

It really is high time that writers and musicians should begin to make themselves popular in the way that pictorial artists and purveyors of knowledge have done. The school of naturalism sought out the people at their work-place – now let real writers seek them out during their leisure hours. I do not mean the people seen as a mob – there are already enough literary pen-pushers writing for them, but they have nothing to do with art – I mean those hundreds of ordinary people who have intellectual needs and whose taste is capable of refinement. In Paris little clubs of young painters, musicians and writers [...] threw open to the public the lively evening entertainments with which they had until then amused only themselves. [...] Cabarets sprang from the ground like mushrooms; in Montmartre and the Quartier Latin they can now hardly be counted. [...]

   In circles of our younger generation of artists the wish has been expressed ever more strongly to attempt the experiment of artistic variety shows in Germany. Several years ago I was stimulated into thinking about this question, and into forming my own plans, not by the Parisian examples but by the fantastic plans of the marvellous Scandinavian poet Holger Drachmann[1] and by Bierbaum's novel *Stilpe*.[2] In the course of the last two years I have repeatedly received written and spoken enquiries whether I would not undertake the establishment of a 'cabaret'. And since public opinion, as far as one can judge from the press, also gave me a heartwarming vote of confidence, I decided I could no longer hold back from setting about the difficult task.

   I consider the undertaking difficult for three reasons: first of all because, generally speaking, our German public lacks the taste for the Bohemian and I suppose too the fine artistic instinct which distinguishes the cultured classes of the Romance nations. Secondly, because our writers and musicians do not possess the talent to perform their works effectively themselves. In the whole of Germany, including the German-speaking nation of Austria, I know hardly half a dozen writers – apart from myself – who would not do themselves serious harm by reading their own works, and I know hardly any greater number of composers who are only moderately capable of singing their own songs. [...] And the third but not least important difficulty arises, I detect, from censorship, which has recently become very sensitive. It may happily overlook a word or smutty joke too many uttered by the most lightly clad muse and grant the law-abiding citizen his pleasure in slender girls' legs and dainty lace underwear, but will anxiously snatch away the stick of the honest fool when he waves it at those who are too high up or points it at generally acknowledged injustices. I also do not consider that we in Germany need to complain about lack of freedom for the printed word. [...] What we creative artists complain about is the exaggerated fearfulness of the police towards words spoken on the stage, for those writers suffer most that take most seriously their vocation as preachers of morals and dressers of wounds. [...] But I find it psychologically wrong to suppress free laughter: [...] the open paw slapping its thigh with laughter is much more harmless than the clenched fist in the pocket. Affronts against things that deserve respect, caused by cheeky laughter, will soon be rendered harmless by the exercise of good taste: ridicule has a fatal effect only when it attacks objects that assume undeserved dignity. Ridicule destroys, but not laughter. Laughter is always liberating, but it destroys malice and hatred, and that is surely something of value. [...]

Now it is my firm conviction that the difficulties which I have just enumerated need not discourage us from the attempt to present genuine art to our educated German public in the style of the variety show. [...] The necessary intimate relationship between the public and the artists will rapidly establish itself at the centre of intellectual life. They already exist in Vienna, Berlin and a few other towns, where the general and detailed attention of the press to the theatre has maintained steady contact between public and artists. And this contact will become even closer when our young writers and composers abandon the prejudice of phoney elitism and themselves mount the intimate stage and speak to their community in the pleasant conversational tones of a small space. The public will soon select itself. For the uneducated taste, the noisy style of the music-hall, with its coarse sensual attractions, will still appeal more strongly than the quiet magic of serious art. [...]

We want to try to adopt the free, ironic standpoint of the experienced man of the world, we want to try to interview court officials and ministers of state in their shirt sleeves over a glass of wine and to catch the opinion of the ordinary man in the street when he expresses it, far from the verbiage of the noisy mass meeting, straight from the heart to his friends. [...]

The Muse of Cabaret will appear in a long dress and will not be afraid to put on a tragic mask from time to time. But she will much prefer to lift her skirts and show her dainty feet, and in the music of our cabaret compositions the most frequently recurring leitmotiv will be the clink of wine-glasses and the carefree tra-la-la.

---

[1] Holger Drachmann (1846–1910): Danish novelist and poet.

[2] In Otto Julius Bierbaum's (1865–1910) novel, *Stilpe*, the hero founds a literary cabaret called 'Momus'. The project fails, and Stilpe becomes an alcoholic music-hall comedian who finally hangs himself in the middle of his act.

68(b)   The opening of Schall u. Rauch, 23 January 1901

In Huesmann, *Wettheater Reinhardt*, p. 114

The programme for the opening of the Schall u. Rauch, 1901.

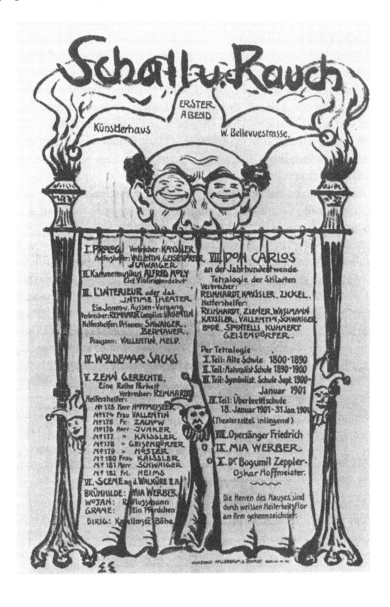

69   Georg Fuchs and his 'theatre revolution': the Munich Art Theatre, 1908

Robert Brussel, 'La saison à Munich – le Künstler-Theater', *Le Figaro*, 233, 20 August 1908. Reprinted in Georg Fuchs, *Die Revolution des Theaters. Ergebnisse aus dem Münchener Künstler-Theater* (Munich: Müller, 1909), pp. 236–42

In 1908 the writer Georg Fuchs (1868–1948) founded the Munich Art Theatre (Künstlertheater), designed by the architect Max Littmann (1862–1931), who had already built the Residenztheater in Munich. The main intention was to create a theatre which would involve practising artists and sculptors in the experimental staging of classical works. The most important elements of this progressive style were the rejection of crude naturalism, the restoration of the fluidity of performance (set-changes were effected in less than three minutes), and the imaginative use of the shallow 'relief' stage, divided into three sections, as described by the French critic Robert Brussel, below.

When the curtain rises one sees a proscenium stage, a second middle stage and a third shallow stage at the back,[1] sometimes all on the same level, sometimes at different heights. At the sides, always visible, stand two square towers of wood, each with a door and a window, without ornamentation or panes. They are connected at the top by a mobile bridge, which supports a complete lighting-rig and which can be raised or lowered at will. When it is lowered to its furthest point and the front curtains are slightly closed, the dimensions of the stage are considerably reduced, and this in itself creates the setting for a very intimate interior. The second stage is defined at the sides either by a mobile frame supporting curtains – when an interior scene is to be played on the second stage – or by two walls, when one wants to suggest a more open space. These two walls are also mobile; they can either disappear completely into the wings on trucks or otherwise be moved together to create the horizon. By means of these walls it is possible to represent a street, a church, a prison, a town-gate or a castle. In the left-hand wall can be seen a low door and a window. The simplest accessory, e.g. a fountain in *Faust* or an archway as in *Twelfth Night*, is enough to transform the set.

The third stage to the rear is separated from the back-cloth by an empty space, which can be filled with decorative scenery, e.g. a staircase or a ramp representing the foot of a sloping road.

Four back-cloths, which are mechanically drawn to left or right, provide the horizon for all shows.

What principles have led to the creation of this theatre, and what needs does it satisfy? [. . .]

'True drama', states Adolf von Hildebrand,[2] 'must make the audience experience *dramatic* life: what is important about the décor is not to reproduce *an exact image* of the setting in every detail, but to create as strong an *illusion* as the drama does itself. The prerequisite of "dramatic life" is *poetic truth*, not *reality*. [...] There are some spectators who are like children who have been given a doll that looks too real and so whose imaginations have nothing more to invent. The *crude reality* of the doll destroys their little world of imagination and they do not know what to do with this useless toy.'

Basically, this is the thinking behind the whole system: *to stimulate the imagination of the audience by suggestion.* [...]

I saw two works at the Künstlertheater: *Twelfth Night* by Shakespeare[3] and *Faust I* by Goethe.[4] [...]

In Shakespeare's play the back-cloth represents a seascape throughout. Georg Fuchs explained this unchanging vista: the play is a 'legend of the sea'. It is the sea that determines all the action, the shipwreck of Viola and Sebastian, and hence the love of the Duke of Illyria and Olivia; so it is the sea which presides over the development of the action.

The arrival of Sebastian and that of Viola have as their setting the town-gate. The two walls mentioned above are pulled together, joined by a curved arch. At the back the sea can be seen and, in the dip behind the third stage, a sail. The second stage is raised and is joined to the front stage by steps. The two towers (the bridge is hidden in the borders) suggest the ends of two houses, and so the town-gate of a port is complete.

The scene in which Toby, Andrew and the Clown get drunk is created as follows: the two walls with a gap between them suggest a bay window giving on to a dimly lit sky. The second stage is slightly raised and is furnished with a long table and two benches, the two towers seem to form part of an enormous hall in a mansion, a diffused light covers the characters, and once more the impression is complete. [...]

In the production of Goethe's *Faust I* the prologue alone would justify the experimentation of Georg Fuchs. It is not exactly easy to represent heaven. Numerous clouds, chubby angels swathed in pink and blowing trumpets, a venerable old God, a mixture of Neptune and Santa Claus, that is what is usually offered. Here there is nothing of this. The back-cloth, quite white, is brilliantly lit. The rear stage is raised, suggesting a high relief on which the three archangels stand out. These are played by very tall actors, whose height is increased by small platforms hidden beneath the folds of yellow cloth falling from their belts. Their arms are bare, their chests covered with heavy brown breastplates, their heads motionless, their eyes raised and steady. They hold colossal swords on the horizontal and lean on heavy brass wings, the ends of which sink from sight into the gap behind the third stage. It is simple and powerfully effective. [...]

The actors are always lit from below and above. They are always presented in *relief*, this is one of the happiest inventions of the new theatre. The scene of Faust and his famulus possessed, from this point of view, supreme beauty. The two dark silhouettes stand out against the dark background of a hilly landscape by night, the dialogue continues, and the story of the poodle, nearly always comic, here acquires a mysterious energy and an unequalled sense of the fantastic. [...] The performance of the actors seems to be freer than on ordinary sets. Freed of multiple superfluous effects, they seem to maintain greater concentration on the text and interpret it more faithfully and with greater emotion. [...]

Why should this dramatic conception not be the beginnings of a popular theatre? Why should it not point the way for small provincial towns whose resources are limited?

---

¹ The total depth of the three stages was approximately eight metres.
² Adolf von Hildebrand (1847–1921), sculptor and painter, was one of the designers at the Künstlertheater.
³ This production was designed by Julius Diez (1870–1957), a painter and, later, Professor of Art at the Munich Art Academy.
⁴ This production was designed by Fritz Erler (1868–1940) and directed by Albert Heine (1867–1949).

70   Fuchs and 'the theatre of the future', 1905

Georg Fuchs, *Die Schaubühne der Zukunft* (Berlin: Schuster & Loeffler, n.d. [1905]), pp. 65–6

Georg Fuchs wrote two major works on the theatre, both of which were to prove very influential, for example on Meyerhold. These were *Die Revolution des Theaters* (The Revolution in the Theatre, 1909) and *Die Schaubühne der Zukunft* (The Theatre of the Future, 1905), from which the following extract, 'Speaking to actors', is taken.

When you have full intellectual and linguistic command of the author's text, you have merely done the preparatory work: absorbed the material. Now you must create, create yourself into the figure intended by the author, not by reducing it to some unique and accidental character but by striving for universality and beauty. You will need your whole body. You are wrong if you think that the face is the most important means of expression. If you assume that with the decline of bourgeois barbarism field-glasses will disappear from the home of ceremonial art, then you will no longer be so eager to try out your stock grimaces. [...] Remember that the art of the actor is derived from the dance. [...] The closer an actor approaches to the rhythmic motion of the limbs in dance, the more perfect will be his creation, even though he should never completely become a dancer.

71   Wedekind on acting, 1910

Frank Wedekind, *Schauspielkunst, Ein Glossarium,* (Munich: Müller, 1910). Reprinted in
Gesammelte Werke (Munich: Müller, 1920), vol. VII, pp. 299–324

Frank Wedekind (1864–1918) was the major dramatist of the anti-naturalist movement
which led directly to expressionism. An actor himself, he was strongly opposed to the flat,
untheatrical style of naturalist acting. In its championing of the rhetorical style of Schiller's
tragedy, this document provides a striking contrast with the extract from *The Rats* by
Hauptmann (56).

(a) 'On the misery and death of German theatre' [pp. 19–21]

Actors, whose art is beyond the reach of criticism, whose ability stands
absolutely unchallenged and who have a decisive influence on the fate of today's
dramatic writing, rush out of the performance of *The Bride of Messina*[1] in which
they have just played the leading roles and cry: 'This Schiller! What a bungler!
What an idiot! Just ask the audience what a dreadful impression this miserable
Schiller text made on them! What a scribbler! What would it have been like
without us!'

Not one of them has the least awareness of the vast historical charade which
Schiller constructs in his mighty verse, compared with which Ibsen's *Master
Builder,*[2] which they worship as a divine revelation because for the last twenty
years they have not learned to perform anything more demanding, is a trivial
piece of eccentricity.

So Schiller, too, becomes a fellow sufferer by moreover parodying himself: it is
not that the hero must succumb while the idea triumphs. No one is interested in
the idea. The play must succumb while the production triumphs.

How is this possible?

Actors, who nowadays are regarded as exemplary, have no backbone or
stamina. They are unsurpassable in theatrical moments and episodes and so are
dearly loved by their directors. They need not be ashamed of their ability to rattle
off drawing-room comedies, but it induces them simply to dispose of the fire and
passion of a playwright as though holding a conversation. Then the critics
scream: the playwright writes lifeless German! – Sadly, such actors have lost the
gift of presenting greatness as something natural, of remaining overwhelmingly
simple, of convincingly portraying heartfelt emotion and depth of feeling with
power and spirit. If they speak simply, naturally and with feeling, then nobody
understands what they say, because they have neglected vocal technique for the
last twenty years. If they try to appear powerful, heroic and spirited, then every
word sounds so deliberately emphatic, strained and self-conscious that all
naturalness is lost. The modern actor turns each of God's creatures who are not

naturalistic mental cripples into bloodless and extravagant products of the writing-desk.

This is the art of theatre which opens up an unbridgeable yawning gap between playwright and audience.

¹ *Die Braut von Messina* (1803). See 56, note 1.
² *The Master Builder* received its first full performance in Berlin (1893).

(b) 'Transition' [pp. 7–8]

The works of naturalist playwrights owed their rapid dissemination not least to the advantage that they were child's play to perform. This is not to object to their literary and social qualities. The actor stuck his hands in his pockets, placed himself with his back to the audience next to the prompter's box and waited completely relaxed until he had understood the line that the prompter was calling out to him. If he misunderstood the line, then it did not matter much, because those who were listening were mainly the stage-hands playing skat and tarot behind the scenery. The audience however placed no greater demands on the actor than not to have the mood spoilt by the spoken word.

Actors who celebrated their triumphs in this art are no longer of value to us. Plays now deal with more serious problems and nourish a higher form of art than that of naturalism.

(c) 'For the public' [pp. 36–8]

When I appeared recently in Düsseldorf, the other actors shook their heads and shrugged their shoulders because I rolled my 'r' on my tongue,¹ because I did not turn my back on the audience and because I did not conceal my plays behind gauze curtains. Or, put simply, because I proceeded on the barbaric assumption that the audience wanted to see and hear something for their money. I am completely convinced that for the last twenty years our literary theatre has, first, been too little theatre and, secondly, been far too literary. I am convinced that for twenty years literary theatre has offered far too little enjoyment and far too little entertainment. And that is why I am an object of horror to all snobs and philistines.

By the way, I know two actors who share my views in these matters: Josef Kainz² and Josef Jarno.³ [...] Both share one gift that is very rare at the moment, namely to perform a role as though riding a steeplechase. The routine performance of a cliché actor entrances the audience by simply cutting out every obstacle with the blue pencil and playing only the remaining banalities. This is the way for years people have coped with my *Court Singer*.⁴ On the other hand, the great and celebrated actor stops at every obstacle as though it were a labour of Hercules and indulges in wild orgies of never-ending pauses. When and how he arrives at his goal is not of the least interest to him. After all, naturalism has taught the public such patience that it is less likely to snap than the most efficient pair of braces.

[1] Traditional 'stage-German' requires a uvular 'r' (as in French). The lingual 'r', trilled on the tip of the tongue (as in Italian), is associated with the South and is therefore often felt to be outlandish and comic in North Germany.
[2] Josef Kainz (1858–1910): see **48** and **49**.
[3] Josef Jarno (1866–1932): Hungarian by birth, began career in Austria 1885, came to Berlin 1889, performed at Deutsches Theater, 1894–7, Director of Josefstädtertheater in Vienna 1899–1918.
[4] Der Kammersänger (1899), Wedekind's comic piece about the pressures on a highly successful singer.

(d) 'Perforce directing' [p. 48]

The expression 'perforce directing' was coined by Wilhelm von Scholz,[1] whom I here publicly thank for it.

The perforce director is a man who does not allow any stage-play, however powerful it may be, to put him in the shade.

In one of my plays the perforce director was afraid that one of the most effective scenes would indeed put him in the shade. What was to be done? He found the solution by meaninglessly bringing on to the stage a real live donkey. The experiment was a great success. My play flopped, but the donkey received rave reviews.

[1] Wilhelm von Scholz (1874–1969): Director of Stuttgart theatre 1914–23 and author of plays of the Neuklassik, e.g. Der Jude von Konstanz (The Jew of Constance, 1905).

72(a) Hugo Ball: Wedekind as actor, 1914

Hugo Ball, 'Wedekind als Schauspieler', Phöbus, Monatsschrift für Ästhetik und Kritik des Theaters, ed. H. Eckenroth, Munich, 1914, I, 3, pp. 105–8. Reprinted in Paul Pörtner, ed., Literatur-Revolution 1910–1925 (Darmstadt: Luchterhand, 1960), vol. I, pp. 338–40

As Dramaturg at the Kammerspiele in Munich, Hugo Ball (1886–1927) promoted the work of Wedekind and the expressionists. He is probably best remembered as a co-founder of the Dadaist Cabaret Voltaire in Zurich during the First World War. In this pyrotechnical piece Wedekind is considered as a performer in the new unrestrained, 'ecstatic' style that was to become characteristic of expressionist acting.

The day will dawn when it is part of one's education to be an actor, when acting will be practised like a sport. [. . .] Such a time will smile when they hear that it was an issue for us whether Wedekind was an actor or not. Everyone is an actor who sets foot in public on a stage or platform to give of his best *coram publico*. The art of transformation is unimportant, ever since we have all spiritually become actors. [...] We don't give a damn whether Herr Schulze can also be Herr Müller, or whether Fräulein Schmidt can turn into Fräulein Huber. We no longer care. We want new legs. New hips. New heads. A new structure of body and soul.

Wedekind's shortcoming: the art (i.e. the control) of invective. Throwing bombs will soon be more modern and will replace him.

Acting as cruel as hara-kiri (they'll say then): he slit open his soul. Destroyed the wall between inside and outside (a wall called 'shame'). Between public and private. Ripped and lacerated himself. Barbarism. Flagellation. And invited us in as spectators. Cursed sadistically, spat out jokes and scorn. And always his intellect, the intellect of an executioner. Running berserk like an Ancient Goth in this self-revelation – unspeakable. (Remind yourselves one day of *Censorship*,[1] when he played Buridan. 'Wedekind the clown.' Your laughter stuck in the throat. Or when he played Hetmann:[2] for the first time we saw Don Quixote in the realm of ideas.)

You're not always carried away by him. Hypnotized rather. He has cramp in his brain. Cramp (in his body). Cramp (in the throat), in his legs. And in the ... Everything a wood-carving, rough and angular and indestructible. Gargoyles off the cathedrals of Rheims and Amiens. Wood-carving by Riemenschneider. The floor creaks when he speaks. His nose is sharp and impudent. When he meets a tram in the street, it is the tram that gives way. Suspicious, touchy, embarrassed. Or tactless, brutal, sarcastic. Naïve as a pony and mad as a fool.

[1] *Die Zensur* (1907), a play by Wedekind, subtitled 'A Theodicy'.
[2] *Karl Hetmann* or *Hidalla* (1903–4, premièred 1905), a play by Wedekind.

72(b) The final scene of Wedekind's *Spring Awakening*

From Reinhardt's production at the Deutsches Theater Kammerspiele, Berlin, 1906, with
Wedekind as the Man in the Mask.

73   Stylized acting: the influence of the Orient, 1912

Bernhard Kellermann, 'Japanische Schauspielkunst', *Theaterkalender*, 1912, pp. 43–7

The importance of oriental theatre in the development of European theatre in this century
has been considerable (one thinks especially of Artaud and Brecht). Here, already in 1912,
the novelist Bernhard Kellermann (1879–1951) draws lessons for the anti-naturalist
theatre of his day, especially in terms of acting style.

Everyone knows that Japanese theatre is different from ours. The European stage
is more concerned with reality, truth, intensity, the spiritual and the aesthetic; the
Japanese with appearance, externals, images, illusion. European theatre reveals
man, Japanese theatre the ghost of man. At least that is how it seems at first
glance! [...]

[The Japanese actor] does not individualize, he does not seek psychological
motivation, he presents the typical and the type, in the correct understanding that

man, seen at his most basic, loses all individual characteristics. He presents man larger than life. [...] That is why I began by saying that the Japanese stage only *seems* to be concerned with externals, images and illusion; for one of these colossal visions alone often tells us more about the essence of man than a very carefully performed production on a European stage. [...]

The first actors were marionettes. [...] Not so much a psychological as a pictorial art, which allows psychology to be hinted at and reveals it like a flash of lightning at single climactic moments, not so much human as superhuman and heroic. [...] The masks of Japanese actors are works of art, and European theatre practitioners could learn a great deal in this respect from their slant-eyed colleagues.

IV   Two prescriptions for expressionist acting

74   Friedrich Kayssler: 'It is the soul that acts', 1912

Friedrich Kayssler,[1] 'Die Seele ist es, die da spielt', *Theaterkalender*, 1912, pp. 55–9

It is the soul that acts roles, not the body. The body is an instrument, a mouthpiece, a means of expression, a tool. The soul is – well, without the soul there is nothing. [...] How crude theatre is as an art-form. How rough, how barbaric. How desperately seldom do we ever think – in the midst of this wild round of *coups de théâtre*, of dust, greasepaint and the sweat-laden renown of a night [...] – how seldom do we think of – the soul. [...] And one day there will be a higher form of theatre, in which the soul will hold sway – and the spirit.

[1] See 67(a), note 3.

75   Paul Kornfeld calls for 'theatricality in the theatre', 1916

Paul Kornfeld, 'Nachwort an den Schauspieler', in *Die Verführung* (Berlin: S. Fischer Verlag, 1916)

Paul Kornfeld (1889–1942) wrote *Die Verführung* (The Seduction) in 1913. When he sent the manuscript to the Fischer Verlag in 1916 he appended an 'Afterword to the actor', since he was clearly concerned that the melodramatic nature of the plot and its heightened dialogue might seem simply absurd if the piece were played in a naturalistic, so-called 'hands-in-the-pocket' style. His advice was taken by the director Hartung and the leading actor Feldhammer at the play's première in Frankfurt am Main in December 1917, and this contributed to its instant public and critical success. Running to five editions by 1921, the play is nevertheless not one of the strongest pieces of expressionism for the stage. However, Kornfeld's 'Afterword', which urges the theatre to acknowledge its own theatricality, is not only an important document for its own time: it also looks forward to Brecht's bold distancing effects, the recognition that the stage is an artificial representation of real life. While Kornfeld's mode of expression is predictably heightened and there is much that Brecht would have found questionable, the insistence on an unspontaneous, generalized and clear depiction, free from the ambiguities of naturalistic performance, anticipates Brechtian theory, and in the final sentence, urging the actor to dispense with agonized writhing in his death-scene, one may perhaps see already the rejection of self-indulgent emotionalism and the 'silent scream' of Mother Courage over the corpse of Swiss-Cheese.

I do not know whether this drama will ever be performed on stage. It is written for the theatre. If it is never performed, I will accept any reasons for this but one: that its style is not theatrical. I would neither contradict nor agree with the suggestion that it is not worthy of being presented to a wider audience, but I would protest strongly if it were said that it is worthy but not suitable.

The prerequisite for this is that the director and actors do not force upon it a style which runs counter to its essential nature. But, given the way acting has developed over the last few decades, this danger is all too apparent, and, given the type and character of most of the dramas published over the last few decades, so-called 'modern' plays, then the situation is twice as dangerous for a contemporary (hence also 'modern') dramatist. This is why it seems essential to address the following words to the actor. [...]

The actor in this play should not make an effort to appear as though the thought or word to which he has to give expression only came to him at the very moment he utters it. If he has to die on stage, he should not visit a hospital beforehand to find out how to die, nor go to a public house to see how people behave when they are drunk. Let him dare to spread his arms wide and to speak a lyrically soaring speech in a way that he would never speak in real life. He should not be an imitator nor seek his models in a world alien to the actor. In short, he should not be ashamed to perform, he should not deny the theatre, he should not try to pretend to a reality, which, on the one hand, will anyway be unsuccessful, and on the other, would be suitable for the theatre only when dramatic art has been reduced to a state of banality – a state where quality may or may not occur, whether such plays try to achieve their effects through feelings, moral exhortations, or through an imitation of physical reality and of everyday psychology together with a liberal sprinkling of aphorisms.

The actor, who creates characters by experiencing his own feelings or by personally identifying with the situation he has to present, using gestures appropriate to this experience, will come closer to the truth than if he were to recall the behaviour of people filled with such feelings or facing an identical situation. Indeed, if he banishes this recollection totally from his memory, then he will find that his expression of an emotion that is not real, and whose cause is merely imagined, is purer, clearer and stronger than that of someone whose emotion is real and whose cause is real; for human emotion can never be clear and unambiguous, since man is never One, and even if he were, he is One in a constantly changing flow. If he imagines himself overcome by a single emotional experience, there are still innumerable psychic facts which falsify this feeling. The surroundings of the present and the legacy of the past cast their shadows over it. Some people perform for their own benefit, and so it is that the actor, merely through playing, is more truthful in his expression than many who are actually experiencing their fate. Various concerns inhibit them from full expression of their feelings, untold memories affect the present, and thousands of different events shine their beams across the experience. So at any moment they can only be the ever-changing sum of different emotions. But the actor is free of all this; he is not a complex but always only One, without falsification, and so he can only be clear and unambiguous. And if he is the embodiment of this One, and if he expresses this One alone, then he can do so totally and unstintingly; and in his creation he will find the intensity of unalloyed feeling.

So let the actor abstract from the attributes of reality and be nothing but the representative of thought, feeling and fate!

The melody of a grand gesture says more than the most perfect form of what is called naturalness could ever achieve.

The actor should think of opera, where the singer, dying, still sounds forth a top C, and with the sweetness of his melody says more about death than if he were to twist and writhe in agony; for it is more important that death is a misfortune than that it is horrible.

Russia, 1848–1916

Edited and translated by LAURENCE SENELICK

Introduction

Throughout the nineteenth century, realism in the arts was associated with a liberal political agenda and social progress. Close observation of life and the reproduction of its details were taken to be preliminaries to a reform of society. Consequently, 'civic' critics like Belinsky interpreted even the fantastic grotesque of Gogol' as 'realism' in order to enrol an important artist in the cause.

In a theatre hampered by stringent censorship and patronized by a sparse public often uninterested in Russian culture, realism was to be found more in acting than in playwriting or staging. Even in the eighteenth century, the actor Dmitrevsky, who knew the work of Garrick and Lekain, was acclaimed for his 'realism', although descriptions make it clear that his style was formal and declamatory. Mikhail Shchepkin praised the amateur actor Prince Dmitry Meshchersky, whose performances were so lifelike that he seemed not to be acting. But Shchepkin himself distrusted over-specificity in the creation of character, and preferred a generic emotional authenticity which had a more universal appeal.

This type of 'romantic realism' worked well in sentimental melodrama and comedy, as well as in Molière and Shakespeare; but it came up against an obstacle in the 1860s with the advent of *bytovaya drama*, the school of 'everyday life'. Such dramatists as Ostrovsky and Potekhin drew their tableaux from previously neglected strata of Russian society, the manners and mores of peasants and merchants; they put on stage dialects, customs and folklore which required a more ethnographic approach. Actors who could adapt themselves to the new repertoire attained stardom, but historians have exaggerated the import of this realistic drama. Popular though it was, its popularity was matched, and often surpassed, by that of sensation drama and comic opera from the West, although reformers deplored these imports as un-Russian and meretricious.

Between 1880, when the Imperial monopoly on theatres in the capitals was cancelled, and the outbreak of the 1917 Revolution, the Russian theatre underwent a heady creative ferment. Private theatres sponsored a conscientious drive towards artistic homogeneity and perfection which required the authority of a director. This move culminated in the Moscow Art Theatre which gained its reputation with veristic productions but constantly experimented with new forms. Millenarian philosophical and mystical movements tried to promote the notion of theatre as communion; avant-garde literary movements rejected naturalism and experimented with new modes of staging and performance. This thirst for experimentation was at first endorsed and supported by the Bolsheviks, but by the middle of the 1920s the torrents of creativity were being dammed (and damned) by Party ideologues. Under Stalin, the earlier Russian equation of realism and progress would be reinvented as 'socialist realism' and prescribed for all theatrical endeavours.

I   Mikhail Shchepkin's advice to actors, 1848–1854

Mikhail Semënovich Shchepkin (1788–1863) is generally taken to be the father of realistic acting in Russia. Born a serf on an estate in the Ukraine, he had, by 1825, become the leading actor in the provinces and was invited to join the Imperial Theatre in Moscow, where he managed to pay for his emancipation. His best roles were the Mayor in Gogol''s *The Inspector*, Famusov in Griboedov's *Woe from Wit*, the title-role in the French melodrama *A Sailor*, and the heroes of Molière. Shchepkin was dedicated to a form of 'idealized realism', in which genuine emotion was harnessed to the requirements of a role, without recourse to ethnographic specificity. Although he never managed to form his ideas on acting into a coherent code, his correspondence is peppered with influential advice. Through his students, he virtually created a new school of virtuosic, realistic acting in Russia.[1]

---

[1] See Laurence Senelick, ed., *National Theatre in Northern and Eastern Europe, 1746–1900* (Cambridge University Press, 1991), documents 223a and 224.

76   Letter to S. V. Shumsky, 27 March 1848[1]

Mikhail Semënovich Shchepkin zhizn' i tvorchestvo, eds. T. M El'nitskaya and O. M. Fel'dman (Moscow: Iskusstvo, 1984), vol. I, pp. 197–8

What would be the meaning of art if it weren't achieved through hard work? Profit by your opportunities, work hard, improve your God-given talents to the best of your ability, do not spurn criticism, but try to probe its deeper meaning; and, as a check on yourself and the advice you get, always keep nature in sight. Get under the skin of your character, so to speak, study his particular ideas well, if he has any, and do not overlook the social influences on his past life. When all this has been analysed, then whatever situations may be drawn from life, you will not fail to depict them truthfully. You may perform poorly at times, barely adequately at other times (this often depends on your state of mind), but you will perform truthfully. [...]

[...] you should observe all ranks of society, without prejudice to any, and you'll see that there is good and bad everywhere, and this will enable your acting to give each class its due. That is, when playing a peasant you won't be able to

maintain polite decorum when overjoyed, and when playing a gentleman who's
out of temper you won't start shouting and waving your arms like a peasant.

[1] The occasion of the first two letters was the foundation of a new theatre in Odessa staffed by young
actors of the Moscow Maly Theatre whom Shchepkin had recommended. Sergey Vasil'evich
Shumsky (1821–78), his favourite pupil, later became a leading member of the Maly troupe; despite
an unprepossessing appearance and a speech defect, he was an actor of wide range and depth of
penetration.

77   Letter to A. I. Shubert, 27 March 1848[1]

El'nitskaya and Fel'dman, eds., *Shchepkin*, vol. 1, pp. 199–200

It is much easier to play everything mechanically, for nothing is needed but
reason – and gradually you will come as close to joy and sorrow as an imitation
can come to the truth. But the empathetic actor is something else again; he is faced
with an indescribable chore. He must begin by effacing himself, his personality,
his whole individuality, and turn himself into the character intended by the
author; he must walk, talk, think, feel, weep, laugh, as the author wishes – to
achieve this, without effacing yourself, is impossible. [...] Suppose you're playing
a French peasant girl, for instance, but you laugh and cry like yourself,
Aleksandra Ivanovna, so it doesn't work. You may say it's utterly impossible to
get this right. No, it only involves hard work! You may say, why bother with
perfection, when there is a much, much easier way of pleasing the public? In that
case, I must remark, what's the point of art? Therefore, my dear, study things
scientifically and don't pretend. If you happen to see two actors, both working in
good faith, one cold, intelligent, lifting make-believe to the highest level, and the
other with a passionate soul, a divine spark [...] you will discover the vast gulf
that lies between genuine feeling and pretence.

[1] Aleksandra Ivanovna Shubert (1827–1909) began as a soubrette and later became a popular
comedienne at the Moscow Maly and St Petersburg Alexandra Theatres. Her memoirs are a valuable
source of information about backstage intrigue and Shchepkin's home life.

78   Letter to P. V. Annenkov, 12 November 1853[1]

El'nitskaya and Fel'dman, eds., *Shchepkin*, vol. 1, pp. 223–4

Real life and thrilling passions, in all their authenticity, should be revealed lucidly
in art, and real feeling admitted only so far as the author's conception allows. Let
the feeling be as true as it can be, but if it exceeds the bounds of the general
concept, there is no harmony, which is the *general* law of every art form. [...]
Naturalness and genuine feeling are indispensable to art, but only in so far as the

general concept allows. All art consists in observing and being grounded in this point.

---

[1] The occasion of the letters to Annenkov was the Russian tour of the French tragedienne Rachel, which sparked a lively debate over the merits of neo-classic declamation versus those of native Russian acting. Pavel Vasil'evich Annenkov (1813–87), editor of the influential journal *Sovremennik* (The Contemporary) and literary arbiter, had been publishing a series of critiques of Rachel in *Moskvityanin* (The Muscovite).

79   Letter to P. V. Annenkov, 20 February 1854

El'nitskaya and Fel'dman, eds., *Shchepkin*, vol. 1, pp. 223–4

The main thing I have to say is that [Rachel] showed clearly how necessary it is to study. Yes! The actor must certainly study how to recite any speech, without leaving it to chance or, as they say, to nature, because nature's version of a character and mine are entirely opposite, and if one creates a role along the lines of one's own personality, the characteristics of the individual one is acting are lost.

II   The Meininger in Russia, 1885 and 1890

The troupe of the Duke of Saxe-Meiningen, under the direction of Ludwig Chronegk,[1] toured to St Petersburg and Moscow in 1885 and again in 1890, when it was acclaimed by audiences and critics alike. The carefully organized *mises en scène*, with their drilled crowd scenes, were singled out for praise. They provided much food for thought to Aleksandr Nikolaevich Ostrovsky (1823–86), Russia's leading dramatist and proponent of a national theatre, and Konstantin Sergeevich Alekseev, an avid amateur actor later to take the stage-name Stanislavsky.

[1] Ludwig Chronegk (1837–90), German actor of Jewish extraction, who became *Regisseur* and *Intendenzrath* (see 42(b), note 7) of the Duke of Saxe-Meiningen's theatre at Weimar. He revolutionized the German stage by his expert handling of crowds and his attention to historical detail. (See 27, 52, 53.)

80   Ostrovsky appraises the Meiningen troupe, 1885

Extracts from his theatrical journal, 5 April 1885; in A. N. Ostrovsky, *Polnoe sobranie sochineny* (Moscow: Iskusstvo, 1973–80), vol. x (1976), pp. 297–301

[The Meiningers'] acting does not produce that full, soul-satisfying impression one derives from a work of art. What we saw them do is not art but technique, i.e. professionalism. These were not plays by Shakespeare and Schiller, but a series of living pictures taken from these plays. [...]

I was thrilled by the disciplined, easy and skilful execution of a command. It is obvious that the stage-manager Chronegk is a cultivated man of taste, but it is the crucial flaw of the Meiningen troupe that the stage-manager can be seen in everything. It is obvious that even the leading players act under orders and according to plan, and because orders cannot impart what one requires of leading players, i.e. talent and feeling, they are disconnected with the crowd, lag behind it, become inferior to it. [...] When Julius Caesar first appeared in the mob on the square, when he entered surrounded by lictors, it was striking, the likeness was amazing; it was the spitting image of Caesar as he lived. But when he began to speak and then throughout the rest of the play, this wishy-washy, unimpassioned, lifeless actor was more like an untalented and stodgy schoolmaster than the mighty Caesar. [...]

What can a right-thinking man find in the Meiningers' success that might instruct the Russian theatre? Just this: since the Meiningers owe most of their success to the excellent stage-management of Chronegk and the Russian soldiery [who were recruited as extras], what one needs for complete success in producing a play are good stage-managers with aesthetic taste and all-round education and well-trained performers. [...] A well-trained soldier is always superior to provincial and amateur actors. [...] A soldier performs a studied gesture on stage with utter precision and aplomb. But the amateur histrion does nothing on stage, stares at his hands and feet which do not obey him. [...] Therefore when a crowd in motion is required for great historical dramas, they must be composed of ballet supers and soldiers, and then the crowd will come to life. [...] Chronegk was ecstatic over the capabilities of the Russian for stage art; he said, 'If you've got soldiers like this, what actors you must have!' Only feelings of patriotism prevented us from objecting that, with the closure of the dramatic school,[1] our soldiers have surpassed our actors.

[...] The Administration would do well not to mimic the Meiningers: art will not profit by it, but expenses will double. Before squandering enormous sums on productions, one should know how to perform the play coherently.

[1] The Dramatic division of the Theatrical School of the Imperial Theatres had been closed in 1871. Ostrovsky long militated for its re-opening.

81   Stanislavsky imitates the Meininger, 1890

K. S. Stanislavsky, *My Life in Art*, trans. J. J. Robbins (Boston: Little, Brown, 1924), pp. 198–202

It seemed to me that we amateurs, together with our director,[1] were in the same predicament as Chronegk and the Meiningen Players. We also wanted to give luxurious performances to uncover great thoughts and emotions, and because we did not have ready actors, we were to put the whole power into the hands of the stage-director. He had to create by himself, with the aid of the production, scenery, properties, interesting *mises en scène* and the stage imagination. This is why the despotism of the Meiningen stage-directors seemed to me to be grounded in necessity. I sympathized with Chronegk and tried to learn his methods of work. [...] The restraint and cold-bloodedness of Chronegk were to my taste and I wanted to imitate him. With time I became a despotic stage-director. Very soon the majority of Russian stage-directors began to imitate me in my despotism as I imitated Chronegk. [...] These directors of the new type became mere producers who made of the actor a stage-property on the same level with stage-furniture, a pawn that was moved about in their *mises en scène.*

[1] In 1888 Stanislavsky co-founded the amateur Moscow Society of Art and Literature with Aleksandr Filippovich Fedotov (1841–95), whom he described as a 'genuinely talented director'. There, Fedotov directed him in leading roles in Pushkin's *Covetous Knight* and Pisemsky's *Bitter Fate.*

III Acting and staging before 1898

82 A. K. Tolstoy on staging *Tsar Fëdor*, 1868

A. K. Tolstoy,[1] 'General Remarks', in 'Project for Staging *Tsar Fëdor Ioannovich*', in *Sobranie sochineny* (Collected Works) (Moscow: Pravda, 1969), vol. III, pp. 494–536

Full and naked truth is a subject for science, not art. Art should not *contradict* truth, but it does not accept it *as it is in its entirety*. It takes from each phenomenon only its typical features and discards any inessentials. That is what distinguishes painting from photography, poetry from history and, to some degree, drama from a dramatic chronicle. [...] Painting (when it deserves the name) discards everything fortuitous, everything insignificant, everything *indifferent* in the original, and preserves only its essence. It elevates a unique phenomenon of nature into a type or an idea; in other words, it *idealizes* it and thus lends it beauty and meaning. The dramatist does the same thing with a historical subject; the dramatic actor is under an obligation to do the same: to invest the dramatist's idea with flesh and blood. Just as his characters in the drama are not reproductions of living persons but are the ideas of those persons, so the dramatic actor in his performance must refrain from anything that fails to create the essence of his role; he must carefully seek out and reproduce all its typical traits. His acting must accord with nature, but not imitate it. No doubt Julius Caesar sometimes happened to cough and sneeze as all mortals do, and a performer who included coughing and spitting as part of his role would not be diverging from nature, but his realism would diminish the idea of Julius Caesar whose essence lies not in sneezing, a trait he shared with other Romans, but in the traits pertinent to him alone. The performer of a serious role must remember that, within the bounds of the dramatic framework, each of his moves and intonations has a meaning; he must not allow himself anything superfluous or miss out anything essential. In short, he must himself be permeated with the *idea* which he represents and constantly keep himself up to it, keeping in view the *ideal* and not the real truth. [...]

The coordination of roles, which we call by the unattractive name 'ensemble' but which might be denoted by the word 'co-operation', is pre-eminently the work of the director. It is so important that in his absence any artistic performance is inconceivable. A painter, sculptor, architect or poet can depend on himself alone; but the dramatic actor, like the musician who takes part in a symphony, depends on his colleagues as they depend on him. The slightest discrepancy will produce a dissonance, discord, a false note, and the responsibility lies with the director, who is the conductor of the troupe.

[1] Aleksey Konstantinovich Tolstoy (1817–75), poet, novelist and dramatist, had written a monumental blank-verse trilogy about seventeenth-century Russia, *The Death of Ivan the Terrible* (1863), *Tsar Fëdor Ioannovich* (1868) and *Tsar Boris* (1869). When he heard that the stage censorship would not pass *Tsar Fëdor* for performance, he published a 'Project' in *Vestnik Evropy* (European Herald), 12 (1868), to explain the style and characters in the play. An opponent of Ostrovsky's school of 'everyday life' drama, Tolstoy directed some of his general remarks at the article 'Last Word on Russian Historical Drama' by Ostrovsky's champion Apollon Grigor'ev which appeared in *Russky Vestnik* (Russian Herald), 7 (1868). *Tsar Fëdor* was first staged at Suvorin's Theatre of the Literary-Artistic Circle in St Petersburg in 1898.

83   Lack of realism in provincial staging

P. A. Strepetova,[1] *Vospominaniya i pis'ma* (Memoirs and letters) (Moscow-Leningrad: Iskusstvo, 1934), pp. 266–7 and 269–70

Not only in the 1860s but even much, much later, directors were supposed to exist only in the theatres of big university towns such as Kiev, Khar'kov and Kazan. In mere district towns, not to mention county seats, this function was entirely absent or existed in name only as at Smirnov's in Yaroslavl.[2] In Samara the ordinary scenarius who checked the punctuality of entrances and arranged the stage was deemed the director. It goes without saying that such a person was too illiterate to handle the staging of a play and, anyway, that fell outside the sphere of his duties. Plays seemed to stage themselves: one experienced actor or another would give advice – and the job was done. Nor had we any notion of dress-rehearsals. How could there be dress-rehearsals when there were seldom more than three ordinary rehearsals, and most of the time we were lucky to get two. [...]

They weren't particularly fussy about costumes for us. For instance, a seventeenth-century Frenchwoman's costume consisted entirely of a one-piece gown, adorned with nothing but a white powdered wig and a black 'beauty spot' or two stuck to the cheek, according to the actress's desire or zeal. Men's costume was somewhat more elaborate: besides the powdered wig, a black cloth pelerine would be sewn to an ordinary modern black surtout; high oil-cloth gaiters with tops were adapted to one's own polished boots – and the Marquis was ready. And if a big cut-glass star of incredible size blazed in splendour on the actor's right breast, it meant he was about to portray some Choiseul or Duke of Somerset or, at the very least, the President in *Love and Intrigue*.[3] Two such enormous cut-glass pancakes, one on each breast, denoted their wearer as a member of a royal family, some prince of the blood, in short, a personage of rank beyond the merely exceptional and very, very grand indeed.

[1] Polina (Pelageya) Antip'evna Strepetova (1850–1903): an actress expert at portraying temperamental lower-class women. Her best roles were Lizaveta in Pisemsky's *Bitter Fate* and Katerina in Ostrovsky's *Thunderstorm*. She played in the provinces from 1865 to 1873, before eventually joining the troupe of the Alexandra Theatre in St Petersburg (see **86**).

[2] V. A. Smirnov was an entrepreneur in Yaroslavl, one of Russia's oldest theatre cities, 1855–80. When critics complained that his repertoire was too old-fashioned and stilted, he pointed to his sold-out houses.

[3] Schiller's domestic tragedy *Kabale und Liebe* (1784) had been on the Russian stage in the translation of S. A. Smirnov since 1810.

84   Directing in the provinces, 1871–1872

V. N. Davydov,[1] *Rasskaz o proshlom* (Story of Days Gone By) (Leningrad-Moscow: Iskusstvo, 1962), pp. 93–4

As a director, [Medvedev[2] in Kazan in 1871–2] knew so well how to take an actor in hand, enthuse and inspire him, that even the most untalented came to life and did their job intelligently. He did not use sophistry or worry it out of himself as many modern directors do, but tried to make the theatre a reflection of truth. And he was right. Man acts within a context, but he appears as the centre of life, the master of this context. That's why in the theatre the human being must take pride of place. [...]

All the director's attention must be focused on [the actor and] must see to it that the actor is sincere and moves the audience to tears and laughter, sorrow and delight. When this fails to happen, you have a circus or a sideshow, what you please, but not a theatre. The old directors understood this and therefore did most of their work with the actors. [...] Medvedev had already begun to usurp the actors' right to organize the staging itself, as had others including Yablochkin,[3] with whom I once chanced to work in Odessa, who completely relieved the actors of the right to organize the staging. But in those days directors didn't wrack their brains to cook up a more wonderful spectacle or turn the theatre into a problem in geometry, but created honestly, truthfully, allowing each his own, recognizing that the staging is only background in the picture. [...] Naturalism was not achieved, but superfluous convention was also shunned. [...] Lightning was depicted by a simple flash of lycopodium powder, which flared out of an iron box right under the actor's nose, and rain was portrayed by means of the plain noise of dried peas shaken and poured out, without having to operate a hydraulics plant along the footlights. Nevertheless, the actor knew how to make the spectator feel both the force of the thunderclap and the terror of the lightning and whatever his character was going through because of the rain and storm. [...] The audience of bygone days was forgiving and paid no heed if the tragedian, as he pompously and heroically got out of a boat, knocked over a whole bank of the Dnieper or Volga with its bushes and boulders, or if the moon came out in front of the trees and shone so low that the performer could touch it with his hand.

[1] Vladimir Nikolaevich Davydov (né Ivan Nikolaevich Gorelov, 1849–1925) was a leading actor at the Alexandra Theatre, St Petersburg, from 1880 to 1924, having worked extensively in the provinces from 1867. He was the original Ivanov in Chekhov's play (1887).

[2] Pëtr Mikhaylovich Medvedev (1837–1906), a provincial actor and impresario who became a director in 1890. His troupes, particularly in Kazan from 1866, were renowned for their strong acting talent, and his memoirs are rich in anecdotes about the stage outside the capitals.

[3] Aleksandr Aleksandrovich Yablochkin (1821–95): stage-director at Tiflis (1846–51), Odessa (1879–80) and chief régisseur of the Alexandra Theatre (1868–95). An expert at crowd scenes, he was noted for his mounting of historical dramas and operettas.

85   The rise of realism in the 1890s

Yu. M. Yur'ev,[1] *Zapiski* (Notes) (Leningrad-Moscow: Iskusstvo, 1963), vol. II, pp. 134–7

Starting in the middle of the 1890s – in other words, the first years of my stage career – a gradual fermentation began to ripen in the theatre. [...] Such a ferment did not occur all at once. Even my teacher Aleksandr Pavlovich Lensky[2] in his pedagogical work and early directorial experiments had been reacting against routine and stagnation on stage. But in 1898 K. S. Stanislavsky and V. I. Nemirovich-Danchenko[3] came on the scene as pioneers in the struggle against the obsolescent forms of our theatre, by organizing their own theatre which was eventually called the Moscow Art Theatre.

Stanislavsky and Danchenko were protesting against the old style of acting and that conventional theatricality which even the most talented stage figures often indulged in at that time.

Such a brilliant actress as O. O. Sadovskaya,[4] distinguished by remarkable naturalness and truth-to-life, could not, for instance, break the habit of speaking monologues 'to the house' – a habit ingrained in her by many years of stage practice. Whatever the situation, she used to take a chair, plant it in front of the footlights facing the audience, sit down – and converse in her normal tones, addressing herself straight to the auditorium. She couldn't help it! ...

Or take V. N. Davydov.[5] Wasn't he one of the brightest and most powerful proponents of the realistic school? He would be playing, say, Chebutykin in *Three Sisters*, when in the course of the act he had to do a Russian folkdance to the tune of 'Ah, you gates, gates of mine' – and what do you think? He would perform his dance as a separate turn in a music-hall ... Faithful to his early experience, inculcated in the plays of Vl. Tikhonov and V. A. Krylov,[6] Davydov, without batting an eyelash, would step out on the apron, divorcing himself from the rest of the action, and cut every sort of amusing caper, not at all native to Chebutykin's character. No wonder after such a music-hall turn, applause and shouts of encore were forthcoming. And this in a Chekhov play! [...]

In the first years of my theatrical career the habit of 'making an exit' survived. This means that, in the course of a play, whenever an actor effectively ended his scene in the middle of an act and withdrew to the wings emphatically and artificially, applause would burst forth in his wake, and he would immediately return and bow, even though the action came to a standstill and those actors still on stage froze in position as they were, awaiting the end of these inappropriate ovations. [...]

A. A. Potekhin,[7] a respected dramatist and to all appearances a man not devoid of culture, in his capacity as administrator and artistic director of the Alexandra Theatre in the 1880s, started a special book, in which he put down who 'made an exit' and how many he had made. This served to measure an actor's success and was taken into consideration when casting roles in new productions and influenced an actor's salary when his contract was renewed.

[1] Yury Mikhaylovich Yur'ev (1872–1948) was the leading man at the Alexandra Theatre, St Petersburg, from 1893. He appeared in two of Meyerhold's best productions, as Molière's *Dom Juan* (1910) and as Arbenin in Lermontov's *Masquerade* (1917).

[2] Aleksandr Pavlovich Lensky (né Vervitsiotti, 1847–1908), actor and director, associated with the Moscow Maly Theatre from 1876 to his death. A co-founder of the New Theatre (affiliated with both the Maly and the Bol'shoy, 1898–1903), he trained young actors to subordinate their performances to the harmony of the production. See Senelick, ed., *National Theatre in Northern and Eastern Europe*, document 249.

[3] See pp. 208–26, below, and Senelick, ed., *National Theatre in Northern and Eastern Europe*, documents 258–62.

[4] Ol'ga Osipovna Sadovskaya (née Lazareva, 1849–1919), an actress of the Maly Theatre, specialized in old women's roles from an early age, and was noted for her expertise in colloquial speech. Chekhov wanted her to play Ranevskaya in *The Cherry Orchard*.

[5] See 84, note 1.

[6] Vladimir A. Tikhonov (1857–1914), comic dramatist, and Viktor Aleksandrovich Krylov (1839–1906), playwright-of-all-work, were bywords as hacks and popular play-doctors.

[7] Aleksey Antipovich Potekhin (1829–1908), a major dramatist of peasant and middle-class life in the realistic mode, became head of the repertoire section of the Alexandra Theatre in the early 1880s.

86   *The Power of Darkness* at Suvorin's Theatre, 1895

B. Varneke,[1] 'Vospominaniya P. A. Strepetovoy' ('Memories of P. A. Strepetova'), in *Sobranie P. A. Strepetova* (Strepetova Anthology) (Moscow, 1934), pp. 460–3

About a month after it opened in 1895, Suvorin's Theatre[2] put on Tolstoy's *The Power of Darkness*[3] a day before the play was to go on for V. V. Strel'skaya's[4] benefit on the Alexandra stage. And this competition of the old State Theatre with the young private one, and the author's name and the play itself, attracted to both productions the attention of all who were interested in theatre. It was especially difficult to get into Suvorin's theatre, and *The Power of Darkness* was successful enough to play some ten times before I managed to procure a pass and be convinced there was cause for excitement. First of all, there was E. P. Karpov's[5] staging: he succeeded in the details of the huts' furnishing and the clothes of the peasants to show a real village. The everyday, strictly reticent speech of the actors and their manners forced us to believe that the spectators were seeing not ladies and gentlemen in fancy dress but real live peasants. [...] Strepetova[6] totally outdid the other actors, and in all her scenes the spectators watched no one but her. First of all she offered the amazing make-up of a famished dog, avid for any crust. In her deathly pale face, wound round with a dark kerchief, greedy vulpine eyes smouldered ominously. Having blacked out most of her teeth, she left two fangs, yellowing within the vacant rictus of a mouth that did not always close firmly. Even on her first entrance as a guest of her son who was still working as a hired hand, Strepetova, by a myriad of tiny details, emphasized how dazzled she was by Anisya's wealth and why she moves to marry her son to Anisya. She indefatigably ran her eyes over all the walls and corners, with a fingernail tested the durability of the upholstery [...] she knew how to fit the most subtle nuances to the simplest words, endlessly varying the singsong aspect of the speech and, playing her whole role in a minor key, made the least note reach the spectators in the furthest seats. With each of her words she held them in suspense and completely subject to her will. It seemed as if everyone was afraid of breaking that silence with the slightest movement or sound, a silence which accompanies only the greatest manifestations of artistic creativity. This tension was stretched to its limit in the cellar-door scene, when Nikita goes to smother the baby. Matrëna uttered her horrible words in a real snake's hiss, twisting her wiry body into an awful contortion.

The curtain came down for the intermission, but the spectators silently sat in their places as if rooted to the spot, as if each of them had just suffered cruel torture. The only time I had ever experienced such a profound shock in the theatre was when Ermolova played *The Maid of Orléans*.[7] The romanticism of a poetic legend and the naked truth of our villages gave two great artists an equally profound foundation for the greatest creations of tragic technique.

[1] Boris Vasil'evich Varneke (1878–1944), author of standard histories of Russian theatre.
[2] Aleksey Sergeevich Suvorin (1834–1912), millionaire publisher of the conservative newspaper *Novoe Vremya* (New Times), founded the privately owned Theatre of the St Petersburg Literary-Artistic Society (1895–1917). It began with the highest dramatic standards, but gradually widened its repertoire to include melodramas, problem plays and farces.
[3] Lëv Nikolaevich Tolstoy's tragedy of peasant life, *The Power of Darkness* (1886), had been offered to the actress Savina for a benefit performance in 1887, but it was forbidden by the censorship. The first production took place at Antoine's Théâtre Libre in Paris in 1888. See 29.
[4] Varvara Vasil'evna Strel'skaya (1838–1915), an actress on the Alexandra stage from 1857 to her

death, made her name in Molière and vaudevilles, but moved on to character roles of merchants' wives and matchmakers, 'drawn from nature'; admired by Stanislavsky.

5 Evtikhy Pavlovich Karpov (1857–1926), director and playwright, began his directorial career staging plays with peasants and factory workers before moving to the Alexandra in 1896 as chief stage-director; staged the first production of Chekhov's *The Seagull* (1896).

6 See **83**, note 1.

7 Mariya Nikolaevna Ermolova (1853–1928), leading tragedienne at the Moscow Maly Theatre, first played Jeanne d'Arc in Schiller's tragedy in 1884. It became her trademark role, performed for eighteen years. For a description, see Senelick, *National Theatre in Northern and Eastern Europe*, document 248a.

IV   The Moscow Art Theatre, 1898–1905

The principles on which the Moscow Art Theatre (MAT) was founded[1] were not wholly in evidence in its first year of operation, owing to high costs, inadequate space and the rawness of the actors. Instead of a theatre at popular prices, it was the resort of the professional classes and the intelligentsia; instead of a democratic ensemble, it was an oligarchy headed by its two directors, the wealthy amateur actor Konstantin Sergeevich Alekseev, known as Stanislavsky (1863–1938) and the dramatist and pedagogue Vladimir Ivanovich Nemirovich-Danchenko (1858–1943). The opening production, A. K. Tolstoy's blank-verse chronicle *Tsar Fëdor Ioannovich*, translated the techniques of Meiningen staging to Russian subject matter; but it was noted that only Ivan Moskvin, in the title role, distinguished himself as an actor. The eclecticism of the rest of the season revealed the company's inadequacies. It was on the brink of failure when the Art Theatre 'found itself' in its revival of Anton Chekhov's *The Seagull* (*Chayka*), a play which had suffered a disastrous opening night at the Alexandra Theatre in St Petersburg in 1896. Stanislavsky and the actors devised a kind of atmospheric or lyric realism, heavily reliant on sound effects, pauses, modulated psychologized acting and mood (*nastroenie*), which established *The Seagull* as a masterpiece of modernism. Chekhov, somewhat to his own surprise, became the house dramatist, and the MAT produced the premières of *Uncle Vanya* (*Dyadya Vanya*), *Three Sisters* (*Tri sestri*) and *The Cherry Orchard* (*Vishnëvy sad*), and a revival of *Ivanov*. Another new playwright who became identified with the MAT, although politically and temperamentally he was an unlikely ally, was Maksim Gor'ky, whose first plays *The Lower Middle Class* (*Meshchan'e*) and *The Lower Depths* (*Na dne*) enabled the theatre to show that it was capable of slice-of-life presentations illustrative of a social conscience.

However, the aims of the directors grew increasingly divergent. Stanislavsky sought picturesque production techniques and opportunities for unusual staging; Nemirovich wanted the theatre to advocate progressive causes and great literature. Although it soon became the foremost theatre in Russia, the MAT was attacked in 1902 by the symbolist poet Valery Yakovlevich Bryusov (1873–1924) in an article called 'Unnecessary Truth' which appeared in the journal of the *World of Art* movement. He assailed realism in the theatre as meaningless in a conventionalized art-form. In response to this and other criticism, the MAT tried to join the fashionable trend towards symbolism with productions of Maeterlinck, Hamsun and Leonid Andreev, only to find their traditional style inadequate. Seeking an innovative means of acting and staging such plays, Stanislavsky founded the Studio on Povarsky Street in 1904, with the former MAT actor Vsevolod Emil'evich Meyerkhol'd (Meyerhold, 1874–1940) as artistic director and Bryusov himself as literary adviser. Unfortunately, the Studio never opened to the public, ostensibly because the uprisings of 1905 made the streets unsafe, but more because Stanislavsky was dissatisfied with the static and hieratic solutions Meyerhold had found.

[1] See Senelick, ed., *National Theatre in Northern and Eastern Europe*, Section IX (Russia).

87   Stanislavsky prepares *Tsar Fëdor*, 1898

K. S. Stanislavsky, *My Life in Art*, pp. 312–13 and 317–18; translation revised by L. Senelick

First of all we began to study the costumes of the epoch of *Tsar Fëdor*, for that was to be our first production. The accepted stereotype for boyar costumes was especially conventionalized. True, there had been attempts to give it new glory in the productions for members of the royal family,[1] for *Tsar Fëdor* was not at first permitted to be played for the general public.[2] But this attempt at rejuvenation expressed itself only in the use of rich materials and finish, which in most cases far from resembled the costumes of old Russia and reminded one more of fashionable modern dress. So far as style and cut went, they remained the same that we had come to know as the standard products of theatrical tailors. There are nuances in lines and cut which are never noticed by ordinary tailors, but which are most typical of one epoch of costume or another. [...] It was this secret, this *je ne sais quoi* of costume that we sought. We read and studied all the books obtainable in Moscow that dealt with Russian costume, we looked for engravings, old armour and monastic and churchly robes, that could be found in the city in rich profusion. But we were unable to copy those archaeological models, and we began to look for old embroidery, ancient Russian head-dresses, and so forth. I organized an expedition to various cities to visit second-hand dealers and to see peasants and fishermen in the villages, for I knew that the latter kept much that was old and valuable in their trunks. [...] We brought home a great deal of loot at a rather small price. [...] Part of the troupe, headed by Nemirovich-Danchenko, remained to rehearse at Pushkino, while I, the designer Simov, my assistant stage-director Sanin, my wife, a *costumière* and several actors went [to several ancient cities like Yaroslavl, Rostov, Yaroslavsky, Troitse-Sergievo] in search of material.[3] [...] We had struck on the true path. The new gimmick of 'dazzling the bourgeoisie' with luxury was found, and it was important, for we were forced for the time being to conceal the defects and immaturity of our actors by the splendour of their costumes.

[1] Boyar costume, heavily embroidered with gems and pearls, was popular fancy dress at court balls. The Tsar's brother, the Grand Duke Konstantin Aleksandrovich, was an avid amateur actor, and spent lavishly in mounting his productions.

² Although written in 1867–8, *Tsar Fëdor* was not licensed by the censor for performance until 1898, when permission was granted to both Suvorin's Theatre in St Petersburg (see 86, note 2) and the Moscow Art Theatre to stage it with cuts. (See 82, note 1.)

³ Viktor Andreevich Simov (1858–1935), the Art Theatre's leading stage-designer 1898–1912 and 1925–35, was responsible for scenery and costumes of Chekhov, Gor'ky and *Julius Caesar*. Aleksandr Akimovich Sanin (né Shenberg, 1869–1956), a member of the amateur Artistic and Literary Society, co-directed *Tsar Fëdor* with Stanislavsky and played Lup-Kleshin in it; he later worked with Evreinov and Diaghilev. Mariya Petrovna Lilina (née Perevoshchikova, 1866–1943) married Stanislavsky in 1889; an actress of great wit and versatility, she created Sonya in *Uncle Vanya*, Natasha in *Three Sisters* and Anya in *The Cherry Orchard*. The other members of the excursion were the actress M. F. Andreeva, the actor G. S. Burdzhalov, and A. A. Zhelyabushky, a board-member of the Artistic and Literary Society.

88   Researching *Tsar Fëdor*, 1898

I. Vinogradskaya, *Zhizn' i tvorchestvo K. S. Stanislavskogo – letopis'* (Moscow: Iskusstvo, 1971), vol. I, pp. 230–31

The illustration shows two pages from Stanislavsky's working album for *Tsar Fëdor*. The left-hand page shows sketches and notes on boyar costumes, and the right-hand page a sketch of the women's quarters in the Kremlin Palace.

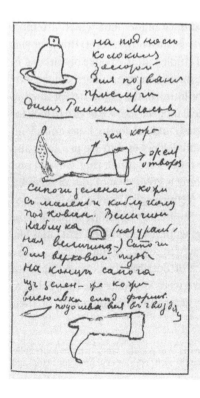

89   A journalist attends *Tsar Fëdor*, 1898

Zritel (Spectator), 'On the opening of the Art Theatre at Popular Prices', *Kur'ër* (The Courier, Moscow), 285 (1898)

Almost at the very entrance to the Art Theatre at Popular Prices I ran into one of our theatre critics ... 'Going in?' I asked. But the critic only waved his hand dismissively. 'No, I'd be better off paying another visit to the Armoury Museum.' [...]

When I entered the auditorium, the dramatic action was already under way. On stage, behind a wooden lattice, a boyar feast was going on, with all the accessories, in all points exactly like Makovsky's boyar feast.[1] Even Prince Shuysky (Mr Luzhsky)[2] wonderfully reminded me of the grey-bearded boyar merrily laughing in Makovsky's picture.

The first tableau ended. The bed-curtains closed (the curtain at the Art Theatre at Popular Prices is supplied by travelling bluish-green bed-curtains, sewn with very effective white embroidery).[3] The lights went on in the auditorium. One could see the audience. The theatre was full to bursting, but the assemblage was far from that audience which is usually deemed 'Tout-Moscou' or first-nighters. In the first rows and boxes in the first tier, true, a few conspicuous representatives of the world of 'Moscow gentry' stood out in splendour, but beside them sat persons who had nothing in common with a first-night audience. [...]

[...] the official intermission came only after the third tableau. Somewhat wearied by long sitting, deafened by shouting crowds after the Meiningen recipe, blinded by the bright colours of the brocade, golden and bejewelled costumes in the style of Karelin's famous historical pictures,[4] the audience poured into the foyer. The soft light of electric lamps newly illumined the compartmented, inviting, smart lobby of the Hermitage Theatre.[5] The audience was quick to share its impressions. 'Isn't it real, isn't it wonderfully staged', a caressing baritone resounded behind my back. I turned around. The words were spoken by one of the Muscovite Maecenases who, it seems, had so much faith in the Art Theatre at Popular Prices that he had even become a shareholder.[6]

[...] About one in the morning, weary with what I'd seen and heard, I abandoned the Art Theatre at Popular Prices, but the 'Meiningenitis' was still at fever pitch.

---

[1] Konstantin Egorovich Makovsky (1839–1915), painter of huge historical genre pictures. His painting *The Boyars' Wedding Feast* was sold in New York in 1936 for $2,500 and now hangs in the De Young Museum, San Francisco.

[2] Vasily Vasil'evich Luzhsky (né Kaluzhsky, 1869–1931), an actor with the Artistic and Literary Society before becoming a charter member of the MAT; later roles included Sorin in *The Seagull* and the Professor in *Uncle Vanya*.

[3] One of the MAT's innovations was to have a curtain that drew apart, rather than rising and falling. After 1898, in their new house in Kammerherr Lane, the curtain was embellished with an art-nouveau seagull.

⁴ Andrey Osipovich Karelin (1837–1906), painter and photographer.
⁵ A derelict music-hall in Carriage Row, connected with a pleasure garden, had to be totally refurbished by the MAT. They did not move into their own splendidly equipped building until 1902.
⁶ Probably Savva Timofeevich Morozov (1862–1905), a self-made banker and industrialist, who offered the MAT a gift of 10,000 rubles on the understanding that he would be sole donor and principal shareholder in the theatre.

90   Stanislavsky prepares *The Seagull*, 1898

Stanislavsky, *My Life in Art*, pp. 321–2; translation revised by L. Senelick

Just as soon as I was alone with the script of the play, I ceased to like it and was bored by it. And yet I had to write the *mise en scène* and prepare the plans for the play, for in those days I was the only one in the theatre closely acquainted with that kind of work. Unconvinced, my mind in turmoil, with the unpleasant prospect of the duty of working on a play that did not interest me, I was allowed to leave Moscow and stay at the estate of one of my brothers, where I was to write the plans and send them to Moscow, whence they were to be taken to Pushkino, where the preparatory rehearsals were taking place. [...]

Everything was written into the stage-director's copy of the play – how, where and in what way one was to understand the role and the hints of the author, which tone of voice to use, how to act and move, where and how to change position. There were special drawings in accord with the principle worked out at the time for all the business of entrances, exits and changes of position. There was a description of the scenery, costumes, make-ups, manners, ways of walking, methods and habits of the roles played. I had three or four weeks to carry out all this difficult and extensive work on *The Seagull*.

91(a) The director's score for *The Seagull*, 1898

The Seagull produced by Stanislavsky, ed. S. D. Balukhaty, trans. D. Magarshack (London: Dennis Dobson, 1952), p. 245

As Stanislavsky explains in 90, he prepared the *mise en scène* of *The Seagull* in its minutest details during the 'three or four weeks' preceding rehearsals. The elaborate ground plan was drawn with precision for the benefit of the actors as well as for the technical crew.

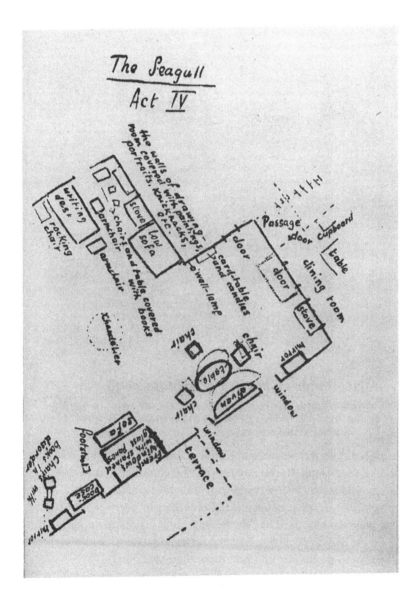

91(b) Pages from Stanislavsky's stage-director's copy of *The Seagull*, 1898

264 THE SEAGULL

MASHA: So you recognised me? *(Presses his hand.)*
TRIGORIN: Married?
MASHA: Ages ago.
TRIGORIN: Happy?[59] *(Exchanges bows with DORN and MEDVYEDENKO, then approaches KONSTANTIN diffidently.)* Your mother has told me that you've forgotten the past and are no longer angry with me.[60]

KONSTANTIN *holds out his hand to him.*

MISS ARKADINA *(to her son)*: Boris has brought you the magazine with your new story.
KONSTANTIN *(accepting the magazine, to TRIGORIN)*: Thank you. It's very kind of you, I'm sure.

They sit down.

TRIGORIN:[61] Your admirers want to be remembered to you . . ,[62] You'd be surprised how interested they are in you in Petersburg and Moscow. They're always asking me all sorts of questions about you. What you are like, how old you are, whether you are dark or fair. For some reason they all assume that you can't be young. And no one knows your real name as you write under a pseudonym. You're as mysterious as the Man in the Iron Mask.[63]
KONSTANTIN: Will you be staying long?
TRIGORIN: No, afraid not. I'm thinking of leaving for Moscow tomorrow. I'm anxious to finish my novel and I've promised to contribute something to a collection of short stories. As you see, it's the old, old story.

While they are talking, MISS ARKADINA *and* PAULINE *place a card table in the middle of the room and open it out;* SHAMRAYEV *lights candles and sets chairs. A game of lotto is brought out of the bookcase.*[64]

TRIGORIN: I'm afraid the weather hasn't been very kind to me. The wind's ferocious. If it drops by the morning I'll do a bit of fishing in the lake. And come to think of it, I might as well take a walk round the garden too.

* Stage direction crossed out by Stanislavsky. (S.B.)

PRODUCTION NOTES 265

59. Masha shrugs her shoulders. Trigórin looks at Konstantin, who lowers his eyes. Miss Arkádina stops looking at herself in the mirror and watches the two of them, standing with her back to the audience. *An awkward pause,*[*] during which the conversation of the group up stage can be heard (it is here that I would make them burst out laughing suddenly at some of Dorn's witticisms).
Meanwhile Sorin raises himself painfully in his bath-chair, takes the box of chocolates, unwraps it, and starts eating the sweets one after another, though he is forbidden to eat sweets.
60. A pause of five seconds. Konstantin at last decides to shake hands. Trigórin takes his hand, while Miss Arkádina walks up to them and embraces her son impulsively; Konstantin takes the magazine from Trigórin, carries it to the writing desk where he opens it. After Trigórin has left Masha, Medvyédenko crosses over to her and sits down beside her.
61. Konstantin crosses over to the writing desk, sits down by the rocking chair and opens the magazine. As he walks off, Miss Arkádina and Trigórin exchange glances. Miss Arkádina motions to Trigórin to continue his conversation with Konstantin. She even gives Trigórin a push in the direction of Konstantin. Trigórin goes while Miss Arkádina, watching her son, crosses over to Sorin's bath-chair and leaning against it, gazes at Konstantin.[†]
62. Trigórin speaks, leaning with his hands on the writing desk. Konstantin opens the magazine and turns the pages.
63. Konstantin motions to Trigórin to sit down. He sits down on the edge of the writing desk.
64. Dorn and Shamráyev fetch the card table and open it up. Medvyédenko gets up to help them. Masha remains sitting on the divan. Pauline brings the candles, puts them on the table, then lights them.
* Underlined in ink. (S.B.)
† Crossed out; (In the meantime Pauline and Shamráyev [near the divan in the background] light the lamp.)

92   A favourable review of *The Seagull*, 1898

Prince A. I. Urusov,[1] *Kur'ër* (The Courier), 3 (3 January 1899), reprinted in A. I. Urusov, *Stati ego o teatre, literature i iskusstve* (His articles on theatre, literature and art) (Moscow: I. N. Kolchëv, 1907), vol. II, pp. 34–8

28 December. The Art Theatre at Popular Prices was entirely sold out at the première of *The Seagull*. In the auditorium one could sense that special nervous tension so seldom to be observed: an unusual keenness on the part of the audience, a passionately concentrated attention to every word on stage. The stillness was wonderful. They were not only watching a play: they were hearkening to it and grasping it. It seemed at moments as if life itself were speaking from the stage – no theatre can give more than that. [...]

The Moscow press has already noted that the success of *The Seagull* in Moscow, independent of the drama's poetic spell, has been brought about by the thorough-ness of the staging. While rendering full justice to the artistic quality of the director's contribution and the stylishness of the performance, I think it necessary to point out a few minor flaws.

First I consider the red lighting at the top of Acts I and IV unsuccessful. It is utterly phoney and endows everything with the unnatural coloration of a fireside glow. Such lighting, dim and sinister, prevents us from hearing and seeing. In Acts I and II, to set up a large bench directly in front of the footlights, so that the characters sit in a row with their backs to the audience – en rang d'oignons – may be innovative and daring, but not quite successful. The actors hunch together in embarrassment, constrained to speak to one another askance, twisting them-selves into profiles – otherwise they can't be heard – while their silhouettes, lit by the footlights, present no specially attractive spectacle. Act IV was performed too 'ponderously'; it should go more quickly with fewer of the pauses which Mr Meyerhold and Miss Roksanova[2] abused. [...]

[...] Miss Knipper and Mr Stanislavsky were remarkably superior to the Petersburg 'originals'.[3] The former plays her whole role with exceptional brilliance, refinement and naturalism. Only in the climactic moment, the great scene in Act III, does she weaken a bit during the reconciliation with her son: the pathetic notes sound insufficiently sincere, when she ought to be deeply sincere, despite the artificiality of her nature. [...] Mr Stanislavsky as a true actor is completely transformed in The Seagull. He is immeasurably superior to, subtler and more interesting than Mr Sazonov,[4] in whom I have never noticed any special capabilities other than routine and stage know-how. Mr Stanislavsky in tone and manner is very reminiscent of one of our best novelists.

[1] Prince Aleksandr Ivanovich Urusov (1843–1900), critic for a number of periodicals, was a proponent of naturalistic theatre as prescribed by Zola.
[2] Vsevolod Meyerhold later created Tusenbach in Three Sisters; see 95, 103, 104, 110–15, 123, 124. Mariya Lyudomirovna Roksanova (née Petrovskaya, 1874–1958), a former student of Nemirovich-Danchenko, whose performance as Nina was loathed by Chekhov and his friends, left the MAT in 1902, but returned to its Fourth Studio in 1923, and later acted at the Kamerny Theatre.
[3] Ol'ga Leonardovna Knipper (1868–1959), a former student of Nemirovich-Danchenko, who married Chekhov in 1901. One of the MAT's stars, she created Masha in Three Sisters, Ranevskaya in The Cherry Orchard and Natasha in The Lower Depths. Chekhov objected to Stanislavsky's perfor-mance of Trigorin, finding it too elegant and romantic.
[4] Nikolay Fëdorovich Sazonov (1843–1903), essentially a farce and operetta actor, who performed a wide range of roles at the Alexandra from 1868.

93   *The Seagull*, Act IV, Moscow Art Theatre, 1898

Collection Laurence Senelick. Original in Moscow Art Theatre Museum

The photograph shows the dim lighting and some actors sitting with backs to the audience: two innovations which attracted the audience's complaints. Left to right: I. A. Tikhomirov as Medvedenko, V. V. Luzhsky as Sorin, V. E. Meyerhold as Treplev, O. L. Knipper as Arkadina, K. S. Stanislavsky as Trigorin, M. P. Lilina as Masha, E. M. Raevskaya as Polina, A. R. Artëm as Shamraev, A. L. Vishnevsky as Dorn.

93

94   An unfavourable review of the *The Seagull*, 1898

Moskovsky listok (Moscow Leaflet) 28 December 1898

One could feel in the characters' deportment, their movements, their words, every sound of their voices, a forlornness and abnormality that bordered on madness. The wind whistling in the chimneys, the slow measured pealing of the church-bell, the semi-darkness that prevailed on stage, the sound of a gunshot with which the play's hero Konstantin Treplëv ends his stage-life harmonized with this in tone.

95   Meyerhold comments on realism in *The Seagull*

A. K. Gladkov, 'Meyerkhol'd govorit' ('Meyerhold speaks'), *Novy Mir* (New World), 8 (1961), p. 221

You ask me whether there was naturalism in the Art Theatre *Seagull* and think you've posed me a 'trick' question because I detest naturalism and yet, with trepidation, I played my favourite role in that play. I suppose there were individual elements of naturalism but that's not important. The main thing is, there was a poetic nervous system, the concealed poetry of Chekhov's prose, instilled in the theatre thanks to Stanislavsky's brilliant directing. Before Stanislavsky, all they ever played in Chekhov was the plot, but they forgot that in his plays the sound of rain on the window-pane, the clatter of a falling bucket, dawn peeping through the shutters, mist over the lake are (as previously they had been only in prose) associated with human behaviour. At the time this was a discovery, but 'naturalism' is what it looked like when it became a cliché. And all clichés are bad: naturalistic ones or 'Meyerholdian' ones.

96   Stanislavsky prepares *The Lower Depths*, 1902

K. S. Stanislavsky, *My Life in Art*, pp. 395 and 397; translation revised by L. Senelick

As usual whenever I began work, I was in a helpless muddle, rushing from local colour to emotion, from emotion to image, from image to production. I even pestered Gor'ky in my search for creative material. He told me how he had written the play, where he had found his types, how he had wandered in his youth, how he had met the originals of the characters in his play. I ran from Gor'ky to those 'ex-human beings' who furnished him with material for his writing.

We arranged an excursion in which many of the actors in the play, Nemirovich-Danchenko, Simov and I took part. Under the leadership of the writer Gilyarovsky,[1] who had studied the life of tramps, and who always helped them out with money and advice, we went one night to Khitrov Market. This was a large part of town which housed tramps exclusively.[2] [. . .]

The excursion to Khitrov Market, more than any discussion or analysis of the play, awoke my fantasy and my imagination. There was nature which one could mould to one's heart's delight; there was live material for the creation of human beings, *mises en scène*, images, models and plans. Everything had a real basis and fell into its proper place. Making the sketches and the *mise en scène*, or showing the actors any of the scenes, I was guided by living memories and not by invention or guesswork. But the chief result of the excursion was the fact that it revealed to me the inner meaning of the play.

---

[1] Vladimir Alekseevich Gilyarovsky (1853–1935), known familiarly as Uncle Gilyay, was a provincial barn-stormer who went into journalism: his various memoirs are a rich fund of anecdotes about the pre-Revolutionary Russian stage.

[2] The excursion took place on 22 August 1902. According to Nemirovich-Danchenko, 'The flop-houses themselves provided us with little material. They are set up in regimentally serried straight lines and uncharacteristic in atmosphere. But their types helped us a good deal. At least after meeting them I finally felt ground beneath my feet, solid ground' (Letter to Maksim Gor'ky, 27 August 1902, in Vl. I. Nemirovich-Danchenko, *Izbrannye pis'ma* (Selected letters) (Moscow: Iskustvo, 1979), vol. 1, p. 305).

97   Simov's design for Act III of *The Lower Depths*, Moscow Art Theatre, 1902

Collection Laurence Senelick. Original in Moscow Art Theatre Museum

98   Nemirovich-Danchenko criticizes Stanislavsky's acting in *The Lower Depths*, 1902

Letter to K. S. Stanislavsky, September–December 1902, in Nemirovich-Danchenko, *Isbrannye pis'ma*, vol. 1, pp. 305–8

Probing the psychology of your personality as an actor, I note that you had great difficulty surrendering yourself to the role [of Satin], and this is because, first, you don't believe in the audience's sensitivity and think that it has to be beaten over the head all the time, and, second, you don't want to use almost any of your lines to create anything. And it gets tedious listening to you because throughout the dialogue, your mimicry and gesture have already made it clear to me, the spectator, what you mean to say or act out, but you still keep on acting out the details for me, even though they don't much interest me in their essence. This takes place not only on individual lines, but even in the middle of monologues and cues. [...] What if you were the one to deliver the monologue about the land of righteousness?[1] You would probably chop it up into several parts – and overact. And it wouldn't get across to the audience so lightly. For the whole splendour of the play's tone is this *brisk lightness*. And if people say that would make it seem like a Maly Theatre production, I would confidently reply that's a lie. On the contrary, playing a tragedy (*The Lower Depths* is a tragedy) in such a tone is an absolutely new phenomenon on the stage.

[1] This speech, which occurs in Act III, is spoken by the ambiguous pilgrim Luka, played by Ivan Moskvin.

99   A critical attack on superfluous realism, 1902

V. Bryusov, 'Nenuzhnaya pravda' ('Unnecessary Truth'), *Mir iskusstva* (World of Art, 4, 1902); reprinted in *Sobranie sochineny* (Collected works) (Moscow: Khudozhestvennaya literatura, 1975), vol. VI, pp. 62–72

Contemporary theatres strive to reproduce life as truthfully as possible. They think they are pursuing their vocation worthily if they put everything that exists in reality on the stage. The actors try to speak as they do in drawing-rooms, the set-designers paint landscapes from nature, the costume-designers cut their costumes to accord with archaeological data. Even so, there still remains a certain something the theatres are incapable of imitating. The Art Theatre even set itself the goal of reproducing this certain something. [...] Instead of a three-sided 'box-set', a room was set on the stage on an angle, with other rooms visible through open doors, presenting the spectators with a whole apartment. [...] If there were a wind, the window curtains fluttered, etc., etc.

First, it must be said that these are very timid innovations. They seem auxiliary and leave untouched the basic traditions of the stage. And until the traditions that constitute the essence of stage presentation are changed, no modifications of detail will bring the theatre any closer to reality. All theatres, including the Art, strive to make everything on stage visible and audible. Stages are lit by footlights, overhead lights and back lights, whereas in reality light either falls from the sky or comes through a window or issues from lamps or candles. The Art Theatre does not dare illumine the stage with one lamp alone. [...]

The stage is by nature conventional. [. . .] When an avalanche of cotton batting comes crashing down on stage, the spectators ask each other: how did they do that? If Rubek and Irene simply went backstage, the spectator would more readily believe in their destruction than now, when straw-stuffed dummies and armfuls of cotton batting tumble before their eyes.[1] 'It faded on the crowing of the cock', they say in *Hamlet* after the Ghost appears. That's enough to let the spectator imagine the cock crowing for himself. But in *Uncle Vanya* the Art Theatre makes a cricket chirp.[2] [. . .]

It is time for the theatre to stop imitating reality. [. . .] The stage must do all it can by means of the most efficient imagery to paint in the spectator's imagination the stage picture required by the play's plot. If a battle is absolutely necessary, it is awkward to send out a dozen extras or even a thousand of them with property swords: perhaps a musical rendition by the orchestra would strike the spectator as more rewarding. [. . .] There's no need to eliminate the stage picture, but it should be deliberately conventional. It should be, so to speak, stylized. [. . .]

[. . .] The dramatist must provide the actor with the possibility to express spiritually everything that is physical. Something in the direction of creating a new drama has already been accomplished. The most remarkable attempts of this kind are the plays of Maeterlinck and the late dramas of Ibsen.[3] It is striking that it was precisely when staging them that the contemporary theatre revealed its impotence with exceptional clarity.

[1] The avalanche occurs at the end of Ibsen's *When We Dead Awake*; the MAT's production opened on 28 November 1900 with V. I Kachalov as Rubek and M. G. Savitskaya as Irene.

[2] In the last act. During rehearsals in October 1899, Stanislavsky had said, 'Notice how Chekhov himself sedulously describes these "crickets". For him they are an integral symbol. All Russia is in these dreary crickets' (Nikolay Éfros, *Moskovsky Khudozhestvenny teatr, 1898–1923* (Moscow Art Theatre) (Moscow-Petrograd: Gos. izdatel'stvo, 1924), pp. 232–3).

[3] By 1902, the only attempts to stage late Ibsen in Russia had been the MAT's failed *Hedda Gabler* (1899) and *When We Dead Awake*. Maeterlinck had been played in Petersburg: *Intérieur* at Suvorin's Theatre and productions of *Monna Vanna* with Vera Kommissarzhevskaya and Lidiya Yavorskaya (1902).

100   Stanislavsky prepares Act III of *The Cherry Orchard*, 1903

Stanislavsky archive, 19 November 1903; published in Vinogradskaya, *Stanislavskogo*, vol. I, pp. 446–7

MOOD. Wholly unsuccessful ball. Few persons. Despite all efforts, they didn't manage to attract many people. Barely hauled in the stationmaster and the postal clerk. A shop-assistant in a jacket and red tie, a very young boy (old lady's son) dancing with the tall skinny daughter of the priest's wife. Even Dunyasha's been recruited. Half the dancers don't know the figures of the quadrille, let alone the *grand rond*. So it doesn't come off. Pishchik had got into difficulties. He has to teach a lot of people so that something will come of it. Besides, Pishchik's own acquaintance with the steps isn't extensive. Sometimes he doesn't have a large enough stock of French phrases and gives the calls in Russian. For instance: 'Chinese chain, promenade, arms across, spin your partners', etc., expressions often heard at middle-class weddings and evening parties. To each command they add 'Je vous en prie' (with the accent on 'en'). The crowd watching the dancers is even scantier. It is scattered in the doorways, back to the audience. We can see: the priest's wife, an old military man and his wife, an old lady in black. Yasha is standing by the door jamb watching the dancers. Firs is in the hallway looking dignified in a tailcoat, as he used to look in days gone by. Appearance and manner are those of a real major-domo.

In the billiard-room Epikhodov and the overseer from a neighbouring estate – a kindly old German with an imperial and a pipe – are playing billiards. The noise of balls clicking goes on non-stop all night. Silence reigns throughout the party guests. You'd think they were there for a funeral. The dances end – and everyone subsides, scatters along the walls. They sit and fan themselves. As soon as someone livens up, moves rapidly or talks loudly, everyone gets embarrassed, and the party responsible for the noise, ashamed of the racket he's made, gets even more embarrassed and quiet.

101 Diaghilev reviews Maeterlinck at the Art Theatre, 1904

S. P. Dyagilev,[1] 'Novoe v Moskovskom Khudozhestvennom Teatre' ('Something new at the Moscow Art Theatre'), *Mir iskusstva* (World of Art), 8–9 (1904), pp. 161–4; reprinted in *Sergey Dyagilev i russkoe iskusstvo* (Moscow: Izobrazitel'noe isskustvo, 1982), vol. I, pp. 189–92

The primary significance of the Moscow Art Theatre is that it can 'dare' such feats as would cost dear any other less popular and authoritative initiator of sometimes very risky enterprises. Not only do people forgive this theatre everything, but they even try to believe in the sincerity and earnestness of its undertakings, however extravagant they may be.[2] [...]

As for Maeterlinck, the Art Theatre remained true to itself; it offered an exceptionally virtuosic spectacle with a plethora of talented contrivances; all evening long there was not a single crude or shocking touch, and this is particularly difficult with Maeterlinck, who is too intimate.

The Blind unfolded a picture which sticks in the memory, and for all its apparent realism it stands somewhere outside of time. The sea, the trees, the horrible figure of the dead man, the dog, moving in its absurdity – all this glides by without touching us like a shadow horrible in its coldness. This frigid picture was splendidly conceived.

I will not say, however, that no faults could be found. I think it might be possible to stylize these horrible figures even more and, principally, to maintain a strict monotone, a uniform flatness in their auditory, one might even say musical, aspect. [...]

For the most part, the largest proportion of blunders was tolerated in *The Intruder*: an arid wooden set immediately made impossible any kind of mysterious contemplation whatever; then a series of crude symbols – the scrape of the scythe, the net curtains blowing in the air – profoundly contradicted Maeterlinck's very subtle symbology which strays eternally between reality and fraud.

[1] The World of Art (*Mir iskusstva*) was a loosely knit group of St Petersburg aesthetes, among them the artists Lëv Bakst, Aleksandr Benua (Benois) and Nikolay Rèrikh (Roerich). The driving force behind the group was Sergey Pavlovich Dyagilev (Diaghilev, 1872–1929), general editor of its journal from 1898 to 1905. In its pages, he emblazoned critical tenets which were, roughly, anti-realistic and 'art for art's sake', a doctrine which ran counter to the traditional Russian insistence on art's social purpose. Diaghilev's critical attacks targeted the management and policies of the Imperial Theatre from which he had been sacked; he also propagandized for Maeterlinck and Chekhov although he considered them *vieux jeu*.

[2] The season of evenings of three Maeterlinck one-acts, *Les Aveugles*, *Intérieur* and *L'Intruse*, in translations by the symbolist poet Konstantin Balmont', opened on 2 October 1904. For the first time in the theatre's career, Simov was not used as designer; the sets were by the Armenian artist Vardkes Akopovich Surenyants. Most of the critics were far more negative than Diaghilev and condemned the MAT for straying from accustomed modes.

102   Stanislavsky's score for *The Drama of Life*,[1] 1905

Stanislavsky archive, Moscow Art Theatre; excerpts in Vinogradskaya, *Stanislavskogo*, vol. I, pp. 517–26

(Note to Teresita's line: 'You've got a white spot on your arm. Wait a bit.' (*Takes out her handkerchief and cleans Kareno's forearm.*))

Teresita gazes on him with love-stricken eyes, has an uncontrollable urge to stroke his hand. Now she rails at fate. Rises and tremulously drags herself along, as if to an idol – touches and tenderly cleans his hand. Then for a long time and without interruption she tenderly strokes it, trying to press the hand to her breast. Her face becomes radiant. She is in a kind of languor. He notices none of this. He has given her his pale beautiful hand, is dreaming, carried away. He has turned over on to his stomach.

To be played smoothly, tenderly, consistently, like an idyll. See pose p. 18, sketch E.

(Note to Kareno's line: 'What I want to do is so simple, if you think about it. I want to learn from things, I want to eavesdrop at people's doors. Does that strike you as so fantastic?')

Teresita, back to the audience, raises her eyes to him, her face becomes radiant. She is literally praying to him, dragging herself to him. The pose of an ecstatic idol-worshipper. Suffers from a conflict with her vices in her striving for the ideal.

Kareno is once more forgetful of everything, is borne aloft in dreams. Entirely illumined by ideas. Rays of the sun pour over his transparent parasol. Teresita, still in the same prayerful pose, tries to reach him. The less she succeeds, the gloomier she becomes, and suffers all the more. See pose, p. 18, F.

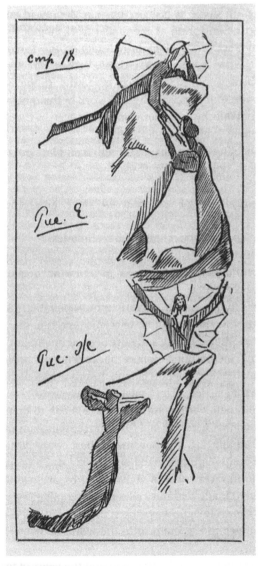

---

[1] In July 1905, Stanislavsky began preparing a director's score for *The Drama of Life* by Knut Hamsun, whose production was intended to be a 'revolution in art'. He saw the play as a mixture of two tones, the realistic and the mystical; the latter was to be performed majestically and quietly like a service of worship. His sketches were attempts to combine stateliness of decorative pose with psychologically justified motivations. His notes make a striking comparison with those for *The Cherry Orchard* (100).

103   Meyerhold founds the Theatre Studio, 1905

V. E. Meyerkhol'd, 'Teatr (k istorii i tekhnike)' (Theatre (towards a history and technique)'), in *Teatr: kniga o novom teatre* (St Petersburg: Shipovnik, 1908), pp. 3–14; translation by Edward Braun in *Meyerhold on Theatre* (London: Methuen, 1969), pp. 39–48

The so-called 'Theatre Studio' was due to open in Moscow in 1905. Over a period of almost six months (in spring at the model workshop of the Art Theatre, in summer in Dupuy Park at the Mamontov Estate on the Yaroslavl Road, and in autumn at the theatre by the Arbat Gate), actors, directors, designers and musicians assembled by Stanislavsky were preparing for the opening of the new theatre with extraordinary energy. But the work of the theatre was destined to remain unseen – not only by the general public but even by the close circle of those interested in this new dramatic undertaking.

[...] The first meeting of the Theatre Studio took place on 5 May, and at this very first meeting the following points were made:

1. Contemporary forms of dramatic art have long since outlived their usefulness.

2. The modern spectator demands fresh techniques.

3. The Art Theatre has achieved virtuosity in lifelike naturalism and true simplicity of performance, but plays have appeared which require new methods of production and performance.

4. The Theatre Studio should strive for the renovation of dramatic art by means of new forms and new methods of scenic presentation.

[...] The Theatre Studio became a theatre of experiment, but it was not so easy for it to break away from the naturalism of the Meiningen school. When the fateful day came and our theatre 'shed its blooms before it had a chance to flourish', Valery Bryusov wrote in *Vesy* [The Scales] (January 1906):

'In the Theatre Studio various attempts were made to break away from the realism of the contemporary stage and to embrace stylization whole-heartedly as a principle of dramatic art. In movement there was plasticity rather than impersonation of reality; groups would often look like Pompeian frescoes reproduced in living form. Scenery was constructed regardless of the demands of realism; rooms were made without ceilings; castle pillars were twined around with some sort of liana; dialogue was spoken throughout against a background of music, which initiated the spectator into the world of Maeterlinck's drama [*La Mort de Tintagiles*].

'But at the same time, theatrical tradition and the years of teaching of the Art Theatre exercised a powerful influence. Actors achieved a stylization of gesture worthy of the dreams of the Pre-Raphaelites, yet in their speech they still strove for the intonation of normal conversation; they attempted to express emotions in the same way as they are expressed in real life. [. . .] The Theatre Studio demonstrated to everybody who made its acquaintance that it is impossible to build a new theatre on old foundations.'

104   Meyerhold distinguishes between naturalistic theatre and the theatre of mood, 1908

Meyerkhol'd, 'Teatr', pp. 14–28; Braun, *Meyerhold*, pp. 23–33

The Moscow Art Theatre has two aspects: the Naturalistic Theatre and the Theatre of Mood. The naturalism of the Art Theatre is the naturalism adopted from the Meiningen Players; its fundamental principle is the *exact representation of life.*

[. . .] The naturalistic theatre has created actors most adept at the art of 'reincarnation', which requires a knowledge of make-up and the ability to adapt the tongue to various accents and dialects, the voice being employed as a means of sound-reproduction; but in this plasticity plays no part. The actor is expected to lose his self-consciousness rather than develop a sense of aestheticism which might balk at the representation of externally ugly, misshapen phenomena. The actor develops the photographer's ability *to observe the trifles of life.* [. . .]

The naturalistic theatre teaches the actor to express himself in a finished, clearly defined manner; there is no room for the play of allusion or for conscious understatement. That is why one so often sees overacting in the naturalistic theatre; it knows nothing of the power of suggestion. [. . .] In the theatre the spectator's imagination is able to supply that which is left unsaid. It is this mystery and the desire to solve it which draw so many people to the theatre. [. . .] Thus the spectator in the theatre aspires – albeit unconsciously – to that exercise of fantasy which rises sometimes to the level of creativity. [. . .]

Whereas naturalism has involved the Russian theatre in complicated stage techniques, the theatre of Chekhov (the other aspect of the Art Theatre), by revealing the power of *atmosphere* on the stage, has introduced that element without which the Meiningen-style theatre would have perished long ago. [. . .] The secret of Chekhov's mood lies in the *rhythm* of his language. It was the rhythm which was captured by the actors of the Art Theatre during the rehearsals of that first production of Chekhov. [. . .]

In the first two productions, *The Seagull* and *Uncle Vanya*, when the actors were still free, the harmony remained undisturbed. Subsequently, the naturalistic director first based his productions on 'the ensemble' and then lost the secret of performing Chekhov.

Once everything became subordinated to the 'ensemble', the creativity of every actor was stilled. The naturalistic director assumed the role of a conductor with full control over the fate of the *new tone* which the company had discovered; but instead of extending it, instead of penetrating to the heart of the music, he sought to create atmosphere by concentrating on external elements such as darkness, sound effects, properties, and characters.

Although he caught the speech rhythms, the director lost the secret of conducting (*The Cherry Orchard*, Act III) because he failed to see how Chekhov progresses from subtle realism to mystically heightened lyricism.

Having found the key to Chekhov, the theatre sought to impose it like a template on other authors. It began to perform Ibsen and Maeterlinck 'à la Chekhov'.

V Symbolism and the 'Crisis in the Theatre', 1902–1908

The influence of Nietzsche's *Birth of Tragedy* and Maeterlinck's plays made a deep imprint on Russian intellectuals. Impelled by the milleniarism of the *fin de siècle*, many thinkers and writers called for a new theatre that would promote communion between performer and public, exalting the spectator to a higher realm. The dominant voice was that of Vyacheslav Vasil'evich Ivanov (1866–1949), poet and classicist, who envisaged the playwright as a hierophant who would put the audience in touch with the sphere of *realiora*, true reality, by reviving the Dionysian origins of the theatre. His call for choric participation and ritual enactments was echoed by numerous followers, especially the so-called 'mystical anarchists', including Aleksey Remizov. But attempts to write Russian symbolist drama and stage it appropriately were not very successful, and the failed Revolution of 1905 dashed the hopes of many who had seen art as the path to the New Jerusalem.

Nevertheless there was a consensus that naturalism was bankrupt and that the theatre, as currently constituted, was an irrelevant vestige of the past. Some, like the decadent author Fëdor Sologub (né Fëdor Kuz'mich Teternikov, 1863–1927), called for a mandarin drama performed by human puppets, a direct emanation of the playwright's persona. His emphasis on a unique point of view was distilled by the young director Nikolay Nikolaevich Evreinov (1879–1953) into a theory of monodrama that would fuse the spectator's psychology with that of the play's protagonist. Others, like Bryusov, insisted that the theatre be stripped of extraneous production values and handed back to the actors. The poet Andrey Bely (né Boris Nikolaevich Bugaev, 1880–1934) was not untypical in renouncing his own experiments with symbolist drama, mocking the Dionysian approach, and declaring the theatre an obsolescent halfway house situated between the present and the life of the future.

Many of these writers, along with the Bolshevik ideologue Anatoly Lunacharsky and the 'World of Art' member Aleksandr Benois, contributed to the important anthology *Theatre: A Book about the New Theatre* (1908) that stated the more radical position. It added fuel to the controversy over the 'Crisis in the Theatre', and was countered by another anthology of that title, whose contributors rejected human puppet-shows and mystery plays as the way out. In both cases, general opinion held that the theatre was seriously disaffected from the most important issues of modern Russian life.

105   Ivanov projects a 'Theatre of the Future', 1904

V. Ivanov, 'Novye maski' ('New Masks'), *Vesy* (The Scales), 7 (1904) and *Po zvëzdam* (To the Stars) (St Petersburg, 1909); trans. as 'The Theatre of the Future' by Stephen Graham, *English Review* X (March 1912), pp. 634–50; translation revised by L. Senelick

VII

One cannot possibly be blind to the fact that the thirst for a new and as yet undisclosed theatre is an indefinite and vague one, as is also the general dissatisfaction with the existent theatre. Therefore the artists who are to reshape the theatre must anticipate and articulate the demands of society, struggling not so much for the sake of their own personal creativity as for the very principle and essence of change itself. They must understand not only their own ordinary souls but their innermost souls; not only their own intentions but the deeper and fuller intentions of the Muse.

Stage art is dynamic, and drama, evolving throughout history and before our eyes, is energy expressing itself. It is not merely struggling to enrich our minds by new forms of beauty, but also striving to enter our soul-life and become an active factor there. [...]

According to Nietzsche, the drama was born of the soul of music, or to put it more precisely and historically, from the choric dithyramb.[1] In this dithyramb everything was dynamic. Each participant in the liturgical chorus was an active molecule in the orgiastic life, the life of the Dionysian Communion. From the ecstatic ceremonial around the victim of sacrifice arose the Dionysian art of choric drama. The victim, at first real but afterwards fictitious, was the protagonist – the hypostasis of the god of the orgy himself, describing within the ecstatic circle the suffering of the hero who is devoted to destruction. The choral dance was primordially the communion of the sacrificers and the participants in the sacrificial mystery. [...]

VIII

The new theatre tends once more to a dynamic beginning. Is this not indicated in the drama of Ibsen, where accumulated electrical energies condense into suffocating heat and then burst in the demoniac magnificence of a few proprietary words, but without clearing the atmosphere of its threatening tension? Or in the theatre of Maeterlinck, where we are led away into a labyrinth of mystery and abandoned before heavily locked doors? Or in the Wagnerian drama of Tristan and Isolde.[2] [...]

More generally remarked of all, perhaps, is the principle of dynamism in the so-called realistic theatre, which wishes to banish the hero from the stage and put in his place 'Life' itself – the great process of becoming. Those who go to contemplate these living-picture-like exhibitions of daily life know in advance that the new knot of life-powers to be tied before our eyes is not tied for the first time, and they disregard the catastrophe because they know that the action on the stage is only a fraction of the great general drama of living, in which they are themselves serious actors. [. . .] The dark abysses of the soul are lit up momentarily with torches, and the spectators look down at the running light illumining the bottomless immeasurability. [. . .] This is almost the Dionysian tremor, and the 'frenzy on the verge of the dark abyss'.

And if the theatre is to be dynamic once again, let it be so right through. [. . .] Sufficient dramatis personae, we ourselves desire to act. The spectator must become an actor, and participate in the action. The crowd of spectators must mingle in the choric body as in the mystical communion of the ancient 'orgy' and 'mystery'. [. . .]

XII

Thus the synthetical-drama-form which we have deduced demands (1) that the scenic action arises from the orchestral symphony, that the symphony be the hidden and dynamic foundation of the action, the termination of the dramatic episodes interrupting it – for the Apollonian vision of the myth rises out of the sea of orgiastic agitation and vanishes once more into the same emotional depths, brightening them with its wonder as each cycle of musical purification is achieved – (2) that the chorus become part of the symphony and part of the dramatic action – (3) that the actors speak, and not sing from the stage.

The pit of the theatre must be cleared away to make room for the choric dance and the choric play. Sloping gradually upwards from the pit on three sides will be tiers of seats; and on the fourth side, i.e. in front of it, will be the stage. The orchestra will either remain unseen in the hollow assigned to it in the theatre of Wagner,[3] or be disposed in other places. The conductor (coryphæus) of the instrumental orchestra will stand in the gaze of all the people, clothed in a dress matching the dresses of the chorus, holding in his hand the magic wand and waving it with the rhythmic gestures of the all-powerful magician and mystagogue. [. . .]

XVI

[. . .] The theatres of choric tragedy, comedy and mystery should become the homes of creative and prophetic self-expression. In them will be finally solved the problem of the mingling of actors and onlookers in one organic body. Then the living and creative forces in the chorus will cause the drama to devolve, not outwardly but inwardly, not as a spectacle of outsiders, but as a great communion of all within the theatre walls.

Only then, may we add, will real political freedom exist, when the choric voice of the masses will be an authentic referendum of the true will of the people.

[1] Friedrich Nietzsche's *Die Geburt der Tragödie aus dem Geiste der Musik* (1872) suggested that the modern equivalent was Wagnerian music-drama.
[2] A German troupe had brought *Tristan und Isolde* to St Petersburg in 1898 with Jean de Reszke and Félia Litvinne. The first Russian production took place at the Maria Theatre, St Petersburg, in 1899.
[3] Wagner called for a 'mystic gulf' between spectator and spectacle, in lieu of the orchestra pit; he instituted it at the Bayreuth Festspielhaus, placing the orchestra out of sight.

106   Remizov proposes a 'New Drama', 1903

A. Remizov,[1] *Krashennyya ryla. Teatr i kniga* (Painted Snouts. The Theatre and the Book) (Berlin, 1922), pp. 80–82

The 'New Drama' sets as its task the creation of that kind of theatre which, in a series of movements turbulent with philosophy and art, would progress with them in their thirst for new forms to express eternal mysteries and a sense of our existence and the earth, which has nourished man on the agony of the cross, in wretchedness and heavenly ecstasy. [...]

By fulfilling such a purpose, the theatre will be raised to the very acme, vast distances will be reflected in the human eye, dark depths will open at the foothills, – the mystery will be enacted. Both actor and spectator, as one being, an illuminatus, will be submerged in a single action, a single feeling. The voices of the soul, dim and strange, heard only at fateful moments, will blaze forth with fiery tongues. And the earth will be illumined with the anguished smile of a martyr.

The theatre is not an amusement and entertainment, the theatre is not a copy of human wretchedness, the theatre is a cult, the theatre is a Mass. [...] The 'New Drama' must run counter to the whole pack of catchpennies, all the claptrap and nid-nod [of the outworn theatre], and it awaits a new actor, one unbesmirched by the rouge of things learned by rote, one whose open heart has suffered greatly and whose soul dares.

[1] Aleksey Mikhaylovich Remizov (1877–1957), a habitué of the Green Lamp salon run by Zinaida Gippius, composed synthetic versions of mystery plays and folk dramas.

107   Sologub conceives a 'Theatre of a Single Will', 1908

'Teatr odnoj volej' ('Theatre of a Single Will'), in *Teatr: kniga o novom teatre* (1908); trans. in Laurence Senelick, ed., *Russian Dramatic Theory from Pushkin to the Symbolists* (Austin: University of Texas Press, 1981), pp. 132–46

I think the first obstacle to be overcome [...] is the performing actor. The performing actor draws too much of the spectator's attention to himself, and obfuscates both drama and author. The more talented the actor, the more insufferable his tyranny over the author and the more baneful his tyranny over the play. To depose this attractive but nonetheless baneful tyranny, two possible remedies exist: either transfer the central focus of the theatrical presentation to the spectator in the pit or transfer it to the author backstage.

[...] The drama is the product of a single concept just as the universe is the product of a single creative idea. Fate in tragedy or chance in comedy turns out to be none other than the author. [...]

Here is how I envisage the theatrical spectacle: the author or the reader who stands in for him – or best of all, a reader, impassive and calm and unruffled by an author's shyness in the presence of spectators who may shout praise or blame at him (both equally unpleasant) and have perhaps brought their latchkeys for high-spirited whistling – sits near the stage, somewhat to one side. Before him a table, on the table the play which is about to be presented. The reader begins at the beginning:

He reads the title of the drama. The author's name.

The epigraph, if there is one ...

Next the cast list.

The author's preface or commentary if there is any.

Act I. Setting. Names of the characters discovered on stage.

Entrances and exits of the actors, as they are designated in the playscript.

All stage-directions, not omitting even the slightest, be it but a single word.

And even as the reader reads beside the stage, the curtain parts, on stage the setting indicated by the author is revealed and lighted, the actors come on stage and do what the author's stage-directions prompt them to, as they are read aloud, and speak what the playscript sets down. If an actor forgets his lines – and when does he not forget them! – the reader reads them, as calmly and as loudly as all the rest. [...]

[... W] hy shouldn't the actor resemble a marionette? It's no humiliation for a man. Such is the unalterable law of universal play-acting that man is like a wonderfully constructed marionette. And there is no way he can avoid this or even forget it. [...]

[...] The actor ought to be cool and collected, every one of his words ought to ring out evenly and resonantly, every one of his movements ought to be slow and graceful. The performance of a tragedy ought not to remind us of the flashing images in the cinema. Relieved of this irrelevant and annoying flashing, an attentive spectator should travel the very long road to an understanding of tragedy. [...]

In line with this, perhaps, the lighting design is both pertinent and wholly functional: the spectator should perhaps be shown only what he is meant to see at any given moment, with all the rest submerged in darkness – just as in our consciousness, everything impending that does not immediately catch our attention falls outside the threshold of consciousness. [...]

The action of a tragedy will be accompanied by and interspersed with dance. [...] The rhythm of liberation is the rhythm of dance. The pathos of liberation is the joy of the beautiful, undraped body.

The dancing spectator of either sex will come to the theatre and at the threshold he or she will doff the coarse, philistine clothing. And trip it in the light-footed dance.

So the throng which came to look on will be transfigured into the choric round dance, come to participate in the tragic action.

108   Bely criticizes symbolist proposals, 1908

A. Bely, 'Teatr i sovremennaya drama' ('Theatre and Modern Drama'), in *Teatr: kniga o novom teatre* (1908); trans. in Senelick, *Russian Dramatic Theory*, pp. 149–70

The most recent theorists of drama, perhaps correctly, establish a bond between the modern conditions of the dramatic enactment and the conditions for the rise of ancient drama. [...] The theatre, it appears, should become a temple. But why should the theatre become a temple, when we have both temples and theatres? Divine worship takes place in a temple. So does the sacrament. 'Let the sacrament be performed in the theatre as well', so say the latest theorists of drama. But what are we to understand by 'sacrament'? [...] We understand the connection between ancient Greek drama and the religious cult of Dionysos. But in Greece the drama developed by moving away from religion. Drama was emancipated from religion. The legacy we received was an emancipated drama. [...]

If [what they tell us] *is* the case, give us a goat to immolate! But what are we to do with a goat, once we have had Shakespeare? If this implies some kind of new divine service, tell us the name of the new god! [...] If the name of this new god is not given us, if the religion of such a god is wanting, all intrinsic statements about the path of modern drama, the new theatre as a temple, remain figurative statements which change nothing in the modern theatre. [...]

Suppose that we, the spectators, have reverted to the choric element. And, moreover, that the choric element indulges in dances of prayer. Then, however, the distance of our states of prayer from a life unrecreated through prayer will be emphasized with particular acuity. For life will overwhelm prayer. [...] we shall enter the theatre-temple, drape ourselves in white garments, crown ourselves with garlands of roses, to act out a 'mysterium' (whose theme is ever the same: a godlike man struggles with fate): at the proper moment we shall take another by the hand and dance. Picture yourself, reader, in this role for just a moment. Is that us spinning around the sacrificial altar – an art-nouveau lady, a stockbroker, a working man and a member of the Privy Council? I am sure that our prayers will not tally. The art-nouveau lady will pray to some poet in the image and likeness of

Dionysos, the working man will pray for a shorter workday, while the senior civil servant – to what star does his gaze aspire? No, it is far better to whirl round in a waltz with a pretty young miss than to lead a choric dance with a senior civil servant. [...]

The director is now the autocrat of the theatre. He towers over actors, spectators and dramatists. He segregates them from one another. Thus he usurps the author's prerogatives and meddles in the creative act. [...] Simultaneously he must contend with the actors, correct the author's mistakes by means of his staging and instruct the audience in a new life – such is the task of the modern director; and naturally, it is impossible to fulfil this task. Hence the duty is imposed on the director to be a mystagogue of the crowd. [...]

The modern theatre will be wrecked against either the Scylla of the Shakespearian theatre or the Charybdis of the cinema.

The sooner the better!

109   Evreinov introduces monodrama, 1908

N. N. Evreinov, *Vvdenie v monodramu* (Introduction to Monodrama) (St Petersburg: *Sovremennoe iskusstvo*, 1908); trans. in Senelick, *Russian Dramatic Theory*, pp. 183–99

Now by 'monodrama' I mean to denote the kind of dramatic presentation which, while attempting to communicate with the spectator as fully as it can the protagonist's state of mind, displays the world around him on stage just as the protagonist perceives the world at any given moment of his existence on stage. [...]

In other words, the external spectacle must be an expression of the internal spectacle.

Monodrama requires each of the spectators to stand in the protagonist's shoes, to live his life, i.e. to feel as he feels and share an illusion of thinking as he thinks, and therefore to be the first to see and hear the same thing the protagonist does. The cornerstone of monodrama is the protagonist's on-stage emotional experience producing an identical co-experience in the spectator, who, through this act of co-experience, becomes one with the protagonist. To induce the illusion in the spectator that he is turning into the protagonist is the chief task of monodrama. [...]

And therefore I would very much insist that the protagonist be designated by the simple but expressive first-person pronoun 'I'. [...] The spectator should know from the playbill itself with whom the author invites him to share experience and in whose image he, the spectator, must appear. [...] Let us suppose that the protagonist, the one designated in the playbill as 'I', has begun to squint; the result is darkness; the spectator experiences this result, because the lighting man at that instant in the monodrama turns out the footlights and the border lights and the strip lights, everything; however, by proceeding from effect to cause, i.e. from one's one sensation of darkness to whatever caused it, the spectator by the gradual power of imagination will realize that the darkness was caused not by switching off the electric current to the stage but by his, the spectator's, closing his eyes.

VI Kommissarzhevskaya and Meyerhold, 1905–1907

Vera Fëdorovna Kommissarzhevskaya (1864–1910) was a leading ingénue at the Alexandra when she quit to form her own theatre with a 'progressive' repertoire of Gor'ky, Naydënov and Ibsen. She became renowned for her portrayal of sensitive, oppressed women, striving for the truth; under the direction of Akim Volynsky, she developed an other-worldly quality which made her attractive to the symbolists. She, in turn, founded a salon to fuse Vyacheslav Ivanov's mystical doctrine with social purpose, and opened a new theatre in Officer Street, 'a wooden amphitheatre, white walls, grey cloth – pure as the inside of a yacht and bare as the inside of a Lutheran chapel' (Osip Mandel'shtam). Vsevolod Meyerhold became its artistic director with a mandate to create a symbolist repertoire; he also followed a personal agenda of realizing principles of decorative stasis and rhythmical action. Following Bryusov, he described this as *uslovny teatr*, 'stylized' or 'conventionalized' theatre. Despite some outstanding successes – Maeterlinck's *Sœur Béatrice*, Sologub's *The Triumph of Death* and Blok's *The Little Showbooth* (the last two without Kommissarzhevskaya's participation) – the regime was attacked on all sides. The actress's public complained of obscurantism and sterility; the intellectuals berated the inconsistency of the production values. In the middle of the second season (1907), Kommissarzhevskaya dismissed Meyerhold; working henceforth with her half-brother Fëdor Kommissarzhevsky, Nikolay Evreinov and Valery Bryusov, she still clung to mystical idealism. Her enterprise failed and, after a disastrous tour to America in 1908, she died of smallpox in Tashkent while travelling to raise money for a projected theatrical university.

110 Kommissarzhevskaya as Meyerhold's Hedda Gabler, 1906

Yury Belaev, quoted in D. Tal'nikov, *Kommissarzhevskaya* (Moscow-Leningrad: Iskusstvo, 1939). p. 323

I failed to recognize her. I knew that for the sake of art she was capable of great sacrifices, but a true self-sacrifice stood before me; this Hedda Gabler, at whose sight the reviewers had cried 'Green! Green!', was as enigmatic as the depths of an onyx. From her russet hair, the intricately heavy splendour of her green gown, the long pointed toes of her slippers and the red-polished fingertips one could intuit the enchantress, who might at any moment transform herself into a lizard, a serpent, a naiad. This was not Hedda Gabler, but, as it were, her wraith, her symbol. [. . .]

She froze one to ice with her severe and heartless gaze, with her inordinately tense and cadenced voice. If only there had been one smile or one catch in the throat.

111   Meyerhold defines stylized theatre, 1908

Meyerkhol'd, 'Teatr', pp. 33–55; Braun, *Meyerhold*, pp. 49–64

I should like to mention two distinct methods of establishing contact between the director and his actors. [...]

1. A triangle, in which the apex is the director and the two remaining corners, the author and the actor. The spectator comprehends the creation of the latter two through the creation of the director. This is method one, which we shall call the 'Theatre-Triangle'.

Spectator

2. A straight, horizontal line, with four theatrical elements (author, director, actor, spectator) marked from left to right, represents the other method, which we shall call the 'Theatre of the Straight Line'. The actor reveals his soul freely to the spectator, having assimilated the creation of the director, who, in his turn, has assimilated the creation of the author.

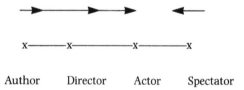

[...] In order for the straight line not to bend, the director must remain the sole arbiter of the mood and style of the production, but, nevertheless, the actor's art remains free in the 'Theatre of the Straight Line'. [...] *Above all, drama is the art of the actor.*

[...] the director and actors intuitively established the following principles during the course of preliminary rehearsals:

A. Diction

1. The words must be coldly 'coined', free from all tremolo and the familiar break in the voice. There must be a total absence of tension and lugubrious intonation.

2. The sound must always be 'reinforced'; the words must fall like drops into a deep well. [...]

B. Plasticity

1. [...] The essence of human relationships is determined by gestures, poses, glances and silences. Words alone cannot say everything. Hence there must be a *pattern of movement* on the stage to transform the spectator into a vigilant observer. [...] Words catch the ear, plasticity the eye. Thus the spectator's imagination is exposed to two stimuli; the oral and the visual. [...]

2. [...] The unsightly clutter of the naturalistic stage was replaced in the New Theatre by constructions rigidly subordinated to rhythmical movement and to the musical harmony of colour masses. [...] It was necessary to focus the spectator's entire attention on the actors' movement. [...]

The human body and the objects surrounding it – tables, chairs, beds, cupboards – are all three-dimensional; therefore the theatre, where the main element is the actor, must find inspiration in the plastic arts, not in painting. The actor must study *the plasticity of the statue.*

[...] The stylized theatre [...] aims at a deft mastery of line, grouping and costume colour, which even when static creates an infinitely stronger impression of movement than the naturalistic theatre. [... I]t anticipates the revival of the dance and seeks to induce the active participation of the spectator in the performance, [and clearly] is leading to a revival of the Greek classical theatre.

112   Kommissarzhevskaya as Sister Beatrice, 1906

In Braun, *Meyerhold,* opp. p. 49

The last act of Maeterlinck's *Sister Beatrice.*

113   Kommissarzhevskaya dismisses Meyerhold, 1907

Inberg, 'Plokhoy anekdot' ('A bad joke'), in A. Zonov 'Letopis' teatra nad Ofitserskoy'
('Chronicle of the Theatre on Officer St'), in *Alkonost* (The Mythic Bird) (St Petersburg,
1911), vol. I, pp. 72–3

Everyday life is dead – for me that is an axiom of art. And if I broke with Meyerhold,
it was certainly not because I felt nostalgia for realism or was disappointed by
symbolist drama or conventionalized theatre. I was simply alarmed by the blank
wall, the impasse to which – I saw clearly – Meyerhold persistently led us. I saw
that in this theatre, we the actors had nothing to do. I felt the dead knots with
which Meyerhold was tightly binding us. [. . .] With every rehearsal I noticed the
fruitlessness of my own and my colleagues' work. Meyerhold stubbornly strove for
'flatness' and 'immobility' and we had a flop, a deserved flop. *Pelléas* opened my
eyes to something more important.[1] I saw that we gradually had turned the stage
into a laboratory for director's experiments. The spectators stared at us in
bewilderment, shrugged in incomprehension and finally – went away. The thread
between us and the audience was deliberately broken. Which means, the entire
meaning of our work disappeared. [. . . F]or us to have lost the spectator made it
clear that we had come to a precipice, a blank wall.

[1] In Meyerhold's production of *Pelléas et Mélisande* (1907), the heroine was portrayed as a passive
puppet in the hands of Fate. Aleksandr Mgebrov, a young actor in the cast, recalled 'the actors did
not play *Pelléas et Mélisande*, they performed a religious rite' (A. A. Mgebrov, *Zhizn' v teatre* (A Life in
the Theatre) (Leningrad: Academia, 1929), vol. I, p. 373).

114   Kommissarzhevskaya discusses drama, 1908

'Not politics, only drama – Komisarzhevsky', *New York Times* (1 March 1908), p. 10

I do not believe in ultra-realism – in what you might call naturalism. Life is not
really as brutal as that, and people are not such animals. There must be something
more elevated on the stage, something higher and more artistic. In my work I
strive for a combination of symbolism and realism – not the underlying significance of things. Oh no! Naturalism is not the real art! [. . .]

The real drama is not the drama of the present or the drama of the past. It is the
eternal drama – perhaps the drama of the future, who knows? It is the drama not
of one locality, but the drama of all the world: the international drama. In Russia
now too much of the drama is given over to politics and temporary and local
conditions.

115   Aleksandr Blok's eulogy of Kommissarzhevskaya, 1910

A. A. Blok,[1] 'Vera Fëdorovna Kommissarzhevskaya', *Rech'* (Speech), 12 February 1910

[We the symbolists] were of course all in love with Vera Fëdorovna Kommissar-zhevskaya, unbeknownst to ourselves, and we were in love not only with her, but with what shone behind her restless shoulders, with that towards which her sleepless eyes and ever-thrilling voice summoned us. 'Please, you have forgotten nothing. You are simply a bit ashamed. People don't forget such things . . . Give me my kingdom, master builder. My kingdom on the table.'

Never shall I forget the demanding, capricious and triumphant voice with which Kommissarzhevskaya pronounced those words as Hilda in Ibsen's *Master Builder*.[2] Can *such a thing* be forgotten? I remember her slight, quick figure, in the semi-dusk of the backstage alley, her hastily flung greeting before her entrance on stage. [. . .] She was all rebellion and all springtime, like Hilda. [. . .]

The death of Vera Fëdorovna is disturbing and alarming; for all its monstrous suddenness and undeserved cruelty it is a beautiful death. For it is not death, not ordinary death, of course. It is another new message for us – for us to stand staunchly on guard.

[1] Aleksandr Aleksandrovich Blok (1880–1921) began as a symbolist poet, but disappointed by the failed Revolution of 1905 attacked mysticism with irony in his *Lyrical Dramas*. Meyerhold staged his *Little Showbooth* at Kommissarzhevskaya's theatre with great *éclat* (1906), and in 1908 the poet translated Grillparzer's *Die Ahnfrau* for her.
[2] She had first played Hilda Wangel in her Theatre in the Passage in 1904.

VII New directions for the Moscow Art Theatre, 1909–1917

Although Nemirovich-Danchenko pursued fresh approaches to social purpose and literature, first through Andreev's allegory *Anathema* and then through a dramatization of Dostoevsky's *Brothers Karamazov*, Stanislavsky became more convinced that the answer lay in a new means of stimulating the actor's imagination and fortifying his inner life. At the insistence of Isadora Duncan, he contracted with Edward Gordon Craig to mount a production of *Hamlet*. After three years of intense but sporadic work, an imperfect mixture of Craig's monodramatic ideas and the MAT's psychologized acting opened to contradictory reviews. Stanislavsky then invited Benois to stage colourful (albeit realistic) versions of Molière and Goldoni, whose frivolity disgusted Nemirovich. Rebuffed at his attempt to win converts to his newly developed 'system' of acting from the regular MAT company, Stanislavsky, with the help of his assistant Sulerzhitsky, founded another Studio, this one staffed by young students, including Mikhail Chekhov, Evgeny Vakhtangov, Serafima Birman, Ryszard Boleslawski and Mariya Uspenskaya. Their work in the Studio would later be imported, in various forms, to acting schools and rehearsal halls in Poland, England and North America.

116 Nemirovich-Danchenko defends realism, 1909

Discussion with performers before rehearsing Leonid Andreev's *Anathema*, in Vl. I. *Nemirovich-Danchenko o tvorchestva aktĕra: khrestomatiya* (Nemirovich-Danchenko on the actor's creativity: an anthology) (Moscow: Iskusstvo, 1973), pp. 59–63

I find that in the last few years our theatre has fallen short of its purpose – progressive ideology [*ideynost'*].

Fallen behind plays of progressive ideology – in the best sense, not in the sense of street-corner uprisings. The work we are doing now and the audiences we are serving have made us dreadful Octobrists.[1] [. . .]

We must stop shilly-shallying in search of form, which we have been doing for five or six years now. Everywhere people are talking about the crisis in the theatre, symbolism, stylization, realism, etc. At all the big debates they always start by cursing the Art Theatre. [. . .]

After last year I reached the conclusion that if they want to destroy realism, which adheres in the very composition of this theatre, they would have to dismantle the whole theatre, disband its workers, etc. The trouble arises when realism dwindles into something petty like naturalism. The ideal is realism honed to the point of symbolism. [...]

The whole company and its stage-director are the best in the world. What we lack is a striving for progressive ideology; we approach a play with our soul on a petty plane and so we become petty naturalists. If we were to approach it with a great idea and the soul of an artist on a sublime plane, the minutiae would drop away and life itself would help us create something superior.

¹ A political party of right-wing liberals that came into being after the Imperial Manifesto of 1905 granted a constitution. Nemirovich's sympathies lay further to the left, with the Constitutional Democrats or Cadets.

117   Stanislavsky and Gordon Craig discuss *Hamlet*, 1909

Transcription into English by Ursula Cox and Mikhail Lykiardopoulos, 29 April 1909; copybooks at the Bibliothèque Nationale, Paris; in L. Senelick, *Gordon Craig's Moscow Hamlet: A Reconstruction* (Westport, Conn.: Greenwood Press, 1982), pp. 62–71

CRAIG [...] In Hamlet's monologue in the second scene, Act I, beginning: 'Not seems, madam; nay, it is; I know not seems', [...] only the first two lines and [...] the last two lines are important. All the rest of the monologue must be pronounced more as music, so that the thought becomes so much lost in the sounds that the audience simply *does not follow* the thought except in the above-mentioned four lines. How this music is done will depend on the individuality of the actor. [...]

I want all this (*points to the scene*) to be in no way realistic. [...] All the tragedy of Hamlet is in his isolation. And the background of this isolation is the court, a world of pretence. [...] And in this golden court, this world of show, there must not be various different individualities as there would be in a realistic play. No, here everything melts into a single mass. Separate faces as in the old masters of painting must be coloured with one brush, with one paint. [...]

STANISLAVSKY I understand what you say about monodrama. Let us try by every means to make the public understand that it is looking at the play with the eyes of Hamlet; that the king, the queen and the court are not shown on the stage such as they really are, but such as they appear to Hamlet to be. And I think that in the scenes where Hamlet is on stage we can do this. But what are we to do with the characters when Hamlet is not on the stage?

CRAIG I should like Hamlet to be on the stage always, in every scene, all through the play; he can be in the distance, lying, sitting, in front of the people acting, at the side, behind, but the spectator ought never to lose sight of him. I want the public to feel the connection between what is going forward on stage and Hamlet. So that the public should feel as keenly as possible all the horror of Hamlet's position.

118(a)Egorov's design for *Hamlet*'s first court scene, 1909

In N. N. Chushkin, *Gamlet-Kachalov: iz stsenicheskoy istorii Gamlet Shekspira* (Moscow: Iskusstvo, 1966), facing p. 64

Egorov worked from field research in Germany and Denmark in 1909. An archaeological approach, copying Cranach, is evident.

118(b)Craig's design for *Hamlet*'s first court scene, 1909

In N. N. Chushkin, *Gamlet-Kachalov*, facing p. 192

Gordon Craig's conception of the first court scene in *Hamlet*, with the Court a mass of gold and the Prince in profile, down left of centre. This was the design realized in production.

119   Bryusov reviews the Craig–Stanislavsky *Hamlet*, 1912

V. Bryusov, 'Gamlet v Moskovskom Khudozhestvennom teatre' ('Hamlet at the Moscow
Art Theatre'), *Ezhegodnik Imperatorskikh teatrov* (Yearbook of the Imperial Theatres), vol.
II (1912), pp. 43–58; trans. in Senelick, *Russian Dramatic Theory*, p. 180.

A conventionalized staging requires conventionalized acting; the Art Theatre failed to
understand this. [. . .] Instead of a court there was a hint of a court; in
correspondence with this we should have heard not a shout but a hint of a shout.
The platform was indicated by parallelepipeds disappearing aloft; lifelike movements, lifelike gestures should have been indicated by conventionalized gestures,
like those we see in old Byzantine icons. A house without windows, doors and
ceilings, the monochromatic denuded walls, even the stone graveyard itself with
its square pillars would not have seemed strange and inappropriate if we had seen
them filled with substantially 'conventionalized' creatures, with conventionalized
gestures and vocal intonations.

120   Nemirovich-Danchenko on the director's function

Vl. I. Nemirovich-Danchenko, *My Life in the Russian Theatre*, trans. J. Cournos (London:
Geoffrey Bles, 1937), pp. 155–60; translation revised by L. Senelick

You must know that a director is a triple-faced creature:
    1) the interpretive director: he instructs *how* to act; so one might call him the
actor-director or pedagogue-director;
    2) the mirror director, reflecting the individual qualities of the actor;
    3) the organizing director of the whole production.
[. . .] No matter how deep and rich in content the director's role may be in the
shaping of the actor's creativity, it is absolutely essential that not a trace of it be
visible. [. . .] In this then lies the first and most significant difference between the
new and the old theatre: a single will reigns in our theatre. The production is
permeated with a single spirit. [. . .]
    Later, when Stanislavsky had transferred his director's attention from the outer
to the inner, he occupied himself, together with his assistant Sulerzhitsky,[1] with a
precise definition of the elements of an actor's creativity. The so-called Stanislavsky 'system' found its approximation at this time. There appeared his now
popular expression 'transparent action'. It answers the question I put earlier:
where should the actor's temperament be directed? The deepest essence of a play
or role was defined in the word 'seed', more particularly the seed of the scenes, the
seed of a fragment.

---

[1] Leopol'd Antonovich Sulerzhitsky (1872–1916), former architect, seaman and Tolstoyan, became
Stanislavsky's personal, privately paid assistant in 1900, at the suggestion of Gor'ky and Chekhov.
He was responsible for much of the success of the MAT's *Blue Bird* (1908) and the Gordon Craig
Hamlet (1912) and ran the First Studio from 1913. Many of Stanislavsky's inchoate ideas on acting
took shape with Sulerzhitsky's help and support.

121   Sulerzhitsky's principles for the First Studio, 1914

From Sulerzhitsky's diary (22 September 1914), in L. A. Sulerzhitsky, *Povesti i rasskazy, stat'i i zametki o teatre, perepiska, vospominaniya o L. A. Sulerzhitskom* (Tales, articles and notes on theatre, correspondence, memoirs of him) (Moscow: Iskusstvo, 1970), pp. 351–3

[Stanislavsky] dreams of someday establishing a class where the *whole company* of the Art Theatre will daily arrive at, say, half an hour before rehearsals or between them, and where these exercises will be performed precisely and strictly according to the 'system' by everyone, the way singers sing vocal exercises (his analogy), no matter what parts they sing.

The exercises should be individually:

to relax the muscles,

to bring oneself into the circle of concentration,

to confirm oneself in faith, naïvety,

to learn to bring oneself into any *affective condition* whatever,

to learn to bring oneself to the sensation of what [Stanislavsky] calls 'I am' in the various complexes of circumstances of different kinds that might exist, etc.

to establish a living objective,

to use all these means to awake in oneself an efficient condition for work, etc.

Moreover, all these tasks must be attractive, must *interest the will*, because, according to his *invariable expression*, 'one cannot command the creative will – one can only coax it'.

[. . .] STANISLAVSKY What good are words? Without words one can present all sorts of feelings more subtly. For instance, which actress has presented more subtle feelings on stage than Duncan?[1] If you compare Duncan with Duse, I prefer Duncan. The theatre must attain that art, must develop it so that everything will be presented without words.

SULERZHITSKY That's entirely wrong. The dramatic theatre is that species of dramatic art whose means are not only *emotion* but *thought*, ideas; and when thought enters in, when the actor must make the audience experience not only *emotion* but *thought*, *words* are indispensable, and besides, *words* by themselves, apart from serving hand-in-glove with other auxiliary means of expressing *thoughts and ideas*, are also capable of beauty. [. . .]

One must find *what* to teach the actor so that he knows how to take fire from the *ideas* of a work, just as Duncan found the way to teach her art. [. . . Stanislavsky's] system is a system for the accurate re-living o feelings. In that sphere it is the ultimate point of development of stage-art as an art of re-living, the ultimate, uttermost point of development of the theatre of emotion. It completes a whole era in the life of the theatre. [. . .]

Now the theatre must develop further in the direction of producing ideas by means of *emotion*, which will no longer be *an end in itself* on stage, but a *means* towards producing ideas.

[1] Isadora Duncan (1878–1927) had brought her barefoot, liberated *plastique* in dance to St Petersburg in 1904; it became a revelation for Russian artists, conservative and avant-garde alike. She returned regularly from 1907 to 1913, and lived in the Soviet Union 1921–4, marrying the poet Sergey Esenin.

VIII Innovation and experimentation, 1907–1917

Despite the perceived 'Crisis in the Theatre', the period between the two Revolutions of 1905 and 1917 was remarkably fertile in theatrical experimentation. Among the most important movements were:

Reconstructivism, a turn to the pre-realistic theatre of the past and reproducing its most striking features. Evreinov's productions at the Antique Theatre in St Petersburg were perhaps the most archaeologically accurate. Meyerhold, a director at the Imperial Theatres, adapted the practice in mounting Molière's *Dom Juan* at the Alexandra Theatre and Gluck's *Orfeo* at the Maria Theatre, carefully selecting the salient feature from the past to stimulate the audience's imagination.

Theatre of Miniatures, which grew out of the greenroom high jinks of the professional theatre. Some, like Nikita Baliev's *The Bat* in Moscow, were essentially revues, using literary material and classical music. Others, like Meyerhold's *The Strand* and *Interlude House* in St Petersburg, were seriously intended arenas for experimentation; Meyerhold was exploring the roots of the actor's creativity in the grotesque and *cabotinage* (by which he meant the presentational skills of the itinerant performer). Still others were cabarets on the models of Ernst von Wolzogen's Berlin *Überbrettl*, staging satire and parody for a sophisticated audience. The best of these was A. R. Kugel''s *The Crooked Mirror* in St Petersburg, directed by Evreinov: one of its favourite targets was extremism in directing. Evreinov's *The Fourth Wall*, for instance, reduced naturalism *ad absurdum* and in the process blasted a number of fashionable theatres and directors.

Theatricality, Evreinov's theory that the theatrical instinct lies at the base of all human behaviour and is as natural an appetite as sex. A secular version of the symbolists' desire for communion, theatricality required that life, not the stage, become more theatrical, and thus improve.

Syntheticism, the brain-child of Fëdor Fëdorovich Kommissarzhevsky (1882–1954). Opposed to the MAT's naturalism and to Meyerhold's puppet-actors, Kommissarzhevsky, working at Nezlobin's Theatre and his own Studio in Moscow, proposed that each production be predicated on the idiosyncratic style of the playwright. All elements in the production – pictorial, musical, psychological – must be fused into an integral statement by the director. He applied this principle to Molière, Ostrovsky and Goethe with considerable taste and verve.

Futurism, both a continuation and a refutation of symbolism, dating in Russia from 1910. Anti-mystical and anti-philistine at once, the futurists painted their faces, held nonsensical gatherings and issued outlandish manifestos to *épater le bourgeois* before war broke out. Their more serious aesthetic was to renew the Russian language and eradicate foreign influence from its poetry. Their most striking theatrical event was *Victory over the Sun* (1913), a collaboration of the composer Mikhail Matyushkin, the designer Kazemir Malevich and the poet Aleksey Kruchënykh, often considered the first realized use of cubist principles in the theatre.

Constructivism, although not to become a major theatrical mode until after the Revolution, made its initial appearance in the productions of the Kamerny (Chamber) Theatre, Moscow. The Kamerny had been founded by Aleksandr Yakovlevich Tairov (né Kornblit, 1885–1950) in 1914; he was a dogged opponent of naturalism and, using his wife Alisa Koonen as star, promoted a theatre of marvels, in which the actor would unite the virtuosity of singer, dancer, juggler and acrobat in a harmonic and musical whole.

122   *The Miracle of Théophile* re-created at the Antique Theatre, 1907

E. Stark, *Starinny teatr* (The Antique Theatre)[1] (St Petersburg: Tret'ya strazha, 1922), pp. 27–8

This production, despite its overall archaism, was charming. The designer I.Ya. Bilibin[2] gave it a setting of rare beauty and restraint in the style of a twelfth-century miniature. The whole performance was permeated in proper proportion with primitivism and this too bespoke the enormous effort that went to achieving a definite unity of tone in speech and to imparting to the actors' gestures the necessary simplicity. [...] When the curtain rose, all the characters were already seated in their places: in the upper level, depicting heaven, the Holy Ghost; in the middle, symbolizing earth, the Cardinal on the left with his attendant Théophile on the right, and at the very edge his friends Pierre and Thomas; at the bottom the magician Saladin. In the bottom right-hand corner was located a person who fulfilled an unusual function: to proclaim aloud the author's stage-directions. [...] He not only reported on the characters' movements, but even elucidated their inner emotional reactions:

'Then Théophile departs from Saladin and thinks to repudiate the Cardinal is no laughing matter. He speaks:'

[...] This was remarkably characteristic and greatly caught the audience's fancy, especially since the actor who played the 'prologos' had not only a stylish figure and comported himself handsomely, but also knew how to invest his voice with a total lack of affect when pronouncing stage-directions. As a result, even this 'enactment', so alien to the modern theatre, so simple and naïve in form and content, left an impression of something wrapped in the subtle afflatus of poetry.

[1] The young director Evreinov and an administrator of the Imperial Theatre, Baron Nikolay Drizen, founded the Antique Theatre (*Starinny teatr*) in St Petersburg in 1907, to reconstruct theatrical

forms of the remote past. A season of medieval French plays, including *The Three Magi*, Rutebeuf's *Miracle de Théophile*, and *Le Jeu de Robin et Marion* were presented in 1907/8; after a hiatus, a Spanish season was offered in 1911/12; a projected *commedia dell'arte* season was not realized. Evreinov had hoped for an audience in costume, interacting with the performers, but this never happened. The experiment fell between the two stools of archaism and aestheticism, but it had practical effect in channelling the minds of directors and designers to past theatrical conventions for inspiration.

2 Ivan Yakovlevich Bilibin (1876–1942), graphic artist, closely associated with the World of Art; his earliest work for the theatre was the Antique Theatre, but he later became a frequent designer of operas set in medieval Russia.

123   Meyerhold on staging drama of the past, 1910, 1913

V. E. Meyerkhol'd, *O teatre* (On theatre) (St Petersburg, 1913), pp. 121–8; translation in Braun, *Meyerhold*, pp. 98–104

[I]n producing a work from a past age of the theatre it is by no means obligatory to stage it *according to the archaeological method*; in the process of reconstruction there is no need for the director to bother with the exact reconstruction of the architectural characteristics of the stage of the period in question. An authentic play of the old theatre may be staged as a *free composition* in the spirit of the theatre in which it was originally staged, but on one inflexible condition: from the old theatre one *must* select those architectural features which best convey the spirit of the works. [...]

There are plays, such as Sophocles' *Antigone* and Griboedov's *Woe from Wit*, which may be perceived by the modern spectator in the light of his own time. It is even possible to perform both these plays in modern dress; the hymn to freedom in the first and the conflict of generations in the second are expressed with a clear, persistent leitmotiv and both retain their tendentiousness, whatever the setting.

On the other hand, there are works which cannot be understood properly by the modern spectator unless he is able both to grasp all the subtleties of the plot and to penetrate the intangible atmosphere which enveloped both the actors and audience of the author's day. There are plays which cannot be appreciated unless they are presented in a form which attempts to create for the modern spectator conditions identical to those which the spectator of the past enjoyed. Such a play is Molière's *Dom Juan*. [... W]hen a director sets about staging *Dom Juan*,[1] his first task is to fill the stage and the auditorium with such a compelling atmosphere that the audience is bound to view the action through the prism of that atmosphere. [...]

The stage to be divided into two parts:

1. The proscenium, constructed according to architectural principles exclusively for 'reliefs' and the figures of the actors (who perform only on this area). The proscenium to have a forestage projecting deep into the auditorium. No footlights. No prompt-box.

2. The upstage area, intended exclusively for painted backdrops, is not used by the actors at all, except in the finale (downfall and immolation of Juan), and even then they will appear only on the dividing line between the two areas.

[1] Meyerhold's production of *Dom Juan* at the Alexandra Theatre in 1910 removed the footlights and the drop curtain, added a semi-circular apron over the orchestra pit, set up a conspicuous prompter and 'blackamoor' proscenium servants to change the set, and kept the lights on throughout except for the final confrontation.

124   Meyerhold calls for theatricality, 1911–1912

V. E. Meyerkhol'd, *O teatre*, pp. 143–73; translation from Braun, *Meyerhold*, pp. 119–42

[T]he mask, gesture, movement and plot are ignored by the contemporary actor. He has lost sight of the traditions of the great masters of the art of acting. [...]

In the contemporary theatre the comedian has been replaced by 'the educated reader'. [...] The cult of cabotinage, which I am sure will reappear with the restoration of the theatre of the past, will help the modern actor to rediscover the basic laws of theatricality. Those who are restoring the old theatre by delving into long-forgotten theories of dramatic art, old theatrical records and iconography, are already forcing actors to believe in the power and the importance of the art of acting. [...] The actor may get bored with perfecting his craft in order to perform in outdated plays; soon he will want not only to act but to compose for himself as well. Then at last we shall see the rebirth of the *theatre of improvisation*. [...]

The art of the grotesque is based on the conflict between form and content. The grotesque aims to subordinate psychologism to a decorative task. That is why in every theatre which has been dominated by the grotesque the aspect of design in its widest sense has been so important (for example, the Japanese theatre). Not only the settings, the architecture of the stage, and the theatre itself are decorative, but also the mime, movements, gestures and poses of the actors. Through being decorative they become expressive. For this reason the technique of the grotesque contains elements of the dance; only with the help of the dance is it possible to subordinate grotesque conceptions to a decorative task.

125   Evreinov insists on theatricality, 1912

N. N. Evreinov, Teatr kak takovoy (St Petersburg: Sovremennoe iskusstvo, 1912), pp. 77–86; translation from *The Theatre in Life*, ed. and trans. A. Nazaroff (London: George G. Harrap, 1927), pp. 135–52

Everything in the theatre is, and *must be*, conventional. [...] When I hear the theatre should be a temple, a school, a mirror, a tribune, or a pulpit, I answer: 'No. It should be just a theatre' [...], a self-sufficient artistic entity synthesizing, if necessary, all arts, making them serve its own ends and creating its own spiritual values, which are precious to us not because they serve this or that idea, or illustrate some moral doctrine, but because they are *theatrical*. There is 'beauty for beauty's sake'. There is also 'the theatre for the theatre's sake'. And only such a theatre is the real theatre.

Both *pure realism* and *pure symbolism* are irreconcilable with the true nature of the theatre: the former, because it aims at a useless duplication of life (and to duplicate life does not mean to serve art: it means to kill art); the latter, because it is in its very essence hostile to the direct and straightforward enjoyment of the visual perception. Professing, as I do, the principle of idealized theatricality, I advocate *conventional realism*, or *stage realism*, that is to say, the free imaginative creation of stage images which command belief to the spectator's receptive mind.

126   Kommissarzhevsky's philosophy of directing, 1915

F. Kommissarzhevsky, *Teatral'nyya prelyudii* (Theatrical Preludes) (Moscow, 1916), pp. 5–18

The theatrical spectacle is an integral artistic production *which must be conceived and fashioned by a single individual*. The director is not a dictator with a cat-o'-nine-tails. The director is the one who absorbs all the rest into himself *primus inter pares*. He has to have perspicacity and knowledge and animation. And *all* the participants in the spectacle are required to subject themselves willingly, passionately to the basic and cardinal methods of his work-plan. [...]

The director must reveal on stage the individual essence of an author in his interpretation.

Having penetrated the inner essence of a work, he must create an idea, a concept for the production, and express it inwardly and outwardly on stage.

The spectator–auditor must receive the concept *from everything that exists and acts on stage*, beginning with the nature of the psychological movement and the nature of the actor's 'inner experience', and ending with the way the curtain is raised and lowered.

[...] All this must be created by the same person who conceived the production, i.e. the director. And full harmony is necessary both between him and the designer (if the director does not act as designer too) and between the director and all the participants in the performance without exception. [...] The style of the scenery and the manner in which it is painted, like the style and manner of any artistically painted work, must without fail speak to the spectator of a certain definite artistic concept. And this designer's concept must express the concept of the director and actors and should be connected with them. For instance: I was staging *Prince Igor* for S. I. Zimin's opera.[1] The sets were painted in the spirit of icon-painting. This icon-painting was acknowledged to be indispensable to the general concept of the production, as an external expression of Russian romantic mysticism, which I also feel in *The Lay of Igor's Armament*[2] and at the base of all the scenes in Borodin's opera, except for those laid in the Polovtsian camp. But to express this romantic mysticism, mere scenery was not enough. It had to be justified by the character of the entire action on stage: by the psychology of the characters and their behaviour, by the patterns of their movements and groupings.

[1] Sergey Ivanovich Zimin (1875–1942) organized his own private opera in Moscow in 1904, absorbing most of the troupe of M. M. Ippolitov-Ivanov's private opera in the process. It was taken over by the State in 1917.

[2] *Slovo o polku Igoreve*, an epic masterpiece of Kievan Russia, describing a disastrous raid by the Russian princes against a Turkic tribe; probably written around 1200, though some think it a Romantic forgery.

127   A critic rejects the theatre, 1913

Yuly Aykhenval'd,[1] 'Otritsanie teatra' ('Rejecting the Theatre'), in *Slova o slovakh: kriticheskie ocherki* (Words on words: critical essays) (Petrograd: Izd. byvsh. M. A. Popova, 1923?), pp. 32–8

I think that the theatre in our time is undergoing not a crisis but a closure – not empirically, of course, but in the sense that its paradoxical nature, its lack of justifying principles, is being manifested. The stage, 'that monstrosity', is becoming increasingly irrelevant to the modern reader, the highly cultured elite. Its illusion fails to grip him, and the theatre's efforts, its shifts and dodges, are fatally wrecked upon the refined consciousness of the modern spectator. [...]

[...] The theatre is a spurious and illegitimate kind of art. It does not, after all, belong to the noble family of fine arts. It is not illustrious (although once associated with a religious cult). The delight of the plebs, the plaything of children, a pseudo-art, it responds to no pure aesthetic feeling in us. [...]

Art is above time, whereas the theatre, like life which it partially presents, is within time. [...] However talented the actor, he performs someone else's bidding, he executes someone else's theme; the actor is devoid of initiative. [...] The theatre illustrates, but that play would be very bad indeed which absolutely required the good offices of the stage to reveal its inner essence. [...] All that is very subtle and spiritual, *recherché* and psychological will fail to yield to embodiment on stage. A fairy tale or dream play cannot support the cumbersome realism of the footlights and so fades, folds in upon itself like a mimosa, from coarse contact with the property-man. [...]

The diminution of the author by the director, the criminal constriction of the playwright's autocracy, not only fails to bring about the theatre's independence, but simply exposes its lack of independence. The very need for a director (a need

which, without certain limitations, is incontestable), his very indispensability
[. . .] if only backstage, rocks the foundations of the theatre as rational entity. Who
is this third party? What are his necessary relations to the play? If he is himself an
individual, a creator, does not the playwright impede him? Does he not impede the
playwright? And does it not seem inevitable that he will constrict the actors?

[1] Yuly Aykhenval'd (1872–1928), a widely read critic and theatrical reviewer for *Russkaya mysl'*
(Russian thought), took the 'Crisis in the Theatre' to be a token of its irrelevance and imminent
demise. His lecture 'The End of Theatre' (later retitled 'Rejecting the Theatre') was frequently read
and republished. The practical effect of this attack was to compel workers in the theatre to close
ranks. It provoked a volume, *V sporakh o teatre* (Debating the Theatre, 1914), in which Nemirovich-
Danchenko, Kommissarzhevsky and other luminaries undertook to confute Aykhenval'd. Evreinov,
whom Aykhenval'd had taken to task in his lecture, replied in an impassioned article, a 'polemic
from the heart', in the avant-garde journal *Strelets* (The Bowman).

128   The first performance of *Vladimir Mayakovsky*,[1] 1913

A. A. Mgebrov,[2] *Zhizn' v teatre* (Leningrad: Academia 1929–32), vol. II, pp. 278–80

A crowd had already gathered in the auditorium. [. . .] I sat down next to Velemir
Khlebnikov.[3] He's a futurist too. The lights went down and the curtain went up. A
half-mysterious light lit the stage which had been draped with cotton or calico;
that and a high backdrop of black cardboard constituted almost all the scenery.
What this cardboard was supposed to represent neither I nor anyone else
understood, but the strange fact of the matter was – it made an impression; there
was substance to it, movement . . . It was as if I saw represented on this cardboard
a very real impression of a city I had seen at some time or other.

The participants in the play filed out from behind the curtains one after another.
The participants were cardboard: living dolls. The public tried laughing, but the
laughter died out. Why? Because it wasn't funny at all. [. . .] And when the
laughter died out that first moment . . . you could sense at once that the audience
was strangely alert.

Mayakovsky made his entrance. He was wearing no make-up and his own suit.
He seemed above the crowd, above the city, for he is the city's own son and it has
raised a monument to him. What for? Because, apparently, he is a poet. 'Mock me
if you will,' he seemed to be saying. 'I stand among you as a monument. Laugh . . .
I am a poet. My wealth and my solace are love. I am a force striving upwards,
whereas you are the foothills below. [. . .]'

Of course, Mayakovsky didn't actually say any of this, but it seemed to me as if
that was what he was saying. When he sat down on a cardboard cut-out
representing a stump, the thousand-year-old man started to speak. All are
cardboard dolls – they are his dreams, the dreams of a human soul, alone,
forgotten, persecuted in the chaos of movement.

'Don't go, Mayakovsky', the audience shouted mockingly as he, absent-mindedly, emotionally, gathered into a big sack all the tears and newspaper pages, his cardboard toys and the audience's mockery – into a big, burlap sack; he gathered them up as if to set out for eternity, the endlessly vast expanse of space. [...]

Of course, it was badly performed, the actors mispronounced words and didn't understand what they were saying, but they had, it seemed to me, something that came from the depths. The audience weren't such rude listeners that their whistles and catcalls managed to drown out everything that came across. Twice I was moved to tears and emotionally overwrought.

[1] Vladimir Vladimirovich Mayakovsky (1893–1930), art student and Bolshevik, while still in his teens signed the futurist manifesto 'A Slap in the Face of Public Taste' (1912). Convinced that the theatre had to be revived by the cinema, he worked on a tragedy and a screenplay simultaneously: the tragedy took its title from a censor who thought the author's name was the play's, and it was first performed at the Luna-Park Theatre in St Petersburg on 2 December 1913 on a double-bill with Kruchënykh's futurist 'opera' *Victory over the Sun* (see 129 and 130). A short two-act play in verse, it was directed by its author who also played the Poet; the abstract sets and costumes were by P. N. Filonov and I. S. Shkolnik.

[2] Aleksandr Avel'evich Mgebrov (1884–1966) had acted at the MAT (1907), Kommissarzhevskaya's theatre (1908–11) and Evreinov's Antique Theatre (1910–12); his memoirs are an entertaining account of the backstage reality of many of the innovations of the time.

[3] Velemir (actually Viktor) Vladimirovich Khlebnikov (1885–1922): 'trans-mental' poet and founder of Russian futurism, whose complex theories renounced symbolism and ideas for the associative power of sounds and etymologies.

129   The meaning of *Victory over the Sun*, 1913

A. Kruchënykh,[1] *Nash vykhod* (Our Way Out, unpublished memoirs), in Camilla Gray, *The Great Experiment: Russian Art 1863–1922* (London: Thames and Hudson, 1962), p. 186

The scenery and stage-effects were as I expected and wanted. A blinding light from the projectors. The scenery by Malevich[2] was made of big sheets – triangles, circles, bits of machinery. The actors' masks reminded one of modern gas-masks. The *Likari* [*Visagers*, a futurist coinage] reminded one of moving machines. Malevich's costumes were cubist-like,[3] made of cardboard and wire. They transformed the human anatomy, and the actors moved, held and directed by the rhythm dictated by the artist and director. What particularly struck the audience in the plays were the songs of the Coward (in vowels) and of the Aviator (entirely in consonants). Professional actors sang. The public demanded an encore, but the actors were shy and did not come out. The choral song of the Gravediggers, which was composed with unexpected intervals and dissonances, was performed to a completely furious public. (The point of the opera is to destroy one of the greatest artistic conventions, the sun in the given instance. In men's minds there exist certain means of human communication which have been created by human thought. The futurists wish to free themselves from this ordering of the world, from these means of thought communication, they wish to transform the world into chaos, to break the established values into pieces and from these pieces to create anew.)

[1] Aleksey Eliseevich Kruchënykh (1886–1968), in his pamphlet *Trio* (1913), had queried, 'A word is wider than its meaning ... Each letter, each sound has its relevance ... Why not renounce ideas, why not write with idea-words, with words freely made?'

[2] Kazimir Severinovich Malevich (1878–1953) was strongly influenced in his attempt to develop a new pictorial language by the European avant-garde and native Russian folk-art, combining cubism with devices from the icon and the twopence-coloured woodcut.

[3] Several Russian artists, such as Vladimir Tatlin, had seen cubist works in Paris, but cubist paintings were also on view in the Shchukin collection in Moscow and at various Russian exhibitions before 1915.

130   What the spectator saw in *Victory over the Sun*, 1913

From an interview given by Malevich and Matyushin[1] to *Den'* (Day) (December 1913); translation in Gray, *The Great Experiment*, pp. 189–90

The curtain flew up, and the spectator found himself in front of a second one of white calico on which the author himself, the composer and the designer were represented in three different sets of hieroglyphics. The first musical chord sounded, and the second curtain parted in two, and an announcer and troubadour appeared and an I-don't-know-what with bloody hands and a big cigarette. He began to read the prologue. The prologue ended. Old war-cries sounded, and the new curtain again divided in two. From above, a piece of cardboard was lowered, covered all over with war-like colours. On it, two life-like warrior figures of two knights were depicted. All this in a blood-red colour. The drop-curtains were abandoned. Now the action begins. The most diverse masks came forward and walked off. The back-cloths were changed, and the moods changed. Ear-splitting noises sounded and gun-shots rang out.

[1] Mikhail Vasil'evich Matyushin (1861–1934) had been associated with World of Art; a painter as well as a composer, he later invented the concept of 'zorved' (roughly, 'visuknow'), an amalgam of physical vision and spiritual intuition.

131   *Thamyris the Cithærist* at the Kamerny Theatre, 1916

A. Koonen,[1] *Stranitsy zhizni* (Pages of life) (Moscow: Iskusstvo, 1975), pp. 228–32

Thamyris the Cithærist[2] [...] precisely initiated the tragedy side of the Kamerny Theatre's repertoire, while, for the first time on stage, constructivism, which later became a substantial aspect of theatrical practice, was utilized.

In his first discussion [...] Tairov[3] spoke of the form of the production and [...] the 'scenic atmosphere'. 'On stage there must reign an absolute harmonic unity of emotion, rhythm and all the formal structures', he said. [...]

Let me remind you of Annensky's nearly forgotten play. Its theme is the destruction of an audacious musician who has flung a challenge at the gods. The son of a Thracian king, devoted to playing the cithæra, he invites the Muses to a competition and loses the match. Angered by the mortal's audacity, the Muses deprive him of sight and musical talent, and the gods condemn him to eternal wandering.

While he was working out the inner content of each image in the play, Tairov also doggedly searched for the speech and movement that would define the character and form of tragedy. [...] 'Speech in tragedy should be very simple, strictly subservient to emotion, but necessarily observant of the verse rhythm,' he explained. [...] Tairov advised: in those passages where the text is exceptionally complex, do not stress it, but strengthen the general emotional and plastic expressivity of a given moment. This had a beautiful result. [...] In certain passages Tairov began to translate the stanzas into demi-song and recitative. This turned out to be absolutely organic psychologically. [...]

Ékster's[4] design, which on opening night had the effect of a detonating bomb, was, strange as it may seem, unreservedly accepted both by exacting connoisseurs and peevish bourgeois critics. [...] For the first time, the stage space was rhythmically organized. There are two principles in *Thamyris*: the boisterous, Bacchic Dionysian one and the sublime harmonic Apollonian one. These two principles determined the rhythmic structure of constructivism. Curiously, the spectator definitely associated the heaps of cubes on stage with heaps of rocks in a savage landscape, and the conical shapes with pyramidal poplars or cypresses. As Tairov had promised, constructivism offered the actors splendid opportunities. The dances of the mænads and satyrs, arranged to a syncopated rhythm, made a great impression on the spectator with their boldness and lovely movement. A similar powerful and profound impression was produced by the slow, gliding gait of the blind Thamyris, and his regal movements were emphasized by the gentle, broad flight of stairs.

[...] Salzmann's[5] lighting seemed absolutely organically connected with the artistic style of the production. It filled the whole scenic space. The lighting used no footlights or soffits or spotlights – the light was limpid, sometimes bright and gay, sometimes overcast. At first, Salzmann's lighting perplexed us actors. When his lights poured on stage for the first time in rehearsal, it made the usual theatrical make-up seem quite unacceptable. The actors seemed to be painted for a shabby fairground showbooth. Then Tairov got the idea of graphic make-up. Only the eyes and eyebrows were emphasized, the facial complexion remained natural, one's own. Because the actors' bodies were largely naked, another idea dawned on him – to emphasize the relief of the muscles with subtly shaded lines [which made] the bodies seem larger and especially powerful.

[. . . The première took place on 2 November 1916.] A tense stillness in the auditorium, no outward signs of approbation. We couldn't figure out if it were a success or not. When it ended, the audience was in no hurry to leave, but heatedly exchanged impressions. [. . .] Imagine our amazement when the next day unanimously laudatory notices appeared in the press.

[1] Alisa Georgievna Koonen (1889–1974), actress and co-founder (with her husband, Tairov) of the Moscow Kamerny (Chamber) Theatre (1914).
[2] Innokenty Fëdorovich Annensky (1856–1909), classical scholar, critic and poet, made his living as a school inspector. His last play, *Thamyris the Cithærist* (*Famira-Kifared*, 1906), was the only one to be staged.
[3] Aleksandr Yakovlevich Kornblit, known as Tairov (1885–1950) was one of the most original of this century's directors. He founded (with his wife, Alisa Koonen) the Moscow Kamerny Theatre, rejecting both Stanislavsky's and Meyerhold's approaches, striving to attain musicality and plasticity in his productions. He helped to introduce Western plays to the Soviet stage (Wilde, Shaw, O'Neill).
[4] Aleksandra Aleksandrovna Ékster (née Grigorovich, 1884–1949): a painter who attempted to reform scene and costume design in the direction of 'architecturality'; at the Kamerny 1916–21. She emigrated to the West in the mid-1920s.
[5] Alexander von Salzmann (b. 1870), a Russian painter and virtuoso of technical lighting, who had been working in Hellerau with Appia and Dalcroze from 1910. Inspired by Fortuny's ideas of reflected light, he became the principal executant of Tairov's desire for 'chromatic energy' in stage-lighting.

132   Evreinov parodies naturalism in a cabaret, 1915

N. N. Evreinov,[1] *P'esy iz repertuara 'Krivogo Zerkala'* (Plays from the Crooked Mirror Repertoire) (Petrograd: Academia, 1923), pp. 47–80; translation in L. Senelick, ed., *Russian Satiric Comedy* (New York: Performing Arts Journal Press, 1983), pp. 96–9

The Director appears before the curtain. He is in evening dress, with white gloves, impeccably shaven and coiffed, and beaming with complacency.

[. . .] Today's première, ladies and gentlemen, is the total liquidation of old-fashioned, conventional art, steeped through and through with falsity! Today's première is a triumphal victory for unadorned truth in the theatre. Today's première is the greatest event in the universal history of dramatic art. [. . .]

(*He exits. The orchestra plays the overture to 'Faust'. [. . .] At the conclusion of the overture an unendurable silence ensues, during which the conductor leaves his place and a second curtain rises.*

On stage, almost at the footlights themselves, towers the notorious fourth wall. It is constructed with all the realism of the stone-mason's art and observes all the archaeological findings relating to German architecture of the late Middle Ages. The half-light of early morning. The stage is empty. In one of the windows on the second storey we can see the flickering light of an oil lamp; judging by the two or three retorts, globe and skull visible on the window-sill, it is the window of Doctor Faust's study. As a matter of fact, his dishevelled shadow flashes by! Then, at last, his characteristic old man's cough is heard! . . . As if in response to it, somewhere far, far away, the bell of the townhall rings out, tolling five o'clock in the morning. The light gradually grows brighter. At the right we can hear the drunken singing (in Middle High German) of the guild artisans to the theme from the first chorus in 'Faust'. [. . .])

(From right to left passes a band of youths who have been up all night carousing, while one of them plays a Dutch chorus on a fiddle.)

((After ten minutes of more details from everyday medieval German life) the auditorium is filled with the stench of saltfish, onions and pork. [. . .])

(Marguerite and Martha appear right. Both in dresses made of ticking. Marguerite, barefoot, holds a spinning-wheel. They stop just in front of the study window of Faust who, having heard Marguerite's bawdily vulgar laugh, reappears in the window, this time holding the poisoned chalice.)

MARGUERITE   *(admiring the spinning-wheel)* Ach, Gott! mag das meine Mutter sein!

MARTHA   O, du glückliche Kreatur! . . .

MARGUERITE   Ah, seh Sie nur! Ach, schau Sie nur! . . .

MARTHA   Geht! Ist schon Zeit!

MARGUERITE   *(slowly exiting with Martha, sings, playing the spinning-wheel)* 'Es war ein König in Thule.'

---

[1] *The Fourth Wall (Chetvërtaya tsena)*, Evreinov's favourite among his own plays for the Crooked Mirror, had three targets: the attempts of the Moscow Art Theatre to create veristic sets, costumes and psychological realism; Lapinsky's Theatre for Musical Drama, which tried to demolish outworn conventions in opera and make the productions as naturalistic as possible; and Kommissarzhevsky's *Faust* at Nezlobin's Theatre, in which Mephistopheles was portrayed as Faust's *alter ego*. In this skit, a producer, intent on innovation, stages Gounod's opera by eliminating the music, translating recitative into Middle High German, combining Mephistopheles and Faust (played by an aged actor who is made to live on the set) and, finally, erecting a fourth wall.

Scandinavia, 1849–1912

Edited and translated by INGA-STINA EWBANK

I The development of a national theatre in Norway

In nineteenth-century Norway – a sovereign territory under the Swedish king since the end of Danish rule in 1814 – the search for a truly national theatre was part of a larger nationalist movement seeking independence from foreign, and particularly Danish, language and culture. It was not until 1899 that Nationaltheatret was established in Christiania (Oslo), in the magnificent building which still stands midway between the Royal Palace and the Parliament, flanked by the statues of Henrik Ibsen and Bjørnstjerne Bjørnson. Until the early 1860s, the country's leading theatre, the Christiania Theatre, was generally perceived as being at best passive, at worst antagonistic, in its attitude to nationalist endeavours. The Christiania Theatre company had been formed in 1827 by a Swede, Johan Peter Strömberg; and when their first playhouse burned down, a new theatre was built in Bank Square in 1837. Almost inevitably, its architect and designer were Danish, as were its actors; but the first production was Andreas Munch's pseudo-historical play *The Youth of King Sverre* – the winner in a play competition arranged in order to open the Christiania Theatre 'in a fashion worthy of the nation, with the performance of an original Norwegian dramatic work'. Yet, in its first season the theatre gave 101 performances of 60 different plays, only 2 of which were Norwegian, as against 18 Danish and 30 translated from the French. A repertoire of short runs was necessary in a town of (in 1837) no more than 25,000 inhabitants (as against Copenhagen's c.120,000 and Stockholm's c.80,000). There was little or no native dramatic heritage to draw from, and for financial reasons the theatre management was none too keen on new Norwegian plays; the authors had to be paid fees, whereas translated drama could be had for free. The economical situation was precarious, often hand-to-mouth, as the Norwegian Parliament remained unwilling, on principle, to subsidize theatre.

Some of these preconditions were slow to change: when Bjørnstjerne Bjørnson reported in 1866 on his first season as artistic director of the Christiania Theatre, in which there had been 140 performances of altogether 60 plays, 31 of them new in the repertoire, he lamented that 'our theatre-going public is too small', and that in consequence even great and famous plays could only expect four or five performances (*Aftenbladet*, 25 June 1866). But the proportion of Norwegian plays, though still inevitably small, had by then increased (and included three of Bjørnson's own plays); and there were a number of accomplished Norwegian actors and actresses to speak the national language.

The Christiania Theatre had depended in its early years on Danish acting talent. It was only in 1850 that its first Norwegian actors were engaged: the same year as Ole Bull (1810–80) founded the Norwegian Theatre in Bergen, and two years before the opening of the Christiania Norwegian Theatre (which, to avoid confusion, will hereafter be referred to by its Norwegian name, the Norske Theater). Both these were, as their names indicate, programmatically nationalist in the way the Christiania Theatre was not. The Norske Theater went bankrupt in the 1862/3 season, and the eventual absorption of its actors into the Christiania Theatre marks the end of what had become known as *Theaterstriden* (the War of the Theatres) and the beginnings of a national theatre in Christiania – always remembering that Bergen had the first truly Norwegian theatre.

The 1850s saw the height of the War of the Theatres. The artistic director of the Christiania Theatre from 1851 until he was dismissed in the midst of the 1862/3 season, was Carl Peter Borgaard (1801–68) who, as a Dane, had many opponents among the nationalists. The directorate was accused, generally, of lacking an ideology and, more specifically, of malpractices which suggested an anti-Norwegian bias. The strength of feeling can be gauged from the polemics in contemporary newspapers, not least in the contributions by the two young men who were to become their country's foremost dramatists, Bjørnstjerne Bjørnson (1832–1910) and Henrik Ibsen (1828–1906), both of whom also at various times worked as artistic directors or stage-instructors at each of the three theatres.

Two separate, if related, issues produced two particularly embattled moments. In May 1856 the Christiania Theatre took on an inexperienced Danish actor, Ferdinand Schmidt, nominally for a 'guest performance' but clearly with a view to permanent engagement. This brought to a head the nationalist resentment at seeing new, untrained Danish actors being employed where Norwegian ones might have been given a chance. Bjørnstjerne Bjørnson led two loud and vigorous demonstrations in the theatre: on the second night, 8 May, the sound of 600 whistles greeted the unfortunate Schmidt. In 1858 the theatre refused to put on Ibsen's *Vikings at Helgeland*, although Borgaard had earlier accepted it; and this provoked Ibsen to a violent attack on the policies of the theatre with regard to original Norwegian drama.

In subsequent decades, the two Bjørnsons, father and son, were hugely influential in 'nationalizing' the choice of plays and the language spoken in the Christiania Theatre. Although he was its director only for a short period, 1865–7, Bjørnstjerne Bjørnson's historical plays, and in the 1870s and 1880s his realistic prose plays (the earliest antedating Ibsen's), became important in the repertoire. When, in 1870, a group of leading actors revolted against the direction of the theatre, he directed the dissident company in the old Norske Theater, where they played until 1873. They returned when the Swedish director Ludvig Josephson was appointed to direct the Christiania Theatre (1874–7); he staged a number of plays by Bjørnson and by Ibsen, including *Peer Gynt* (ur-première) in a production which ran for thirty-seven performances. The consolidation of a genuinely Norwegian company was continued under the long directorship (1879–99) of Hans Schrøder; but the really influential force in the late 1880s and early 1890s was Bjørn Bjørnson (1859–1942), who joined the company in 1884, after eight years of working experience in European theatre in Vienna, with the Meiningen company, and in Switzerland, Paris and Hamburg. His concerns for the Norwegian language and for a realistic style of acting are exemplified in the excerpt from his reminiscences of *The Old*

Theatre (136). As the first director of Nationaltheatret he was to lead Norwegian theatre into its 'Golden Age' – a period of greatness which owed nearly everything to the ensemble of Norwegian players built up, and the Norwegian plays written, since 1850. (See Laurence Senelick, ed., *National Theatre in Northern and Eastern Europe, 1746–1900*, Cambridge University Press, 1991), esp. document 112.)

133   Ibsen's case for a Norwegian theatre, 1858

Henrik Ibsen, 'Et Traek af Christiania Danske Theaters Bestyrelse', *Aftenbladet*, 10 March 1858[1]

I learned that the controlling body of the theatre had come to a decision – God knows when – the point of which was: 'that the financial situation of the theatre, and its prospects in the near future as regards income in relation to already committed and inevitable expenses, are such that they do not allow the theatre during the current season to pay fees for original works; consequently it will not be possible to perform the play submitted by Mr Ibsen, *The Vikings at Helgeland*,[2] in the current season'.

There is more to this remarkable decision than meets the eye. The controlling body of the Christiania Theatre has here plainly and clearly announced its policy. [...] The point here is not the rejection of a play already accepted; what is important is the theatre's own declaration that 'in the near future' it will be unable to support, encourage or indeed have anything to do with Norwegian dramatic literature.

Now, if it was only the financial *means* that were missing, it would not be so bad; this could always be put right; but what is missing is the *will*.

For, if the directorate had had the smallest spark of interest in staging the play in question, they could of course – instead of taking that decision – have turned to me with a request that the payment of my fee be deferred until the times were more favourable.[3]

But apparently the directorate have foreseen my willingness to accept such an arrangement, and have therefore preferred the other way out, as being more in agreement with their policy.

It was to this same theatre that a speaker in Parliament gave the testimony that it was an institution which welcomed Norwegian dramatic works, and performed them well – a testimony that provided one of the reasons for voting a subsidy of *Nothing* to the Norwegian Theatre![4] [...]

But it is good that that Christiania Theatre has at last spoken out; for some twenty years now it has insisted on defending its ever-more-ailing existence; step by step and inch by inch, and protected by prejudice and the indifference of the public, it has surrendered the broad basis on which it rested originally. [...]

But it is, as I said, good that this declaration has at last been made; the peace in our dramatic world must and will now be broken, and the public must take a stand *for* or *against*; for the present situation is untenable. *Either* we must have a Norwegian theatre which understands and has the power to act in the interest of national art, *or else* we must, one and all, support the so-called national stage: we must, one and all, flock there when, in the future, it treats us three times a week to translations raked up from all the corners of the earth.[5] No more national sympathies! [...]

And yet the time has now come when an influential national stage could be founded. If the Danish theatre, with its foreign predilections, its undemocratic impact, did not stand as an obstacle in the way, then it would be possible to build a company out of the best Norwegian talents at the three theatres[6] – a company which realized the idea of a national theatre, a theatre which worked hand in hand with the literature that is now coming into being among us. Whereas this literature is now barred not only from its own stage but also from that of the Norske Theater, in that the Christiania Theatre prevents the merging of those talents which are absolutely necessary for the production of a truly artistic result.

[1] Also reprinted in *Henrik Ibsen: Samlede Verker* (*Hundreårsutgave*), eds. Francis Bull, Halvdan Koht and Didrik Arup Seip (Oslo: Gyldendal, 1928–57), vol. XV (1930), pp. 190–202.

[2] This heroic saga play was eventually performed on 24 November 1858 at the Christiania Norske Theater, where Ibsen was then artistic director. Its first performance at the Christiania Theatre was on 11 April 1861.

[3] This practice prevailed when, as often happened, the Christiania Theatre's finances were precarious. As late as 1876 Edvard Grieg was told in May that he would have to wait until the beginning of the next theatre season to be paid for the music he had composed for the production of *Peer Gynt* which had been playing since 24 February.

[4] In 1854 there was some Government support for a grant of 2,000 Spd to the Christiania Theatre (1 speciedaler = 4 kroner (about 40 pence) in 1996 currency). Simultaneously the Norske Theater and the Bergen Theatre had applied for, respectively, 1,000 and 2,000 Spd. A parliamentary committee recommended, and Parliament unanimously agreed (a) that it was impossible to subsidize all three theatres, (b) that the Christiania Theatre should have preference, but (c) that it would be wrong to 'burden the State with expenses of a kind not justified by a higher and indisputable necessity'. In the end, therefore, all the theatres received '*Nothing*' (submissions and replies quoted in T. H. Blanc, *Christiania Theaters Historie 1827–1877* (Christiania: Cappelen, 1899), pp. 157–8; and by the same author, *Norges første nationale scene* (Christiania: Cappelen, 1884), pp. 221–9). In an emotional article in *Morgenbladet*, 21 June 1857, Bjørnson pleaded with Parliament not to turn down, yet again, the application for theatre subsidy.

[5] cf. Bjørnson's description of the typical repertoire (135).

[6] The three theatres are, of course, those named in note 4, above.

134   Ibsen's case opposed by Richard Petersen

Richard Petersen, in *Christiania-Posten*, 21 March 1858[1]

Mr Ibsen is, as a dramatist, a great nonentity whom the nation can feel no impulse to cherish and protect. *The Feast at Solhaug*[2] is far too short of freshness and originality [...] and the work that followed, *Lady Inger*,[3] is lacking in idealism and poetry to such a degree that one can only be amazed at it. Every single character in that play is marked with the stamp of baseness, and the development of characters takes place not through action but in monologues. [...] Given all this, Mr Ibsen must understand that the public is not keenly looking forward to his *Vikings*, and that these are not the times to allow on stage a play that is apparently of only middling merit. [...]

The cry for things Norwegian and the satisfaction with things Norwegian show a lack of taste which puts great obstacles in the way of proper intellectual activity in this country.[4] [...] Norwegian dramatic literature cannot really be said to have begun to exist. [...] After this, Ibsen can never more come to the Christiania Theatre.

[1] Richard Petersen (1821–1908), in 1858 a copying clerk in a government department and later a prison governor, was also the drama critic of *Christiania-Posten*, a paper regarded as the ally of the Christiania Theatre. Ibsen, in his reply to Petersen, which stretched over three issues of *Aftenbladet* (25 and 31 March and 10 April), called him 'the critical bondslave of *Christiania-Posten*'. In 1864, as a member of the board of directors of the Christiania Theatre, he was to dissent from the board's decision to offer Bjørnson the post of artistic director: 'It seems to me a dangerous experiment to place this impetuous young poet at the head of the Theatre' (letter of 11 April 1864, in Statsarkivet, Oslo; see also Øyvind Anker, 'Ibseniana og Bjørnsoniana fra Kristianiateaterns arkiver', *Edda*, 43 (1956), 111–60).

[2] Ibsen's ballad play, written in 1855 and first performed at the Norwegian Theatre in Bergen on 2 January 1856 – his first success in the theatre. It had six performances at the Christiania Theatre in 1856, opening on 13 March.

[3] Ibsen's historical tragedy, written in 1854 and first performed at the Norwegian Theatre in Bergen on 2 January 1855, was refused by Borgaard in 1857. Ibsen staged it himself at the Christiania Norske Theatre on 11 and 13 April 1859; and it was finally performed at the Christiania Theatre in 1875 to mark Ibsen's birthday, 20 March.

[4] This was a common line with the Norwegian literary establishment, many of whom regarded the depature of Danish actors as spelling doom for the Norwegian theatre: see Ibsen's 1859 poem, 'Åpent brev' ('Open Letter', translated by John Northam, *Ibsen's Poems*, Norwegian University Press, 1986, pp. 49–52), which is part of his row in verse with the 'poet' H. Ø. Blom.

135   Bjørnstjerne Bjørnson champions indigenous theatre, 1858

Bjørnstjerne Bjørnson, Letter in *Bergensposten*, 28 March 1858[1]

The outrageous attack on Norwegian playwrights, in support of the Danish stage, which has been made in *Christiania-Posten*, must be reversed, if there is to be any meaning in what we are doing – indeed, if there is to be any meaning in being a nation. But it has to be done with every possible respect for the Danish company that, until now, have served their guiding idea with rare faithfulness. It has to be done with a thank-you for everything until now – only, we have to add that now there is a different guiding idea, which also demands different servants.

The Christiania Theatre, as a home for the arts, has been founded on Scribean comedy, Danish vaudeville and partly (but only partly) on Oehlenschläger's tragedies.[2] All this is now old and has become obsolete, just as Christiania-Danish actors have become obsolete. [...] Oehlenschläger's tragedies will always be there, but like those tall signposts which stick out above the snow. We shall play them now and then in order to remind ourselves of where we used to be. [...]

Ibsen's play [*Vikings at Helgeland*] is *dramatically* (whatever else my opinion of it may be) *the foremost so far written in Norway*. [...] The reason why it is not to be performed this season cannot possibly be that it would not be a success. [...] I am dumbfounded when I think of these people, with such incredible insolence, declaring it lacking in that theatrical power which holds an audience. It is not Borgaard; it cannot possibly be Borgaard, but the cruder business sense of the Norwegian board of directors.[3]

[1] Also reprinted in Chr. Collin and H. Eitrem, eds., *Bjørnstjerne Bjørnson: Artikler og Taler* (Kristiania and Kjøbenhavn: Gyldendal, 1912) pp. 158–67.

[2] This is largely borne out by the lists of plays staged in the period. Adam Oehlenschläger (1779–1850), Danish Romantic poet and dramatist, was generally seen as Scandinavia's answer to Shakespeare and Goethe.

[3] Referring to the fact that fees had to be paid to Norwegian playwrights.

136   Bjørn Bjørnson remembers the Christiania Theatre

Bjørn Bjørnson, *Det gamle teater: Kunsten og menneskene* (Oslo: Aschenhough, 1937), pp. 17–18 and 98–9

I stood in front of the main entrance and looked at [the old Theatre]. When it was built, many years ago, I thought, it was definitely seen as a palace. A building worthy of our art. But those who appeared in it at that time – the actors – were chiefly Danish. It didn't occur to the Norsemen that it was possible to speak Norwegian on stage, 'ungraceful and harsh' as it was, compared with the supple Danish language, dancing gracefully on tiptoe. My father had told me a great deal about those student days when the young, led by him, exploded in the famous and notorious battle of the theatre where they screamed and shouted and whistled against the Danish tongue in our theatre.[1] [...]

He told me, in Vienna, about Lucie Wolf,[2] our Norwegian actress. She sprang like an apparition, young and beautiful, on to the virtually Danish-speaking stage in Christiania. Danced in, on tiptoe, more gracefully than anyone before her. Danced in, to Norwegian rhythms and with a ringing Bergen voice. It seemed to the small town like an unimagined joy. [...]

The whole town was in love with her. Then she married a Danish actor.[3] To those who felt that we had given Denmark more than enough of what was ours, it felt almost like an act of treason.

But on the Norwegian stage they went on speaking Danish. [. . .] I told the most Norwegian theatre director they had had: my father, who had let it pass. In Vienna I told him [i.e. how strange it sounded].

'So that's how it is, Bjørn. So the ear alone is not enough. You have to hear with your feelings. And I couldn't do it. Strange.'

I promised myself, as I stood in front of the theatre, that I would make them speak the harshest Norwegian consonants I could dig up.

I kept my promise. Not without a gentle resistance from some of my colleagues. When I left Christiania Theatre after nine years, *Verdens Gang*[4] published a thanks to me from the harsh consonants because I had given them a chance. [. . .]

Schrøder and I discussed *The Wild Duck*[5] for ages. For this we *had* to have elbow-room. We had a brilliant cast.

'We must work our way from the centre outwards. Speech by speech – to make it a work of art on stage. Worthy of the text.'

It was the first Norwegian production of a modern play since I came [to the theatre]. Elbow-room meant a French one-acter and various other pieces.[6]

We managed to give *The Wild Duck* twenty rehearsals. Something just about unheard of at this impoverished theatre which had to run panting from play to play as best it could. We were all entranced. It went without saying that we rehearsed on Sundays as well. After church, at noon. Mrs Gundersen[7] said to me:

'I never thought I'd do this. I go to church every Sunday. And all Sunday, except for the evening, I have this need to do my own thing. I'm religious, but not a kill-joy. Last night I was so tired I didn't have the strength to say my prayers. I just folded my hands and said: "Good night, Lord". And went happily to sleep.'

---

[1] On 'the War of the Theatres', see 133–135.

[2] Bjørn Bjørnson went to Vienna in 1877 to study music but soon transferred to the drama school of the Konservatorium. His father visited him during this formative period. The long career of Lucie Wolf, née Johannesen (1833–1902), is virtually an epitome of Norwegian theatre history in the second half of the nineteenth century. She acted at three major theatres, and was directed by Ibsen, both in Bergen and in Christiania, and by both Bjørnsons. Her musical talent brought her fame, early in *syngespil* and vaudeville and later in serious opera; but at the Christiania Theatre, which she had joined in 1853, she came to take a series of major Ibsen parts. She was Lona Hessel in *Pillars of Society* from 1879 to 1899; Ibsen especially asked for her to play Gina in *The Wild Duck*, 1885; and at the National Theatre she played Mrs Stockman in *An Enemy of the People*, 1899.

[3] Nicolai Wolf (1824–75), who, trained at the Royal Theatre in Copenhagen where he also made his début (1848), was attached to the Christiania Theatre from 1852 to 1874 – a reminder that, despite the pressure to replace Danish with Norwegian as a theatre language, the hostility to Danish actors was not universal.

[4] Infuential liberal newspaper published in Christiania, weekly (1868–85) and daily (1885–1923).

[5] Ibsen's *Wild Duck* opened at the Christiania Theatre on 11 January 1885, two days after the ur-première at the Norwegian Theatre in Bergen. Before embarking on the production, Schrøder sent a telegram to Ibsen in Rome, which elicited from the playwright a famous letter of advice on the casting, lighting and theatrical mode ('truth to nature and an air of reality') of the play (20 November 1884; in *Samlede Verker*, XVIII, pp. 46–8).

[6] Plays, that is, which the company could put on with a minimum of rehearsal while concentrating their efforts on *The Wild Duck*.

[7] Laura Gundersen (1832–98) made her début in 1850 at the Christiania Theatre as the first and for some time only Norwegian player there. Except for the years 1870–2, when she joined a dissident group, led by Bjørnstjerne Bjørnson, playing at the old Norske Theater, her whole long career was tied to the Christiania Theatre, where she was particularly famed for tragic roles, such as, in Shakespeare: Lady Macbeth, Ophelia, Desdemona, Volumnia, Hermione (and also Portia); in Ibsen: Lady Inger, Hjørdis (*Vikings at Helgeland*), Ellida Wangel (*The Lady from the Sea*). Ibsen suggested her for the role of Mrs Sørby in *The Wild Duck* (see note 5, above). In 1888 he 'gladly' agreed to her request to put on Act IV of *Brand* (then unperformed in its entirety in Norway) as part of the jubilee celebration of her actor-husband Sivard Gundersen (see 137), and in 1896 he sent her flowers on the occasion of her hundredth performance in the role of Hjørdis. (See Blanc, *Christiania Theaters Historie, passim*; and Ibsen's letter of 20 March 1896, in *Samlede Verker*, vol. xviii, p. 381.)

137   Members of the Christiania Theatre Company move to the National Theatre, 1899

Drawing by Olaf Gulbransson[1]. From A. Rønneberg, *Nationaltheatret gjennom femti år* (Oslo, 1949)

[1] As a cartoonist, Olaf Gulbransson (1873–1958) had his finger on the pulse of Norwegian political and cultural life (see the illustrated catalogue of the 1962 exhibition of his work at the National Gallery, Oslo). He won European fame and spent most of his life in Germany, where he became an Honorary Professor at the University of Munich.

[2] This kindly caricature captures, against the background of the characteristic façade of the Christiania Theatre, the spirit, in both senses of the word, with which its actors and actresses moved on to form the core of the National Theatre company. The new beginning did not rule out continuity,

especially as Bjørn Bjørnson (not in the drawing), who had both acted and directed at the Christiania Theatre (see pp. 262–3 and 136), was the first director of Nationaltheatret, 1899–1907, and returned for a second period, 1923–7. The tradition of ensemble playing, to an audience familiar with many of the players, was assured.

³ The drawing also catches, in the present of 1899, both the past and the future of Norwegian theatre, so dependent on a number of remarkable actors and actresses. Theatre careers here caught in characteristic individual *gestes* stretch back as far as 1853 and forward to 1947.

⁴ The drawing depicts, from left to right: Jens Wang, Per Winge, Sofie Parelius, Jens Selmer, Gyda Christensen, Egil Eide, Johanne Dybwad, Ludvig Müller, Hans Schrøder, Sivard Gundersen, Lucie Wolf, Ludvig Bergh.

Jens Wang (1859–1926): appointed 'scene-painter' at the National Theatre ahead of the move, in 1898, he was to remain attached to that theatre until 1918, when he opened his own atelier – from which he continued to supply scene-designs to theatres in Christiania and elsewhere. His appointment at the Christiania Theatre in 1889 had been epoch-making, as until then Norwegian theatres had mainly recruited designers from abroad, particularly from Denmark.

Per Winge (1858–1937): conductor of the Christiania Theatre's orchestra since 1894, he did not join in the new venture but went instead to conduct at Centraltheatret, 1899–1902.

Sofie Parelius (1823–1902): after a début at the Christiania Norske Theater in 1852, she had been a mainstay of the Christiania Theatre since 1855 and was to make her last appearance at the National Theatre in May 1900. Among the parts she carried over to the new theatre was that of Aase, which she had first played, to Bjørn Bjørnson's Peer, in a shortened (first three Acts only) version of *Peer Gynt* in 1892.

Jens Selmer (1845–1928) excelled in comic and tragi-comic parts. At the Christiania Theatre, which he joined in 1865, he had been a natural for Old Ekdal in *The Wild Duck* and Foldal in *John Gabriel Borkman*; at the National Theatre, where he stayed until 1908, he added Engstrand in *Ghosts* to his repertoire.

Gyda Christensen (1872–1964) made her début at the Christiania Theatre in 1893 and acted at the National Theatre (where she also directed operas and promoted dance drama) until 1920, though with three years out, 1915–18, to work with Max Reinhardt at the Deutsches Theater, on ballet and pantomime. She moved, via Centraltheatret, to the New Theatre in Oslo, where she was chief director throughout the Second World War years. As talented and versatile as she was long-lived, she is possibly the only actress to have played the title-role in both *The Merry Widow* and *Hedda Gabler*.

Egil Eide (1868–1946) began his career at the Bergen Theatre in 1894 and moved to the Christiania Theatre in 1898. By the time he retired from the National Theatre, in 1934, he had, among other achievements, left his mark on a whole series of Ibsen parts, from Julian in *Emperor and Galilean* to Rubek in *When We Dead Awaken*, and had played the title-roles in *Richard III, Othello, Macbeth* and *King Lear*. One of the great Norwegian actors of the twentieth century, he was also the first Norwegian Brand (1904).

Johanne Dybwad (1867–1955) had a legendary career, both as actress and as director. Like so many, she came to the Christiania Theatre (1888) from a début at the Bergen Theatre (1887); she ended her career at the National Theatre as Aase in *Peer Gynt* on 8 December 1947. She was an innovatory Ibsen director, including a *Rosmersholm* with herself as Rebekka West and a *Ghosts* with herself as Mrs Alving; but her reach was also across world drama, and – typically – when she directed *Six Characters in Search of an Author* the part of the theatre-director was sex-changed so that she could play it.

Ludvig Müller (1868–1922) had been attached to the Christiania Theatre since 1897 and had a reputation (caught by the cartoonist) for 'a fine but fragile talent as a romantic lover'. His career at the National Theatre was short; he went via Centraltheatret to be director of the Trondhjem Theatre, 1913–16.

Hans Schrøder (1836–1902), seen washing his hands of the new venture, had been the somewhat conservative director of the Christiania Theatre since 1879 (see p. 262).

Sivard Gundersen (1842–1903) made his début at the Christiania Theatre in 1862 and soon established himself as a leading actor in serious drama, playing such parts as Haakon in Ibsen's *Pretenders*. He and his wife Laura (see 136, note 7) were one of several notable acting couples: she died a year before the move to the National Theatre; and his background position in the drawing bespeaks the end of a career which had included such roles as Othello, Macbeth and Faust.

Lucie Wolf (1833–1902): her long career is outlined in 136, note 2. Appropriately, after forty-six years as a leading actress with the Christiania Theatre, she also leads the procession to the new theatre, having played Lona Hessel (*Pillars of Society*) in the very last performance at the old, and with Ibsen in the audience, on 15 June 1899.

Ludvig Bergh (1865–1924) had been with the Christiania Theatre since 1890, playing mainly in comedy; he was to become director of the National Theatre in Bergen from 1909 until 1924.

II Directing plays in Denmark and Norway after 1850

The distribution and delimitation of duties in Danish and Norwegian theatre productions of the period were often problematic. It took Bjørnstjerne Bjørnson almost a year (1864) to persuade the management of the Christiania Theatre of the need for a full-time artistic director with the power to control all aspects of a production; and even then his working conditions were such that he was glad to leave after two seasons (1867). It was only in the later years of the Christiania Theatre and with the opening of the National Theatre (see 137) that the artistic importance of a powerful (i.e. empowered) director was fully realized in the Norwegian theatre. But in the 1850s and 1860s, in both Denmark and Norway, the director held the managerial and executive power while artistic duties were relegated to subordinate posts. Thomas Overskou, 'stage-instructor' under Johan Ludvig Heiberg's directorship of the Royal Theatre (see 141), saw himself as in the service of Heiberg, even as he was anxious to prove that the post of stage-instructor is tantamount to that of a 'régisseur'. Norwegian theatres shared this sense of hierarchy and worth: Carl Peter Borgaard (see p. 262) was appointed director of the Christiania Theatre in 1851 at an annual salary of 1,200 speciedaler (see 133, note 4), while Ibsen was paid 200 speciedaler a year as a stage-director in Bergen. Even the great Johanne Luise Heiberg (see 142), when she returned (1867) to the Royal Theatre in Copenhagen to direct plays, perceived her task as a power struggle.

138 Ibsen warns against working in the theatre, 1867

Henrik Ibsen, letter to Bjørnstjerne Bjørnson, 28 December 1867. *Samlede Verker*, vol. XVI, p. 203

My dear Bjørnson! Do you really want to tackle the theatre again?[1] Of course you have a task to perform there; but remember that you have a more urgent task in your own writing. [. . .] For a writer, to work in the theatre is to go through a daily act of abortion;[2] civic law has punishments for such things; I don't know whether the Lord is more liberal.

---

[1] Ibsen is writing, from his self-chosen exile in Rome, to Bjørnson who had left the post of artistic director of the Christiania Theatre at the end of the 1866/7 season but was to resume negotiations (which in the end came to nothing) with the Theatre in 1868. He is writing from experience: six years at the Norwegian Theatre in Bergen (1851–7), where he was initially employed to 'assist the theatre as dramatic author' but was soon also made 'stage-instructor'; five years as director at the

Norske Theater in Christiania (1857–62) and a year as 'artistic adviser' at the Christiania Theatre (1863–4) (see p. 262).

² That is, his creative ideas 'die unborn'. Since leaving Norway and the theatre, Ibsen had written *Brand* (1866) and *Peer Gynt* (1867).

139   Defining the duties of the 'Stage-Instructor' at the Norwegian Theatre in Bergen, 1852

'Instrux for det norske Theaters tvende Instructeurer', DNT Kopibok, 1850–60, Bergen Museum Manuscript Collection. no. 230¹

§ 1. *The Role-Instructor*² is required to be present in the theatre daily from 9.00 a.m. to 12 noon to conduct the reading-rehearsals and to use the remaining time for the study of individual parts, as needed, and for the general instruction and development of members of the company, always provided that this can be done without let and hindrance to the Stage-Instructor's rehearsals of plays. It is also part of his duties, during the same hours, to study parts with beginners.

With regard to reading-rehearsals he is to pay particular attention to the following:

1. That all obstructions to a rapid and satisfactory stage-rehearsal are removed, with regard both to language and to the meaning of words.
2. That the cast is given all necessary explanation of historical context and background, and that the correct interpretation of parts is ensured.
3. That the diction is correct.
4. That members of the cast memorize their parts carefully and well enough to be able to appear without scripts or books at the first stage-rehearsal.

§ 2. *The Stage-Instructor*³ is required to be present in the theatre for as many hours daily, Sundays and holidays included, as are needed for an exhaustive and careful instruction on stage, in order that each play be ready for public performance at the time determined by the management. Thus, once he has found the cast to be adequately prepared, he is to continue the instruction from the point reached at the last reading-rehearsal; furthermore he is to prepare draft timetables for stage-rehearsals and may return members of the cast to further reading-rehearsals when he finds this necessary.

Further duties of the Stage-Instructor are:

1. To organize the scenic arrangements for each play (costumes and scenery included) and altogether to be responsible for its staging (groupings, entrances, exits in appropriate postures, etc.).

2. To observe the facial expressions and gestures of each member of the cast in order to make sure that the bodily language answers to the words and the nature of the part.

3. To promote the necessary interplay between members of the cast and to define for each member of the cast, in each shifting situation, his place in the action as a whole.

§ 3. Before work on any new play begins, both Instructors should confer with each other in order to attempt to reach agreement concerning the interpretation of the individual characters, and where no agreement can be reached, the matter is to be put before the management for decision.

§ 4. Furthermore, before the management casts the parts in a play, the Instructors should confer and seek to agree on a proposal for casting which they submit jointly; but if a difference of opinion arises, each Instructor is to submit a separate proposal.

§ 5. If the Role-Instructor so wishes, the last stage-rehearsal before the dress-rehearsal is to be held between the morning hours of 9.00 and 12 and in his presence; moreover it is self-evident that he is free to be present at stage-rehearsals in order to supervise, within the limits of his duties, the observance of the instructions he has given the cast.

---

[1] These documents, together with letters and other evidence of Ibsen's struggles and frustrations with management and actors, have been translated by James Walter McFarlane in *The Oxford Ibsen* (Oxford University Press, 1960–77), vol. I, pp. 607–84. The excerpt (independently translated) given here has been selected to show the underlying assumptions (a) that the tasks are strictly matters of *instruction*, and (b) that, in the division of duties between 'role-instructor' and 'stage-instructor', the text of the play and its realization on stage can be so far separable.

[2] As stage-instructor, Ibsen was regarded as subordinate to the role-instructor, Herman Laading (1813–1904), who managed to combine his theatre duties with running a grammar school.

[3] In addition to his duties as stage-instructor, Ibsen also supplied a play annually to be performed on the anniversary of the opening of the theatre, 2 January: *St. John's Night, The Burial Mound, Lady Inger, The Feast at Solhaug* and *Olaf Liljekrans*, in that order. The management of the theatre entrusted him with a study trip to Copenhagen and Dresden in 1852 (April–July/August) for the purpose of acquiring practical theatre knowledge and finding texts suitable for performance and books with illustrations from which properly authentic sets could be designed. In both Copenhagen and Dresden he saw plays; in the Danish capital he was looked after by Thomas Overskou, met Johan Ludvig Heiberg (then director in charge of the Royal Theatre) and saw Johanne Luise Heiberg act. On his return he tackled his duties with the conscientiousness (rather than imagination) which they seemed to demand (see **140**).

140   Ibsen's stage-plan for *Dragedukken*,[1] 1852

Henrik Ibsen, sketch in his *Regiebok* for 1852 (manuscript in the Theatre Museum, University of Bergen)

Ibsen's *Regiebok* for 1852 contains notes and sketches for the eleven plays produced at the Norwegian Theatre in Bergen during the 1852/3 season. Envold Falsen's[2] *Dragedukken: A vaudeville in four acts*, is the third play thus prepared by Ibsen, but was the first to be staged (6 October 1852). Ibsen's practice was to begin his notes for each act with a half-page plan of the stage, showing the position of the wings and side shutters, curtains, prompt-box, built sets and stage furniture, indicating stage right ('H') and left ('V') as determined by the actor facing the audience. For the earlier plays he also makes a detailed plan, as here, of characters' entrances, exits and movements, indicating these with dotted lines identified by letters and indices (for main characters: here 'j″' and 'j‴', referring to Jacob in scenes i and ii; and 'k' for the Grocer [Kraemmer], who does not move from his doorstep) and by numbers (for crowd characters). In Act II, sc. ii of *Dragedukken*, a policing patrol and a group of watchmen sweep across the stage; these are identified as, respectively, 'Runden 2ᵉ Sc:' and 'Vegter i 2ᵉ Scene'. Acts I, III and IV are set in the Shoemaker's house and are less interesting, in terms of stage-movements, than Act II which builds up to a crowd scene and a crescendo of character involvement.

Ibsen's notes under the drawing explain the letters used to identify parts of the set and items of stage furniture as follows:

A street.

A. The grocer's house with a door to the street and steps, as well as a window in the second storey.
B. House with window in the second storey. a. A shed over a well.
C. Inn with door and steps. Window in second storey.
D. House with window in both storeys.
b. c. & d. Lanterns.

Ibsen's set follows Falsen's stage-directions at the beginning of Act II: '*A Street at night. The stage is illuminated only by a few lanterns which shed a dim light here and there. At the side where Jacob enters is the Grocer's house, and close to it a shed over a well. Jacob enters, anxiously, with the basket under his arm.*' Every item is functional and derived from the text: Jacob repeatedly hides in the well-shed ('a'); the singing revellers rowdily emerge from the inn ('C') in scene v and try to climb on to it, knocking over the lantern ('b') in the process and thus alerting the watchmen (numbered positions) and bringing citizens out to watch at all the windows.

---

[1] The title is untranslatable – a *dragedukke* (or *dragdokke*) is, in folklore, a benevolent spirit who draws riches to a house – but also holds the central conceit of the play and the plot. The 'hero', Jacob, is a shoemaker whose wife has just given birth to twins: a catastrophe in this already large and very poor family. Jacob decides to leave one of the twins on the doorstep of the rich and childless Grocer, not knowing that his wife has substituted a wooden doll (*dukke*) for the child in his basket. The Grocer intercepts Jacob and as a punishment forces upon him yet another basket containing a baby left on his doorstep earlier the same night! Jacob returns home with both baskets, to find that only the

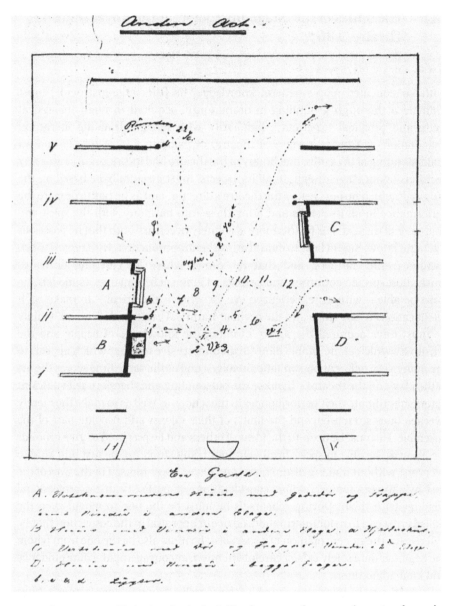

second contains a real baby, but that it also holds a large sum of money and promise of a regular supply of more. Thus his key-line: 'It was a *dragedukke* I was carrying, for it has brought money into the house' (*Envold Falsens Skrifter*, ed. L. S. Platou (Christiania: Lehmann, 1821), vol. I, p. 273).

[2] En(e)vold (de) Falsen (1755–1808), Danish lawyer and prominent statesman in Norway, translated and adapted a number of plays; *Dragedukken* (1797), one of his few originals and a popular and lasting success, is a *syngespil* (vaudeville) with music by Friedrich Ludwig Aemilus Kunzen (1761–1817). Realistic in its depiction of a poor Copenhagen shoemaker's life, it yet also begins and ends with songs, and the action is a pretext for more songs: solos, duets and choruses.

141   The duties of the 'Stage-Instructor' at the Royal Danish Theatre, 1867

Thomas Overskou,[1] *Den danske Skueplads og Staten. Meninger og Forslag* (Copenhagen: Stinck, 1867), pp. 52–5

With an educated man's general knowledge, he [the stage-instructor] must combine a thorough grounding in dramaturgy, acquired through theoretical study and practical experience; familiarity with foreign dramatic literature; imagination and taste; a sense of theatre, of painting and of music; and an understanding of the entire machinery of the theatre and its use. As of course any decisions about stage-design, in all its aspects, must essentially be based on the proposals which he puts before the theatre's director, and as he has to prepare the performance in all its details and bring these into harmony with the spirit and character of the text, it is furthermore absolutely necessary both that he possesses a general knowledge of how to mount an authentic production, with regard to set, costumes and manners, and that he knows where he can find drawings illustrating specific countries and periods.[2] Using such drawings as models, he must be able – with an experienced eye for what is theatrical – to make such modifications as the stage and the peculiar nature of each work demand. Finally he must have acquired the agility of mind, the knowledge of people and the sensitivity which alone enable him – in an unobtrusive manner which appeals to the many very different personalities involved and at the same time serves the art of the play and the theatre – to make the outstanding and therefore self-sufficient actors subordinate their performances to the whole, as well as to make the merely average ones stretch beyond the limits of their talents and become part of the ensemble. He must be open to the ideas of others and be prepared to give grounds for his own, be able to speak firmly without being stubborn, be just and kind to everyone without making distinctions, and never lower himself in the eyes of the cast by showing temper, selfish considerations or partiality in his professional dealings with them. During rehearsals he must be the one to whom even the skilled artist can turn for information, advice or appraisal in the conviction that he will receive the sincere opinion of a specialist; he must also be the one from whom the beginner dare safely expect careful attention, encouragement, polite guidance and kind admonition.

[...] If the stage-instructor does his job properly, then it follows from what has been said that [...] the post of costume-designer – an extra burden on the theatre's budget – disappears, as completely superfluous.

The post of régisseur should also be incorporated into that of the stage-instructor. [...] If we notice that the person we call stage-instructor is at all theatres abroad called régisseur and is in charge of everything to do with the stage, then there is no ground for dismay [...]: it is one and the same post under two names. [...] Under Heiberg's directorship my duty, as stage-instructor, was to arrange and direct all preparations for staging, and to organize, announce and supervise all rehearsals. In consequence it was my responsibility – quite rightly, as it was I who had to arrive at a complete overview of all the requirements for the performance – to compose the instructions, after which I had to make decisions concerning design and properties in consultation with the scene-painters and the machine master; to arrange the overall design of costumes and to consult the wardrobe master, the tailor and the actors about the individual costumes; with operas or vaudevilles, to familiarize myself with the music; and to work out the details of the staging. Since Heiberg rightly required the stage-instructor to be present at all theatrical activity for which he was responsible, I had to arrive, each evening when we were playing, half an hour before the performance began, to check that all the actors had arrived; and then to signal to the cast, by ringing the greenroom bell, the beginning of each act; to order the raising of the curtain; and generally to supervise the entire performance, with the exception of ballet and dance. The tasks were thus many, but in no way unmanageable. The staging had to be thought out and worked out at home; and if some of the works that were being prepared were large and difficult, involving many rehearsals which required intensive attention and doing some scenes over and over again, until they were right, this was true for far from all of them. Some rehearsals consisted simply of repetitions, to refresh actors' memories before the evening's performance; and when works were performed that had already been played a few times, it was enough for the stage-instructor to be in the building and to be available in case of any emergency. This gave plenty of time, during the acts, to hold meetings with other staff members about the staging of new plays and, as Heiberg was usually present in the evening, to give out announcements and information and to discuss his plans for repertoire and casting. Any business connected with the stage but not referred to above, was taken care of by the Theatre Secretary.

[1] Thomas Overskou (1798–1873) turned theatre historian after a varied career in the theatre. He began (1821) as an actor in minor comic parts and developed into a prolific writer and translator of comedies and vaudevilles. When Johan Ludvig Heiberg became director of the Royal Theatre (1849), Overskou was appointed 'stage-instructor', sharing his duties uneasily with the actor Thomas Hoedt. He was dismissed by Heiberg's successor and eventually became director of the (private) Casino Theatre in Copenhagen.

[2] To find such illustrations, to promote 'authentic' set designs, is one reason why the Norwegian Theatre in Bergen sent Ibsen abroad in 1852 (139, note 3).

142   An actress as 'Stage-Instructor' in Copenhagen, 1867–1874

Johanne Luise Heiberg, *Et Liv Gjenoplevet i Erindringen* (Copenhagen: Gyldendal, 1891–2), vol. III (1892), pp. 312–23

There was a general agreement that the theatre[1] needed new talents to exercise genuine leadership in the study and producing of drama; for at this time straight plays had been pushed aside by opera and ballet,[2] and it was felt that things had come to this pass because plays had been carelessly studied and ineptly staged. Voices from among the general public were forever exclaiming: 'It's not worth going to see plays any more; we have to stick to opera!' – and the low attendance figures at performances greatly dismayed the actors. That my appointment brought new life was felt not only by the actors but also by the management and the general public, whose interest was freshly roused, so that audiences again came streaming in.

Of course I knew very well that my apointment as stage-instructor – the unusual phenomenon of a lady taking up this position – would not please those who had themselves hoped to be considered. I had also anticipated that many a minor actor would have it rammed into him that it was below the dignity of a man to be subordinated to a woman and to have to obey her orders; but those who said this had forgotten that, during the many years I had been active as an actress,[3] it had often actually been I who influenced how the plays were staged – and this had not only been tacitly accepted, but I had been expressly urged, time and time again, to give advice and assistance at rehearsals. [...]

My method as stage-instructor was to come to the first rehearsal with the entire production planned out, act by act, scene by scene; and I made sure that everything – scenery, props, etc. – was completely worked out and ready. This method demanded a great deal of hard work in advance. But the advantage is, first, that you have familiarized yourself with the play, down to the smallest detail, as no one else has, so that you can give a satisfactory answer to any question from the players; and that all that talking, on and on, all that sensible advice – now from one, now from another who usually says the opposite – becomes unnecessary; and that thereby much waste of time at rehearsals, much bandying of ideas to and fro, is avoided, as the players are bound to feel that none of them are as much inside the play as a whole as you are, and that they therefore have to submit to you. Once you begin to listen to what Peter thinks and what Paul wants, then there is no end to it, and the whole thing dissolves into quarrelling and posturing. This I was spared, throughout the seven years that I directed the rehearsal of plays. Very rarely did any of the players suggest any substantial change to what I had decided in advance, albeit I did not entirely escape suggestions from the players concerning what the playwright had meant or not meant – but they were suggestions which were so easy to see through that they could without any difficulty be dismissed.

[...] Ibsen's *Pretenders* was perhaps of all major plays the most difficult to stage,[4] especially with the cast available: in this play nearly every single part demands an actor or actress of the first rank. Added to this, the scene-changes present the designer and the stage-instructor with almost insurmountable difficulties, unless they are prepared to resort to the method which has unfortunately become common practice in all theatres abroad – that is, to lower a curtain while the most complicated scene-changes take place, and thus to tear an act into rags and tatters and continually to break the illusion, telling the audience through the use of the curtain that the work of the actors has to be interrupted to let that of the stage-staff begin, to the sound of hammering and other noises, behind the curtain. I count it an achievement never to have made use of this inartistic method, not even in *The Pretenders*, where the temptation to do so was undoubtedly great; but I discovered [...] a different solution to the problem of difficult scene-changes, one which proved so effective that it has been used ever since in our theatre, as preferable to interrupting the action with a curtain. For the most difficult scene-changes I had the stage in complete darkness, and during this black-out the new scenery was put in place, and only when this was completed was the stage lit again. Much was gained by this, for it is not attractive, nor helpful to the illusion, to see walls, trees and other essential parts of the scenery come sliding down, helter-skelter, from the heavens – not to mention how the legs and arms of the stage-staff often appear on view in such scene-changes and draw laughter from the audience. The drawing of a curtain interrupts the action, and members of the audience, not knowing how long this interruption will last, start talking to each other, and silence and concentration are lost and dispersed. But when there is a black-out, then the audience's attention is sharpened into suspense, wondering what there will be to see when it is no longer dark; and they remain inside the illusion. It has also become obvious that scenery never makes more impact than at the moment when darkness is followed by light.

I was practically alone in my desire to stage Ibsen's great play. All the actors, except Mr Emil Poulsen,[5] who was to play Bishop Nicolas, were against the production, and the management shook their heads at the thought of how it would go down with the audience; so it took great persistence, determination and courage on my part not to give the whole thing up. In the end, however, I was proved right, as the play had a most wonderful reception. [...]

As with *The Pretenders*, so I had to fight against resistance to *The League of Youth*,[6] to Shakespeare's *Cymbeline* and other important plays – the clearest proof of how low the artistic spirit in the theatre was at the time!

¹ The Royal Theatre in Copenhagen. For Mrs Heiberg's career there, see p. 285.
² cf. 143.
³ i.e., 1826–64. Ibsen celebrated the great actress in his 'Rhymed letter to Mrs Heiberg' of 1871.
⁴ Mrs Heiberg's production of *The Pretenders* opened at the Royal Theatre on 11 January 1871. It was reviewed, enthusiastically, in *Faedrelandet* on 14 January, and Ibsen wrote to thank the reviewer but also to point out that 'during my stay in Copenhagen last summer, I explained to the director of the theatre that my play neither could nor should be performed in its entirety. With his approval I therefore prepared a shortened version, in which the Bishop's death-scene was quite extensively abridged, and moreover I gave my express consent to any further cuts being made in rehearsals, if such should be found necessary. If the theatre has not after all made use of the shortened version which I provided, then I have been treated very badly, and this would also explain what would otherwise seem inexplicable – that is, that the performance lasts so long' (*Samlede Verker*, vol. XV, p. 338). Mrs Heiberg, on the other hand, reports how, with the author's consent, she cut the ending, and also how, on her own initiative, she modified it to make it less 'undramatic'.
⁵ Emil Poulsen (1842–1911) was a leading actor at the Royal Theatre and eventually (1891) joined its governing body. He played Helmer to Betty Hennings's Nora in the world première of *A Doll's House*, 21 December 1879, having already played Bernick in *Pillars of Society* (18 November 1877), and was over the next few decades to play a series of leading roles in Ibsen plays, such as Dr Stockmann in *An Enemy of the People* (1883), Hjalmar Ekdal in *The Wild Duck* (1885), Eilert Løvborg in *Hedda Gabler* (to Betty Hennings's Hedda, 1891) and Solness in *The Master Builder* (1893).
⁶ Ibsen's *The League of Youth* opened at the Royal Theatre on 16 February 1870.

143   A new and larger Danish Royal Theatre, 1874

P. Hansen,[1] *Den danske Skueplads*, (Copenhagen: Ernst Bojesens Kunstforlag, n.d. [1890–6]), vol. III, pp. 270–1

The Danish Royal Theatre was the home of opera and ballet as well as drama. Renovated in 1857 (when Hans Christian Andersen wrote a prologue for the re-opening), the old building was replaced by a new and larger one in 1874.

For the authors and artists of the theatre the move into the new building has created working conditions which are materially an improvement but artistically an impoverishment. The greater audience capacity[2] and higher ticket prices[3] have quite considerably raised both the part of the income which goes to royalties and the percentage of the gross income on which they are calculated. But at the same time the theatre, built virtually with the dimensions of an opera house, has proved to be very ill-suited to the spoken repertoire which always has been, is, and should continue to be the most important part of the artistic activity of the national theatre. The stage is so wide and high that part of the effect of the speaking voice is lost, and so deep that a crowd which, in the old theatre, made a mass impact, here looks thin and ineffectual.

¹ Hans Christian Peter Hansen (1840–1905): journalist, minor poet and noted literary translator (especially of Goethe's *Faust*, 1881–9); wrote a number of studies of Danish literature, including a book on J. L. Heiberg (1867) and a two-volume *History of Danish Literature* (1886). His magnum opus is the *Illustrated History of the Danish Stage* which, while it draws heavily on the work of Thomas Overskou (see 141), is less biased than the accounts given by that embroiled and embittered man of the theatre.

[2] The new building could hold *c*.1,540 spectators; the old *c*.1,350.
[3] The average price per seat had gone up from 1.66 kroner in the old theatre to 2.07 kroner in the new.

144(a) Creating a set

Jul. Lehmann,[1] 'Bag Taeppet' ('Behind the Curtain'), in Hansen, *Den danske Skueplads*, vol. III, pp. 433–7

The stage [. . .] is a large square space; in our Royal Theatre it is 32 ells high, 44 ells wide and 35 ells deep.[2] The floor slopes down towards the auditorium,[3] out of consideration for the audience in the stalls. [. . .]

The sets are constructed from painted canvas. To the audience[4] they should look like complete pictures; but they are nonetheless composed of many and very different parts. Among those, some *hang*, others *stand*. In the former category are *flats* [*taepper*], *cut-cloths* [*buetaepper*] and *soffits* [*soffiter*]. [. . .] The flats form whole surfaces which represent either air and sky or distant views; they are used to separate the set from the background. The cut-cloth has been cut in one or more places, leaving a view of the part of the stage which is behind it. It is used particularly in landscapes to represent groups of trees, whose branches then meet at the top; in architecture it can, for example, be painted like a traverse, resting on free-standing pillars. Soffits (an Italian word: that which is fastened underneath something) are thin strips of canvas which are used to finish the set on top. They can represent, according to need, sky, foliage, tapestries or tops of houses. Standing objects of décor are stretched on light wooden frames. They are either fastened as wings to tall uprights, *wing chariots*, which are situated on both sides of the stage and can be pushed backwards and forwards on rails on the floor – or they are *flats* and *screens* which, with the aid of supports, are screwed into the floorboards wherever they are needed. Nearest the auditorium, in front of the whole set, is always the so-called *frame* [*Drapperi*], consisting of two wings – one on each side of the stage – connected at the top by a soffit. It is painted to look like red curtains with many folds and is intended to form the frame around the stage picture.

The plan of the Gurre set in *Seven Sleepers' Day*[5] [*Syvsoverdag*] shows that it consists of no fewer than twelve different pieces. Starting at the back, there is the air piece (no. 1) and in front of it a low flat (no. 2) which marks the distant hills separating the sky from Gurresø. In front of this, closer to the audience, is another flat (no. 3) which suggests a still distant headland with shrubs on it, jutting out into the sea. On the far left, placed to form an obtuse angle, is a screen (no. 4) representing a group of slender trees, with the sky and air visible between their trunks. On the left side the set is then completed by wing no. 9 and flat no. 10. The wing is a group of trees similar to the one behind it, but somewhat larger; it ends with some low shrubs which are continued by the flat. In the centre of the plan we find the two flats, no. 5 and no. 12, the first of which depicts a headland, not unlike no. 3 but closer to us and therefore seen in more detail, while the second represents the grassy shore of the sea. The right side is occupied by no. 6, the ruin – which can be made to vanish, so that the castle becomes visible behind it – and nos. 7, 8 and 11, forming together a boscage with a few high trees rising out of it. In the picture of the complete set, such as it is seen by the audience [144(c)], it should be easy to recognize the separate items enumerated here.

[1] Julius Lehmann was appointed 'stage-instructor' (see **139–142**) at the Royal Theatre in 1893. He had previously held the same position at Folketheatret, had been one of the three who formed the new administration of the Dagmar-Theatre in 1889, and had had a curtain-raiser, *Afdansning*, performed at the Royal Theatre in 1884.
[2] A Danish ell ('alen') = 0.627 metres.
[3] The Danish word, 'Tilskuerpladsen' (literally, 'the area for the spectators'), unlike the English, stresses the visual aspect of theatre.
[4] Here, as in the last sentence of the excerpt, the Danish word, 'Tilskuerne', strictly means 'the spectators'.
[5] See **144(b)**. The play, a vaudeville comedy by Johan Ludvig Heiberg, was written for a gala performance, in honour of the coronation of King Christian VIII, on 1 July 1840. It was revived in 1872 and stayed in the repertoire for fifty performances.

144(b) The plan of the Gurre set for Heiberg's *Seven Sleepers' Day*

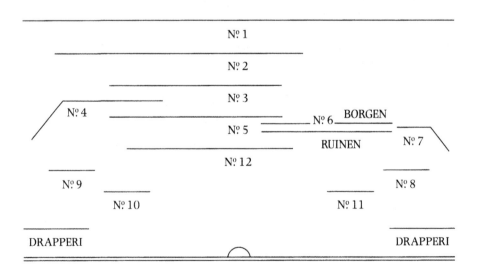

144(c) The Gurre set for *Seven Sleepers' Day*, as seen by the audience

144(d) A transformation scene: *Seven Sleepers' Day*

Johan Ludvig Heiberg, *Syvsoverdag* (1840), Act II, in *Samlede Skrifter* (Copenhagen: J. H. Schubothes Boghandling, 1833–41), vol. VII (1841), pp. 207 and 212–13

As a typical *vaudeville*, Heiberg's play depends on music and spectacle as much as on words, and combines contemporary and topical material with the legendary and fantastic. There are three groups of dramatis personae: a modern family, the fourteenth-century King Valdemar and his court, and the Prospero-like magician Phantasus with an entourage of sylphs, elves, ondines and gnomes. According to legend, the seven Ephesian Christians fell into their two-hundred-year-long sleep on 27 July, known as Seven Sleepers' Day; but Heiberg set the action of his play on 27 June and the night following, in order to lead up to the coronation of Christian VIII which took place on 28 June 1840. With similar freedom he uses the conceit of the seven sleepers to form the basis of the transformation of present into past, and vice versa.

ACT II

By the ruins of Gurre Castle[1]

In the background a mound, surrounded by trees and bushes, in which a partly excavated ruin can be seen. Towards the foreground, on each side, dense clumps of bushes. It is evening; the sun is setting. [...]

Scene Two

Phantasus, *with a staff in his hand, enters from behind the mound in the background; he circles the mound and comes to the front of the stage.*

PHANTASUS
Now sets the sun on Seven Sleepers' Day
And now's the time for me to call to life
Those visions hovering in the summer night
Like slender spiders' web in moonlight beams.
Ye visions, I will show you, not as dreams,
No, just the opposite, as real life.
A long-since vanished time I now invoke;
So long since gone, it can't be said to *be*,
But to *become*, at my command;
And it shall rise, in order that the past
May form a happy union with the present,
And give to it a real and abiding life.
    (*Points with his staff.*)
Arise, thou ancient castle, from thy ruin!
    (*He draws a circle with himself as the centre, while saying:*)
Seven-sleepers, awaken from your sleep!
    (*Exit* Phantasus)

A brief melodrama[2]

during which the old castle of Gurre rises out of the ruins. A circular wall, with a gate, conceals its lowest parts.

---

[1] Gurre, in northern Sealand, was the favourite castle of King Valdemar – known as 'Atterdag' (variously interpreted as 'New Day', pointing to him as a restorer of Denmark, and as 'There Will be a Day Tomorrow') – and the place where he died in 1375.

[2] The word 'melodrama' is used in the original in the sense of a musical interlude during which a scene-change takes place.

III Royal theatres become national

A consequence of the radical constitutional reform which began in Denmark in 1848 was that control of the Royal Theatre moved from the court to government and ultimately parliament. From 1849, repertoire and budget had to be approved by the Minister for Culture. The Director of the Royal Theatre (as it continued to be called) from 1849 to 1856 was Johan Ludvig Heiberg (1791–1860), scholar, philosopher, publicist, poet and the greatest Danish writer of comedies after Holberg. His wife, Johanne Luise Heiberg, née Pätges (1812–90), was for four decades (1826–64) the Royal Theatre's leading actress and at a later period (1867–74) its stage-director (see **142** and **145**). Her posthumously printed *Reminiscences* give first-hand evidence – coloured, of course, by her temperament and experiences – of the problems facing the director in the transitional period, caught between royalty and parliament, between actors, audiences and the press, and between his own artistic aims and the absolute need to make the theatre a paying 'business'.

In Sweden, constitutional reform was more gradual, as was the *embourgeoisement* of the Royal Theatre, which from the 1850s received annual subsidies both from parliament and from the king. As in Denmark, the 1850s witnessed a lively debate about the function of a national theatre. K. A. Lindblad's pamphlet, *The Theatre Question: Should Sweden continue to support a Royal Theatre, a National Theatre?* (Stockholm, 1856), typically insists that theatre must be 'part of the general education necessary to a civilized nation'. In the chapter on the Royal Theatre, 'A National Educational Institution', in his collection of satirical vignettes published in 1882 as *The New Kingdom*, August Strindberg attacks the Theatre for having deviated from the aim of being a national stage, a home for national drama.

145 The Danish Royal Theatre under a new constitution, 1849
Johanne Luise Heiberg, *Et Liv Gjenoplevet i Erindringen* vol. III, pp. 6–13

Account had now to be kept of everything to do with this 'business' and for every decision, however unimportant, permission had to be obtained from the Minister. Hence a continuous stream of papers flowed between the Minister and the Director, adding not a little to his daily labour. [...]

In the Theatre a number of changes had now to be implemented which were bound to make the new Director unpopular. First of all, as the State had now taken over the Theatre which had belonged to the King, it became important to make the 'business' yield as much as possible – not artistically but financially. For this reason the system of reserving free places in the stalls for members of the court was abolished. Imagine what this meant! All these gentlemen, the flower of the court, who for years had been in the habit of congregating in the stalls, every evening throughout the season, partly to convey, listen to and discuss the news of the day, coming and going, in and out, during the performance, banging the doors behind them, as if it was all put on for them, and them alone; they would enter noisily, their swords clanging, after dining at the Palace, talking loudly to the right and the left – so that you could often follow their conversation from the stage – now clapping, now booing, depending on what they were told by their leaders – for all these elegant judges the entrance was now closed; all this 'fine set' was now mercilessly shown the door as persons not authorized to be in the Theatre. An absolute furore broke out among these birds who for so long had been allowed to make their nests in the centre of the Temple and were now driven out! Even the domestic staff of the court had had the free use of a box in the Upper Circle every evening, and this was similarly cancelled. And who was the villain? The new Theatre Director, of course. He alone had propagated this unheard-of insult. For them – as for the entire court, and the audience, and the actors – it was impossible to grasp so quickly that all aspects of the absolutist State were going through a radical change. Everybody knew that something new had happened, in that a constitution had been given to the people; but everybody thought that this new thing could or should not affect him personally, nor his traditional privileges. The most illustrious members of the court were similarly accustomed, from time immemorial, to regarding the Theatre and everything connected with it as something over which they had rights, as their property, since it was called 'the Royal Theatre'. When the royal family wanted to see a play, there would be a command – often at short notice – to withdraw the performance which had been announced and replace it with the one they wanted to see – which meant a great burden on all involved and often a loss of the income that had been counted on. When there were concerts at court, the Theatre's singers and orchestra were obliged to participate, however much the Theatre needed them for that evening's performance. When there were masquerades, costume balls or plays at court, the Theatre's wardrobe was ransacked and no thought given to whether just those costumes were meant to be used the same evening. All these court rights were now abolished, to the great indignation of high and low. So little was even the Lord Chamberlain, Lewetzau, able to grasp what had now become the duty of the new Theatre Director that he, who had always been devoted to Heiberg, now wrote him bitter notes rebuking him for the changes and regarding himself as personally insulted by him. [...]

As with the court, so with the actors. Imaginative and open to new impressions, they had greeted the idea of liberty in Denmark with spontaneous warmth, indeed with ecstasy. They were, one and all, friends of liberty; but that this liberty would at many points have to impinge on their own situation in the Theatre, they would or could not understand. On the contrary, they thought that all restrictions were now gone, that all they had to do now was to win the support of the one Director (instead of several, as before) for their plans and demands, and then there would be no limit to what could be achieved in this lovely Golden Age of Liberty. That the new Theatre Director was tied by the new state of things as no one had been before him, did not occur to them.

Being part of a system of duties and obligations is something that actors have always found difficult to understand and accept, and it is therefore equally difficult for them to understand that others can accept it. How often have I heard them reply, when it was said: 'This or that can no longer be done; what would the Minister, what would Parliament, say to this?' – 'Ah, Parliament! What do we care about Parliament! It's none of its business!' – Now, as the Theatre was almost entirely separated from the King and the court, many a royal grace and favour naturally disappeared. There was no longer any question of those privileges which had been enjoyed: ex gratia payments, travel grants, or special requests from the Directorate to the King for the secret payment of the odd debt. If anything out of the ordinary was to be done now, the Minister had to give his agreement, and – worse – Parliament had the apparently incredible lack of delicacy to make public announcements of things which nobody should really know about. [...] When the Ministry – in the same cause of higher income for the Theatre as had led it to abolish free places and the like – now also abolished the right of actors to take on private engagements for the summer, on the grounds that the Theatre suffered considerable losses in the last few months of each season through actors refusing to learn new roles because they were busy learning their roles for private summer performances – well, then the actors became disgruntled with the new age and found its conditions highly embarrassing.

With the public, Heiberg quickly made himself unpopular through two decisions which caused excessive displeasure. Like all of us artists, he had often been dismayed at the malpractice of allowing the admission of quite small children into a theatre of high artistic standards. Often a whole scene, a whole act, indeed the effect of a whole play, had been ruined when – in a moment of pathos and achieved dramatic illusion – there would suddenly be the voice of a child, crying and calling out loud: 'I want to go home!', and so provoking laughter. [...] What it means to an actor who, carried away by the illusion, has also been able to carry others away, to be suddenly disturbed by such a noise – well, you have to be an actor yourself fully to understand this. Heiberg therefore refused admission to the National Theatre to children under ten years of age. [...] The alarums and excursions created by this prohibition were truly ridiculous. Although it had been announced in all the papers – and, if I remember right, on the posters too, in the beginning – that no child under ten would be admitted to the theatre, the mothers still brought them; and when they were stopped at the entrance, there were the most violent scenes of weeping and other spectacles. Heartbreaking notices appeared in the papers attacking the cruel, heartless man who persecuted the little ones; Heiberg received anonymous letters, both polite and crude, in which he was called a barbarian, etc. But his decision was not revoked, to the benefit of silence in the theatre, and to the great satisfaction of the actors.

The other decision was to close to all unauthorized persons the gate through which the carriages take the ladies of the Theatre to and from rehearsals and performances. This decree greatly displeased another part of the public, namely the young gentlemen of the leisured classes who were in the habit of turning up after the performance, cigars in their mouths, to wait for the actresses and ballerinas so as to have another look at them when they stepped into their carriages – indeed sometimes to leap on to the back of a carriage in order to demonstrate their admiration. They would even pay the coachman, secretly, not to use his whip to get rid of the added burden. It was not very pleasant, in the dreary darkness, to be taken home by a servant who had let himself be bribed; for, once the man was there, who could be sure that he had not persuaded the coachman, with whom he had an understanding, to drive somewhere else? The history of the Theatre tells us that such things could happen. The closing of the gate put a stop to all that. [...]

As with the court, the actors and the public, so with the newspaper editors. They, too, would not realize that many things looked different in the new dispensation. Thus Mr Ploug[1] rebuked Heiberg again and again for having betrayed his former belief that the auditorium should be rearranged, to make the parterre, the cheapest area, take up most of the ground floor, next to the orchestra. Heiberg announced this opinion in 1840 and had not changed it in 1849; but the constitutional reform of 1848 forced him to abandon the idea of realizing it, since it was impossible to carry out a restructuring which would considerably lessen the Theatre's income. From the very beginning Parliament took a hostile attitude to the Theatre; and the sentiments – anti-art, not to say brutal – which were forever being uttered on the floor were all directed towards decreasing the subsidy as far as possible, if not abolishing it altogether. In such a situation it would have been foolish to think of cutting down the daily takings in the interest of art. Now, couldn't Mr Ploug have said this to himself, time and time again, and so spared us his attacks? I cannot believe that he couldn't, as he himself took an active part in our political life. Can he possibly have failed to notice that, despite all the hollow rhetoric about Art, High Art, National Art, etc., – each theatre director's worth is judged by whether his box-office is flourishing or not? A deficit of a few thousand crowns at the end of a season would infallibly signal the sacking of the director, whether or not he had put on original works by native dramatists,[2] whether or not he had given new authors the chance to show their strengths, and so on. [...]

Why has there been more peace, more silence, more discipline in the treatment of the private theatres?[3] There is no reason to believe that the directors and artists in these theatres are more principled, unbiased, disinterested individuals than those at the National Theatre, where one newspaper scandal has followed another, under the various directors. No, but in dealing with the private theatres the papers have limited themselves – God knows why – to what should be their only concern: judging the public activity, and letting the director look after the rest. It could be objected that they have more of a right to meddle with details at the National Theatre, since this institution is supported by the State, and since therefore every citizen pays his mite towards it.

[1] Carl Ploug (1813–94): Danish poet, politician (member of the assembly which formulated the new Basic Law) and editor, until 1881, of the liberal newspaper *Faedrelandet*.
[2] Heiberg's aim was to create a national repertoire, and in his seven years as Director no less than forty-five Danish plays were put on.
[3] The chief 'private' – i.e. not State-subsidized – Copenhagen theatres in the 1850s were the Casino Theatre, founded in 1848, and Folketheatret ('the People's Theatre'), founded in 1857.

146   August Strindberg caricatures the 'Swedish National Institution of Higher Education', 1882

August Strindberg, *Samlade Verk*. Nationalutgåvan, vol. XII, ed. Karl-Ake Kärnell (Stockholm: Almqvist & Wiksell, 1983), pp. 102–14

The clock strikes eleven in the office of the Board of Directors of the National Theatre.[1] A handful of young actors, due at rehearsal, have to leave, after waiting for an hour to see the National Director of His Royal Majesty's Court Chapel[2] and Theatres.

Presently the Secretary appears; he has not been able to turn up sooner, as he also works in the Pensions Department of the Civil Service. Having explained to the porter that no one in the directorate will be available before two o'clock, he settles down at his desk and starts to compose a leader for the court newspaper. The subject given him by the Board of Directors is:

'A National Institution of Higher Education'. And he wrote:

'It is not the first time that sacrilegious hands have reached out towards the sacred precincts of national culture and the creation of Gustav III.'[3] The pen stopped. [...] 'Let me think,' said his brain.

'Too late,' said the pen. But his brain went on thinking. 'Royal creator? Royal memorial? Too many royals, when I was supposed to talk about national culture and education. Besides, the peasants acknowledge only one Creator – so far anyway.' But he had written it. So the pen took in more ink and began again to spew out:

'Do we not complain about the lack of a native dramatic literature? How could we complain if we no longer had a National Theatre (he first wrote 'Royal', but crossed it out) to nurse the tender plants, as it has been doing hitherto, and without which there would not have been a single name to record in the history of our country's drama!'

'That's a lie,' said the brain. [...]

Now the nation's Adviser on Dramatic Repertoire arrived from the National Board of Ships' Pilots, where he was employed in the secretariat, bringing a play which he wanted to have put on at once. The wife of the Director of Pilot Postings had dramatized a short story from the French fashion magazine *Le Printemps*, and the Adviser on Dramatic Repertoire had touched it up and entitled it *The Duchess*. There was an excellent part for 'the Duke' and six changes of costume for the Duchess. Everything pointed to a success, and the Secretary had no objections to make. The National Cashier, who had just arrived from the Department of Defence and who served in the directorate of the Theatre as a 'connoisseur', was consulted; and, after seeing the title and the list of dramatis personae, he swore that the play was good for twenty-five performances. He promised his support. In due course there arrived, from the Office of the Exchequer, the National Treasurer of the Royal Theatre whose job it was to supervise the National Secretary; and also, from the Cashiers' Office of the Bank of Sweden, the National Superintendent of Swedish Dramatic Literature. There were no further arrivals until half past two, by which time *The Duchess* had been accepted for performance, the parts distributed, and the Director arrived from the Lord Lieutenant's Office. Business had now to be done quickly, as the Director had to be in the Lord Chamberlain's Office by four o'clock.

First he read the leader for the court newspaper and changed every 'royal' to 'national'. Then he approved *The Duchess* for performance.

The National Superintendent of Swedish Dramatic Literature next reported that he had completed the scenario for the play about compulsory military service which the Government had ordered,[4] whereupon the Director asked to hear a synopsis of it. [...] The play was at once accepted for performance because of its patriotic message, but it must not be put on before the parliamentary recess.

The National Cashier submits two new plays which his sister-in-law has translated, and the National Adviser approves of them.

The National Treasurer now remembers that there is a coal-basket[5] full of uncollected manuscripts of Swedish plays. The Director asks the Adviser if he has read them, and when he says yes, the porter is ordered to carry the coal-basket up to the attic. Why Swedish original manuscripts should be kept in a coal-basket is still a mystery. [...]

Håkan Olsson, MP, had had a few good years and managed to save some money; he had long felt a deep desire for education but had not had the time to acquire this commodity – which did not actually seem to make people any better, only more conceited, judging by his educated fellow MPs.

During the debate concerning theatre subsidy he had realized that there was a national institution of education which, bearing the name of The Royal Theatre, was the pride and delight of all Stockholmers. According to some gentlemen, it was the best and cheapest institution for the acquisition of national education, and its beneficial effects were immeasurable, besides which it would be a blot on the nation's escutcheon if it did not pay the annual debts of the Theatre.

Now, Mr Olsson had been to many other theatres and found both pleasure and edification, but he had never really felt educated. On the contrary, in the company of a crowd of young clerks he had felt very uneducated, as they kept asking him whether he had seen Miss Rose as Cocotte or Mr Anatole as Monsieur Jean and he had to reply, to his embarrassment, that he had not. As his finances improved, and stirred by the information given by the educated clerks, he was seized by this deep desire for national education, and he decided to share it with his wife and daughter.

He therefore bought tickets to the small National Theatre[6] and waited with great excitement to see how national education would fall upon himself and his family and make them into enlightened patriots. The play is *Monsieur Jean*, a comedy in three acts, translated from the French original by Cassacko (one of the Adviser's pseudonyms). The curtain rises on an endless Brussels carpet, interrupted only by a few sofas and a stove with an ornate clock above it.[7]

The Maid enters, wearing a silk dress; she holds and reads a rose-coloured billet-doux and says something inaudible. Monsieur Anatole enters through another door and kisses her over her shoulder. Monsieur Anatole is wearing a gold-knobbed cane, a lorgnette, a contraption for rolling cigarettes, and an enormous watch chain. [...] Anatole rolls himself a cigarette and says something to the Maid. The Marquise enters, and gives a wink to the Maid who immediately understands and removes herself. They are alone.

'Monsieur!'

'Madame la Marquise!'

Anatole puts away the cigarette contraption and grasps his cane.

'What gives me the honour of such an early visit?'

Anatole beats his trousers with his cane.

'To be honest, my dear Marquise, I don't know what right you have to ask this question.'

'Your absence would give you the right to ask me why your presence does not give me the right to ask you!'

('What dialogue: charming!' Faint applause!)

Anatole walks diagonally across the Brussels carpet, puts on his lorgnette, beats a sofa with his cane and says with his back turned to the Marquise:

'Because I love you.'

The Marquise turns her back to him and wraps the train of her dress around her feet; then she turns her head, while her body remains immobile, and positions her face over her back, her chin resting on her spine, and says with a sphinx-like smile:

'The weather is beautiful today.'

Anatole begins to laugh convulsively and takes out his cigarette contraption again. The Marquise draws in her train and begins to leave; she stops in the middle of the carpet and opens her mouth as if to say something, but says nothing and exits.

A loud applause calls her immediately back in to receive the homage of the audience. [...]

In the second act the entire Drama School of the National Theatre plus all the walk-on actors who are paid less than 2,000 crowns per year are gathered round a colossal billiard table at the Marquise's. [...] The Drama School exists, and the Marquise enters, followed by Jean. [...] Jean rushes out. [...] Anatole rushes in. [...]

'Hah, I see that you are hiding something from me, and I swear you have his letter in your bosom! Give it here!'

[...]

But the Marquise throws herself at him and takes the letter back. Now begins a very exciting scene. Anatole throws himself at the Marquise, flings her backwards over a sofa and puts his knee on her chest. The Marquise kicks him in the stomach while uttering half-suffocated screams of anguish and surreptitiously putting the letter in her mouth. [...] Anatole strikes her in the face and calls her 'cochonne'. The Marquise declares that she has swallowed the letter, whereupon Anatole rolls himself a cigarette and exits. Curtain. Curtain calls.

Håkan Olsson is delighted but pleads a sudden attack of nausea and leaves after giving his ladies permission to complete their national education on their own until the show is finished.

He goes down to the restaurant and meets a few other MPs who have been invited to supper by famous actors from the National Theatre [...] and both Jean and Anatole are hosts. [...]

After supper Jean made a brilliant speech full of Gustav III's creation, sacred precincts, sacrilegious robbers and shameful blots.

Håkan Olsson replied:

He didn't like going to the Opera, as he didn't understand foreign languages (Hear, hear!); he wasn't going to vote for a penny for the National Opera, since there was no such thing [. . .], but he would vote for the Dramatic Theatre. He who had led a quiet and isolated life in the country and never had a chance to consort with the best sort of people, he could learn so much from seeing a play at the National Show Place, because it showed him how the best sort of people live and think. The Theatre, gentlemen, is an educational institution; it is a dangerous weapon and must therefore not be left in the hands of the uneducated; therefore the State ought to be in charge and keep a careful watch so that the weapon is not turned against the Government.

[1] The Royal Theatre (The Opera) and the Dramatic Theatre were jointly called the Royal Theatres (not the National Theatres, although Strindberg's nomenclature – and his piece as a whole – points to what ought to be the name *and* function of these theatres). The 'Smaller Theatre' was acquired, on the instigation of King Karl XV, in 1863 and, as the Royal Dramatic Theatre ('Dramaten'), put under the same directorate as the Royal Theatre. The latter increasingly became the home of opera and music drama, while the more intimate space (600 seats) made 'Dramaten' suitable for modern French drama – Augier, Dumas *fils* and Sardou – whose plots and style are parodied by Strindberg.

[2] 'Chapel': the Director would be concerned with vocal and instrumental music.

[3] The Royal Theatre (The Opera) was founded by Gustav III in 1773.

[4] Strindberg was against compulsory military service and felt that the Government was driving it through against the wishes of parliament.

[5] 'Coal-basket': the word Strindberg uses denotes a kind of flat wicker receptacle, used to carry coal and other coarse material – an indication of how he saw native Swedish plays rubbished by the directors of the Royal Theatres.

[6] i.e. the Dramatic Theatre (see note 1, above).

[7] In other essays of the 1880s Strindberg criticizes the Swedish 'national' theatre in similar terms. Thus in 'The Literary Reaction in Sweden', first published in *Tilskueren*, May 1886: 'The theatre, which can be an educator, can also be a bad educator. In such [directorial] hands as Hedberg's and Wijkander's our royal stage became a private court theatre where mainly French comedy was played. We have been brought up on French comedy, and it has had many good sides; it has dealt with reality, but it has been bourgeois-aristocratic. Its heroes have always had an income of at least 12,000 francs, and the action has always taken place on a Brussels carpet' (August Strindberg, *Samlade Skrifter* [ss], ed. John Landqvist (Stockholm: Albert Bonnier, 1912–20), vol. XVII (1913), p. 214).

IV Old and new traditions of acting

In Scandinavian theatres, the 1880s saw a decided movement towards naturalism in acting styles. The letter by Ibsen on presenting the character of Rebekka West in *Rosmersholm* as 'a living, real human being' (**148**), sketches a method not far removed from Stanislavsky's. But Ibsen's hint at the complexities which bedevil the 'presenting and representing' of this character also points to the new problems offered by his more symbolical drama of the late 1880s and 1890s.

In the Danish Royal Theatre, continuity of earlier traditions, as illustrated in the excerpt below from Edvard Brandes' book on *The Art of Acting in Denmark* (1880) (**147**), prevailed side by side with a new realism. Despite its royal name, the theatre largely supported itself on a bourgeois and conservative audience who were prepared to accept the new in small doses, but who also still wanted their vaudevilles and plays by Heiberg and Holberg (see **141–145**). Edvard Brandes' account of how the young Olaf Poulsen, auditioning for a student place at the Royal Theatre, is hijacked by the Holbergian actor Phister who moulds him in his own image, shows the limitations – but, to be fair, also the strengths – of such tradition. The two Brandes brothers, Georg (1842–1927) – more famous and lastingly influential – and Edvard (1847–1931), were both radical critics of Danish culture, theatre and literature; both were eventually to support Strindberg's attempts to find a stage for his naturalistic drama (see **152(a)** and **152(b)**). Edvard, himself a minor playwright, was very active in theatre polemics, and particularly critical of such practices in the Royal Theatre as those which shaped the acting career of Olaf Poulsen (1849–1923). The constraints of that career markedly contrast with the freedom of his older brother Emil's (see **142**, note 5): as a leading character actor in the Royal Theatre between 1862 and 1900, Emil Poulsen came to develop a naturalistic style of his own, playing in all of William Bloch's important Ibsen productions, beginning with *An Enemy of the People* in March 1883. Yet, Olaf Poulsen, as hinted at in Brandes' second paragraph, was not to be limited to Holberg parts; he became the company's chief and versatile comic character, capable, for example, of a moving realization of Old Ekdal in Bloch's production of *The Wild Duck* in 1885, in which Emil Poulsen played Hjalmar Ekdal.

147   Olaf Poulsen's acting début

Edvard Brandes, *Dansk Skuespilkunst: Portraetstudier* (Copenhagen: Philipsen, 1880), pp. 318–19

[Phister][1] immediately dismissed the pupil he was in the process of instructing, and managed to set Poulsen up with a small salary. The young man was given a written statement to say that he was offered engagement with special reference to Holbergian comedy.

It would perhaps have been better for Poulsen if Phister had not been there. He would have gone to one of our secondary theatres,[2] would very soon have become its leading comic actor and been given twice or three times as many parts as he had at the Royal Theatre during the same period. He would have had his talent tested and stretched in every direction, and would perhaps in due course have stood on the National Stage as a mature artist. Instead Olaf Poulsen has for a long time been sentenced to being the slavish copy of another, still living artist: to be Phister all over again.

It was in truth a sad business, and it was almost impossible for him, whatever he did, to please the audience. [...] Each time he was given a new role, it was one of Phister's old ones; as he was playing it, people said how like Phister he was, and at the end they said that Phister had been much funnier. [...]

On the other hand, I would be the last to deny that Poulsen's schooling by Phister has been thoroughly useful to him. It has disciplined his natural talent, which is anything other than classically inclined. At a smaller theatre Poulsen could very easily have sacrificed his given talent to his desire to score laughter and applause as an immediate reward – he is still a little too sensitive on this point. He could have come to take his art altogether too lightly. As it is, Phister has strengthened in him that love of Holberg which he had had since boyhood, and taught him a respect for the study of classical roles which only a very few actors in our theatre possess to the same extent.

[1] Joachim Phister (1807–96), attached to the Royal Theatre, Copenhagen, from 1852, was part of the theatre's backbone, as a classical performer in Holberg comedies. His third wife, Louise Phister (1816–1914), was attached to the Royal Theatre for sixty years.

[2] For example, the Folketheater (founded 1857), or the Casino (founded in 1848), which had its heyday under the direction of Theodor Andersen, 1869–84, with particular strength in comedies and operettas. The Dagmar-Theatre, which was to become Copenhagen's leading 'secondary', or 'private' (i.e. not State-funded) theatre, was not to open until 1883.

148   Ibsen writes to Sofie Reimers on how to play Rebekka, 25 March 1887

Henrik Ibsen, letter to Sofie Reimers, 25 March 1887,[1] *Samlede Verker*, vol. XVIII, pp. 130–31

To be able to give you any guidance I would have to be there to see how you have conceived of the part.

The only advice I can give you is to read through the whole play thoroughly several times, and to note carefully what the other characters say about Rebekka. Our actors often used to make the big mistake, at least in earlier times, of studying their parts in isolation and without paying proper attention to the character's position in, and relation to, the play as a whole. [...]

For the rest, you must draw on your studies and observations of real life.

No declaiming. No theatrical emphasis. No bombast at all! Express each mood in a way that is believable, natural, true to life. Never think of this or that actress whom you have seen. But stay close to the life that moves all around you and present a living, real human being.

I don't think Rebekka's character is difficult to penetrate and understand.

But there are difficulties in presenting and representing this character because it is so complex.

However, I have no doubt that you will overcome these difficulties, as long as you simply make real life, and real life alone, the foundation and starting point for your creation of Rebekka's personality.

---

[1] Sofie Reimers (1859–1932) had made her début at the Norwegian Theatre in Bergen in 1879, and was attached to the Christiania Theatre from 1881, and to the National Theatre from its opening in 1899 until her death. She replaced Laura Gundersen (see 136, note 7) in the part of Rebekka West in the Christiania Theatre production of *Rosmersholm* which opened on 12 April 1887, and wrote to Ibsen for advice.

V Strindberg discusses realism and naturalism, 1882 and 1889

Strindberg's Preface to *Miss Julie* is well known and available in most of the published translations of the play. Composed more or less immediately after the play, in August 1888, it is both a naturalistic manifesto and a means of demonstrating that the play he has written is a model for the drama of the present, and of the future.

The two Strindberg documents here reproduced are not so well known; together they present his rapid development from a position of advocating a realism, particularly in the theatre, which he defines in Hamlet's words as holding 'the mirror up to nature', to a naturalism which itself seems to be moving into expressionism: 'the great naturalism which seeks those points where the great battles take place, which loves seeing what you don't see every day ...'. Both essays construct themselves as part of a European, rather than national or local, argument.

149 A Strindbergian definition of realism, 1882

August Strindberg, 'Om realism. Några synpunkter' ('On realism. Some viewpoints'), *Ur dagens krönika*, 2 (1882)[1]

'Realism' is what we call that movement within all spheres of art where the artist seeks to achieve the intended impression, that is illusion, by representing the most important of the multitude of details of which the picture is composed.

In the past, authors could make an impression through general suggestions, because the generation who listened to them had had their senses educated so as to make them receptive to such methods of representation. On the new generation, brought up with the 'exact sciences' – the natural sciences, mathematics – the general suggestions of the old authors make no impression; this is not a fault in the young, but a characteristic quality.

The author of these 'viewpoints', when he reads in an old-fashioned poem of a rose and a butterfly, cannot envisage these abstract concepts of *genus*: his eye suffers until it can focus on the species.

Nor, therefore, can such an image make the symbol clear, the inward, the spiritual, 'the evanescence of love', for when the sense impression is vague, the thought becomes imprecise. [...]

297

The new realists have been accused of having lost their ideals. This is only apparently true, in so far as ideals are the highest, that which stands outside and above the mundane.

We who are young were brought up by parents born in an era which respected faith and honesty. We were then thrust into a new era which worshipped success at any price. We experienced the new age of fraud and are living in the midst of an epoch the name of which comes from America: humbug.

So we lost our faith in the reward of worth; virtue was no merit; honesty was less than practical, honour was lovely but ludicrous! Our gentlemen idealists have betrayed us, hence we abandoned them!

We have lost our faith in the Order of the Seraph[2] – true, but we still believe in God!

The realists have been accused of preferring what is ugly.

It is true that we who have been brought up on French comedy at our court theatre[3] have been given the idea that people cannot be presented on stage unless they have twenty thousand francs of annual unearned income [. . .]; we have lost faith in these ideals of society, with their starched shirt-fronts and six yards of train to their dresses; they have taught us to be nauseated by the kind of beauty that exists at the expense of others.

It is these others, the poorly dressed, that we dare love, sometimes commiserating with them, sometimes admiring them, even at the risk (much feared) of not being regarded as belonging to the better sort of persons.

Our realists have been accused of being something worse still: naturalists.

To us, this is an honorary title! We love nature, we turn in nausea from the new social conditions, from the police state, from the military regime which claims to defend the nation but merely protects those in power; because we hate what is artificial and contrived, we love to call each spade a spade, and we believe that societies will collapse unless sincerity, the first covenant on which societies rest, is restored.

There is also another accusation, which has become the magic formula of the opponents and their means of dismissing the whole issue as with a 'hocus-pocus', and this is the accusation that the realists love dirt! The world's two greatest authors of dirt, the former coachman and the former shop-assistant,[4] later known as William Shakespeare and Charles Dickens, two of the greatest benefactors of the human race, can stand up to such accusations.

We insignificant ones may answer quite briefly: Why are ye then dirty, gentlemen ideals-of-our time? For we realists still hold to the old faith that the end of literature, as of the theatre, 'both at the first and now, was and is to hold, as 'twere, the mirror up to nature; to show virtue her own feature, scorn her own image, and the very age and body of the time his form and pressure'.[5] [. . .]

The realists have also been rebuked for insisting on tackling a question which the idealists regard as unimportant, namely the relationship between the sexes.

The question is insisted on, it is true, by those who realize that this relationship is one of the most important factors in human life, and because this relationship is just at present being inquired into, and the position of the two parties clarified. But the realists pursue the matter at the deepest level, take it seriously and find the question too solemn to be dealt with in comic form![6]

[1] This originally non-partisan journal, founded by A. Ahnfelt and published in Stockholm, 1881–91, came to be an organ for radical social, political and aesthetic criticism in Sweden in the 1880s. The essay is reprinted in *SS*, vol. VII, pp. 191–200.

[2] The Order of the Seraph (*Serafimerordern*), instituted by the Swedish King Fredrik I in 1748, is the country's highest honour. Strindberg uses the phrase to symbolize hierarchy.

[3] cf. Strindberg's attack on the 'court theatre' of the time (**146**).

[4] Strindberg takes certain liberties with facts: Shakespeare is reputed to have held horses outside the theatre, and Dickens worked in a blacking factory.

[5] *Hamlet*, Act III, sc. ii, lines 21–4. Strindberg quotes from the standard Swedish translation by Karl August Hagberg (1810–64) whose twelve volumes of *Shakespeare's Dramatic Works* appeared in 1847–51.

[6] cf. Strindberg's discussion of *The Father* (**153(a)** and **153(b)**).

150   Strindberg reviews the contemporary theatre, March 1889

August Strindberg, 'Om modernt drama och modern teater' ('On Modern Theatre and Modern Drama'), *Ny jord*, 2, 3 (March 1889)[1]

The current crises in the theatre have prompted two conclusions: on the one hand, that theatre is a dying art-form; on the other, that this form of art has merely fallen behind and needs modernizing in tune with the times, in order to resume its fairly modest place as a cultural force. It cannot be denied that there is something archaic about the theatre as it is still constructed: the size of a circus, the stage enclosed behind a Graeco-Roman triumphal arch decorated with emblems and grotesque masks, reminiscent of the centuries BC. The red draperies, the resplendent curtain, the place of the orchestra which is still the same as in antiquity, the trap-doors leading down to where Charon waits, the elaborate machinery for bringing down gods to conclude the fifth act – all this takes you back to ancient times when the theatre was the site of religious and national festivals; and the masses still seem to come to the theatre expecting to be shown a piece of world history or at least some pictures from their own country's past to rouse memories of great and important events. We therefore cannot blame the national theatres for wanting to keep this role, even as they open their gates to jubilee celebrations and offer an assembly hall where the nation's leaders meet the people's delegates to receive their homage – or something else.

This persistent idea of the theatre as primarily a festive space – an arena where splendidly dressed warriors, princes and ladies appear *en masse*, and where mysterious, preferably inexplicable, events take place in palace halls, wild forests or castle moats – is so rooted that, for a play to be a success, it generally has to conform to this genre. [...] In due course, the drama of naturalism will regard Zola's *Thérèse Raquin*,[2] and thus the year 1873, as its first milestone. [...]

With *Thérèse Raquin*, the great style, the deep excavation into the human mind, had for a moment attracted attention, but no successors seem to have the courage to appear. It is true that, since 1882, claims have been made for Henry Becque's *Corbeaux* as a pioneering work.[3] I think this play is a mistake. If art is to be, as has been said, a corner of nature seen through a temperament,[4] then there is certainly a piece of nature in Becque's play but the temperament is missing. [...] Here we have the longed-for *ordinary* situation, the *typical*, the generally human, which is so banal, so flat, so boring, that after four hours of torture one has to ask the old question: what's this to me? This is objectivity, so beloved by those who lack a subject, by those with no temperament, those who ought to be called soulless!

This is photography which includes everything, even the grain of dust on the lens of the camera; this is realism, a working method elevated to a form of art, or the small art which does not see the wood for the trees; this is mistaken naturalism which believes that it is merely a matter of copying a corner of nature in a natural manner, but it is not the great naturalism which seeks those points where the great battles take place, which loves seeing what you don't see every day, which rejoices at the struggle of natural forces, whether those forces are called love and hatred, the spirit of revolt or social instincts, which is indifferent to whether something is ugly or beautiful, as long as it is great. It is this grand art which we have found in *Germinal* and *La Terre*,[5] which we glimpsed for a moment in *Thérèse Raquin*, and which we expected to see again, firmly established in the theatre – but which did not arrive with Becque's *Corbeaux* or Zola's *Renée*,[6] rather it was to rise and gain ground little by little through the opening of the new stage which, under the name of Théâtre Libre,[7] is active in the very heart of Paris. [...]

In the new naturalistic drama a thrust towards the significant motif was immediately noticeable. This meant that it tended to deal with the two poles of existence: life and death, the act of birth and the act of death, the battle for one's wife, for subsistence, for honour – all these struggles, with their battlefields, their screams of agony, their wounded and dead, through which one could sense the quickening southerly winds of the new philosophy of life as a struggle [...].

[...] The taste of the age, the fast-moving, hectic age, seems to favour the brief and expressive play [...].

One scene, a *quart d'heure*, seems increasingly to be the model for contemporary drama, and it has ancient antecedents. For it can claim to descend – yes, why not?

– from Greek tragedy, which consists of a concentrated happening in a single act, if we regard the trilogy as three separate plays. [. . .]

In the proverb[8] we are given the heart of the matter, the entire situation, the battle of souls, in Musset at times approaching tragedy, without having to be distracted by alarums and excursions or processions of extras. With the aid of a table and two chairs[9] it was possible to represent the most intense conflicts which life offers; and it was in this art-form that all the discoveries of modern psychology could first be popularly presented.

Could it not be that this is an emancipation of art, a renaissance, a deliverance from a formidable aesthetic which was making people miserable, which wanted to transform the theatre into a political riding-school, into a Sunday school, into a prayer-meeting? It may be!

Let us then also have a theatre where we can shudder at the most gruesome, smile at the ridiculous, play with toys; where we can see anything and not take offence when we are shown what has hitherto been hidden behind veils of theology and aesthetics, even if it means breaking old rules of propriety; let us have a free theatre, where one is free to do anything, except lack talent and be a hypocrite or an idiot!

And if we are not given such a theatre, I suppose we shall still survive!

[1] Strindberg was a frequent contributor to *Ny jord*, a short-lived monthly journal, edited by the Danish journalist and author Carl Johan Behrens (1876–1946), from January 1888 to June 1889. The essay is reprinted in *SS*, vol. XVI (1913), pp. 281–303.

[2] See 21.

[3] Henry Becque (1837–99), though committed to a 'théâtre vrai', opposed the extremes of naturalism in terms which clearly fit, among others, Ibsen's *Ghosts* and Strindberg's *The Father* and *Miss Julie*: 'I have never been very fond of assassins, hysterics, alcoholics, of martyrs of heredity or victims of evolution' (*Souvenirs d'un auteur dramatique*, Paris, 1895).

[4] Strindberg translates Zola's definition of a work of art: 'a corner of nature seen through the temperament of the writer' (cf. **54**, note 1).

[5] Strindberg seems to have in mind Zola's novels, *Germinal* (published in March 1885) and *La Terre* (November 1887), since adapted versions did not reach the stage until April 1888 and January 1902 (see **31**), respectively.

[6] Zola wrote *Renée* as a play in 1880–1, a modern version of the Hippolytus/Phaedra myth, drawing on his novel *La Curée* (1872). Rejected by the Théâtre-Français and other theatres, it opened at the Vaudeville in April 1887 and ran for thirty-eight performances.

[7] André Antoine's Théâtre Libre opened on 30 March 1887 (see **26–30**).

[8] The 'proverbes' of Alfred de Musset (1810–57), so called because the titles and motifs were taken from proverbs, unpopular in their own age of Romantic theatre, were by now being seen as forerunners of experimental plays being staged at the Théâtre Libre. (See S. M. Waxman, *Antoine and the Théâtre Libre* (Cambridge, Mass.: Harvard University Press, 1926), pp. 4–8).

[9] This was Strindberg's own favourite formula, both for naturalistic theatre – on completing *Creditors* in August 1888, he prided himself on the creation of 'a new naturalistic tragedy, still better than *Miss Julie*, with three characters, a table and two chairs, and no sunrise!' (*August Strindbergs Brev*, eds. Torsten Eklund and Björn Meidal (Stockholm: Bonnier, 1948–91), vol. VII (1961), p. 105) – and for the kind of simplified staging, prioritizing the spoken word, which, twenty years later, he wanted to see at the Intimate Theatre: 'A table and two chairs! The ideal!' he wrote to Falck (see **153(b)**) in March 1908 (*Brev*, vol. XVI (1989), p. 232).

VI   Correspondence between Strindberg and Zola, 1887

In September 1887 Strindberg sent a *cri de cœur* to Zola. *The Father*, which Strindberg wrote in February 1887, had been rejected by the royal theatres in Stockholm and also by August Lindberg, the most adventurous of contemporary Scandinavian directors (see **153(b)**, note 2). His usual publisher, Bonnier, would not touch the play, and it was 15 September before a provincial publisher, Österling, brought it out. It was unfavourably reviewed, largely as a document of misogyny, in the Swedish press. At this point Strindberg, refusing to abandon the belief that he had written an important naturalistic tragedy in tune with the 'formula' proposed by Zola, notably in *Le Naturalisme au théâtre* (1881), himself translated *The Father* into French and sent a copy to Zola with a letter asking for criticism. Having received no reply, he wrote again on 26 November, which provoked Zola's response.

151(a) Strindberg sends his own French translation of *The Father* to Zola

August Strindberg, letter to Zola, 29 August 1887. Original in Bibliothèque Nationale, Paris.[1]

Sir,

I do not claim to be an author known to you, but the literary career which I have pursued since 1869, as the acknowledged leader of the experimental and naturalist movement in Sweden, and the consequences thereof which I have had to suffer, from the obligatory court action to voluntary exile,[2] and finally the honourable retreat into being a serial novelist for the *Neue Freie Presse* in Vienna,[3] inspire me with some confidence that you might take the trouble, in a moment of leisure, to read the enclosed work.

The isolation in which I live, the absolute lack of a literary milieu, have driven me to commit this indiscretion at the risk of being disagreeable to you.

The great interest which you take in the 'theatre of the future' also gives me the hope that you might be kind enough to take note of an effort in the direction you, with a master's hand, have indicated.

As you will see, I take the liberty of submitting to your enlightened judgement a drama composed with an eye to the experimental formula, with the intention of bringing out the internal action at the expense of external theatrical effects, of reducing scenery to a minimum, and of preserving the unity of time as far as could be done.

Without wishing to abuse your well-known kindness, without any intention of presuming on your glorious name, I present myself only in the hope of receiving a word of good and severe criticism, after years of deadly silence.

In the hope, Sir, that you will not be offended by my strange request, and that you will be so good as to honour me with a reply in due course, I ask you to accept my sincere gratitude and my strong admiration.

Auguste[4] Strindberg

[1] Reprinted in *Brev*, vol. VI (1958), pp. 262–3.

[2] In the early 1880s Strindberg was the leader of a group of young radicals which he named 'Young Sweden' (Unga Sverige); he soon proved to be more radical than any of them. His voluntary exile began in September 1883; he came back to stand trial for blasphemy (of which he was acquitted) in November 1884, and returned abroad until 1889. The letter to Zola was written from Lindau in Bavaria.

[3] *Neue Freie Presse*, a democratic daily paper with a prestigious cultural section, had published two of Strindberg's short stories and asked him to write a novel for serial publication, which he never did. In 1887, however, the paper published four of his semi-fictional explorations into human psychology, later gathered under the title of *Vivisections*.

[4] Strindberg, writing in French, Frenchifies even his name.

151(b) Zola's disappointing reply

Emile Zola, letter to Strindberg, 14 December 1887[1]

Dear Sir and Colleague,[2]

[...] Your drama has interested me greatly. Its thought content is bold, its characters are very audaciously portrayed. You have made the subject of a man's doubt of his paternity yield powerful, disturbing effects. Lastly, your Laura is a real woman in her pride, in the recklessness and in the mysteriousness of her qualities and her faults. She will remain imprinted on my memory. In short, you have written a curious and interesting work in which there are, especially towards the end, some very fine things. To be quite honest, I am somewhat uncomfortable with the shortcuts in your analysis. You know perhaps that I am not fond of abstraction. I like it when characters have a complete social identity, when one can rub shoulders with them, when they breathe the same air as we do.[3] And your Captain who does not even have a name, and your other characters, who are almost reasonable beings, do not give me the complete sense of life which I demand. But here, between you and me, we have most probably a question of race. As it is, I repeat, your play is one of the rare dramatic works that have profoundly moved me.

I am your very devoted and very sympathetic colleague,

Emile Zola

[1] The text is as given in Strindberg's own translation of *The Father* into French, published as *Père. Tragédie en trois actes. Précédée d'une lettre de M. Émile Zola* (Hälsingborg: Österling, 1888); the same source is used in B. H. Bakker, ed., *Émile Zola. Correspondance* (Montreal: University Press), vol. VI (1987), p. 220.

[2] Zola's original phrase, 'Monsieur et cher confrère' balances distance and colleagueship.

[3] A Zolaesque criterion: he can prefer an acknowledgedly mediocre contemporary playwright to Shakespeare because the modern play 's'agite dans l'air que je respire' ('Le Naturalisme au théâtre', in *Œuvres Complètes*, ed. Eugène Fasquelle (Paris: Bernouard, n.d.), p. 121).

VII Strindberg tries to found an experimental theatre in Copenhagen, 1888

A theatre for his own plays had at various times been a dream of Strindberg's, but the refusal of publishers, reviewers and theatre directors to recognize the importance of his naturalistic plays sharpened the dream into plans, however unrealistic. At the end of May 1887 he went to Copenhagen, where Edvard Brandes had been one of the very few critics to praise *The Father*, and through Brandes he learned of Antoine and the opening, in March of that year, of the Théâtre Libre. On 3 June he wrote to the Swedish actor-director August Lindberg (see **153(b)**, note 2) proposing a joint venture: a small touring company, playing 'only plays by August Sg and none of his earlier repertoire. I will write the plays so that no costumes, sets or props need to be carted around'. A maximum of 30,000 crowns would be needed as capital, he writes, and shares in the company would be offered for sale (*Brev*, VI (1958), pp. 215–16). Not surprisingly, nothing came of this, nor of his hope, the following spring, to found in Stockholm 'a miniature Théâtre Libre with eight actors and four hundred seats in the auditorium' (*Brev*, vol. VII (1961), p. 39). But by this time *The Father* had been performed at the Casino Theatre in Copenhagen (see p. 307), and the Danish capital seemed to him to offer more of a milieu for a Strindberg theatre than did its Swedish counterpart. On the anniversary of the première of *The Father* he claimed to have 'founded the Scandinavian Experimental Theatre' (*Brev*, vol. VII, p. 157), and in order to make this notional theatre into a reality he proceeded to place the advertisements reproduced below. The idea was to start with *Miss Julie* and *Creditors*, Strindberg's wife Siri playing the leading parts, and to widen the repertoire to include suitable plays by other playwrights. The response to the notice in *Politiken* (**152(a)**) was poor: 'I have now read twenty-five submitted plays and found only one that could be acted', he wrote on 1 December (*Brev*, vol. VII, p. 187). In the end the repertoire would have to be provided by himself alone.

Strindberg had no illusions of providing a popular theatre: 'An Experimental Theatre in Scandinavia can exist only as a touring one since the elite is so small and has to be looked for in the capitals, the university towns and the largest cities', he wrote in the letter just quoted; and earlier he had outlined the itinerary of such an elitist company: 'We would open with two subscription performances in Copenhagen, then Gothenburg, Christiania, Bergen, Helsinborg, Malmö, Kristianstad, – NB not Stockholm [he adds 'because of ill-will and meanness!']. High prices and small houses – so that only the elite can come – only stalls and dress circles to be sold – galleries to be blocked off – so that the rabble can't get in and laugh at us' (*Brev*, vol. VII, p. 161).

The advertisement in *Dagens Nyheter* (**152(b)**) produced no sponsor, and financially the venture was doomed from the start. Strindberg had hoped to work with willing amateur actors for next to nothing, on the argument that 'The Théâtre Libre uses amateurs, and Lessing once (Hamb. Dramat.) suggested the same way out' (*Brev*, vol. VII, p. 162). In the end he left the organization almost entirely to Siri and to the Danish author and amateur actress Nathalie Larsen (who relieved Siri of the part of Tekla in *Creditors*). Two male actors, both having been associated with the 1887 production of *The Father*, were drawn into the venture: Hans Riber Hunderup (see **153(a)**, note 2) and Gustav Wied (1858–1914). The lady organizers managed to rent the Dagmar-Theater and planned to open on 2 March 1889, with a double bill of *Miss Julie* and *Creditors*, but on 1 March police arrived at the theatre to inform them that the censor had decided to ban *Miss Julie*. This play was then replaced by two Strindberg one-acters, and the Scandinavian Experimental Theatre opened with a triple bill on 9 March. A week later, after a mixed reception, they took the same bill across the Sound to Malmö, and there, after one performance and with no money left, ended the short life of Strindberg's experimental theatre. Meanwhile, *Miss Julie*, with Siri Strindberg in the title-role, had had its world première as a private performance, on 14 March, at the Students' Union of the University of Copenhagen.

152(a) Newspaper announcement for a Scandinavian Experimental Theatre

Announcement in *Politiken*, 17 November 1888[1]

As my intention is very shortly to open a Scandinavian Experimental Theatre modelled on the Théâtre Libre in Paris, I hereby invite the submission of plays for performance. These can be of any kind, but should preferably have a contemporary setting, be relatively short and not require elaborate machinery or a large cast.

---

[1] The announcement was published in Danish, presumably translated by Edvard Brandes to whom Strindberg sent his Swedish draft in a letter of 15 November 1888 (original in the Royal Library, Copenhagen; see *Brev*, vol. VI, pp. 158–9). *Politiken* was a Copenhagen daily newspaper, an organ for the radical left, founded by Edvard Brandes and V. Hørup in 1884, and with Georg Brandes and Bjørnstjerne Bjørnson among its contributors.

152(b) Front-page advertisement for the Experimental Theatre

Dagens Nyheter, 26 November 1888[1]

Financial sponsor

wanted for Scandinavian Experimental Theatre. Required capital relatively modest and may be managed, if desired, by sponsor in the capacity of the Theatre's Director of Finance. Write to: August Strindberg, Holte (Denmark).

---

[1] The advertisement represents a somewhat edited version of Strindberg's draft, which is contained in his letter to his brother Oskar on 20 November 1888. Instead of the 'relatively modest' capital, Strindberg specified 'around 10,000 crowns' (see *Brev*, vol. VII, p. 173).

VIII Naturalism and beyond: Strindberg on The Father, 1887 and 1908

The ur-première of *The Father* took place at the Casino Theatre, Copenhagen, on 14 November 1887. The Swedish première was at the New Theatre (Nya Teatern) in Stockholm on 12 January 1888. At the Intimate Theatre in Stockholm, August Falck staged the play for seventy-seven performances, opening on 4 September 1908, himself playing the Captain. There is a marked contrast between the advice Strindberg gives in connection with the 1887 and 1888 productions, on the one hand, and his instructions to Falck in 1908, on the other.

153(a) Strindberg calls for understated naturalism in the performance of *The Father*, 1887

August Strindberg, letter to Axel Lundegård,[1] 17 October 1887

Who will play the Captain, and what woman will want to play Laura?[2] The play can easily be ruined, become ridiculous! I suggest, although I rarely interfere in these matters, that the role of the Captain is given to an actor with a cheerful temperament so that, with the self-consciously superior, self-ironic and some-what sceptical tone of a man of the world, he[3] may face his destiny with a certain courage, fatally tangled in spider-webs which the laws of nature prevent him from tearing apart.

A deceived husband is a comical figure in the eyes of the world, and particularly in those of a theatre audience. He must show that he knows this, and that he too would laugh as long as it involved someone else!

This is what is modern about my tragedy, and woe unto me and the fool who in 1887 goes and plays it like *The Robbers!*[4] No screams, no sermons. Gentle, calm, resigned: the way an otherwise strong spirit encounters the destiny of modern man in the shape of an erotic passion.

---

[1] Axel Lundegård (1861–1930), Swedish author and journalist, based in Copenhagen (where he wrote for *Politiken*), had been asked by Hunderup (see note 2, below) to translate *The Father* into Danish and negotiate with Strindberg about the performance of the play. Lundegård published the letter in his book, *Några Strindbergsminnen* (Stockholm, 1920), from where – the original lost – it was reprinted in *Brev*, vol. VI, pp. 282–3.

[2] The Captain was played by Hans Riber Hunderup, the soon-to-be-bankrupt director of the Casino Theatre, and Laura by his wife-to-be, Johanne Krum.

'he' refers, as does the whole sentence as it progresses, more to the Captain than the actor: Strindberg
overrides rules of syntax in his involvement with the character he has created.
Schiller's *Sturm und Drang* play, *Die Räuber* (1780).

153(b) Strindberg's advice to the director, 1887

August Strindberg, letter to August Falck, Sr,[1] 23 December 1887

I just heard from August Lindberg[2] that you have decided to put on *The Father*.

As you know, I haven't much understanding of details of staging, and I don't like to interfere with the work of the actors. So I am just sending you a few general comments, based on what we have learned from the production here. Here goes:

General observation: Do the play the way Lindberg has done Ibsen: thus: not tragedy, not comedy, but something in between. Don't play it too fast, as we did at first here at the Casino. Instead, let it ease its way forward slowly, steadily, until it gathers speed of itself towards the last act. Exception: the speeches of the Captain when his *idée fixe* has taken root. They have to be spoken quickly, abruptly, spat out, continually breaking up the mood of the scene.

To be remembered: the Captain is not a coarse soldier, but a scholar who rises above his profession, [...] gentle in the first act, a good child; hardens, becomes furious and finally mad.

A detail: when he enters in the third act, he is in his shirt-sleeves (Jaeger shirt), has the books under one arm and the saw under the other.

If Laura is played by a young and beautiful woman, she should be hard, as her appearance softens the impact, and this will motivate her influence over her husband; if she is played by an older woman, the maternal aspect will have to be emphasized and the hard quality underplayed somewhat. [...]

Have sent off a copy in which I have made cuts. Cut more if you like. You are bound to hear in rehearsal if something doesn't sound right.

The throwing of the lamp demands careful preparation. The lamp used here was made of basketwork; the glass is fastened with putty so that the lamp can be thrown without the glass falling off; it is thrown past Laura's head through the open door, but not until she has backed out, so that the audience is left in ignorance of whether it hit her or not. Laura screams and the stage is blacked out.

[...]

Laura has an opportunity for significant action in the first scene of Act III, when she sits down at the same secretaire where the Captain sat. If, sitting there, she repeats or imitates some gesture of the Captain's (e.g. holds the pen with her lips while speaking, always assuming that the Captain did the same), then you produce an effective contrast.

[1] Per Johan August Falck (1843–1908). Swedish actor, director and theatre administrator (and father of August Falck, the founder and actor-manager of the Intimate Theatre; see 155–156(c)).

had been attached to the New Theatre (Nya Teatern) in Stockholm since 1874. He was one of the leaders of the company which rented the theatre for the 1887/8 season, during which the Swedish première of *The Father* took place, Gustaf Ranft playing the Captain and Ottilia Littmarck, Laura.

[2] Johan August Lindberg (1846–1916): talented actor/director; toured Sweden, Norway and Denmark with his own company in 1882–4, 1888–93 and 1894–7. His series of Ibsen productions includes his pioneering *Ghosts* – the first in Scandinavia – which opened at Hälsingborg (Sweden) on 22 August 1883.

154(a) An expressionist conception of *The Father*, 1908

August Strindberg, note to August Falck, Jr, 25 April 1908[1]

The Father is to be played as a tragedy! Large, broad strokes, loud voices!

Alexandersson[2] is to show the lioness she didn't show in *Easter*. She is to be the Tragédienne, but at the same time contemporary, modern; not tame, not the Comédie,[3] not to fear eruptions and wild passions, great hatred and lust for power, like a fury from hell –

[...]

Let the passions loose, shout and scream but don't get hoarse, don't hold back on hell!

Invite people (artists, theatre people) to every rehearsal, and ask them to 'say something'. [...] Don't play to an empty house, or the dress-rehearsal and first night will smell of rehearsal!

[1] On August Falck and the Intimate Theatre, see 155.

[2] Karin Alexandersson, one of the actresses who stayed with the Intimate Theatre from beginning to end, played the Mother, Mrs Heyst, in *Easter*, which opened on 16 April 1908 and became the most successful of this company's productions, with 182 performances in all. She also played Kristin in the Intimate Theatre's *Miss Julie*.

[3] 'Not the Comédie', i.e. not in the style of the Comédie-Française.

154(b) A non-representational set for *The Father*, 1908

August Strindberg, note to August Falck, 1 April 1908

If we use the drapery stage[1] for *The Father*, the play will be lifted out of its heavy everyday sphere and become high tragedy; the characters will become sublimated, ennobled, and will seem to belong to another world. [...]

We have sunk – regressed into what used to be called Molander,[2] or realism, naturalism, all of which is now passé. Nowadays it's called Michaelson![3] It's my fault: I get tired sometimes and have a relapse!

[1] Strindberg refers to the experiment with a simplified 'drapery stage' which had proved successful in the Intimate Theatre's production of *Queen Christina* (which opened on 27 March 1908). In this, reddish brown curtains of heavy velvet, in a lighter shade where they served as backdrop and darker where functioning as side wings, replaced painted flats; and to suggest a change of scene, emblematic objects were placed on barriers, one on each side of the stage. To Strindberg this neutral

permanent set was a 'discovery' and a 'miracle', and he was forever after to push *'draperibanan'* – the drapery stage – as the ideal to which scenic art should aspire.

² Johan Harald Molander (1858–1900) directed plays in Stockholm and Helsinki in the 1880s and 1890s. Known for the Meiningen-inspired stress on ensemble playing and the detailed realism of acting and décor in his productions he was responsible for an epoch-making staging of Strindberg's *Master Olof* at the Svenska (formerly Nya) Teater in 1897. He was the father of Olof Molander who was to become the supreme Swedish director of Strindberg plays in the twentieth century.

³ Knut Gottlieb Michaelson (1841–1915), playwright, businessman and director, was appointed to lead the new Royal Dramatic Theatre, and chose to open it with a new production of Strindberg's *Master Olof.*

154(c) *The Father* at the Intimate Theatre, 1908

Original in the Strindberg Museum, Stockholm

The first première of the Intimate Theatre's second season was *The Father*, which opened on 4 September 1908. The photograph shows the final moment of the play, as the Pastor pronounces his 'Amen' over the collapsed Captain/Father, while the wife and mother takes sole possession of the daughter: 'My child! My own child!' The cast is, from left to right: Fanny Falkner as the daughter, Berta; Karin Alexandersson as the wife, Laura; Anna Flygare as the Nurse; August Falck as the Captain; Gösta Gustafson as the Pastor; and Anton de Verdier as the Doctor.

Falck records how, working on the play, the company came increasingly to feel the need for 'an ordinary realistic stage space'. They wanted to stress 'the enclosed room, the suffocating milieu, the individual's struggle against his environment' (August Falck, *Fem år med Strindberg* (Stockholm: Wahlström & Widstrand, 1935), p. 208); and Strindberg let himself be persuaded to abandon the idea of the 'drapery stage'. The photograph shows the set closely adhering to the directions in the text as printed in 1887.

IX The Intimate Theatre and its actors, 1907–1910

155 Plan of the Intimate Theatre, 1907

Sketch by Alrik Kjellgren. Original (in colour) in the Strindberg Museum, Stockholm

The Intimate Theatre at Norra Bantorget, Stockholm, provided for the three years of its life – from November 1907 (when it opened with *The Pelican*) to 11 December 1910 (when it closed with performances of *Queen Christina* at 1.30 p.m., *The Father* at 4.30 and *Miss Julie* at 8.00) – a stage for the plays of August Strindberg. A wider repertoire – national and international – had originally been envisaged; in the end it was the decision of August Falck – the initiator, manager, director and leading actor of the theatre – to stage Maeterlinck's *L'Intruse* (23 September 1910) that precipitated a break with Strindberg, who withdrew his financial support and poured abuse over Falck.

A theatre for his own plays, to which the Swedish stage had, with a few exceptions, remained hostile (despite a growing interest in France and Germany), had long been an unfulfilled dream of Strindberg's (cf. p. 305). He took a lively interest in European developments in staging, and in particular saw Reinhardt's work as a model: 'Last year Reinhardt ... opened the Kammerspiel-Haus, the name of which suggests the secret programme: the idea of chamber music translated into drama [see **67**]. The intimate style, the significant *motif*, the sophisticated treatment. Last autumn the Hebbel Theater opened in almost the same spirit, and all over Germany theatres have grown up, bearing the name of "Intimes Theater"' (*Memorandum to the Members of the Intimate Theatre from the Director* (1908), in SS, vol. L, pp. 11–12¹). August Falck had come to his attention as the director of a successful touring production of *Miss Julie* – the first Swedish production of this play – and when the young director arrived in Stockholm (where *Miss Julie* opened at Folkteatern on 13 December 1906), the joint planning for an Intimate Theatre began. By the time a theatre building was actually found, in June 1907, and the high rent – 15,000 crowns per year – agreed to, Strindberg had written all his Chamber Plays.

The physical features of the building, the tenth theatre actively playing in Stockholm at the time, are indicated by the plan reproduced below. Located in an apartment block (completed in 1905), wedged between Norra Bantorget and Västmannagatan, the auditorium, foyers and box-office occupied part of the ground floor facing Norra Bantorget; the carpenter's shop, the twenty individual dressing-rooms and the greenroom (in the semi-basement), as well as the director's office (first floor), were entered from Västmannagatan. In the costly fitting out of spaces, originally advertised for renting as shop, store-room or factory premises, Falck (encouraged by Strindberg) paid much attention to audience comfort. There were separate foyers for ladies and gentlemen, the former with furniture in yellow silk, the latter equipped as a smoking-room. In the auditorium seats were of light mahogany, well upholstered; there were white walls and a soft, green carpet, and the ceiling lights were hidden under a yellow silk canopy. Only (free) soda water was available; no alcohol: the sustenance was to be spiritual.

Intimacy did indeed dominate auditorium and stage. There was seating for 161 persons (including two boxes of three seats each). The stage measured 6 by 4 metres, with cramped spaces for storing scenery and props at either side. Copies of Böcklin's 'The Island of the Living' and 'The Island of the Dead', made at Strindberg's request by the theatre's painter, Carl Kyhlberg, hung on either side of the proscenium (cf. the end of *The Ghost Sonata*). In this setting, Falck's company gave altogether 1,025 performances (or 1,147, if we count double programmes as two) of 24 different Strindberg plays (Falck's figures in *Fem år*), with varied success and under constant financial strain.

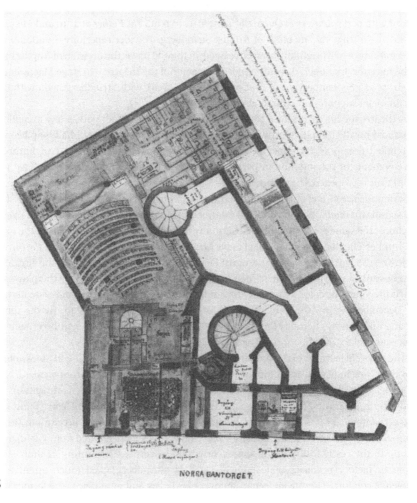

NORRA BANTORGET.

The young and small company at the Intimate Theatre, under the direction of August Falck (who also played a large number of leading roles – too many for a director-manager, Strindberg thought), worked extremely hard. The repertoire grew rapidly, and rehearsals and performances filled days and evenings. Sometimes there were marathon performances, such as on 21 February 1909, when *Easter* was performed at 1.30 p.m., *Miss Julie* at 4.30 and *There are Crimes and Crimes* at 8.00. Between 1908 and 1910 there was also an intensive touring activity, carried on simultaneously with their Stockholm performances. A constant theme in Falck's account of the history of the Intimate Theatre, *Fem år med Strindberg*, is the lack of appreciation his company found in Stockholm, as against the enthusiasm and admiration met on tours in other Scandinavian countries.

Falck was basically a naturalist, and the small stage did not easily lend itself to experiments in non-illusionist staging. Tensions, as well as occasional felicities (such as the 'drapery stage' for *Queen Christina* (see 154(b)), sprang from his relationship with Strindberg. Ironically, on a stage especially intended to house Strindberg's Chamber Plays, these turned out to be among the least successful. The popular successes were the naturalistic plays: *Miss Julie* and *The Father*, and apparently on the same terms, *The Dance of Death*. *Swan White* succeeded as a Maeterlinck-inspired fairy tale; and only the acclaimed production of *Easter* suggests that the Intimate Theatre created an understanding audience for later Strindberg.

Strindberg never attended public performances of his plays, being too painfully involved with his own creations and with their effect on an audience. He found rehearsals painful, too. But, Falck writes, 'we discussed the plays carefully before they went into rehearsal. And after the dress-rehearsals [which Strindberg did attend] he used to give us notes' (*Fem år*, pp. 59–60). At the beginning of the second season he attempted for a short while to fill more formally the function of a director – and the first *Open Letter to the Intimate Theatre* (1908) marks his taking up of this office – but gave up after sitting in on four rehearsals of *The Father*. He disliked the idea of long rehearsal times, as he felt that they bred excessive self-consciousness in actors; whereas Falck was a hard taskmaster, claiming for example that *The Dance of Death* was given eighty rehearsals. The gist of Strindberg's letters, notes and memoranda to the director and cast tends to be that the roles 'play themselves'. His belief in the spoken word – and he was forever instructing the actors (in writing) in the proper speaking of his words – was also his philosophy of acting: 'When the actor's whole being has absorbed the role, it lives in every muscle, nerve and sinew. From the word springs the gesture, of itself; not a muscle is lifeless. Without this connection, arms and hands hang there dead, mere things. But if the words come from the heart, the hands will follow the movement of the mouth, so that you don't have to think about it' (*Brev*, vol. XVI, p. 278).

---

[1] During 1908 and 1909 Strindberg dedicated altogether four pamphlets, of which the *Memorandum* was the first, to the Intimate Theatre. Only the last bore the title, *Open Letters to the Intimate Theatre*, under which they have all become known since their publication, together with a fifth and related pamphlet (*Shakespeare's 'Macbeth'*), as vol. L (Stockholm, 1919) of Strindberg's *Samlade Skrifter* (*SS*).

156(a) Alrik Kjellgren, 1927

Alrik Kjellgren,[1] 'Intima minnen från första Intiman', *Scenen*, 13, 23–4 (1–15 December 1927), 744–6

No allowance was made [by reviewers and critics] for the pace at which we worked – often giving five performances on a Sunday, two in Uppsala and three in Stockholm – nor for the sheer technical difficulties offered by the small stage.[2] It was rather like playing under a magnifying glass: any exaggerated gesture, any excessive emphasis, was twice as noticeable here as it would have been on a large stage. Even an experienced actor could look amateurish before he had time to get used to the small movements demanded by the small stage. Undoubtedly the severe criticism we received had an adverse effect on many an acting talent who lost faith in himself or herself and stopped growing. But, despite everything, our effort may be said to have been the first embryonic attempt to create, through Strindberg, a Swedish theatre tradition.

[1] Alrik Kjellgren (1883–1964) was a member of the Intimate Theatre company from beginning to end, 1907–10, and later became an administrator at the Royal Dramatic Theatre.
[2] The stage measured 6 × 4 metres (see 155).

156(b) Maria Schildknecht, 1952

Maria Schildknecht,[1] 'Strindberg och Intima Teatern', *Hörde Ni*, 19 August 1952, 633–8

How differently Strindberg's mind worked when he had a pen in his hand as against when he was supposed to direct our actual work on stage. In the hands of a great director or a gifted actor his plays and his roles can become fantastic creations, as we have often seen; but Strindberg gave his actors the advice, indeed one might say the command, simply to read what the text says, not to try to create anything themselves [...] and thus he killed the very life nerve in his plays.

He understood the essence of the theatre, the nature of theatre, only when he was writing, but then, it is true, he understood it all the more profoundly.

[1] Maria Schildknecht (1881–1977) joined the Intimate Theatre in its second season; after its closure she had a long career as one of the leading actresses of her generation. She was married to Helge Wahlgren (see 156(c)). The article is the record of a radio broadcast.

156(c) Helge Wahlgren, 1928

Helge Wahlgren,[1] 'Strindbergs egen teater', *Ord och Bild*, 37 (1928), 45–56

Contrary to what has been written, both at the time and later, Strindberg did not exercise a crucial influence on the way his plays were performed. At times he himself even complained that the instructions he gave were not always followed. This is simply further proof of how far he was from realizing what a director's work involves – believing that young people allow themselves to be instructed by something as intangible as brief notes.

Thus, during the first couple of years, critics often drew attention to the subdued mode of performance, the monotonous delivery, sometimes calling it 'stylizing'; the opinion was that the plays were not acted but read, and this was attributed to Strindberg's influence, probably against the background of his pronouncements [...] about following the text. It is true that Strindberg in his brief notes gave advice such as: 'Don't agonize over the part, don't analyse it, but learn it by heart and then it comes of itself'; but on another occasion he wrote: 'Don't think of the stage as a platform from which you preach but as a place where you represent people.'[2] He repeatedly warned against stylizing, and in *Julius Caesar* he goes so far as not even to insist on faithfulness to his own text: 'I have told my actors: tamper with a speech if it makes it come more naturally; patch it up if you like, but make sure that there is cut and thrust in the dialogue.'[3] This doesn't fit with all that talk about the veneration of Strindberg which was supposed to be holding the actors back out of reverence and fear of asserting themselves at the expense of the author. The subdued tone was simply the result of the small stage and the small auditorium with the audience so close to the actors [...]; it was also the result of the tendency to self-effacement and hesitancy in insecure and inexperienced actors.

[1] Helge Wahlgren (1883–1958) made his début as Pelléas in Falck's production of Maeterlinck's *Pelléas and Mélisande* at the Malmö Theatre in 1907 and followed Falck to the Intimate Theatre where he stayed until the end; from acting he eventually turned to directing and had a long and distinguished career at the Gothenburg Stadsteater, where he became known for his dislike of a director's theatre and his self-effacing devotion to the texts of the plays he chose to stage.

[2] Letter from Strindberg to Wahlgren, 2 February 1908 (*Brev*, vol. XVI, p. 173), in which the actor is praised for his performance as the Judge in *The Link* (première on 31 January 1908) but criticized as the Student in *The Ghost Sonata* (première on 21 January 1908).

[3] The third *Letter to the Intimate Theatre* (*SS*, vol. L, p. 139). See also Strindberg's essay on 'The Concept of Stylizing' in the fifth *Letter*.

X   *Strindberg on the staging of* To Damascus *and* A Dream Play

'In this dream play, as in his earlier dream play, *To Damascus* [1898], the author has sought to imitate the disconnected but apparently logical form of a dream. Anything can happen, everything is possible and probable. Time and space do not exist.... The characters split, double, multiply, evaporate, densify, disperse, assemble.' Thus Strindberg in a prefatory note to *A Dream Play* (1901) which implicitly points out the discrepancy between, on the one hand, the demands of his post-naturalistic art and, on the other, traditional methods of staging. The documents below record his view of success and failure in the first Swedish productions of the two plays, and his thinking, during the time of the Intimate Theatre, on ways of staging these plays.

Emil Grandinson's production of *To Damascus* at the Royal Dramatic Theatre, which opened on 19 November 1900, was a milestone in Swedish theatre history. The initial idea of achieving simplicity and flexibility by projecting scenery had to be abandoned; but the effect of a pilgrimage through a landscape more internal than external was gained by the use of a raised and arch-framed inner stage, producing a structure similar to the Munich *Shakespearebühne* which Strindberg much admired. (His essay on *Hamlet* in the second *Open Letter to the Intimate Theatre* contains a discussion and, in the original, 1908, edition a reproduction of a photograph of that stage.) Electric light had been introduced at 'Dramaten' in 1898, and the employment of space and lighting apparently gave a hallucinatory quality even to the backdrops painted by the traditionalist scene-painter Grabow.

When, seven years after it was written, Strindberg finally found a director, Victor Castegren, to tackle *A Dream Play*, that director's willingness to experiment was not matched by the attitude of the theatre management and the availability of equipment. Strindberg records the 'materialization phenomenon' achieved in the production which opened at the Swedish Theatre on 17 April 1907. He continued to struggle with the problem of 'de-materialized' productions of this play and *To Damascus*, at times seeing a solution to it in the use of the 'drapery stage' as in the Intimate Theatre production of *Queen Christina* (see **154(b)**). Falck realized the inadequacy of his stage and cast for such a task, but Strindberg continued to urge him on with plans and sketches, the gist of which was to avoid photographic realism and laborious scene-changes. In the design for *A Dream Play*, (**157(b)**) he envisaged a permanent set with the various locations, in and out of which the action flows, suggested by symbols painted on side flats. The Intimate Theatre never did put on *A Dream Play*, and when Falck finally mounted *To Damascus I*, on 18 November 1910,

Strindberg was at war with him, and the end of the theatre was in sight. The sketch reproduced here – one of many with which Strindberg bombarded Falck – suggests a neutral stage with the stations of the wandering of the Unknown and the Lady represented by stark symbols, in a form of simultaneous staging.

157(a) Strindberg praises Grandinson's staging of *To Damascus*

August Strindberg, 'Goethe's *Faust*', in *Öppna Brev till Intima Teatern* (Stockholm: Björck & Börjesson, 1909), pp. 56–8[1]

Grandinson[2] made a beautiful job of staging *To Damascus*. The play could never have been put on if we had aimed at simplification. Composed in a strictly contrapuntal form, Part I (which is what was played) consists of altogether seventeen tableaux. But, allegorizing the pilgrimage, the drama moves forward to the ninth tableau, which takes place in the Asylum; then the exiled couple turn around and make their weary way back, and at the same time the settings are reversed so that the drama ends at the street corner where it began. To make these scene-changes swift, a smaller stage was constructed within the main stage and framed by an exceptionally beautiful arch, painted by Grabow.[3] There was no need for side wings; we played against a series of backdrops suspended one behind the other and raised, as needed, by a silent pulley. Instead of unnecessary lowerings of the curtain, blackouts were used. [. . .]

Once Mr Castegren[4] had managed to get [*A Dream Play*] accepted at the Swedish Theatre, we began to discuss how to turn dream into stage image without materializing it too much. We first tried the sciopticon – something we had already tried at the Royal Dramatic Theatre in connection with *To Damascus*. Sven Scholander[5] [there] succeeded in projecting a backdrop large and clear enough, but since there had to be darkness in front of the backdrop for it to be seen, the actors were not visible enough. Another drawback was that the electric light showed through the fabric, though this could be remedied by placing the lights below the level of the stage floor. We were in a hurry, and gave up. [. . .]

Now, concerning *A Dream Play*, I had stated in the text that it should be performed with unchanged sides of 'stylized murals suggesting at the same time room, architecture and landscape'.[6] I had implied: backdrop to be changed as needed. Castegren travelled to Dresden, where they had recently used the sciopticon for *Faust*. He bought the apparatus, but when it was tried out back here (without me being invited to attend), it did not live up to its promise. As Mr Ranft[7] did not want to hear of the *Damascus* system of an arch and backdrops, there was no choice but to 'go to Grabow'.

Castegren [. . .] now applied all his inventiveness and energy to realizing *A Dream Play*, defying all those who resist anything new. I have thanked him, but have also told him that the production was not a success, because it made the dream image too material. [...] The constant scene-shifting disturbed the actors' concentration[8] and necessitated endless intermissions; apart from the fact that the entire performance became a 'materialization phenomenon' instead of the intended opposite (de-materialization). We are now intending to make a new attempt with *A Dream Play* at the Intimate Theatre, and this time to go all the way.[9] Instead of painted sets, which *in this case* are incapable of rendering amorphous and floating mirages, we intend to seek the effect of colours alone. We have discovered that our red plush drapery can be made to take on all nuances of colour, from azure blue through molten metal to purple, simply through the use of varied lights. And we have decided to replace the colourless costumes of our own age with colourful costumes from all ages, as long as they are beautiful, because in the dream there is no question of reality, which gives us every right to prefer Beauty to Truth.[10]

[1] The essay is part of the fifth *Open Letter* and is reprinted in *SS*, vol. L; see pp. 286–9.
[2] Emil Grandinson (1863–1915) was senior director at the Royal Dramatic Theatre, 1900–10.
[3] Carl Ludvig Grabow (1847–1922), traditionalist scene-painter, was stage-designer at a number of Stockholm theatres, while attached to the Royal Dramatic Theatre since 1890.
[4] Adolf Victor Teodor Castegren (1861–1914), actor and director at a number of theatres in Sweden and Finland, became director at the Swedish Theatre in 1906.
[5] Sven Scholander (1860–1936), more famous as a composer and singer of ballads, was also a photographer.
[6] Stage-directions at the head of the first scene (after the Prologue, which was added in 1906).
[7] Albert Adam Ranft (1858–1938), theatre magnate of unequalled power on the Stockholm scene, owned and ran the Swedish Theatre from 1898 until it burned down in 1925.
[8] Strindberg uses the word '*andakt*', literally 'pious devotion', suggesting the kind of 'concentration' he expects from actors in *A Dream Play*.
[9] The intention was never realized.
[10] Strindberg uses the German nouns '*Schönheit*' and '*Wahrheit*'.

157(b) Strindberg's design sketch for *A Dream Play*, 1909

August Strindberg, sketch of design for *A Dream Play*, from Falck, *Fem år*, p. 273

Under the sketch, Strindberg has written the following explanatory notes:

> *The Dream Play*[1]
> *A permanent set.*

Backdrop. Billowing clouds.[2] The castle is visible only when lit from behind.
Side flat 1. Hollyhocks.
Side flat 2. The door. Above it the masts of the brig.
Side flat 3. Fingal's Cave or the organ. Above it a cypress = Italy.
Side flat 4. A piece of furniture from the Lawyer's room. Italian cypress.
Side flat 5. Iron stove = Skamsund (Quarantine) or the home of the Lawyer. Above it a
barrier (ditto). Tops of masts.
Side flat 6. Hollyhocks.

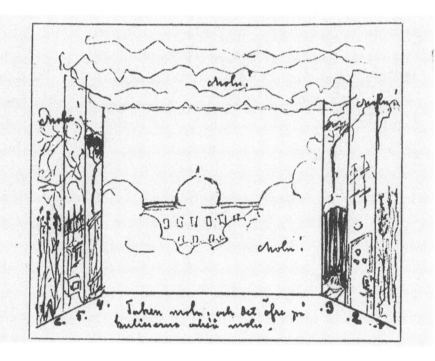

---

[1] Although published as *A Dream Play*, Strindberg generally refers to the work as *The Dream Play*.
[2] Clouds ('*moln*') dominate the stage image. In the space representing the stage floor, Strindberg has written: 'The ceiling, clouds; and the upper part of the flats also clouds'.

157(c) Strindberg's design sketch for *To Damascus*, *c.*1909

August Strindberg, sketch of design for *To Damascus, Part I*, from Falck, *Fem år*, p. 327

From (reader's) left to right, Strindberg's notes identify the side areas as follows: 'Church'; 'Hotel Room'; 'The Rose Chamber'; 'The Asylum'; 'The Kitchen'; 'Inn and Post Office'. The backdrop is described, at the top, as 'permanent'. High up on the (reader's) left is 'The whole mountain black!'; on the right 'The whole mountain white!' Midway is 'The Sea', and 'The Wrecked Ship' (with its masts 'like three white crosses': stage-direction in text, tableau 14). At the lower level, left to right: 'The Smithy/*Black*'; 'The Road'; 'The Miller/*White*'.

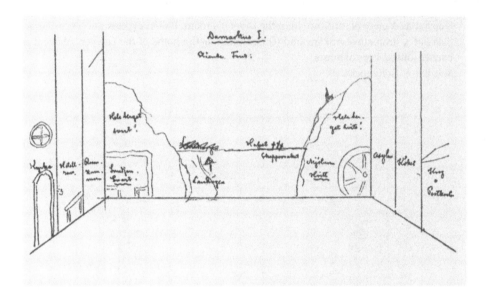

England, 1850–1914

Edited by LOUIS JAMES *and* MARION O'CONNOR

Introduction

A. 1850–1880 (by Louis James)

English theatre in the 1850s was rich in performance and spectacle. From 1850 to 1859, Charles Kean, as Manager of the Princess's Theatre, Oxford Street, dazzled London with his extravagant Shakespearian revivals. His production of *The Corsican Brothers* (1852), adapted by Dion Boucicault from the novel by Dumas *père*, depended upon ingenious stage-effects and introduced a new 'gentlemanly' style of melodramatic acting. It was a fashionable success – Queen Victoria went to see the play four times in two months.[1] Across the river in Lambeth, Astley's Amphitheatre was packed nightly to see such spectacles as J. H. Stocqueler's *The Battle of the Alma* (1853), which was staged, with 400 extras, barely a month after the actual event.[2] In the East End of London, George Dibdin Pitt's sensational melodramas were attracting over three and a half thousand to the Britannia Theatre each night.

American subjects were fashionable, partly in response to Harriet Beecher Stowe's *Uncle Tom's Cabin* (1851–2), a best-selling novel that became the source of scores of stage adaptations.[3] Charles Reade's *Gold* (Drury Lane, 1853) and Boucicault's *The Octoroon* (Winter Garden, 1959), two of the most popular plays of the decade, were set in America, and the flagging interest in English temperance drama was revived with transatlantic imports imports such as William W. Pratt's *Ten Nights in a Bar Room* (1858).

What was lacking was a major English 'literary' playwright. Many writers produced material which worked well on the stage, but few plays had literary quality. The most successful British author was the Irishman Dion Boucicault (1822–90), whose talent was for plotting and stage-effect rather than creating character or exploring significant themes. As plays tended to work to formula, the playwright's status was low, and he was accordingly paid little. The West End was dominated by plays imported from France or America, and as late as 1879,

[1] See George Rowell, *Queen Victoria goes to the Theatre* (London: Elek Books, 1978), p. 58.
[2] See A. H. Saxon, *Enter Foot and Horse* (New Haven: Yale University Press, 1968), pp. 144–6.
[3] See introduction to Stephen Holland, ed., *Colin Hazlewood, 'The Christian Slave'* (M.A. thesis, University of Kent, Canterbury, 1983).

Matthew Arnold was to lament, with some exaggeration, that 'we in England have no modern drama at all'. Everything notable on the stage, he believed, had come from abroad.[4]

In spite of Queen Victoria's enthusiastic patronage of the theatre, for the first two decades of her reign, the stage in England held a dubious social status. Many of the middle classes still held Puritan attitudes condemning plays as lies, and theatres the haunt of the devil – many playhouses were indeed frequented by prostitutes and pick-pockets up to the late 1840s.[5] The acting profession was considered 'low', and no respectable paterfamilias would have wanted his child to take up a career on the stage. Further, at a time when domesticity was increasingly valued among the middle classes, theatres were not organized for domestic outings. Programmes usually started between 6.00 p.m. and 7.00 p.m. and continued until midnight, offered a mixed bill, and expected an expert but rowdy response from the audience. Many parents preferred to buy toy theatres so that their children could act out the current dramatic success at home.[6]

By the 1850s, the theatre was becoming 'respectable'. As Britain's prosperity increased, the Puritan ethic relaxed, and the middle classes, as Arnold noted, returned to play-going. Even without this, the size of the theatre-going public would have increased. The population of England and Wales grew rapidly, from some 18 million in 1851 to nearly 23 million in 1871.[7] The greater part of this growth was in the towns, and between 1860 and 1870, ten new theatres were built in London, and others were refurbished. Improved transport brought provincial and suburban play-goers into the West End. In 1866 Henry Wigan declared that London audiences were 'constituted of an entirely different class; Londoners are in a very great proportion supported by the population *viagère*'.[8] Outside London, the rising prosperity of the northern cities was also reflected in theatre building – entertainment palaces like the refurbished Theatre Royal at Leeds, which opened in 1876 in extravagant style as the New Grand Theatre and Opera House with seating for 2,700.[9]

The theatres in turn changed to accommodate a new style of audience.

[4] Matthew Arnold, 'The French Play in London', *Nineteenth Century* (August 1879), pp. 238–40.
[5] As late as 1865, on the opening of the New Theatre Royal, Nottingham, the theatre was attacked as a place where 'false impressions are made. False principles are inculcated . . . Wherever these piles are reared, they pollute the vicinity'. The Reverend Wilfred Baguley, quoted in Richard Iliffe and Wilfred Baguley, eds., *Victorian Nottingham* (Nottingham: Nottingham Historical Film Unit, 1972), vol. VII, pp. 48–9.
[6] See George Speaight, *Juvenile Drama*, (London: Macdonald, 1946), *passim*.
[7] Out of town, S.C. Rep., Theatrical Licences and Regulations, 1866 (hereafter *SC 1866*), 4591.
[8] Liverpool was the most active centre outside London, in 1879 served by seven theatres, including the Amphitheatre, which held an audience of 5,000. See *The Entertainment Directory, and Playgoer's Guide*, 1879 (hereafter *ED 1879*).
[9] See Victor Glasstone, *Victorian and Edwardian Theatres* (London: Thames and Hudson, 1975), *passim*.

Progressively, the cheap benches of the pit were eased out, and the central auditorium taken over by expensive stalls. Performances started later, for those who wanted to come after dinner. Shows were also shorter, offering at most one or two main plays, with an afterpiece. Priced out of the West End, many of the working-classes moved out to local theatres such as the Britannia in Hoxton; or to the music halls,[10] while younger audiences sought out the many 'penny gaffs' – improvised theatres offering sensational cheap shows for the cost of a penny.[11] Music halls, which grew out of the old singing-saloons, started with Morton's Canterbury Hall in 1850. These made their profits from the sale of refreshments, while offering a miniaturized version of the earlier omnibus theatre programmes. The entertainment could include short versions of plays, though with time limitations that were jealously monitored by the theatre proprietors. By 1866, in London, audiences at the music halls outnumbered theatre-goers by some three to one, with a similar growth in the provinces.[12]

In the 'legitimate' theatre, larger audiences, shorter programmes, and higher entrance charges enabled more lavish styles of production. In scenery, the old system of two-dimensional flats, working along grooves in the stage, was superseded by intricate systems of scenery both 'flown' above the stage and supported by blocks and poles raised from beneath. There was much concern with stage spectacle.[13] Charles Kean turned to exhaustive historical research for his elaborate Shakespearian productions. Dion Boucicault built such plays as *The Corsican Brothers* (1851) and *Arrah-na-Pogue* (1865) around complex stage mechanisms. While it is not true to say that 'realism' on the stage emerged only in this period, enormous attention was paid to devising authentic scenic effects, aided by continuous improvements in theatre lighting.[14] With more time for rehearsal, groupings and crowd scenes were carefully devised. The expensive productions necessitated longer runs: in 1855 Charles Kean's elaborate production of *King Henry VIII* at the Princess's ran for 100 nights; in 1860 Boucicault's *The Colleen Bawn* at the Adelphi ran for 230. The period saw the rise of actor-managers like Charles Kean at the Princess's (1851–9), Marie Wilton and Squire Bancroft at the Prince of Wales (1865–80), and Henry Irving at the Lyceum (1878–99). Following the earlier reforms of Macready at Drury Lane and Covent Garden, these took control over all aspects of production. Boucicault, and later the

---

[10] See Peter Bailey, ed., *Music Hall: The Business of Pleasure* (Milton Keynes: Open University Press, 1986), *passim*.
[11] See Paul Sheridan, *Penny Theatres of Victorian London* (London: Dennis Robson, 1981).
[12] Appendix to *SC 1866*, pp. 295, 313; estimate based on numbers of music halls and theatres recorded in *ED 1879*.
[13] See Michael Booth, *Victorian Spectacular Theatre 1850–1910* (London: Routledge and Kegan Paul, 1981).
[14] See Terence Rees, *Theatre Lighting in the Age of Gas* (London: Society for Theatre Research, 1978).

Bancrofts, organized companies touring with their productions, challenging the dominance of the old provincial circuits.[15]

Acting styles changed, too, although this was an uneven process, and many of the leading actors, including Barry Sullivan, Wilson Barrett and Henry Irving, remained of the 'old school'. The earlier style of acting was based on laboriously learned conventions of speech and gesture;[16] it was strenuously physical and included the skills of singing, dancing and fencing; and it relied on audience response. G. F. Cooke interrupted a tragic Shakespearian scene to scold a hushed Liverpool audience with – 'Ladies and gentlemen, if you don't applaud, I can't act.'[17] This melodramatic style became 'gentlemanly' in the acting of Charles Kean and Charles Albert Fechter at the Princess's Theatre. In his revolutionary *Hamlet* (1861), Fechter removed the histrionic conventions surrounding the play, and combined melodramatic intensity of feeling with a modified style and close interpretation of the text.[18] Moving completely away from the old acting method was the meticulously produced understatement of the 'cup-and-saucer' comedies of T. W. Robertson. Starting with *Society* (1865), these appeared in the Bancrofts' luxurious Prince of Wales Theatre, where audiences watched intimate theatre which critics like Henry James scorned for its limited moral scope and minimal level of acting,[19] but which prepared the way for Ibsen and Chekhov.

The 'new', more naturalistic, form of drama demanded a silent audition. The playwright and comedian J. B. Buckstone complained in 1874 that 'anyone who shouts "bravo" is looked upon as a lunatic, and the very best English art is now presented before an audience of richly-attired and kid-gloved mutes'.[20] Old-style play-goers like Thomas Erle considered the audience at the fashionable Princess's as anonymous 'as a file of policemen who are distinguishable only by their numbers'.[21]

Both acting and playwriting improved in social status. The playwright had played a minor role in early nineteenth-century drama, based as it was on stock conventions of plot and character. Crummles' advice to Nicholas Nickleby would have served in the 1840s for most writers even at the main patent theatres: 'Invention! What the devil's that got to do with it! ... Just turn that [French play]

---

[15] Richard Fawkes, *Dion Boucicault* (London: Quartet Books, 1979), pp. 123–4; Michael Booth, *Theatre in the Victorian Age* (Cambridge University Press, 1992), pp. 18–19.

[16] The earlier conventions are detailed in William Leman Reid's popular *The Road to the Stage* (revised from 1827 original by Leman Thomas Reid, London: J. Onwyn, 1835); similar directions were still being given as late as Henry Neville's (Robert Brierley's) 'Gesture', in Hugh Campbell, R. F. Brewer and Henry G. Neville, *Voice, Speech and Gesture* (London: Deacon, 1895).

[17] Bram Stoker, *Personal Reminiscences of Henry Irving* (London: William Heinemann, 1907), p. 47.

[18] See Kate Field, *Charles Albert Fechter* (London: Osgood, 1882; reprinted 1969).

[19] See, for example, *The Scenic Art of Henry James*, ed. Alan Wade (New Brunswick: Rutgers University Press, 1948), pp. 122–3.

[20] J. B. Buckstone, 'Actors and Audiences', *The Era Almanack* (1874), p. 79.

[21] Thomas W. Erle, *Letters from a Theatrical Scene-Painter* (London, 1880), p. 105.

into English, and put your name on the title-page.'[22] Payment for plays had
shrunk, from the times of the Regency, to levels that could not attract serious
literary talent: £10 (about £200 today) for a three-act play was usual, although a
well-known author might get as much as £70. Douglas Jerrold, as resident
dramatist at Elliston's Surrey Theatre, received £5 a week in 1829, and only £50
for *Black-Ey'd Susan*, one of the most popular and frequently produced plays of the
nineteenth century (Crummles paid Nicholas but £1 a week at Portsmouth).
Although both literary and performing rights in published work were protected
within the Empire by the 1842 Literary Copyright Act (5 & 6 Victoria C.45),
publishers such as John Dicks paid a pittance for the purchase of all rights to the
plays published in popular acting editions.[23]

As the situation changed in the 1860s, and managers vied to attract the
middle-class audiences back into the theatres, a popular playwright could find his
work at a premium. Dion Boucicault who, as successful author, actor, and later
theatre manager, held an unusually strong position, demanded (and got) half-
shares in the profits wherever his plays were produced. In 1866 Wigan cited
Boucicault's claim to be receiving between £600 and £800 a week for *The Streets
of London* and *Arrah-na-Pogue*.[24] In addition, Boucicault's touring companies
netted £500 a week from *The Colleen Bawn*. He also acted in the United States and
entered into lucrative contracts with American managers. Increased links with
the United States and across the Empire mark this period, with actors and whole
productions travelling overseas.

The middle decades of the nineteenth century, then, saw drama in England
entering into an era of expansion, innovation and prosperity. Yet Arnold was
premature in heralding a new 'national theatre'. The most popular play of the
period was H. J. Byron's comedy *Our Boys* (1875), which ran for 1,362
performances on its first production at the Vaudeville. If middle-class critical
attention was focused on the Princess's and Prince of Wales's theatres, the largest
playhouse in London was not in the West End, but the working-class Britannia,
Hoxton, with 3,923 seats.[25] The Britannia offered a mixed fare of stirring
melodramas and Shakespeare festivals, produced with all the histrionic energy of
the Edmund Kean tradition.[26] As with other aspects of culture during this period,
the theatre was marked by a growing split between the intellectual and the
'popular'.

[22] Charles Dickens, *Nicholas Nickelby* (1839), ch. 23.
[23] See Michael Booth et al, *The Revels History of Drama in English* (London: Methuen, 1975), vol. VI, pp.
46–57.   [24] *SC 1866*, 4614.
[25] 'Hoxton and Whitechapel Theatres,' *The Builder*, 16 (25 September 1850), pp. 644–5; (6
November 1858), pp. 654–5.
[26] For performances at the Britannia, see Dickens's 'Amusements of the People', *Household Words* (30
April 1850); on audience, see Clive Barker, 'The Audiences of the Britannia', *Theatre Quarterly*, 9, 3
(1978), pp. 101–8.

B. 1880–1914 (by Marion O'Connor)

In some respects the state of English theatre at the end of the nineteenth century was continuous with that of the middle of the century. Theatre construction had continued apace – especially, for the West End, in the 1880s. The Savoy Theatre, which opened on 10 October 1881, and Daly's Theatre, which opened on 27 June 1893, were respectively first and last in a series of twelve new West End theatres built in as many years. There were no permanent closures of West End theatres during those twelve years, so the cumulative capacity of those dozen theatres at their respective openings represents an expansion of the West End by the same number of seats – 12,711.[27] Over the next eleven years, however, more than twenty new theatres went up in London suburbs, the newly built bedrooms of the expanding metropolitan workforce. And the new suburban theatres were bigger than the new West End theatres: the Savoy and Daly's were, at 1,300 and 1,512 seats respectively, among the largest of the dozen new West End theatres of the 1880s and early 1890s, only the Shaftesbury (1,670 seats), Lyric (1,400 seats) and Empire (1,400 seats but 450 standing places) being larger; but the capacity of the Camberwell Metropole at its opening (1894), for example, was 2,050, while that of the Poplar Hippodrome (1905) was 2,500.[28]

Unlike the West End theatres, most of which were in the hands of actor-managers presenting as-long-as-profitable runs of plays starring themselves and their consorts, the suburban theatres were built and owned by businessmen. (In this respect, and in the frequency with which a group of theatres was owned or controlled by a single individual or partnership, the brief lifespan of the London suburban theatres anticipated developments in the West End theatre after the First World War.) The suburban theatres gave place mainly to touring companies that brought local residents cut-rate productions of West End successes.[29] Built as mass distribution centres for a down-market product, the suburban theatres soon lost their audiences: they went away to the moving pictures and never came back.

Where the suburban theatres sought the custom of local tradesmen, the new West End theatres of the 1880s and early 1890s sought the patronage of the privileged. When the Bancrofts took over the management of the Haymarket Theatre, refurbished it and reopened it in January of 1881, their much-contested closure of the pit and concomitant expansion of the stalls not only improved their

---

[27] This is the sum of their seating capacities as reported in a paper handed in by T. G. Fardell, chairman of the Theatres and Music Halls Committee of the London County Council, to the House of Commons Select Committee on Theatrical Licensing at its meeting on 28 March 1892. The figures for Daly's and the Duke of York's (then called Mrs Wyatt's) Theatres were only projections for buildings then under construction.

[28] For the capacities of the suburban houses, I follow the figures in their respective entries in Diana Howard, *London Theatres and Music Halls 1850–1950* (London: The Library Association, 1970).

[29] On the suburban theatres, see the exchange in *The Theatre*, n.s. 4, vol. [xxx] (October–November 1897), pp. 155–7 and 226–9.

profit margin but also raised the social profile of their audiences. The logical culmination of the Bancrofts' move can be seen in the seating plan of the Little Theatre (1910), the penultimate theatre built in the West End before the First World War. A conversion of (appropriately enough) a building belonging to the private bankers Coutts & Co., the Little Theatre had only 309 seats, two thirds of them stalls and one third balcony and boxes.[30] The Little Theatre was unusual in both its extreme smallness and its total exclusion of impecunious theatre-goers: most turn-of-the-century West End theatres retained the old divisions of auditoria. But the lines of division came to be all but fortified. Separate entrances and staircases for each section of the audience were in part warranted by safety regulations: separate rest-room and refreshment areas were not. However, the provision of separate facilities as well as separate access ensured that the evening-dressed patrons of the stalls need never cross the paths of the street-dressed occupants of gallery benches. The latter were, of course, at the greater distance from the stage, but opera glasses were affixed only to seats in the stalls and dress-circle. These sections of the auditorium, together with their respective lobbies, bars and cloakrooms, were distinguished by sumptuous décor and comfortable furnishings. They mirrored, and were measured against, the reception rooms in wealthy households. As the trade press reported of Daly's Theatre on its first opening night, 'The style of most theatres is based on the idea of a drawing-room; Daly's rather recalls the more solid dining or banqueting apartment.'[31] In some theatres – notably the Criterion under Charles Wyndham's management from 1879, the St James's under George Alexander's from 1890, and the Garrick under John Hare's from 1889 to 1896 and again under Arthur Bourchier's from 1900 to 1910 – the mirror trick took in the stage as well as the interior decoration of the auditorium. For it was for these houses and managements that 'society drama', the new English playwriting of the last decades of the nineteenth century, was written by Henry Arthur Jones, Oscar Wilde, Arthur Wing Pinero and Alfred Sutro.

As the social catchment area of the consumers of theatre moved up-market, so did the social status of its producers. The symbolic moment was Henry Irving's acceptance in 1895 of the first theatrical knighthood, but other indicators abound. The class backgrounds of actors, for example, rose sharply between 1880 and 1914.[32] Among actresses the trend is similar but less pronounced: their

---

[30] Figures for the capacity of the Little Theatre at its opening are from Howard, *London Theatres*. p. 137.

[31] *The Era*, 1 July 1893, reprinted in Raymond Mander and Joe Mitchenson, *The Lost Theatres of London* (London: Rupert Hart-Davis, 1968), p. 54.

[32] For this sentence, the next clause, and several points further on in this paragraph, see Michael Sanderson, *From Irving to Olivier: A Social History of the Acting Profession in England 1880–1983* (London: Athlone Press, 1984), pp. 12–17. See also Michael Baker's excellent study, *The Rise of the Victorian Actor* (London: Croom Helm, 1978).

collective status is perhaps less clearly signalled by the social level from which they entered the profession than by the social level for which they left it. Actresses married into the aristocracy at a rate sufficient to fill an appendix to one of the trade annuals and to provoke leading articles in one of the quality weeklies.[33] The 'less fortunate' could turn to the Theatrical Ladies Guild, founded in 1893 'to provide, by temporary loan of suitable clothing, for distressed actresses, choristers, extras, dressers, and cleaners, during the period of their confinement'.[34] The Guild was one of a significant number of self-help and/or self-improvement organizations within the London theatre at the turn of the twentieth century. (The fact that two of these groups were connected to the established Church, and another to Roman Catholicism, points to the elevation of the reputation of the theatre at the time.) Several of these organizations – notably including the oldest, the Royal General Theatrical Fund – perpetuated the practices of working-men's clubs and trade unions. With the formation of the Actors' Association in February 1891 in Manchester, not London (to which it did, however, move in the following month), theatrical performers were on their way to professionalization, or unionization. The choice between these alternatives was contentious,[35] the definitive issue being the status of the actor-managers. Construed as a professional association, the Actors' Association needed the most powerful and prestigious exponents of the profession. Construed as a trade union, the Actors' Association represented labour and had no place for management. The trade unionist camp broke away for a few years (1907–10) of independent existence as the Actors' Union, and meanwhile the actor-managers started their own Society of West End Theatre Managers. The suburban theatre managers had their own association from 1894.

The various sets of regulations which controlled late Victorian and Edwardian theatre were perceived as more or less cumbersome, more or less out-of-date, depending on the interests of the perceiver. Least contentious, but perhaps of greatest consequence, were the regulations governing the licensing of theatrical buildings. In London these were from 1843 under the direct and somewhat lax supervision of the Lord Chamberlain, but from 1878, with the passage of the Metropolis Management and Buildings Acts Amendment Act (41 & 42 Victoria C.56), the metropolitan authorities were also made responsible for determining and enforcing requirements as to structure, equipment and practice in places of public entertainment within the county of London. In direct consequence of the

---

[33] See John Parker, ed., *The Green Room Book for 1905*, and 'Stage Morals and Stage Marriages', *The World*, 29 March 1910, p. 535, and 5 April 1910, p. 575.

[34] *The Dramatic Review*, 21 November 1893, p. 120. See also the illustrated articles about the Guild in L. Carson, ed., *The Stage Yearbook* (London: Carson & Comerford, 1909), pp. 52–6.

[35] See, for example, Gertrude Kingston, 'Trades Unions and the Censor', in L. Carson, ed., *The Stage Yearbook* (London: Carson & Comerford, 1908), pp. 9–11.

new legislation, the 1880s saw several theatres in London's East End close, never to re-open, while every other theatre in the metropolis had to make a number of changes – ranging from four at St George's Hall to thirty-two at Astley's Circus – to meet the new requirements. These requirements grew ever more exhaustive over the next decades, for the threat of fire did not so much disappear as change its shape when, with the 1881 opening of the Savoy Theatre, the first London theatre to be wholly illuminated by electricity, gas lighting began to disappear from theatres.

One provision of the 1843 Theatres Act (6 & 7 Victoria C.68) which was frequently challenged in the late nineteenth and early twentieth centuries was the restriction of licences for the performance of stage-plays solely to premises licensed as theatres. It would have been in the interests of the managers of music halls, which had both bigger audiences and lower overheads than the theatres, to secure licences for the presentation of stage-plays. However, it was in the interests of the actor-managers that such licences should remain their exclusive prerogative. Two House of Commons Select Committees – in 1866 and 1892 – resolved in favour of the status quo. The provision of the 1843 Act for the pre-censorship of plays as part of their licensing for performance in theatres was also considered but left unchanged by the 1866 and 1892 Select Committees, and then again by a Joint Committee of the House of Commons and the House of Lords in 1909. The pre-censorship of dramatic text could perhaps be said to have limited the actor-managers' notional repertoires, but in practice such a system protected them, and they almost unanimously supported it. Between 1874 and 1911 the Examiners of Plays in the Lord Chamberlain's Office in the Royal Household were, successively, E. F. S. Pigott, formerly a barrister and then a journalist, and G. A. Redford, formerly a bank manager: such censors spoke for the preferred market. Moreover, the issue of a licence could even be regarded as official ratification of a manager's decision as to whether or not a play were suitable for public performance. The people for whom pre-censorship created problems, and from whom the protests were loudest, were primarily the playwrights, and also the more adventurous critics.

For the playwrights, however, the last decades of the nineteenth century brought an appreciable improvement of status. The royalty system of payment for playscripts had become the rule, and the fixed percentage was soon modified into a sliding scale of royalties. Of still greater consequence, were changes in the copyright laws. As it stood at mid-century, British law contained both a muddle around performance rights – as distinct from copyright construed as covering the multiplication of copies – and also a large loophole through which it was possible for pirates to dramatize other people's novels. (In 1888, for example, West End theatre-goers could see both a pirated *Little Lord Fauntleroy* at the Princess's and

The Real Little Lord Fauntleroy at Terry's.[36]) Moreover, it gave British playwrights no protection abroad. From 1886 on, a series of International Conventions tidied up copyright among European nations; and after 1891 dramatic copyright was also protected by law in the United States of America. In 1901 W. S. Gilbert – who at his death ten years later left an estate valued at £111,971[37] – observed: 'What with provincial rights, American rights, and colonial rights, one or two successes now make a man practically independent, place him above the necessity of doing hack work ... and enable him to give time and thought to his art, and scope to his ambition.'[38] The ambition of some of the most vocal and visible turn-of-the-century playwrights was for their work to be read – whether as literature, to which Henry Arthur Jones aspired, or as socio-political agitation, to which George Bernard Shaw laid claim. From the early 1890s they published their plays, often with prefaces and with stage-directions expanded into character sketches and scene descriptions which seemed to have been pasted in from novels.

The new factors in English theatre and drama at the end of the nineteenth century are twinned: the importation and attempted domestication of 'serious' continental drama, notably Ibsen's; and the successive attempts, again cued by if not copied from continental precedents, to establish institutions which might generate such drama in England. The initial appearance of a play by Ibsen on an English stage was as late as 15 December 1880, when an abridged translation of *Pillars of Society* was performed at the Gaiety Theatre, and until the end of that decade, further productions were few and attracted little attention. Then, beginning with Janet Achurch's and Charles Charrington's startlingly successful production of *A Doll's House* at the Novelty Theatre in the summer of 1889, came a spate of productions and ancillary brouhaha, including parodies.[39] Interest peaked in 1893, which saw eight London productions, including the first production of one of Ibsen's plays by a leading West End management. By the end of the 1890s a fashionable journal could write off Ibsen as passé: 'Ibsen appears to be "dead", both for the study and the stage, in England, leaving only the deep impress of his vogue upon the work of our own few dramatic authors.'[40]

It is difficult to assess 'the deep impress of [Ibsen's] vogue' upon English

---

[36] For an account of the rival dramatizations of *Little Lord Fauntleroy*, see William Archer, 'The Season in London', in Edward Fuller, ed., *The Dramatic Year 1887/8* (London: Sampson Low, Marston, Searle & Rivington), pp. 28–30.

[37] George Rowell, *The Victorian Theatre 1792–1914* (1956), second edition (Cambridge University Press, 1978), p. 165.

[38] William Archer, *Real Conversations* (London: William Heinemann, 1904), p. 118.

[39] See Tracy C. Davis, 'Spoofing "The Master": Parodies and Burlesques of Ibsen on the English Stage and in the Popular Press', *Nineteenth-Century Theatre Research*, 8, 2 (Winter 1985), pp. 87–102; and Penny Griffin, 'The First Performance of *Ibsen's Ghost, or Toole-up-to-date*', *Theatre Notebook*, 33, 1 (1979), pp. 30–37.

[40] Percy Cross Standing, 'The London Stage', *The Idler*, 15 (February–July 1899), p. 566.

playwrights between 1880 and 1914. Certainly the drama being written by the later date looks very different from that of a quarter of a century before. But it does not look much like Ibsen's. It lacks Ibsen's characteristic configurations and dramatic structure, his dramatic depths and the impression that what is being represented is ultimately some terrible bias woven deep in the human condition rather than little warps in the fabric of late-nineteenth-century provincial bourgeois society. That impression is a function of Ibsen's language, which is above all what is missing from the English drama written in his wake. There is nothing in the insular output to match either the verbal textures of Ibsen's dialogue or the visual language prescribed, with great precision, by Ibsen's stage-directions. The English analogues (for example, the business and the lines around Paula's mirror in Pinero's *The Second Mrs Tanqueray*) are by comparison embarrassing in their strain to sustain great significance. Yet it is largely to Ibsen's credit that significance is even sought. A reviewer of the 1880 performance of *Pillars of Society* noted of its unknown author that 'he is the leading dramatist of Norway ... usually selecting national subjects of strong domestic interest' and judged that 'the play seemed to contain materials which in an altered form would make it successful with English audiences'.[41] And it would indeed be Ibsen's dramatic materials – the serious representation of those areas of middle-class life in which major ideological crises were underway – which mattered to the vociferous would-be reformers of English drama at the end of the nineteenth century.[42]

In London, the array of attempts at setting up institutions to foster new English drama all went on in the interstices of the actor-managers' theatre and can be divided into three approximately successive kinds, according to the size of the gap each filled. The first kind, filling the smallest gap, was the use of matinées for trial productions. (Originally, as well as etymologically, a morning performance, the matinée could not be attended by the working-classes either then or when it moved to the afternoon. The rapid spread of matinée slots around the performance schedules of West End theatres in the 1870s is another reminder of the exclusion of those classes from those theatres.) By the 1880s, the principal use of the matinée slot was to milk successful productions. In addition, however, matinée performances of new work were staged in West End theatres both by unknown playwrights seeking showcases and/or securing their legal rights, and by managements testing the market. Notable among the latter category were John Hollingshead at the Gaiety (where, in 1880, Britain's first-ever production of a

---

[41] W. H. Rideing in his *Dramatic Notes: An Illustrated Year-book of the London Stage 1880/1* (London: David Bogue, 1881), pp. 68–9.
[42] Shaw asserted that Ibsen's addition of discussion to the well-made play had radically altered its form. But his analysis applies rather better to his own plays than to its ostensible object. See 'The Technical Novelty of the Plays', in *The Quintessence of Ibsenism* (1891), second edition (London: Constable & Co., 1913), pp. 187–205.

play by Ibsen was given only a single matinée performance) and Herbert Beerbohm Tree at the Haymarket (where, in 1893, the first such production by a major West End management was initially scheduled for matinée performances only) and later at Her Majesty's.

In so far as it involved the established managements, the trial of new work at matinée performances was mainly a matter of maximizing the use and profits of their theatre buildings. The fostering of new work was, at most, a desirable side-effect. In the 1890s, however, the institution of the play-producing society gave top priority to the discovery of new drama, or in some cases the resuscitation of very old drama. The play-producing society consisted of a group of subscribers whose annual membership fees secured them tickets to that year's productions, which the fees were supposed to underwrite. This arrangement had two advantages: it provided capital and it eluded pre-censorship. Strictly speaking, a subscription system of ticketing was covered by the law, but in 1886, when the Shelley Society staged *The Cenci* at the Islington Grand Theatre, and then again in 1891, when the newly formed Independent Theatre (the first of the play-producing societies) staged Ibsen's *Ghosts* at the Royalty Theatre, all the relevant authorities proved willing to pretend that the performances were private and outside the terms of the 1843 Theatres Act. The Independent Theatre, which lasted from 1891 to 1898, the equally short-lived (1897–1904) New Century Theatre and the rather hardier (1899–1939) Stage Society were the most important of the play-producing societies dedicated to the fostering of new English drama, of which the Stage Society did manage to discover rather a lot. And some of the societies dedicated to the staging of classical English drama – notably, the Elizabethan Stage Society (1894–1905), the English Drama Society (1905–9) and, after the First World War, the Phoenix Society – made influential innovations in non-realistic staging, sustained acting traditions and revived dramatic ones.

The play-producing societies, while numerous, had small and often overlapping membership lists.[43] Dependent on hiring theatre buildings and halls on dark nights and at matinées, they were itinerant undertakings and as a rule gave only a few performances of their productions. Important as they would prove in the long run, the societies initially made little difference to a theatrical system in which the choice of dramatic fare was determined mainly by a play's potential as an audience-attracting vehicle for the talents of the actor-manager who staged it, and in which the definition of success was the achievement of 100 performances. The twin problems of the star system and the long run had long been damned as

---

[43] The largest was the Stage Society's 1,571 memberships in 1910/11. See James Woodfield, *English Theatre in Transition 1881–1914* (London: Croom Helm, 1984), pp. 55–73.

deleterious (above all in their consequences for the training of actors),[44] and in the first decade of the twentieth century, a succession of short-term managements in London attempted seasons from which, by various stratagems and to various degrees, stars and long runs were excluded. The only one of these attempts to survive more than a season was the enormously influential co-management of the Court Theatre by Harley Granville Barker and John Vedrenne from October 1904 to June 1907, continued at the Savoy for a single further season. After them came, more or less disastrously, Lena Ashwell's management of the Kingsway (the Novelty rechristened to chime with the thoroughfare newly built in its environs) in 1907/8, Charles Frohman's at the Duke of York's and Gertrude Kingston's at the Little in 1910, and then Barker's and Lillah McCarthy's there in 1911.

What these attempts ultimately proved was that the interstices of the West End theatre could not long accommodate permanent companies playing either in repertory from a stock of productions or for short runs of quickly revivable productions. Such a project, tagged 'the repertory ideal', was regularly voiced as the programme to be carried out by a national theatre, the recurrent dream of theatre reformers after Arnold. The repertory ideal was realized and sustained only outside the West End – in fact, outside London. By the last decades of Victoria's reign, the star system and the long run had reduced English provincial theatre to a very-far-flung suburban theatre, a network of temporary venues for touring companies playing to audiences unable to patronize the real West End thing. Yet it was in the new urban centres of the Midlands and the North that the repertory ideal was embodied in institutions of more than a few seasons' endurance – at the Manchester Gaiety (1907–19), the Liverpool Repertory Theatre (1911–39), and the Birmingham Repertory Theatre (1913ff), together with the Glasgow Repertory Theatre (1909–14) in Scotland. Among these companies there is such a continuity of personnel, many of whom were already veterans of at least one of the London ventures, that they can be said to have constituted a 'repertory movement'.[45] That movement did restore to Britain a *geographically* national theatre, but as a rule only the middle classes of the nation would find it 'irresistible'.

[44] See, for example, George Alexander, 'On Theatrical Apprenticeship', *The Theatre*, n.s. 4, xxi (January 1893), pp. 54–5; and Leopold Wagner, 'Should the Touring System be Abolished?', *The Theatre*, n.s. 4, vol. [xxx] (September 1897), pp. 130–33.

[45] See Anthony Jackson and George Rowell, *The Repertory Movement: A History of Regional Theatre in Britain* (Cambridge University Press, 1984) for the most up-to-date study.

I *Theatre buildings and theatre organization*

158 Theatre architecture and class differentials, 1888

James George Buckle, *Theatre Construction and Maintenance* (London: The Stage, 1888),
pp. 9–11 and 21–5

Writing as an architect and in the wake of the horrendous fire which had destroyed at least
127 lives at the newly built Exeter Theatre Royal on 5 September 1887, Buckle was
primarily concerned with safety. His book is subtitled 'a compendium of useful hints and
suggestions on the subjects of planning, construction, lighting, fire prevention, and the
general structural arrangements of a model theatre' and dedicated to Wilson Barrett as 'a
manager who has displayed an earnest desire to adopt reforms conducive to the public
safety and convenience' (see **166**). Buckle's hints and suggestions have been shaped by
expectations about the social conduct, and the physical comfort, proper to the occupants of
seats in the several parts of theatre auditoria. These expectations both convey information
about notional audience behaviour and betray the class assumptions which are built into
late-Victorian and Edwardian theatre buildings.

Seat Dimensions and Auditorium Capacity [pp. 9–11]

When calculating the money-holding capacity of a proposed building, the
following dimensions will be found to constitute a fair average width of seat per
individual – stalls, 20 to 24 inches; dress circle, 20 to 22 inches; upper circle, 18 to
20 inches; pit, 16 to 18 inches; amphitheatre, 16 inches; gallery, 15 inches. In
addition to the actual seating, allowance must be made for the standing-room.
Standing is most undesirable, but when permitted should not exceed one single
row at the back of each circle or section of seating. [. . .]

The auditorium should be cosy and *not too large*. In large theatres, which are not
desirable for dramatic representations, some of the auditors are removed so far
from the stage that the performers are almost inaudible and their facial expression
entirely lost. [. . .] It is desirable that the most remote spectator should not be more
than 75 feet from the stage, nor the angle of vision exceed 45 degrees. Neither
manager nor architect should sanction a seat being fixed unless it permits a good
view of the performance. Having regard to the convenience and adaptability for
dramatic representations, the following accommodation cannot probably be

much exceeded – stalls, 200; pit, 600; first circle, 250; second circle, 350; amphitheatre, 100; gallery, 500: total, 2,000.

Stalls [pp. 21–2]

In some theatres the stall floor is level, but it is better 'stepped' up, rather than on the rake. These steppings should not be less than 2 inches, nor exceed 4 inches, in height.

The width of the seats and area allotted to each person will depend upon the price and degree of luxurious comfort. The width may vary from 20 inches to 24 inches; and the distance from back to back should never be less than 3 feet. It is not unusual to find the same description of seat fitted to the stalls and the dress-circle. This is not desirable, as the occupants of the stalls are generally looking up, and require to lounge in their seats, which should therefore be deeper, and the inclination of the back several degrees more than the dress-circle seats. In all cases the seat should, as far as possible, permit the occupant to comfortably accommodate himself to the angle of sight. [...]

A separate entrance from the street to the stalls is very desirable.

Pit [pp. 21–3]

Managers regard the pit as the 'back-bone' of the theatre. [...] The pit seats are generally continuous, and may be with or without back-rails. The width [i.e., depth] of the seat need not exceed 9 inches or 10 inches, but if fitted with back-rails the seat will have to be increased in width [depth] to 12 inches or 13 inches. When the seats are 'marked off' by painted lines or strips of webbing 18 inches should be allowed to each person. [...] The distance from back to back of the seats should be not less than 2 feet 2 inches, but when fitted with back-rails not less than 2 feet 4 inches. In the latter case a centre gangway will be desirable, otherwise gangways at each side of the pit, not less than 3 feet 6 inches wide, will be sufficient, as the occupants generally walk over the seats. [...] The height from the pit floor to the soffit of the first circle front should not be less than 9 feet, if an appearance of comfort is desired for the occupants of the pit.

Dress Circle [pp. 23–4]

The seats may be similar to the stalls, but should have less depth of seat and inclination of back. It will further be an advantage to have the seats 1 inch or 2 inches higher than those in the stalls. The width of the steppings upon which the seats are fixed should not be less than 3 feet.

The height of the risers will vary according to the distance of the circle from the stage [...] but it is desirable to increase the height of the back rows 2 inches or 3 inches more than the front rows demand. These extra inches in height will make all the difference between 'seeing' and 'not seeing' during a performance at matinées when ladies are permitted to wear their bonnets.

Upper Circle [p. 24]

Unless chairs are used the seats may be continuous, with back-rails, and divided by arm-rests or strips of white webbing. The seats should be 15 inches in width, and not less than 18 inches allowed to each person.

The steppings on this tier should be reduced to 2 feet 6 inches in width.

Amphitheatre [pp. 24–5]

When the front rows of the gallery circle are appropriated as an amphitheatre, a permanent division separates these seats from the gallery. This part of the theatre is invariably approached from the gallery staircase, but a separate means of entrance is desirable.

Gallery [p. 25]

In planning this part of the theatre care should be taken not to place seats from which a view of the stage cannot be obtained. Discomfort in the gallery will create disturbance, and consequent annoyance to the whole house.

The steppings forming the gallery will vary according to the height above and distance from the stage. The general width is about 2 feet, but 2 feet 3 inches is more desirable, and the height of the riser 1 foot 6 inches. In no case should the height of the riser exceed the width of the stepping. This will represent a rake of 45 degrees, the utmost limit that either safety or convenience will admit. The seats should be continuous, and about 9 inches wide [deep], raised on blocks 2 inches or 3 inches deep, and slightly overhanging the nosing of the steppings. The seats may be marked off by an incision or painted line.

Gangways [p. 25]

The number of seats in a row should never exceed twelve without an intervening gangway. The *minimum* width of gangway should equal two seats in the respective section of the auditorium; e.g., stalls, 4 feet; pit, 3 feet; dress circle, 3 feet 4 inches; upper circle, 3 feet; gallery, 2 feet 4 inches. These latter should be double gangways, having dividing hand-rails firmly secured to the guard-rails fixed round the circle front.

Theatres retain individual characteristics throughout this period, often specializing in a house style – for example, the Adelphi was noted for its melodrama, the Gaiety for burlesque – and increasingly attracting a distinct class of audience. Plays therefore need often to be seen in the context of the theatre in which they were produced. The following entries give details of some representative theatres together with information contemporary readers wished to know.

159(a) The Adelphi Theatre, Strand, London

From *The Entertainment Directory, and Playgoer's Guide* (1879), p. 9

The Adelphi Theatre, 409–412 Strand, opened as the 'Sans Pareil' on 27 November 1806: it became the major purveyor of sensational melodramas in the West End.

A large handsome theatre, situated on the north side of the Strand, within a short distance of Charing-Cross. The present building . . . was opened for the first time on 27 December 1858. The total length of the building is 114ft 6in; length from back of boxes to proscenium, 48ft; [. . .] height from pit to ceiling, 57ft; length of stage, 56ft; width of ditto, 66ft 6in. Seats 1,560. The form of entertainment given consists principally of melodrama – always well played, and for which the house has long been famed – farce and occasionally burlesque. Pantomime at Christmas. Open all the year round. Doors open at 6.30. Commence at 7.00 p.m.

Admission: Private boxes, 21s, 42s, 84s; stalls 7s; dress-circle 5s; upper circle, 3s; pit 2s; amphitheatre, 1s; gallery, 6d.

Proprietor, Benjamin Webster. Lessees and Managers. A. and S. Gatti.

159(b) Astley's Theatre and Circus, Westminster Bridge Road, London: the circus ring

From *The Illustrated London News*, 14 April 1842

Astley's was a major phenomenon of Victorian theatre, surviving under differing managements until it was finally closed, under 'Lord' John Sanger in 1893. Patronized by all levels of society from costermongers to royalty, Astley's mixed circus and spectacular theatre in a way disappearing by the end of the century.

INTERIOR OF "ASTLEY'S" AMPHITHEATRE.

The fourth Astley's theatre – the three previous ones having all been destroyed by fire – is a very handsome and large structure and was erected about the year 1842 [opened Easter Monday, 1843]. It seats 3,780 persons, and is the largest equestrian establishment in London. Dramas and spectacles, in which horses are introduced, are the principal forms of entertainment at this house. Pantomime at Christmas. Open almost all the year. Commence at 7.

Admission: Private boxes, 21s to 5 guineas; dress-circle, 4s; pit stalls 2s; amphitheatre, 1s 6d; pit 1s; gallery 6d. Lessee and Manager, George Sanger.

(From *The Entertainment Directory* (1879), p. 11)

159(c) The Britannia Theatre, Hoxton, London, 1858

From *The Illustrated News of the World*, 25 December 1858

The largest London theatre in its time, the Britannia was built in 1858 from the Britannia Saloon, built at the back of the tavern at 188 High Street, Hoxton, in 1841 (see **162**). In 1923 it became a cinema.

INTERIOR VIEW OF THE BRITANNIA THEATRE, HOXTON.—(AFTER AN ORIGINAL SKETCH BY OUR OWN ARTIST.)

One of the largest theatres in London. Built on the site of the old Britannia Saloon, it seats 3,923 persons. To witness the interior of this theatre on a Boxing-night, and to watch the mass of human beings crammed in to see the first performance of the pantomime, is perhaps one of the sights of London. The sensational drama is played here, and the visitor may always rely upon seeing the pieces well mounted. Open all the year round.

Commence at 6.45.

Admission: Stage boxes, 2s each person; boxes and stalls, 1s; pit and box slips, 6d; gallery, 3d. Half-price[1] at 8.30.

Proprietress and Manageress, Sarah Lane.

(From *The Entertainment Directory* (1879), pp. 11–12)

1 See **162**, note 1.

159(d) Covent Garden Theatre and Opera House, Bow Street, London

From *The Entertainment Directory* (1879), pp. 12–13

This was the third Covent Garden theatre; the first was built in 1732. It has basically survived in this form.

A very noble and imposing building erected for the proprietor, Mr Gye, from the designs of Mr Barry, the celebrated architect, in 1856, on the site of the old theatre. [...] Seats 3,000. Italian opera [...] is given here from the end of March, or the commencement of April, until the end of July. The remainder of the year, up till Christmas, Promenade concerts are given. Pantomime at Christmas. Doors open (during the opera season) at 8 o'clock, and the opera commences at half past. During the pantomime season, 6.30. Commence at 7 o'clock.

Admission (Opera Season): Orchestra stalls, 1 guinea; side boxes on the first tier, 3 guineas; upper boxes, 52s 6d; pit tickets, 7s; amphitheatre stalls, 10s 6d and 5s; amphitheatre, 2s 6d; the remaining part of the house is let to subscribers. Private boxes, pit tier, £5 15s 6d; private boxes, first tier, 5 guineas.

Admission (Pantomime Season): Private boxes, from 10s 6d to 4 guineas; orchestra stalls, 10s; dress-circle, 5s; upper boxes, 4s; pit, 2s 6d; amphitheatre stall, 3s; amphitheatre, 1s.

Proprietor, F. Gye. Lessees (winter season) A. and S. Gatti.

159(e) Drury Lane Theatre (Theatre Royal, Drury Lane), London

From *The Entertainment Directory* (1879), p. 14

The first Drury Lane Theatre opened in 1732. The theatre described here is the fourth, and present, building, opened in 1812.

Play-goers may have their particular houses to which they resort, But *all* go to 'Old Drury'. It is the 'National' theatre of England. [...] The present building was erected by B. Wyatt, and opened 16 October 1812, with a prologue from the pen of Lord Byron, *Hamlet* being the opening piece. It has entrances to the pit and gallery, both in Russell Street and in Vinegar Yard; and its principal entrance, which has a large portico, is in Bridges Street. The length of the building from east to west is 237ft, and its width from north to south is 130ft. It is made of brick, and will seat 3,800. [...] The entertainment given is always of the best, and is principally composed of the spectacular and historical drama. The pantomime produced here at Christmas, and for which the house has such a worldwide reputation, is always on the most stupendous and superb scale. Sometimes Italian opera is given here during the summer months. Open (with the exception of a short summer recess) all the year round. Doors open at 6.30. Commence at 7 o'clock.

Admission (Dramatic Season): Private boxes, from 1 guinea to 4 guineas; stalls, 7s; dress-circle, 5s; first circle, 4s; balcony, 3s; pit, 2s; lower gallery, 1s; upper gallery, 6d.

Proprietors, a Company. Lessee and Manager, Frederick B. Chatterton.

159(f) Prince of Wales Theatre, Tottenham Street (from 1905, The Scala, Charlotte Street), London

From *The Entertainment Directory* (1879), p. 22

This is THE fashionable house of London, and is without doubt the most luxuriously comfortable and sumptuously decorated theatre in Europe. It was originally called the 'Queens', but, after its interior was entirely altered and re-modelled, it was opened under its present name, by special permission, on Saturday evening, 25 April 1865, under the management of Miss Marie Wilton (now Mrs Bancroft). It is mainly supported by the aristocracy, and is the best managed theatre in the kingdom. The pieces played consist of the very cream of comedy, and the visitor may always rely on seeing here the very best of works interpreted by the very best of *artistes*. With the exception of a short summer recess the theatre is open all the year round. It seats 814. Doors open at 7.30. Commence at 8 o'clock.

Admission: Private boxes, 21s, 31s 6d and 42s; stalls, 10s; dress-circle, 6s; boxes, 4s; upper boxes, 3s; pit, 2s 6d; amphitheatre, 1s. No fees.

Lessee and Managers, Sydney and Marie Bancroft.

159(g) Princess's Theatre, Oxford Street, London

From *The Entertainment Directory* (1879), pp. 22–3

Charles Kean as Manager, 1850–9, made the Princess's the most brilliant and fashionable theatre of the decade, and led the development of more 'respectable' theatres, drawing out-of-town audiences. First opened in 1840, the theatre was refurbished in 1869. It closed in 1902.

First opened with Promenade Concerts, 30 September 1840. A handsome building, largely associated with the name of Charles Kean, who held the reins of management here for many seasons, and startled the world with the magnificence of his productions. The theatre seats 1,580, and drama is the staple entertainment provided. A pantomime is sometimes played here at Christmas. Open all the year round. Doors open at 6.30. Commence 7 o'clock.

Admission: Private boxes, from 21s to 63s; stalls, 7s; dress-circle, 5s; upper boxes, 3s; pit, 2s; amphitheatre, 1s; gallery, 6d.

Lessee and Manager: Walter Gooch.

159(h)New Grand Theatre and Opera House, Briggate, Leeds

From *The Entertainment Directory* (1879), p. 77

The Grand Theatre, Leeds, was built by Wilson Barrett at a cost of £65,000, and opened in 1878. With its perfect sightlines and advanced backstage facilities, the Leeds Grand became the model for theatre-building in the provinces.

Size, total height from cellar floor to ceiling, 118ft.; depth from footlights to back wall, 75ft; between side walls, 72ft. Seats comfortably, 2,700 persons. Proprietors, a Company. Lessee and Manager, Wilson Barrett.

159(i) Alexandra Theatre, Lime Street, Liverpool

From *The Entertainment Directory* (1879), p. 79

Opened in 1866. Size, 64ft. from back of boxes to curtain. The whole of the staircases are composed of stone – the principal one being 10ft 6in wide, and its corridors are tiled and fireproof. Holds 2,200.

Lessee and Manager, Edward Saker.

160   The very model of a modern music hall: the Coliseum, London, 1905

From the programme in the Theatre Museum for the opening of the Coliseum, 4 January 1905

The Coliseum was widely publicized for its stage equipment, which is advertised in the first two of the following paragraphs of self-description. Equally remarkable is the omission, throughout all of these paragraphs, of the words 'music hall' and 'variety': only in the information about the schedule of performances are there clues that these will not be performances of stage-plays. The building being virtually indistinguishable from a contemporary West End theatre save by reference to the entertainments given in it, the programme describing it is evidence of the way in which turn-of-the-century music hall was taking its cues from West End theatre managements. See Felix Barker, *The House That Stoll Built* (London: Frederic Muller, 1957) and Victor Glasstone, *The London Coliseum* (Cambridge & Teaneck, N.J.: Chadwyck-Healey, 1980).

The London Coliseum is something entirely new in theatrical enterprise. In extent, design and decorative features it has been described by the leading newspapers as a palace of pleasures, colossal and magnificent. By means of the triple electric revolving stage, invented by Mr Oswald Stoll, grand spectacular effects are produced.

All roads lead to the new playhouse in St Martin's Lane, for the theatre is close to and visible from Charing Cross. It occupies an area of about an acre. The stage weighs 160 tons, and is over 10,000 square feet in extent. Its three revolving tables can be turned at a speed of over 20 miles an hour.

Beautiful gold and coloured mosaics and magnificent marble and alabaster are the chief features of an imposing decorative scheme.

Above the Great Tower, on which bold carved figures represent Art, Music, Science, and Literature, is an iron revolving globe, about twelve feet in diameter, from which 500 electric lamps spell out to the public the word 'Coliseum'.

The management have instituted a new order of things in more ways than one. The Coliseum is the only theatre in Europe which provides lifts to take the audience to the upper parts of the building. The lifts are intended primarily for elevation to the handsome Terrace Tea Room, under the management of Fuller's, Limited, of Regent Street, in whose able hands has been placed the refreshment catering throughout the building. The two electric lifts – identical with those supplied for the use of His Majesty the King at Epsom and Doncaster – are in the Grand Salon.

From the Grand Salon, ladies pass through two draped archways into the Ladies' Boudoir, which is beautifully fitted.

Through the Grand Salon is the Royal entry. Immediately on entering the theatre, a Royal party will step into a richly furnished lounge, which, at a signal, will move softly along a track formed in the floor, through the Salon, and into a large foyer, which contains the entrance to the Royal Box. The lounge car remains in position at the entrance to the box, and serves as an ante-room during the performance.

Large handsomely-draped openings divide the Grand Salon from the Grand Staircase. From the ground floor or entrance level the marble staircase is continued down to the large Baronial Smoking Hall, for the use of all parts of the house.

There are spacious tea rooms in every tier – the Terrace Tea Room, Grand Tier Tea Room, and Balcony Tea Room. There are also Confectionery Stalls and an American Bar. Dainty Snacks at moderate charges can be obtained all day in the theatre. Five o'clock tea between the three to five and six to eight performances will be a speciality.

The Terrace Tea Room (which is for the use of Private Box and all Stall patrons) can be reached by the Grand Staircase, or by lift from the Grand Entrance. The Grand Tier Tea Room [...] is on the Grand Tier Staircase. The Balcony Tea Room, on left of Balcony, is on [the] Balcony Entrance Staircase.

In each tea room there is a kiosk (Ticket Office and Information Bureau) where seats for the next performance and transfer tickets are to be obtained.

To the left of the Grand Entrance on entering there is an Information Bureau. Physicians and others expecting urgent telephone calls or telegrams, should leave a notification of the number of the seat they are occupying. If a message comes they will be instantly informed. Brief messages may be typed at and despatched from this Bureau. Telegrams will also be despatched, and stamps sold.

There is a Public Telephone, and a District Messenger call. A Pillar Box will be found in the Grand Entrance Hall. Large cloak-rooms and retiring rooms, fitted with every accommodation, are provided on the latest and most improved principles. There are no fees.

The prices of the seats are as follows: Boxes (4 persons), 21s, Extra Seats, 5s; Royal Box, 42s, Extra Seats, 10s; Orchestra Stalls, 4s; Royal Stalls, 3s; Grand Tier Stalls, 2s; Grand Tier, 1s; Balcony, 6d.

All the seats are comfortable, richly upholstered, and provided with arm rests. Every seat in the house is numbered and reserved, and can be booked in advance. There are four performances daily, and each lasts exactly two hours. The first commences at 12 o'clock noon. The second commences at 3 o'clock p.m. The third commences at 6 o'clock p.m. The fourth commences at 9 o'clock p.m. The first and third performances are alike; so are the second and fourth. During the one hour intervals between the performances, a band will play in the Terrace Tea Room.

Lost Articles – Articles found by visitors to the Coliseum should be left in the Business Offices on the Royal Stalls tier. Enquiries for articles lost should be made at the above offices.

Toilet Rooms – On every floor.

Complaints – In the event of incivility or inattention on the part of any of the staff, complaints should be addressed to the Acting Manager, Mr John Donald.

161   Theatrical provision in Liverpool, 1902

'W.J.W.', illustration to R. J. Broadbent, 'The Theatres of Great Britain: No. 2, Liverpool', *The Playgoer*, 1, 3 (January 1902), p. 159

The histories of the eight Liverpool theatres whose turn-of-the-century exteriors are recorded in these sketches serve as a reminder that the vitality of the late-Victorian stage was not restricted to London's West End. Most of them were built, or rebuilt, in the last years of the nineteenth century, and most of them were large: the Shakespeare (built 1888, capacity 3,000); the Grand Opera House (rebuilt 1895, capacity 2,000); the Lyric (1897, 2,000); the Star (formerly a music hall, a theatre from 1898, capacity 2,000). Henglers Circus had a capacity of 5,000, and only the Prince of Wales's Theatre (converted from a hotel in 1861) seated fewer than 2,000. On the other hand, by the beginning of the Edwardian period, none of these buildings housed a stock company any longer, and most were but touring venues.

II   Audiences

162   Dickens at the Britannia Saloon, Hoxton, 1850

Charles Dickens, 'The Amusements of the People', *Household Words*, 30 April 1850

Dickens's delight in popular melodrama goes back to childhood days when he avidly attended performances at the Theatre Royal, Star Hill, Rochester. In this popular account of the Britannia, he uses the imaginary 'Joe Whelks' to distance himself from a world that would have been alien to many middle-class readers. The Britannia Saloon was rebuilt as a 'Theatre' in 1858 (see **159(c)**).

The saloon in question is the largest in London (that which is known as the Eagle, in the City Road, should be excepted from the generic term, as not presenting by any means the same class of entertainment), and is situated not far from Shoreditch Church. It announces 'The People's Theatre', as its second name. The prices of admission are, to the boxes, a shilling; to the pit, sixpence; to the lower gallery, fourpence; to the upper gallery and back seats, threepence. There is no half-price.[1] The opening piece on this occasion was described in the bills as 'The greatest hit of the season, the grand new legendary and traditionary drama, combining supernatural agencies with historical facts, and identifying extra-ordinary superhuman causes with material, terrific and powerful effects'. All the queen's horses and all the queen's men could not have drawn Mr Whelks into the place like this description. Strenghtened by lithographic representations of the principal superhuman causes, combined with the most popular of the material, terrific and powerful effects, it became irresistible. Consequently, we had already failed, once, in finding six square inches of room within the walls, to stand upon; and when we now paid out money for a little stage-box, like a dry shower-bath, we did so in the midst of a stream of people who persisted in paying theirs for other parts of the house in despite of the representations of the Money-taker that it was 'very full, everywhere'.

The outer avenues and passages of the People's Theatre bore abundant testimony to the fact of its being frequented by very dirty people. Within, the atmosphere was far from odoriferous. The place was crammed to excess, in all parts. Among the audience were a large number of boys and youths, and a great many young girls grown into bold women before they had well ceased to be children. These last were the worst features of the whole crowd and were more prominent there than at any other sort of public assembly that we know of, except at a public execution. There was no drink supplied, beyond the contents of the porter-can (magnified in its dimensions, perhaps), which be usually seen traversing the galleries of the largest Theatres as well as the least, and which was here seen everywhere. Huge ham sandwiches, piled on trays like deals in a timberyard, were handed about for resale to the hungry, and there was no stint of oranges, cakes, brandyballs, or other similar refreshments. The theatre was capacious, with a very large, capable stage, well lighted, well appointed, and managed in a business-like, orderly manner in all respects; the performances had begun so early as a quarter past six, and had been then in progress for three-quarters of an hour.

It was apparent here, as in the theatre we had previously visited, that one of the reasons for its great attraction was its being directly addressed to the common people in the provision made for their seeing and hearing. Instead of being put away in a dark gap in the roof of an immense building, as in our once National Theatres, they were here in possession of eligible points of view, and thoroughly able to take in the whole performance. Instead of being at a great disadvantage in comparison with the mass of the audience, they were here *the* audience, for whose accommodation the place was made.

[1] 'Half-price' was charged for admission halfway through the traditional extended performance, which could last from 6.30 to 11.00 p.m.

163   Audience behaviour, 1874

Clement Scott, 'Talkers at the Play', *Era Almanack*, 1874, pp. 78–9

Scott was attacking not only bad behaviour, but what he saw as the trivializing of theatre-going itself.

There is surely much sound sense and weight in the arguments of those who insist that our fathers, who settled down to the play, refreshed with a strong cup of tea and a round of toast, required, on the whole, a different entertainment from that desired by the modern play-goer, who repairs to the theatre during the process of digesting the heaviest meal of the day, and is sulky at the notion of throwing away at the theatre-door a half-smoked cigar or hastily accomplished cigarette. So much for one point. The old and experienced actor, on the other hand, ascribes the changed tone totally to the abolition of the favourite pit with seats right up to the orchestra, and he falls to vilifying the luxury and the ease of the modern stalls. That was the time for applause, he will say; those were the days for enthusiasm, excitement, and breathless interest, when a perfect sea of faces rolled in even and undisturbed to the footlights, when the truly critical portion of the public paid for its seats, when flirting and philandering and chattering and affectation never disturbed the genius of the dramatist or the art of the actor, when the slightest disturbance or annoyance would be put down by the iron will of the people, and when, at any rate, there was fair play and no favour. In the autocratic days of the pit there was, no doubt, more hissing, but at the same time more applause. [...] The change in the dinner hour and the introduction of the stalls we all admire so thoroughly, have both something to do with this chattering and magpie annoyance – a scandal which can only be stopped by a vulgar disturbance on the part of the audience or a determined attack instigated by some plucky actor. Nowadays there is no end to this irritating chatter. Young men, heated with a hastily eaten dinner at the club [...] come into the stalls when the play is half over. [...] What do they care about the comedy or the drama, the skilful construction here or the rare intensity there?

164(a) An evening at a Whitechapel penny gaff, 1874

James Greenwood, *The Wilds of London* (London: Chatto and Windus, 1874; new edition 1881), pp. 19–20

James Greenwood specialized in reportage of low-life: here he attends an East End theatre patronized almost entirely by teenage costermongers. Doors opened at 6.30 p.m., and the main play of the evening was *Gentleman Jack, or the Game of High Toby.*

In a few minutes the doors were opened, and we were admitted – the box customers on payment of twopence, and the pit customers at the rate of a penny each. It was not a commodious building, nor particularly handsome, the only attempt at embellishment appearing at the stage end, where for the space of a few feet the plaster wall was covered with ordinary wallpaper of a grape-vine pattern, and further ornamented by coloured and spangled portraits of Mrs Douglas Fitzbruce in her celebrated characters of 'Cupid' and 'Lady Godiva'. [...] The stage itself was a mere platform of rough boards; the seats in the pit were of the same material. The boards that were the box seats, however, were planed. [...]

[The performance began with a carroty-haired man in an African wig singing blackface songs, then 'the star of the evening, Gentleman Jack, came in with a bound'.]

It was Mrs Douglas Fitzbruce fully equipped for the 'High Toby game'. She wore buckskin shorts, and boots of brilliant polish knee-high and higher, and spurs to them; her coat was of green velvet slashed with crimson, with a neat little breast pocket, from which peeped a cambric handkerchief; her raven curls hung about her shoulders, and on her head was a three-cornered hat, crimson edged with gold; under her arm she carried a riding whip, and in each hand a pistol of large size. By way of thanking her friends in the boxes and pit for the generous greeting (it is against the law for actors to utter so much as a single word during the performance of a 'gaff' piece) she uttered a saucy laugh (she could not have been more than forty-five), and, cocking her firearms, 'let fly' at them point blank as it seemed; however, the whistling and stamping of feet that immediately ensued showed that nobody was wounded – indeed, that the audience rather enjoyed being shot at than otherwise.

[The account continues with the description of a highwayman melodrama in dumbshow, complete with real coach appearing on the stage. The 'dumbshow' was to evade the regulations of the Theatres Act (6 & 7 Victoria C.68) which required all 'stage-plays' to be licensed by the Lord Chamberlain's Office, London.]

164(b) An evening at a Whitechapel gaff

From Greenwood, *The Wilds of London*

AN EVENING AT A WHITECHAPEL "GAFF."

165   Genteel good manners among Edwardian audiences, 1904

Mrs Alec [Ethel Brilliana] Tweedie, *Behind the Footlights* (London: Hutchinson & Co., 1904), pp. 163–4

In its discernible expectation of a female readership and in its recurrent citation of women's experiences in and of the theatre, Mrs Tweedie's book reflects the increasing importance of women as consumers of theatre, especially at matinées. The book also betrays her class assumptions on its every page, as in the following remarks about audiences' needs for comfort and norms of behaviour.

The stage is conservative in many ways; for instance, that tiresome plan of charging for programmes still exists in England in some theatres, and even good theatres too. Programmes cost nothing: the expense of printing is paid by the advertisements. Free distribution, therefore, does not mean that the management are out of pocket. Why, then, do they not present them gratis? As things are it is most aggravating. Suppose two ladies arrive; as they are shown to their seats, holding their skirts, opera bags and fans in their hands, they are asked for sixpence. While they endeavour to extract their money they are dropping their belongings and inconveniencing their neighbours: in the case of a man requiring change the same annoyance is felt by all around, especially if the play has begun.

Programmes and their necessary 'murmurings' are annoying, and so is the meagreness of the space between the rows of stalls. There are people who openly declare they never go to a theatre because they have not got room for their knees. This is certainly much worse in Parisian theatres, where the seats are high and narrow as well; but still, when people pay for a seat they like room to pass to and fro without inconveniencing a dozen persons en route.

Matinée hats and late arrivals are sins on the part of the audience so cruel that no self-respecting person would inflict either upon a neighbour. But some women are so inconsiderate. [. . .] A gentlewoman never wears a picture hat at the play; if she arrives in one she takes it off. In the same way a gentleman makes a point of being on time. People who offend in these respects belong to a class which apparently knows no better, a class which complacently talks, or makes love, through a theatrical entertainment!

III Finances

166 Wilson Barrett's Company on tour, 1870–1871

Courtesy of the Harry Ransom Humanities Research Center, University of Texas at Austin

Wilson Barrett's Company toured the north of England for the 1870/1 season. Their account books provide useful information on the organization of a provincial tour. From 25 to 30 July 1870 they played the Theatre Royal, Middlesbrough, alternating *East Lynne* with *Harriet Routh*,[1] accompanied by various short farces. The company took £78 10s 0d, of which a third was due to the theatre proprietor (John Jameson), for providing various services (see 'terms third' below).

Terms third for theatre gas posting band carpenters cleaners police etc.

July 25th	£	s	d
Fares from Sunderland 13½ third 2 second[2]	2	14	6½
Cartage of luggage to and from station		14	2
1,000 day bills Mon and Tues – Reid Middlesbrough	1	1	0
50 demy oblong slips ditto		3	6
200 circulars ditto		7	6
25 D. C. Posters – Jordison Middlesbrough		8	0
Advertisement in Echo six insertions		12	0
200 envelopes		1	6
Ewart's expenses[3]		7	5
Dramatic author's fees, twelve nights	1	10	0
July 29th			
Check takers[4]	1	7	0
Lawrence properties	1	4	11½
Porterage of box and beer for carpenters		9	0
Telegrams		3	0
Company[5]	21	11	0
700 day bills – Jordison, Wed and Thurs		17	0
700 day bills – Jordison, ditto Fri		17	0

	£	s	d
27 slips tonight, ditto Sat		2	0
3,000 tickets	1	0	0
July 30th			
Supers		2	0
100 daybills – Jordison	1	1	0
Expenses [sub-total]	36	13	7
Third [of receipts] for Jameson	26	9	4
Total Expenses	63	2	11
Receipts [calculated separately]	78	10	0
Balance in hand	15	7	1

[1] No authors given. The version of *East Lynne* was probably by J. Oxenford (1866).
[2] Wilson Barrett and his wife travelled second class, the rest of the company, third.
[3] Barrett's agent.
[4] On the doors.
[5] Payments ranged from £5 0s 0d to Barrett himself, to £1 10s 0d for actors with minor parts.

167   Playwrights' royalties in the 1890s

'What Playwrights Earn', *The Idler*, 8, 45 (October 1895), pp. 285–7

The author begins with the present, citing 'the interest lately shown in the official statement of the earnings of the unhappy dramatist now languishing in Wandsworth Gaol', and then looks back from Wilde to the bad old days before royalties. He then sets out the way the royalty system had come to operate in the last decades of his century.

Mr W. S. Gilbert was one of the first to insist upon 'payment by results', obviously the fairest method to be devised. If a play be enormously successful, the author should reap a proportionate harvest. If a failure, he should, in reduced fees, indirectly shoulder his share of the loss. Hence a sliding scale has been adopted, which works in this fashion: An author of established – but not pre-eminent – reputation will take 5 per cent upon all takings, until an amount sufficient to cover the weekly expenses of the theatre is reached. This, of course, varies enormously. The Lyceum curtain cannot be raised at a cost of less than £170 a performance. A 'society' play like *The Masqueraders* or *Vanity Fair*[1], played at a 'society' house, will cost the manager £500 to £700 a week. A heavy melodrama like *The Swordsman's Daughter* will cost more; a farce like *The New Boy*[2] much less.

Then the holding capacities vary. Two hundred pounds can be squeezed into the Adelphi pit alone; but barely that sum into the whole of Terry's. The Haymarket and St James's, crammed, can bring in some £225 to £240 a night. The Lyceum holds £420; Drury Lane still more; the Gaiety about £300.[3] Taking the average, however, an author at a reputable London house would receive 5 per cent on all receipts up to, say, £500 a week, with the joyful possibility [...] that, with six evening performances and two matinées, these might be swelled to £1,200, £1,500 or even £2,000. In such an event, his 5 per cent would not apply.

Under the sliding scale arrangement, with the increase of receipts, his weekly solatium increases too. Thus upon receipts of over £500, and under £800, he would expect $7\frac{1}{2}$ per cent; of £800 to £1,000, 10 per cent; and in a few cases, Mr W. S. Gilbert's, Mr Pinero's, Mr H. A. Jones's, and Mr Grundy's, for example, as much as 15 per cent would be levied upon takings in excess of that sum. Then, in addition to London, there are the provinces, Africa, Australia and America, with all their well-nigh inexhaustible supplies of gold and play-goers. Even the Continent furnishes a 'paying claim', until the prospect eventually opened up is that of El Dorado itself. [...] An author's confession is enough. Eight years and more ago, Mr Henry Arthur Jones, in pleading before the Playgoers' Club for the free development of his genius, paralysed his hearers by stating that already his share of *The Silver King*[4] had brought him £10,000, and that play is running to this day. [...] To *The Private Secretary*[5] [...] the author, or rather adapter, Mr Charles Hawtrey, was manager also, and his profits have been placed at £100,000. *Charley's Aunt*[6] [...] can boast a writer, Mr Brandon Thomas, who has now received fees upon over seven thousand performances! At an absurdly low estimate, this means at least £30,000. [...] These are the big figures, and there is, of course, another side to the picture. Few authors, for instance, would refuse a commission to write a play for £200 or £300, but that is largely because success or failure is little better than a 'toss-up'.

[1] With George Alexander and Mrs Patrick Campbell in the leading roles, Henry Arthur Jones's *The Masqueraders* opened at the St James's Theatre on 28 April 1894 and played 139 performances. George W. Godfrey's *Vanity Fair* opened at the Court Theatre on 27 April 1895 and played 120 performances. (For detailed information about dates, casts and reviews, both for these productions and for London productions of the other plays cited in this document, see J. P. Wearing, *The London Stage 1890–1900: A Calendar of Plays and Players* (Metuchen, N. J., and London: Scarecrow Press, 1976), vol. I.)

[2] *The Swordsman's Daughter* was Brandon Thomas's and Clement Scott's adaptation of *Le Maître d'armes*, by Jules Mary and Georges Grisier. Opening on 31 August 1895, the adaptation played 80 performances at the Adelphi. Arthur Law's *The New Boy*, starring Weedon Grossmith, opened at Terry's Theatre on 21 February 1894, and transferred on 16 April 1894 to the Vaudeville, where it played until 2 March 1895.

[3] The respective capacities of these theatres were reported to the 1892 parliamentary select committee as follows: Adelphi 2,135; Terry's 531; Haymarket 924; St James's 1,000; Lyceum 1,835; Drury Lane 2,500 (estimated figure, the lessee having refused to give the information required by the committee); and Gaiety 1,360.

⁴ *The Silver King* played for 289 performances in its first production, by Wilson Barrett at the Princess's Theatre in 1882, and the following year it was staged at Wallack's Theatre in New York. The extent of Henry Arthur Jones's authorial share in this acclaimed, lucrative and frequently revived melodrama was contested both by his collaborator, Henry Herman, and by Barrett.

⁵ *The Private Secretary* was Charles Hawtrey's adaptation of Gustav von Moser's *Der Bibliothekar*. First performed at the Cambridge Theatre Royal in 1883, the adaptation was in the following year brought to London, where it played until 1886. Having been successfully revived by Hawtrey at the Comedy Theatre for 138 performances in 1892, *The Private Secretary* was staged again by Hawtrey in the autumn of 1895, when this document was published, and played for 56 performances at the Avenue Theatre.

⁶ When this document was published, the first London production of Brandon Thomas's *Charley's Aunt* was in the middle of its very long run, eventually totalling 1,469 performances. After a try-out at the Bury St Edmunds Theatre Royal early in 1892, the three-act comedy had opened in London at the Royalty Theatre in December of that year and at the end of January 1893 transferred to the Globe, where it would play until December of 1896.

168   Matinées: trial productions on the cheap, 1891

Alfred Cecil Calmour, *Practical Playwriting and the Cost of Production* (Bristol: J. W. Arrowsmith, and London: Simpkin, Marshall, Hamilton, Kent & Co. Ltd. [1891]), pp. 54–9

The following advice for aspiring dramatists was originally delivered to a meeting of the Playgoers' Club.

Should he ultimately fail in placing his play, I should advise him to muster his friends and give a morning performance at a theatre. [...] The cost of a morning performance is not very great. I had a play [*Wives*] tried at the Vaudeville Theatre some years ago [8 March 1883], and, although my cast included actors of reputation, my expenses came to only seventy-odd pounds. For the benefit of the uninitiated I give the following statement as furnished to me by my acting-manager.

	£	s	d
License for play	2	2	0
Rent of theatre	15	0	0
Salaries	28	4	6
Messenger	0	2	0
Advertisements	7	3	6
Willing & Co. (posting)	1	0	0
Nagle (boardmen)	2	16	0
Carpenters	3	8	4
Aubert (printing)	2	0	0
Austin & Rogers (for floral decorations)	2	2	0
S. Lyon (extra furniture)	2	0	0
Clarkson (wigs)	0	4	2
Band	3	5	0

	£	s	d
Money and check takers	1	0	0
Properties	0	17	6
Cleaners and dressers	0	7	0
Gasman	0	4	6
Simmonds (for hire of costume)	0	10	0
TOTAL	72	6	6

The production of *The Widow Winsome* [at a matinée on 27 November 1888] at the Criterion cost me about £90, and, later, the trial of *Cyrene* [at a matinée on 27 June 1890] at the Avenue cost over a hundred. But both of these were costume plays, and in the former case £17 and in the latter £27 had to be paid for the hire and purchase of dresses. The original production of *The Amber Heart* [at a matinée on 7 July 1887] – with the [Lyceum] theatre rent-free – cost me £200, but out of that I spent some £80 on advertising, an absurdly large sum to spend upon one performance. With the aid of a fine company, I have in nearly every case got my money back.

But the young author must not give a performance with the delusive hope that he will get his money back from the general public. If he be fortunate enough to get his friends to cover his expenses by taking tickets, so much the better; but the paying play-goers do not come to see new plays produced at matinées. The one great drawback to the experimental performance is the difficulty of getting the company together; and, having got them together, to induce them to attend rehearsals.

IV Regulations

169 Rules and regulations for the acting profession, 1860s
From Anon., *The Actor's Handbook* (c.1860), pp. 14–15

These are the first ten of twenty-one regulations quoted in a standard acting handbook; similar lists were often appended to contracts issued by the major theatres. See 1, 2, 42.

1. GENTLEMEN, at the time of rehearsal or performance, are not to wear their hats in the greenroom, or talk vociferously. The greenroom is a place set apart for the quiet and regular meeting of the company, who are summoned thence by the call-boy, to attend on the stage. The manager is not to be applied to in that place on any matter of business, or annoyed with any complaint. For a breach of any part of this article, 1s will be forfeited.

2. The calls for all rehearsals will be put up by the prompt between the play and farce and earlier, on evenings of performance. No plea will be received that the call was not seen, in order to avoid the penalties of Article 5.

3. Any member of the company unable, from the effects of stimulants, to perform, or to appear at rehearsal, shall forfeit a week's salary, and be liable to be dismissed.

4. For making the stage wait, 5s.

5. After due notice, all rehearsals must be attended. The greenroom clock or the prompter's watch is to regulate time; ten minutes will be allowed (the first call only) for difference of clocks, forfeit 2s for each scene – every entrance to constitute a scene; the whole rehearsal at the same rate.

6. A performer rehearsing from a book or part, after proper time has been allowed for study, shall forfeit 10s.

7. A performer introducing his own language, or improper jest, not in the author, or swearing in his part, shall forfeit 10s.

8. Any person talking aloud behind the scenes, to the interruption of the performers, shall forfeit 10s.

9. Every performer concerned in the first act of a play, to be in the greenroom, dressed for performance, ten minutes before the time of beginning, as expressed in the bills, or to forfeit 1 os. The performers of the second act to be ready when the curtain falls in the first act. In like manner with every other act. Those performers who are not in the last acts of the play, to be ready to be in the farce, or to forfeit 1 os. [...]

10. Every performer's costume to be decided on by the manager, and a performer who makes any alteration in dress without the consent of the manager, or refuses to wear the costume selected, shall forfeit 1 os.

170   A managerial protest against legal tangles, 1897

From John Hollingshead, '"Tom Fool's" Legal Status'. *The Theatre*, 1 September 1897, pp. 136–8

John Hollingshead (1827–1904) was Manager of the Gaiety Theatre from its opening in 1868 until 1886. The blunt style of this plea for parliamentary simplification of the legislation controlling theatrical production and dramatic publication is characteristic of narratives he published during his years of management, which include accounts of various entanglements in the web of relevant laws.

Considering the numbers and importance of the dramatic, musical and variety professions – the capital invested in their theatres, 'palaces', and workshops – and above all the annual amount which a blood-sucking Government draws from them in the shape of Imperial and local taxes, it is high time that they had at least one Act of Parliament for their comfort and guidance, drawn clearly enough to be read by a Board School pupil studying as a servant-of-all-work, and interpreted clearly enough to avoid appeal and extra costs by the densest judge ever known to us. It was bad enough when 'the profession' was regarded by some as a fortuitous concourse of 'rogues and vagabonds' [...] but it is worse now, in the days when they have a status, when they are the pets of society, and on the road to swell the ranks of the peerage, to see them treated like fools and children, tossed about in an everyday lawsuit at the mercy of 'custom' as interpreted by old play-goers, managers and 'experts'. [...]

The law of contracts [...] is the foundation and protection of trade – but not a thing to be seriously looked at in connection with theatres and music halls. [...] I will state a case. I engage Mme Adelina Patti. I pay her £1,000 to sing on Saturday, and another £1,000 to sing on Monday. On the Sunday, the day in between, she goes to Mr Alfred Rothschild's, and sings before a very large and distinguished party, including royalty. I engage Mme Bernhardt, and pay her £80 a performance. I have often done so. She gives two performances of heavy plays in hot weather on the Saturday, and receives ... £160. On the Sunday, when she ought to be resting and preparing for another arduous performance on Monday, she is at Lady Jeune's or Baroness Hirsch's, working like a 'nigger'. This is surely, in spirit, a breach of contract, in spite of phrases like *dies non*, or any other courthouse mumbo-jumbo.

Our laws affecting the dramatic profession, especially the licensing laws, are a disgrace to civilization. The 'sketch', which forms the chief pabulum of nearly all the music halls, is utterly and hopelessly illegal. The balls, promenade concerts, circuses, etc., which find a place, from time to time, at Covent Garden Theatre, are no more covered by the [...] patent of Charles II [...] than a prize-fight, a bullfight, or a public execution would be covered. The theatre, for the time being, becomes a 'disorderly house'. Everybody knows it. The Lord Chamberlain retires behind a royal screen, and the police authorities 'wink the other eye'. Our licensing laws are only fit to govern the entertainments (cannibal or otherwise) of African savages.

171   Safety requirements and other regulations, 1886–1895

From Albert Ambrose Strong, *Dramatic and Musical Law* (London: The Era, 1898), pp. 146–9

Under the terms of the 1843 Theatres Act (6 & 7 Victoria C.68), the Lord Chamberlain, who was an official of the royal household, was responsible for licensing all London theatre buildings other than the two patent houses (Drury Lane and Covent Garden) and also all theatres in royal residences. He was also responsible for licensing dramatic texts for performance throughout the country. The following list of regulations proclaims itself as pertaining to the theatres licensed by the Lord Chamberlain, and regulations 1 to 12 do prescribe for the premises, principally in respect of fire-preventive measures. (Far more stringent and exhaustive safety regulations were, additionally, enforced by the London County Council, to which the 1878 Metropolis Management and Building Acts gave authority over all theatre buildings, including those already licensed by the Lord Chamberlain, within the county of London.) However, regulations 13 to 16 and 18 to 20 refer to the Lord Chamberlain's licensing of plays: regulations 15, 16, 19 and 20 were even printed as memoranda on the backs of licences for performance, such as the one reproduced below (172).

Regulations as to theatres under the jurisdiction of the Lord Chamberlain

   1. All doors and barriers to open outwards, or to be fixed back during the time when the public are within the Theatre.
   2. All gangways, passages and staircases, intended for the exit of the

audience, to be kept entirely free from chairs or any other obstructions, whether permanent or temporary.

3. An ample water supply with hose and pipes to be available to all parts of the House, where possible on the high-pressure main.

4. All fixed and ordinary gas-burners to be furnished with efficient guards. Movable and occasional lights to be, where possible, protected in the same manner, or put under charge of persons for lighting, watching and extinguishing them. A separate and independent supply of light for the stage and auditory.

    No white metal gas-pipes to be used in the building.

5. The footlights or floats to be protected by a wire guard. The first ground-line to be always without gas, and unconnected with gas, whether at the wings or elsewhere. Sufficient space to be left between each ground-line, so as to lessen risk from accident to all persons standing or moving among such lines.

6. The rows or lines of gas-burners at wings to commence 4 feet at least from the level of the stage.

7. Wet blankets or rugs, with filled buckets or water-pots to be always kept in the wings; and attention to be directed to them by placards legibly printed or painted, and fixed near them. [...]

8. Hatchets, hooks, or other means to cut down hanging scenery in case of fire to be always in readiness.

9. The regulations as to fire to be always posted in some conspicuous place. [...] A report of any fire, or alarm of fire, however slight, to be at once sent to the Lord Chamberlain's Office.

10. Counterweights, where possible, to be carried to the walls of the building, and cased in. The rope attached to them to be constantly tested.

11. An annual inspection is made of all Theatres. It is expected that all alterations suggested for the safety and convenience of the public will be carried out before the issue of the Annual Licence.

12. No structural alterations to be made in the Theatre without the sanction of the Metropolitan Board of Works. Plans of such alterations to be sent to the Lord Chamberlain's Office.

13. A copy of every new piece, or alterations of old pieces intended to be produced, to be forwarded for Licence to the Examiner of Plays seven clear days before such intended production. No alteration of the text when licensed for representation to be permitted without sanction.

14. Copies of all playbills to be sent to the Lord Chamberlain's Office every Monday, and whenever a change of performance is announced.

15. Notice of the change of title of a piece to be given to the Examiner of Plays.
16. The name and private address of the actual and responsible manager to be printed in legible type at the head of each bill.
17. Admission to be given at all times to authorized officers of the Lord Chamberlain's Department, and of the Police.
18. No profanity or impropriety of language to be permitted on the stage.
19. No indecency of dress, dance, or gesture to be permitted on the stage.
20. No offensive personalities or representations of living persons to be permitted on the stage, nor anything calculated to produce riot or breach of the peace.
21. No exhibition of wild beasts or dangerous performances to be permitted on the stage. No women or children to be hung from the flies, nor fixed in positions from which they cannot release themselves.
22. No masquerade or public ball to be permitted in the Theatre.
23. No encouragement to be given to improper characters to assemble, or to ply their calling in the Theatre.
24. Refreshments to be sold in the Theatre only during the hours of performance, only to the audience and company engaged in the house, and only in positions which do not interfere with the convenience and safety of the audience.
25. No smoking to be permitted in the auditorium.
26. Theatre Licences are granted for one year, from 29 September. Licences are granted also for shorter periods, but all Licences cease on the day above-mentioned.
27. No public entertainment to be given in the Theatre on the days excluded from the Licence.
28. Applications for Licences, with the names and addresses of the actual and responsible Manager and of his two proposed sureties, who must be resident householders and ratepayers, must be forwarded to the Lord Chamberlain's Office seven clear days before the day for which the Licence is required.
29. Theatre Licences are granted, after consultation with the Metropolitan Board of Works so far as the structural condition of the Theatres is concerned, only for buildings in which the above Regulations can be carried out, and on the express condition that these and every other reasonable and practicable precaution against fire or the dangers arising therefrom are adopted.
30. The Manager is held solely and entirely responsible for the carrying

out of the above Regulations, for the management of his Theatre before and behind the curtain, and for the safety of the public and the members of his company.

31. All exits from the Theatre must be plainly indicated by placards, and kept always available for the use of the audience.

32. The service of light for the auditorium and entrance passages must be separate from that for the stage.

172 Licence allowing the performance of *Love and Halfpence*, 24 January 1888

Licence in the Poel Collection, Theatre Museum

Although the Lord Chamberlain licensed plays for performance, the decisions as to whether or not to issue a licence, and what, if any, excisions or alterations to require as conditions of that licence, were taken by his Examiner of Plays.

During the Earl of Lathom's tenure of the office of Lord Chamberlain from 1886 to 1895, the Examiner of Plays was Edward F. Smyth Pigott, whose testimony to the 1892 Parliamentary Select Committee is exemplified below (173). Both men signed the licence, which was issued to the manager: the playwright is not even named. The invisible author of *Love and Halfpence* was William Poel (1852–1934), whose subsequent innovations in the staging of Shakespearian and early modern English drama would earn him some fame and, eventually, a considerable following long after his juvenile efforts at playwriting had been (justly) forgotten. St George's Hall, here licensed for the performance of Poel's own play, was also the venue for performances of some of his Shakespearian productions. The building was used for various late-Victorian and Edwardian entertainments, notably including amateur productions.

It having been represented to Me by the Examiner of All Theatrical Entertainments that a Manuscript entitled *'Love and Halfpence' being a Play in one act*, does not in its general tendency contain any thing immoral or otherwise improper for the Stage I The Lord Chamberlain of HER MAJESTY's Household do by virtue of my Office and in pursuance of the Act of Parliament in that case provided Allow the Performance of the said Manuscript at your Theatre with the exception of all Words and Passages which are specified by the Examiner in the endorsement of this Licence and without any further variations.

Given under my hand this *24th day of January 1888*

Edward F. S. Pigott

Lathom
Lord Chamberlain

To the Manager of the *St George's Hall*

173   The censor speaks in defence of his office, 23 May 1892

E. F. S. Pigott's testimony to the 1892 Parliamentary Select Committee from *Report from the Select Committee on Theatres and Places of Entertainment* (London: Eyre & Spottiswoode for H Majesty's Stationery Office, 1892); facsimile reprint by Irish University Press, Shannon, 1970

In March of 1892 a select committee was appointed by resolution of the House of Commons, 'to inquire into the operation of Acts of Parliament relating to the Licensing and Regulation of Theatres and Places of Public Entertainment, and to consider and report any alterations in the law which may appear desirable'. The recommendations of the committee with regard to the licensing of buildings preserved the legal distinction between theatres and music halls, and the recommendation with regard to the licensing of plays recapitulated the conclusion of an 1866 select committee 'that the censorship of plays has worked satisfactorily, and that it is not desirable that it should be discontinued'. The Committee heard the testimony of some thirty-seven men, including managers of theatres (Henry Irving, John Hare, Edward Terry) and of music halls (James Graydon, William Bailey), artistes, solicitors, architects and civil servants. Playwrights were represented only vicariously, through journalists (William Archer, Joseph Comyns Carr, Clement Scott). The censor spoke for himself, after the critics had had their say, on 23 May 1892. His explicit statements of allegiance to the interests of managers are almost as unforgettable as his opinions about Ibsen.

Mr Edward F. Smyth Pigott called in and examined

5178 What is the designation of your office?
Examiner of Stage Plays. I would ask the Committee to allow me to protest against the term of 'censor', because [. . .] to many minds it represents the Star Chamber and the Inquisition, and all manner of ancient institutions; whereas my office is simply that of examiner.

5179 Will you please give me as much of your memorandum as you think has not been already covered by the evidence that we have heard?

[5183] I should say that this memorandum which I hold in my hand was written nine years ago. As far as the principle is concerned it holds good now, but, of course, there have been some changes in numbers and in the statistics. The licensing of stage-plays implies certain qualification [*sic*] for the office, which can scarcely be looked for in a local functionary. A large proportion of the new stage-plays licensed for representation in the course of the year are submitted by the managers of provincial theatres. I should think at the present day two fifths of the plays submitted for license for the year (and I receive now about 300 plays a year) come to me from the provinces. [. . .] Then with regard to Ireland: the Licencer's jurisdiction does not extend to Ireland; but, so far as my experience goes, the very few plays that are played in Ireland first have been licensed by the managers for English theatres, and have been submitted for future representation before they were done in Ireland. And then of the other plays, the great majority of them [...] have been performed in England first. For instance, in the year 1882, 154 new stage-plays were produced in London alone, and 113 in the provinces. Four new stage-plays were produced in Ireland. Two of these, however, were subsequently played in Great Britain. [...] Plays produced with success in London are carried by travelling companies through all the principal theatres in the country; plays produced with success at any one of the principal provincial theatres are generally performed afterwards in London or at other theatres in the country. Manifestly, then, no single local authority is competent to license new stage-plays for representation, 'at any theatre in Great Britain'. [...] At the present time there are in London (this was written in 1883) alone thirty-eight licensed theatres, and four in course of construction, while in Great Britain there are not less than 286 theatres and public halls licensed for theatrical performances. Under the Regulation of Theatres Act, every new stage-play must be submitted to the Lord Chamberlain for examination and licence. The reading of plays is entrusted to the examiner of all theatrical entertainments, who belongs, *ex officio*, to Her Majesty's household, and who is selected on account of the qualifications indispensable for the post. It is his business and duty [...] to administer those clauses of the Act which concerns his department in the most liberal spirit, with the discernment and discrimination that belong to a wide knowledge of the world, and that cultivated sympathy with literature and art, which is equally regardful of public morality and public decency, and of the freedom and dignity of a liberal profession and a noble art. [...] As a servant of the Crown he prevents scandals of which public opinion would otherwise demand a rigorous repression. [...] The principles on which the Examiner of Plays consistently acts, are: to eschew even the faintest semblance of a frivolous or vexatious interference with managers; not to fritter away official influence upon details; to act as much as possible by personal intercourse, or confidential correspondence with managers; and, in some cases even, unofficially, with the authors of plays; in short to avoid all unnecessary friction. If I may be pardoned for appealing to personal experience, my official relations with managers of theatres, metropolitan and provincial, have been constantly harmonious and agreeable; we have given each other credit for the best intentions and the best motives, and the result has been reciprocal goodwill. Some scandals, however, I have been obliged and enabled to prevent. [... **5184**] Some half-a-dozen manuscripts (mostly adaptations from French pieces) have been rejected as offensive to public decency (I should say, perhaps, a dozen more since then [1883]). In some other instances, the modification of certain questionable scenes, situations, or passages of dialogue, has been required. [...] It should be understood that of the pieces of all descriptions produced at theatres through-out Great Britain a portion are written by obscure literary nondescripts, without name or fame. Between these and the few dramatic authors, properly so-called, whose names belong to English literature, there are a legion of unknown professional adaptors, whose industry consists in translating the latest and riskiest productions of the Boulevards from bad French into worse English. These gentlemen are apt, I believe, to complain of not enjoying an unrestricted licence in their importations of obscenity. [. . .]

5204 That the censorship, or the examinership of plays, should continue is for the benefit of all parties?
The only opinion I care for in the matter is the opinion of the people I am immediately concerned with, that is the managers; and they all seem to be in favour of it, and I do not see why I should dispute that opinion at all. The only assailant of my office that I have seen that has come before the Committee is Mr Archer. I know nothing of him at all, but I find he has had an experience of 15 years. Well, for a man of my age [68] I am sorry to say that is a very limited experience. [. . .] Of course Mr Clement Scott who, I am happy to find, is on my side, represents a much longer period, and for every reader that Mr Archer represents he represents a thousand. Mr Archer, I understand, said my office was calculated to repress dramatic talent. In my 18 years I have had more than 5,000 plays in my hands, so that there is a great deal of dramatic talent; whereas, I may say with regard to the Independent Theatre which was founded not only to supersede the censorship but to dispense with all questions of profit and loss [see **193**], that one of their own promoters told me they cannot get a play written for them for love or money.

5227 [. . .] On one point that Mr Archer mentioned, about the repression of dramatic talent, I have answered that to some extent in telling you the number of plays that I have had before me; but I imagine from what I hear from some of Mr Archer's juvenile admirers that he means the plays of Ibsen and other foreign dramatists of that school. All I can say is this: I have studied Ibsen's plays pretty carefully, and all the characters in Ibsen's plays appear to me morally deranged. All the heroines are dissatisfied spinsters who look on marriage as a monopoly, or dissatisfied married women in a chronic state of rebellion against not only the conditions which nature has imposed on their sex, but against all the duties and obligations of mothers and wives; and as for the men they are all rascals or imbeciles.

5228 Have you not passed some of Ibsen's plays?
Yes, but I have not seen that they have kept the stage or put a penny into anybody's pocket. I make allowance for Mr Archer because he has some interest in the plays; he is a translator of Ibsen's plays, and therefore I suppose has a certain interest in their being produced.

174   William Archer's obituary for the censor, E. F. S. Pigott, 1895

From *The Pall Mall Budget*, 2 March 1895, reprinted in W. Archer, *The Theatrical 'World' of 1895* (London: Walter Scott Ltd., 1896), pp. 66–73

After more than twenty years as Examiner of Plays, E. F. S. Pigott died in February 1895. Both George Bernard Shaw and William Archer wrote hostile obituaries. Shaw's, published under the title 'The Late Censor' in *Saturday Review* (2 March 1895) and reprinted in his *Our Theatres in the Nineties* (London: Constable & Co., 1932) vol. 1, pp. 48–55, contrives to include an attack on Clement Scott, the *Daily Telegraph* critic who opposed the Ibsenites. The following excerpt from Archer's obituary shows him still smarting from the remarks, here patronizing and there insinuating, which Pigott had made about Archer when he gave evidence to the 1892 House of Commons Select Committee (173).

The late Mr Pigott was probably the least ridiculous Censor we ever had. [...] Well might Mr Pinero and Mr H. A. Jones lay wreaths on his coffin; they may esteem themselves fortunate if they find half such an accommodating autocrat in his successor. For Mr Pigott's tact [...] was precisely the quality that served their turn. [...] Mr Pigott was far too wise, and too sincerely convinced of the necessity of a Censorship, to make his office unpopular. The powerful playwright, the playwright with an actor-manager behind him, might do or say pretty much what he pleased. For the showman who approached our autocrat in the character of managing director of a wealthy syndicate, his bounties were infinite. Hence the possibility of *The Second Mrs Tanqueray*, *The Masqueraders*, and *The Case of Rebellious Susan* on the one hand, *The Gaiety Girl* and *Go-Bang* on the other. It will be fortunate indeed for Mr Pinero and Mr Jones, for Mr 'Owen Hall' and Mr 'Adrian Ross', if his successor's 'tact' should prove equally sensitive.[1]

It is sometimes supposed that my opposition to the Censorship springs from [...] my championship of Ibsen. Mr Pigott himself said as much before the Select Committee of 1892, and even hinted that I had a pecuniary interest in the matter. [...] I have not, and never have had, any pecuniary interest, definite or contingent, in any representation of a play of Ibsen's except one single afternoon performance which took place fifteen years ago, and to which the Censor offered no opposition. When this was pointed out to Mr Pigott, he omitted to apologise or withdraw his innuendo. [...] Perhaps apologies are contrary to the regulations of the Lord Chamberlain's Department. [. . .] One may surely, without suspicion of base or personal motives, oppose the system which places a great and beautiful art, absolutely and without appeal, in subjection to the 'tact' of a Mr Pigott.

But in any case, no one can reasonably complain of Mr Pigott's treatment of Ibsen. He vetoed one play – *Ghosts* – and he could not possibly do otherwise. To have licensed it would have been simply to abdicate his office. [. . .] The Censorship exists for the protection of certain institutions, which *Ghosts* roundly attacks. [. . .] To blame Mr Pigott, then, for vetoing *Ghosts* would be tantamount to blaming him for not resigning his office. (By the way, *Ghosts* was never officially presented to him; but he was approached on the subject and was found to regard the play as hopelessly inadmissible.) All Ibsen's other plays that were submitted to him he licensed without a murmur. [. . .] Yet stay! I should not say that he licensed them 'without a murmur'. When the MS of *Hedda Gabler* was submitted to him, he wrote to the management to the effect that a formal licence would follow in due course, but that they must first send him the end of the play. 'The manuscript submitted,' he said (I quote from memory), 'ends with the phrase, "People don't do such things!" which cannot be the real conclusion.' Poor bewildered gentleman! It would be curious to know what terrible impropriety he imagined that the grim old Giant of the North had kept lurking up his sleeve. I believe, too, that he advised, without insisting on, the suppression of a single line in *The Pillars of Society*; otherwise, he kept his 'kindly blue pencil' entirely in abeyance, so far as Ibsen was concerned. This was a case in which his tact, his opportunism, was really beyond reproach.

[1] Both Arthur Wing Pinero's *The Second Mrs. Tanqueray* and Henry Arthur Jones's *The Masqueraders* were first staged, in May 1893 and April 1894 respectively, by George Alexander during his prestigious management of the St James's Theatre. Jones's *The Case of the Rebellious Susan* was first staged in October 1894 by the actor-manager Charles Wyndham during his long association with the Criterion Theatre. Archer thus points to Pinero and Jones as examples of 'the powerful playwright . . . with an actor-manager behind him'.

Adrian Ross and Owen Hall were musical comedy librettists, the former for *Go-Bang* (1894) and the latter for *A Gaiety Girl* (1893). (See **195**.) Like many other West End musical comedies, *A Gaiety Girl* was produced by the entrepreneur George Edwardes, managing-director of the limited company which from 1888 controlled the Gaiety Theatre.

175   Playwrights challenge the pre-censorship of their work, 1907

Letter to *The Times* from 71 dramatic authors, 29 October 1907, from G[ertrude] M. G[odden], *The Stage Censor: An Historical Sketch 1544–1907* (London: Sampson Low, Marston & Co., 1908), pp. 125–8

In 1907 the Examiner for Plays, then G. A. Redford, refused licences to Edward Garnett's *The Breaking Point* and Harley Granville Barker's *Waste*. Barker and John Vedrenne had that year completed three seasons of co-management at the Court Theatre in Sloane Square, where their policies and productions had won great acclaim (to be transformed in time into enormous influence). The autumn of 1907 saw them transfer their partnership and project to the Savoy Theatre in the West End, *Waste* having been advertised for a November production there before it was refused a licence. The literary world echoed with protest, and a deputation to Downing Street demanded the abolition of Redford's office. They spoke for sixty-seven men and four women (a startling proportion) over whose signature the following letter was published in *The Times* for 29 October 1907. The signatories included all thirteen of the living English dramatists who had had work premièred in the Vedrenne–Barker seasons at the Court, and also most of the well-established and no longer controversial dramatists of the time – J. M. Barrie, W. S. Gilbert, H. A. Jones, A. W. Pinero, A. Sutro. (The only conspicuous absentee was Sydney Grundy.) The writers did secure the appointment, two years later, of a Joint Select Committee of the House of Lords and the Commons to consider the censorship, but their decision was in favour of its continuance, and it was not terminated until 1968.

The Prime Minister has consented to receive during next month a deputation from the following dramatic authors on the subject of the Censorship of Plays. In the meantime, they desire to enter a formal protest against this office, which was instituted for political, and not for the so-called moral ends to which it is perverted; an office autocratic in procedure, opposed to the spirit of the Constitution, contrary to common justice and to common sense.

They protest against the power lodged in the hands of a single official, who judges without a public hearing, and against whose dictum there is no appeal, to cast a slur on the good name and destroy the means of livelihood of any member of an honourable calling.

They assert that the Censorship has not been exercised in the interests of morality, but has tended to lower the dramatic tone by appearing to relieve the public of the duty of moral judgement.

They ask to be freed from the menace hanging over every dramatist, of having his work and the proceeds of his work destroyed at a pen's stroke by the arbitrary action of a single official, neither responsible to Parliament nor amenable to law.

They ask that their art be placed on the same footing as every other art.

They ask that they themselves be placed in the position enjoyed under the law by every other citizen.

To these ends, they claim that the licensing of plays shall be abolished. The public is already sufficiently assured against managerial misconduct by the present yearly licensing of theatres, which remains untouched by the measure of justice here demanded.

V Professions and trades

176 London company structures and salaries in the 1890s

Charles Booth, *Life and Labour of the People in London*, Second Series: Industry (London: Macmillan, 1904), vol. IV, pp. 121–8

Booth accredits his account of theatrical employees to C. H. de'E. Leppington, who had first published his findings in the *National Review* for April 1891. They were updated to 1896 for inclusion in Booth's massive *Life and Labour*.

In command of all the persons employed behind the curtain [...] is the stage-manager. Below him there is an assistant stage-manager, who is often prompter as well, and a call-boy. These form a department by themselves and are [...] potential actors. In most cases they have already acted on the stage and in all cases they would be pleased to do so. Then there are the actors and actresses and other performers, and finally those who are not, and with certain reservations never wish to become, actors; such as the carpenters and scene-shifters, the box-office staff and the attendants in the auditorium. In London the acting or business manager never acts. He is responsible solely for those parts of the theatre which are situated in front of the curtain.

However distinct the actor's sphere may be from that of the super[1] and the other employees, there is a certain amount of interchange between them. In the minor theatres [...] there is no hard-and-fast rule to prevent an intelligent assistant behind the scenes from taking a small part and thus working his way up; and [...] the humbler actors are sometimes glad while out of an engagement to fill an inferior post at the box-office or as prompter. In point of remuneration there is not much to choose between the money earned by a skilled mechanic and a subordinate actor. If anything, the mechanic as such earns the larger sum of the two, and only takes to acting if he finds that he has a decided gift for it.

We will begin with employees other than actors. And first we note that there are two great departments, the heads of which [...] have power to engage and discharge their subordinates, while they are themselves responsible directly to the stage-manager. These are the stage-carpenter, and the property-master, to whom in large theatres may be added the wardrobe-mistress. When a play is to be brought out, these officers are furnished with a list of the various articles which will be required in their departments for each scene, and it is their business to provide them.

Let us take first the stage-carpenter and his department. His remuneration is pretty high (£3 to £5 per week). [...] It is his business to construct and fit together the different parts of the scenery, to be afterwards painted by the scene-painter. As he is expected to give his whole time, he is not paid for overtime. Whilst a new play is being prepared and introduced on the stage he has to work night and day, but so long as a play is running he has a comparatively easy berth. With an assistant carpenter he superintends the shifting of the scenes. [...] The head stage-carpenter takes charge of one side [of the stage], and his assistant of the other; and during the performance each is responsible for the scenery on his own side.

Besides the assistant stage-carpenter, paid 40s to 50s a week, who, like his principal, is a permanent officer, there are jobbing carpenters who specially devote themselves to theatrical work, and who go from theatre to theatre wherever they hear that men are wanted. For such men work is very uncertain; for a few days, or perhaps a week or two, they have as much work as they can get through, and then, for weeks, they are without a job. Under stage-carpenters receive 8d or 8½d per hour, and a few 9d. Very few make the regulation 9½d. The Theatrical and Music Hall Operatives' Trade Union with about 750 members out of an estimated total of 1,500 who might belong, has a rule to the effect that 'theatrical carpenters shall be paid not less than the standard rate of the London Building Trades' Federation', but it is not strictly enforced.

Scene-shifting is not a trade by itself, and scene-shifters do not go through an apprenticeship. But it requires considerable accuracy of eye and dexterity of hand to adjust the different parts of the scenery exactly in place with the minimum of noise and the maximum of speed. And the furniture and fittings must retain in each subsequent performance the positions assigned them at rehearsal.

The gas-man, who is under the control of the stage-manager, has to perform the very important duty of seeing that the light is cast on the stage so as to make the scenery and actors appear as real as possible, and that it is properly regulated for effects of twilight, chiaroscuro, etc. The lime-light apparatus may be worked from the flies, or from perches placed on either side of the proscenium, or even from the stage itself.

The property-master [...] has to find, or prepare, the various properties needed. Under this name are included furniture, actors' costumes (in theatres where there is no wardrobe-mistress), and all odds and ends which may chance to be required in the course of a play.

The property-master must be a man of resource who can effect hasty repairs, and, if need be, himself make the simpler articles. [...] The property-master often has men to assist him, and they, like himself, must be all-round men. They may be called upon to make anything, from a stage razor to a railway train. Perfect finish is unnecessary, but there must be a semblance of perfection. Success of effect depends on shape and colouring, and wire-workers and house-painters have consequently a certain preference; an elementary acquaintance with [. . .] carpentry, upholstery and mechanics should also be added. By profession, indeed, the property man is jack of all trades. For the best men 5s per day of eight hours is usual, and for second-class men 4s. They are engaged in their greatest numbers before the actual production of a piece, and just about Christmas, overtime is almost inevitable. It is paid at the rate of time and a half. There is a great variation in the numbers of men employed at different seasons. One master stated that whereas he might only have four men in the autumn he would employ sixty during the six weeks preceding Christmas, and that, during these weeks, the men often earned double money owing to the amount of overtime. The London demand is not alone responsible for this sudden rush, for many of the properties used in provincial pantomimes are made in and sent out from the metropolis. The assistants of the master-carpenter, property-master and gas-man are divided into bodies of night-men and day-men. Night-men only come at night and shift the scenes and properties between the acts of a performance, while day-men, arriving in the morning at about 10.00 or 10.30 to attend to repairs during the day, generally remain on during the evening. Day-men, who are practically carpenters' labourers, receive 4s a day and 2s for every night for which they are on duty. Night-men are paid almost invariably 2s per performance.

The wardrobe-mistress [. . .] is [. . .] custodian of the costumes; and either single-handed or with the aid of one or more needle-women, does the necessary repairing, and sometimes adapts costumes designed for one piece to the exigencies of some other. The same person who is needle-woman by day is often dresser by night, and in this way earns a double wage. Prominent actors, especially if they are also managers, have their own dressers, who are, so to speak, specialized valets or ladies'-maids. The dresser has sometimes to assist in the [. . .] process of 'making up'. The actors do most of this themselves, however. The number of actors on whom one dresser can attend will depend, of course, on the amount of elaboration which their toilettes may require. Half a dozen is very common. His tips are an important auxiliary to the dresser's money, for he usually gets a shilling a week from each gentleman he dresses, in addition to his standing wages of 6s to 12s per week, and this system of tipping has survived all attempts to put it down by prohibitory rules.

Scene-painters – A scene-painter is sometimes attached to the permanent staff of a theatre, and sometimes he is engaged for the job. More often the chief part of the scenery is contracted out to a 'scenic artist' with a studio of his own, and only the finishing touches or smaller pieces are executed in the theatre painting-room.

An artist with his assistant and a colour grinder were formerly included in the regular staff of every theatre, and in exceptional cases are so still. But during the last ten years the tendency has been to contract the work out more and more, so that at the present day the work of scene-painting has become almost entirely detached from the theatre, and forms a small industry by itself. It is said that the County Council do not favour painting-rooms in a theatre for fear of fire, but this can only be accepted as a partial reason, since distemper and not oil or turpentine is the usual medium for the colours. The real explanation lies probably in the saving of expense. Long runs of one piece are now of so frequent occurrence that it would not pay to maintain even one artist upon the regular staff throughout the year. Hence a manager saves money in the end by giving the work out even though he pays rather more for the actual painting of any one piece of scenery. The industry gives employment altogether to under one hundred persons of whom about twelve may be employers. [...] Scene-painters are all time-workers. The majority of them are men who have attended regular art schools, or even still do so. A few are formally indentured to master scene-painters. The ordinary hours are from 10.00 a.m. to 7.00 or 8.00 p.m. for six days a week. Some stop at 2.00 on Saturdays, but it is not usual. An artist permanently attached to a theatre will receive £10 per week, assistant artists from £2 to £4, and beginners about 30s. [...] Colourmen are practically first-class labourers and earn from 24s to 28s throughout the year. [See 177]

Front Staff – The 'front' staff [...] comprises check-takers (or ticket collectors), and attendants, who with a fireman and one or two cleaners complete the table of persons usually employed in a theatre. [...] Members of the front staff are often engaged and paid by contractors who [...] rent from the theatre manager the right of selling programmes and refreshments. The employees here are drawn from the ranks of those who in the daytime are working as clerks, drapers, and stationers' assistants, and usually receive 2s per performance. [...]

It must be remembered that, with the exception of the heads of the various departments, none of the persons already mentioned look upon theatrical work as the sole business of their lives. House painters and decorators, bricklayers' labourers, Covent Garden porters, even dockers in the East End, masons and printers' labourers and general labourers of all sorts are drawn upon by the theatre at night after their other work is done. Theatres are busiest during the Christmas holidays, when work for many of these men is slackest, and this employment helps not a few to tide over the period of enforced idleness in their own trade.

---

[1] 'Super' – a colloquial abbreviation of 'supernumerary', defined by the *Oxford English Dictionary* as 'a person employed in addition to the regular company, who appears on stage but does not speak'.

177 (a) Scene painting, 1889

William Lewis Telbin, 'Art in the Theatre', *The Magazine of Art*, 1889, pp. 195–201

William Telbin begins by regretting the change from the earlier nineteenth-century practice of each theatre employing a staff of resident scene-painters, to 'contract' work, in which a painter is hired for a fixed commission to create scenery for a particular play.

When the scene-painter receives his commission from the manager, he receives with it some sort of particulars of what is wanted. Some managers can graphically illustrate their requirements; others, not possessing this happy faculty, give the key to the idea and requirements of the situation by word of mouth. [. . .] The most satisfactory way to proceed is to spend time on the model (which is a representation of the stage to scale), and thoroughly to understand from it what you propose doing – not only the 'practice-abilities', but also your composition, colour and scheme of lighting. Any alterations considered necessary are then easy to make. For according to the scale – perhaps half an inch to the foot, pieces of paper in the model representing canvas and framework – a piece which in the model represents, say, a tree or a column fifteen inches high, would, in the actuality, be thirty feet in height; to re-make or to alter and repaint this would mean considerable labour and expense.

The model completed, after being duly inspected and approved by the management, the master-carpenter comes to see it with respect to the construction of it mechanically, and to hear your suggestions as to setting and striking in something like reasonable time (English time, not French). At the English plays we wait only while the scene is being changed; at the French, while the actresses' dresses are – the interval is theirs! When all is understood, he traces the various portions of the model, and from the duplicates constructs the actual scene, one foot to every half-inch of the model.

A few days after almost acres of framework and bales of canvas are brought in; one great surface is stretched on the frame, and having been duly prepared, upon it you first start – this generally represents the back of the scene. Then you paint the different pieces in order until you arrive at the foreground, gaining in strength as you advance.

The model completed, the scene painted, for a day or two the stage is given up entirely to the artist for the scene to be set and lighted. [. . .] The best scene ever designed and painted can be ruined by injudicious lighting; for the illumination is the last and most important touch to the picture – its very life.

177 (b) Modelling a scene

From a drawing by W. Telbin[1]

[1] William Louis Telbin (1846–1931) designed for the Manchester Theatre Royal before coming to London, where he worked for various theatres, including Covent Garden, the Lyceum and St James's.

177 (c) The Covent Garden Theatre painting-room

From a drawing by W. Telbin

178   Mrs Kendal's condemnation of performers' self-advertisement, 1884

From *The Times*, 24 September 1884, pp. 7–8

Madge Kendal (1848–1935) was born Margaret Robertson, one of the playwright T. W. Robertson's (see 180 and 181) many younger siblings. She made her first public appearance on the stage before her sixth birthday and did not retire from it until after her sixtieth. When, on 23 September 1884, she addressed the third Social Sciences Congress on the subject of 'The Drama', she and her husband William Hunter Kendal were in the middle of a successful decade of partnership with John Hare in the management of the St James's Theatre. An incarnation of her profession's moral probity and social respectability, Mrs Kendal does not appear to have been gifted with a sense of irony sufficient to recognize the incongruity of herself making a speech against actors making speeches.

Perhaps the most remarkable thing which has come over the drama is the fact that there is at last a recognized social position for the professional player. [. . .] I must now turn to the other side of the question and tell you in what ways the drama of the present day has deteriorated and [. . .] is likely still further to deteriorate. No true lover of the dramatic art can look with satisfaction on the many ways in which it is now advertised. Neither the painter nor the poet thinks it advisable to fill the columns of the daily papers with the monotonous repetition of what this or that critic has said of his work, or to keep his name constantly and with wearisome persistency before the public. The extent to which some carry out this system, and the pains which are taken over it, is [*sic*] simply beyond all description. An insatiable thirst for newspaper paragraphs is always tormenting them. [. . .] With people thus constituted even affliction is turned to what they consider profitable account, and at a dull period an illness is regarded as a positive boon. (*Laughter.*) This absurd mania, I am sorry to say, is peculiar to the members of the theatrical profession. [. . .] It is done in manifold ways – in what are known as 'receptions' at theatres, in railway station demonstrations, by photography, by speech-making; and one and all are degrading to the drama. (*Hear, hear.*) As a cloak for incapability, such means may, perhaps, be excusable, but true art in every branch advertises itself. Advertisement nowadays is an art, but it is not the art of acting. This state of things has given rise to a flippant, and what may be termed a personal style of theatrical journalism, which is greatly to be deplored, and certainly to be discouraged. The so-called theatrical papers, in which the leading artists of the stage are alluded to by their Christian names, and where insolent and generally untrue gossip and tittle-tattle takes the place of honest criticism, are absolutely debasing to the profession. The unfortunate outcome of all this is that the actor's capability is too often gauged by the amount of publicity that is given to every little action of his or her life. An unthinking section of the public is hungry for news of this description, and incompetent but 'knowing' actors and their managers take advantage of it.

179   Irving denounces gossip journalism, 1898

From *The Era*, 19 February 1898, p. 12

Addressing the Playgoers Club at its fourteenth annual dinner, held on Sunday 13 February 1898, Henry Irving, who three years earlier had received the country's first theatrical knighthood, took up the same subject as Mrs Kendal (178). He, however, acknowledged the difficulty of public speaking (an activity in which he frequently engaged) against theatrical publicity.

Some people who were intended by nature to adorn an inviolable privacy are thrust upon us by paragraphers and interviewers, whose existence is a dubious blessing, until it is assumed by censors of the stage that this business is part and parcel of theatrical advertisement. Columns of this rubbish are printed every week, and many an actor is pestered to death for titbits about his ox and his ass and everything that is his. Occasionally you may read solemn articles about the vanity of the actor, which must be gratified at any cost, as if vanity were peculiar to any section of humanity. But what this organized gossip really advertises is the industry of the gentlemen who collect, and the smartness of the papers in which it is circulated. 'We learn this', 'We have heard that', 'We have reason to believe' – such forms of intolerable assurance give currency too often to scandalous and lying rumours which I am sure responsible journalism would wish to discourage. But this, I fear, is difficult, for contradiction makes another desirable paragraph, and it is all looked upon as excellent copy. Of course, gentlemen, the drama is declining – it has always been declining since the time of Roscius.

180   Old and new acting styles, 1879

From George Comer, 'The Actor of the Period', *Era Almanack*, 1879, p. 44

Under the old custom of long stock seasons, and playing different pieces every night, a man, whatever his capabilities, was pretty sure to become thoroughly versed in every detail of his profession, and to acquire an ease and confidence apparently quite unattainable by the present race of tyros. The pieces, too, had a great deal more of what is technically called 'business' than is the case the present day. A man had not only to remember the words of his part, but a great deal remained for him to *do* on the stage – struggles, combats and what not. He thus became far more experienced, and as a consequence considerably more self-possessed. His movements would be natural, his gesticulation finished and appropriate, and his delivery well studied; in refreshing contrast to the ungainly, inexperienced youth who now passes as an actor. The late T. W. Robertson[1] may be said in a manner to have inaugurated a new school of acting. His unequalled modern comedies established a demand for a different type of player; one not so much of experience and ability, as a showy-looking person, capable of comporting himself with some amount of ease when in evening dress, and who evinced some acquaintance with the amenities of polite life. To dress well and speak the Queen's English correctly are all that is required for taking part in the majority of the present class of plays.

[1] Thomas William Robertson (1829–71), whose comedy *Society* (1865) established a new intimate style of 'cup-and-saucer' drama. See **181**.

181   Robertson's comedies and the 'natural school of acting'

Marie Effie Bancroft, *Recollections of Sixty Years* (London: John Murray, 1909), pp. 83–4

Squire Bancroft (1841–1926) and his wife Marie Effie (née Wilton 1839–1921) opened the old Queen's Theatre (nicknamed the 'Dust Bowl'), transformed into the fashionable Prince of Wales's, in 1865: their productions of Tom Robertson's domestic comedies were seen as heralding a new style of 'realistic' drama, although the sentimental content, as this extract suggests, limits its claims to 'realism'.

Looking back, as my wife and I often do, through the long vista of more than forty years, it's still easy to understand the great success of this comedy.[1] The Robertson comedies appeared upon the scene just when they were needed to revive and renew intelligent interest in the drama. Nature was Robertson's goddess, and he looked upon the bright young management as the high-priest of the natural school of acting. The return to Nature was the great need of the stage, and happily he came to help supply it at the right moment.

In this connection I may quote from a brilliant pen on a novel scene in *Society*, which was acted by my wife and myself. 'Then came an idyll, evolving amidst the trees of a London square. What! love – youthful, tender, tremulous love – in the very heart of this city of mud, fog, and smoke! Love, so near that you might touch his wings! That was the kind of impression it evoked.'[2]

[1] T. W. Robertson, *Society*, produced at the Prince of Wales's in November 1865. See **180** and **182**.
[2] The 'brilliant pen' cannot be traced.

182   The taste for realism, 1883

Philip Beck, *The Theatre* (1 September 1883), pp. 127–31

The present has been styled the Age of Progress, but it might with equal truth be termed the Matter-of-Fact Age. This being the case, it is only natural that this matter-of-fact feeling should find expression in our amusements as in other concerns of our daily life. Indeed, Realism on the stage is but the application of this same matter-of-fact principle, which demands that objects should not seem to be that which they are not, but that they should actually be what they seem. And, so, as the stage is the clearest reflex of the time, it is in matters dramatic that we first recognize the realistic tendency of today, although it exists co-equally in other directions.

It is not here claimed for Realism that it is of modern birth. It is merely held that its rapid growth and great development are of a comparatively recent date. Who, twenty-five years ago, would have bestowed upon the series of incomparable comedies of modern life from the pen of the late T. W. Robertson, the scrupulous care, that attention to the most minute detail, that unstinted expenditure of time, trouble, and money, lavished upon them by the Bancrofts at the old Prince of Wales's Theatre? Who, fifty years since, could have conceived that series of superb revivals, replete with archaeological research and artistic instinct, faithful echoes of the past, truthful transcripts of by-gone times, could reach the point attained by the productions of the late Charles Kean at the Princess's, and even in a superlative degree in our own day by Henry Irving at the Lyceum. [...]

Nor [...] would the British public nowadays rest content with the real pump and two washing-tubs which the immortal Vincent Crummles purchased cheap at a sale, and of which he thought so highly as to commission Nicholas Nickleby to write a new drama, especially with a view to their introduction in the last act, placed in the centre of the stage, and accompanied with an appropriate illumination of blue fire.[1] On the contrary, it now demands entire rows of real tubs, with real soap, real thumb blue, real washing-powder, and real hot water for the mutual drenching of two real irate females.[2]

The recent visit of the Saxe-Meiningen company taught a lesson in the management of stage crowds.[3] That the lesson was conned with advantage may be readily demonstrated by a reference to the quarrel between the rival houses of Montague and Capulet, which formed one of the prominent features of the revival of *Romeo and Juliet* at the Lyceum last year. Here were some fifty or sixty men inducted into the mysteries of *carte* and *tierce*[4] to add to the realism of one scene – an undertaking, in the magnitude of its design and perfection of execution, without parallel. Different in its means and effect, but alike in its aim, striving after true realism, was the street crowd manipulated with so much skill in *The Lights o'*

London.[5] It is impossible to obliterate the impression created by this bit of living London lifted straight from the street and placed before the footlights.

Vast improvement, too, has been manifested in those mimic combats so essential to many melodramas and tragedies. Time was, and not long since, when a combat generally consisted of what is technically known as round eights, singles, three, broken fives, primes (pronounced preams), double primes, and passes. Very popular was a mysterious combination known as the 'Glasgow tens'; so also was another desperate encounter, carefully arranged, and called 'The Gladiators', this last being a combat fought to music, each blow being struck to its accompanying note or chord in the orchestra. Nor must the glory of the transpontine drama be forgotten, the sailor combats of the T. P. Cooke[6] time, when Jack Tar – armed literally to the teeth – with a combat sword in each hand for use, and a third between his teeth for ornament, encountered and overcame with ease eight 'piratical skunks', seven slain with bloodless slaughter, the eighth contemptuously discomfited with a 'quid o' bacca'. *Nous avons changé tout cela.* Taught by McTurk,[7] many actors now fence brilliantly – 'one, two, and the third in your bosom', and for the broadsword combat of yore, they now receive instruction in the regulation cuts and thrusts.

[1] Charles Dickens, *Nicholas Nickleby* (1839), ch. 24.
[2] The reference is to Charles Read's long-running version of Zola's *L'Assommoir* (Drink), first staged at the Princess's Theatre, 27 May 1879. (See also 23.)
[3] The Meiningen Players visited Drury Lane from May to June 1881. The precision of their meticulous ensemble playing had an impact throughout Europe. (See also 51, 52 and 53.)
[4] Sword fighting terms.
[5] G. R. Sim's popular melodrama was first produced at the Princess's Theatre on 10 September 1881.
[6] Thomas Potter Cooke (1786–1864) was an ex-sailor who came to prominence in Douglas Jerold's *Black-Ey'd Susan* (1829) and specialized in naval parts. His final appearance was at Covent Garden in 1868.
[7] McTurk has not been identified – possibly a character in a contemporary play.

VI   Equipment

183   Stage-directions and equipment: a specialized vocabulary lesson for amateurs, 1881

'Stage Whispers' and 'Shouts Without': a Book about Plays and Playgoers, Actors and Actresses (London: 'Judy' Office [1881]), pp. 40–41

This slim volume, ascribed to Charles Henry Ross, is addressed to amateurs. Under the title 'The Names of Things Behind the Curtain', it gives its uninitiated readers a specialized vocabulary lesson which maps out the notionally standard stage furnishings of a late-Victorian theatre immediately before the introduction of electricity.

I will take it for granted that everybody knows that in stage-directions the actor's R. H. is the spectator's left, and that the Prompt Side is on the spectator's right-hand side, and the O.P. or Opposite Prompt, means the spectator's left. The opening between the proscenium and the first wing is therefore either 1st Entrance R. or L., the opening between the first and second wings 2nd Entrance R. or L., and so on, the entrance farthest from the spectator being termed Upper Entrance. A door in the middle of the scene crossing the stage is the Centre Entrance, and entering by it, say in a procession, an actor may be directed to *exit* C.R. or C.L.

A rolling scene is generally called a *Cloth*, and is worked from the *Flies* by the *Flymen*, as are also the *Act Drop* and green curtain, and *Sky*, *Wood*, or *Chamber Borders*. Scenes on a wooden framework divided into two or more sections are pushed on and formed by the *Stagemen*, *Wingmen*, or *Flatmen* where there is a large staff, and are called *Flats*.

The *Mazarine* (i.e., *Mezzanine*) *Floor* is that beneath the stage dividing the upper part of the cellar from a receptacle for lumber below. The *Cellarmen* work the traps from the mazarine floor at a given signal by the cellar-bell from the prompter's box. Thus – First pull, 'Ready', means that the man below must remove the slides covering the trap above; second, 'Go', and then, according to circumstances, up comes the actor by the *Ghost* or *Star Trap*.

A *Vampire Trap* is one that closes suddenly. They are tightly secured below until wanted, when, the bolts and bars being withdrawn, a sprite slips through like an eel, and is caught in a blanket below, or in some cases [...] into a kind of tunnel lined with brushes [. . .] to avoid a shock. Vampires are also fitted into flats. A *Slider* is an oblong trap running flush with the floor of the stage, which opens in the centre to raise spirits or fairies. [. . .] A *Sloat* is a trap on which fairies ascend or descend gradually from stage to clouds, or vice versa.

A scene, half of which is let down from the flies and meets the other half pulled up through the stage, is called a *Rise-and-Sink*. The scene with portions cut away to show another scene beyond is a *Cut-out Scene* or *Cut-cloth*, and wings cut in the same way are *Profile Wings*.

The technical name for the footlights is *Floats*. *Battens* means the rows of lights crossing the stage from R. to L. The *Wing Lights* are placed perpendicularly in each wing. *Ground Rows* are lights crossing the stage floor from R. to L. behind a set piece or water piece.

Grooves are the slides in which the wings are fixed, being made of strips of wood, and the interspaces are termed *Cuts*. *Rake* is the name given to a slanting platform with footholds such as you may see outside a show at a fair leading up to the 'parade'; and in 'sets' it is sometimes also called a *Return Piece*. Up a series of rakes gallops the untamed fiery steed bearing the undaunted Mazeppa[1] through the rocky gorges. It may be less dangerous than would be a slippery rock itself, but it would be quite dangerous enough for me.

---

[1] Mazeppa is the eponymous hero of a poem published by Lord Byron in 1819 and of its dramatizations, which had been popular in equestrian theatres like Astley's for half a century before the publication of *'Stage Whispers' and 'Shouts Without'*. The spectacular high point of *Mazeppa* on the equestrian stage was a zig-zag gallop up risers. See Anthony D. Hippisley Coxe, 'Equestrian Drama and the Circus', in *Politics and Performance in Popular Theatre*, eds. D. Bradby, Louis James and B. Sharratt (Cambridge University Press, 1980), pp. 109–18; and Saxon, *Enter Foot and Horse*.

184   Technical stage innovations at the Lyceum, 1863

Charles Dickens, 'Fechter's Stage Innovations at the Lyceum', *All the Year Round*, 31 October 1863, pp. 229–34

Charles Albert Fechter (1824–79) managed the Lyceum from 1863 to 1869. Like other actor-managers of the time, he supervised many different aspects of stage presentation.

We must keep at present to the main-deck – the stage that is visible to the public when a play is acted. The first thing that strikes you in examining this, is, that it is traversed completely from side to side by certain narrow slits, through which you can see down into the second stage below. There are two dozens of these slits in parallel lines. Having observed them, and wondering what they are for, you notice a number of strong upright poles rising out of the stage, where the wings are ordinarily placed; going up to one of them you see, on examination, that though it is a pole above the stage, it has a broader lower member – part and parcel of it – which descends through one of those slits already described, into the 'between-decks' below. Descending a companion-ladder, you post off to see what becomes of it after it has passed through the slit, and then one glance reveals the simple plan by which the scenes are pushed backwards or forwards to their positions on the stage. That broad flat piece is received in a travelling crane below, which runs on wheels along an iron tramway, and moves so easily that a child might move it with but little exertion. These iron tramways are laid along the floor of the second stage, exactly underneath the slits above; it will be obvious that the pole which descends through the slit may, by means of the travelling crane which runs along the tramway, be pushed to any part of the stage where it (the pole) is wanted.

Here, then, is the formidable operation of scene-shifting reduced to the most simple of proceedings. Formerly, all that will now be done under the stage was done *on* the stage. There were grooves – raised grooves on the stage – into which the scene was lifted in two halves by staggering carpenters; then the other grooves descended from above, into which the tops of the two halves of the scene fitted – not without a very visible crack up the centre. The reader has often from his place at the side of the theatre seen those upper rows of grooves fall over with a flop when they were wanted. The scene at length got successfully, though not without much resistance, into these grooves, and was pushed forward noisily and awkwardly by the carpenters, and was generally successful in retaining a perpendicular position, and not showing *much* of the bare lights and general shipwreck behind. Under the new system no such pushing, struggling, splitting and joining will ever be beheld; and among its many advantages, one may specially be mentioned. The old necessity of having raised grooves on the stage, in which the bottom of the scene might slide, prohibited the possibility of pushing any scene or object more than a certain distance from the side. These grooves could never be carried far on to the stage, lest the actors should tumble over them. Now this is not the case, according to the new system. [. . .] Those slits, or portions of slits which are not required for any particular performance, are filled up with wooden slides prepared for the purpose, so that no flaw whatever appears on the stage's surface.

185(a) Theatre lighting in the 1860s

'Theatre', *Chambers's Encyclopaedia* (1868), p. 390

Stage lighting was developed during the 1860s and 1870s in line with other scenic innovations, notably by Fechter at the Lyceum (see **184**) and then at the same theatre by Henry Irving (1878–99).

The house, or auditorium department, is generally lighted by means of a large lustre or sun-light in the centre of the ceiling, and much of the effect of the building depends on how this is managed. There are also usually smaller lights round one tier of the boxes at least. The proscenium is lighted by a large lustre on each side, and by the footlights, which run along the whole of the front of the stage. These are sometimes provided with glasses of different colours, called mediums, which are used for throwing a red, green, or white light on the stage, as may be required. The stage is lighted by rows of gas-burners up each side and across the top of every entrance. The side-lights are called *gas-wings*, or *ladders*; and the top ones, *gas-battens*. Each of these has a main from the prompt-corner. They can be pushed in and out, or up and down, like the scenery. There is also provision at each entrance for fixing flexible hose and temporary lights, so as to produce a bright effect wherever required. The mediums for producing coloured light in the case are blinds of coloured cloth. Another means of producing brilliant effects of light is the lime-light, by which, together with the lenses of coloured glass, bright lights of any colour can be thrown on the stage or scenery when required.

185(b) Introduction of electrical stage lighting, 1881

From 'Savoy Theatre', *The Times*, 29 December 1881, p. 4

An interesting experiment was made at a performance of *Patience* yesterday afternoon, when the stage was for the first time lit up by the electric light, which had been used in the auditorium ever since the opening of the Savoy Theatre.[1] The success of the new mode of illumination was complete, and its importance for the development of scenic art can scarcely be overrated. The light was perfectly steady throughout the performance, and the effect was pictorially superior to gas, the colours of the dress – an important element in the 'aesthetic' opera – appearing as true and distinct as by daylight. The Swan incandescent lamps were used, the aid of gaslight being entirely dispensed with.[2] The comparative safety of the new system was pointed out to the audience by Mr D'Oyly Carte, the manager of the Savoy Theatre, who enveloped one of the lamps in a piece of highly inflammable muslin. On the glass being broken and the vacuum destroyed, the flame was immediately extinguished, without even singeing the muslin.

[1] The Savoy opened on 10 October 1881.
[2] The intensity of light was controlled by adding resistance from coils of iron wire to the copper circuit.

VII Mise en scène

186 Charles Kean stages *Richard II*, 1857

Playbill for production of *Richard II* at the Princess's Theatre, 1857. By courtesy of the Pettingell Collection

Charles Kean (1811–68), as manager of the Princess's Theatre 1851–9, staged spectacular and influential Shakespearian productions based on meticulous historical research into setting, costume, music and ritual.

In the present Stage representation I have endeavoured to produce a true portraiture of medieval history. The Lists at Conventry – the Fleet at Milford Haven – the Castles of Pembroke and Flint – the Garden, where 'Old Adam's likeness' startles the Queen with his 'unpleasing news' – the Great Hall at Westminster, rebuilt by Richard, in his pride of kingly sway, and afterwards selected as the place where unkinged Richard was constrained 'with his own hands to give away his crown' – the Royal Chambers and the Royal Prison – are all either actually restored, or represented in conformity with contemporaneous authorities. Between the third and fourth acts I have ventured to introduce the triumphal entry into London of the 'mounting' Bolingbroke, followed by the deposed and captive King, 'in grief and patience'; thus embodying in action what Shakespeare has so beautifully described in the speech of York to his Duchess, towards the close of the play.

The few sentences intervening amidst the clamorous acclamations of the mob in this Historical Episode *are selected from the Chronicles which relate to the circumstances of that remarkable event*, and are added with the view of reviving, as far as possible, a scene that actually occurred in London upwards of four hundred and fifty years since. The entire *tableau* may be considered as an historical picture, in which the creations of the painter's art are endowed with animated reality.

The increasing taste for recreation wherein instruction is blended with amusement, has for some time been conspicuous in the English public; and surely, an attempt to render dramatic representations conducive to the diffusion of knowledge – to surround the glowing imagery of the great Poet with accompaniments *true* to the time in which he writes – *realizing* the scenes and actions which he describes – exhibiting men as they once lived [. . .] can scarcely detract from the enduring influence of his genius. Repeated success justifies the conviction that I am acting in accordance with the general feeling. When plays, which formerly commanded but occasional repetition, are enabled, by no derogatory means, to attract audiences for successive months, I cannot be wrong in presuming that the course I have adopted is supported by the irresistible force of public opinion, expressed in the suffrages of an overwhelming majority.

CHARLES KEAN

CONTRASTING STYLES OF THEATRICAL PRESENTATIONS

187(a) Playbill for *The Great Fire of London* and *The Wandering Jew*, June 1850

Samuel Atkyns, *The Fire of London* and *The Wandering Jew*, playbill for the Bower Saloon, Lambeth, 3, 7 and 8 June 1850. By courtesy of the Pettingell Collection

The plays were based on two sensational novels of the time – W. H. Ainsworth's *Old St Paul's* (1841) and Eugène Sue's *The Wandering Jew* (1844–5) respectively. The 'Benefit' Nights mentioned at the bottom of the playbill (see p. 392) refer to the system by which an actor took the entire receipts of an evening, supplementing what were often inadequate salaries. By 1850 this tradition was dying out.

BOWER SALOON.

Licensed by the Lord Chamberlain

Lessee and Manager, Mr J. Biddle, 71, Hercules Buildings, Lambeth.

Third and Last Week of Mr. S. ATKYNS

On MONDAY, FRIDAY, and SATURDAY, June 3rd, 7th, and 8th, 1850,

Will be performed an Historical and Romantic Drama, with novel and extraordinary effects, (written by Mr S. ATKYNS) entitled THE GREAT

FIRE OF LONDON!

Or, the MYSTERY AND THE MURDER!

The Earl of Raymond	Mr BURROUGHS	Barnaby Bruone
Thomas, a master Baker	Mr BALL	Robert Winter
Edward Montague	Mr SYMONDSON	Lord Mayor
Stephen Sylvester (Host of the Lamb Tavern)	Mr MACKNEY	Jacob Brandon
Solomon Eagle		Mr B. DODSON
Isabel Herbert	Miss Ellen GORDON	Eve Elliott
	Mrs Herbert	

Mr WILSON ... Vincent ... Mr BOLTON
(his assistant, afterwards a Sailor) ... MR S. ATKYNS
Mr H. YOUNG ... Ralph Marshall ... Mr CRAUFORD
(his Partner in Trade and Crime) ... Mr Stacy TEMPLETON
Simon Sumpkins ... Mr BIDDLES
Miss WARDE ... Margaret ... Miss ADELAIDE
Miss JEFFERSON

View of Old London the Southwark Side
The linen arrives...the Plot to destroy the City...Mrs Herbert's Apartment...Mother & Daughter the escape from Danger...the Countryman

The Combat, Tavern & Baker's Shop in Pudding Lane
The Lamb and Wheatsheaf...a Wolf in Sheeps clothing...the Partner's Crime...the Villain and the Isle

A STREET NEAR FINSBURY
The abduction...the Pursuit...the Assassination...Interior of the Baker's Shop...the Midnight Robber...the Murder...Burial of the Victim's Body...the Fire Bell

STREET NEAR LONDON BRIDGE
Consternation of the Citizens at the Progress of the

GREAT FIRE OF LONDON!

A SPLENDID BALL ROOM!!
Wedded Bliss...Grand assemblage of Guests

THE BALL!
Parlor in the Lamb Tavern, The Sailor the Citizen

GLOOMY GARRET IN THE TAVERN.
The Murder and the Ruffian...Perilous adventure...the Rescue, Terrific Struggle...the Knife

Dark Chamber and Vaults beneath the Tavern!
THE TRAP DOOR...APPALLING DISCOVERY.

THE UNHALLOWED GRAVE!
Discovery of the Skeleton—Seizure of the Murderer. Grand Tableau.

To be followed by

A LAUGHABLE FARCE!

Supported by the entire strength of the Company.

The whole to conclude with the Favorite Romantic Drama, (written by Mr S. ATKYNS) of the

WANDERING JEW!

OR, THE
VETERAN, THE BRUTE TAMER
AND THE
ORPHAN GIRLS!

Marquis de Rosengol	Mr BURROUGHS	Lord Lockwit
Morok, a Brute Tamer	Mr SYMONDSON	Karl
Dagobert, the Veteran, Protector of the Orphan Girls		
Claude and Paula	Messrs H. YOUNG and BOLTON	
Rose and Blanche (the Orphan Girls)	Miss Ellen GORDON and Miss ADELAIDE	

...Mr MACKNEY ... Jenkins, a Valet ... Mr CRAUFORD ... Maurice Flash ... Mr FORD
...his assistant ... Mr H. DODSON ... Burgomaster of Mockeron ... Mr BIDDLES ... Old Brandon ... Mr JOHNS
The Wandering Jew ... MR S. ATKYNS ... Justin, a young Peasant ... Mr JONES
Gronedt of women ... Messrs Wilks, James, Walton &c
Jeanette, ... Mrs WARDE ... Lady Lockwit ... Miss JEFFERSON

Watermill and distant View of Mockeron!
The Veteran Soldier and the Orphans on their Journey...a Veterans' grief...the Soldier of many Fights...the Orphan's Love for the Old Soldier

THE BRUTE TAMER'S LOFT.
Morok is seen to ascend...the surprise, the raised Pistol...the interview...they are coming...oh, sure the description

The Seizure. The Threat and the Robbery.
Murder, the Horses alarmed...Morok, the Prophet...the proposal to know the thieves...the capture...the Property restored...he bids he confined &c

THE DEN OF ANIMALS.
Pleasant reflections...the brutal and the spotted tiger...Dagobert's alarm at missing the Horses...the Beasts may be devouring them...the Old Soldier rushes to the rescue of his Horses

Court Yard of the Inn. The Brute Tamer
Sudden appearance of Dagobert...the Dead Horse...the Insulted and the Pamphlet...there he goes

THE DESOLATE CHAMBER, or SLEEPING ORPHANS
The Window opens...an axe grasp by through...the Soldier's Knapsack robbed of its contents...the alarm...the orphan's flown...the Orphans' tale...the Knapsack the search

The Discovery—The Lost Papers!
Arrival of the Burgomaster...top minister and the second...the Old soldier demands justice for the insult of his companion...his favorite Horse...the

THE DYING MOTHER'S CHARGE, THE DEFENCE.
The whisper...one hundred Justice...anger of Dagobert...the demand for the Passports...Triumph of the Brute Tamer...the Old soldier of France...fate of the Burgomaster...the secret confession

The Soldier & the Orphans
The Exiled Mother...the prayer for Protection...the Hustle of Flint...the Arrest...the Struggle...Bravery of Dagobert

Sudden Appearance of the Wandering JEW!
THE BANKS OF THE RHINE
The Soldier and his charge...the poison...we near the...wither !...on the bank of providence is stretched he's to save on...the Ferryman...the appeal...the Report...the Purchase

The Wandering Jew the Brute Tamer
The revengeful Brute Tamer...the intended seizure...the sisters in danger...the Parchment and the Seal

Burning of the Palace. Destruction of Morok

Tuesday, for the Benefit of Mr Dean. Wednesday, Benefit of Mr Williams Thursday, Benefit of Mr Templeton

On MONDAY, Next, will be Produced an entire

New Nautical Drama, Mr J. F. YOUNG will appear

Doors open at half-past Six, commence at Seven Precisely. Boxes - 6d Pit - 4d, Gallery - 2d. Harley, Printer, 4, Gibson Street, Waterloo Road.

187(a)

187(b) Playbill for *Society*, November 1865

Playbill for T.W. Robertson, *Society*, The Prince of Wales's Theatre, 11 and 13
November 1865. By courtesy of the Pettingell Collection

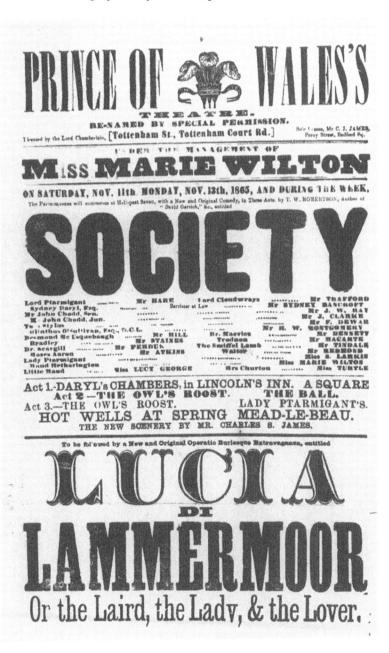

THE STAGING OF SENSATION DRAMA

188(a) A sensation scene in *Arrah-na-Pogue*, 1868

Playbill for Dion Boucicault's *Arrah-na-Pogue*,[1] 2 March 1868, showing a sensation scene. By courtesy of The Theatre Musuem, V&A, London

¹ Dion Boucicault (1822–90) established his reputation as a writer of elaborately staged spectacular melodramas. *Arrah-na-Pogue* (1865) was based on events in the Fenian rebellion of 1798, and built on the popularity of his earlier Irish play, *The Colleen Bawn* (1860). The key 'sensation' scene added after the first production showed Shaun the Post, a genial rogue character portrayed by Boucicault himself, escaping from the British by scaling a castle wall up large moving 'flats'. The play's climactic trial scene, and certain of the characters, were used by Bernard Shaw in his own melodrama, *The Devil's Disciple* (1897).

188(b) Stage-directions for a transformation scene in *Arrah-na-Pogue*

Stage-directions for text of *Arrah-na-Pogue* (New York: De Witt (1865)), pp. 5–7. By courtesy of the Pettingell Collection

1. Act III sc. iii opens in a prison cell, at the end of which Shaun escapes through a broken window. As the gaslight is lowered, the black flat masking the battlement machinery is brought downwards, revealing the ivy-covered battlements.

2. The lower wall sinks slowly through the stage with Shaun climbing up at the same time that the flat is lowered.

3. As the lower flat falls, it reveals the upper battlements, which in turn sink through the stage floor, Shaun continuing to climb the ivy.

4. The upper wall finally comes to rest, having revealed the upper battlements.

SCENE V. – Court-room in Castle, interior in 5th grooves.

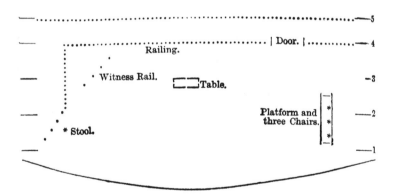

Closed in R. and L. On 4 g. a screen of wainscotting eight feet high. The flat is the Wall. All the side sets and wall of dark oak panelling. Long table, with a drum at L. end, and papers on it, writing materials, chair behind it for CLERK. L. side front, a platform, raised one foot, covered with red cloth, with three large chairs. The railing along R. side is to keep the MOB back. D. in F., side, practicable.

ACT III. – SCENE I. – Interior in 3d grooves.

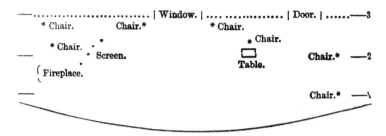

Closed in R. and L. Ample curtains to window. The D. in F. is practicable; back with wall-piece, carpet down.

SCENE II. – Same as Scene 4th, Act 2d.

SCENE III. – Same as Scene 3d, Act II. (Or may be set on 2d groove, the fireplace then being placed tranversely in R. proscenium E., to give more working-room for following changes.

The stage for the last three scenes of Act III.

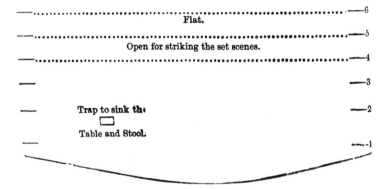

2d groove set, painted a dead black, to form a frame, to mask the working of following change.

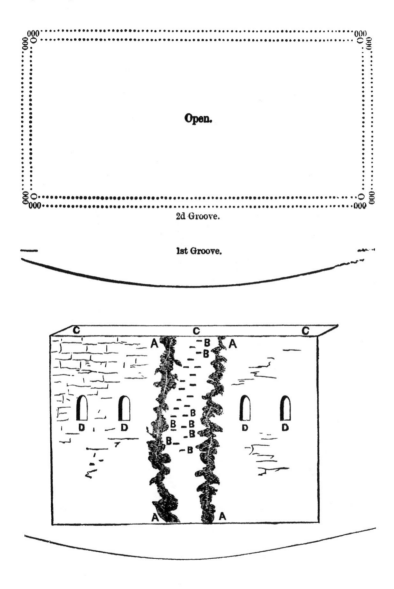

Flat (A), in 3rd grooves to descend. A, A, A, A, outlines of a mass of ivy to cover practicable steps, marked B, B,; SHAUN is discovered halfway up, therefore no steps on lower half of flat; darken the shadows around the steps to hide them. Wall of old gray stone, mossy, etc. The top joins the platform, C. (two feet wide), which laps on the bottom of flat (B) and helps to bring it down in continuous descent. All the face to the audience is in shadow, the light being up at back. D, D, D, D, are arched windows.

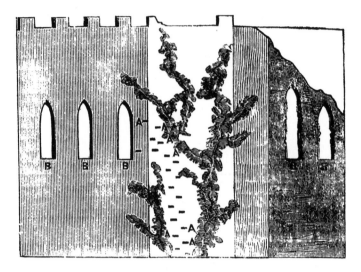

Flat B (inner cut of 3d grooves) to descend. Walls on Flat A, crenellated top edge. A, A, steps as before. B, B, B, B, B, arched windows; the two L. are very ruined, as is all that third of the flat. R. windows practicable. Ivy as before, up the centre, to hide the steps.

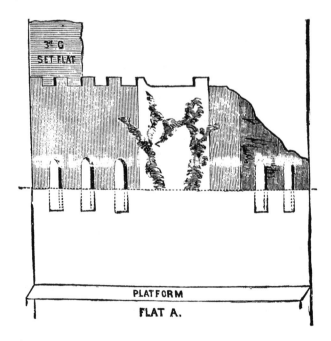

View of Flat B, when it has stopped, half sent down.

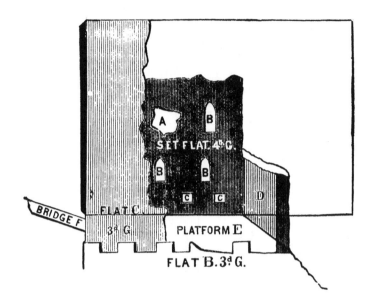

View from the front when Flat B has been sent down, to show the appearance of the set in 3d and 4th grooves, in 3d entrance, R. side and C. L. side is open. The set flat in 4th groove is a wall, ruined top and edges, with gaps (as at A), arched windows (as B, B, B), and small windows (C, C), for cannon, which are on platform E. Platform is practicable for two men's weight, and is reached by bridge (F) from R. 3 E., off. All this set sinks. The up-stage side of 4th groove flat has steps, so that SHAUN is seen climbing along without, past the gap and windows, to exit up R. corner. Flat C on third groove masks the R. end of the set platform, etc. It is a ruined wall.

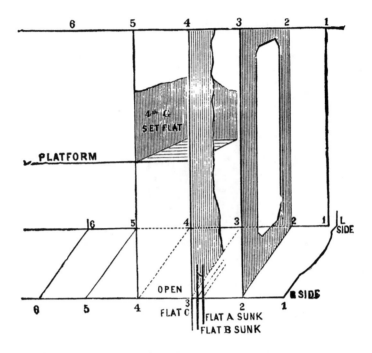

View from R. side, on stage, when Flat B has been sent down.

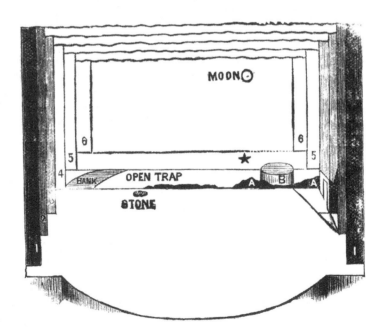

View of the stage from the front when all the changes after Scene III have been made. Landscape on flat is a full moon on a broad lake. R. side a promontory runs out far into the water, with precipitous descent. This connects with the set bank in 4th E., which is practicable. The canvas of the water is brought forward at the base of the flat, to the 5th G., to enable the appearance of space to the water to be more faithfully given. L. side this canvas is transparent, as usual, for the moonbeam glittering-surfaced drum to turn under it and show the reflection through, for the play of the waves (marked *) where the line of light strikes. R. and L. 4th, 5th and 6th borders and sinks, sky; wings on those grooves, sky and water blue. R. side, 1st wing, dark masonry, sink, dark colour; 2d wing stone work, ruined, sink sky; 3d wing, ruined stone work at foot, tree above, sink, sky. L. side, 1st wing, same as R. 1st wing; 2d and 3d, plain; L. 2 E., ruined wall; L. 3 E., a wall with a pract. door. Trap open, R. C., on 4th E. line; the shadow of the cliff is deepened here to hide it; line the front of trap, upper side on 5th groove, with dark blue hangings. A, A. a line of profile ruined wall, tapering from breast-high to stage level. A. loose stone R. C., fallen from it. B, the top of a tower. Limelight for moonlight in L. U. E.

188(c) The staging of East End sensation drama

W. T. Travers, *London by Night*, Act I, sc. iii, Britannia Theatre, 11 May 1868. By courtesy of the Pettingell Collection

Such crude designs (see p. 402 and **188(d)**), sketched into a working prompt-book, illustrate how inseparable stage machinery was from the action in sensation drama. Divided house sets had appeared as early as Edward Fitzball's *Johnathon Bradford* (1833). The trap-door was developed into a central feature of Dibdin Pitt's *Sweeny Todd* (1847).

The stage-directions accompanying this first sketch state 'Interior of Mme Bellefleur's. The scene is divided into two compartments open to the audience. Between these passage to C. leading to door.'

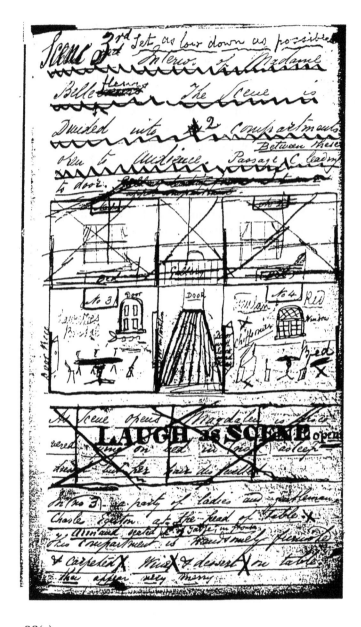

188(c)

188(d) Traps

W. T. Travers, *London by Night*, Act III, sc. i, Britannia Theatre, 11 May 1868. By
courtesy of the Pettingell Collection

Directions accompanying this second sketch (see also **188(c)**) state, 'Trap. Old Tumble
down apartment composed of wooden beams – ''The old house on the Banks of the River'',
[placed in] 3rd. grooves.'

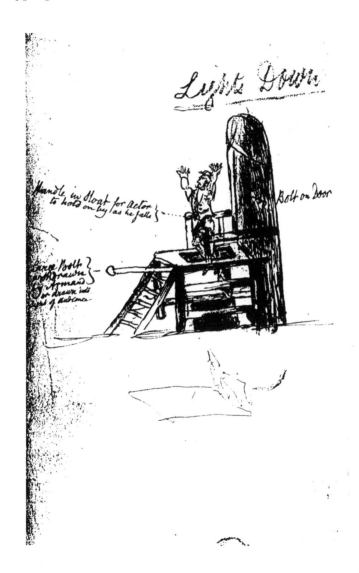

189   The Princess's Theatre pantomime, 1874

From *The Graphic*, 3 January 1874

190   Irving's revival of *The Corsican Brothers*, 1880

From Bram Stoker, *Personal Reminiscences of Henry Irving* (1906), vol. i, pp. 159–61

In September 1880, early in his two decades of management at the Lyceum Theatre, Henry Irving (1838–1905) revived Dion Boucicault's *The Corsican Brothers*, which had been staged by Charles Kean at the Princess's Theatre in 1852. Boucicault's dramatization (via a French dramatization) of Dumas's narrative afforded Irving ample occasion for the extravagant spectacle and carefully executed effects which his productions soon came to typify. Irving himself played the dual role of the Corsican twins, as Charles Fechter and Charles Kean had done before him.

The Corsican Brothers [. . .] requires picturesque setting. [. . .] There are two scenes in it which allow of any amount of artistic effort, although their juxtaposition in the sequence of the play makes an enormous difficulty. The first is the scene of the Masked Ball in the Opera House in Paris; the other the Forest of Fontainebleau. [. . .] Each of these scenes took up the whole stage, right away from the footlights to the back wall; thus the task of changing from one to the other, with only the interval of the supper at Baron de Montgiron's to do it in, was one of extraordinary difficulty. The scene of the Masked Ball represented the interior of the Opera House, the scenic auditorium being furthest from the footlights. In fact it was as though the audience sitting in the Lyceum auditorium saw the scene as though looking in a gigantic mirror placed in the auditorium arch. [. . .] The Opera House was draped with crimson silk, the boxes were practical and contained a whole audience, all being in perspective. The men and women in the boxes near to the footlights were real; those far back were children dressed like their elders. Promenading and dancing were hundreds of persons in striking costumes. [. . .] This great scene came to an end by lowering the 'cut' cloth which formed the background of Montgiron's salon, the door leading into the supper-room being in the centre at back. Whilst the guests were engaged in their more or less rapid banquet, the covered scene was being obliterated and the Forest of Fontainebleau was coming down from the rigging-loft, ascending from the cellar and being pushed on right and left from the wings. Montgiron's salon was concealed by the descent of great tableau curtains. These remained down from thirty-five to forty *seconds* and went up again on a forest as real as anything can be on the stage. Trees stood out separately over a large area so that those entering from side or back could be seen passing behind or amongst them. All over the stage was a deep blanket of snow, white and glistening in the winter sunrise. [. . .] Of many wonderful effects this snow was perhaps the strongest and most impressive of reality. The public could never imagine how it was done. It was *salt*, common coarse salt which was white in the appointed light and glistened like real snow. There were tons of it. A crowd of men stood ready in the wings with little baggage-trucks [. . .] silent with rubber wheels. On them were great wide-mouthed sacks full of salt. When the signal came they rushed in on all sides each to his appointed spot and tumbled out his load, spreading it evenly with great wide-bladed wooden shovels.

One night [. . .] the Prince of Wales came behind the scenes as he was interested in the working of the play. It was known he was coming, and though the stage-hands had been told that they were not supposed to know that he was present they all had their Sunday clothes on. It was the first time His Royal Highness had been 'behind' in Irving's management. [. . .] That night the men worked as never before; they were determined to let the Prince see what [. . .] could be done at the Lyceum. [. . .] That night the tableau curtains remained down only *thirty seconds* – the record time.

191   A double bill at the Lyceum: *The Cup* joins *The Corsican Brothers*

From Percy Fitzgerald, *The World Behind the Scenes* (London: Chatto and Windus, 1881), pp. 43–6 and 50–2. Differently ordered, these paragraphs also appear in Fitzgerald's *Henry Irving: A Record of Twenty Years at the Lyceum* (London: Chapman and Hall, 1893), pp. 151–3 and 159–61

Several months into the run of his production of *The Corsican Brothers*, Irving put Tennyson's one-act *The Cup* into the bill as a curtain-raiser. In this production he, in the role of a wicked Galatian nobleman, played opposite Ellen Terry (1847–1932) in the role of a Roman matron/priestess. Terry, Irving's leading lady throughout his management of the Lyceum, had been touring when the run of *The Corsican Brothers* began.

The performances of *The Cup* and *The Corsican Brothers* [. . .] offer a specimen of that fitting and sumptuous style of revival which is directed, not by outlay of money, but by refined taste and judicious direction. Not less remarkable is the perfect organization, which alone could marshal the work of the night. [. . .] No sooner has the drop-scene fallen [on the penultimate scene of *The Cup*] – and a person always 'stands by' at each side to take care that the huge roller is kept clear of any careless spectator – than a busy scene sets in. Men emerge from every side; the hills and banks, the steps leading down the hill, the massive pedestal that flanks the entrance to the temple on the right and approaches are lifted up and disappear gradually; the distant landscape mounts slowly into the air; the long rows of [gas] jets are unfastened and carried away. In three or four minutes the whole is clear. Then are seen slowly coming down what appear three long, heavy frames or beams – two in the direction of the length, one across the whole breadth of the stage. These are about four feet high, and, touching the ground, form a sort of enclosure open on one side. They form the pediment or upper portion of the temple meant to rest on the pillars. Soon busy hands have joined these three great joists by bolts and fastenings; the signal is given, and it ascends again. Meanwhile others have been bringing out from the 'scene dock' the pillars and their bases, ranging them in the places marked in the ground for them; and as the great beams move slowly up, they hoist with them the columns, attached by ropes which pass through; the place of each pedestal is marked on the floor. In a few moments everything is fitted and falls into its place with a martial exactness. Then is seen slowly descending the other portions of the roof, sky-borders, etc., all falling into their places quietly. [...] We have glimpses in the galleries aloft of men hauling at ropes and pulleys or turning 'drums'; other men below are bearing in the altars and steps with the enormous idol at the back over twenty feet high. [...] The whole 'building' now stands revealed and complete, some twenty feet high. [...]

When the curtain had fallen on *The Cup*, the temple was taken to pieces, reversing the order in which it was put together, – the roof portion ascended into the air; the pillars, pedestals, etc., were all carried away to the store-room on the right, or 'scene dock'; and the stage is once more clear, when the first scene of the Corsican château is set. Here [...] we have the elaborate carved chimney-piece, solid doors with jambs a foot deep, and bolts and locks. [...] All this carving is [...] represented by papier-mâché. At the back is an open gate or arch, through which entrance is made, and through which is a view of the open country. [...] It is curious to note the gaunt and effective trees of the forest, which form the background, cut out in profile and attached to gauze, so that they can be rolled up like a scene. [...]

But it is in the next act that the series of elaborately set scenes succeeding each other entail the most serious difficulties, only to be overcome in one way, viz., by the employment of an enormous number of persons. There is the great Opera House scene, which stretches back the whole length of the stage, followed almost immediately by the supper scene, with its two rooms also stretching back; to be succeeded again by the remarkable forest scene, equally extensive. [...] The rich 'tableau curtain' comes in aid here, but [...] the curtain is only dropped for a few moments, to be raised again at once. Still, by multiplying hands and organization the changes could be made in a few seconds. Few modern scenes are more striking than that of this Opera House lit [...] with its grand chandelier and the smaller clusters running around. [...] Yet nothing can be more simple than the elements of this Opera House scene. From the audience position one would fancy it was an elaborately built and costly structure. It is nothing but two light screens pierced with openings, but most artfully arranged and coloured. At its close down comes the rich curtains, while behind them descends the cloth with the representation of the lobby scene in the Opera House. This is followed by the double rooms of the supper party, a very striking scene. Two handsomely furnished rooms, Aubusson carpets, piano-forte, nearly twenty chairs, sofas, tables, clocks, and a supper-table covered with delicacies, champagne bottles, flowers, etc. Now it has been mentioned that this is succeeded almost instantly by a scene occupying the same space – that of the forest, requiring the minutest treatment, innumerable properties, real trees, etc. Here is what takes place. [. . .] So soon as the 'curtains' are dropped the auxiliaries rush on; away to the right and left fly the portions of the Parisian drawing-room; tables, chairs, piano, sofa vanish in an instant. Men appear carrying tall saplings fixed in stands; one lays down the strip of frozen pond, another the prostrate trunk of a tree – every one from practice knowing the exact place of the particular article he is appointed to carry. Others arrive with bags of sand, which are emptied and strewn on the floor; the circular tree is put in position, the lime-light is ready. The transformation was effected [. . .] in thirty-eight *seconds*, by the stage-manager's watch.

192   Irving's expenses for *The Corsican Brothers*, 1880

From [Moy Thomas] in the *Daily News*, 25 October, 1880, p.2, reprinted in Fitzgerald, *The World Behind the Scenes*, pp. 48–50, and also in William H. Rideing, ed., *Dramatic Notes: An Illustrated Yearbook of the London Stage 1880/1* (London: David Bogue, 1881), pp. 44–5

Aside from the shock value of the figures which it presents as Irving's expenses in mounting *The Corsican Brothers*, Thomas's analysis of the figures is a reminder of the consequences which such expenses carried for dramatic repertoires. The causal connection would be reiterated by many other observers of English theatre in subsequent decades.

The costly nature of theatrical enterprise in these days could not perhaps be better shown than by the instance of the present revival of *The Corsican Brothers* at the Lyceum Theatre. The mere painting of the scenery [. . .] must necessarily constitute a serious item; but perhaps quite as heavy a one [. . .] will be the salaries of the little army of attendants who are nightly required for the rapid and silent setting and changing of scenes. The economical but comparatively rude system of 'wings' and grooves is on this occasion entirely dispensed with [. . .] and scenes are constructed so solidly and with so many details that without minute division of the work, and almost military precision in the movements of the workmen, 'waits' would become intolerably long. For these reasons no fewer than 90 carpenters, 30 gasmen, and 15 property men, in all 135 persons, are permanently engaged in the mere task of arranging and conducting the scenes. It may here be worth mentioning that the handsome 'tableau curtain' made for this occasion, containing a thousand yards of crimson silk velvet, cost £740. Without such special items, but taking into account the frequent rehearsals during the eight weeks that the theatre was closed to the public, the expense of putting this drama on the stage could hardly have been less [...] than £5,000. We may observe that the usual custom of our stage is to pay salaries of all employees during the period of rehearsal. The performers, however, are usually expected to devote themselves gratuitously to this necessary preparation – at least to the extent of a fortnight's attendance. The long 'runs' which so many good friends of the stage deplore as prejudicial to dramatic art are really a necessary concomitant of the elaborate scenic illustration which the public taste now seems imperatively to demand in theatres of the higher class; for it is of course only by the sustained popularity of a performance that a manager can possibly be reimbursed for such an enormous outlay. We are betraying, we hope, no secret when we say that the total working expenses of the Lyceum Theatre at this time reach the large amount of £140 a night. The receipts, we believe, have not fallen far short of £230 at any night or day performance of *The Corsican Brothers*, but it will be perceived from all this that our modern system renders the management even of one of the most prosperous of theatres an undertaking requiring no small amount of courage and confidence in the future.

VIII Repertoires

193 The Independent Theatre's 'private' production of Ibsen's *Ghosts*, 1891

Playbill in the Theatre Museum. Also reproduced in 'Michael Orme' [Mrs. J. T. Grein], *J. T. Grein: The Story of a Pioneer* (London: John Murray, 1936), p. 76

The first of the English play-producing societies was the Independent Theatre, and its initial production was Ibsen's *Ghosts*. As the play had already been performed at the Théâtre Libre in Paris and at the Freie Bühne in Berlin, its selection was a declaration of radical allegiances. The play not having been submitted to the Lord Chamberlain's office for a licence for performance, it was also a challenge to the pre-censorship. Lord Lathom, however, did not pick up the gauntlet but rather chose to acquiesce in the fiction that the performance was a private one. No subsequent production of the London Independent Theatre in its seven years of activity would match the sensation of the single performance of its inaugural one, nor did it ever again find it necessary to dodge the pre-censorship. And, as the Examiner for Plays would remark with some satisfaction less than a year after the production of *Ghosts* (see 173), 'ORIGINAL Plays by English Writers of Distinction' proved hard to find. Continental translations dominated the productions of the Independent Theatre, especially in its early years, although these did bring both G. B. Shaw's *Widower's Houses* in 1892 and George Moore's *The Strike at Arlingford* in 1893, plus a revival of Webster's *The Duchess of Malfi*, directed by William Poel, in 1892.

THE INDEPENDENT THEATRE OF LONDON,

(THÉÂTRE LIBRE)

Founder and Sole Manager . - - *J. T. GREIN.*

The object of the Independent Theatre is to give special performances of plays which have a

LITERARY AND ARTISTIC,

rather than a commercial value.

THE INDEPENDENT THEATRE

Will open on FRIDAY, March 13th, 1891, *when a* <u>PRIVATE</u> *Invitation Performance of*

''GHOSTS,''

By HENRIK IBSEN,

(Translated by WILLIAM ARCHER), will be given at the

ROYALTY THEATRE,

The Repertoire will consist of several ORIGINAL Plays by English Writers of Distinction, AND THE FOLLOWING TRANSLATIONS:

" DON JUAN," from the French by MOLIÈRE.   " EMILIA GALOTTI," from the German by LESSING.

" THE DOMINION OF DARKNESS," from the Russian by TOLSTOI.

" THE WILD DUCK," from the Norwegian by H. IBSEN.   " THE FATHER," from the Swedish by A. STRINDBERG.

" THE GAUNTLET," from the Norwegian by BJORNSTJERNE-BJORNSON.

" SOEUR PHILOMENE," from the French by DE GONCOURT, (Dramatised by ARTHUR BYL & JULES VIDAL).

" LE BAISER," from the French by TH. DE BANVILLE.

" HONOUR," from the Dutch by W. G. VAN NOUHUYS.   " NAPOLEON," from the German by K. BLEIBTREU.

MEMBERSHIP:

TERMS OF MEMBERSHIP (including admission to Stall and Dress Circle at the five <u>following</u> performances) of the Independent Theatre Society, £2 10s.

The Independent Theatre will be maintained by Membership, and by VOLUNTARY CONTRIBUTIONS *which will be gladly received by,* Mr. J. T. GREIN, 84, Warwick Street, Belgrave Road, S.W.

None but *Members* or invited *Guests* can be admitted to the performances of the Independent Theatre.

The five performances will take place in the following order :

March 13th,   April 24th.   May 29th,   June 26th,   September 11th, 1891.

Alterations will be duly notified to all Members and Donors.

[P.T.O.

194   Women as victims, 1893

From W. A. L. Bettany in *The Theatre*, n.s. 4, 22 (1 July 1893), p. 16

The dramatic trivialization of women was not confined to theatres which specialized in musical comedies. A playful paragraph about roles which Cyril Maude (1861–1951) and Winifred Emery (1862–1924) played together in 1890 and 1891 is a reminder of the extent to which, in the classic dramatic tradition and in the new society drama alike, women were defined solely in relation to men. Even leading ladies were effectively limited to roles which presented women not only as sexual objects but usually also as victims.

It is a strange fate that compels Mr Maude so often to play the part of evil genius to his wife. He abducted her in *Joseph's Sweetheart*,[1] he was a miserly old man who wanted to marry her in *Clarissa*,[2] he tried to defame her character in *The Crusaders*,[3] he endeavoured to murder her husband in *Handfast*,[4] and he was her false lover in *School for Scandal*.[5]

[1] *Joseph's Sweetheart* was Robert Buchanan's five-act dramatization of Fielding's *Joseph Andrews*. Maude created the role of Lord Fellamar when the play was first performed, at the Vaudeville Theatre on 8 March 1888; and in December Emery succeeded Kate Rorke in the role of Joseph Andrews' sweetheart, Fanny Goodwill.

[2] *Clarissa*, Buchanan's dramatization of Samuel Richardson's novel, opened at the Vaudeville Theatre on 6 February 1890. Maude played Solmes, the parental choice for the unwilling hand of Clarissa, played by Emery.

[3] In Henry Arthur Jones's *The Crusaders*, which opened at the Avenue on 2 November 1891, Emery created the role of Cynthia Greenslade, a young and pretty widow; and in January 1892 Maude took over the role of Palsom, Vice-President of the London Reformation League.

[4] *Handfast*, by Henry Hamilton and Mark Quinton, was first staged at the Prince of Wales's Theatre on 13 December 1887. The review in the *The Era* (17 December 1887, p. 14) praised Maude for his 'strikingly clever impersonation of the weak but vicious Austin Woodville', a role which he repeated in the revival at the Shaftesbury Theatre on 16 May 1891, when Emery played the heroine Beatrice Culver, AKA Mrs Mervyn Woodville, Mrs Jocelyn Woodville, *and* Mme de Ligniac.

[5] Sheridan's *The School for Scandal* was 'revived provisionally pending the production of the new play [*Clarissa*, see note 2 above] by Robert Buchanan' at the Vaudeville Theatre on 11 January 1890. Maude played Joseph Surface to Emery's Lady Teazle.

195   The West End considers the woman question, 1894

From *The Era*, 8 December 1894, p. 10

During the first half of the 1890s, the shock waves initiated by the first English productions of Ibsen's plays were registered in the West End mainly by an extreme preponderance of productions of plays centring on women. Late in 1894, a gossip column in the theatrical trade press took note of the feminized fare on offer in the West End that week.

The girls certainly have it all their own way on the modern stage. With *The Gaiety Girl* not at the Gaiety because *The Shop Girl* is there, and *The Wrong Girl* at the Strand,[1] where one hopes she may prove the right girl, one would think that they might be satisfied; but the Comedy and the Avenue insist on being up to date with

The New Woman and *The Lady Slavey*.[2] *The Case of Rebellious Susan*[3] also proclaims itself . . . 'a case of *cherchez la femme*', and *Mirette*[4] was evidently 'written round' a pretty girl. What is one *New Boy*[5] among this galaxy of femininity?

[1] Opening at the Prince of Wales's Theatre on 14 October 1893, the musical comedy *A Gaiety Girl* had a run of just under eleven months there and a further two months at Daly's, totalling 393 performances. Now touring, it would be revived at Daly's in 1899. *The Shop Girl*, another musical comedy, had but recently (24 November 1894) opened at the Gaiety, where it would run for 547 performances. But *The Wrong Girl* flopped at the Strand, where it had opened on 21 November 1894 and would survive only 33 performances. (For these productions and all others cited in this document, dates and performance figures are taken from J. P. Wearing, *The London Stage 1890–1900*, vol. 1 (Metuchen, N. J., and London: Scarecrow Press, 1976).)

[2] Sydney Grundy's *The New Woman* had a respectable run of 173 performances at the Comedy, where it opened on 1 September 1894. *The Lady Slavey*, a musical comedy, did less well at the Avenue, opening on 20 October 1894 and running for 94 performances.

[3] Henry Arthur Jones's comedy, *The Case of Rebellious Susan*, starring Charles Wyndham and Mary Moore, opened at Wyndham's Criterion Theatre on 3 October 1894 and ran for 164 performances.

[4] *Mirette* opened at D'Oyly Carte's Savoy Theatre on 3 July 1894 and, having just exceeded 100 performances, closed there two days before the publication of this document.

[5] Arthur Law's *The New Boy* played for two months at Terry's from 21 February 1894 before transferring to the Vaudeville, where it had a long run.

Italy, 1868–1919

Edited and translated by LAURA RICHARDS

I The condition of the Italian theatre in the late nineteenth century

For complex social and political reasons, the Italian theatre in the second half of the nineteenth century presents rather different characteristics to those of most other European theatres at this time. Italy became a unified state only in 1861, and Rome became its capital only in 1870. Fusing the economic, cultural and administrative structures of the seven pre-unification states presented the new national politicians with major problems, and these problems were accentuated by the poverty of the new state, the backwardness of many regions and the high percentage of illiteracy in the population as a whole. As the most social of the arts, theatre was particularly affected by these conditions. The organization of both drama and theatre in the period was dominated by attempts to give some sort of national unity to an art-form that had traditionally been regional in a peninsula where half a dozen cities aspired to the title of cultural capital.

Fragmentation and itinerancy were the theatre's most salient features, for companies had to travel widely and frequently from city to city, often carrying sets, props and wardrobe with them. The economics of the profession were precarious, no government subsidy was available, private patronage was limited, and the support of the predominantly conservative audience was unreliable (see 197). Dramatic writing did not escape the general financial exigencies governing the profession: few native dramatists were able to earn a living by their writing, and many had recourse to translation and adaptation of French boulevard drama in order to survive. The influence of Goldoni on comedy was ubiquitous. Dialect drama remained vigorous in the regions although it, too, reflected the influence of contemporary boulevard theatre. The one area of dramatic writing that obtained central-government support was that which could be construed as contributing to the development of a national drama, written in Italian rather than in dialect, and treating of issues relevant to Italian history, customs and culture. Government competitions and prizes were launched to ferret out such drama, but in so far as these succeeded at all they produced mainly a literary output that rarely achieved successful performance in the theatres. Theatre buildings and their technical facilities reflected the generally low condition of the profession (see 200). Only by the last decade of the century did this condition begin to change for the better.

196   A view of the Italian theatre in the 1880s

Yorick,[1] *Teatro e governo* (Florence, 1888), pp. 12–16

In the past thirty years, which have been so restless and embattled,[2] the Italian theatre, considering the conditions from which it emerged, does not seem to justify the complaints and lamentations of the pessimists.[3]

The list of actors who have achieved fame includes the names of Ristori, Salvini, Ernesto and Cesare Rossi, Domeniconi, Dondini, [...] Morelli, Bellotti Bon, Emanuel, Pezzana, Cazzola, Tessero, ... and a whole troop of minor players who are nonetheless not unworthy of praise.[4] The Italian school, thanks to the work and ability of its most illustrious members, has triumphed in Paris, London, Madrid, Barcelona, Brussels, St Petersburg and even in the two Americas.

The list of the dramatists who have been applauded, admired and praised by audiences and critics over the last thirty years runs to more than a hundred names – not just a sufficiency but an excess – and at least provides evidence of the activity and vitality of our theatre. Some will have lasting status, like Giacometti, Gherardi Del Testa and Paolo Ferrari; others will remain for long in the memory and affections of the public, like Marenco, Giacosa, Torelli, Suñer, Cossa, Bersezio, Castelvecchio and Napoleone Giotti.[5] [...]

Today, and in the face of the evidence it would be pointless to deny it, actors and authors live in a different climate, and address their efforts to a different outcome. Notwithstanding that complaints are still heard, and are perhaps more vociferous than ever, one hundred and twenty-seven acting companies, the list of which can be read month by month in the Milanese journal *L'Arte Drammatica* [...] do manage to tour Italy and keep open about four hundred theatres for prose drama, not always with great success it is true, but unquestionably in conditions no worse than in the past.[6]

A new law [...] has ensured that as far as possible dramatists receive proper remuneration for their labours.[7] Some of these dramatists [...] in the course of a few years have been able to earn from a five-act play, or even a one-act piece, an income not less than 25,000 lire.[8] [...]

The earnings of an actor or actress particularly favoured by audience approval have risen recently in Italy to reach 40,000 lire a year for a *prima attrice* and 25,000 lire for a *primo attore*, sums at which any of the most celebrated and famous artists of the last century and the first half of this would have raised their eyebrows in astonishment. Of course these are exceptional cases,[9] but as we go down the ladder it cannot be denied that generally salaries have increased in proportion, nor likewise can we deny that there has been an enormous increase in expenditure on staging and the proper setting out of plays. Thus among the one hundred and twenty-seven companies mentioned above a few (two or three perhaps) cost the actor-manager a sum not less than 400 lire a day in salaries, travelling expenses, overheads for the use of theatres, taxes and other charges. Others cost no more than 300 lire, and progressively less as we go further down the ladder. Overall, however, for upkeep, travelling, and the use of the theatres, the Italian audience must be paying no less than 800,000 lire a month. An art which manages to draw 10 million lire a year from the pockets of private citizens does not seem to me to warrant that much commiseration.

[...] Many actors among us today are accustomed to a certain refinement and elegance in their way of living: many are able to educate their children outside the theatre in the country's best colleges, preparing them for the liberal professions or for military careers. Nowadays our actors are well received in society, are courted and deservedly valued, and, thanks to the benevolent admiration of some politician, have honours bestowed on them. They have little in common with those irregular bands of proverbial *commedianti* described and celebrated in the verse and prose of the past.

All this leads me to conclude that despite the iniquity of the public[10] and the indifference of governments,[11] so much bewailed and condemned in all possible tones, the Italian theatre has come a very long way in just a few years and, at least as far as material considerations go, the lamentations about decline and ruin are altogether premature and exaggerated.

[1] Yorick was the pseudonym of Pier Coccoluto Ferrigni (1836–95), theatre critic for the journal *La Nazione* in Florence from 1868. A somewhat conservative critic, Ferrigni was a great admirer of the dramatist Paolo Ferrari (the Italian Dumas *fils*) and quite failed to appreciate the originality of an actress like Duse.

[2] Italian unification in 1861 had not meant the end of wars and unrest in the peninsula. Apart from the wars for independence and unification (1859–60), Ferrigni is referring here to the government's repressive action against brigandage in southern Italy in the two years following unification, to its actions against Garibaldi's attempt to conquer Rome (1862 and 1867), and to the 1866 war against Austria which Italy fought on the side of Prussia. He alludes also to the conquest of Rome in 1870, to the separation of the Catholic Church from the Italian state which followed the war, and to the frequent demonstrations and activities in connection with the position of Trieste, which remained an Austrian possession until the end of the First World War.

[3] One of the most vociferous was the writer, dramatist and politician Ferdinando Martini, who in a controversial article, 'La fisima del teatro nazionale' (The Obsession with the National Theatre), published in 1888 (see Martini, *Al teatro* (Florence 1895), pp. 140–72), had denied the existence of an Italian national theatre, and criticized as pointless state attempts at cultural intervention (e.g. competitions and subsidies) to promote an art for which as yet natural talent was lacking.

[4] For Ristori, Salvini and Ernesto Rossi, see **204**, **205**, **206(a)** and **206(b)**; for Cesare Rossi, see **215**, note 3; for Domeniconi, see **199**, note 4; Cesare Dondini (1807–75) was a celebrated *brillante* (comic actor) and character actor, and was for several years manager of his own company; for Morelli, see **199**, note 7; for Bellotti Bon, see **199**, note 5; for Emanuel, see **214(a)**, note 3; Clementina Cazzola (1832–68) was at nineteen *primattrice* in Dondini's company, where she first acted alongside Tommaso Salvini with whom she later lived. She was considered the best Italian actress of mid-century after Ristori; for Pezzana, see **199**, note 9; for Tessero, see **199**, note 8.

[5] The work of few of these dramatists is remembered or performed in the Italian theatre today. Paolo Giacometti's best play, *La morte civile* (Civil Death, 1861) was made famous by Tommaso Salvini's celebrated interpretation of its protagonist, Corrado (see **206(a)** and **206(b)**). Giuseppe Giacosa (1847–1906) wrote what are arguably the two best plays of Italian *verismo*, *Tristi amori* (Sad Loves, 1887) and *Come le foglie* (Like the Leaves, 1900). Paolo Ferrari (1822–89) was highly popular in the 1870s for his thesis dramas *à la* Dumas. Achille Torelli (1841–1922) is remembered for the play

I mariti (The Married, 1867), and Vittorio Bersezio (1828–1900) wrote plays on social themes, the best of which is *Le miserie d' monssu Travet* (The Miseries of M. Travet, 1863), written in the Piedmontese dialect and one of the masterpieces of Italian dialect theatre. Pietro Cossa (1830–81) wrote several verse dramas of which the best known was *Nerone* (Nero, 1872), later set to music by Mascagni.

6 It was calculated in 1871 that there were 957 theatres in Italy, divided among 711 *comuni* (municipalities). These were classified into theatres of I, II and III *ordine* (categories) (see G. Azzaroni, *Del teatro e dintorni* (Rome, 1981), pp. 286–307).

7 The first Italian copyright law was passed in 1865, followed by a second in 1875. The provisions of both were absorbed within a third law (*testo unico*) in 1882, which lasted until 1926 (see Azzaroni, *Del teatro e dintorni*, pp. 45–57).

8 But this applied to very few dramatists indeed. The majority of writers still encountered a lot of hostility from actor-managers reluctant to pay the percentage determined by the copyright law, especially when touring abroad, the managers objecting that audiences went to see the actors and not the plays.

9 These were very few exceptions indeed. In 1888 the average annual salary of a lead actor was about 10,000 lire. For an actor's point of view on the level of salaries paid, and the professional expenses these had to cover, see L. Bellotti Bon, *Condizioni dell'arte drammatica italiana* (Florence, 1875), cited in V. Pandolfi, *L'antologia del grande attore* (Bari, 1954), pp. 105–6. Current values are hard to calculate, but, very approximately, 25,000 lire in 1890 would have been the equivalent in 1991 to £54,650 (source ISTAT).

10 For an actor's opinion of the attitudes of Italian audiences, see T. Salvini, *Ricordi, aneddoti e impressioni* (Milan, 1895), pp. 184–7.

11 The post-unification Italian governments, apart from promoting competitions and opening one or two acting schools, offered theatre no kind of subsidy whatsoever. Only in 1921, on the eve of the Fascist takeover, did the government award a *premio* (prize) of 120,000 lire to Virgilio Talli's Drammatica Compagnia di Roma del Teatro Argentina (see Azzaroni, *Del teatro e dintorni*, pp. 23–45).

197   A French critic's impressions of the Italian theatre, 1900

Henri Lyonnet,[1] *Le Théâtre en Italie* (Paris, 1900), pp. 3–6

In Spain a new play is born in Madrid; in Portugal, in Lisbon; this is almost invariably the rule. In Italy, however, a new work may appear in Milan, in Rome, in Turin, in Florence, or in Venice. An Italian company, no matter how good, never has a permanent home, but tours from month to month visiting all the main cities one after the other. [...]

All Italian theatre artists without exception have to adapt to this 'wandering-jew' kind of existence – even La Duse, Novelli, Zacconi, Tina di Lorenzo, etc.[2] [...]

Each distinguished artist in Italy manages a company which takes his name.[3] [...]

We do not find in Italy, as far as the theatre or anything else is concerned, a capital around which everything is centred, and the old political divisions of the country have left deep marks.[4] In our view there is a great disadvantage in this, for both authors and dramatic works, to say nothing of stage-design which, given the constant travelling, is reduced to the minimum.

A company which is frequently on the move can easily enough carry its costumes along with it. But when in the course of a month it is a matter of changing a show every night, taking along very cumbersome décor is no minor problem. Hence a sparseness of design equalled nowhere else. What else is one to do in a country where theatre is done so much on the cheap and where a respectable company will spend on design and costumes a mere 15,000 francs? I shall not speak of the less important companies which start their tours with just a few thousand francs' worth of costumes and décor.

The theatrical season begins at the start of Lent, and each company knows about a year in advance where it is going, for it is necessary to arrange beforehand with the theatre proprietors bookings for the best theatres.[5] An impresario who opens at the Constanzi theatre in Rome, for Lent, will be in Venice in the spring, in Genoa in the summer, and in Turin in the autumn, and he may still go on to visit Leghorn, Naples or Florence.[6] Thus one should not be surprised to find that a consequence of this communal wandering life is that most of the company players intermarry.[7] It is not unusual to see, as in the dénouement of a Scribean comedy, that the *jeune premier* has married the *soubrette*, or the businessman prosaically wed the *ingénue*, from the recurrence of the same names on the theatre posters.

[1] Henri Lyonnet (1852–1933), a French journalist and theatre historian, wrote several studies of the French and other European theatres. His *Le Théâtre en Italie* is a valuable source of information on Italian performers and stages at the turn of the century.

[2] These were among the major players of the age and are referred to in more detail throughout this section.

[3] Lyonnet mentions 222 theatrical enterprises in all (pp. 313–14). The companies were for the most part of two kinds: '*di complesso*' (ensemble) and '*a mattatore*' (star-dominated). The first preserved the traditional structure based on '*ruoli*' (a term dating back to the *commedia dell'arte*, and signifying those parts for which an actor or actress was thought particularly suited by physical, vocal and personality attributes) and for the most part offered a mediocre repertory of vaudeville and *pochades* (short light comedies, of farcical emphasis, invariably marked by intrigue and elements of the bawdy, and invariably performed with small casts). The second relied upon the prestige and popularity of the lead player and had the characteristics and defects of the actor-manager 'star' system: texts selected to highlight the 'star's performance, and arbitrarily cut and altered to ensure that all other roles were subordinated to that of the lead; makeshift rehearsals which often the 'star' did not bother to attend, and so on.

[4] No very useful distinction could then be made between the capital, Rome, and the major provincial cities, like Milan, Turin, Naples and Florence, as far as cultural activity in particular was concerned. To some extent this remains the case today, the main *teatro stabile*, for example, being in Milan, not Rome, as too is the most important Italian opera house, La Scala.

[5] Until 1928 the theatrical year ran from the first day of Lent to the last day of Carnival (i.e. Shrove Tuesday, the day before Ash Wednesday) the following year. The theatrical season at this time usually began on 26 December and closed on Ash Wednesday. But there were also unofficial short seasons in the course of the year. From 1928 the *anno teatrale* ran from 1 September until 31 August of the following year, but usually companies were formed for a maximum period of 6 to 8 months.

[6] An impresario was often an actor-manager whose personal money underpinned the economy of the company (see, for example, the remarks of Salvini, *Ricordi*, pp. 175–83).

[7] Until the twentieth century most Italian players were born into the profession, hence the familiar phrase '*figli d'arte*', 'children of the profession'.

198   A scene from R. Simoni's *La vedova*, 1903

Biblioteca Teatrale Burcado, Rome. Photo: Oscar Savio

The extent to which Italian theatre companies continued into the twentieth century to be family concerns is well illustrated in this scene from R. Simoni's *La vedova* (The Widow), produced in 1903. The players here, from left to right, are Amelia Dondini Benini, Ferruccio Benini and Italia Benini Sambo.

199   Tommaso Salvini on the profession, 1885

A letter by Salvini[1] cited in Celso Salvini, *Tommaso Salvini nella storia del teatro italiano e nella vita del suo tempo* (Rocca San Casciano, 1955), pp. 334–5

Notwithstanding his own success, Salvini, the greatest Italian actor of the age, here expresses to a journalist friend reservations about the wisdom of pursuing a career in the Italian theatre.

My dear Checchi,[2]

Although I am extremely grateful to you for the news you give me about the success of my son Gustavo,[3] I should have much preferred to be told that he had brought off a trade or bank deal for three or four million at the appropriate commission of one or two per cent.

This should not surprise you: like all who know me, you must be aware of the growing antipathy I have for my son's single-minded pursuit of a career in the theatre.

I was left an orphan and without means at fifteen and was obliged to carry on in my present profession in order to survive. I had then been in it only a short time, and had of necessity to commit myself to it out of self-respect rather than inclination. Later the encouragement I received from audiences and the great success I enjoyed endeared it to me, and it would be ungrateful of me to complain about it. However, if I consider the present state of the art, how could I, or can I, approve my son's wish to dedicate his life to it?

His transient triumphs of today do not deceive me; I think of the future. The example of so many illustrious artists who at the end of their careers found themselves, or now find themselves, in dismal circumstances proves my point. Domeniconi was obliged to call on the charity of his artistic colleagues to avoid dying in a hospital.[4] Bellotti Bon,[5] after a splendid artistic career in the theatre of forty years, during which his achievements both as actor and actor-manager were outstanding, committed suicide. Majeroni[6] is still forced to choose between lunch or a meagre dinner.

Morelli,[7] Tessero,[8] and Pezzana[9] certainly do not offer splendid examples of prosperity, and the countless numbers whom I do not know personally, but who turn to me and to others for aid, or seek benefit performances, speak for themselves. What more can I say? 'Very well,' I hear you reply, 'but what about yourself? What about Ristori? And Rossi?'[10]

My response is that in the first place exceptions just prove the rule. Further, if Ristori, Rossi and I had been able to count only on our Italian earnings we would have been very hard up indeed.

'Why then,' you will say, 'could others not go abroad too in search of fame and fortune?' My dear friend, this is now becoming, if not actually impossible, certainly very difficult. Abroad they are understandably beginning to advance their own national artistic achievements. Those who hope to succeed abroad are on a losing game. Pezzana and Tessero did rather poorly in South America, yet you will not deny that they are both excellent actresses.[11] [...] And if you don't know it already, let me explain to you the position of an artist who undertakes to lead a dramatic company in a permanent theatre: he has to pay personal tax, business tax, tax on nightly receipts, theatre opening tax, tax on bills and posters, and has the responsibility for settling the taxes of each player in the company. There is more than enough in this to make one ill. And the public? They are not prepared to pay more than one lira, yet are demanding, critical audiences, all too willing to condemn authors and actors.

[1] For Tommaso Salvini, see **206(a)**.

[2] Eugenio Checchi was a journalist and critic. He wrote under the pseudonym 'Tom' for *Il Giornale
d'Italia*, and at the time of this letter was editor of *Fanfulla della Domenica*, a weekly journal, where
Salvini's letter appeared in the summer of 1885.

[3] Gustavo Salvini (1859–1930) was the son of Tommaso Salvini and the actress Clementina Cazzola.
Despite his father's hostility, Gustavo became an actor and eventually formed his own company,
which enjoyed artistic if not overmuch financial success.

[4] Luigi Domeniconi (1786–1867) was a prominent actor-manager in the middle decades of the
nineteenth century. His first company included in 1847 Ristori (see **204(a)**, note 1) and Tommaso
Salvini. He was obliged to retire from the stage in 1863, after suffering a succession of strokes, and,
as Salvini remarks, it is a measure of the hardship endured by many of even the most distinguished
in the profession that he spent the remainder of his life in poverty. Salvini helped to raise a collection
for him among his acting colleagues.

[5] Luigi Bellotti Bon (1820–83) was a major actor-manager of the period. In 1873 his over-ambitious
formation of three separate companies led him into financial difficulties. He went further and
further into debt, and shot himself to escape his creditors. For similar sentiments see Bellotti Bon
(1875) in Pandolfi, *L'antologia del grande attore*, pp. 105–11.

[6] Achille Majeroni (1824–88) was a leading actor-manager whose own playing is described by Luigi
Rasi as 'good without being outstanding' (see Rasi, *I comici italiani* (Florence, 1897–1905)).

[7] Alamanno Morelli (1812–93) trained under the great early nineteenth-century Italian actor,
Gustavo Modena, and was one of the first Italian actors to play Hamlet (in 1850). In 1840 he had
acted Macbeth. Like Bellotti Bon, and others, he sought to improve the conditions of the Italian
stage particularly after 1860, when he managed his own company and encouraged contemporary
Italian dramatic writing.

[8] Adelaide Tessero (1842–92), niece of Ristori (see **204(a)**, note 1), acted with Bellotti Bon and
Morelli, before forming her own company in 1881.

[9] Giacinta Pezzana (1841–1919), one of the leading Italian actresses of the late nineteenth century,
performed with Cesare and Ernesto Rossi (see **205**, note 1) among others. A particularly celebrated
role was her performance of the mother in *Thérèse Raquin* (with the young Duse in the title-role), in
Naples in 1879.

[10] For Ristori, see **204(a)**, note 1, and for Rossi, see **205**, note 1.

[11] In 1886, on her return from a tour of South America, Eleonora Duse complained that she had not
covered her expenses (see W. Weaver, *Duse, A Biography* (London, 1984), p. 58).

200   Italian theatre technology at the end of the nineteenth century

Cronache teatrali di Giovanni Pozza, 1886–1913, ed. G. A. Cibotto (Vicenza, 1971), pp.
201–6

Giovanni Pozza was one of the first professional theatre critics to be employed by a
newspaper in Italy. He wrote for the *Corriere della sera* in Milan between 1887 and 1914.
This article was written about an exhibition mounted at the Teatro La Scala as part of 'Le
Esposizioni Riunite di Milano' (The United Exhibitions of Milan) in 1894 (see *Illustrazione
italiana*, May 1894).

Our theatre technology has made very little progress indeed over the last fifty
years. We still use backdrops, wings, traverses, hand-pulleys and practicables
laboriously put together on trestles. Our old stages, built as they are without side
exits, without sufficient width and depth below stage, with their enormous

prosceniums, have not allowed our theatrical technique to do better. To modify any of our stages one would need to build it again from scratch – and who can contemplate that in the present circumstances?[1]

Stage-design too is fully justified in complaining of the awkward way in which our stages are built. There was a time when this art was the glory of Italy.[2] As long as the perspective effects of a single painted canvas sufficed to create illusion for the spectator our stage-designers were unequalled. But today a single cloth is insufficient. One needs several spaced cloths, one in front of the other, composite sky-pieces (not skies made up of transversal strips), rippling waves, rising and setting moons, trees and columns detached from the background, unbroken side walls, concealed wings, light distributed and graduated according to the hour and the place – these are all things which require a space that usually is not available, an arrangement of capstans and pulleys that invariably is not possible, a lighting apparatus that often simply does not exist, or if it does, cannot be utilized, and finally a degree of research and labour which theatre managements, municipalities, and organizations by common accord have no wish to recompense according to their worth.

I hesitate to specify the cost of a complete scene at La Scala as I do not recall the exact figure. What I do recall very well is that the sum is derisory. La Scala would not have stage-designers if it did not give them access throughout the year to its huge design rooms – that is if it did not provide them with the opportunity to earn extra money working for foreign theatres during the summer. What can one expect of these artists when they are scarcely paid the cost of their paints and brushes? Ferrario,[3] a hard-working and productive designer, accomplished in imagination and execution, gave La Scala a wealth of ill-recompensed labour. But having exhausted in its service his great fund of fantasy and ingenuity, disgusted and dejected, he left the theatre to launch a school of stage-design. Zuccarelli, who succeeded him, and was a worthy successor, is perhaps already tempted to follow his example.

It is crucial that this system be changed, and that Italian stage-designers be given the means to live and work. It is a difficult and indispensable art which calls for great knowledge and constant observation of reality, an art exposed to the direct criticism of the audience and as noble as any other of the theatrical arts. If, as is said, it will not be possible to pay in a more honest and decent way until scenery is preserved (and today it is washed out as soon as the performances of the production are finished) there is only one thing to do: save the scenery.

This small and inexpensive reform would not be to the advantage of the stage-designers only. Such a reform would make it much easier and quicker to restage the production and, further, fine designs and paintings would not be pointlessly destroyed, paintings like those we have so admired, and whose loss we have regretted, as we have looked at the collections of sketches exhibited by Ferrario and Zuccarelli.

Of our theatrical techniques the most advanced and developed is that of prop-making and costume. Thanks to fine artists, and encouraged by the insatiable demands of the audience, it has truly reached a high level of industry and perfection. In only a few years it has become capable of withstanding foreign comparison and competition.

This craft triumphs in the large Pompeian gallery.[4] One can say that the success of the theatre exhibition is due entirely to it. It has brought to the exhibition a glittering richness of materials, trimmings, feathers, armoury and jewellery; and with the ingenious device of the 'collective exhibitions' has transformed the display of its products into a spectacle which is particularly exciting the curiosity and admiration of visitors. In three side-branches of the gallery, where the lights have been taken out, it has built fifteen stages lit by their own footlights, placing on these stages life-size figures representing characters from different works.

The rear of each stage is filled with painted scenery; furniture and props are disposed around the characters, so that looking at them one has the illusion of watching a performance. Here we find the suicide scene in *La Gioconda*; further on, a scene from *Semiramide*; then one of *Cristoforo Colombo*; one of *Manon Lescaut*, others of *Otello, Falstaff, Amico Fritz*; and further on a Goldonian scene from *Il Cavaliere di Spirito*. [...]

In these plastic pictures, particularly remarkable is the artistic and historical aspect of the costumes. In costume-design we move from the pictorial fantasy of Edel[5] to the more severe and more scrupulous truth of Hohenstein. Thus we have followed the general trend of the time, which is so eager for exactitude as to have imposed on art that scientific method of analysis and reconstruction that is called *verismo*. For its own part, theatrical prop-making has not only banished from its workshops papier-mâché, but by using metal to make metal objects, is increasingly trying to reproduce exactly the forms characteristic of different times so that scenic spectacle in a modern theatre can be regarded as true historical reconstruction.

The influence of foreign theatres – particularly German – and the artistic taste of our foremost music publisher, Ricordi,[6] have contributed much to the development and refinement of *mise en scène* in Italy as elsewhere. It is not so long ago, and to the advantage of impresarios, that a gilt throne and a fifty-strong chorus dressed as Roman soldiers sufficed to stage all the Latin, Greek and Babylonian melodramas of Metastasio.

The exhibition of costumes presented by the publishers Ricordi and Sonzogno is extraordinarily rich and interesting. Almost all the designs bear the signatures of Edel and Hohenstein – the artists who gave us in succession the most lavish *mises en scène* that our theatres can boast in the last fifteen years – and they show very clearly their very distinct talents. While in the first the feeling for colour and materials is most prominent, to the extent that no one has bettered his ability to invest choreography with fantastic shapes and colours, in the second we find signs of deeper study, a more delicate selection, and a closer relationship between costume and character.

Looking at these costume-designs one has an impression not only of how much has been done already to give proper artistic authority to our theatrical productions, but also how much remains to be achieved.

We have managed to find the costumes, but have not yet found those who can wear and carry them. As a crowd, our extras and chorus still give the impression of being in mere masquerade, and the more the designers and costumiers cover them in silk and velvet, the worse it is. Such is the inelegance and carelessness in the dressing of our crowds that one could almost think them proud of it. One can still see at La Scala each evening wigs askew, dresses awry, ladies poorly combed and gentlemen with week-old beards, helmets worn like caps, capes worn casually – a complete lack of care and good taste, an undisciplined vulgar gaucheness, which destroy all illusion and render grotesque the very lavishness of the *mise en scène*.[7] It is high time this gross defect of our productions was remedied. Our theatres need better-selected and better-trained crowds, and require intelligent and exacting directors who know how to make themselves obeyed.

---

[1] Several theatres were restored or rebuilt in the first decades of the twentieth century, e.g. the Teatro Quirino in Rome was radically rebuilt in 1914.

[2] Italian architects, scene-designers and machinists were the great Renaissance stage innovators in these fields, and Italians dominated theory and practice in the European theatre for more than 250 years. Notable among the practitioners were Giovan Battista Aleotti, Giacomo Torelli and the Vigarani in the seventeenth century, and Giovanni Niccolo Servandoni and various members of the Mauri and the Galli-Bibiena families in the eighteenth. Italian ideas were spread by publications like Sebastiano Serlio's *Le Second Livre d'architecture* (Paris, 1545), Nicola Sabbattini's *Pratica di fabricar scene e machine ne'teatri* (Ravenna, 1638), Andrea Pozzo's *Prospettiva* (Rome, 1693) and Ferdinando Galli-Bibiena's *L'architettura* (Parma, 1711).

[3] Carlo Ferrario (1833–1907) worked at La Scala between 1853 and 1881, and again from 1887. He is particularly remembered for his designs of Verdi's operas. The most fashionable Italian designer of the second half of the nineteenth century, he championed the new realism, as did his successor, Zuccarelli.

[4] One of the rooms in La Scala.

[5] Alfredo Edel (1856–1912) was an internationally known Italian painter and costume-designer, who also worked in London and Paris, where he lived from 1890.

[6] The publishing house Ricordi and its rival Sonzogno were involved in running La Scala throughout most of the 1890s (see J. Rosselli, *The Opera Industry in Italy from Cimarosa to Verdi* (Cambridge University Press, 1984), p. 175).

[7] This was a frequent complaint. See, for example, Jarro's review of Ernesto Rossi's *Giulio Cesare* in *La Nazione*, cited in E. Rossi, *Quarant'anni di vita artistica* (Florence, 1887–8), vol. III, pp. 207–9.

201   A state competition for playwrights, 1888

G. Costetti, *Il teatro italiano nel 1800* (Rocca San Casciano, 1901; reprinted Bologna, 1978), pp. 489–90[1]

The tradition of drama competitions had begun in the Kingdom of Piedmont and Sardinia in the 1850s. After the unification of Italy in 1861, the Ministry of Education took over responsibility, and competitions were held annually until 1877. There were no more until this competition of 1888.

A competition is announced for two prizes: the first for 10,000 lire, the second for 5,000 lire,[2] to be awarded to the two best original plays by Italian authors staged in Italian theatres between the date of announcement of the competition and 31 December 1889.

Only plays of three acts or more are eligible for the 10,000 lire prize; there is no minimum requirement for the number of acts in plays competing for the 5,000 lire prize.

All plays which have already been considered for other prizes are excluded from the competition, as too are plays first performed before the date of this announcement.

In order to qualify for the aforementioned prizes, these original Italian plays must have been staged in the main theatres of at least three of the following cities: Rome, Bologna, Florence, Genoa, Milan, Naples, Palermo, Turin, Venice; and these cities must include: Florence, in recognition of the fact that the prize was instituted there, and Rome, as it is the capital of the kingdom.[3] They must, too, have been staged at some time between the date this competition was announced and 31 December 1889.

Rome, 22 February 1888

[1] Giuseppe Costetti (1834–1928) was a dramatist and theatre historian. His many plays, now largely forgotten, were very popular in the first three decades after unification, and were widely performed by some of the best-known Italian players. His fundamental critical study, *Il teatro italiano nell' 800* (1901), is an invaluable source of information, and a full account of the various drama competitions in the second half of the nineteenth century can be found there, pp. 457–518.

[2] A reasonable sum: in the late 1880s the average annual salary of a lead actor was roughly 10,000 lire.

[3] It was not overly difficult for dramatists to get their plays staged, as most companies were anxious to increase their repertory of Italian drama, and so reduce their dependence on foreign, especially French, plays – a dependence very marked throughout the period. It was rather more difficult to get a play staged in three different cities as invariably box-office considerations forced actor-managers to drop those plays which had achieved little initial success.

202   An actor's contract, 1868

E. Scarpetta, *Cinquant'anni di palcoscenico* (Fifty Years on the Stage) (Naples, 1922), pp. 91–2

Eduardo Scarpetta (1853–1925) was a Neapolitan actor, actor-manager and dramatist, and one of the main figures in the history of nineteenth-century dialect theatre in Italy. His farcical comedies in Neapolitan dialect were often skilful reworkings of French *pochades* (see 197, note 3) and vaudevilles within a Neapolitan context. At his best, as in the highly original *Miseria e nobiltà* (Poverty and Nobility), first staged in 1887, Scarpetta achieved a perfect blend of tradition and modernity, and he is rightly considered the father of the modern Neapolitan theatre. This was Scarpetta's first contract with an acting company.

I, the undersigned Eduardo Scarpetta, acknowledge to be from this time contracted with the acting company led and directed by the owner and impresario of the [Teatro San Carlino],[1] Signor Salvatore Mormone, in the capacity of an all-round actor of secondary roles, not excluding small parts and those of little or no importance.[2]

I likewise undertake to supply my own basic foreign costumes, and have no right to expect these from the impresario.[3]

I also undertake to take part in all rehearsals and to turn up at the time and place designated by the impresario, Signor Mormone, or whosoever is acting on his behalf.

If, at the impresario's bidding, the company travels outside Naples and performs in other theatres, I, the undersigned, agree to go with it, expecting in recompense only travel and lodging expenses.[4]

I equally undertake to dance, paint my face and be flown in the air should any productions require it, and finally agree to undertake anything required of me, such as to sing solo or chorally in vaudevilles.

In payment the impresario guarantees the said Eduardo Scarpetta seventeen lire per month, payable at eight lire and fifty *centesimi* fortnightly, beginning a fortnight from the coming 27th of this month of October.

Naples, 22 October 1868

[1] The Teatro San Carlino in Naples specialized in popular entertainment. In 1868 its major star was the actor Antonio Petito (1822–76), the last famous Pulcinella. Scarpetta created a mask that was an updating of the traditional Pulcinella – a down-at-heel Neapolitan, Don Felice Sciosciammocca.
[2] Right to the end of the nineteenth century many of the traditional acting roles, deriving often from the *commedia dell'arte*, prevailed in Italian companies. Young Scarpetta was engaged as *generico di secondo filo*; other roles were those of *primattore* (lead actor), *primattrice* (lead actress), *brillante* (comic actor), *amoroso* (lover), *padre nobile* (heavy father), *caratterista* (character actor), etc. The advent of naturalism eventually limited and gradually eliminated the importance of roles. See pp. 52, note 1, 119 and 126.
[3] All actors were obliged to provide their own costumes. See 3.
[4] Usually actors had to pay their own travel expenses (see a typical actor's contract cited in Azzaroni, *Del teatro e dintorni*, pp. 262–4). See also 2(a) and 42(n) to 42(q).

203   Eduardo Scarpetta in the part of Peppeniello in his own comedy, *Miseria e nobilità*, 1888

Biblioteca Teatrale Burcardo, Rome. Photo: Oscar Savio

First staged on 8 January 1888, at the Teatro San Carlino, Naples. In addition to exploiting Scarpetta's own talents, the play was written to include a part for the actor's eight-year-old son, Vincenzino.

II   The realism of the Italian international acting 'stars'

'Unfortunately, the most artistic race in the world is not able to pay largely for its pleasure, and Italian actors and singers are almost of necessity wanderers and exiles.'[1] Among these 'wanderers and exiles' four figures stood out and were universally praised as being among the greatest artists of the century: Adelaide Ristori, Ernesto Rossi, Tommaso Salvini and Eleonora Duse. The two most prominent features which characterized the work of all four were in line with the two fundamental reforms promoted by the celebrated actor Gustavo Modena[2] in the 1840s: first, the pursuit of truth and sincerity in performance, and the need to make acting as close as possible to the representation of psychological reality, and, second, the championing of a theatre that was artistically, morally and socially committed.

The plays they acted in were mainly nineteenth-century melodramas (most of them adaptations from the French) and heavily adapted versions of Shakespeare, in which, however, their performances profoundly impressed public and critics alike for the psychological truth in the portrayals. The close identification of the actor with the character he or she performed was, from Modena onwards, what all the foremost Italian players sought.[3] Some of the most perceptive accounts of all four of the major Italian touring 'stars' were written by foreign critics, as the brief selection below indicates.

[1] Henry James, *The Scenic Art* (London, 1949). p. 29.
[2] Gustavo Modena (1803–61) was a highly influential reformist actor and actor-manager. A committed patriot, he took part in the revolution of 1848 and afterwards was forced into exile. Both Rossi and Salvini worked with him in their early years, as did Bellotti Bon (see **199**, note 5).
[3] Rossi, for example, wrote in his reminiscences that a true artist was the actor who could 'subordinate his own physical and moral qualities to the many and different characters whom he set out to interpret and present on the stage ... and to effect this transformation in such a perfect way as to succeed in showing the *living character*'. Rossi, *Quarant'anni di vita artistica*, vol. III, (1888), pp. 97–8.

204(a) Adelaide Ristori: a stylish performer, 1875
The Nation, 18 March 1875, reprinted in James, *The Scenic Art*, pp. 28–31

Madame Ristori,[1] as an actress, is before all things stately, and her stateliness surmounts the disadvantage of a superlatively shabby *mise en scène*, a meagre company, and a somewhat surprised welcome. She apparently – very wisely – confines herself to a limited round of characters, and she offers us only one part in which she has not hitherto appeared.[2] Fortunately, the parts left in her repertory are the strongest ones, and those which have done most to make her famous. She is indissolubly associated with the picturesque stage-figures of Medea and Mary Stuart, and though the strong colouring of these representations has suffered somewhat from the chill of years, they keep their place, in all essentials, among the most accomplished pieces of acting of our time. There are, indeed, things in each of them which it is safe to say the stage has never seen surpassed. Those who remember Madame Ristori twenty years ago may be conscious that here and there the execution drags a little; but young spectators should be assured that in witnessing the last act of *Mary Stuart*, or certain of the great points in *Medea*, they are looking at a supreme exhibition of the grand style of acting.[3] No one whom we have seen, or are likely to see in this country, can interpret tragedy in the superbly large way of Madame Ristori – can distribute effects into such powerful masses. [. . .] Madame Ristori has the fortune to come of the great artistic race – the race in whom the feeling of the picturesque is a common instinct, and the gift of personal expression so ample that, even when quite uncultivated, it begins where our laborious attempts in the same line terminate. [. . .]

Madame Ristori's great merit – a merit that abundantly covers her defects, such as they are – is one that is perhaps especially appreciable here. She has *style*. The quality is so rare upon the English-speaking stage – especially, it is painful to observe, among the actresses – that one should make the most of any suggestion of it. It is the result in Madame Ristori of a combination of fine elements – her admirable stage-presence, her incomparable language, and the peculiarly *masterly* way – the firmness, the certainty, the assurance – with which she deals with her part. Her Mary Stuart is full of style; the whole manner in which the part is 'composed' to the eye is one of the great things of the stage. The intellectual conception, we think, is not particularly elevated; it is the natural woman simply – the woman of temper, the woman who talks loud, who struggles, hates, revenges, who is quite untouched by what Matthew Arnold calls 'sweet reasonableness'.[4] But the part is superbly worn, and the last act is rendered as no one but Madame Ristori could render it. The expression of dignity here reaches a great height. No one but Madame Ristori could manage the farewell to her weeping servants, could gather the group about her, and handle it, as one may say, with that picturesque majesty. It is realism, especially in the closing moments, of a downright pattern; but it is realism harmonized by a great artistic instinct.

[1] Adelaide Ristori (1822–1907) was the most famous Italian actress of the mid-nineteenth century. She was *primattrice* from 1841, and from 1846 to 1851 acted in the Compagnia Domeniconi which had also enlisted the young Tommaso Salvini. In 1853, she joined the Compagnia Reale Sarda with the then enormously high annual salary of 20,000 lire, plus a share in the Company's profits. In 1855 she visited Paris for the first time, winning an enthusiastic reception, and being favourably compared to the great Rachel. After the dissolution of the Compagnia Reale Sarda in 1856, for thirty years she toured in Italy and abroad, including Britain and the United States, where her Lady

Macbeth was particularly admired. From 1885 onwards she appeared on the stage only on very special occasions.

[2] The part was the title-role in *Lucrezia Borgia* by Victor Hugo (1833).

[3] *Medea* was a version of the Greek story by Ernest Legouvé, an Italian translation of which was first played by Ristori at the Théâtre Italien in 1856. Schiller's tormented heroine Mary Stuart was one of Ristori's most celebrated roles.

[4] See Ristori's own account of her main roles in *Studies and Memoirs* (London, 1888), and *Memoirs and Artistic Studies of Adelaide Ristori* (London, 1907).

204(b) Adelaide Ristori in the lead role in Paolo Giacometti's *Elisabetta d'Inghilterra*, 1862

Biblioteca Teatrale Burcardo, Rome. Photo: Oscar Savio

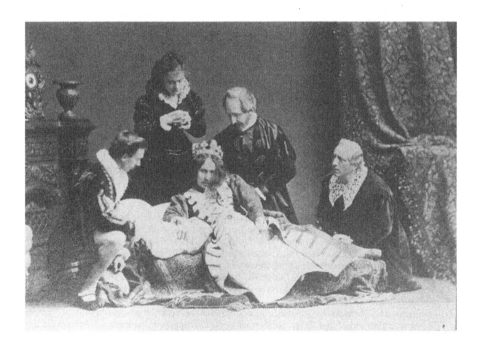

205   Ernesto Rossi's Romeo, 1876

New York Tribune, 5 February 1876, reprinted in James, *The Scenic Art*, pp. 53–4

[Ernesto Rossi][1] has lately appeared as Romeo, and though he has attracted less attention in the part than in some others, it is the one in which he has given me most pleasure. He has scandalously mutilated the play, but there is a certain compensation in the fact that what he has left of it sounds wonderfully well in

Italian. [...] It is singular that Rossi should play best the part that he looks least; for a stout middle-aged man one would say that Romeo was rather a snare. But it is with Romeo very much as with Juliet; by the time an actor has acquired the assurance necessary for playing the part, he has lost his youth and his slimness. Robust and mature as he is, Rossi does it as a consummate artist; it is impossible to imagine anything more picturesquely tender, more intensely ardent.[2] As I have said, he has done very much what he chose with the play, but it is not to be denied that in one or two cases he has almost made his modification pardonable. He makes Juliet come to her senses in the tomb and discover her inanimate lover before Romeo has utterly expired. Besides enabling the hapless couple to perish in each other's arms, this gives Rossi an opportunity for a great stroke of dumb-show – the sort of thing in which he decidedly excels. He has staggered away from the tomb while the poison, which he has just drunk, is working, and stands with his back to it as Juliet noiselessly revives and emerges. He returns to it, finds it empty, looks about him, and sees Juliet standing a short distance off, and looking in the dim vault like a spectre. He has been bending over the empty tomb, and his eyes fall upon her as he slowly rises. His movement of solemn terror as he slowly throws up his arms and continues to rise and rise, until, with his whole being dilated, he stands staring and appalled, on tiptoe, is, although it is grotesque in description, very well worth seeing. Rossi's speeches are often weak, but when he attempts an acutely studied piece of pantomime, he never misses it. This superiority of his pantomime to his delivery seems to me to fix him, in spite of his great talent, in the second line of actors.[3]

[1] Ernesto Rossi (1827–96) early in his career acted with Gustavo Modena, who taught him how to make a psychological study of character and to divest himself of many stage mannerisms by developing a more natural technique. From 1864 he had his own company and in 1866, visiting Paris, the general acclaim of the critics helped to establish his international reputation. From then on he toured mainly abroad with a repertory which became increasingly Shakespearian: his major roles being Othello, Hamlet, Romeo, Macbeth and King Lear. Rossi's observations on Shakespeare and Shakespearian plays, as well as his translation and adaptation of *Julius Caesar*, are in his *Studi drammatici* (Florence, 1885).

[2] In his memoirs, Salvini wrote 'I do not believe there ever was an artist who could utter the words *I love you* as Ernesto Rossi said them'. *Leaves from the Autobiography of Tommaso Salvini* (London and New York, 1893), p. 152.

[3] Although widely praised by many critics, Rossi was also often accused of interpolating too much 'business', 'lacking style', abandoning himself to the role, and failing to keep it under control. In such respects he was adversely compared to Salvini who could brilliantly orchestrate a part. Eleonora Duse, after seeing Rossi in *King Lear* and *Hamlet* in 1887, called him 'a tooth puller', 'a horror as an actor, a charlatan as a man' (cited in Weaver, *Duse*, p. 68).

206(a) Tommaso Salvini's tragic expressiveness

Pall Mall Gazette, 27 March 1884, reprinted in James, *The Scenic Art*, pp. 187–9

La morte civile[1] is a heavy, melancholy piece, with very little richness of texture – though in this respect it does not compare unfavourably, surely, with the usual pabulum of the London play-goer – and that, giving, with its faults, occasion for the most perfect representation of moral suffering that our generation can have seen, it has been promptly shelved as not being sufficiently amusing. To witness 'La morte civile' is a very serious affair, I admit; the manner in which Salvini[2] plays it is a constant challenge of the attention. The ripeness and richness of his acting give every tone and gesture their place in a conception extraordinarily complete: the whole thing has a surface as firm and polished as the glaze of a precious porcelain. The Othello is more brilliant, but it has not more truth, and does not surpass the Corrado in the supreme merit of the latter creation – the expression of life. The manner in which life is produced in 'La morte civile' is one of the most wonderful triumphs I have seen in the actor's art; we seem to touch it, to feel the depth of its throbs, the warmth of its breath, to live, ourselves, in the given situation, rather than to watch and follow, in a greater or lesser degree of detachment. Like everything that Salvini does, it is an expression of pure feelings, and no expression was ever at once more real and more beautiful. The beauty that his admirable artistic organization gives to everything he does is a matter apart from the truth of his inspiration, apart from the mastery that great experience has given him; but they add to his genius that quality that converts the happy confidence of the spectator into what I ventured just now to call a luxury. No other word will express this sense of the degree to which nature has been generous to the great Italian actor, and of such qualities of voice and glance, such a magnificent apparatus of expression, being in themselves a high entertainment. The facility, the immediacy, with which he produces his great effects, has an extraordinary charm. Throughout 'La morte civile' his splendid voice carries, as it were, the whole drama; without a note of violence, of effort, deep and intensely quiet from beginning to end, it reflects the finest shades of concentrated emotion, and goes to the depths of the listener's mind.[3] The facility of execution is as delightful as the conception is simple and sincere. The long speech in which Corrado relates to Don Fernando and the malicious priest the circumstances of his incarceration and those of his escape, is an extraordinarily vivid and interesting piece of acting, and a striking example of Salvini's power to lift great weights – the length of the recital constituting a direct presumption against its success, and violating every prejudice of the English spectator, who often seems to carry to the theatre – and with reason, perhaps, when one thinks what he is sometimes exposed to – an insurmountable distrust of human speech. The part of Corrado is also a capital example of the simple way in which Salvini conceives his characters. They present themselves to him – as they naturally do to the Italian imagination – as embodiments of feeling, without intellectual complications; the creature to be represented appears a creature of passion, of quick susceptibility, of senses lying close to the surface, in whom expression is immediate and complete. The picture given in 'La morte civile' is a picture of suffering pure and simple, or of suffering illumined at most by one or two fitful rays of reflection and resistance. Nothing could be more natural, almost more sensual (for it is the torment of the whole sentient being, sick with suffering), more Italian – at any rate more expressive and more alien to the English theory of how a man should meet trouble.

[1] *La morte civile*, written in 1861 by Paolo Giacometti, concerns an escaped convict who, on realizing that his wife loves another man and that his daughter believes herself to be this man's child, commits suicide. Both the play's thesis, the need for divorce, and Salvini's interpretation of the protagonist Corrado, made the play immensely successful both in Italy and abroad. Zola admired the play and was greatly impressed by the force and truth of Salvini's interpretation, especially in the death scene of the last act.

[2] Tommaso Salvini (1829–1915), *primo attore* from 1854, was distinguished for the exemplary care he put into the analysis of the characters he played. An actor-manager from 1867, he toured Italy and increasingly (from 1871) abroad, with quite phenomenal success, particularly as Othello (see **207**), of which he was perhaps the most striking and controversial interpreter of the nineteenth century. He retired from the stage in 1903.

[3] Salvini was universally praised for the richness, range and sonority of his voice.

206(b) Tommaso Salvini as Corrado in Paolo Giacometti's *La morte civile*

Biblioteca Teatrale Burcardo, Rome. Photo: Oscar Savio

207   Tommaso Salvini prepares to perform Othello

Konstantin Stanislavsky,[1] *My Life in Art* (London, 1924), pp. 273–4

The relations of Salvini to his artistic duties were touching. On the day of a performance he was excited from the very morning, ate very little, and after dinner retired into solitude and received no guests. The performance would begin at eight o'clock, but Salvini was in the theatre at five, that is three hours before the performance began. He went to his dressing-room, removed his overcoat, and began to wander about the stage. If anyone approached him he would talk a little, then leave his companion, sink into thought, stand in silence, and then lock himself in his dressing-room. After a while he would issue in his bathrobe or a make-up coat, and after wandering about the stage and trying his voice on some phrase, or rehearsing a gesture or a series of movements necessary for his role, he would again retire to his dressing-room, put the Moorish make-up on his face and glue his moustaches and beard. Having changed himself not only outwardly but inwardly, he would walk out on the stage again, his footstep lighter and younger than before. The stage-hands were beginning to set up the scenery. Salvini tried to talk to them. Who knows, perhaps Salvini imagined then that he was among his soldiers, who were putting up barricades and fortifications against an enemy. His strong figure, his military pose, his eyes attentively fixed on some far-off object seemed to add truth to his supposition. Again Salvini would retire into his dressing-room and come out in a wig and underdress of Othello, then with a girdle and scimitar, then with a turban on his head, and at last in the full costume of Othello. And with each of his entrances it seemed that Salvini not only made up his face and dressed his body, but also prepared his soul in a like manner, gradually establishing a perfect balance of character. He crept into the skin and body of Othello with the aid of some important preparatory toilet of his own artistic soul and body.

Such preparatory work before every performance was necessary for the genius after he had played the part of Othello many hundreds of times, after he had spent ten years in the preparation of the part alone. It was not in vain that he confessed in his reminiscences that it was only after the hundredth or two-hundredth performance that he understood what Othello was and how to play the part well.[2]

---

[1] Stanislavsky saw Salvini perform in the Imperial Great Theatre in Moscow in 1891.
[2] Salvini's disciplined approach to each performance made Stanislavsky realize how much Russian actors needed 'spiritual baggage'. Salvini was a fundamental influence on the Russian director's later elaboration of his acting 'method'.

208(a) Eleonora Duse eulogized by G. B. Shaw, June 1895

George Bernard Shaw, *Our Theatres in the Nineties* (London, 1932), vol. I, pp. 144–5, 150–52 and 161. Courtesy of The Society of Anthors on behalf of the Bernard Shaw Estate

When [Eleonora Duse][1] comes on the stage [Drury Lane],[2] you are quite welcome to take your opera-glass and count whatever lines time and care have so far traced on her. They are the credentials of her humanity; and she knows better than to obliterate that significant handwriting beneath a layer of peach-bloom from the chemist's. The shadows on her face are grey, not crimson; her lips are sometimes nearly grey also; there are neither dabs nor dimples; her charm could never be imitated by a barmaid with unlimited pin money and a row of footlights before her instead of the handles of a beer-engine. The result is not so discouraging as the patrons of the bar might suppose. Wilkes, who squinted atrociously, boasted that he was only a quarter of an hour behind the handsomest man in Europe: Duse is not in action five minutes before she is a quarter of a century ahead of the handsomest woman in the world. I grant that Sarah's elaborate Mona Lisa smile, with the conscious droop of the eyelashes and the long carmined lips coyly disclosing the brilliant row of teeth, is effective of its kind – that it not only appeals to your susceptibilities, but positively jogs them. And it lasts quite a minute, sometimes longer. But Duse, with a tremor of the lip which you feel rather than see, and which lasts half an instant, touches you straight on the very heart; and there is not a line in the face, or a cold tone in the grey shadow that does not give poignancy to that tremor.

[...] In *La Dame aux camélias*, for instance, it is easy for an intense actress to harrow us with her sorrows and paroxysms of phthisis, leaving us with a liberal pennyworth of sensation, not fundamentally distinguishable from that offered by a public execution, or any other evil in which we still take a hideous delight. As different from this as light from darkness is the method of the actress who shows us how human sorrow can express itself only in its appeal for the sympathy it needs, whilst striving by strong endurance to shield others from the infection of its torment. That is the charm of Duse's interpretation of the stage poem of Marguerite Gautier. It is unspeakably touching because it is exquisitely considerate: that is, exquisitely sympathetic. No physical charm is noble as well as beautiful unless it is the expression of a moral charm; and it is because Duse's range includes these moral high notes, if I may so express myself, that her compass, extending from the depths of a mere predatory creature like Claude's wife up to Marguerite Gautier at her kindest or Magda at her bravest, so immeasurably dwarfs the poor little octave and a half on which Sarah Bernhardt plays such pretty canzonets and stirring marches.

¹ Eleonora Duse (1858–1924) was a *figlia d'arte* and had a difficult beginning to her acting career. Her first notable role was as Thérèse Raquin at the Teatro dei Fiorentini in Naples, in 1879. In 1880 she joined Cesare Rossi's Compagnia della Città di Torino, of which she soon became *prima attrice*. While acting in Turin she first saw Sarah Bernhardt perform, and was fired to emulate her by interpreting the French actress's repertory in her own personal style. From the mid-1880s, first in partnership with Cesare Rossi, then as manager of her own company, Duse toured extensively both in Italy and abroad, and quickly established a reputation as a great 'star' actress, perhaps the greatest of the age. While the originality of Duse's acting technique was much admired both in Italy and abroad, and was highly influential, her contribution to the Italian theatre went further. On the one hand she encouraged new dramatists, notably the work of D'Annunzio, Verga and Praga, and successfully acted in Ibsen; on the other, she anticipated many aspects of modern stage practice.

² In London in June 1895, Duse performed at the Theatre Royal in Drury Lane, while at the same time Sarah Bernhardt was acting at Daly's Theatre. They had similar repertories (Dumas's *La Dame aux camélias* and *La Femme de Claude*; Sudermann's *Heimat*).

208(b) Eleonora Duse in the lead role in Gabriele D'Annunzio's *Francesca da Rimini*, 1901

Biblioteca Teatrale Burcardo, Rome. Photo: Oscar Savio

209   Adelaide Ristori assesses Eleonora Duse's star quality

From an interview with Adelaide Ristori in *Illustrazione Italiana*, April 1897, pp. 230–34

The journalist Leone Fortis interviewed Ristori in Rome on 15 March 1897, and in the course of the interview asked her about the main differences between the great actresses of the past and the young lead actresses of the present.

'You talked to me, dear friend, about the great actresses of the past, about Internari, Marchionni, etc.; can you tell me the main difference between those actresses and the young lead actresses of today?'

La Ristori did not hesitate a moment before answering: 'The difference,' she said, 'is very easily identified: in the past the actress wholly transformed herself into the character she represented, while today young actresses, starting with La Duse, try to make the character suit their means, their physique, their personalities, and even their physical and artistic defects. [. . .]

'La Duse possesses the rare merit of creating for herself a very unique personality, an aesthetic individuality quite unlike that of any great artist now or in the past in that she knows how to exploit all her physical defects, including her neuroses, in order to extract from them effects which are, or seem, new and create a novel impression on the audience.

'Her voice is rather weak and occasionally grating, and she has invented a totally personal way of acting, very fast, very quiet, which does not allow for any vocal outburst, and she hides well this harshness of tone, making it appear the result of emotional excitement.

'She is not a real beauty, but she has undeniably the merit of being one of the few women who can acknowledge this, and she has created for herself a bizarre, eccentric and strange *persona*, extremely pale, that sort of pallor that justifies the much criticized line in *Ballo in maschera*: "radiant of pallor", a *persona* that is easily altered and recomposed; a *persona* that, as soon as the artist appears on the stage, captivates the spectator and monopolizes his attention.

'She is thin, a *fausse maigre* as the French say, but this allows her in love and seduction scenes to assume an air of languid abandonment, of swooning away, that in her appears to be the product of passion, and immediately engages the sympathy of the audience.

'One does not succeed in this without great talent, and her achievements account for the enthusiasm she excites in Italian and foreign audiences.

'As it is, La Duse is an artist who is more admired by the mind than felt in the heart, an artist who subjugates her audience, who communicates to the audience her nervous tension so that one continues to think of her after leaving the theatre. These qualities and defects of La Duse make her particularly powerful in stage-business that requires profound emotional expression to be conveyed through the visage or through the physique. These qualities and defects make her a powerful actress in the expression of neurotic feeling, and this is the secret of her appeal.

'However, at times she tends to abuse these effects.

'She has a certain bizarre way of gesticulating which has something about it of the mechanical, a certain lifeless abandonment of her arms by the side of her tired and defeated body, a certain way of lifting the arm up and keeping it up with an almost mechanical rigidity, a certain way of raising her opened hands with all five fingers separated, a gesture which in any actress who tried slavishly to imitate her would seem an unbearable baroque effect, but done by her creates an effect which you cannot ignore.

'From all this I draw the conclusion that La Duse is an actress of great talent and much originality, but she is not at all a naturalistic artist, as some of her over-enthusiastic admirers have claimed.

'Duse has created for herself her own mannerisms, she has created a kind of convention peculiar to her: according to this "she is the modern woman" with all her maladies of hysteria, anaemia and neuroses, and with all their consequences. She is, then, the *fin-de-siècle* woman, and for this reason she has gathered in her repertoire a complete collection of such abnormal women, with all their weaknesses, fantasies, vacillations, outbursts, languors – from Marguerite Gautier to Fedora, from la femme de Claude to the protagonist of Sudermann's *Heimat*, from Francillon to the second Mrs Tanqueray of Pinero.

'But the real defect of Duse is this: the character always remains the same.

'I do admit though that in order to absorb, if I may use that word, the types of the various characters she represents, fusing them with her own personality, I allow that a great deal of talent, a lot of work and a lot of study is needed, the same it cost me when I attempted, more or less successfully, to transform myself into the various and often very different characters of my repertoire, letting the artist disappear so that the character can emerge. And that is why I admire La Duse and recognize her extraordinary merit.'

III Verismo

With the exception of a handful of plays, Italian drama in the 1860s and 1870s is of indescribable mediocrity. It ranges from romantic dramas, through melodramas *à la* Sardou and sentimental historical or pseudo-historical tragedies, to comedies of manners, farces and thesis plays *à la* Dumas *fils*. For all the proliferation of plays, complaints about the lack of a truly Italian drama abound: 'We have always, and this is the problem', wrote Fernando Martini in 1888, 'more or less imitated the French. If we had tried to learn from them the secret of an art in which, from Molière to Augier, they were superior to everyone else, we need do nothing but praise ourselves: instead we have studied them too little and imitated them in too servile a manner, even in that which has nothing to do with art.'[1] Martini's complaint is perhaps excessively pessimistic: in January 1884 Cesare Rossi's company had staged Verga's *Cavalleria rusticana*, which from the time of its first-night success was considered one of the most innovative of modern Italian plays; although it failed on its first night, equally innovative was Giuseppe Giacosa's *Tristi amori*, staged by the Compagnia Nazionale in Rome in 1887.

In effect these two plays pointed up, as Pullini remarked, in *Teatro italiano del novecento*, the two distinctive aspects of Italian naturalism (*verismo*): the popular, region-based, lyrical and choral naturalism of *Cavalleria*, and the bourgeois naturalism of *Tristi amori*. With Verga, Giacosa, Bracco, Capuana, Rovetta, Praga and others, from the 1880s onwards Italy too could boast that it had reputable dramatists. The prime influence on this new writing was that of French naturalism, particularly after *Thérèse Raquin* was seen throughout Italy from 1879. Nonetheless Italian *verismo* now had its very distinctive features which set it somewhat apart from mainstream European naturalism.

In the theatre, although no phenomena equivalent to the Théâtre Libre in France, or the Moscow Art Theatre in Russia, appeared in Italy, *verismo* provided an excellent schooling for actors, helping to free them of melodramatic and outworn traditional techniques, and encouraging naturalness and spontaneity in performance.

[1] F. Martini, *Lettere 1860–1926* (Milan, 1934); letter to Salvatore Barzilai, 6 December 1888.

210 The first night of Giovanni Verga's *Cavalleria rusticana*, 1884

A review by Eugenio Torelli-Viollier in *Corriere della sera*, Milan, 15 January 1884; cited in Federico De Roberto, *Casa Verga e altri studi verghiani* (Florence, 1964), pp. 209–10

Cavalleria rusticana is a one-act play that portrays certain scenes from Sicilian life.[1] It concerns a young woman who, having been seduced by a young man, and realizing that he is now pursuing a married woman, denounces him to the woman's husband. The husband revenges himself by killing his wife's lover. The dialogue, a faithful reproduction from life, and the 'local colour' cleverly calculated, conveys to the audience a profound impression of truth. [...]

All the actors gave sound performances, but Signora Duse, whom I saw for the first time, showed herself to be a first-class artist. In the role of the seduced and abandoned girl who denounces her lover, throughout she displayed control, discipline and simplicity, without resorting to a single cry or violent gesture, yet she created highly emotional effects and moved the spectators to tears. The work is wholly theatrical, completely of the stage, and all the effects are thoroughly theatrical and scenic. There is nothing in it that is literary or romantic. Rhetoric is quite absent. *Cavalleria rusticana* gives promises that Verga is a true and powerful dramatist.

[1] Giovanni Verga (1840–1922) was a novelist and dramatist. His short stories (*Vita dei campi*, 1880, and *Novelle rusticane*, 1888) and novels (*I Malavoglia*, 1881, and *Mastro Don Gesualdo*, 1888) portray many aspects of Sicilian life and class relationships and are considered masterpieces of Italian *verismo*. His first staged play, the one-act *Cavalleria rusticana*, was performed in 1884 and it was followed by several others, the most interesting of which were *La lupa* (1896) and *Dal tuo al mio* (1903). *Cavalleria rusticana* was based on a short story in *Vita dei campi* and was innovative in both form and content. It was staged in Turin by Cesare Rossi's Compagnia della Città di Torino on 15 January 1884 and, contrary to Verga's fears, was a great success. It was set to music by Mascagni in 1890, to a libretto by Targioni Tozzetti.

211   Giovanni Verga analyses his own writing in *In portineria*, 1885

A letter from Verga to L. Capuana in G. Verga, *Lettere a L. Capuana* (Letters to L. Capuana), ed. G. Raya (Florence, 1975), pp. 207–9

I wanted the play[1] to be strictly of an 'intimate' nature, a play of subtle interpretation, as things really are in life; and in this sense it was another step in my search for the 'truth'. I wanted the passions to be subdued and the plot to be simple, not only to make it contrast with *Cavalleria rusticana*, but also in order to reproduce truthfully and sincerely the different *milieux* I had set out to portray. Although the picture was very different, too, in what one might call the technique of the form, the purpose was the same: to aim at portraying another facet of working-class life, to do for the lower urban classes what I had done in my treatment of Sicilian peasants.[2] [...]

In this, as in the work I am writing at the moment, I am attempting once again to depict what is called 'society'. I expect I shall be damned for this work as well, because my method will still be the same and is the product of an old conviction of mine, that education or, if you will, something like it, has smoothed away edges, flattened differences, given a uniform veneer to the way sentiments, passions, manifest themselves. Not that these are any the less strong at times, but they are more delicately expressed and must be more delicately portrayed by the writer and rendered by the actor with great attention to nuance.

The whole thing, then, is a matter of interpretation:[3] interpretation by the writer, by the actors and also, you see, by the audience, who should bring to this experiment a degree of observation, of love and, I would also add, of collaboration.

You might object that this is a poor start indeed, and that so far we have only one capable interpreter: La Duse. Certainly she is the only person who can make the second act of *Portineria* acceptable to the public. But is that reason enough to abandon our convictions? Better to be damned. Time will tell.

[1] *In portineria* was written soon after *Cavalleria rusticana* and staged at the Teatro Manzoni in Milan on 16 May 1885. It was a two-act play based, like *Cavalleria rusticana*, on a love triangle.

[2] In contrast to *Cavalleria rusticana*, which had an *al fresco* setting, *In portineria* was set in the porter's living quarters in a block of flats in Milan.

[3] Verga stressed the need for subtle interpretation by actors and he disliked the arbitrary changes they made to his texts. He was outraged, for example, at the liberties taken with *Cavalleria rusticana* and *La lupa* by Giovanni Grasso's company when it produced them in Paris (see letter to Rod, 21 January 1908, in *Lettere al suo traduttore*, ed. F. Chiapelli (Florence, 1954), p. 245). Verga was always sceptical of the artistic merits of theatre: 'I have written for the theatre, but I do not believe drama to be an art-form superior to the novel. On the contrary, I consider it to be an inferior and primitive form for some reasons which I shall call technical. Two in particular: the need for the actor as intermediary between the author and his audience; the need to write not for an ideal reader, as is the case with the novel, but for a body of spectators, and that obliges one to think in terms of an average intelligence and taste, an "average reader" as the English say.' (Cited in Ugo Ojetti, *Alla scoperta dei letterati* (Florence, 1946), pp. 70–71.)

212   Luigi Capuana champions dramatic *verismo*, 1887

Letter to F. De Roberto[1] cited in *Verga, De Roberto, Capuana*, Exhibition Catalogue, Catania, 1955

I am laughing in advance at the disappointment of audiences and critics. They will expect from Capuana,[2] the ferocious *verista* as they call me, a *verista* play in the way they understand it, virtually pornographic [...] but they will find it the most elevated and wholesome thing in the world. It seems to me that I have made no concessions whatsoever to theatrical *convention* or to fashion. [...]

It will present performers with great problems, given that our precious actors lack the habit of learning their parts by heart. [...] But they will be absolutely obliged to speak, and not declaim, for that will be impossible: not a single word is declamatory. [...] The characters are all taken from life, without being ordinary and vulgar, the action takes place in a bourgeois *milieu*. [...] In short, as a subject it is something new for Italy: in formal terms I think it altogether new anywhere.

[...] Even Becque sacrifices too much to *theatrical convention*. The action of *Nanette*, for example, is so condensed that it lies uncomfortably within one act, and in the three acts of *La Parisienne* there are five monologues, and some of these are so long they occupy an entire page.

In my play there is not a single monologue, not even of one syllable, and no *aside*.

[1] A Sicilian, like Verga and Capuana, Federico De Roberto was a novelist and a dramatist of *verismo*. His novel, *I Vicerè* (1894), is a penetrating psychological study of a noble Sicilian family in the nineteenth century. His best play, the one-act *Il rosario*, was first staged at the Teatro Manzoni in Milan on 29 November 1912.

[2] Luigi Capuana (1839–1915) was a novelist, dramatist and critic, and a highly influential champion of *verismo*.

213   The Théâtre Libre in Milan, 1892

Cibotto, ed., *Cronache teatrali di Giovanni Pozza*, pp. 166–8

Although we are kept regularly informed of artistic developments in Paris, many among us have a very distorted idea as to the aims and purposes of the Théâtre Libre.[1] It is commonly believed that the Théâtre Libre is a theatre devoted to the representation of the most naturalistic audacities of literary sensuality.

Nothing is further from the truth. The Théâtre Libre does include in its repertoire a few works which are perhaps a little too detailed in their reproduction of intimate life, but the purpose for which the theatre was created is an eminently artistic one.

M. Antoine – its founder – intended with this theatre to offer young French authors a chance to prove themselves, for they are too frequently excluded, for non-artistic reasons, from the great Parisian theatres. But that is not all. He wished also to organize a company educated in the ways of an ensemble and not dominated by the capriciousness and vanity of 'star' players. And this is not all. By offering competition he aims to reduce ticket prices, which speculation has currently pushed to a high level so that dramatic art can again become a popular art. In Italy we do not need a Théâtre Libre – or need it only to reduce ticket prices.[2] Our acting is generally natural and coordinated. There is no shortage of theatres for our young authors. Do you know how many 'new' plays were performed in Milan between January and the end of November this year? *One hundred and four*, of which only *twenty-nine* were by foreign authors. Altogether two hundred and seventy-three acts; don't you think this is good enough?

It is natural, then, that the aims of the Théâtre Libre should have been misunderstood by some among us – and that was the reason the public went last night to the Manzoni hoping to find there what they did not find. In fact the plays seemed not just respectable but moralistic; and the *troupe*, the famous *Antoine troupe*, made up of former amateur actors, was generally thought a good company of actors and actresses not so very different from one of our own. Nothing remarkable then, nothing distinctive.

But this is true only at first sight. Last night's performance did have something different, and what was distinctive could not escape those who watched attentively.

The two plays were acted in a way rarely seen on our stage. I mean with an assurance, an intonation, a careful study of even the most minor details, which only our dialect companies can sometimes succeed in achieving.

Evidently M. Antoine is not only an excellent actor, but a conscientious and zealous director, too, inspired by a noble artistic sense. He succeeded in offering us in both plays – and unhampered by the rather poor *mise en scène* – a complete environment; and he achieved this by way of painstaking attention to each particular element.

His colleagues, with one or two exceptions, were interpreters and not actors, always careful not to disturb the harmony of the ensemble, the levels of dramatic perspective, never stepping out of character in their intonation, gestures and expression.

[1] Antoine's Théâtre Libre visited Milan in December 1892, performing, at the Teatro Manzoni, E. Brieux's *Blanchette*, and *La Tante Léontine* by M. Boniface and E. Bodin.
[2] When attempts came to be made to establish *teatri stabili* the provision of cheap ticket prices was an important consideration.

214(a) Ermete Zacconi epitomizes Italian naturalist acting, 1895

From articles by Leporello[1] in *Illustrazione Italiana*

Zacconi[2] is most appreciated as an actor. A pupil of Emanuel,[3] he has learned from his teacher how to develop a role gradually and intelligently. By breaking a long tradition, that inveterate habit that has made of our actors so many improvisers, he has pushed the analysis of every role, every character, every pathological peculiarity, to the limits of the possible. More endowed with vocal timbre than his teacher, he has been a supreme interpreter where the effect of a particular situation can best be conveyed by nuances of tone. No one knows better than he how to bring to the surface a thought hidden in a beautiful phrase, or to give colour to a speech as it rises to a crescendo.

I have mentioned what has been good, must I also mention what is bad? I said that he takes character analysis to the limits of the possible; I must add that sometimes, too, he goes beyond what is proper. Consider the role of Oswald in Ibsen's *Ghosts*. He has no doubt studied in real life that disease which brings Oswald to imbecility, and just as he saw it in life so he reproduces it on the stage, with terrifying results. But in order to give reality to stage fiction, he reveals too soon the symptoms of that disease growing in Oswald's body. Absorbed in his own character, he has paid insufficient attention to the other characters. Why is it that Mrs Alving notices the dreadful disease consuming her son only at the end of the play, when from the start of the final act Oswald's speech is no more than the babble of a paralytic and imbecilic creature? In his attempt to be scrupulously realistic, Zacconi ceases at times to be credible.

13 January 1895

Zacconi is [...] the artist of sorrow: even over his smile there is a veil of sadness – in life, as on the stage. Like Gringoire, the protagonist of Banville's[4] poetic drama, one of his most perfect interpretations, he has received from nature and his innate talent a mission to reveal to those who are fortunate the miseries of the unfortunate: from the unbalanced excitement of Oswald in *Ghosts* to the morbid sensitivity of the blind man in Maeterlinck's short piece *The Intruder*, he presents the live and pulsating hidden anguish within a numerous and wide-ranging assortment of artistic creations. Even in those who are most light-hearted he reveals the sorrow that is hidden in all men. [...]

For this reason he is the best interpreter of that Scandinavian art in which the physical and intellectual imbalance of individuals has to correspond to an exaggeration of the organic imbalance of society. Eleonora Duse was the first who tried to show Ibsen to us with some success.[5] Zacconi was the first to make us truly know, understand and wholly accept him.

[...] From [Emanuel] he learned the art of giving a distinctive physiognomy to each character, whereby the personality of the actor disappears, is transformed, and a complete reincarnation takes place. [...]

As actor, actor-manager and director he holds today virtually undisputed supremacy.[6] Perhaps only one actor can challenge him, an actor who preceded him in distinction, another Ermete – Novelli:[7] and Novelli is his opposite – an artist of joyfulness.

17 February 1895

---

[1] Leporello was the pseudonym of the theatre critic Achille Tedeschi.

[2] Ermete Zacconi (1857–1948), a *figlio d'arte* like Duse, after a long and difficult novitiate in third-rate companies, joined, in 1884, Giovanni Emanuel's company for two years, an experience which served to discipline his natural acting talent. From 1894 he managed his own company and became one of the most acclaimed actor-managers of the time, not only in Italy but also abroad. In 1911 he visited Paris where he successfully presented a number of plays at the Théâtre Antoine. H. Lyonnet provides a sympathetic account of his work in *Le Théâtre en Italie*. Between December 1894 and March 1895 at the Teatro Manzoni in Milan, Zacconi staged *Lonely People* by Hauptmann; *I diritti dell'anima* (Rights of the Soul) by Giacosa; Ibsen's *Ghosts*, *Little Eyolf* and *An Enemy of the People*; Maeterlink's *The Intruder*; Tolstoy's *The Power of Darkness*; Dumas fils's *La Dame aux camélias*; and many other plays. He also directed (without acting in them) Sheridan's *The School for Scandal* and Goldoni's *I rusteghi* (The Boors).

[3] Giovanni Emanuel (1848–1902) was an actor-manager famous for his naturalistic Shakespearian

performances (Othello, Lear). He toured to Latin America and Russia. He also left many valuable prompt-books.

⁴ *Gringoire*, by Théodore de Banville, was first produced at the Théâtre-Français on 23 June 1866 with Coquelin in the title-role.

⁵ She staged *A Doll's House* in 1891.

⁶ Later in his career Zacconi was also a successful film actor and transferred to the screen some of his greatest stage successes like *Spettri* (Ghosts, 1917), *Il Cardinale Lambertini* (1934) and *Processo e morte di Socrate* (1940).

⁷ See p. 461 and p. 463, note 2.

214(b) Ermete Zacconi in the part of Oswald in Ibsen's *Spettri*

Biblioteca Teatrale Burcardo, Rome. Photo: Oscar Savio

215   Contractual arrangement between the dramatist Luigi Capuana and the actor-manager Francesco Pasta

Letter of 1891 from Capuana to Pasta,[1] cited in G. Oliva, *Capuana in archivio* (Roma, 1979), pp. 357–8

Dear Cav. Pasta,

An unforeseen necessity prompts me to approach you with the following suggestion. In about a month I could let you have my play *Malia*, of which you already know both the content and to some extent the form. I can straight away promise to let you have either exclusive rights on the play for one year or partial rights as far as certain performance places are concerned.[2]

Before I contact Cesare Rossi[3] or La Duse (to whom I spoke about the play last time she visited Rome), I should like to know with some urgency if you find my suggestion acceptable. I have never dealt with actor-managers on such a matter before; but I guide myself by my considerable experience of dealing with the publishers of my books; and I imagine that a manager like you would not have difficulty in accepting an arrangement which has so often been acceptable to publishers to the satisfaction of both parties. I never fail to meet my obligations. It would then be a question of signing in advance the contract for the play *Malia* (to be handed over in a month's time) and of deciding the terms and the exclusive rights for the performance places. On signing the contract you would pay me a sum of money which I would guarantee with a one-month bill in your favour. Giannotta in Catania, Paggi in Florence, other publishers in Milan, I repeat, have made similar agreements with me and have gone through the same procedure. For commercial or administrative reasons, I could renew the bill for three further months, that is until the performances of the play would have repaid you the sum advanced, as would be the case if you yourself were to take the percentage due to me from the box-office takings each night until the debt was repaid in full. The sum I would wish to receive in advance is 1,000 lire, which would be guaranteed by a promissory note. Cesare Rossi, two years ago, came to the same arrangement with me in the case of *Giacinta*.[4]

If possible, I should like an early answer so that I can turn elsewhere should you not be interested. If you are interested, all you would have to do would be to send me two copies of the contract: one signed by you, the other to be signed by me. The conditions could be the same as for the production of my *Giacinta* in Catania: that is from the gross box-office nightly returns (including returns from subscriptions) the daily costs of the company would be deducted. The sum remaining would be divided equally between the two of us. Alternatively, we could observe the copyright law as it operates in the case of literary works.[5] I can see no difficulty in that. In return for the favour of the advance, I would be willing to grant you the rights for any performance place you might want. I hope that both the nature of the work and my name will be excellent guarantees for the completion of the arrangement. It is understood that should the play fail to achieve in one year the success necessary to recoup the sum you have advanced, then I will be obliged to reimburse you myself.[6]

Respectfully yours,

Luigi Capuana

[1] Francesco Pasta (1839–1905), after a successful career as a lead actor, took up actor-management in 1882. The title Capuana uses before Pasta's name is a complimentary form of address: *Cavaliere*.

[2] The practice varied according to the preferences of writers and actor-managers.

[3] Cesare Rossi (1829–98) was a notable support and lead actor in a number of companies, including those of Ernesto Rossi (1857–60) and Bellotti Bon (1860–71). In 1877 he took up actor-management, and from then until 1885 he ran a semi-permanent company at the Teatro Carignano in Turin: the Compagnia della Città di Torino (see **220**, note 5). His *prima attrice* was Duse, with whom he went into joint management in 1885–6.

[4] Capuana here contradicts his claim earlier in the letter never to have dealt with an actor-manager before. Duse refused 'for personal reasons' to act in *Giacinta*, disliking the play's morally dubious subject-matter. Rossi's company staged the play at the Teatro Sannazzaro in Naples on 18 May 1888.

[5] For copyright law in Italy, see **196**, note 7.

[6] *Malia* was first performed at the Teatro Nazionale in Rome in December 1891. A peasant drama, it was originally written in Italian then translated into Sicilian dialect, in which form it was first performed in 1903.

IV   The theatre of Gabriele D'Annunzio

The reaction against 'naturalism' in the Italian theatre came about several years after the naturalistic aesthetic had been challenged in France by Paul Fort, Lugné-Poe and others. It was most pronounced in the work of Gabriele D'Annunzio[1] and Eleonora Duse.[2] The former was already well established by the mid-1890s in Italy and abroad as poet and novelist, and he now turned to playwriting with the deliberate intention of rejecting what he felt to be the banalities of the 'naturalistic' theatre, and sought to widen the horizons of the Italian theatre by opening it up to the influences of literary and artistic mysticism and symbolism already strongly felt elsewhere in Europe.

La Duse was an actress of technical skill and profound sensitivity who in the 1890s, particularly after stage experience with Shakespeare and Ibsen, rejected much of her old repertoire, and driven by an almost messianic sense of purpose, tried to establish in Italy a new and more serious theatre characterized by spiritual depth and intellectual complexity. Duse and D'Annunzio first met in 1895 and combined their talents in the service of this new theatre. Their initial intention was to build an open-air theatre on the banks of Lake Albano, near Rome, where they would stage classical drama and plays D'Annunzio intended to write. Nothing came of these plans, but the project encouraged D'Annunzio to write, and Duse, though momentarily discouraged by the fact that he gave his first play, *La città morta* (The Dead City), to Sarah Bernhardt, staged a number of his dramas, beginning with the one-act *Sogno di un mattino di primavera* (Dream of a Spring Morning) in Paris, 15 June 1897, at the Théâtre de la Renaissance.

D'Annunzio's novel, *Il fuoco* (The Flame of Life, 1900), contains as explicit a statement of his dramatic theory as he ever attempted, and something of the ambitious nature of the venture he and Duse projected in the late 1890s is indicated there, and clearly shows his indebtedness both to Wagner and the French symbolist movement.[3] Prominent, too, is a powerful strain of nationalism, a reassertion of the primacy of Italian art in a field in which it had not excelled since the Renaissance. D'Annunzio's dramatic theory was derivative and his practice fell far short of his ideal, but the fact that an Italian dramatist had succeeded in getting his first two plays staged by the two most famous actresses of the time, and in Paris, the artistic capital of Europe, secured for him international critical attention and gave a fillip, however short-lived, to Italian theatre as a whole. His achievement signalled both the need for, and the possibility of achieving, a resurgence of Italian drama that had for long been French-dominated and artistically negligible.

Duse was a keen champion of D'Annunzio's *teatro di poesia*. Between 1898 and 1904 she dedicated her talent and money to promoting his work, although her success with it was erratic, and often it was her artistic reputation alone that brought partial acceptance or interest from an Italian public largely indifferent, when it was not downright hostile, to change of any kind. Only in 1901, with *Francesca da Rimini*, did she record her first unqualified success with a play by D'Annunzio. Her productions of D'Annunzio's work were characterized by the care and precision devoted both to staging and costuming, thanks not least to the author's dictatorial insistence on such matters. That Duse spent a particularly large sum on the production of *Francesca da Rimini* was perhaps not unconnected with the fact that D'Annunzio himself supervised the production, enlisting some of the finest Italian design and technical staff in order to reconstruct the medieval world of the play (although some critics nonetheless complained of historical inaccuracies). Thanks to the joint efforts of D'Annunzio and Duse, for the first time Italian theatre-goers were given the largely unfamiliar example of staging that functioned wholly in the service of the author's idea.

[1] Gabriele D'Annunzio (1863–1938), Italian poet, novelist, dramatist and adventurer. Despite the skills of Bernhardt and Duse, audiences found D'Annunzio's plays verbose, static and undramatic.
[2] See 208(a), note 1.
[3] *Il fuoco* is set in Venice in 1883 and deals with the love affair between a poet, Stelio Effrena (in effect D'Annunzio himself) and an actress, Foscarina (most certainly Duse). It enjoyed a *succès de scandale* for its explicit autobiographical details, not least its definition of the actress as an 'older woman'. The novel was translated into English as *The Flame of Life*.

216   D'Annunzio's conception of an ideal theatre, 1900

Gabriele D'Annunzio,[1] *Il fuoco* (Milan, 1900), pp. 157–61 and 286–9

(a) 'Drama is nothing if it is not a rite or a message,' Daniele Glauro said wisely. 'It is necessary for a performance again to become as solemn as a ceremony, combining the two elements which make up any religion: a living person who embodies on the stage the world of a Revealer like a priest at an altar, and the presence of a silent multitude as in a temple ...'

'Bayreuth,' interrupted Prince Hoditz.

'No, the Gianiculum,' cried Stelio Effrena, emerging suddenly from his vertiginous silence. 'A Roman hill. On the Roman hill we shall not have the wood and brick of High Francony, but a theatre of marble.'[2] [...]

'Don't you admire Richard Wagner's work?' asked Donatella Arvale with a slight frown, which for a moment made her inscrutable face almost hard.[3] [...]

'Richard Wagner's work,' he replied, 'is rooted in the Germanic spirit, its essence is wholly northern. His reform has something akin to that attempted by Luther. His drama is but the supreme expression of the genius of a race; it is but the magnificent quintessence of the aspirations of national poets and composers from Bach to Beethoven, from Wieland to Goethe. If you could imagine his work on the shores of the Mediterranean among our light olive groves, among our lissom laurels, and under the glory of the Latin sky, you would see it pale and fade. But as he himself says, the artist has the gift of seeing the final perfection of a world not yet given shape, and the prophet-like gift of rejoicing at this in desire and hope. Therefore, I announce the advent of a new or reborn art which, in the strong and sincere simplicity of its lines, in its rigorous grace, in the ardour of its spirit, in the pure power of its harmonies, should continue and crown the immense ideal edifice of our own chosen race. I rejoice in being a Latin; and – forgive me, dreamy Lady Myrta, forgive me, sensitive Hoditz – I see a barbarian in any man of different blood.'

'But Richard Wagner too, developing the thread of his own theories, takes his starting point from the Greeks,' said Baldassare Stampa who, just back from Bayreuth, was still full of its ecstasies.

'A very uneven and confused thread,' the *maestro* answered. 'Nothing could be further from the *Oresteia* than the *Ring* cycle. The Florentines of the House of Bardi penetrated far more deeply into the essence of Greek tragedy.'[4]

(b) 'Further, have you ever considered that the essence of music lies not in the sounds?' asked the mystical doctor.[5] 'It lies in the silence that precedes and follows them. The rhythm appears and lives in these intervals of silence. Every sound and every melody awakens in the silence that precedes and follows it a voice that can only be heard by our spirit. Rhythm is the heart of music, but its beats can only be heard in the pauses between the sounds.' [...]

'Do you remember that image that Schiller uses in the Ode he composed in order to celebrate Goethe's translation of Mohammed, that image he uses to signify that on the stage the only thing that can have life is an ideal world? The chariot of Thespis, like the boat on the Acheron, is so flimsy that it can only take the weight of shades or human images. On the common stage those images are so distant that any contact with them seems impossible, like contact with phantoms of the mind.[6] They seem distant and alien. But in making them appear in the rhythmic silence, in making music accompany them to the threshold of the visible world, I can make them seem closer, because I throw light on the mysterious recesses of the will that produces them. Do you follow me? Their intimate essence is there, revealed and put in close communion with the soul of the crowd which can feel, under the ideas expressed by voice and gesture, the profundity of the musical themes that correspond to the ideas in the symphonies. In short, I show them images painted on a veil and, at the same time, what happens beyond the veil. Do you understand? And, by means of the music, the dance and the lyrical song, I create around my heroes an ideal atmosphere in which the whole world of nature throbs, so that in each of their acts there seem to converge, not only the powerful forces of their predetermined destinies, but the most obscure influences of surrounding things, of the elemental souls which live in the great tragic circle.'[7]

Ideally, just as Aeschylus' creations carry in them something of the natural myths out of which they came, so in the same way I wish my creations could be felt to throb in the torrent of savage forces, to ache from contact with the earth, become one with air, water and fire, with the mountains, with the clouds, in their melancholy struggle against a fate that must be overcome, for I wish Nature to be around them as the ancient fathers saw her as a passionate actress in an eternal drama.'

[1] D'Annunzio expresses his ideas in the classic form of a dialogue. Stelio Effrena, the artist protagonist, is a mouthpiece for D'Annunzio himself.

[2] This first passage is strongly nationalistic in tone, and in it D'Annunzio praises the achievements of Italian Renaissance theatre practitioners and theoreticians, seeing in them the true heirs of the Greek concept of total theatre that so influenced his own ideas about the direction modern Italian drama should take.

[3] D'Annunzio was a great admirer of Wagner's work and the shadow of the great composer dominates the whole of *Il fuoco*.

[4] Camerata dei Bardi, or Camerata Fiorentina, was the name given to those gatherings held in Florence before and after 1580 in the house of Giovanni de'Bardi, Count of Vernio.

[5] In this second passage D'Annunzio stresses the importance of music in drama. In his opinion, it was not proper to subordinate drama to music, as Wagner had done, but rather the music should primarily precede and conclude a dramatic work.

[6] D'Annunzio's stance is distinctly anti-naturalistic. The general ideas expressed here have much in common with those of Edward Gordon Craig, who D'Annunzio later came to know and admire, calling him '*Il novatore Britanno*', 'the Briton innovator' – a curious expression reflecting D'Annunzio's liking for obsolete and bizarre words and expressions. In 1901 D'Annunzio wrote to the critic Giovanni Pozza: 'those who object, "In daily life one does not talk like this", show that they do not understand what tragic art really is, indeed what art in general is. It is time to open a breach in the great prejudice that surrounds us, it is time to re-affirm the privileges of poetry.' *Cronache teatrali di Giovanni Pozza* (1971), p. 347.

[7] This vision of a total theatre D'Annunzio came close to realizing in the production of the plays he wrote in French. Those were *Le Martyre de saint Sébastien* (first produced at the Théâtre du Châtelet on 22 May 1911, with Ida Rubinstein in the main role, designs by Bakst, choreography by Fokine, music by Debussy); *La Pisanelle, ou la mort parfumée* (first produced at the Théâtre du Châtelet in June 1913, Ida Rubinstein in the main role, design by Bakst, music by Pizzetti); *Le Chèvrefeuille* (first produced at the Théâtre de la Porte-Saint-Martin, Paris, in December 1913). See G. Gullace, *Gabriele D'Annunzio in France* (Syracuse, 1966), pp. 83–97.

217   D'Annunzio writes to Zacconi about modern tragedy, 1899

Letter from D'Annunzio to the actor Ermete Zacconi,[1] in G. Zacconi, *Ricordi e battaglie* (Milan, 1946), pp. 225–7

Corfu, 5 March 1899

Let us now talk of the tragedy [*La gloria*] I am about to complete and that will not *live* on the stage unless helped by your magic art.[2]

This tragedy differs from my earlier ones: it is grander, more emotional, more torrid. One might call it a 'national' tragedy, because it portrays a tragic moment in the life of a people, and the violent actions and reactions between the soul of the people and the will of a hero.

A modern, complex tragedy, in which it might be possible to recognize the features of some well-known personality.[3]

All essence, all expression is concentrated in the person of the protagonist, from heroism to fear, from oratorical flights to confused babble, from life at its most intense to the most fearful contractions of death.

There is in it, furthermore, a singular feature which will not, I hope, displease you: the apparition of a gigantic character in the second act, of a Dictator, the last support of a dying world which falls as he falls.[4]

The scene has a fierce, grandiose simplicity. Only you can do it. If my tragedy can be staged, you will have to undertake two 'parts', as ancient tragic actors did in Aeschylus' time, when they played the protagonist and the deuteragonist.

You will not mind too much, I hope, dying twice – and in two different ways.

I have called this tragedy *La gloria* and it will be ready in a few days. I can send you the first acts straight away.

In the first, second and third acts there are some choral scenes, that is scenes with many characters, crowd scenes; such scenes you can stage inimitably.

What do you think, then, of my plan to stage, perhaps on tour, both *La Gioconda* and *La gloria*? For this a great effort is needed, an effort of which only you are capable, because *La gloria* rests entirely on your robust shoulders.

Thus this experiment would have a profound and vast meaning. It would mean the following: 'An Italian writer with a theory of his own about the essence of a theatrical work has written a few plays in his own language, in an undertaking both sincere and determined. Today we present this undertaking to the public so that it can judge the vitality of the innovation. And this short experiment also includes a hope – a hope that tomorrow other and younger talents will emerge, and that this attempt at a more noble art will prove fruitful for our theatre.'

I thank Eleonora Duse and Ermete Zacconi who are so graciously allowing me to see my work, elsewhere already making its way, come alive on the Italian stage. *La gloria* at the Théâtre des Nations, the *Sogni* cycle at the theatre in Munich and in Vienna.

---

[1] For biographical details on Zacconi, see **214(a)**, note 2.

[2] Between the autumn of 1898 and the spring of 1899, D'Annunzio wrote two dramas, *La Gioconda* and *La gloria*, which he hoped Duse and Zacconi would stage in various Italian cities. Duse was all too aware that Zacconi's acting style was not exactly suited to D'Annunzio's dramas, but she liked the actor personally and his reputation as player and manager made him a valuable partner. *La Gioconda* was performed at the Teatro Bellini in Palermo on 15 April, and repeated in various Italian cities with various degrees of success. *La gloria*, after its first performance at the Teatro Mercandante in Naples on 27 April, an outright fiasco, was not revived. D'Annunzio was very resentful of the Neapolitan audience, which he blamed for the play's failure.

[3] Audiences saw in the play veiled references to the Italian contemporary political scene and thought one of the characters portrayed was the politician Francesco Crispi. D'Annunzio had been a member of the Italian Parliament in 1897–8.

[4] The protagonist of this, as of all D'Annunzio's fiction and drama, is an exceptional figure who

cannot, according to Nietzschean terms, be measured against the normal criteria of good and evil. *La gloria* made some appeal to Italian audiences later during Fascism, and certain critics saw in its protagonist an anticipation of Mussolini.

218(a) Duse rehearses D'Annunzio's *La Gioconda*, November–December 1906

From *Duse on Tour (Guido Noccioli's Diaries 1906–7[1])*, ed. Giovanni Pontiero (Manchester, 1982), pp. 53–5

Florence, 30 November 1906

At three o'clock in the afternoon a rehearsal of *La Gioconda*[2] in the salon of the Grand Hotel. The Signora is taciturn and deathly pale. Grey hairs straggle wildly from her broad plumed hat, which frequently slips to the back of her head causing her to readjust it with a hasty, almost aggressive gesture. Before her, an enormous wall mirror reflects in frontal view her surprisingly agile figure and thin, emaciated face, with those large eyes that at times assume a strange expression, never witnessed in any other woman. It reminds me of the masterly description of Foscarina given by the author of *Fuoco*.[3] Meantime, while the rehearsal proceeds rapidly with few interruptions, the Signora studies herself in the mirror in silence – one might even say in darkest gloom. Suddenly she speaks: 'You go on rehearsing. I am leaving. Tomorrow at the same time there will be a rehearsal of *La Gioconda* for Signorina Rossi and Signorina Zucchini.' And off she goes.

[1] Guido Noccioli was a young actor in Duse's company in 1906–7. His account of this experience in his diaries, as well as in letters written to his teacher, Luigi Rasi, director of the Academy of Dramatic Art, offer a unique insight into Duse's practice as actor-manager and director.
[2] *La Gioconda* was the only play by D'Annunzio that Duse kept in her repertory after 1904. In her last tour in 1923–4, she revived *La città morta*.
[3] See p. 453, note 3.

Florence, 1 December 1906

At three o'clock the Signora is already waiting in the salon. She starts rehearsing her scenes with Signorina Luciana Rossi (who plays the role of Francesca Doni) and the Signora makes a number of interesting suggestions. She is in good form and introduces some quite felicitous nuances. She advises Signorina Rossi to wear something *more seemly and becoming* in the last act.

She then goes on to rehearse her scenes with Sirenetta (played by Signorina Clelia Zucchini, a young pupil of Teresa Boetti Valvassura). The actress slowly begins to read her part, without any vigour or expression. Just as if she were 'rehearsing in her underclothes' to use an Italian stage expression. The Signora watches her with a grim expression on her face and says nothing.

Signorina Zucchini continues with her *cantilena*, self-absorbed and impassive.

The Signora intervenes: 'Signorina, are you rehearsing for your own benefit, or for mine?'

The young actress looks dismayed and is silent. Whereupon the Signora, suddenly roused, exclaims: 'Put some life into it, Signorina! You are like marble! Put some life into it. Put some soul into it, for Heaven's sake!'

This exclamation is beautifully phrased – an exclamation worthy of Eleonora Duse's exquisitely modulated voice. La Zucchini begins to recite her part once more, unfortunately in the same dull fashion. This exasperates the Signora, who jumps to her feet. Shaking with rage, she upbraids the little actress with a torrent of abuse.

Among other bitter accusations, she rails: 'Perhaps you have been deceived into believing that you are a fine actress. Nothing could be further from the truth, Signorina, so get the idea out of your head. Your acting is hopeless! Pitiful! You are nothing better than a pretty child (and even that is questionable) who cannot act any part she is given. Get this sad fact into your head and start studying. If I am obliged to study, then you can study too. The other evening in Vienna, your disastrous performance caused me to break out in a cold sweat, and you completely ignored my pleas for more life. Hopeless! As dense as stone! You are heartless! Totally insensitive.'

Now La Zucchini mutters: 'That is not true, Signora.' And she bursts into a flood of tears. The Signora replies: 'Go on, cry, cry! It will do you some good. Tears wash away a great many sorrows.'

Then when the girl continues to sob, she sternly adds: 'That's enough now! A little weep can be interesting but too much is irritating.' But since the Signorina remains inconsolable, the rehearsal is postponed until the next day.

In taking her leave, the Signora says to La Rossi pointing to La Zucchini: 'Try to calm her down. Take her for a nice walk. It is such a lovely day!'

Florence, 2 December 1906

A rehearsal in the theatre with sets, furniture and lighting for *La Gioconda*. The Signora finds furniture for the first two acts quite distasteful. She says over and over again: 'No, no, that simply won't do. It is horrendous. Everything must be changed!' Even the drapes for the third act are altered. Initially, she requests lots of statues; then these are nearly all eliminated. The tapestries too must be changed.

The property man, Luigi Bergonzio, trying to excuse himself, explains: 'But, Signora, this is the same scenery we used last time!' This is enough to enrage her: 'How dare you speak to me about the last time! That is a *cowardly* explanation that I refuse to accept!'

As God decrees, the drapes too are changed. Now everything is in order. Just as well. In the fourth act, the lighting for the back-cloth strikes her as being inadequate. She exclaims: 'It is far too dark, far too dark!' She could be right! But it looks all right to me.

I try to get her to agree and, little by little, I succeed. The rehearsal ends there, and we go off to get some sleep.

Florence, 3 December 1906

This morning an urgent summons to the Grand Hotel. The Signora hands me some drapes in old brocade and some magnificently bound books that are to be used for this evening's performance. At the theatre, I find the most exquisite pieces of furniture, chosen by the Signora herself from an antique dealer. Later on, the performance is given before an enthusiastic audience. The theatre is full. The Signora is extremely nervous. The furnishings, as usual, are modified at the last minute. The speed with which La Duse makes decisions only to change her mind is quite perplexing.

Throughout the entire evening, the expression on her face is one of great tension. Everything in her behaviour betrays her disquiet, anxiety, fever. She acts extremely well, but not consistently with the same brilliance. It is clear that this evening's performance is marred by her nervous state. In the scene in Act III with Gioconda, she loses control, but in the final act with Sirenetta, she is truly divine! Leo Orlandini (in the part of Lucio Settala) is frankly disappointing. The narration at Act II could hardly be declaimed more poorly, but the audience applauds. And once the audience is satisfied, everyone is satisfied. After all, is the theatre-going public not perhaps one *Great Ignoramus?* Although not entirely suited to the role, Elisa Berti Masi has played the part of Gioconda with a certain charm. This evening La Zucchini, in the role of Sirenetta, scales some miraculous heights. After the performance, as the Signora is leaving the theatre, she meets the young actress and embraces her, saying: 'Brava, well done!' Perhaps in order to make up for the harsh reproaches of the other day.

218(b) Duse in *La Gioconda*

A scene from Gabriele D'Annunzio's *La Gioconda*, with La Duse in the main part.
Biblioteca Teatrale Burcardo, Rome. Photo: Oscar Savio

V   The teatri stabili *and reform*

Duse was not the only player and manager of the time who wished to effect a reform of the theatre. Attempts of varying importance and significance were made by others in these years, aimed at correcting the worst defects of the itinerant and 'star' management system. One such actor-manager was Francesco Garzes, whose lavishness on productions was exceptional, encouraged as it was by the designer, Antonio Rovescalli, as well as by the acclaim his productions received.[1] Among other attempts to combat the essentially itinerant nature of Italian theatre, was that of another famous actor-manager Ermete Novelli, who founded the *Casa di Goldoni* in 1900 at the Valli Theatre in Rome.[2] This should have been 'the first stone of a permanent national theatre', but the undertaking lasted for only two years.

More culturally demanding than Novelli, and inspired by a more profound sense of the need to reform the Italian theatre, was the actor-manager Virgilio Talli.[3] His work marks the beginnings of the modern director in Italy, and he is perhaps the only figure in the period who can stand comparison with Duse. Like her, he understood the novelty of D'Annunzio's ideas and was responsible for the first staging of that dramatist's *La figlia di Jorio* (Jorio's Daughter) in 1904, a production enthusiastically acclaimed for its lavishness, precision of detail and unity of conception. In the choice of his repertory between 1900 and 1918, Talli showed himself well aware of the best that had been written in Italy and abroad, and his productions were throughout carefully orchestrated. He was one of the first seriously to challenge the tradition of the *'figli d'arte'* that was so closely linked to the 'star' system.

However, it was not so much actors and actor-managers as critics and authors who promoted the three main attempts at theatrical reform between the end of the century and the outbreak of the First World War: the creation of permanent theatre companies in Turin, Rome and Milan. The most ardent supporter of the permanent company was the Roman critic Edoardo Boutet, who argued, in his *Cronache drammatiche* and *Cronache teatrali*, for the establishment of permanent companies, under the overall control of an artistic director who would determine choice of repertory, hiring of actors, casting and interpretation of the plays. The inadequacies of the traditional stage he sought to banish included the excesses of 'star' actors and their arbitrary *'soggetti'*,[4] the domination of commercial rather than artistic considerations in the choice of plays, and the general lack of respect for theatre audiences evident in the excessive length of intervals and the inadequate discipline of the performers.

The first practical initiative in the direction of reform took place not in Rome, but in Turin, in 1898, with the inauguration of the Teatro d'Arte di Torino, under the direction of the critic Domenico Lanza. The Teatro d'Arte charged moderate entrance prices, seeking to attract a large and socially rather heterogeneous audience to its culturally ambitious repertory of Italian and foreign classics and the best work of the naturalistic playwrights. At first the venture enjoyed considerable success, but it survived only a year, brought to an end by internal disputes and financial difficulties caused largely by erratic public support.

Late in 1905, on the initiative of the Society of Authors in Rome, and with financial support from various bodies, the Drammatica Compagnia di Roma was founded, based at the Teatro Argentina, with Edoardo Boutet as its Artistic Director. Like the Teatro d'Arte of Turin, it was an ensemble company with few famous names. Unlike the Teatro d'Arte, however, the Drammatica Compagnia di Roma was socially and politically committed, at least initially, producing, for example, the work of Hauptmann, Sudermann and Hervieu. This repertory was very much the initiative of Boutet. After a year, however, the artistic direction of the company was put in the hands of the actor Ferruccio Garavaglia.[5] The first period of the Compagnia from 1905 to 1908, was notable for the high quality of its plays and presentation, and its reputation was such that it helped to convert many spectators and critics to the idea of a permanent repertory company. In 1908, however, first Boutet, and then Garavaglia departed, a going all the more unfortunate in the case of Garavaglia in that only a few months before he left he had obtained great success with D'Annunzio's *La nave* (The Ship, 1908), the most spectacular production of a play that had been seen in Italy for many years. From 1908 to 1917 the Compagnia Drammatica survived under a number of directors, but after the Teatro Argentina was taken over by Virgilio Talli's company in 1918 the Compagnia continued only in a semi-permanent way until it disbanded in 1921.

In Milan, meanwhile, the author, critic and dramatist Marco Praga[6] had formed in 1912, with the financial support of Count Giuseppe Visconti di Modrone, the Compagnia Stabile del Teatro Manzoni. Praga invited the well-established actor-manager company, Falconi–Di Lorenzo,[7] to play there. Unfortunately, the lead actor and actress gradually became dissatisfied with Praga's aims, while Praga himself compromised more and more on the matter of repertory. In 1914 Falconi and Di Lorenzo broke with Praga who hired a new company that included the actress Irma Gramatica. This played with moderate success until February 1917, when Count Visconti withdrew his financial support and Praga himself resigned the artistic directorship.

In addition to the phenomenon of the *teatri stabili* there was that of the 'minimal' or 'sectional' theatre companies, founded mainly between 1910 and 1913. These were small companies, directed for the most part by dramatists, which contributed productions of mainly one-act plays to the programmes of mixed spectacle offered by some theatres. These *teatri minimi* had experimental and avant-garde ambitions and their utility, as well as their novelty, lay in the fact that they took drama to an audience less affluent, and supposedly less sophisticated than that catered for by the *stabili*. Again Rome, Turin and Milan are the cities where the *minimi* mainly developed. In Rome, the dramatist Nino Martoglio founded such a company to perform in the Teatro Metastasio in 1910–11 with a repertory of Italian and foreign one- or two-act plays.[8] Martoglio staged, among other pieces, *La giara* (The Jar) and *Lumie di Sicilia* (Sicilian Limes), the one-act plays with which Pirandello, already an established novelist, entered the theatrical field. Other 'minimal' theatre companies worth mentioning are Teatro Trianon, Turin, under the dramatist Gerolamo Nani; Teatro Stabilini, Milan; Quattro Fontane, directed by the actor Cesare Dondini; and Teatro per Tutti, at the Sala Umberto, under the direction of the dramatist and critic Lucio D'Ambra, Rome, 1912–13.

In no real respect, however, can any of these ventures, *stabili* or *minimi*, be seen as comparable to the repertory theatres led by directors which had been established by this time in France, England, Germany and elsewhere.

[1] Francesco Garzes (1848–94) was an actor-manager, journalist and dramatist influenced by the Meiningen company.

[2] Ermete Novelli (1851–1919) made his first significant mark after entering the Bellotti Bon company in 1877 to play in the role of *promiscuo* (all-round actor) and *brillante* (comic actor).

[3] For detailed accounts of the *teatri stabili* and *minimi*, see A. Camilleri, *I teatri stabili in Italia 1898–1918* (Bologna, 1959), Federico Doglio, *Il teatro in Italia* (Rome 1976), to both of which I am indebted here. Virgilio Talli (1858–1928) was an Italian actor, company manager and stage-director, who worked with most of the leading players of his day and was particularly vigorous in staging modern drama.

[4] '*soggetti*': ad lib insertions by actors and actresses.

[5] Ferrucio Garavaglia (1870–1912) was an Italian actor and company manager.

[6] Marco Praga (1862–1929) was an Italian dramatist and critic. Although few of his comedies and social dramas are now performed, he enjoyed a considerable reputation in his day, and as theatre critic for *Illustrazione Italiana* throughout the 1920s exercised great influence. While director of the Compagnia del Teatro Manzoni he staged Pirandello's *La ragione degli altri* (Other People's Reason), 1915.

[7] Armando Falconi (1871–1954) was an Italian comic and character actor, who managed his own company (1905–12) with his actress wife, Tina Di Lorenzo (1872–1930).

[8] Nino Martoglio (1870–1921) was a Sicilian dramatist.

219   A scene from D'Annunzio's most successful verse play, *La figlia di Jorio* (1904), directed by Virgilio Talli

Biblioteca Teatrale Burcardo, Rome. Photo: Oscar Savio

220   Aborted attempt at creating a national theatre: La Casa di Goldoni, Rome, 1899–1901

G. Costetti,[1] *Il teatro Italiano nel 1800* (Rocca San Casciano, 1901; reprinted Bologna, 1978), pp. 453–6

Two years ago [1899], during a banquet given in Rome for Ermete Novelli,[2] the eminent actor rose and announced his intention of founding at the Teatro Valli, La Casa di Goldoni[3] [an equivalent of] the glorious Maison de Molière. [...]

However, Rhetoric, that elf of words, had prompted Novelli to promise things which could not be realized. Three similar attempts recently made in Italy, unfortunately, came to nothing. First, La Compagnia Nazionale,[4] that included an outstanding list of players, a director like Paolo Ferrari, and a theatre especially built for the purpose – millions were spent on it, but it failed. Second, Cesare Rossi, who hired the Carignano Theatre at a modest rent and for six months kept a magnificent company there, a company that included as lead actress La Duse, as leading man, Flavio Andò, as *brillante*, Claudio Leigheb, as well as Rossi himself, a born artist and an expert actor-manager. Further, competitions at the Carignano offered prizes for the most successful plays. But two years later, the Turin council exacted a rent that took all the theatre's profits; the action was more than enough to ensure disaster. So that experiment failed too.[5] Third, Francesco Garzes, the favourite pupil of Bellotti Bon, a good actor, a fair dramatist, a gentle soul and a daring spirit, one ever ready to start worthy ventures, brought together an excellent company with La Mariani as lead actress, Virginia Marini as *madre nobile*, and three men, Paladini, Belli Blanes and Reinach. He had new scenery, no prompter, real props, antique furniture, new styles of lighting and the best plays Italian authors could provide. Even this experiment failed and, like Bellotti Bon, Francesco Garzes shot himself in an inn at Chioggia.[6]

The Maison de Molière, i.e. the Comédie-Française, is a very complex, centuries-old institution. It has its own assets, an annual grant, a pension fund, permanent as well as temporary artistic staff, a repertory, an archive, etc. La Casa di Goldoni . . . [founded] at the Valle Theatre on the evening of 3 November 1900, has none of these things, neither assets nor grant unfortunately and, as it is not a legally recognized and approved body, it cannot even take advantage of the insurance fund for dramatic artists which is flourishing. La Casa di Goldoni does have an artistic complement, namely the Novelli Company, which is organized in such a way as to give its very talented actor-manager all the limelight. The company has perhaps expanded in numbers, but it has not been strengthened in its lead roles. Novelli might at least have prepared the repertory before he came to Rome, but clearly he did not even do that as he needed, for example, several days of intensive rehearsals to stage Ferrari's two plays, *Goldoni* and *Parini*.[7] So the attractions of La Casa di Goldoni consist in the establishment backstage of a greenroom for the artists, in the adaptation of two small rooms at the third tier of boxes for smokers, in the elimination of the prompt-box,[8] the footlights, the orchestra and the wings, and in the masking of the electric lights above the boxes. Soft and luxurious rugs and carpets deaden footsteps everywhere in the auditorium, the corridors and the rooms.

Light is evenly distributed on the stage in a realistic way, the scenes are most beautiful, with solid walls for interiors and spacious wingless vistas for wood and road scenes. Furniture and props are expensive and in good taste, there is fine ensemble playing and excellent delivery – an atmosphere of refined art carries from the stage to the auditorium and from the auditorium to the stage. All this is splendid, indeed very splendid. . . but it is not La Casa di Goldoni. It is the Company of Ermete Novelli, or better, it is Ermete Novelli who, for a few months, is giving in Rome productions as only he can give them, but as he has given them before, only then they were given with the orchestra and prompt-box, and without the greenroom and the smoking-rooms. [. . .]

But suddenly now, while attendance remained good even given the high cost of tickets, it seems to Novelli that... the audience is not adequately responding to a project Novelli himself could not, or did not, wish actually to realize.

The great artist picks up the pieces, and instead of producing *Il ricco insidiato* (The Harrassed Rich Man), *Il ventaglio* (The Fan), *Il medico olandese* (The Dutch Doctor) and similar bright jewels by Goldoni, the landlord of the theatre, he reintroduces, at first timidly, then without restraint, those *pochades* [see **197**, note 3], which when the Valli Theatre became La Casa di Goldoni ought certainly to have been banished.[9]

We understand that the audience appreciates these changes in the programme and is rushing to see *Il sistema Ribaudier* (The Ribaudier System) and *Mia moglie non ha chic* (My Wife Has No Style). If I said I was happy, my readers would know I was lying. I will say instead that the audience, no less than Novelli, has decided the matter, because there has never been any question of having La Casa di Goldoni; what we have is a long series of performances given by Novelli and his company, and justly appreciated by the audience. Nothing more and nothing less.

[1] See **201**, note 1.
[2] For Novelli, see p. 463, note 2.
[3] Carlo Goldoni (1707–93) is, with Pirandello, the most famous and the most frequently performed of Italian dramatists. Most of his best work was written in the 1750s and the early 1760s for the Venetian theatres, including *La locandiera* (The Mistress of the Inn), *I rusteghi* (The Boors) and *Le baruffe chiozzotte* (The Chioggian Squabbles). In 1763 he left Venice and the rest of his working career was with the Théâtre-Italien in Paris.
[4] The Compagnia Nazionale Romana was directed by the dramatist Paolo Ferrari (1822–89) and operated in Rome in 1886–7. It was sponsored by a group of Roman aristocrats.
[5] Rossi's Company, the Compagnia della Città di Torino, operated from 1877 to 1885.
[6] For Garzes, see p. 463, note 1.
[7] The full titles of these are *Goldoni e le sue sedici commedie nuove* (Goldoni and His Sixteen New Comedies, 1853) and *La Satira e Parini* (Parini and Satire, 1856). They were Ferrari's best plays, and are still occasionally performed.
[8] In a footnote, Costetti adds that the prompt-box reappeared after a few performances.
[9] Novelli blamed critical hostility and audience apathy for his accumulation of a deficit of 200,000 lire, and he maintained that he had to include comedies and popular farces in the programme in a desperate attempt to reduce it (see E. Novelli, *Foglietti sparsi narranti la mia vita*, Rome, 1919).

221   Marco Praga extols the virtues of the *teatro stabile*, Milan, 1912

M. Praga, *Compagnia Drammatica Italiana del Teatro Manzoni di Milano* (Milan, 1912), pp. 5–17

The purpose is to establish in Italy the bases for true and proper *teatri stabili* in those main cities which have sufficiently large and affluent populations and a demonstrable interest in the 'prose' theatre,[1] and are thus in a position to give birth to such enterprises. [...]

For many years I have wanted to attempt this experiment in Milan, which has always shown such a keen interest in the theatre. But it would have been pointless to ask the state or the municipality for subsidies. Attempts made elsewhere have firmly convinced me that such enterprises cannot depend on patronage: the patron invariably either quickly tires of his role, or, in return for his money, wants to interfere in the venture in ways which are usually neither helpful nor sensible. I have therefore come to believe that the foundation of a *teatro stabile* in Italy, or at least of the first *teatro stabile*, can only be the work of a private individual who is an expert in the art – a company manager, be he actor or dramatist, or any other person, provided he has the experience and possesses the necessary knowledge, and has the money essential for the enterprise and the courage to take risks. [...]

Tina di Lorenzo, [...] with the very warm and cordial support of Armando Falconi, wished to accept my offer and make my plan her own. Thus we decided to form the Compagnia Drammatica Italiana del Teatro Manzoni di Milano. Nor was this name chosen by chance. It indicates that the intentions which guided us marked [...] the beginning of a venture founded on criteria different from those which have governed similar undertakings. It will also be managed in ways not tried elsewhere. [...]

A *teatro stabile*, or a theatre run according to criteria and methods made possible by stability, permits [...] a long, patient, careful preparation of each production. With us the period usually allowed for the actors to get to know each other (the *affiatamento*) – in other words the period given over to rehearsing the company's first shows – will be much longer than is customary. Our actors are obliged to learn each of their parts by heart so that they can act without a prompter. For every serious drama, and every comedy, there will be as many rehearsals as necessary: because it is not enough for the interpreters to have learned their parts; they must know the parts in context. [...]

Therefore we shall not put any work before the audience, even at the cost of keeping the theatre dark on some nights, unless that work has been fully rehearsed. Every dramatist who entrusts us with the production of his play can be sure of twenty or thirty rehearsals, or as many as he himself judges necessary. Nor will these be rehearsals without scenery, furniture and props. [...] they will be full dress-rehearsals, with lighting, as well as with the players in costume and make-up, and thus will give him a clear and concrete view of his work before it faces the judgement of an audience. [...]

I shall say quite simply then that as far as stage-preparation is concerned, we shall always insist on these three essentials of a good *mise en scène:* variety, suitability and solidity. We have adopted a new system of stage-design, devised by the talented and experienced artist Sig. Pietro Spiga, by means of which walls, doors, stairs and every 'prop' have the appearance of being real, and possess a genuine solidity. We have abolished paper scenery, which shakes, shows fold marks, can be torn by the slightest knock, and shows the pin marks where it has been fixed to rickety frames. [...] We have abolished everything that looked false, papier mâché, mere theatre – in short, itinerant theatre, which is ever plagued by the problem that it has to be transported here and there by train, and so has to weigh little and occupy small space. We have banished the old furniture – always the same – borrowed from a second-hand dealer. In short, we have taken as our models the *teatri stabili* of foreign capitals, and as far as stage-setting goes we have turned, and will always turn, to those who are expert in the wholly modern art of interior decoration. We hope to offer the audience an almost perfect illusion of reality. [...]

As far as outdoor scenes (gardens, town squares, beaches, vistas) are concerned, it is impossible to reproduce reality, especially in a small theatre. However, it is possible to give the spectator a pleasant illusion and to avoid offending his eye. But for this the art of the painter is insufficient and one must adopt the latest inventions of theatre technology, like the flies (*capote*) and the cyclorama (*panorama*). We have adopted them, and have placed their execution in the hands of Spiga who has devised a very practical system of his own – and we have entrusted the pictorial side to Rovescalli.[2] [...]

Finally, I must point out that our entire 'prop' and scenic wardrobe will travel with us everywhere, and that our company will perform in various Italian cities with the same scenes, furniture and 'props' with which it will play in Milan.

---

[1] The term '*teatro di prosa*' is used in Italian to distinguish the theatre performing plays from other kinds like the musical theatre (*teatro lirico, teatro di rivista*) and the variety theatre (*teatro di varietà*).

[2] Odoardo Antonio Rovescalli (1864–1936) was a distinguished scene-designer who worked with Duse on the staging of several of D'Annunzio's plays in his early years in the theatre.

VI   *The futurist theatre movement*

The theatre of the futurists was above all a theatre of uncompromising opposition. It stood in opposition to *verismo*, to romantic D'Annunzian theatre, dialect theatre, translated foreign drama, to the *teatri stabili* and to the theatre of the actor-managers; it was equally opposed to traditional scenography and performance, to all current and accepted dramatists and critics, and to the bourgeois audience. Initially the futurist theatre was nothing if not iconoclastic. Its most original theatre manifestos appeared between 1911 and 1916, and they preached not so much reform as a global revolution in theatrical content and means.

The futurist movement was launched by the poet and dramatist F.T. Marinetti[1] in the manifesto he published in *Le Figaro*, 20 February 1909. It attracted not only poets, but painters, sculptors, composers, architects and designers among whom the most celebrated were the sculptor Giacomo Balla, the painter Umberto Boccioni and the composer Luigi Russolo. Futurism advocated the collaboration of all the arts in a synthesis that sought to transform not just art, but life itself. Up to the mid-1930s innumerable manifestos advanced futurist proposals for such a transformation.

The futurist attack was directed at content, which it sought to undermine by use of caricature, parody, ridicule, irony, sarcasm, paradox and grotesque distortion, sparing neither individuals nor institutions. It rejected all traditional dramatic forms, whether comedy, tragedy, historical drama, vaudeville or farce, in favour of a concept of theatre rooted less in verbal structures than in gesture and movement. The futurists sought a dynamic rather than a static theatre in which speed, fragmentation, surprise and simultaneity were the distinctive qualities. Inspired by contemporary experimental fine art, ballet, cinematic techniques and modern technology in general, the futurists tried to advance a new theatrical aesthetic, revolutionary in its use of space and time, in which the actor, rejecting psychological identification and impersonation, employed his physical skills (*fisicofollia* and not *psicologia*) to the point where he became an object in space. They rejected the scenography of naturalistic reconstruction in favour of a more subjective scenography that saw the spectator not as a mere passive onlooker, but as participator and collaborator.

Futurist ideas were widely publicized in the celebrated futurist evenings (*serate*) held in many Italian cities. But they had little success, save for a certain *succès de scandale*, and for the most part audiences received them with incomprehension and hostility. The limitations of the movement cannot wholly be ascribed to the bewilderment of critics and spectators, and the opposition of the established theatre. When the futurists later toured Italian cities with presentations of their synthetic theatre their performance practice was so deficient, organizationally and technically, that their theory seemed more extravagantly frivolous than seriously innovative. Their example, however, was not completely lost on the Italian theatre between the World Wars: it produced some fruit in the 1920s in the Teatro degli Indipendenti of Anton Giulio Bragaglia, whose work encouraged theatrical experimentation and advanced the role of the director in the Italian theatre.[2]

Later, after the experience of the so-called absurdist theatre, the work of the futurists received fresh attention and it has exercised some influence on the development of theatrical theatre in the past two decades.

[1] Filippo Tommaso Marinetti (1876–1944), poet and dramatist. His first play, *Le Roi Bombance*, was staged by Lugné-Poe at the Théâtre de l'Œuvre in Paris, on 3 April 1909.
[2] Anton Giulio Bragaglia (1890–1960), theatre and film director. His most important stage-work was done at the Teatro Sperimentale degli Indipendenti between the wars; see A. C. Alberti, S. Bevere and P. Di Giulio, *Il Teatro Sperimentale degli Indipendenti (1923–1936)* (Rome, 1984).

222   The pleasure of being booed, 1911

First published in January 1911 as '*Manifesto dei drammaturghi futuristi*' (Manifesto of the Futurist Dramatists). Reprinted, with variations, as '*La voluttà d'esser fischiati*' (The pleasure of being booed), in *Guerra sola igiene del mondo* (War, the world's only hygiene), Milan, 1915. In R. W. Flint, ed., *Marinetti, Selected Writings* (London, 1972), pp. 113–15

Among all literary forms, the one that can serve futurism most effectively is certainly the theatre. Therefore we do not want the dramatic art to continue to be what it is today: a mean industrial product subject to the market for cheap popular amusements. We must sweep away all the dirty prejudices that crush authors, actors and the public.

1. We futurists, above all, teach authors to *despise the audience*[1] and especially to despise first-night audiences, whose psychology we can synthesize as follows: rivalry of coiffures and toilettes – vanity of the expensive seat, which transmutes itself into intellectual pride – boxes and orchestra seats occupied by rich mature men with naturally contemptuous brains and very poor digestions, which make any effort of mind impossible.

The audience, varying from month to month, from city to city and from quarter to quarter, subject to political and social events, to whims of fashion, to deluges of rain, excesses of heat or cold, to the last article read in the afternoon, having to its disgrace no other desire but a peaceful digestion at the theatre, can judge, approve or disapprove nothing in a work of art. [...]

2. We especially teach a *horror of the immediate success* that normally crowns dull and mediocre works. The theatre pieces that immediately take hold of each member of the audience, with no intermediaries or explanations, are more or less well-made works that lack any novelty or creative intelligence.

3. Authors should have no preoccupation except *an absolute innovative originality*. All dramatic works built on a cliché or that borrow their conception, plot or a part of their development from other works of art are wholly contemptible.

4. The *leitmotivs* of *amore* and the adulterous triangle, by now overworked, should be entirely banned from the theatre.

Amore and the adulterous triangle on the stage should be reduced to a minor role, accessory and episodic, to the same importance they now have in life itself, thanks to the great achievement of the futurists.

5. Since dramatic art, like every art, can have no other purpose than to force the soul of the audience away from base everyday reality and to lift it into a blinding atmosphere of intellectual intoxication, we despise all those works that merely want to make people weep or to move them, by means of the always pitiful spectacle of a mother whose child has died, or of a girl who cannot marry her lover, or other such insipidities...

6. We *despise* in art, and especially in the theatre, *every kind of historical reconstruction*, no matter whether it takes its interest from a famous hero or famous heroine (Nero, Julius Caesar, Napoleon or Francesca da Rimini), or whether it is founded on the appeal of pointlessly sumptuous costumes and scenery.

The modern drama should reflect some part of the great futurist dream that rises from our daily lives, stimulated by terrestrial, marine, and aerial velocities, dominated by steam and electricity. One must introduce into the theatre the sensation of the Machine's dominion, the great shudders that move the crowd, new currents of ideas, and the great discoveries of science that have completely transformed our sensibility and our mentality as men of the twentieth century.

7. The dramatic art ought not to concern itself with psychological photography, but rather to move toward *a synthesis of life in its most significant lines* ...

8. Dramatic art without poetry cannot exist, that is without intoxication and without synthesis.

Regular prosodic forms should be excluded. The futurist writer in the theatre will therefore employ *free verse*, a mobile orchestration of images and sounds that, passing from the simplest tone, when for example a servant must enter or a door must be closed, can slowly rise to the rhythm of the passions, in strophes by turn cadenced or chaotic, to the moment when victory of a people or the glorious death of an aviator must be announced.

9. One must destroy the obsession for money among writers, because greed for gain has pushed into the theatre writers gifted with the mere qualities of a critic or worldly journalist.

10. We want to subordinate the actors completely to the authority of writers, to free them from domination by the audience, a force that fatally moves them to

search for easy effects and estranges them from any effort towards interpretation in depth. For this reason we must abolish the grotesque habit of clapping and whistling, a good enough barometer of parliamentary eloquence but certainly not of artistic worth.

11. While waiting for this abolition, we teach authors and actors *the pleasure of being booed*.

Not everything booed is beautiful or new. But everything applauded immediately is certainly no better than the average intelligence and is therefore *something mediocre, dull, regurgitated or too-well digested*.

---

¹ Marinetti means the affluent bourgeois audience. The futurists looked favourably on popular audiences, particularly in variety theatre. Audience involvement became a basic tenet of the movement.

223   Marinetti's variety theatre, 1913

First published in *Lacerba*, October 1913; in English in London's *Daily Mail*, 21 November 1913 as 'The Means of the Music Hall' Reprinted in Gordon Craig's *The Mask*, January 1914. In Flint, ed., *Marinetti, Selected Writings*, pp. 116–21

Futurism exalts the Variety Theatre because:

1. The Variety Theatre, born as we are from electricity, is lucky in having no tradition, no masters, no dogma, and it is fed by swift actuality.¹

2. The Variety Theatre is absolutely practical, because it proposes to distract and amuse the public with comic effects, erotic stimulation, or imaginative astonishment.

3. The authors, actors, and technicians of the Variety Theatre have only one reason for existing and triumphing: incessantly to invent new elements of astonishment.² Hence the absolute impossibility of arresting or repeating oneself, hence an excited competition of brains and muscles to conquer the various records of agility, speed, force, complication, and elegance.

4. The Variety Theatre is unique today in its use of the cinema, which enriches it with an incalculable number of visions and otherwise unrealizable spectacles (battles, riots, horse races, automobile and airplane meets, trips, voyages, depths of the city, the countryside, oceans, and skies).³

5. The Variety Theatre, being a profitable showcase for countless inventive forces, naturally generates what I call 'the Futurist marvellous', produced by modern mechanics. Here are some of the elements of this 'marvellous': (a) powerful caricatures; (b) abysses of the ridiculous; (c) delicious, impalpable ironies; (d) all-embracing, definitive symbols; (e) cascades of uncontrollable hilarity; (f) profound analogies between humanity, the animal, vegetable, and mechanical worlds; (g) flashes of revealing cynicism; (h) plots full of the wit, repartee, and conundrums

that aerate the intelligence; (i) the whole gamut of laughter and smiles, to flex the nerves; (j) the whole gamut of stupidity, imbecility, doltishness, and absurdity, insensibly pushing the intelligence to the very border of madness; (k) all the new significations of light, sound, noise and language with their mysterious and inexplicable extensions into the least-explored part of our sensibility; (l) a cumulus of events unfolded at great speed, of stage characters pushed from right to left in two minutes ('and now let's have a look at the Balkans': King Nicholas, Enver-Bey, Daneff, Venizelos, belly-blows and fistfights between Serbs and Bulgars, a *couplet*, and everything vanishes);[4] (m) instructive, satirical pantomimes; (n) caricatures of suffering and nostalgia, strongly impressed on the sensibility through gestures exasperating in their spasmodic, hesitant, weary slowness; grave words made ridiculous by funny gestures, bizarre disguises, mutilated words, ugly faces, pratfalls.

6. Today the Variety Theatre is the crucible in which the elements of an emergent new sensibility are seething. Here you find an ironic decomposition of all the worn-out prototypes of the Beautiful, the Grand, the Solemn, the Religious, the Ferocious, the Seductive, and the Terrifying, and also the abstract elaboration of the new prototypes that will succeed these.

[1] The variety theatre was eminently popular, because of its lack of pretentiousness, the immediacy of its impact, and its strong links with the tradition of dialect theatre. Its main centres were Rome and Naples, but it was implanted in most Italian cities.

[2] In 1921 Marinetti and Cangiullo published a development of this idea in their manifesto 'Il teatro della sorpresa'.

[3] The futurists were among the first to realize cinema's potential as an artistic and popular art-form (see the *Futurist Cinema* manifesto, 1916). In 1926 Marinetti wrote *La cinematografia astratta è un'invenzione italiana*, whose nationalism pleased Mussolini.

[4] These are references to political figures and events in the Balkans. See also Marinetti's novel *Zang Zang Tumb Tumb* (1914) on the Balkan war.

224   'Balance sheet' of the synthetic theatre, 1919

Emilio Settimelli,[1] *Inchiesta sulla vita italiana* (Cappelli, 1919), pp. 137–9

We have given this synthetic theatre in all the main Italian cities except Turin, where the prefects prohibited it, as well as in many of the less important towns. It has engaged the attention of the whole Italian press, has inspired hundreds of imitators among the young and the very young, has caught the interest of the whole European and American press, and has recently, too, been produced in an aristocratic hall on the Champs-Elysées in Paris. In my opinion it is the only attempt at reform made to some effect in the last hundred years.

In fact it has attempted to open up the theatre to a thousand other artistic possibilities by advocating among other things the eruption of all the arts on to the stage, and by raising the hope that theatre might become the most modern and comprehensive of the arts. It has attempted, by means of free publicity, seeking wide acceptance by young people, and imposing itself by means of money on the thick skulls of impresarios, to offer the beginnings of an artistic revolution against those who stifle the theatre. This revolution we shall put into practice as soon as possible, by powerful means and with decisive results.

From a purely artistic point of view the synthetic theatre attempted above all to offer a theatre matching our speed-mad, multifaceted modern soul ...

We reached the point where we could perform fifteen works in a single evening.

There was a mime synthesis, a lyrical synthesis, a highly dramatic synthesis, a synthesis à *Calembour*.

The purpose was, through variety and speed, to place the spectator at the centre of life. He had to be given a total impression of life: its poetry, mystery, drama, smell, strangeness, oddities, witty agility, goodness, brutality, monotony, might, sun, calmness, storm.

What of its defects? As I am speaking frankly here of our strengths, I cannot in truth dodge out of saying something about our weaknesses.

1. Lack of means adequate to such an enormous and important reform.
2. Too much waste of energy, as we took on too many reforms simultaneously.
3. Inadequacy in interpretation.

The lack of adequate means prevented us from giving a more robust structure to our undertaking.

We should have had a company and a theatre of our own.

In particular, not having a purpose-built theatre damaged us a great deal, for this considerably reduced the efficacy of our syntheses.

On occasions it happened that the synthesis lasted a mere three minutes, while the interval between it and the next synthesis was as much as a quarter of an hour.

This tended to generate boredom and impatience in the audience, and a hostile mood was carried over in attitudes to the next synthesis.

Therefore in order to ensure that the number of plays offered in a single spectacle is very large, and the performances of the various points follow each other after an interval of no more than two or three minutes, a revolving stage would be needed. In this way the boredom of waiting would be avoided and the audience, variously and rapidly impressed by the most diverse sensations, would have the illusion of supposing itself to be at the centre of life, and of receiving from every side its vibrations.

A specialized company, too, would have helped to ensure success, for often our syntheses have very striking roles which call for exceptional actors.

But everything, as can be seen, comes back to the lack of money.

Is this actually a fault? There are patrons, there are funds. But nearly always just for vile and imbecilic things.

For the innovators, the courageous, there is not so much as a penny.

But when we have achieved anything it has been by paying, paying, paying.[2]

---

[1] Emilio Settimelli, primarily a journalist, wrote a number of dramatic syntheses, and was keenly interested in the practical application of futurist ideas to theatre (see Remo Chiti, 'I creatori del teatro futurista: Marinetti – Corradini – Settimelli', in M. Verdone, *Teatro italiano d'avanguardia* (Rome, 1970), pp. 35–41).

[2] For an account of the productions and their critical reception see Antonucci, *Cronache del teatro futurista* (Rome, 1975.)

Iberian Peninsula, 1884–1913

Edited and translated by DAVID GEORGE

To the memory of Xavier Fàbregas

Introduction

The Iberian Peninsula comprises two countries, Spain and Portugal, but within Spain there are several distinct language groups, together with their own cultures and literatures. The dominant one is Castilian or *castellano*, more usually known as Spanish. This language is spoken all over Spain as well as Latin America. The other major languages of Spain are Galician, which is close to Portuguese, Catalan (like Galician and Castilian Spanish, a Romance language) and Basque, which is unlike any other Indo-European language. The most important theatrical cultures of the nineteenth and twentieth centuries are those of Castilian Spanish, Portuguese and Catalan, and it is with these three that this introduction and documentary study are concerned.

A common characteristic of the drama written in the Castilian, Catalan and Portuguese languages during much of the second half of the nineteenth century is the continuation of Romanticism, in spite of the efforts of individuals or groups to modernize and renovate the theatre. Another common feature is the general critical agreement (whether by contemporary writers or by critics to the present day) about the poor quality of much of the drama written between 1850 and the 1890s when, at long last, and in however tentative a manner, innovations that had profoundly changed the theatre of other European countries began to make some impression on the Iberian Peninsula. Despite this common characteristic, there are important differences between the theatrical traditions of the three languages, which often reflect social and cultural conditions within the country or regions where these languages are spoken.

Mediocrity was the keynote of drama written in Castilian Spanish between 1850 and the last decade of the century. Criticism of the quality of the drama was widespread in the 1890s, and little of note was written in Castilian in the post-Romantic period. The public could choose between pseudo-Romantic drama – typified by the use of historical material and uncontrolled language – and pseudo-realist plays: neither of these two groups has stood the test of time.

Two of the better dramatists of the period were Adelardo López de Ayala and Manuel Tamayo y Baus, who at least tried to present on stage a psychological study of human passions. To quote D. L. Shaw, 'when all has been said in their disfavour, it should be recalled that no such attempt at renovation was even begun in Britain until the time of Robertson and Pinero years later'.[1] Neither López de Ayala (1828–72) nor Tamayo y Baus

---

[1] D. L. Shaw, *A Literary History of Spain: The Nineteenth Century* (London: Ernest Benn, 1972), p. 80.

(1829–98), however, succeeded in giving new life to the Castilian theatre, and they were not able to bring about a break with Romantic tradition.

The nineteenth century saw a revival of Catalan culture and literature, which had been declining severely for several centuries: this movement is known as the *Renaixença*. There was a revival of interest in, and a nostalgia for, Catalan history, particularly the medieval period when the Catalan–Aragonese Empire was at its most powerful. This interest was reflected in the drama, both in the historical subject-matter (as typical of Romanticism in Europe as it later was, for entirely different reasons, of symbolism) and in the use of archaic language.

Side by side with these historical plays was another completely different, popular dramatic tradition, which was associated with the *sainet*, a short comic piece usually performed after the main play. This type of drama used the language of ordinary people, and its authors tended to despise the archaic nature of the language of more elevated forms of theatre. The best-known writer of *sainetes* in the nineteenth century is Josep Robrenyo (1780–1838), who, among other things, wrote political propaganda plays.

In the eighteenth and early nineteenth centuries, plays in Catalonia had often been performed in private houses or in small theatres, and in the 1850s this tradition was continued in the formation of workshops (*tallers*), in which plays were performed, and political discussions, and also more light-hearted activities such as dances and parties, were held. The 'workshops' produced one of the most famous Catalan dramatists of the nineteenth century, Serafí Pitarra (pseudonym for Frederic Soler, 1839–95). His plays satirized the bourgeoisie in a humorous, even scurrilous fashion. His *Jaume el Conqueridor* is virtually a pornographic parody of one of the figures of Catalan history who had become almost mythical for writers of the *Renaixença*. Pitarra founded a group known as *La Gata*, which performed his plays between 1864 and 1866, and gave rise to works known as *gatades*, which were parodies of the heroic stances and gestures that were common in historical plays of the era and attained great popularity. After 1866, however, Pitarra began to write completely different kinds of plays. The Catalan bourgeoisie grew in importance in the 1860s, and members of this class became more and more irritated by Pitarra's plays. Younger people were becoming more serious in outlook, and were rejecting the 'workshops'. Pitarra's own theatrical work mirrored these social and cultural changes: in 1866 he formed the Teatre Català, which constituted an attempt at creating a National Theatre, and he began to write Romantic plays. He was associated with Catalan liberalism, but became more reactionary after the political upheavals in Spain of the late 1860s and early 1870s. By the mid-1870s, Pitarra was the dramatist of the bourgeoisie, and was writing the same sort of historical and melodramatic material he had parodied in his youth. His growing conservatism was reflected in plays which portrayed the traditional life style of the richer rural classes in Catalonia.

There is no dramatist quite so dominant in Portugal in the period 1850–80 as Pitarra was in Catalonia. Plays reflecting social customs were written in the 1850s, which responded to political attempts made in Portugal from 1851 onwards to improve the standard of living of the lower classes. Dramatists like Mendes Leal (1818–86) and Ernesto Biester (1829–80), who had been fervent advocates of historical drama, began writing in the new style, which anticipated the work of writers like Dumas *fils*. One should note the often paternalistic attitude displayed by the authors of these plays, and the fact that beneath the appearance of wishing to reform society they exhibited essentially conservative attitudes.

Despite the existence of this 'social' drama in Portugal, Romanticism, as was observed earlier, continued to flourish throughout the century in the work of playwrights such as Pinheiro Chagas. Melodrama was commonplace, with its rhetorical language and lack of verisimilitude. Furthermore, the period 1886–92 saw another revival of historical drama, corresponding to a sense of nationalism in Portugal which was associated with a high point in the Portuguese colonization of Africa. However, attempts were made to create a naturalist repertoire in certain anti-clerical plays of the 1870s, such as António Enes's *Os lazaristas* (1875), which met with only limited success. The general quality of Portuguese drama in the nineteenth century, however, was low, a fact lamented by such writers as the great novelist Eça de Queirós in 1871, and later by D. João da Câmara, who, in 1895, commented on the 'terrible mediocrity to which the intellectual level of society had descended'.

AFTER 1880

The lack of adventure, experimentation and quality that characterizes Iberian drama in the period 1850–80 continues well into the twentieth century. It is not until the 1920s and 1930s that the full effects of the theatrical revolution that had taken place in other European countries were felt in Spain. This hapened when Valle-Inclán (1866–1936) and Garcia Lorca (1898–1936), the first dramatists of international stature that Spain had had since the seventeenth century, breathed new life into the Spanish stage. Even these two great playwrights, however, did not profoundly change the commercial theatre, which, following the victory of General Franco in the Spanish Civil War, reverted to conservative, unadventurous type.

It may seem surprising that the social turbulence of the early years of the century in Spain was not reflected in the drama produced, a fact that is partly accounted for by the deep-seated conservatism of Iberian society. The Catholic Church was particularly powerful and able to impose its moral beliefs in many areas. The social questioning and exposure of moral decadence associated with naturalism was anathema to conservative opinion, and helps to explain why theatre owners were reluctant to put on plays that contained anything other than the blandest social comment, a fact complained about by more liberal and progressive critics (see **226** and **227**).

Moreover, as far as theatrical style was concerned, there was little or no experimentation in the commercial theatre. Impresarios preferred to stick with tried and trusted formulae, with mild drawing-room comedy or neo-Romantic melodrama. The likes of Valle-Inclán and Lorca were to complain bitterly about what they saw as the sorry state of the commercial theatre in their country. It was only in the 1920s and 1930s that new styles and attitudes made some, albeit temporary, headway in the commercial theatre.

There were, however, some valiant if limited attempts at innovation in Iberian drama in the period 1880–1918, which will be examined in **230–235**.

I   Naturalism in Iberia: ma non troppo

225   Josep Yxart's ambiguous position on naturalism in a review of Ibsen's *Ghosts*, 1892

Josep Yxart,[1] 'Enrich Ibsen', in *Obres catalanes* (Barcelona, 1895), pp. 206–7; reproduced in Josep Yxart, *Entorn de la literatura catalana de la Restauració*, ed. Jordi Castellanos (Barcelona: Edicions 62, 1980), p. 158

The final scene of *Ghosts* has something repugnant about it. It hurts one when one reads it, and when one sees it on stage it must be really unbearable. At this point Ibsen's play has the same defect for which French naturalism, at the Théâtre Libre, has so often been criticized. The pathological case, which causes physical emotion, that is depressing, immediate and brutal, inhibits the spectator to such an extent that a truly artistic, contemplative, objective emotion does not materialize. But, apart from this, Ibsen, with his vigorous talent as a dramatist, is able to soften some of the cruder elements and to give his play a strange and a very sharp intensity, which is independent of the spectacle's repulsive side. If not in Osvald, then in Mrs Alving there is an inner struggle, a soul.

[1] Josep Yxart (1852–95) was the leading Catalan theatre critic of the late nineteenth century. He wrote both in Castilian and Catalan; 226 is a typical example of his scathing criticisms of Spanish drama, which he sees as banal and backward.

226   Yxart attacks Spain's failure to grasp naturalism, 1894

Josep Yxart, *El arte escénico en España* (Scenic Art in Spain) (Barcelona, 1894), vol. I, pp. 91, 152–3 and 243

Because of this confusion between moral and artistic questions, the ultra-Romantic plays of Echegaray[1] and Cano's melodramas[2] have passed for naturalist works. The result is that we hear the same old cliché over and over again: 'the theatre is no longer a school, but a sterile and cruel photography of our customs', although there is no 'photography' to be seen anywhere; and everything is 'an emaciated and stinking anatomy', although in the Spanish theatre no one has ever dissected anything. [...]

From time immemorial in Spain we have confused drama with fine arts. [. . .]
Our plays consist of a collection of rhetorical devices. Since literature for us means
expressing things in a pleasant manner, which is very different from the style of
speaking that ordinary mortals would use, the language of our plays has become a
convention which would fit perfectly into chivalric literature, and into period
pieces, but which is an anachronism in a play about social habits.

The really modern works consist of an application to drama of naturalist
theories as formulated by Taine in his study on Balzac – which has been called the
'Preface to *Cromwell*' of the positivist aesthetic – and as expressed by Zola in his
Naturalism in the Theatre.

[1] José Echegaray (1832–1916) was one of the most famous Spanish dramatists of the nineteenth
century. Echegaray's plays are, in many ways, Romantic in style and content, although he was
interested in new developments, in the European theatre. His play *El hijo de don Juan* (Don Juan's Son,
1882) is based on Ibsen's *Ghosts* and he uses, appropriately, the legendary Spanish character, don
Juan Tenorio, as the dissolute father from whom the son inherits the disease which causes his
insanity. Echegaray denies that his play is merely a reworking of its much more famous source.

[2] Leopoldo Cano (1844–1934), whose most important work, *La pasionaria* (1883), suggests the
presence of conflict between the interests of the church and the army.

227   The Spanish theatre-going public does not understand naturalism, 1884

Benito Pérez Galdós,' review of Eugenio Sellés's *Las vengadoras*, in *La Prensa* (Buenos
Aires, 25 April 1884), cited in Jesús Rubio Jiménez, *Ideología y teatro en España: 1890–
1900* (Universidad de Zaragoza, 1982), p. 37

Our theatre-going public is still too timid to stand these things, when they are not
translated from French, or performed in French or Italian. For we have agreed
that the worst examples of immorality are true and even artistic, as long as their
theatrical setting is the great and dissolute Paris. But here, in our Spain, perish the
thought that such horrors could occur! And if by some chance they did, for
anything is possible, heaven help the unwary author who portrays them on the
stage. One of the most interesting areas of patriotism is the one that proclaims,
if not the absolutely honourable manliness of our nation, then the need to show
publicly that such manliness does exist.

[1] Benito Pérez Galdós (1843–1920), the most famous Spanish novelist of the nineteenth century, in
general cultivated realism in his novels. He did not start writing plays until fairly late in his career
(his first play was an adaptation of his novel *Realidad* in 1892), and in them he is concerned with
many of the social and religious questions that dominate his novels. Galdós was also an important
theatre critic, and his attitude to the so-called naturalism of *Las vengadoras* may be compared with that of Josep Yxart to naturalism in Spain in **226**.
The Vengeful Women, which depicts a dissolute aristocracy, was the focal point of a fierce debate
about the merits and demerits of naturalism in the theatre.

228   Unamuno on naturalism, 1896

Miguel de Unamuno,[1] 'La regeneración del teatro español', in *Teatro completo* (Madrid: Aguilar, 1973), pp. 1343–73

In *L'Assommoir*, Zola presents us with a typical drunkard, who has been constructed from details taken from clinical memoirs; this is, basically, merely a presentation of personified drunkenness. Of course, since naturalist abstraction comes out of a great number of documents and a greater amount of information, which are more precise, it has more of a 'concrete' feel about it, and produces a greater illusion of a living reality, which, in fact, it is not. Living realities, taken 'live' from objective reality, and bursting with vitality, are presented to us by artists of genius, be they ancient or modern. Anything that is not intuitively observed is a pure abstraction and an alchemy, whether it be taken from scholastic ideology or from paraphysiology.

A similar sort of absurdity is the bringing of scientific determinism into art, where it produces only automata; since it is not necessary for us to see what is determined as such in the infinite complexity of the concrete or the individual, and characters whose actions can be foreseen are in reality puppets. [...]

Symbolism has come from the understanding of the dynamism of ideas, from dynamic ideology. The symbolism of Ibsen is the resurrection of ancient allegory and its insertion into our own lives. [...]

For all its defects, the *género chico*[2] is the most alive and real part of our theatre, and something of the popular spirit which inspired our glorious Golden Age of theatre has taken refuge in the *sainetes*.[3] The *género grande*[4] is divorced from the common people, and does not penetrate into their dramatic lives. It is concerned only with the casuistry of adultery, which really interests no one here and has reached our pepole through an ungainly importation of foreign works.

The ordinary people are abandoning the theatre and going instead to see bullfights, which offer them a more dramatic and alive theatrical performance. [...] The people go to see bullfights, or to similar sorts of entertainment, or they go nowhere at all.

Neither do more cultured people go to the theatre, and they do not go for they too are 'people', because all culture that is deep-rooted returns to the people.

The theatre no longer lives off the people, nor does it look for sustenance in their entrails; it lives off itself.

[1] Miguel de Unamuno (1864–1936), one of the major writers in modern Spain, was an essayist, novelist, poet and dramatist. He influenced profoundly Spanish thought and fiction, and was also a highly influential writer on the theatre.

[2] Literally, 'small genre', this is the genre of one-act comic pieces, or short farces, which were very popular in Spain, especially the *zarzuela*, or operetta.

[3] One-act farce or comedy, or comic sketch.

[4] Literally, 'large genre', this refers to the full-length 'serious' plays performed in the commercial theatre, as opposed to the short comic pieces of the *género chico*.

229   An early twentieth-century Portuguese manifesto in favour of the modern theatre, 1905

'Why *Teatro Moderno?*', manifesto written by the Teatro Moderno company, and first published in 1905. May be read in L. F. Rebello, *O teatro naturalista e neo-romântico (1870–1910)* (Lisbon: Instituto de Cultura Portuguesa, 1978), p. 83

Antoine visited Lisbon in 1896, and again in 1903, in which year he performed several plays at the Teatro D. Amélia. A co-operative was formed in the Portuguese capital, in 1902, to establish a Théâtre Libre (*Teatro Livre*), which would put on educational plays. The experiment lasted some six years, during which time both foreign and Portuguese plays were performed. The *Teatro Moderno* was born from a split within the *Teatro Livre* co-operative, and had as its director Araújo Pereira. The following passage is part of the group's explanation of their *raison d'être*.

For many years there has been no drama company in Lisbon willing to perform educational plays, written from a moral or social point of view. There is a great need for such a company, which would put on plays by young Portuguese authors who are studious and intelligent, yet whose work, however good it may be, has not been appreciated because it has not been performed in the theatre. Such a situation is unjust and iniquitous; even well-known authors find it difficult to have their plays performed in our narrow and timid theatrical environment, and there are many others with great powers of study and intelligence, who could be well known if only their work as dramatists were accepted and submitted to critical appreciation by the public. It has also been recognized for many years that there is a need to transform the theatre, which itself is full of *ficelles*, with absurd preconceptions and age-old prejudices, into a true art-form, which is to say into a modern theatre, as an element of the moral and social education which is necessary.

230   Ignasi Iglésies's portrayal of working-class life in Barcelona, 1902

Ignasi Iglésies,[1] *El cor del poble* (4th edn, Barcelona: Selecta, 1963), p. 124

The dining-room of a third-floor flat in a working-class district of Barcelona.[2] The room is very clean, its walls are recently whitewashed, the ceiling has arched beams painted metallic blue, and the tiled skirting is an ochre yellow.[3] Upstage is an open window, with a curtain drawn to one side, and on the sill are two flowerpots full of white and pink carnations. Through the window one can see indistinctly because of the fine mist a mass of houses and factories with tall chimneys blackened by smoke; in the background the distant shoreline stands out clearly beneath a gloomy sky, made cloudy by the day's smoke; downstage right is the front door, with a knocker and a peephole through which the person who is knocking can be seen; upstage of the front door is the kitchen door. To the left are two more doors, which lead to the bedrooms. Centre stage, a folding pinewood table. An oil lamp hangs from the ceiling over the centre of the table, its shade decorated with an edging of green paper. In a corner, stage right, is a cupboard overflowing with all kinds of chinaware and other assorted utensils. Upstage right of the back wall are two portraits, both with a very simple frame, one of Pi i Margall[4] and the other of Clavé.[5] On the two side walls are two or three framed diplomas and a calligraphic drawing. Conveniently distributed around the stage are several rush chairs, painted black, with yellow borders.

It is late afternoon on Easter Sunday.

[1] Ignasi Iglésies (1871–1928) was born of a working-class family, and his socialist views meant that he was rejected by the bourgeois-dominated Catalan theatre of his day, but was greatly respected by working-class people whose problems he portrayed in his drama. Together with Jaume Brossa and Pere Coromines, he founded the Teatre Independent in 1896, and played the part of Oswald in that company's production of *Ghosts* in Catalan, also in 1896. He was influenced by Hauptmann and Maeterlinck, and once said that the adaptation of Zola's *Thérèse Raquin* to the theatre represented a decisive moment in the development of the theatre, despite the play's lack of success. *El cor del poble* (The Heart of the People, first performed at the Teatre Romea in Barcelona in 1902) is the title of a newspaper in which one of the characters of the play, Fidel, a young man inspired, like many people in Catalonia at the time, by anarchist ideas, has had an article published.

[2] Barcelona (along with Bilbao) was at the turn of the century (and still is today) the main industrial centre of Spain. There were textiles and, as the reference to the smoking chimneys suggests, heavy industry.

[3] Several features indicate that this is a working-class environment, e.g. the whitewashed walls, the arched beams, the pine table and the rush chairs.

[4] Francesc Pi i Margall (1824–1901), radical politician, historian and political philosopher.

[5] Josep Anselm Clavé (1824–74) was instrumental in the formation of working-class choirs in Catalonia. Choral music was (and continues to be) an important feature of Catalan working-class culture, and on Easter Sunday songs known as *caramelles* are sung. In *El cor del poble* Fidel expresses the view that the traditional, sometimes sentimental music of Clavé should be replaced or at least supplemented by songs of a more revolutionary nature.

231   A naturalist set in Joaquín Dicenta's *Daniel*, 1907

Joaquin Dicenta,[1] *Daniel* (Barcelona: Félix Costa, 1913), p. 29

Upstage to the left and to the right one can see the smelting furnaces blazing, and work is in full swing.

These furnaces will be square-shaped and wide, with huge mouths, to which iron plates will act as doors.

An effort should be made to give to the audience the exact impression of a foundry; the spectacle of one of those mining hells where the workers suffocate and roast for hours on end.

Joaquín Dicenta (1863–1917) was the most important social dramatist writing in Castilian at the turn of the century. In addition to being a dramatist, he edited the socialist newspaper *El País*, and the weekly journal of the Germinal Group, the name of which derives from Zola's novel. This group were fervent admirers of Zola's socialist and positivist views, and their naturalism is strongly influenced by the works of the French author. Dicenta's best-known play is *Juan José* (1895). However, social criticism in this play is diluted by an element of Romanticism. *Daniel* (1907) contains harsher and more hard-hitting social criticism, and expresses the misery of mine-workers in the south of Spain.

II   The late arrival of symbolism in the Iberian theatre

232   An atmospheric stage-direction from Valle-Inclán's *Romance de lobos*, 1908

Ramón del Valle-Inclán,[1] *Romance de lobos*, Act I, sc. iii, in *Teatro selecto* (Madrid: Escelicer, 1969), p. 94

A stormy night on a beach. A few women, dressed in mourning clothes, motionless on the rocks and covered with black capes, waiting for the fishing-boats to return. The howling black sea, which breaks on the sandbars, wets those unshod, beggars' feet. The seagulls fly over the beach, and their incessant cawing and the crying of a child, which its mother shelters beneath her cape, are voices of fear which magnify the extraordinary voice of the wind and the sea.

[1] Ramón del Valle-Inclán (1866–1936), poet and novelist as well as a playwright, was the most innovative Spanish dramatist since the seventeenth century. He is perhaps best known for his tragi-comic farces which he called *esperpentos*, written in the 1920s. Valle-Inclán was bitterly critical of the contemporary commercial theatre in Spain, and his plays consistently reveal the influence of symbolism. *Romance de lobos* (Ballad of Wolves, 1908) is part of a trilogy entitled *Comedias bárbaras*. G. Edwards writes of the trilogy's symbolist aesthetics: 'the *Comedias bárbaras* possess a discernible and carefully controlled element of gesture, movement and action which, often replacing words, certainly speaks as loudly as them, enhances the archetypal nature of a character, expresses and reveals emotions, or deepens the mood of a given moment' (G. Edwards, *Dramatists in Perspective: Spanish Theatre in the Twentieth Century* (Cardiff: University of Wales Press, 1985), p. 46; see also John Lyon, *The Theatre of Valle-Inclán* (Cambridge University Press, 1983) for a discussion of symbolism in Valle-Inclán's work). The *Comedias bárbaras* trilogy is set in Valle-Inclán's native Galicia, and reflects the author's detestation of the bourgeoisie and his sadness at the decline of the Galician aristocracy.

233   Illustration by Manuel Fontanals of Martínez Sierra's *Canción de cuna*, 1911

In Gregorio Martínez Sierra, *Un teatro de arte en España: 1917–1925* (Madrid: Ediciones de la Esfinge, 1926), p. 37

Gregorio Martínez Sierra (1881–1948) was a leading exponent of symbolist and poetic theatre (for example in his *Teatro de Ensueño* (Dream Theatre, 1905) and *Canción de cuna* (Cradle Song). The latter is his best-known work, and highlights the position of the woman in what is a traditional and moralistic view of the family. Martínez Sierra's own plays tend

488

towards superficiality and sentimentality, and it is as a director rather than as an author that he was an important innovator, his base being the Teatro Eslava in Madrid. He was responsible for the performance of plays by foreign dramatists (Shakespeare, Molière, Goldoni, Dumas, Ibsen, Shaw, Maeterlinck and Hauptmann). Spanish poetic dramatists, such as Eduardo Marquina and Martínez Sierra himself, were cultivated by the Eslava. Children's theatre was performed there. Composers and dancers (for example, Manuel de Falla and la Argentinita) collaborated with Eslava projects, and several younger Spanish dramatists (including García Lorca) had their plays performed there when more established theatres were turning their backs on them. Martínez Sierra saw theatrical creation as being one of team-work, involving the director, the author, the scene-designer, actors, dancers and composers. Martínez Sierra worked closely with three painters at the Eslava: Manuel Fontanals, Sigfrido Burman and Rafael Pérez Barradas.

234   A symbolist drama: Fernando Pessoa's *O marinheiro*, 1913

Fernando Pessoa,[1] *O marinheiro*, extract in L. F. Rebello, *O teatro simbolista e modernista (1890–1939)* (Lisbon: Instituto de Cultura Portuguesa, 1979), p. 102

FIRST WATCH LADY Tell me now what you dreamed of on the seashore.

SECOND WATCH LADY I dreamed of a sailor who was lost on a distant island. There were a few stiff palm trees on the island, and birds drifted by over it . . . I didn't ever see them pause to rest . . . From the time he was saved from the shipwreck, the sailor lived there . . . As he did not have the means to return to his native land, and as every time he remembered it he suffered, he began to dream of a native land which he had never had; he began to pretend that another land was his, another type of country with different kinds of landscape, different people, a different pattern walking through the streets and leaning out of windows . . . Even now he constructed this false land in his dreams and he never stopped dreaming, by day beneath the short shadows of the palm trees, which were outlined on the sandy, warm ground, at night stretched out on the beach, lying on his back, unaware of the stars.

---

[1] Fernando Pessoa (1888–1935) is the best-known Portuguese poet of this century, writing much of his poetry under various heteronyms. Despite his repeated claims that he was basically a dramatist, he wrote only one complete play, the one-act *O marinheiro* (The Sailor, 1913). He called it a 'static play', and referred to it as 'the most remote thing that exists in literature', adding: 'the most nebulous and subtle work of Maeterlinck is crude and carnal in comparison with it'.

III   The Catalan dimension

Most of the albeit limited influence of naturalism and, particularly, symbolism on the Spanish theatre of the period 1890 to 1918 came via Catalonia. Authors and artists of the *modernista* or Catalan *art nouveau* movement, such as Santiago Rusiñol, reacted against what they considered to be the narrow provincialism of late-nineteenth-century Catalan culture by turning towards northern European models. All kinds of European dramatists, from Hauptmann to Ibsen to Maeterlinck, found favour in Catalonia. The first performance of Maeterlinck's *L'Intruse*, for instance, took place in Catalonia, at the 1893 Modernista Festival organized by Rusiñol at Sitges, to the south of Barcelona.

The whole period from 1890 to the end of the Civil War was one of social and artistic ferment in the Catalan capital, Barcelona. Anarchist activity and civil strife were widespread, the social issues finding expression in, for example, the plays of Ignasi Iglésies (see 230). Architecture and the visual arts also underwent a radical transformation, the architect Antoni Gaudí being one of the most influential figures in twentieth-century European architecture.

Catalan theatre was inevitably affected by the cultural ferment, although as in the case of the rest of Spain, poetry and prose were more in the vanguard of the new movements than drama. An exception to this was Adrià Gual, on whose work we concentrate in the following three documents on the Catalan theatre. The last of these documents (237) illustrates Gual's interest in Wagnerian opera; Barcelona, in fact, was one of the Wagnerian capitals of Europe.

235   Costumes for Adrià Gual's symbolist drama, *Nocturn andante morat*, 1896

Adrià Gual (1872–1943), actor, teacher, director and author, was the most important figure in the Catalan theatre in the early years of the twentieth century. He is best known for his work with the Teatre Intim and the Escola Catalana d'Art Dramàtic, in Barcelona. As well as his own plays, Gual was responsible for staging Catalan translations of many foreign plays by authors such as Ibsen, Hauptmann and Maeterlinck.

Gual's first published work, *Nocturn andante morat* (Nocturn. Andante in Purple) reveals the influence of symbolism, and as the illustration of the costumes shows, contains a pre-Raphaelite element in the form and conception of the female figures.

235

236   Hauptmann's *Drayman Henschel*: an example of 'total theatre' in Barcelona, 1903–1904

Adrià Gual, *Mitja vida de teatre, Memòries* (Barcelona: Aedos, 1960), p. 167

In Gual's memoirs one finds the most complete account in existence of the Catalan theatre of the late nineteenth and early twentieth centuries. The memoirs consist mainly of accounts of plays directed by Gual himself, and contain many interesting observations on directing and performing, which place Gual firmly in the anti-naturalist camp. This passage describes a production of Hauptmann's *Drayman Henschel* during the 1903/4 winter season at Les Arts in Barcelona. Hauptmann's *Weavers* was also performed during this season, as were works by Beaumarchais, Goethe, Molière, Ibsen (*John Gabriel Borkman*), the Catalan dramatist Guimerà, Galdós, Shakespeare (*Twelfth Night*) and Gual himself.

Shortly before his production of *Drayman Henschel*, Gual tells us, the play had been performed in Barcelona by the Italian actor/director Ermetti Zaconni, to whom reference is made in the first sentence of this document. (See 214.) Many people considered Gual's a risky venture, coming so soon after the highly successful Zaconni version. In this passage, Gual explains that in his production he was trying to get away from the emphasis placed by Zaconni on the leading actor.

And this is what our daring enterprise offered the public: the 'play', which the brilliant Italian actor had forgotten about. One could tell from the atmosphere that the audience was well aware of the daring to which I have referred, so much so that I almost went on stage before the performance to explain to them the *raison d'être* of our determination to put on this particular play. However, in the end I thought it better that the play should speak for itself; it was thus that we won the day, and we did not take long to do it.

Within a few moments of the curtain going up, the atmosphere had convinced the public. The careful study that we had made of the play, the way in which we captured the spirit of the characters, the costumes which indicated the class to which they belonged, all this helped to achieve a suggestiveness which magically blotted out the actor's mission, with the result that he was converted into the main instrument of the orchestration which the author had conceived. [...] In the course of the evening all our colleagues, caught up in the atmosphere created by the designs of Alarma and Junyent, formed one single spirit.

237   Gual's lecture to the Barcelona Wagnerian Association, 1902–1906

Adrià Gual, 'L'art escènica i el drama-wagnerià', in *XXV conferències donades a la Associació Wagneriana (1902–1906)* (Barcelona: Associació Wagneriana, 1908), pp. 115–45

In this lecture, one of a series delivered by various lecturers between 1902 and 1906 to the Wagnerian Association of Barcelona, Gual suggests ways of interpreting Wagner's work, and considers how an understanding of Wagner may help a modern theatrical director. Gual stresses the importance of Wagner for his generation, and the need for him to be made more accessible to the general public.

But as the playwrights of the past are no longer with us, we must advise modern directors to improve upon what their predecessors have done.[1] Scenic art will be the result of following with scrupulous devotion the most lively views, and of interpreting the work of past writers in an elevated, intelligent fashion. This is true scenic art; it is related to all the elements which make up the scene, so that nothing is without value. Scenic art consists of painting, lighting, elements of 'construction' – in the broad sense of the word – and costume, which includes dress, footwear, arms, armour and wigs. The art is not that of the painter, lighting technician, carpenter, tailor, etc., but is the sum of all these elements which form a single whole [pp. 124–5].[2]

What must we do, then? Try to find the most accurate solution possible based on principles which seem to be rooted in the very depths of Wagner's work. We must try to penetrate Wagner's work, and to understand it more deeply through the love we have for it. Above all, a good director and painter are necessary. The painter, through his bold composition, based on a slice of nature that will seem real to him, through the exuberance of tones, through the soft but at times harsh intonation, through the corpulent masses and delicate details, through what his work will evoke in its visible whole and through the hints it will give of what is invisible, through these and many other qualities which taken all together will undeniably mean a great effort, he will conjure up the scene in question, and the talents of the artist of the canvas will replace those of the dramatic artist. As we look at the painting, we will even hear the music [pp. 136–7].[3]

[1] Just before the beginning of the above passage, Gual had said that dramatists of previous centuries such as Shakespeare and Goethe were not very precise in their scene descriptions.
[2] The similarity with the theories of Gordon Craig will be noted. In another part of this lecture Gual criticizes the 'lack of absolute direction in the performance of theatrical works' (p. 121).
[3] At the end of the lecture a piano, which was hidden from the view of the audience, played some notes from the *Pilgrim's Chorus*.

Select bibliography

FRANCE, 1851–1919

(unless otherwise stated, place of publication is Paris)

Abraham, Emile, *Les Acteurs et les actrices de Paris, biographie complète* (Michel Lévy, 1861)

Agate, May, *Madame Sarah* (London: Home & Van Thal, 1945)

anon., *La Censure sous Napoléon III* (Savine, 1892)

Antoine, André, *Mes Souvenirs sur le Théâtre Libre* (Fayard, 1921); English trans.: *André Antoine's Memories of the Théâtre Libre*, trans. Marvin Carlson (University of Miami Press, 1964)

Mes Souvenirs sur le Théâtre Antoine et sur l'Odéon (Les Œuvres représentatives, 1928)

Le Théâtre (Editions de France, 2 vols., 1932)

Le Théâtre Libre (Paris-Geneva: Slatkine reprints, 1979)

Asholt, Wolfgang, *Gesellschaftskritisches Theater im Frankreich der Belle Epoque, 1887–1914* (Heidelberg: Studia Romanica 59, Winter 1984)

'Les matinées caractéristiques et le Théâtre des Nations', *Revue d'Histoire du Théâtre*, 34 (1982), pp. 211–36

Astruc, Joseph, *Le Droit privé du théâtre ou Rapport des directeurs avec les auteurs, les artistes et le public* (Mâcon: Protat frères, 1897)

Audebrand, Philibert, *Petits mémoires d'une stalle d'orchestre* (Jules Lévy, 1885)

Bablet, Denis, *La Mise en scène contemporaine, I, 1887–1914* (La Renaissance du livre, 1968)

Le Décor de théâtre de 1870 à 1914 (CNRS, 1975)

Baguley, David, ed., 'Later Nineteenth-Century Theatre', in *A Critical Bibliography of French Literature: The Nineteenth Century* (Syracuse University Press, 1994), pp. 1250–86

Bapst, Germain, *Essai sur l'histoire du théâtre* (Hachette, 1893; reprinted 1971)

Baret, Charles, *Le Théâtre en province: propos d'avant-guerre* (La Renaissance du Livre, 1918)

Baring, Maurice, *Sarah Bernhardt* (New York: Appleton-Century, 1934)

Barish, Jonas, *The Antitheatrical Prejudice*, (Berkeley: University of California Press, 1981)

Bayet, Jean, *La Société des auteurs et compositeurs dramatiques* (Rousseau, 1908)

Becq de Fouquières, L., *L'Art de la mise en scène, Essai d'esthétique théâtrale* (G. Charpentier, 1884)

Béhar, Henri, *Jarry dramaturge* (Nizet, 1980)

Bellanger, Justin, *Entre deux spectacles: esquisses théâtrales* (Dentu, 1879)

La Vie au théâtre: souvenirs de jeunesse (Lemerre, 1905)

Bennett, Arnold, *Paris Nights and other impressions of places and people* (London: Hodder & Stoughton, 1913)

Bernhardt, Sarah, *L'Art du théâtre. La voix, le geste, la prononciation* (Nilsson, 1923)

Ma double vie: mémoires de Sarah Bernhardt (Charpentier-Fasquelle, 2 vols., 1923)

Bernheim, Adrien, *Trente ans de théâtre* (Fasquelle, 4 vols., 1903–8)

Bertaut, Jules, *Les grandes époques du théâtre contemporain* (Cercle de la librairie, 1924)

Berthier, Patrick, *Le Théâtre au 19e siècle* (Presses universitaires de France, 1986)

Blanchart, Paul, *Firmin Gémier* (L'Arche, 1954)

Bogerhoff, Joseph Leopold, *Nineteenth-century French Plays* (2 vols., 1931, 1933)

Braun, Edward, *The Director and the Stage* (London: Methuen, 1982)

Brisson, Adolphe, *Le Théâtre et les mœurs* (Flammarion, 1907)

Bureau, Georges, *Le Théâtre et sa législation* (Ollendorff, 1898)

Cahuet, Albert, *La Liberté du théâtre en France et à l'étranger: histoire, fonctionnement et discussion de la censure dramatique* (Dujarric, Chevalier-Marescq, 1902)

Cain, Georges, *Anciens théâtres de Paris: le Boulevard du Temple; les théâtres du boulevard* (Charpentier et Fasquelle, 1906)

Carlson, Marvin, *The French Stage in the 19th Century* (Metuchen, N.J.: Scarecrow Press, 1972)

Caradec, François and Weill, Alain, *Le Café-concert* (Hachette, 1980)

Carter, Lawson A., *Zola and the Theater* (New Haven: Yale University Press, 1963)

Chandler, Frank Wadleigh, *The Contemporary Drama of France* (Boston: Little, Brown, 1920)

Charle, Christophe, *La Crise littéraire à l'époque du naturalisme: roman, théâtre et politique* (Presses de l'E.N.S., 1979)

Chauveron, Edmond de, *Les grands procès de la Comédie-Française depuis les origines jusqu'à nos jours* (Rousseau, 1906)

Chothia, Jean, *André Antoine* (Cambridge University Press, 1991)

Claretie, Jules, *Profils de théâtre* (Fasquelle, 1904)

 La Vie moderne au théâtre (Barba, 2 vols., 1869–75)

Clark, Barret H., *Contemporary French Dramatists* (Cincinnati: Stewart & Kidd, 1916)

 The Continental Drama of Today (New York: Holt, 1914)

 Four Plays of the Free Theater (Cincinnati: Stewart & Kidd, 1916)

Coquelin, C. *The Art of the Actor* (*L'Art du comédien*, 1894), trans. E. Foferty (London: Allen & Unwin, 1932)

Descotes, Maurice, *Histoire de la critique dramatique en France* (Place, 1980)

 Le Public du théâtre et son histoire (Presses Universitaires de France, 1964)

Doumic, René, *De Scribe à Ibsen. Causeries sur le théâtre contemporain* (Delaplane, 1893)

 Essais sur le théâtre contemporain (Perrin, 1897)

 Le Théâtre nouveau (Perrin, 1905)

Dubech, Lucien, *Histoire générale illustrée du théâtre*, vol. V (Librairie de France, 1934)

Dubois, Jean, *La Crise théâtrale* (Imprimerie de l'art, 1895)

Erichsen, Svend, 'Percée du réalisme dans le théâtre français du XIXe siècle', *Revue d'Histoire du Théâtre*, 31 (1979), pp. 52–80

Esslin, Martin, 'Naturalism in Context', *Drama Review*, 13 (1968), pp. 67–76

Faguet, Emile, *Notes sur le théâtre contemporain*, Lecène-Oudin, 1889, 3 vols.

Féral, Josette, 'Le Signe en procès: l'expérience du théâtre naturaliste', *Cahiers naturalistes*, 56 (1982), pp. 115–30

Filon, Augustin, *De Dumas à Rostand. Esquisse du mouvement dramatique contemporain* (Collin, 1898)

Fort, Paul, *Mes mémoires. Toute la vie d'un poète, 1872–1944* (Flammarion, 1944)

Gascar, Pierre, *Le Boulevard du crime* (Hachette/Massin, 1980)

Germain, Auguste, *Les Dessous du théâtre–Les Agences dramatiques et lyriques* (Perrin, 1891)

Gisèle, Marie, *Le Théâtre symboliste: ses origines, ses sources. Pionniers et réalisateurs* (Nizet, 1973)

Gontard, Denis, *La Décentralisation théâtrale en France, 1895–1952* (CDU/SEDES, 1973)

Got, Edmond, *Journal d'Edmond Got, sociétaire de la Comédie-Française* (Plon-Nourrit, 2 vols., 1910)

Grossman, Manuel, 'Alfred Jarry and the Theater of his Time', *Modern Drama*, 13 (May 1970), pp. 10–21

Guiches, Gustave, *Le Spectacle: trois étapes du théâtre et de la vie parisienne de 1887 à 1914* (Spès, 1932)

Hallays-Dabot, Victor, *La censure dramatique et le théâtre; histoire des vingt dernières années* (Dentu, 1871)

 Histoire de la censure théâtrale en France (Dentu, 1862)

Hays, Michael, 'Nineteenth-Century Theater and Society', *Revue des langues vivantes*, 1 (1978), pp. 56–65

The Public and Performance: Essays in the History of French and German Theater (Ann Arbor, Michigan: U.M.I. Research Press, 1981)

Hemmings, F. W. J., *The Theatre Industry in Nineteenth-Century France* (Cambridge University Press, 1992)

Theatre and State in France, 1760–1905 (Cambridge University Press, 1994)

Henderson, John, *The First Avant-Garde, 1887–1894. Sources of the Modern French Theater* (London: Harrap, 1971)

Hobson, Harold, *French Theatre since 1830* (London: Calder, 1978)

Howarth, W. D., *Comic Drama. The European Heritage* (London: Methuen, 1978)

Sublime and Grotesque: a Study of French Romantic Drama (London: Harrap, 1975)

Jacquot, Jean, ed., *Réalisme et poésie au théâtre* (CNRS, 1960)

Jerrold, Laurence, *The Real France* (New York: Lane, 1911)

Jomaron, Jacqueline, *Le Théâtre en France*, vol. II *De la Révolution à nos jours* (Colin, 1989)

Jullien, Jean, *Le Théâtre vivant* (Charpentier et Fasquelle, 1892; revised, 2 vols., Tresse et Stock, 1896)

Kahn, Armand, *Le Théâtre social en France de 1870 à nos jours* (Lausanne, 1907)

Knapp, Bettina K., *The Reign of the Theatrical Director. French Theater 1887–1924* (Troy, N.Y.: Whitson, 1988)

Knowles, Dorothy, *La Réaction idéaliste au théâtre depuis 1890* (Droz, 1934)

Lagorce, Henri, *Droit théâtral. De la rémunération des artistes* (Laval: Léon Barnéoul, 1903)

Larroumet, Gustave, *Etudes d'histoire et de critique dramatiques* (Hachette, 2 vols., 1892–9)

Legouvé, Ernest, *Soixante ans de souvenirs* (Hetzel, 1893)

Lemaître, Jules, *Impressions de théâtre* (Lecène-Oudin, 11 vols., 1888–1920)

Lugné-Poe, *La Parade: I. Le Sot du Tremplin* (1930); *II. Acrobaties. Souvenirs et impressions de théâtre (1894–1902)* (1931); *III. Sous les étoiles. Souvenirs de théâtre (1902–1913)* (1933) (Gallimard)

Lyonnet, Henry, *Dictionnaire des comédiens français (ceux d'hier). Biographies, bibliographie, iconographie* (E. Jorel, 2 vols., 1908–12)

McCormick, John, *Popular Theatres of Nineteenth-Century France* (London: Routledge, 1993)

Madsen, Børge Gedsø, *Strindberg's Naturalistic Theater: Its Relation to French Naturalism* (New York: Russell & Russell, 1973)

Martin, Jules, *Nos auteurs et compositeurs dramatiques* (Flammarion, 1897)

Matthews, James Brander, *The Theatres of Paris* (London: Sampson Low, Marston, Searle, & Rivington, 1880)

Melcher, Edith, *Stage Realism in France between Diderot and Antoine* (Lancaster, Penn.: Lancaster Press, 1928)

Mortier, Arnold, *Les Soirées parisiennes, par un Monsieur de l'orchestre* (Dentu, 10 vols., 1875–84)

Mounet-Sully, Jean, *Souvenirs d'un tragédien* (Lafitte, 1917)

Muriel, Auguste, *Le Théâtre aujourd'hui* (Michel Lévy, 1855)

Noël, E. and E. Stoullig, *Les Annales du théâtre et de la musique, 1876–1901*

Poizat, Alfred, *Les Maîtres du théâtre, d'Eschyle à Curel*, vol. II (La Renaissance du livre, 1923)

Pougin, Arthur, *Dictionnaire historique et pittoresque du théâtre et des arts qui s'y rattachent* (Firmin-Didot, 1885; reprinted 1985)

Pruner, Francis, *Les Luttes d'Antoine. Au Théâtre Libre*, vol. I (Lettres modernes, 1964)

Quéant, Gilles, *Encyclopédie du théâtre contemporain*, vol. I: *1850–1914* (Les Publications de France, 1957)

Reyval, Albert, *L'Eglise et le théâtre, essai historique* (Bloud et Gay, 1924)

Robichez, Jacques, *Lugné-Poe* (L'Arche, 1955)

R. Rolland et Lugné-Poe. Correspondance 1894–1901 (L'Arche, 1957)

Le Symbolisme au théâtre: Lugné-Poe et les débuts de l'Œuvre (L'Arche, 1957)

Rolland, Romain, *Le Théâtre du peuple* (Albin Michel, 1913)

Roubine, Jean-Jacques, *Théâtre et mise en scène, 1880–1980* (Presses universitaires de France, 1980)

Rouché, Jacques, *L'Art théâtral moderne* (Bloud et Gay, 1910)

Royer, Alphonse, *Histoire universelle du théâtre*, vols. v and vi: *Histoire du théâtre contemporain en France et à l'étranger* (Ollendorff, 1878)

Rudlin, John and Norman H. Paul, *Copeau: Texts on Theatre* (London: Routledge, 1990)

Rueff, Suze, *I Knew Sarah Bernhardt* (London: Frederick Muller, 1951)

Saint-Auban, Emile de, *L'Idée sociale au théâtre* (Stock, 1901)

Samson, Joseph-Isidore, *Mémoires de Samson, de la Comédie-Française* (Ollendorff, 1882)

Santa Vicca, Edmund F., *Four French Dramatists* (Metuchen, N.J.: Scarecrow Press, 1974)

Sarcey, Francisque, *Comédiens et comédiennes: la Comédie-Française* (Librairie des bibliophiles, 1877)
  Comédiens et comédiennes: théâtres divers (Librairie des bibliophiles, 1884)
  Quarante ans de théâtre (8 vols., Annales politiques et littéraires, 1900–2)
  Souvenirs d'âge mûr (Ollendorff, 1892)

Saunders, James B., *La Correspondance d'Antoine: le Théâtre Libre* (Longueuil, Québec: Le préambule, 1987)

Schumacher, Claude, *Alfred Jarry and Guillaume Apollinaire* (London: Macmillan, 1984)

Smith, Hugh Allison, *Main Currents of Modern French Drama* (New York: Holt, 1925)

Soubies, Albert, *Almanach des spectacles (1874–1913)* (Librairie des bibliophiles, 38 vols., 1874–1913)

Taylor, F. A., *The Theatre of Alexandre Dumas fils* (Oxford: Clarendon, 1937)

Thalasso, Adolphe, *Le Théâtre Libre* (Mercure de France, 1909)

Tzara, Tristan, *Seven Dada Manisfestos* (*Sept Manisfestes Dada*, 1917–22, published by Pauvert, 1963) (London: John Calder, 1977)

Veinstein, André, *Du Théâtre Libre au Théâtre Louis Jouvet* (Billaudot, 1955)

Waxman, Samuel M., *Antoine and the Théâtre Libre* (Cambridge, Mass.: Harvard University Press, 1926; also New York: Blom, 1964)

Weiss, Jean-Jacques, *A propos de théâtre* (Michel Lévy, 1893)
  Le Théâtre et les mœurs (Calmann-Lévy, 1887)

Whitton, David, *Stage Directors in Modern France* (Manchester University Press, 1987)

Wicks, Charles Beaumont, *The Parisian Stage: Alphabetical Indexes of Plays and Authors. Part IV (1851–75) and Part V (1876–1900)* (University of Alabama Press, 1967, 1979)

Yerlès, Pierre, 'L'Interrogation sur la mise en scène, en France, autour de 1880', *Cahiers Théâtre Louvain*, 10–11 1970–1, pp. 40–60

Zola, Emile, 'Le Naturalisme au théâtre' (December 1878), in *Le Roman expérimental* (G. Charpentier, 1880; Flammarion, 1971)

GERMANY, 1850–1916

Allen, Richard H., *An Annotated Arthur Schnitzler Bibliography. Editions and Criticism in German, French, and English 1879–1965* (Chapel Hill: North Carolina University Press, [1966])

Appignanesi, Lisa, *Cabaret. The First Hundred Years* (London: Methuen, 1984)

Bab, Julius, *Die Chronik des deutschen Dramas* (2 vols., Darmstadt: Wissenschaftliche Buchgesellschaft, 1972)

Bab, Julius and Handl, Willi, *Deutsche Schauspieler. Porträts aus Berlin und Wien* (Berlin: Oesterheld, 1908) [Contains essays on: Matkowsky, Engels, Vollmer, Bassermann, Sauer, Reicher, Rittner, Lehmann, Bertens, Eysoldt, Kayssler, Moissi, Girardi, Niese, Sonnenthal, Kainz, Medelsky, Baumeister, Ernst Hartmann, Maran, Tyrolt, Lewinsky and Krastel]

Bahr, Hermann, *Josef Kainz* (Vienna: Wiener Verlag, 1906)
  Schauspielkunst, Leipzig: Dürr & Weber, 1923
  Zur Überwindung des Naturalismus: theoretische Schriften 1887–1904, ed. G. Wunberg (Stuttgart: Kohlhammer, 1968)

Bayerdörfer, Hans-Peter, ed., *Literatur und Theater im wilhelminischen Zeitalter* (Tübingen: Niemeyer, 1978)

Behl, C. F. W. and Voigt, Felix A., *Gerhart Hauptmanns Leben. Chronik und Bild* (Berlin: Suhrkamp, 1942)

Benoist-Hanappier, Louis, *Le Drame naturaliste en Allemagne* (Paris: Alcan, 1905)

Blätter des Deutschen Theaters (Berlin: Reiss, 1911–14)

Borchmeyer, Dieter, *Richard Wagner. Theory and Theatre* (Oxford University Press, 1991)

Boyer, Robert D., *Realism in European Theatre and Drama 1870–1920* (Westport: Greenwood Press, 1979)

Brahm, Otto, *Theater, Dramatiker, Schauspieler*, ed. H. Fetting (Berlin: Henschelverlag, 1961)

Braulich, Heinrich, *Die Volksbühne. Theater und Politik in der deutschen Volksbühnenbewegung* (Berlin: Henschelverlag, 1976)

Bühne und Welt (Hamburg: Hanseatische Verlaganstalt, 1898–1914)

Bühnen-Almanach [originally *Almanach der Genossenschaft deutscher Bühnenangehöriger*] (Leipzig: Luckhardt, 1873–1914)

Burckhard, Max, *Theater, Kritiken, Vorträge und Aufsätze* (2 vols., Vienna: Manz, 1905)

Carlson, Marvin, *The German Stage in the Nineteenth Century* (Metuchen: Scarecrow Press, 1972)

Claus, Horst, *The Theatre Director Otto Brahm* (Michigan: UMI Research Press, 1981)

Coghlan, Brian, *Hofmannsthal's Festival Dramas. Jedermann, Das Salzburger Grosse Welttheater, Der Turm* (Cambridge University Press, 1964)

Davies, Cecil W., *Theatre for the People: the Story of the Volksbühne*, (Manchester University Press, 1977)

'The Volksbühne – a descriptive chronology', *Theatre Quarterly*, 2, 5 (1972), pp. 57–64

DeHart, Steven, *The Meininger Theater 1776–1926* (Michigan: UMI Research Press, 1981) [Includes appendix giving complete list of all plays presented at the Court Theatre in Meiningen and on the Meininger tours]

Doerry, Hans, *Das Rollenfach im deutschen Theaterbetrieb des 19. Jahrhunderts*, (Berlin: Gesellschaft für Theatergeschichte, 1926) [Schriften der Gesellschaft für Theatergeschichte 35]

Deutsche Bühne, Die (Leipzig: Schmidt, 1894–8; Berlin: Oesterheld, 1909–14)

Deutsches Bühnenjahrbuch [originally *Neuer Theater-Almanach*] (Berlin: Günther, 1890–1914)

Fiedler, Leonhard, *Max Reinhardt in Selbstzeugnissen und Bilddokumenten* (Reinbek: Rowohlt, 1975)

Fontane, Theodor, *Theaterkritiken*, ed. S. Gerndt (4 vols., Frankfurt/Main: Fontane Ullstein, 1979)

Fuchs, Georg, *Die Revolution des Theaters. Ergebnisse aus dem Münchener Künstler-Theater* (Munich: Müller, 1909)

Die Schaubühne der Zukunft (Berlin: Schuster & Loeffler, [1905])

Fuhrich, Edda and Prossnitz, Gisela, eds., *Max Reinhardt. 'Ein Theater, das den Menschen wieder Freude gibt. . .' Eine Dokumentation* (Munich: Langen Müller, 1987) [Includes chronology of Reinhardt's life and a list of his stage-roles and productions]

Gal, Hans, *Richard Wagner* (London: Gollancz, 1976)

Grube, Max, *The Story of the Meininger*, trans. A. M. Koller, ed. W. Cole (Coral Gates: University of Miami Press, 1963)

Im Theaterland (Berlin: Hofmann, 1908)

Hagemann, Carl, *Moderne Bühnenkunst* (2 vols., Berlin: Schuster & Loeffler, 1912–18)

Hannsen, Hanns, *Beiträge zur Technik der Bühnen-Regie-Kunst* (Leipzig: Xenien, 1908)

Hart, Heinrich, *Gesammelte Werke*, ed. J. Hart (4 vols., Berlin: Fleischel, 1907)

Herald, Heinz, *Max Reinhardt. Ein Versuch über das Wesen der modernen Regie* (Berlin: Lehmann, 1915)

Hern, Nicholas, 'Frank Wedekind: an introduction', *Theatre Quarterly*, 1, 2 (1971), pp. 8–15

Ihering, Herbert, *Von Josef Kainz bis Paula Wessely. Schauspieler von gestern und heute* (Heidelberg: Hüthig, 1942)

Jacobs, Margaret and Warren, John, eds., *Max Reinhardt. The Oxford Symposium* (Oxford: Polytechnic, 1986)

Jhering, Herbert, *Regisseure und Bühnenmaler* (Berlin: Goldschmidt-Gabrielli, 1921)

Kayssler, Friedrich, *Schauspieler-Notizen* (Erste Folge, Berlin: Reiss, 2nd edn., 1919)

Kerr, Alfred, *Gesammelte Schriften* (7 vols., Berlin: Fischer, 1917–20)

Mit Schleuder und Harfe. Theaterkritiken aus drei Jahrzehnten, ed. H. Fetting (Berlin: Henschelverlag, 1981)

Kindermann, Heinz, *Hofmannsthal und die Schauspielkunst* (Vienna: Böhlau, 1969)

Theatergeschichte Europas, vols. vi–viii (Salzburg: Müller, 1964–8)

Knilli, Friedrich and Münchow, Ursula, *Frühes deutsches Arbeitertheater 1847–1918. Eine Dokumentation* (Munich: Hanser, 1970)

Koller, Ann Marie, *The Theater Duke, Georg II of Saxe-Meiningen and the German Stage* (Stanford University Press, 1984)

Kosch, Wilhelm, *Das Deutsche Theater und Drama im 19. Jahrhundert mit einem Ausblick auf die Folgezeit* (Leipzig: Dyksche Buchhandlung, 1913) [Includes chronology of major plays and critical works 1805–1913]

Krauss, Rudolf, *Modernes Schauspielbuch. Ein Führer durch den deutschen Theaterspielplan der neueren Zeit* (Stuttgart: Muth, 4th edn., 1918)

L'Arronge, Adolph, *Deutsches Theater und deutsche Schauspielkunst* (Berlin: Concordia Deutsche Verlags-Anstalt, 1896)

Laube, Heinrich, *Schriften über Theater*, ausgewählt und eingeleitet von E. Stahl-Wisten (Berlin: Henschelverlag, 1959)

Lewinsky, Josef, ed., *Kleine Schriften dramaturgischen und theatergeschichtlichen Inhalts*, ed. O. Lewinsky (Berlin: Gesellschaft für Theatergeschichte, 1910) [Schriften der Gesellschaft für Theatergeschichte 14]

Liptzin, Sol, *Arthur Schnitzler* (New York: Prentice-Hall, 1932)

Löden, Brigitte, *Max Reinhardts Massenregie auf der Guckkastenbühne von 1905 bis 1910. Ein Versuch zu Darstellungsmittel und Regieintention* (Berne: Lang, 1976)

Moormann, M., *Die Bühnentechnik Heinrich Laubes* (Leipzig: Voss, 1921) [Theatergeschichtliche Forschungen 30]

Moritz, Karl, Eulenberg, Herbert and Poppenberg, Felix, *Neue Theaterkultur* (Stuttgart: Strecker & Schröder, 1906)

Newmark, Maxim, *Otto Brahm. The Man and the Critic* (New York: Stechert, 1938)

Noa, Wolfgang, ed., *Josef Kainz, Briefe* (Berlin: Henschelverlag, 1966)

Osborne, John, 'From Political to Cultural Despotism: the Nature of the Saxe-Meiningen Aesthetic', *Theatre Quarterly*, 5, 17 (1975), pp. 40–54

The Meiningen Court Theatre 1866–1890 (Cambridge University Press, 1988)

The Naturalistic Drama in Germany (Manchester University Press, 1971)

ed., *Die Meininger. Texte zur Rezeption* (Tübingen: Niemeyer, 1980)

Otto, Rainer and Rösler, Walter, *Kabarettgeschichte. Abriss des deutschsprachigen Kabaretts* (Berlin: Henschelverlag, 1977)

Pascal, Roy, *From Naturalism to Expressionism: German Literature and Society 1880–1918* (London: Weidenfeld & Nicolson, 1973)

Patterson, Michael, *The First German Theatre: Schiller, Goethe, Kleist and Büchner in Performance* (London: Routledge, 1990)

The Revolution in German Theatre 1900–1933 (London: Routledge, 1981)

Pörtner, Paul, ed., *Literatur-Revolution 1910–1925* (2 vols., Darmstadt: Luchterhand, 1960)

Prütting, Lenz, *Die Revolution des Theaters. Studien über Georg Fuchs* (Munich: Kitzinger, 1971) [Münchner Beiträge zur Theaterwissenschaft 2]

Reimers, Charlotte Engel, *Die deutschen Bühnen und ihre Angehörigen, Eine Untersuchung über ihre wirtschaftliche Lage* (Leipzig: Duncker & Humblot, 1911)

Reinhardt, Max, *Schriften. Briefe, Reden, Aufsätze, Interviews, Gespräche, Auszüge aus Regiebüchern*, ed. H. Fetting (Berlin: Henschelverlag, 1974)

Richter, Helene, *Schauspieler-Charakteristiken* (Leipzig: Voss, 1914) [Theatergeschichtliche Forschungen 27. Includes chapters on Wolter, Josef Lewinsky, Sonnenthal, Kainz, Hohenfels, Baumeister, Ernst Hartmann, Bleibtreu, Olga Lewinsky, Mitterwurzer, Gabillon, Albert Heine, Hugo Thimig and Schmittlein]

Rieder, Heinz, *Arthur Schnitzler. Das dramatische Werk* (Vienna: Bergland, 1973)

Ruprecht, Erich, ed., *Literarische Manifeste des Naturalismus 1880–1892* (Stuttgart: Metzler, 1962)

Ruprecht, Erich and Bänsch, Dieter, eds., *Literarische Manifeste der Jahrhundertwende 1890–1910* (Stuttgart: Metzler, 1970)

Sayler, Oliver M., ed., *Max Reinhardt and his Theatre* (New York: Brentano, 1924)

Schaubühne, Die [later *Die neue Weltbühne*] (Berlin, 1905–14; reprinted Königstein: Athenäum, 1979–80)

Schlenther, Paul, *Theater im 19. Jahrhundert. Ausgewählte theatergeschichtliche Aufsätze*, ed. H. Knudsen (Berlin: Gesellschaft für Theatergeschichte, 1930) [Schriften der Gesellschaft für Theatergeschichte 40]

Schnitzler, Arthur, *My Youth in Vienna* (London: Weidenfeld & Nicholson, 1971)

Seehaus, Günter, *Frank Wedekind und das Theater* (Munich: Laokoon, 1964)

Seidlin, Oskar, ed., *Der Briefwechsel Arthur Schnitzler – Otto Brahm* (Berlin: Gesellschaft für Theatergeschichte, 1953) [Schriften der Gesellschaft für Theatergeschichte 57]

Skraup, Karl, *Mimik und Gebärdensprache* (Leipzig: Weber, 2nd edn., 1908)

Speidel, Ludwig, *Schauspieler* (Berlin: Meyer & Jessen, 1911) [Vol. IV of *Schriften*]

Steinmetz, Hans, *Theatralische Kunst an der Wende vom Naturalismus zur Stilisierung. Betrachtungen über die Entwicklung des Theaters zur bildenden Kunst am Anfang des 20. Jahrhunderts* (Würzburg: Triltsch, 1939) [Dr. Phil. Diss., Münster U.]

Styan, J[ohn] L., *Max Reinhardt* (Cambridge University Press, 1982)

Theater, Das (Berlin: Cassirer, 1903–5). Facsimile reprint, eds. L. Fiedler and E. Fröböse (Emsdetten: Lechte, 1981)

Tinti, Luisa, *Georg Fuchs e la rivoluzione del teatro* (Rome: Bulzoni Editore, 1980)

Tschörtner, H. D., *Gerhart-Hauptmann-Bibliographie* (Berlin: Deutsche Staatsbibliothek, 1971)

Wagner, Renate and Vacha, Brigitte, *Wiener Schnitzler-Aufführungen 1891–1970* (Munich: Prestel, 1971)

Weber, Horst, *Hugo von Hofmannsthal. Bibliographie des Schrifttums 1892–1963* (Berlin: De Gruyter, 1966)

Wedekind, Frank, *Schauspielkunst. Ein Glossarium* (Munich: Müller, 1910)

Wedekind, Tilly, 'Lulu: the Role of my Life', *Theatre Quarterly*, I, 2 (1971), pp. 3–7

Weil, Theodor, *Die elektrische Bühnen- und Effekt-Beleuchtung. Ein Überblick über die Methoden und neuesten Apparate der elektrischen Bühnenbeleuchtung* (Vienna: Hartleben, 1904)

Weilen, Alexander von, ed., *Heinrich Laube. Theaterkritiken und dramaturgische Aufsätze* (2 vols., Berlin: Gesellschaft für Theatergeschichte, 1906) [Schriften der Gesellschaft für Theatergeschichte, 7/8]

Winds, Adolf, *Die Technik der Schauspielkunst* (Dresden: Minden, 2nd edn., 1919)

Zabel, Eugen, *Moderne Bühnenkunst* (Bielefeld: Velhagen, 1911)

Ziemann, Erich, *Heinrich Laube als Theaterkritiker* (Emsdetten: Lechte, 1934) [Die Schaubühne 3 (wongly given on title-page as 4)]

RUSSIA, 1848–1916

Abalkin, N., ed., *Maly Teatr SSSR 1824–1974*, vol. I (Moscow: Vserossiyskoe teatral'noe obshchestvo, 1978)

Adaryukov, V. Ya., *Bibliografichesky ukazatel' knig, broshyur, zhurnal'nykh statey i zametok po istorii russkogo teatra* (St Petersburg: E. Arngold, 1904)

Aganbekyan, A., *Moskovsky Khudozhestvenny teatr 1898–1938. Bibliografichesky ukazatel'*, ed. S. N. Durylin (Moscow-Leningrad: Vserossiyskoe teatral'noe obshchestvo, 1939)

Alekseev, A. et al, eds., *Russkaya khudozhestvennaya kultura kontsa XIX-nachala XX veka (1908–1917)* (Moscow: Nauka, 1980)

Alpers, B., *Aktërskoe iskusstvo v Rossii* (2 vols., Moscow-Leningrad: Iskusstvo, 1945)

Al'tshuller, A. Ya., ed., *Ocherki istorii russkoy teatral'noy kritiki: konets XIX-nachalo XX veka* (Leningrad: Iskusstvo, 1979)

Amiard-Chevrel, Claudine, *Le Théâtre artistique de Moscou (1898–1917)* (Paris: Editions du Centre national de la recherche scientifique, 1979)

Anushkin, Y., *Kamerny teatr* (Moscow-Leningrad: Academia, 1927)

Ashukin, P. S., V. N. Vsevolodsky-Gerngross and Yu. V. Sobolëv, *Khrestomatiya po istorii russkogo teatra XVIII i XIX vekov* (Leningrad-Moscow: Iskusstvo, 1940)

Aykhenval'd, Yuly, *Slova o slovakh: kriticheskie ocherki* (Petrograd: Izd. byvsh. M. A. Popova, 1923?)

Baikova-Poggi, T., 'La théâtralité chez Evreïnov et les futuristes russes', *Revue des études slaves*, 53, 1 (1981)

Balukhaty, S., 'Chayka' v postanovke Moskovskogo Khudozhestvennogo teatra. Rezhissërskaya partitura K. S. Stanislavskogo. (Leningrad-Moscow, 1938); trans. D. Magarshack, *The Seagull Produced by Stanislavsky* (London: Dennis Dobson, 1952)

Benedetti, Jean, *Stanislavski, A Biography* (London: Methuen, 1988)

ed., *The Moscow Art Theatre Letters* (London: Routledge, 1992)

Blok, Aleksandr, 'Vera Fëdorovna Kommissarzhevskaya', *Rech'*, 12 February 1910

Bowlt, John E., *The Silver Age: Russian Art of the Early Twentieth Century and the 'World of Art' Group*, 2nd edn. (Newtonvile, Mass.: Oriental Research Partners, 1982)

'Synthesism and symbolism: the Russian "World of Art" movement', in *Literature and the Plastic Arts 1880–1930*, ed. I. Higgins (Edinburgh: Scottish Academic Press, 1973)

'The World of Art', in *The Silver Age of Russian Culture*, eds. C. and E. Proffer (Ann Arbor: Ardis, 1975)

ed., *Russian Art of the Avant-garde: Theory and Criticism 1902–1934* (New York: MSS, 1976)

Braun, Edward, *Meyerhold: A Revolution in Theatre* (London: Methuen, 1995)

ed. and trans., *Meyerhold on Theatre* (London: Methuen, 1969)

Brodskaya, G. Yu., 'Bryusov i teatr', *Literaturnoe nasledstvo*, 85 (1976)

Brukson, Ya., *Problema teatral'nosti* (Petrograd: Tret'ja strazha, 1923)

Teatr Meyerkhol'da (Leningrad: Academia, 1925)

Bryusov, Valery, 'Gamlet v Moskovkom Khudozhestvennom teatre', *Ezhegodnik Imperatorskikh teatrov*, 2 (1912)

Sobranie sochineny (7 vols., Moscow: Khudozhestvennaya literatura, 1975)

Carnicke, Sharon, 'L'instinct théâtral: Evreïnov et la théâtralité', *Revue des études slaves*, 53, 1 (1981)

Chushkin, N. N., *Gamlet-Kachalov: iz stsenicheskoy istorii Gamlet Shekspira* (Moscow: Iskusstvo, 1966)

Davydov, V. N., *Rasskaz o proshlom* (Leningrad-Moscow: Iskusstvo, 1962)

Derzhavin, K., *Épokhi Aleksandrinskoy stseny* (Leningrad: Academia, 1932)

Kniga o Kamernom teatre 1914–1934 (Leningrad: Academia, 1934)

Dmitriev, Yu., 'Iz istorii russkoy rezhissury 1880–1890-kh godov', in *Teatr i dramaturgiya* (Leningrad: Iskusstvo, 1967)

Doroshevich, V. M., *Staraya teatral'naya Moskva* (Petrograd: Izd-vo Petrograd, 1923)

Drizen, N. V., *Dramaticheskaya tsenzura dvukh èpokh 1825–1881* (Petrograd: Prometey, 1917)

'Meyningentsy v Peterburge', *Stolitsa i usad'ba*, 43 (1915)

Sorok let teatra. Vospominaniya 1875–1915 (Petrograd: Prometey, 1916?)

'Starinny teatr (vospominaniya)', *Stolitsa i usad'ba*, 71 (1 December 1916)

Dukor, I., 'Problemy dramaturgii simvolizma', *Literaturnoe nasledstvo*, 27–28 (1937)

Dyagilev, S. P., *Sergey Dyagilev i russkoe iskusstvo*, (2 vols., Moscow: Izobrazitel 'noe iskusstvo, 1982)

Éfros, N., '"Chayka" A. P. Chekhova na stsene MKhT', in *Ezhegodnik MKhT 1944*, vol. 1

Moskovsky Khudozhestvenny teatr, 1898–1923 (Moscow-Petrograd: Gos. izdatel'stvo, 1924)

'Vishnëvy sad', p'esa A. P. Chekhova v postanovke MKhT. (St Petersburg, 1919)

Evreinov, N. N., *Histoire du théâtre russe* (Paris: Éditions du Chêne, 1947)

'K pereotsenke teatral'nosti', *Zhizn' iskusstva*, 37 and 38 (18 September and 25 September 1923)

P'esy iz reperturara 'Krivogo Zerkala' (Petrograd: Academia, 1923)

Pro scena sua (Petrograd: Prometey, 1914)

'Starinny teatr: ob aktëre srednikh vekov', *Teatr i iskusstvo*, 50 (16 December 1907)

Teatr dlya sebya (3 vols., Petrograd: Sovremennoe iskusstvo, 1915–17)

Teatr tak takovoy (St Petersburg: Sovremennoe iskusstvo, 1912)
Teatralizatsiya zhizni (Moscow: Vremya, 1922)
The Theatre in Life, ed. and trans. A. Nazaroff (London: George G. Harrap, 1927)
Vvdenie v monodramu (St Petersburg: Sovremennoe iskusstvo, 1908)
Evstigneeva, L., 'Nicolas Evreïnov, théoricien et philosophe du comique', *Revue des études slaves*, 53, 1 (1981)
Ezhegodnik Imperatorskikh teatrov (St Petersburg: Tipografiya imp. Spb. Teatrov, 1892–1915)
Ezhegodnik Moskovskogo Khudozhestvennogo teatra (Moscow, 1943–61)
Gerasimov, Yu. K., 'Krizis modernistskoy teatral'noy mysli v Rossii (1907–1917)', *Teatr i dramaturgiya*, 4 (1974)
'V. Ya. Bryusov i uslovny teatr,' *Teatr i dramaturgiya. Trudy Leningradskogo gos. instituta muzyki i kinematografii*, 4 (1974)
Gerould, D. C., 'Andrey Bely: Russian symbolist', *Performing Arts Journal*, Fall 1978
'Sologub and the theatre', *The Drama Review*, 76 (December 1977)
'Valerii Briusov: Russian symbolist', *Performing Arts Journal*, Winter 1979
Gladkov, A. K. 'Meyerkhol'd govorit', *Novy Mir*, 8 (1961)
Golub, Spencer, *Evreinov, the theatre of paradox and transformation* (Ann Arbor: UMI, 1984)
'The mysteries of the self: the visionary theatre of Nikolai Evreinov', *Theatre History Studies*, 2 (1982)
The Recurrence of Fate. Theater and Memory in Twentieth-Century Russia (University of Iowa Press, 1994)
Golobushenko, Yu., *Rezhissёrskie iskusstvo Tairova* (Moscow, 1970)
Gray, Camilla, *The Great Experiment: Russian Art 1863–1922* (London: Thames and Hudson, 1962)
Grits, T. S., *M. S. Shchepkin: letopis' zhizni i tvorchestva*, ed. A. P. Klinchin (Moscow: Nauka, 1966)
Grover, S. R., *Savva Mamontov and the Mamontov Circle 1870–1905. Art Patronage and the Rise of Nationalism in Russian Art*. Ph. dissertation, University of Wisconsin, 1971
Hoover, M. L., *Meyerhold – the Art of Conscious Theater* (Amherst: University of Massachusetts Press, 1974)
Institut istorii iskusstv Ministerstva kul'tury SSSR, *Istoriya russkogo dramaticheskogo teatra*, ed. E. G. Kholodov (7 vols., Moscow: Iskusstvo, 1977–87)
Ivanov, Vyacheslav, *Borozdy i mezhi. Opyty esteticheskie i kriticheskie* (Moscow: Musaget, 1916; reprinted Letchworth: Bradda Books, 1971)
'Novye maski', *Vesy*, 7 (1907)
Po zvёzdam (St Petersburg, 1909)
'The theatre of the future', trans. S. Graham, *English Review*, 10 (March 1912)
Janecek, G., ed, *Andrey Bely, a Critical Review* (Lexington: University of Kentucky Press, 1978)
Kamerny teatr i ego khudozhniki 1914–1934 (Moscow, 1934)
Kazansky, B. V., *Metod teatra (analiz sistemy N. N. Evreinova)* (Leningrad: Academia, 1925)
Kommissarzhevsky, F., *Myself and the Theatre* (London, 1929)
'O garmonii iskusstv na stsene', *Ezhegodnik Imperatorskikh teatrov*, vol. 1 (1912)
Teatral'nyya prelyudii (Moscow, 1916)
Tvorchestvo aktёra i teoriya Stanislavskogo (Petrograd, 1916)
Koonen, Alisa, *Stranitsy zhizni* (Moscow: Iskusstvo, 1975)
Kruchёnykh, A. E., *Pobeda na solntsem* (St Petersburg, 1913); English trans. E. Bartos and V. N. Kirby, 'Victory over the sun', *Drama Review*, 15, 4 (Fall 1971); French trans. V. and J.-C. Marcadé, *Victoire sur le soleil* (Lausanne, 1982)
15 let russkogo futurizma (Moscow, 1928)
Kryzhitsky, G., *Rezhissёrskie portrёty* (Moscow-Leningrad: Tea-kino-pechat', 1928)
'Vospominaniya "Laboratoriya smekha"', *Teatr* 8 (August 1967)
Kugel, A. R., *Utverzhdenie teatra* (Moscow: Teatr i iskusstvo, 1923)
Lapshina, M., *Mir Iskusstva* (Moscow: Iskusstvo, 1977)
Leach, Robert, *Meyerhold* (Cambridge University Press, 1988)
Lo Gatto, Ettore, *Storia del teatro russo* (2 vols., Florence: G. G. Sansoni, 1952)

Lodder, Christina, *Russian Constructivism* (New Haven: Yale University Press, 1983)

Markov, P. A., *Noveyshie teatral'nye techeniya (1898–1923). Opyt populyarnogo izlozhenie* (Moscow, 1924)

'Pervaya studiya MKhT: Sulerzhitsky – Vakhtangov – Chekhov', in *Moskovsky Khudozhestvenny teatr vtoroy* (Moscow, 1925); reprinted in *Pravda teatra: stat'i* (Moscow: Iskusstvo, 1965)

ed., *Teatral'naya èntsiklopediya* (6 vols., Moscow, 1961–7)

Markov, Vladimir, *Russian futurism: a history* (London: MacGibbon and Kee, 1969)

Mayakovsky, V. V., *The Complete Plays of Vladimir Mayakovsky*, trans. G. Daniels (New York, 1968)

Teatr i kino (2 vols., Moscow: Sovetsky pisatel', 1954)

Medvedev, P. A., *Vospominaniya* (Leningrad: Academia, 1929)

Meyerkhol'd, V. E., *O teatre* (St Petersburg, 1913)

Perepiska 1896–1939 (Moscow: Iskusstvo, 1976)

Stat'i, pis'ma, rechi, besedy (2 vols., Moscow: Iskusstvo, 1968)

Teatr: Kniga o novom teatre (St Petersburg: Shipovnik, 1908)

Mgebrov, A., *Zhizn' v teatre* (2 vols., Leningrad: Academia, 1929–32)

Mir iskusstva (St Petersburg, 1898–1914)

Mollica, Fabio, ed., *Il teatro possibile. Stanislavskij e il primo studio del Teatro d'arte di Moscoa* (Florence: La casa Usher, 1989)

Moody, C., 'The Ancient Theatre in St Petersburg and Moscow 1907–8 and 1911–12', *New Zealand Slavonic Journal*, 2 (1976)

'The Crooked Mirror', *Melbourne Slavonic Studies*, 7 (1972)

Moskovsky Khudozhedstvenny teatr v illyustratiyakh i dokumentakh 1898–1938 (Moscow: Izd. Moskovs-kogo ordena Lenina khudozhestvennogo akademicheskogo teatra Soyuza SSSR imeni M. Gor'kogo, 1938)

Moskovsky listok, 28 December 1898

Nelidov, V. A., *Teatral'naya Moskva (sorok let moskovskikh teatrov)* (Berlin-Riga: S. Kretschetow, 1931)

Nemirovich-Danchenko, Vl. I., *Iz proshlogo* (Moscow: Academia, 1938); trans. J. Cournos, *My Life in the Russian Theatre* (London: Geoffrey Bles, 1937)

Izbrannye pis'ma v dvukh tomakh (2 vols., Moscow: Iskusstvo, 1979)

'Po povodu Yuliya Tsesarya u Meyningenerov', *Teatr i zhizn'*, 89 (1885)

Vl. I. Nemirovich-Danchenko o tvorchestve aktëra: khrestomatiya (Moscow: Iskusstvo, 1973)

Nil'sky, A. A., *Zakulisnaya khronika 1856–1894* (St Petersburg, 1900)

'Not politics, only drama – Komisarzhevsky', *New York Times* (1 March 1908)

Ostrovsky, A. N., *Polnoe sobranie sochineny* (12 vols., Moscow: Iskusstvo, 1973–80)

Pavlova, T., 'Teatr F. A. Korsha i zritel'', in *Problemy sotsiologii teatra: sbornik statey*, ed. N. Khrenov (Moscow: Vserossiyskoe teatral'noe obshchestvo, 1974)

Pearson, A. G., 'The cabaret comes to Russia: "Theatre of Small Forms" as cultural catalyst', *Theatre Quarterly*, 36 (Winter 1980)

Pervaya russkaya revolyutsiya i teatr. Stat'i i materialy (Moscow, 1956)

Petrovskaya, I. F., *Istochnikovedenie istorii russkogo dorevolyutsionnogo dramaticheskogo teatra* (Leningrad: Iskusstvo, 1971)

Teatr i zritel' provintsial'noy Rossii vtoraya polovina XIX veka (Leningrad: Iskusstvo, 1979)

Pluchek, V., *Na stsene Mayakovsky* (Moscow, 1962)

Polyakova, M. Ya., ed., *Russkaya teatral'naya parodiya XIX-nachala XX veka* (Moscow: Iskusstvo, 1976)

Prygunov, M. D., *Russkaya stsena za poslednie sorok let 1880–1920* (Kazan, 1921)

Red'ko, A. D., *Teatr i èvolyutsiya teatral'nykh form* (Leningrad: Seyatel', 1926; reprinted Letchworth: Prideaux Press, 1977)

Remizov, A., *Krashennyya ryla. Teatr i kniga* (Berlin, 1922)

'Tovarishchestvo novoy dramy', *Vesy*, 4 (April, 1904)

Rice, Martin P., *Valery Briusov and the Rise of Russian Symbolism* (Ann Arbor: Ardis, 1975)

Ripellino, A. M., *Maïakovski et le théâtre russe d'avant-garde* (Paris, 1965)

Roberts, J. W., *Richard Boleslavsky: His Life and Work in the Theatre* (Ann Arbor: UMI, 1981)

Rodina, T. M., *Aleksandr Blok i russky teatr nachala XX veka* (Moscow: Nauka, 1972)
Rosenthal, B. G., 'Theatre as Church: The Vision of the Mystical Anarchists', *Russian History*, 4, 2 (1977)
Rostotsky, B. and N. Chushkin, '"Gamlet": publikatsiya materialov k postanovke spektaklya v MKhT', *Ezhegodnik MKhT 1944*, vol. 1
'Tsar Fëdor Ioannovich' na stsene MKhT (Moscow-Leningrad: Iskusstvo, 1940)
Rudnitsky, Konstantin, *Rezhissër Meyerkhol'd* (Moscow, 1969); trans. G. Petrov, *Meyerhold the Director* (Ann Arbor: Ardis, 1981)
Russian & Soviet theatre. Tradition & the avant-garde, trans. R. Fermar, ed. L. Milne (London: Thames and Hudson, 1988)
Russell, Robert and Andrew Barratt, eds., *Russian Theatre in the Age of Modernism* (London: Macmillan, 1990)
Samsonov, L. N., *Teatral'noe del v provintsii* (Odessa, 1875)
Sbornik pamyati V. F. Kommissarzhevskoy (St Petersburg, 1911)
Sbornik pamyati V. F. Kommissarzhevskoy (Moscow, 1931)
Shcheglov, I., *Narod i teatr. Ocherki i izsledovaniya sovremennago narodnago teatra v 6 chastyakh* (Petrograd: P. P. Soykin, 1911)
Schchepkin, M. S., *Mikhail Semënovich Shchepkin zhizn' i tvorchestvo*, eds. T. M. Elnitskaya and O. M. Fel'dman (2 vols., Moscow: Iskusstvo, 1984)
Segel, Harold R., *Turn-of-the-century Cabaret* (New York: Columbia University Press, 1987)
Senelick, Laurence, 'Chekhov's drama, Maeterlinck and the Russian symbolists', in *Chekhov's Great Plays*, ed. J. P. Barricelli (New York University Press, 1981)
'Evreinov's *Inspector General*', *Performing Arts Journal*, 22 (March 1984)
Gordon Craig's Moscow Hamlet: A Reconstruction (Westport, Conn.: Greenwood Press, 1982)
'Rachel in Russia: The Shchepkin–Annenkov Correspondence,' *Theatre Research International*, 3, 2 (May 1978), pp. 93–114
Serf Actor: The Life and Art of Mikhail Shchepkin (Westport, Conn.: Greenwood Press, 1984)
'Vera Kommissarzhevskaya: the Actress as Symbolist Eidolon', *Theatre Journal*, December 1980
ed. and trans., *Cabaret Performance: vol. 1: Europe 1890–1920 Songs, Sketches, Monologues, Memoirs* (New York: Performing Arts Journal Publications, 1989)
ed., *National Theatre in Northern and Eastern Europe, 1746–1900* (Cambridge University Press, 1991)
ed. and trans., *Russian Dramatic Theory from Pushkin to the Symbolists* (Austin: University of Texas Press, 1981)
ed. and trans., *Russian Satiric Comedy* (New York: Performing Arts Journal Publications, 1983)
Sobolëv, Yu. V., *Moskovsky Khudozhestvenny teatr* (Moscow-Leningrad, 1938)
Stanislavsky, K. S., *My Life in Art*, trans. J. J. Robbins (Boston: Little, Brown, 1924)
Rezhissërskie eksemplyary K. S. Stanislavskogo, ed. I. Ya. Vilenkin and I. N. Solov'eva (6 vols., Moscow: Iskusstvo, 1980-in progress)
Sobranie sochineny (8 vols., Moscow: Iskusstvo, 1954-9)
Sobranie sochineny, ed. O. N. Efremov et al, (11 vols., Moscow: Iskusstvo, 1988-in progress)
Stark, E., *Starinny teatr* (St Petersburg: Tret'ya strazha, 1922)
Strepetova, P. A., *Vospominaniya i pis'ma* (Moscow-Leningrad: Iskusstvo, 1934)
Zhizn' i tvorchestvo tragicheskoy aktrisy (Leningrad-Moscow: Iskusstvo, 1959)
Stroeva, M. N., *Chekhov i Khudozhestvenny teatr* (Moscow: Iskusstvo, 1955)
Rezhissërskie iskaniya Stanislavskogo 1898–1917 (Moscow: Nauka, 1973)
Sulerzhitsky, L. A., *Povesti i rasskazy, stat'i i zametki o teatre, perepiska, vospominaniya o L. A. Sulerzhitskom* (Moscow: Iskusstvo, 1970)
Sumbatov-Yuzhin, A., *Pervy Vserossiysky s"ezd stsenicheskikh deyateley, ego rezolyutsii i nastroeniya* (Moscow, 1897)
Syrkina, F. Ya., *Russkoe teatral'no-dekoratsionnoe iskusstvo vtoroy poloviny XIX veka: ocherki* (Moscow: Iskusstvo, 1956)

Tairov, A., *Zapiski rezhisséra* (Moscow, 1921); trans. W. Kuhlke, *Notes of a director* (Coral Gables: University of Miami Press, 1969)
    Zapiski rezhisséra: stat'i, besedy, rechi, pis'ma (Moscow: Vserossiyskoe teatral'noe obshchestvo, 1970)
Tal'nikov, D., *Komissarzhevskaya.* (Moscow-Leningrad: Iskusstvo, 1939)
    Sistema Shchepkina (Moscow-Leningrad: Iskusstvo, 1939)
Teatr (Moscow), 5 (May 1993). [Art nouveau/Modernism issue]
Teatr: kniga o novom teatre (St Petersburg: Shipovnik, 1908)
Teatr i iskusstvo (St Petersburg, 1897–1918)
Telyakovsky, V. A., *Vospominaniya* (Leningrad-Moscow: Iskusstvo, 1965)
Tikhvinskaya, L. N., '"Krivoe zerkalo" i monodrama', in *Mir iskusstv*, eds. M. P. Kotovskaya and S. A. Isaev (Moscow: GITIS, 1991)
Tolstoy, A. K., *Sobranie sochineny* (4 vols., Moscow: Pravda, 1969)
Trudy pervogo Vserossiyskogo s"ezda stsenicheskikh deyateley, parts 1 and 2 (St Petersburg: Nadezhda 1898; Moscow: A. A. Levenson, 1898)
Tugenkhol'd, Ya., *Aleksandra Ékster kak zhivopisets i khudozhnik stseny* (Berlin, 1922)
Tvorcheskoe nasledie V. E. Meyerkhol'da (Moscow: Iskusstvo, 1978)
Urusov, A. I., *Stati ego o teatre, literature i iskusstve* (2 vols., Moscow: I. N. Kolchév, 1907)
Uvarova, E., *Estradny teatr: miniatyury, obozreniya, myuzik-kholly (1917–1945)* (Moscow: Iskusstvo, 1983)
Vakhtangov, E. B., *Materialy i stat'i* (Moscow: Iskusstvo, 1959)
Varneke, B. V., *Istoriya russkogo teatra* (3rd edn., Moscow-Leningrad: Iskusstvo, 1939) [The English translation by B. Brasol, *History of the Russian Theatre seventeenth through nineteenth century* (New York: Macmillan, 1951) lacks the notes and bibliographic material.]
Vera Fëdorovna Kommissarzhevskaya. Pis'ma aktrisy, vospominaniya o ney, materialy, ed. A. Ya. Al'tshuller (Moscow-Leningrad: Iskusstvo, 1964)
Veselovsky, A., 'Predstavleniya meyningenskoy truppy', *Artist*, 7 (1890)
Vinogradskaya, I., *Zhizn' i tvorchestvo K. S. Stanislavskogo – letopis*, vol. 1 (Moscow: Iskusstvo, 1971)
Volkov, N. D., *Meyerkhol'd* (2 vols., Moscow-Leningrad: Academia, 1929)
Vsevolodsky-Gerngross, V., *Istoriya russkogo teatra* (2 vols., Leningrad-Moscow: Tea-Kino-Pechat', 1929)
    ed., *Khrestomatiya po istorii russkogo teatra* (Moscow: Khudozhestvennaya literatura, 1936)
Weisbaden, N., 'Une résurrection du théâtre médiéval à Saint-Pétersbourg en 1907–08', in *Mélanges Cohen* (Paris, 1950)
West, J., *Russian Symbolism: A Study of Vyacheslav Ivanov and the Russian Symbolist Aesthetic* (London: Methuen, 1970)
Woodward, J. B., 'From Brjusov to Ajkhenval'd: Attitudes to the Russian Theatre 1902–1914', *Canadian Slavonic Papers*, 7 (1965)
Woroszylski, W., *The life of Mayakovsky*, trans. B. Taborski (New York: Orion Press, 1971)
Yukovsky, Yu., ed., *'Na dne,' materialy i issledovaniya* (Moscow-Leningrad: Iskusstvo, 1940)
Yur'ev, Yu. M., *Zapiski* (2 vols., Leningrad-Moscow: Iskusstvo, 1963)
Znosko-Borovsky, E. A., *Russky teatr nachala XX veka* (Prague: Plamja, 1925)
Zograf, N. G., *Maly Teatr vtoroy poloviny XIX veka* (Moscow: Akad. Nauk, 1960)
Zonov, A., 'Letopis teatra nad Ofitserkoy', in *Alkonost'*, vol. 1 (St Petersburg, 1911)

SCANDINAVIA, 1849–1912

Aarseth, Asbjørn, *Den nationale scene, 1901–31* (Oslo, 1969)
Ahlström, Stellan, *Strindbergs erövring av Paris*, Stockholm Studies in the History of Literature, 2 (Stockholm, 1956)
Anker, Øyvind, *Christiania Theaters repertoire 1827–99* (Oslo, 1956)
    Christiania Norske Theaters repertoire 1852–1863 (Oslo, 1956)
    'Ibseniana og Bjørnsoniana fra Kristianiateaterns arkiver', *Edda*, 56 (1956), pp. 111–60

Johan Peter Strömberg (Oslo, 1958)
Den danske teatermaleren Troels Lund og Christiania Theater (Oslo, 1962)
Ansteinsson, Eli, Teater i Norge (Oslo, 1968)
Arpe, Verner, Das Theater in Skandinavien (Zürich, 1966)
    Das schwedische Theater (Gothenburg, 1969)
Aumont, A. and Collin, Edgar, Det danske Nationalteater 1748–1889. En statistisk Fremstilling (5 vols.,
    Copenhagen, 1896–99)
Bang, Herman, Teatret (Copenhagen, 1892)
Baude, H., 'Stockholms teatrar och teaterpublik vid 1800– talets slut', in Nya teaterhistoriska studier.
    Skrifter utgivna av Föreningen Drottningholmsteaterns Vänner, 12 (Stockholm, 1957)
Bergman, Gösta M., 'Dramaten – från Bollhuset till Nybroplan', in Dramaten 175 år: Studier i svensk
    scenkonst (Stockholm, 1963)
    Den moderna teaterns genombrott 1890–1925 (Stockholm, 1966)
    ed., Svensk teater: strukturförändringar och organisation 1900–1970 (Stockholm, 1970)
Bjørnson, Bjørn, Det gamle teater. Kunsten og menneskene (Oslo, 1937)
Blanc, T. H., Norges første nationale scene (Christiania, 1884)
    Christiania Theaters historie 1827–1877 (Christiania, 1899)
    Henrik Ibsen og Christiania Theater 1850–1899 (Christiania, 1906)
Bloch, Anton, Fra en ander Tid. Erindringer. (Copenhagen, 1930)
Bøgh, Gran, Henrik Ibsen på Ole Bulls Teater (Bergen, 1949)
Borup, Morten, Johan Ludvig Heiberg (3 vols., Copenhagen, 1947–9)
Brandes, Edvard, Dansk Skuespilkunst: Portraetstudier (Copenhagen, 1880)
Brandes, Georg, Henrik Ibsen. Bjørnstjerne Bjørnson (London, 1899)
Christensen, Harald, Det Kongelige Theater i Aarene 1852–1819 (Copenhagen, 1890)
Christiansen, Svend, Klassisk skuespilkunst. Stabile konventioner i skuespilkunsten 1700–1900 (Copen-
    hagen, 1975)
Clausen, Julius, Kulturhistoriske Studier over Heibergs Vaudeviller (Copenhagen, 1891)
Doumic, R., De Scribe à Ibsen (Paris, 1896)
Durbach, Errol, ed., Ibsen and the Theatre (London, 1980)
Elster, Kristian, Skuespillerinden Johanne Dybwad: Til belysning av realismen i skuespilskunsten (Oslo,
    1931)
Fahlstrøm, Alma, To norske skuespilleres liv, og de Fahlstrømske teatres historie 1878–1917 (Oslo, 1927)
Falck, August, Strindberg och teater (Stockholm, 1918)
    Fem år med Strindberg (Stockholm, 1935)
Fredericia, Allan, August Bournonville. Balletmesteren som genspejlede et århundredes idealer og konflikter
    (Copenhagen, 1979)
Friese, William, ed., Strindberg und die deutschsprachigen Länder. Beiträge zur nordischen Philologie, 8
    (Basel and Stuttgart, 1979)
Gravier, Maurice, Strindberg et le théâtre moderne. I: L'Allemagne, Bibliothèque de la Societé des Études
    Germaniques, 2 (Lyons and Paris, 1949)
Hansen, Peter, Den danske Skueplads (3 vols., Copenhagen, 1889–96)
Hedwall, Yngve, Strindberg på Stockholmsscenen 1870–1922 (Stockholm, 1923)
Heiberg, Gunnar, Ibsen og Bjørnson paa scenen (Christiania, 1918)
    Norsk Teater (Oslo, 1920)
Heiberg, Johan Ludvig, Samlede Skrifter (9 vols., Copenhagen, 1833–41)
Heiberg, Johanne Luise, Et Liv Gjenoplevet i Erindringen (4 vols., Copenhagen, 1891–2)
Henriques, Alf, et al, Teatret paa Kongens Nytorv, 1748–1948 (Cpenhagen, 1948)
Ibsen, Henrik, Samlede Verker (Hundreårsutgaven), eds. Francis Bull, Halvdan Koht and Didrik Arup
    Seip (21 vols., Oslo, 1928–57)
    The Oxford Ibsen, ed. James Walter McFarlane (8 vols., London, 1960–77)
Josephson, Ludvig, Våra teaterförhållanden (Stockholm, 1870)
    Teaterregi (Stockholm, 1892)

Just, Carl, *Schrøder og Christiania Theater* (Oslo, 1948)

Lamm, Martin, *August Strindberg* (2 vols. Stockholm, 1940-42). Trans. Harry G. Carlsson (New York, 1971)

Lindberg, Per, *August Lindberg, skådespelaren och människan* (Stockholm, 1943)

Lorentzen, Bernt, *Det første norske teater* (Bergen, 1949)

Lugné-Poe, *Aurélien-Marie, Ibsen* (Paris, 1937)

Lund, Audhild, *Henrik Ibsen og det norske teater* (Oslo, 1925)

Lycke, Lise, *Norges teaterhistorie* (Asker, 1991)

Madsen, Børge Gedsø, *Strindberg's naturalistic theatre: its relation to French naturalism* (Copenhagen, 1962)

Mantzius, Karl, *Skuespilkunstens Historie i det nittende Aarhundrede* (Copenhagen, 1922)

Marker, Frederick J. and Marker, Lise-Lone, *The Scandinavian Theatre: A Short History* (Oxford, 1975)

Ibsen's Lively Art: A Performance Study of the Major Plays (Cambridge, 1989)

Molander, Olof, *Harald Molander* (Helsinki, 1960)

Neiiendam, Robert, *Det Kongelige Teaters Historie*, 1874-1922 (5 vols., Copenhagen, 1921-30)

Nordensvan, G., *Svensk teater och svenska skådespelare från Gustaf III till våra dagar* (2 vols., Stockholm, 1917-18)

Normann, Axel Otto, *Johanne Dybwad: Liv og kunst* (Oslo, 1937; 2nd edn. 1950)

Ollén, Gunnar, *Strindbergs dramatik* (Stockholm, 1948; 4th edn., 1982)

Reimers, Sophie, *Teaterminder fra Kristiania Teater* (Christiania, 1919)

Reque, A. D., *Trois auteurs dramatiques scandinaves – Ibsen, Bjørnson, Strindberg – devant la critique française 1889-1901* (Paris, 1930)

Richardson, Gunnar, *Oscarisk teaterpolitik: De kungliga teatrarnas omvandling från hovinstitution till statliga aktiebolag* (Summary in English) (Gothenburg, 1966)

Rønneberg, Anton, *Nationaltheatret gjennom femti år* (Oslo, 1949)

Schyberg, Fr., *Dansk teaterkritikk indtil 1914* (Copenhagen, 1937)

Stockenström, Göran, ed., *Strindberg's Dramaturgy* (Minneapolis, 1988)

Strindberg, August, *Samlade Skrifter*, ed. John Landqvist (55 vols., Stockholm, 1912-20)

Samlade Verk. Nationalutgåvan, gen. ed. Lars Dahlbäck (Stockholm: 1981-[in progress])

August Strindbergs Brev, eds. Torsten Eklund and Björn Meidal (Stockholm, 1948-[in progress])

Strindberg's Letters, selected, edited and translated by Michael Robinson (2 vols., Chicago and London, 1992)

Open Letters to the Intimate Theatre, trans. Walter Johnson (Seattle and London, 1966)

Strømme Svendsen, Arnljot, *Den Nationale Scene. Det norske repertoire 1876-1964* (Bergen, 1964)

Svanberg, J., *Kungliga teatrarna under ett halft sekel 1860-1910* (Stockholm, 1917)

Törnqvist, Egil, *Strindbergian Drama* (Stockholm, 1982)

Waal, Carla Rae, *Johanne Dybwad: Norwegian Actress* (Oslo, 1967)

Wiers-Jenssen, H., *Billeder fra Bergens ældste teaterhistorie* (Bergen, 1921)

and Nordahl-Olsen, Joh., *Den Nationale Scene: De første 25 aar* (Bergen, 1926)

Wiesener, A. M., *Henrik Ibsen og Det Norske Teater i Bergen 1851-57* (Bergen, 1928)

Wolf, Lucie, *Livserindringer* (Christiania, 1897)

ENGLAND, 1850–1914

Periodicals (including annuals)

The Builder (1842–)

Dramatic Notes (1879-1893)

The Dramatic Review (1885-1894)

The Dramatic Year (1892)

The Era (1838-1939)

The Era Almanac (1868-1919)

The Green Room Book: or, Who's Who on the Stage (1906–1912)
The Illustrated London News (1842–1966)
The Illustrated Sporting and Dramatic News (1874–1925)
London Entr'acte (1869–1874); cont. as Entr'acte (1872–1907)
Nineteenth-Century Theatre Research (Edmonton, Alberta, 1973–)
Play Pictorial (1902–1939)
The Playgoer (1901–1904)
The Stage Directory (1880–1881); cont. as The Stage (1881–)
Stage Society: Annual Reports (1899/1900–1920/21)
The Stage Souvenir (1903)
The Stage Yearbook (1908–1928)
The Theatre (1877–1897)
Theatre Notebook (1946–)
Who's Who in the Theatre (1912–)

Books and articles

Agate, James, A Short View of the English Stage 1900–1926 (London, 1926; reprinted New York and
    London: Benjamin Blom, 1969)
Archer, William, English Dramatists of Today (London: Sampson Low, 1882)
Arliss, George, On the Stage (London: John Murray, 1928)
Arnott, James F. and J. W. Robertson, English Theatrical Literature 1550–1900: a Bibliography (London:
    Society for Theatre Research, 1971)
Bailey, Peter, ed., Music Hall: The Business of Pleasure (Milton Keynes: Open University Press, 1986)
Baker, H. B., History of the London Stage (1904, reprinted New York: Blom, 1969)
Baker, Michael, The Rise of the Victorian Actor (London: Croom Helm, 1978)
Bancroft, Squire and Marie Bancroft, Mr and Mrs Bancroft on and off the Stage, 4th edn. (London:
    Bentley, 1888)
Beauman, Sally, The Royal Shakespeare Company: A History of Ten Decades (Oxford University Press,
    1982)
Booth, Michael, English Melodrama (London: Herbert Jenkins, 1965)
    prefaces and notes to English Plays of the Nineteenth Century (4 vols., Oxford University Press,
    1969–73)
    Theatre in the Victorian Age (Cambridge University Press, 1991)
    Victorian Spectacular Theatre 1850–1910 (London: Routledge and Kegan Paul, 1981)
Booth, Michael R., Richard Southern, Frederick and Lise-Lone Marker and Robertson Davies, The
    Revels History of Drama in English, vol. VI, 1750–1880 (London: Methuen, 1975)
Borsa, Mario, The English Stage of Today (London: John Lane, 1908)
Boucicault, Dion Lardner, The Art of Acting, lecture, reprinted. Dramatic Museum of Columbia
    University, ser. 5, no. 1 (New York: Columbia University Press, 1926)
Bradby, David, Louis James and Bernard Sharratt, eds., Performance and Politics. Aspects of Popular
    Entertainment in Theatre, Film and Television 1800–1976 (Cambridge University Press, 1980)
Bratton, Jacqueline S., Wilton's Music Hall (Cambridge: Chadwyck-Healey, 1980)
    et al., Acts of Supremacy. The British Empire and the Stage, 1790–193((Manchester University Press,
    1991)
    and Jane Traies, Astley's Amphitheatre (Cambridge: Chadwyck-Healey, 1980)
Bridges-Adams, Walter, '[Edwardian] Theatre', in Simon Nowell-Smith, ed., Edwardian England 1901–
    1914 (London: Oxford University Press, 1964), pp. 369–409
Buckle, J[ames] G[eorge], Theatre Construction and Maintenance (London: The Stage, 1888)
Calmour, Alfred C[ecil], Practical Playwriting and the Cost of Production (Bristol: J.W. Arrowsmith; and
    London: Simpkin, Marshall, Hamilton, Kent & Co., [1891])

Cavanagh, John C., *A Bibliography of the British Theatre 1901–1985* (Romsey, Hants.: Motley Books, 1989)

Clarke, Ian, *Edwardian Drama* (London: Faber & Faber, 1989)

Cole, John William, *The Life and Theatrical Times of Charles Kean* (London: Bentley, 1859)

Coleman, John, *Players and Playwrights* (London: Chatto and Windus, 1888)

Cook, Dutton, *Nights at the Play* (London: Chatto and Windus, 1883; reprinted 1971)

Cross, Gilbert B., *Next Week, East Lynne – Domestic Drama in Performance, 1820–1874* (Lewisburg: Bucknell University Press, 1977)

Darbyshire, Alfred, *The Art of the Victorian Stage: Notes and Recollections* (London: Sherratt & Hughes, 1907)

Davis, Jim, ed., *The Britannia Diaries (1863–1875)* (London: Society for Theatre Research, 1992)

Davis, Tracy C., *Actresses as Working Women: Their Social Identity in Victorian Culture* (London, New York: Routledge, 1991)

Donaldson, Francis, *The Actor-Managers* (Chicago: Henry Regnery, 1970)

Donoghue, Joseph, ed., *The Theatrical Manager in England and America* (Princeton University Press, 1970)

Earl, John, and Stanton, John, *The Canterbury Hall and the Theatre of Varieties* (Cambridge: Chadwyck-Healey, 1982)

Elliott, W.G., ed., *Amateur Clubs and Actors* (London: Edward Arnold, 1898)

Elsom, John, *Theatre Outside London* (London: MacMillan, 1971)

    and Nicholas Tomalin, *The History of the National Theatre* (London: Jonathan Cape, 1978)

Erle, Thomas W., *Letters from a Theatrical Scene-Painter* (London: privately printed, 1880)

Fawkes, Richard, *Dion Boucicault* (London: Quartet Books, 1979)

Filon, Auguste, trans. Frederic Whyte, *The English Stage: Being an Account of the Victorian Drama* (London: John Milne, 1897)

'Findlater, Richard' [Bain, Kenneth Bruce Findlater], *Banned: A Review of Theatrical Censorship in Britain* (London: MacGibbon & Kee, 1967)

Findon, B.W., *The Playgoers' Club 1884–1905: Its History and Memoirs* (London: The Playgoers' Club, 1905)

Fitzgerald, Percy, *The World Behind the Scenes* (London: Chatto and Windus, 1881)

Foulkes, Richard, ed., *Shakespeare on the Victorian Stage* (Cambridge University Press, 1986)

    ed., *British Theatre in the 1890s: Essays on Drama and the Stage* (Cambridge University Press, 1992)

Garcia, Gustav, *The Actor's Art*, 2nd edn. (London: Simpkins Marshall, 1880)

Glasstone, Victor, *Victorian and Edwardian Theatres* (London: Thames and Hudson, 1975)

    The London Coliseum (Cambridge: Chadwyck-Healey, 1980)

Goldie, Grace Wyndham, *The Liverpool Repertory Theatre 1911–1934* (Liverpool University Press, 1935)

Harrop, Josephine, *Victorian Portable Theatres* (London: Society for Theatre Research, 1989)

Hogg, Wentworth, ed., *Guide to Selecting Plays; or, Managers' Companion* (London & New York: Samuel French [1882]

Holledge, Julie, *Innocent Flowers: Women in the Edwardian Theatre* (London: Virago, 1981)

Howard, Diana, *London Theatres and Music Halls 1850–1950* (London: The Library Association, 1970)

Howe, P.P., *The Repertory Theatre: A Record and a Criticism* (London: Martin Secker, 1910).

    Dramatic Portraits (London: Martin Secker, 1913)

Hudson, Lynton, *The English Stage 1850–1950* (London: George Harrap, 1951)

Hunt, Hugh, Richards, Kenneth, and Taylor, John Russell, *The Revels History of Drama in English*, vol. VII, *1880 to the Present* (London: Methuen, 1978)

Innes, Christopher, *Modern British Drama 1890–1990* (Cambridge University Press, 1992)

Irving, Lawrence, *Henry Irving: the Actor and his World* (London: Faber. 1952)

Jackson, Russell, ed., *Victorian Theatre* (London: A. & C. Black, 1989)

James, Henry, *The Scenic Art of Henry James: Notes on Acting and the Drama 1872–1901*, ed. Alan Wade (New Brunswick: Rutgers University Press, 1948)

Jenkins, Anthony, *The Making of Victorian Drama* (Cambridge University Press, 1991)

Jerome, Jerome K. *Stage Land* (London: Holt, 1890)

Johnston, John, *The Lord Chamberlain's Blue Pencil* (London: Hodder & Stoughton, 1990)

Jones, Henry Arthur, *Municipal and Repertory Theatres* (London: George Bell & Sons, 1913)

Lewes, George Henry, *On Actors and the Art of Acting* (London: Smith Elder, 1875)

Lewis, Leopold, ed., with an introduction by David Mayer, *Henry Irving and The Bells* (Manchester University Press, 1980)

Loewenberg, Alfred., ed., *A Bibliography of Theatres of the British Isles (Excluding London)* (London: Society for Theatre Research, 1950)

MacCarthy, Desmond, *The Court Theatre 1904–1907: A Commentary and Criticism* (London: A.H. Bullen, 1907)

Mander, Raymond and Joe Mitchenson, *The Theatres of London* (London: Rupert Hart-Davis, 1961; revised 1963)

The Lost Theatres of London (London: Rupert Hart-Davis, 1968)

Matthews, Bache, *The History of the Birmingham Repertory Theatre [1907–1924]* (London: Chatto & Windus, 1924)

McCarthy, Lillah, *Myself and My Friends* (London: Thornton & Butterworth, [1993])

McCormick, John, *Dion Boucicault (1820–1890)* (Cambridge: Chadwyck-Healey, 1982)

McDonald, Jan, *The New Drama 1900–1914* (London: Macmillan, 1986)

Meier, Erika, *Realism and Reality: The Function of the Stage Directions in the New Drama from T. W. Robertson to G. B. Shaw* (Bern: Francke Verlag, 1967)

Meisel, Martin, *Shaw and the Nineteenth-Century Theater* (Princeton University Press, 1963)

Realizations: Narrative. Pictorial and Theatrical Arts in Nineteenth-Century England (Princeton University Press, 1983)

Miller, Anna Irene, *The Independent Theatre in Europe: 1887 to the Present* (New York: R. Long & R.R. Smith, 1931)

Nicoll, Allardyce, *A History of English Drama 1660–1900. Late Nineteenth-Century Drama 1850–1900*, vol. v (Cambridge University Press, 1962)

O'Connor, Marion, *William Poel and the Elizabethan Stage Society* (Cambridge: Chadwyck-Healey, 1987)

Oliver, D. E., *The English Stage: Its Origin and Modern Developments* (London: Ouseley, 1912)

'Orme, Michael', *J. T. Grein: The Story of a Pioneer 1862–1935* (London: John Murray, 1936)

Palmer, John Leslie, *The Censor and the Theatres* (London: T. Fisher Unwin, 1912)

Pearson, Hesketh, *The Last Actor-Managers* (London: Methuen, 1950)

Pemberton, T. E., *The Life and Writings of T. W. Robertson* (London: Bentley, 1883)

Pick, John, *The West End: Mismanagement and Snobbery* (Eastbourne: John Offord, 1983)

Planché, J. R., *Recollections and Reflections* (London: Tinsley Brothers, 1872)

Pogson, Rex, *Miss Horniman and the Gaiety Theatre, Manchester* (London: Rockliff, 1952)

Pope, W. Macqueen, *Carriages at Eleven: The Story of the Edwardian Theatre* (London: Hutchinson, 1947)

Rees, Terence, *Theatre Lighting in the Age of Gas* (London: Society for Theatre Research, 1978)

Report from the Select Committee on Theatres and Places of Entertainment Together with the Proceedings of the Committee, Minutes of Evidence, Appendix and Index (London: Eyre & Spottiswoode for H. M. Stationer's Office. 1892; reprinted Shannon: Irish University Press, 1970)

Report from the Select Committee on Theatrical Licences and Regulations (London: Eyre and Spottiswoode for H. M. Stationer's Office, 1866; reprinted Shannon: Irish Universtiy Press, 1970)

Richards, K. and P. Thomson, *Nineteenth-Century British Theatre* (London: Methuen, 1971)

Ross, Charles Henry, *'Stage Whispers' and 'Shouts Without': A Book about Plays and Playgoers, Actors and Actresses* (London: 'Judy' Office [1881])

Rowell, George, *The Victorian Theatre 1792–1914* (1956; revised edn., Cambridge University Press, 1978)

Theatre in the Age of Irving (Oxford: Blackwell, 1981)

The Old Vic Theatre: a History (Cambridge University Press, 1992)
   ed., *Victorian Dramatic Criticism* (London, Methuen and Co, 1971)
Sanderson, Michael, *From Irving to Olivier: A Social History of the Acting Profession* (London: Athlone, 1984)
Savin, M., *Thomas William Robertson: his Plays and Stagecraft* (Providence: Brown University, 1950)
Saxon, A. H., *Enter Foot and Horse* (New Haven: Yale University Press, 1968)
Scott, Clement, *The Drama of Yesterday and Today* (London: Macmillan, 1899)
Scott, Clement, and Cecil Howard, *The Life and Reminiscences of E. L. Blanchard* (London: Hutchinson, 1891)
Select Committee on Theatrical Licenses and Regulations (1866), reprinted in *British Parliamentary Papers: Stage and Theatre*, 2 (Shannon: Irish University Press, 1970)
Shaw, Eyre Massey, *Fires in Theatres*, 2nd edn. (London: E. & F. N. Spon, 1889)
Shaw, George Bernard, *Our Theatres in the Nineties*, 3 vols. (London: Constable & Co., 1932)
Sheridan, Paul, *Penny Theatres of Victorian London* (London: Dennis Robson, 1981)
Sherston, Erroll, *London's Lost Theatres of the Nineteenth Century* (London: John Lane, The Bodley Head, 1925)
Southern, Richard, *Changeable Scenery* (London: Faber, 1952)
   The Victorian Theatre: A Pictorial Survey (Newton Abbot: David and Charles, 1970)
Speaight, George, *Juvenile Drama* (London: Macdonald, 1946)
Spence, E[dward] F[ordham], *Our Stage and Its Critics* (London: Methuen [1910])
Stephens, John Russell, *The Censorship of the English Drama, 1824–1901* (Cambridge University Press, 1980)
   The Profession of the Playwright: British Theatre 1800–1900 (Cambridge University Press, 1992)
Stoker, Bram, *Personal Reminiscences of Henry Irving* (1906; revised edn. London: William Heinemann, 1907)
Stokes, John, *Resistible Theatre: Enterprise and Experiment in the Late Nineteenth Century* (London: Elek Books, 1972)
Stokes, John, Booth, Michael R., and Bassnett, Susan, *Bernhardt, Terry, Duse: The Actress in her Time* (Cambridge University Press, 1988)
Stowell, Sheila, *A Stage of their Own. Feminist Playwrights of the Suffrage Era* (Manchester University Press, 1992)
Stratman, Carl J., *Britain's Theatrical Periodicals 1767–1920* (New York Public Library, 1972; 2nd edn. 1974)
Strong, Albert A[mbrose], *The Law of Copyright for Actor and Composer* (London: The Era, 1901)
   Dramatic and Musical Law (London: The Era, 1898, 2nd end. 1901)
Taylor, George, *Henry Irving at the Lyceum* (Cambridge: Chadwyck-Healey, 1980)
Thomas, James, *The Art of the Actor-Manager: Wilson Barrett and the Victorian Theatre* (Epping: Bowker, 1984)
Trewin, John Courtney, *Edwardian Theatre* (Oxford: Blackwells, 1976)
Tweedie, Mrs Alec [Ethel Brilliana], *Behind the Footlights* (London: Hutchinson & Co., 1904)
Vernon, Frank, *The Twentieth-Century Theatre* (London: George Harrap, 1924)
Walkley, A. B., *Drama and Life* (London: 1907; New York: Brentano's, 1908)
Watson, Earnest Bradlee, *From Sheridan to Robertson* (Cambridge. Mass.: Harvard University Press, 1926)
Wearing, J.P., *The London Stage 1890–1899: A Calendar of Plays and Players*, 2 vols. (Metuchen, New Jersey and London: Scarecrow Press, 1976)
   The London Stage 1900–1909: A Calendar of Plays and Players, 2 vols. (Metuchen, New Jersey and London: Scarecrow Press, 1981)
Weller, Bernard, *Stage Copyright at Home and Abroad* (London: The Stage, 1912)
Who Was Who in the Theatre 1912–1977, 4 vols. (London: Pitman, 1978)
Wilson, A. E., *Edwardian Theatre* (London: Barker, 1951)
   East End Entertainment (London: Barker, 1954)

Winter, Marian Hannah, *Le Théâtre du merveilleux* (Paris: Olivier Perrin, 1962)
Woodfield, James, A., *English Theatre in Transition 1881–1914* (London: Croom Helm, 1984)

ITALY, 1868–1919

General reference and periodicals

Enciclopedia dello spettacolo (Rome, 1954–66)
Enciclopedia del teatro del '900, ed. A. Attisani (Rome, 1980)
L'arte drammatica (Milan, 1871–1929)

Books and articles

Albini, E., *Cronache teatrali 1891–1925* (Genoa, 1973)
Alexander, A., *Giovanni Verga* (London, 1972)
Alonge R., *Teatro e società del Novecento* (Milan, 1974)
    Teatro e spettacolo nel secondo Ottocento (Rome-Bari, 1988)
Angelini, Franca, *Cultura, narrativa e teatro nell'eta del positivismo* (Rome-Bari, 1975)
    Teatro e spettacolo nel primo novecento (Rome-Bari, 1990)
Antona Traversi, C., *Le grandi attrici del tempo andato* (Turin, 1930)
Antonucci, G. *Cronache del teatro futurista* (Rome, 1975)
Apollonio, M., *Storia del teatro Italiano* (Florence, 1954)
Apollonio, U., ed., *Futurist Manifestos* (London, 1973)
Artioli, U., *Teorie della scena dal naturalismo al surrealismo*, vol. I *Dai Meininger a Craig* (Florence, 1972)
Artisti scenografici italiani 1915–1930, Galleria Nazionale dell'Arte Moderna (Rome, 1981)
Azzaroni, G., *Del teatro e dintorni. Una storia della legislazione e delle strutture teatrali in Italia nell '800*
    (Rome, 1981)
Ballo, G., *Poetiche e sviluppo nella scenografia da Wagner alla scenodinamica* (Varese, 1956)
Barbina, A., ed., *Teatro verista siciliano* (Bologna, 1970)
Barsotti, A., *Verga drammaturgo tra commedia borghese e teatro verista siciliano* (Florence, 1974)
Bartolucci, G., *Il gesto futurista* (Rome, 1969)
Bellotti Bon, L., *Condizioni dell 'arte drammatica italiana* (1875); reprinted in V. Pandolfi, *L'antologia del
    grande attore* (Bari, 1954)
Bisicchia, A., *D'Annunzio e il teatro, tra cronaca e letteratura drammatica* (Milan, 1991)
Boutet, E., *Cronache drammatiche* (Rome, 1899–1900)
    Cronache teatrali (Rome, 1900–1)
    La mia follia (Rome, 1908)
    'Dal teatro per tutti al caffè concerto', *Nuova Antologia* (September–October, 1913)
Bracco, R., *Tra le arti e gli artisti* (Naples, 1918)
Bracco, V., *Teatro verista* (Brescia, 1975)
Calendoli, G., ed., *Teatro di F. T. Marinetti* (Rome, 1960)
Camilleri, A., *I teatri stabili in Italia 1898–1918* (Bologna, 1959)
Canudo, R., *Gabriele D'Annunzio et son théâtre* (Paris, 1911)
Capuana, L., *Il teatro italiano contemporaneo* (Palermo, 1872)
    Libri e teatro (Catania, 1892)
    Gli 'ismi' contemporanei (Palermo, 1898)
    Teatro dialettale siciliano, vols. I–III (Palermo, 1911–12); vols. IV–V (Catania, 1920–21)
Cenni, V., *Arte e vita prodigiose di Ermete Zacconi* (Milan, 1945)
Chiara, P., *Vita di Gabriele D'Annunzio* (Milan, 1978)
Cibotto, G. A., ed., *Cronache teatrali di Giovanni Pozza 1886–1913* (Vicenza, 1971)

Corra, B. and Settimelli, E., *Teatro futurista sintetico* (Milan, 1915–16)
Corsi, M., *Le prime rappresentazioni dannunziane* (Milan, 1928)
Costetti, G., *La Compagnia Reale Sarda e il teatro Italiano 182 al 1855* (Milan, 1893)
  Il teatro Italiano nel 1800 (Rocca San Casciano, 1901; reprinted 1978)
Crispolti, E. and M. L. Dondi Gambillo, eds., *Giacomo Balla* (Turin, 1963)
D'Amico, S., 'Virgilio Talli', *L'idea nazionale*, 9 January 1925
  Tramonto del grande attore (Milan, 1929)
  'Edoardo Boutet e il sogno della Stabile', in *Invito al teatro* (Brescia, 1935)
  La regia teatrale (Rome, 1947)
D'Annunzio, G., *Opere complete* (Milan, 1927–36)
DeMaria, L., ed., *Marinetti e il futurismo* (Milan, 1973)
Doglio, Federico, *Il teatro pubblico in Italia* (Rome, 1976)
  Teatro in Europa: storia e documenti vol. III, (Milan, 1989)
Fagiolo dell'Arco, M., *La scenografia, dalle sacre rappresentazioni al futurismo* (Florence, 1973)
  Balla, the Futurist (Oxford, 1987)
Ferrigni, M., 'La Compagnia Drammatica del Teatro Manzoni di Milano', *La Lettura*, May 1913
Ferrone, Siro, ed., *Teatro dell'Italia unita* (Milan, 1980)
Ferrone, S., ed., *Il teatro italiano, V* (Turin, 1979)
  Il teatro di Verga (Rome, 1972)
Fiocco, A., *Teatro universale. Dal naturalismo ai giorni nostri* (Bologna, 1963)
Flint, R. W., ed., *Marinetti, Selected Writings* (London, 1972)
Fontana, A., 'La Scena', in *Storia d'Italia* (Turin, 1972), vol. I, pp. 793–866
Forgione, M., *La vita e l'arte di Marco Praga* (Padua, 1944)
Fossati, P., *La realtà attrezzata – scena e spettacolo dei futuristi* (Turin, 1977)
Frette, G., *Scenografia teatrale 1909–54* (Milan, 1955)
Fusero, C., *Eleonora Duse* (Milan, 1971)
Grano, E., *Pulcinella e Sciosciammocca* (Naples, 1974)
Gullace, G., *Gabriele D'Annunzio in France* (Syracuse, 1966)
Hulten, Pontus, ed., *Futurismo e futuristi* (Milan, 1986)
Jacobbi, R., *Teatro da ieri a domani* (Florence, 1972)
James, H., *The Scenic Art* (London, 1949)
Jarro, *Sul palcoscenico e in platea* (Florence, 1893)
Kirby, E. T., *Total Theatre* (New York, 1969)
Kirby, M., *Futurist Performance* (New York, 1971)
Lambiase, Sergio and Lanza, D., 'Attorno alla Casa di Goldoni', in *Rivista teatrale italiana* (1901), vol. I
Lapini, L., *Il teatro futurista italiano* (Milan, 1977)
Levi, C., *Profili di attori, gli scomparsi* (Palermo, 1923)
  Il teatro (Roma, 1919)
Lista, Giovanni, ed., *Théâtre futuriste italien* (Lausanne, 1976)
  Giacomo Balla (Modena, 1982)
  La scène futuriste (Paris, 1989)
Livio, G., *Il teatro in rivolta* (Milan, 1976)
  La scena italiana. Materiali per una storia dello spettacolo dell'Otto e Novecento (Milan, 1989)
Lugné-Poe, A., *La Parade: III. Sous les étoiles* (Paris, 1933)
Lyonnet, H., *Le Théâtre en Italie* (Paris, 1900)
  'E. Novelli et le Théâtre en Italie', in *La Revue d'Art dramatique* (1902)
Mangini, G., *Gustavo Modena e il teatro italiano del primo Ottocento* (Venice, 1965)
Martini, F., *Al Teatro* (Florence, 1895)
Meldolesi, Claudio, *Fondamenti del teatro italiano. La generazione dei registi* (Florence, 1984)
Meldolesi, C. and Taviani, F., *Teatro e spettacolo nel primo Ottocento* (Rome-Bari, 1991)
Molinari, Cesare, *L'attrice divina Eleonora Duse nel teatro italiano fra due secoli* (Rome, 1985)
Nazzaro, G. B., *Marinetti e i futuristi* (Milan, 1978)

Novelli, E., *Foglietti sparsi* (Roma, 1919)
Oliva, D., *Il teatro in Italia nel 1909* (Milan, 1911)
　Note di uno spettatore (Bologna, 1911)
Pandolfi, V., *L'antologia del grande attore* (Bari, 1954)
　Spettacolo del secolo (Pisa, 1953)
　Regia e registi del teatro moderno (Bologna, 1961)
　Storia universale del teatro drammatico, vol. II, (Turin, 1964)
Pardieri, G., *Ermete Zacconi* (Bologna, 1960)
　Ermete Novelli (Bologna, 1966)
Passamani, B., ed., *Depero e la scena 1916–1930* (Turin, 1970)
Pirandello, L., 'Eleonora Duse', *Century Magazine*, June 1924; reprinted in E. Bentley, *The Theory of the Modern Stage* (Harmondsworth, 1968), pp. 158–69
Pontiero, G., ed., *Duse on Tour (Guido Noccioli's Diaries 1906–7)* (Manchester, 1982)
Praga, M., *Compagnia Drammatica Italiana del Teatro Manzoni di Milano* (Milan, 1912)
Primoli, J. N., 'La Duse', *La Revue de Paris*, 1 June 1897
Pullini, G., *Marco Praga* (Bologna, 1960)
　Cinquant'anni di teatro in Italia (Bologna, 1970)
　Teatro italiano del novecento (Bologna, 1971)
Rasi, L., *I comici italiani* (3 vols. Florence, 1897–1905)
　La Duse (Florence, 1901)
Ristori, A., *Ricordi e studi artistici* (Turin-Naples, 1887)
Rossi, E., *Quarant'anni di vita artistica* (3 vols., Florence, 1887–8)
Salaris, Claudia, *Bibliografia del futurismo, 1909–44* (Rome, 1988)
Salvini, C., *Tommaso Salvini nella storia del teatro italiano e nella vita del suo tempo* (Rocca San Casciano, 1955)
Salvini, T., *Leaves from the Autobiography* (London and New York, 1893)
　Ricordi, aneddoti e impressioni (Milan, 1895)
　Discorso in commemorazione di Adelaide Ristori (Florence, 1906)
Scarpetta, E., *Cinquant'anni di palcoscenico* (Naples, 1922)
　Dal San Carlino ai Fiorentini (Naples, 1900)
Scrivo, L., *Sintesi del futurismo. Storia e documenti* (Rome, 1968)
Setti, D., *Eleonora Duse ad Antonietta Pisa* (Milan, 1972)
Shaw, G. B., *Our Theatres in the Nineties*, vol. I (London, 1932)
Signorelli, O., *Vita di Eleonora Duse* (Bologna, 1962)
Simoni, R., *Trent'anni di cronaca drammatica* (Turin, 1951)
Stauble, A., *Il teatro intimista* (Rome, 1975)
Symons, A., *Eleonora Duse* (London, 1926)
Talli, V., *La mia vita di teatro* (Milan, 1927)
Tisdall, C. and Bozzolla, A., *Futurism* (London, 1977)
Tosi, G., *Gabriele D'Annunzio à Georges Herelle* (Paris, 1946)
Verdone, M., *Teatro del tempo futurista* (Rome, 1969)
　Teatro italiano d'advanguardia (Rome, 1970)
　Teatro del novecento (Brescia, 1981)
　Il movimento futurista (Rome, 1986)
Verga, De Roberto, Capuana, *Catalogo della mostra*, ed. A. Ciaravella (Catania, 1955)
Verga, G., *Lettere al suo traduttore*, ed. F. Chiapelli (Florence, 1954)
　Teatro (Milan, 1966)
　Lettere a L. Capuana, ed. G. Raya (Florence, 1975)
Vergani, L., *Eleonora Duse* (Milan, 1959)
Viviani, V., *Storia del teatro napoletano* (Naples, 1969)
Wade, Alan, ed., *Henry James, The Scenic Art* (London, 1949)
Weaver, William, *Duse, A Biography* (London, 1984)

Yorick *Teatro e governo* (Florence, 1888)
Zacconi, G., *Ricordi e battaglie* (Milan, 1946)
Zapulla-Muscara, S., *Capuana e De Roberto* (Caltanissetta, 1984)

IBERIAN PENINSULA, 1884–1913

Alarma, S., *Escenografía* (Barcelona, 1919)
Arias de Cossío, A. M. *Dos siglos de escenografía en Madrid* (Madrid: Mondadori, 1991)
Asenjo, A., 'Crónica: la decadencia del género chico', *Comedia y Comediantes*, 15 (1910), p. 3
Batlle, Carles et al, *Adrià Gaul: Mitia Vida de Modernisme* (Barcelona, Diputació de Barcelona, 1992)
Berenguer, A., *El teatro en el siglo XX (hasta 1939)* (Madrid: Taurus, 1988)
Curet, F., *Història del teatre català* (Barcelona: Aedos, 1967)
Díaz de Escobar, N. and Lasso de la vega, F., *Historia del teatro español* (2 vols., Barcelona: Montaner y Simón, 1924)
Edwards, G., *Dramatists in Perspective: Spanish Theatre in the Twentieth Century* (Cardiff: University of Wales Press, 1985)
Fàbregas, X., *Història del teatre català* (Barcelona: Millà, 1978)
Gagen, D., 'Unamuno and the Regeneration of the Spanish Theatre', in *Re-reading Unamuno*, Glasgow Colloquium Papers, 1 (University of Glasgow: Department of Hispanic Studies, 1989), pp. 53–79
Gallén, E., 'El teatre' and 'Santiago Rusiñol', in Comas, A., ed., *Història de la literatura catalana* (11 vols., Barcelona: Ariel, 1980–88), vol. VIII (1986), pp. 379–480
García Pavón, F. *Teatro social en España* (Madrid: Taurus, 1962)
George, D. 'El pan del pobre: a Spanish Version of Hauptmann's *The Weavers*', *Theatre Research International*, 12 (1967), pp. 23–38
Gual, Adrià, *Mitja vida de teatre, Memòries* (Barcelona: Aedos, 1960)
Hall, H. B., 'Joaquín Dicenta and the Drama of Social Criticism', *Hispanic Review*, 20 (1952), pp. 44–66
Lyon, J. *The Theatre of Valle-Inclán* (Cambridge University Press, 1983)
Mainer, J-C., 'Joaquín Dicenta (1863–1917)', in *Literatura y pequeña burguesía en España* (Madrid: Edicusa, 1972), pp. 29–57
Muñoz Morillejo, J. *Escenografía española* (Madrid, 1923)
Pérez de la Dehesa, R., *El grupo 'Germinal': una clave del 98* (Madrid: Taurus, 1970)
Rebello, L. F., *O teatro naturalista e neo-romántico (1870–1910)* (Lisbon: Instituto de Cultura Portuguesa, 1978)
O teatro simbolista e modernista (1890–1939) (Lisbon: Instituto de Cultura Portuguesa, 1979)
Rubio Jiménez, J., *Ideología y teatro en España: 1890–1900* (Universidad de Zaragoza, 1982)
'El teatro en el siglo XIX (II) (1845–1900)', in Díez Borque, J. M., ed., *Historia del teatro en España* (Madrid: Alfaguara, 1988), pp. 625–762
El teatro poético en Espâna: Del modernismo a las vanguardias (Universidad de Murcia, 1993)
Ruiz Ramón, F., *Historia del teatro español, II: Siglo XX* (6th edn., Madrid: Cátedra, 1984)
Siguán, M. 'L'ideari d'Adrià Gual en el marc de la renovació del teatre català i la introducció de Gerhart Hauptmann a Catalunya', in *Antoni Comas. In Memoriam* (Barcelona, 1985), pp. 435–446
Unamuno, M. de, 'La regeneración del teatro español', in *Teatro completo* (Madrid: Aguilar, 1973), pp. 1343–73
Yxart, J., *El arte escénico en Espâna* (2 vols., Barcelona, 1894)
'De teatre', in *Entorn de la literatura catalana de la Restauració*, ed. Jordi Castellanos, Les Millors Obres de la Literatura Catalana, 42 (Barcelona: Edicions 62, 1980), pp. 39–176

General index

Achurch, Janet, 332

acting

necessary prerequisites to become an actor, 23–4; Antoine disappointed by the Meiningen, 81; symbolist 'non-acting', 93, 95–6; typecasting in Germany, 119; Winds's Stanislavskian techniques, 138–40; Kainz analyses his own acting style, 140–4; Saxe-Meiningen's influential principles of staging, 148–52; importance of non-verbal communication in naturalist acting, 157–8; the actor's centrality in Reinhardt's theatre, 170–2; Fuchs on the link between acting and dancing, 181; Wedekind attacks naturalist acting, 182–3; Wedekind judged as actor, 184–5; Oriental influence: stylized acting, 186–7; expressionist acting, 188–9; Shchepkin's advice to actors: to keep nature in sight, to observe, to be truthful, to work hard, 195–7; on the necessity of creating the essence of a role, 201; Russian ham acting, 204–5; subtle acting in *The Power of Darkness*, 206; Nemirovich criticizes Stanislavsky for overacting, 218–19; Meyerhold's stylized acting which 'reveals the actor's soul', 286–7; Kommissarzhevskaya fails to understand Meyerhold's symbolist acting, 238 – but she rejects naturalism, 238; first expression of Stanislavsky's principles on acting, 244–5; the actor at the Danish Royal Theatre, 278–80; acting début of a Danish actor, 295; Ibsen on how to play Rebekka, 296; Strindberg on how to play *The Father*, 307–10; Strindberg on acting, 314–15; Salvini expresses reservations about an acting career, 422–3; Ristori's style and realism, 432; Salvini's tragic qualities, 434–6; Salvini's meticulous preparation before a performance, 438;

Shaw compares Duse and Sarah Bernhardt, 439

actors' contracts

at the Ambigu-Comique, Paris, 24; in Germany, 126–8; in England, 362–3; protest against legal tangles, 363–4; the fifteen-year-old Scarpetta's first contract, 429

Ainsworth, W. H., *The Great Fire of London*, adapted from *Old St Paul's*, 391–2

Albee, Edward, 9, 22

Albert, Prince of Wales, 406

Alexander, George, 329, 359

Alexandersson, Karin, 309, 310

Alexis, Paul: *Mademoiselle Pomme*, 83

'alternative theatre'

Tzara's anti-art Dada manifesto, 105–8; in praise of German cabaret, 175–8; Russian cabaret, 246, and Russian futurism, 246–7, 252–56; Evreinov parodies naturalism, 256–7; Italian futurism: Marinetti's 1911 manifesto, 470–2; a futurist variety theatre, 472–3; synthetic theatre, 473–5

Andreev, Leonid, 7, 208, 240

Annenkov, Pavel V., 197

Annensky, Innokenty F., *Thamyris the Cithærist*, 254–6

Antique Theatre, St Petersburg: *The Miracle of Théophile*, 246, 247–8

Antoine, André, 2, 3, 4, 5, 6, 17, 18, 68, 71; defends his experimental theatre, 79; assesses the Meiningen, 80–1; encourages visual artists, 82; interviewed by a London journalist, 83–4; defines the role of the director, 84–6; stages *La Terre*, 86, 90, 113, 146, 147, 158, 305; in Milan, 446–7; visits Lisbon, 485

Appia, Adolphe, 113, 161, 163; *Die Musik und die Inscenierung*, 113

Archer, William, 368, 370; a censor's obituary, 371–2

Index of main theatres cited

Lightning Source UK Ltd.
Milton Keynes UK
UKOW06f1103091116

287228UK00009B/385/P

9 780521 100793